P9-DBI-954

FOURTH EDITION

THE POLICE

AN INTRODUCTION

FOURTH EDITION

THE POLICE

AN INTRODUCTION

Michael D. Lyman
Columbia College of Missouri

Prentice Hall

Boston Columbus Indianapolis New York San Francisco Upper Saddle River
Amsterdam Cape Town Dubai London Madrid Milan Munich Paris Montreal Toronto
Delhi Mexico City Sao Paulo Sydney Hong Kong Seoul Singapore Taipei Tokyo

Editor in Chief: Vern Anthony
Acquisitions Editor: Tim Peyton
Editorial Assistant: Alicia Kelly
Director of Marketing: David Gesell
Marketing Manager: Adam Kloza
Senior Marketing Coordinator: Allicia Wozniak
Project Manager: Renata Butera
Operations Specialist: Renata Butera
Creative Director: Jayne Conte
Cover Designer: Bruce Kenselaar
Image Permission Coordinator: Kathy Gavilanes
Manager, Cover Visual Research: Beth Brenzel
Manage Manager, Rights and Permissions: Zina Arabia
Cover Art: Getty Images, Inc.
Full-Service Project Management: Saraswathi Muralidhar
Composition: GGS Higher Education Resources, A Division of PreMedia Global Inc.
Printer/Binder: Hamilton Printing Company
Cover Printer: Lehigh Phoenix
Text Font: Times New Roman

Credits and acknowledgments borrowed from other sources and reproduced, with permission, in this textbook appear on appropriate page within the text.

Copyright © 2010, 2005, 2002, 1999 Pearson Education, Inc., publishing as Pearson Prentice Hall, One Lake St., Upper Saddle River, NJ 07458. All rights reserved. Manufactured in the United States of America. This publication is protected by Copyright, and permission should be obtained from the publisher prior to any prohibited reproduction, storage in a retrieval system, or transmission in any form or by any means, electronic, mechanical, photocopying, recording, or likewise. To obtain permission(s) to use material from this work, please submit a written request to Permissions Department, Pearson Prentice Hall, One Lake St., Upper Saddle River, NJ 07458.

Many of the designations by manufacturers and seller to distinguish their products are claimed as trademarks. Where those designations appear in this book, and the publisher was aware of a trademark claim, the designations have been printed in initial caps or all caps.

Library of Congress Cataloging-in-Publication Data

Lyman, Michael D.
  The police: an introduction / Michael D. Lyman.—4th ed.
    p. cm.
Includes bibliographical references and index.
  ISBN-13: 978-0-13-500566-8
  ISBN-10: 0-13-500566-3
  1. Police—United States. 2. Law enforcement—United States. I. Title.

HV8138.L95 2010
363.20973—dc22

                          2009004027

Prentice Hall
is an imprint of

www.pearsonhighered.com

10 9 8 7 6 5
ISBN-10: 0-13-500566-3
ISBN-13: 978-0-13-500566-8

In fond memory of my loving parents:
Roy E. Lyman and Harriet W. Lyman
The best teachers I ever had.

CONTENTS

PREFACE

It could be said that police work touches more lives than any profession, whether directly or indirectly. Certainly, it remains as the cornerstone of virtually all government functions. Yet with almost a century and a half of formalized policing in our history, police work is one of the least understood professions of all. The mystique and misunderstanding surrounding police work generate a certain amount of controversy, hostility, and resentment toward the police. The police view themselves as society's protectors: dedicated professionals who risk their lives, sacrifice time with their families, and work nights and weekends, all out of a sense of devotion to the profession and service to the community. At the same time they are often maligned by the public, criticized by the courts, and scrutinized by the media. This book was written to introduce the reader to the police: who they are and who they are not, what they can and cannot do, and, finally, why their exact role in society remains so unclear to so many.

The Police: An Introduction, third edition, is designed with learning in mind. To that end, a number of pedagogical learning aids have been included in its preparation; for example, chapter objectives that highlight the main points of each chapter and topical vignettes, including "Highlights in Policing, A Closer Look," and "American Policing Under Fire." Each of these discusses specialized and timely topics of interest.

The section at the end of each chapter titled "Improve Your Professional Vocabulary" is designed as a learning tool that identifies key chapter terms. Discussion questions for useful review of chapter material have been updated. Of particular significance are two new appendices included with this new edition. These include: Selected Provisions from the USA PATRIOT Act of 2001 and a Sample Police Academy Curriculum. These will give students a better and clearer understanding of the function of police in a free society.

Additional aids include a helpful instructor's guide and test bank, comprehensive index, and a detailed look at the new Department of Homeland Security as well as the expansion/reorganization of federal law enforcement in the aftermath of September 11. Also included are updated sections on police research and statistics, police liability, racial profiling, domestic violence, women and minorities in policing, changing demographics, the war on terrorism, and private policing.

Finally, many of the points made in the book are illustrated with case examples of recent police stories. The book provides students with the basic framework for understanding fundamental police issues while empowering them to question the conventional wisdom about policing.

The writing of any book represents a considerable commitment of time and energy. But such a project cannot be completed without the help and support of many people: the always helpful people at the National Institute of Justice, Bureau of Justice Statistics, and those professionals at the Federal Bureau of Investigation, Drug Enforcement Administration, and the Police Executive Research Forum. Special thanks to the Columbia Police Department, Columbia, Missouri; Boone County Sheriff's Department and the Missouri State Highway Patrol.

I thank the reviewers of this edition for their insightful comments: G. Harrell, Altamaha Technical College; David Koteras, Canisius College; and Denny Powers, South University. I also thank the reviewers of previous editions: James Albrecht, Sam Houston University, Huntsville, TX; Chuck Brawner, Heartland Community College, Bloomington, IL; David Graff, Kent State University–Tuscarawas, New Philadelphia, OH; Mark Jones, Atlantic Cape Community College, Mays Landing, NJ; and Dana De Witt, Chadron State College, Chadron, NE. I would like to extend individual gratitude to the following people: Detective Mike Himmel of the Columbia, Missouri, Police Department and Carroll Highbarger for providing many of the photos for this book; and Stephanie Faler for her capable assistance in organizing and formatting the manuscript, instructor's manual, and test bank for this book.

I also would like to thank you for using this book to help you better understand your police. Any comments about how this book can be improved in future editions will be greatly appreciated and may be directed to my attention at the following address:

Michael D. Lyman, Ph.D.
Department of Criminal Justice & Human Services
Columbia College of Missouri
1001 Rogers Street
Columbia, MO 65216
(573)875-7472

ABOUT THE AUTHOR

Michael D. Lyman is on the faculty of the Criminal Justice and Human Services Department at Columbia College, Columbia, Missouri. He serves the department as teaching faculty, the departmental liaison for the Master of Science degree in Criminal Justice, and as program director for the Bachelor of Science in Forensic Science degree program. Dr. Lyman has testified as an expert in police practices and procedures in state and federal courts across the country. He has also authored seven books dealing with various aspects of policing, criminal investigation, drug trafficking, and organized crime.

Prior to entering the field of college teaching, Michael Lyman was employed as a criminal investigator for the Kansas Bureau of Investigation and later as a senior agent for the Oklahoma Bureau of Narcotics and Dangerous Drugs. He received both his bachelor's and master's degrees from Wichita State University and his Ph.D. from the University of Missouri–Columbia.

FOURTH EDITION

THE POLICE

AN INTRODUCTION

PART 1

The Basis for Modern Policing

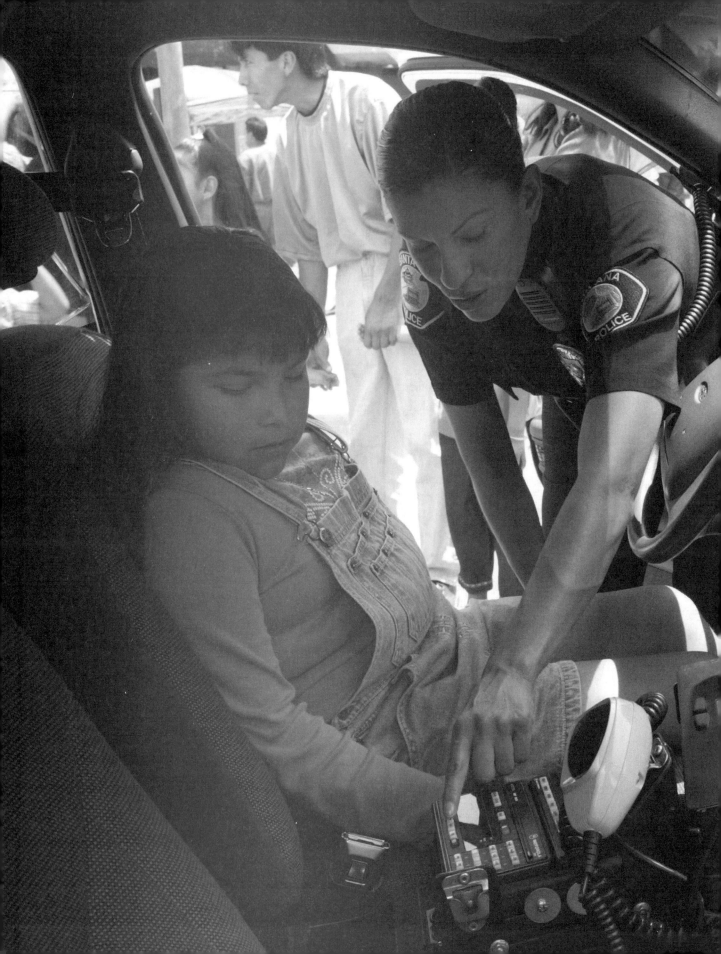

CHAPTER 1

Understanding the Police

This chapter will enable you to:

- Understand how the public and police interrelate with one another.
- Contrast the roles of police with the needs of society.
- Understand the many roles of police in U.S. society.
- Comprehend the complex relationship between the rule of law and the functions of the police in society.

- Discern between the popular image of the police officer and the reality of the police role.
- Understand how individual police officer behavior affects the performance of the police in our communities.
- Appreciate the dynamics of the police subculture and how they contribute to the effectiveness or ineffectiveness of the police officer on the street.

One of the most memorable shooting rampages in American history started just after 7 A.M. on April 16, 2007, in Blacksburg, Virginia. Seung-Hui Cho, a 23-year-old English major armed with 9mm Glock 19 and .22-caliber Walther P22 handguns, started his violent morning by killing two students at the West Amber Johnston Hall on the campus of Virginia Polytechnic Institute and State University (Virginia Tech). He then stopped by his dorm room before heading to a local post office, where he mailed a package to the headquarters of the NBC television network in New York City. The parcel contained 28 self-made video clips, a 23-page written statement, and more than 40 still photographs of himself, some of which showed him posing menacingly with the two firearms.

Cho was far from finished. He returned to the campus and headed for Norris Hall; after chaining the doors to the building shut, he continued upstairs. "He stepped in and assumed the shooting position and then took aim," remembered Guillermo Colman, who was sitting in the first row of his advanced hydrology class at the time. "His face was a complete blank stare. It seemed very mechanical." Cho opened fire in four different classrooms, methodically shooting each of his victims two to three times. Law enforcement officials believe that he did not stop until he heard the sound of the shotguns that campus police were using to break the chains on the doors. Cho then placed one of his weapons to his head and committed suicide.

Looking back, the red flags concerning Seung-Hui Cho seem so numerous. His writing assignments were laced with gory and violent imagery. "[His] plays had really twisted, macabre violence that used weapons I wouldn't have thought of," remembered one classmate, adding that he and his friends had "serious worry about whether [Cho] could be a school shooter." Eventually, Cho's manner became so descriptive that his creative writing professor removed him from class. During the fall of 2005, two female students complained to Virginia Tech police that Cho was harassing them. That same semester, a doctor at nearby Carilion St. Albans Psychiatric Hospital determined that Cho was "mentally ill" but not an imminent threat to himself or anyone else.

For all his disturbing words and behavior, Cho had broken no law; therefore, Virginia Tech had no grounds to remove him from school. The rampage at Virginia Tech raises a number of other concerns as well. Why was Cho, whom the physician had determined to be mentally ill, nonetheless, able to purchase firearms from a local gun shop and pawnbroker? Why did the police fail to identify Cho as a suspect and warn the Virginia Tech community during the two-hour window between the shooting incidents?

The Virginia Tech incident illustrates the unpredictability of crime and the difficulty the police had in predicting it, enforcing it, and ensuring public safety.

The uniformed men and women who patrol American streets are the most visible presence of government in the United States. They're joined by thousands of plainclothes officers who share various law enforcement responsibilities. Whether they're members of the local or state police, sheriff's departments, or federal agencies, the more than 700,000 sworn officers in the country play key roles in U.S. society. Citizens look to them to perform a wide range of functions, including law enforcement, crime prevention, maintenance of order, and community services. However, the public's expectations of the police are not always clear as many citizens form judgments about the police. Those judgments have a strong impact on the way the police function.

The police are required to maintain order in a free society, and in performing this function, police officers are given a great deal of authority. Using their powers to arrest, search, detain, and use force, they can interfere with the freedom of any citizen. If they abuse their powers, they can threaten the basic values of a stable, democratic society.

Police work represents a field of endeavor in which the public has certain public-safety expectations. Included in these are assumptions that criminals will be caught and that methods employed by police to do so will be lawful. In the minds of many people, the police occupy a strangely unique place in our society. Their very existence represents a contrast between a controlling governmental force and an otherwise free and democratic society. Consequently, a job well done is often viewed as a "responsibility" of the police rather than a societal fringe benefit provided by them.

THE GOVERNMENT, THE POLICE, AND THE PEOPLE

Perhaps no branch of government is as visible and controversial as that of the police. While fulfilling a unique social niche, the police exist in a very distinctive and unique environment. This environment is dynamic. It changes with the ebb and flow of politics, social mores, culture, law, and intellectual influences throughout society.[1] To a very great extent, this unique environment dictates whether the police will act informally or formally in any given situation; it will have a bearing on whether the police choose to enforce a law; and it will also play a large part in the manner in which the police intervene should they choose to do so.

The forces that play the greatest role in shaping U.S. police are the government and society. Because of this mutual interdependence, the terms *government* and *society* are often referred to interchangeably. But, in fact, they are unique in their own ways. We can see from examining societies around the globe that many societies exist without government; however, governments cannot exist without the support of societies.

For generations, well-known scholars have examined the unique relationship between government and society. Great political minds of the 1700s and 1800s, in particular, considered the role of government in society. For example, philosophers John Locke, Thomas Hobbs, and Jean-Jacques Rousseau developed essays on the ideal relationship between government and society. Over time, these works have become known as *social contract theory*. Social contract theory explains the relationship between government and society and, in particular, government's relationship with its citizens. According to this theory, members of society are assumed to have entered into an agreement to create government to acquire security and order for the entire society.[2] By entering into such a "social contract," citizens forego certain natural rights and empower government with the power to maintain social stability and protect the collective interests of its populace.

As a trade-off for the right to use physical force, citizens expect the government to provide an effective system for regulating conduct and creating mechanisms by which conflict among citizens can be arbitrated. While an assumption is made that citizens and the governments they create will observe the spirit of the social contract, deviations are common. Behaviors committed against the social good, whether by citizens or government, that violate the spirit of the social contract require control and, in many cases, punishment.

Democratic systems of government observe a number of unique principles that distinguish them from other forms of government. The very concept of democracy includes observance of such fundamental principles as respect for the rule of law, individual rights, civil rights, human dignity, constitutionalism, social justice, and majority rule. These principles are held in the highest regard, with a second priority for social control also being observed. So, in terms of the social contract, democratic societies view the government as the minor party in the contractual arrangement and emphasize the process that achieves order and stability over the ends themselves. These principles make democracy a unique political form of government and policing society a difficult challenge.[3]

CRIME AND THE POLICE

In the twenty-first century, crime and the threat of victimization remain a perennial concern. But whether crime is on the increase or decrease, it remains a constant in our society, and to many it is one of the most important social issues confronting our communities today. With this in mind, some important questions can be asked: Are our police adequately prepared to deal with crime in a modern society and if not, what is needed? How does the frequency and type of crime affect what the police do? No simple answer can be offered to either question because crime has complex causes, comes in so many varieties, and is impossible to eradicate totally.

To a great extent, these questions are the essence of the study of policing. Although the police do much more than enforce the law, their role in society is integral in preserving the American dream—whatever we perceive that to be. As the roles, functions, and purposes of the police are discussed throughout the remainder of the book, the terms *police* and *law enforcement* will be used interchangeably because they both represent the same general types of organizations in our society. The enforcement of the law is one of the most significant mechanisms for social control.

If one stops to think about it, there is no function of government that more directly controls the activities of citizens than the police. This contact and control is constant whether experienced through direct police–citizen contact or by the mere perception of police presence in the community.

To many people the term *law enforcement* brings to mind uniformed officers driving boldly marked police cars. To a certain extent this is an accurate perception, but it lacks clarity. Law enforcement can include local municipal police as well as county sheriffs, state highway patrol troopers, and even federal agents, all of whom are charged, in one way or another, with the responsibility of enforcing laws and maintaining order. But our law enforcement officers are only one governmental mechanism used to maintain prescribed standards of conduct. Others include

- Campus police
- Housing authority officers

- Transit police
- Coroners or medical examiners
- Marine patrol agencies
- Conservation officers

Today's police officer faces a number of problems that his or her counterpart 20 years ago did not. Racial tensions have escalated, and incidents of violence have risen both on the street and in the home. The proliferation of both drugs and guns is also much higher today than for the police officer of generations gone by.

THIS BOOK'S THEME

Americans look toward the police for a number of things. First, the police are their first-line defense against crime. They are also whom the public can turn to for order maintenance and public peace. The orientation of this book is especially appropriate for the study of police in contemporary U.S. society, as it is important for people to be aware of the role of the police in detecting and countering crime. But it is also important for people to have an understanding of the relationship between crime, the fear of crime, and the role of the police in suppressing it while at the same time observing the rights of citizens. As a result, the materials presented in this book support the following theme:

> The police in a contemporary society work at the pleasure of the people they serve, and because of this they face a unique challenge. Those who are fearful of an overbearing and abusive police system suggest that police power can and should be restricted. On the other hand, citizens who are the most fearful of crime argue that neighborhoods are in need of more police officers who are afforded more authority with which to identify and arrest lawbreakers. This presents a dichotomy, for these views conflict. In a democracy, to ensure effectiveness, police must be responsive to the public's fear of crime while counterbalancing that response with a fair application of the law.

PREVENTING CRIME BY POLICE

What Works

- **Extra police patrols in high-crime hot spots** reduce crime in those places.
- **Repeat offender units** reduce the time on the streets and thus the crimes of known high-risk repeat offenders by monitoring them and returning them to prison more quickly than when they are not monitored.
- **Arresting domestic abusers** reduces repeat domestic abuse by employed suspects as well as offenders living in neighborhoods where most households have an employed adult.

What Doesn't

- **Neighborhood watch programs organized with police** fail to reduce burglary or other target crimes, especially in higher-crime areas where voluntary participation often fails.
- **Arrests of juveniles for minor offenses** cause them to become more delinquent in the future than if police exercise discretion to merely warn them or use other alternatives to formal charging.
- **Arrests of unemployed suspects for domestic assault** cause higher rates of repeat offending over the long term than nonarrest alternatives.
- **Increased arrests or raids on drug markets** fail to reduce violent crime or disorder for more than a few days, if at all.
- **Storefront police offices** fail to prevent crime in the surrounding areas.
- **Police newsletters with local crime information** failed to reduce victimization rates in Newark, New Jersey, and Houston, Texas.[4]

DEFINING THE POLICE

Thus far we have been talking about the police as if that word meant something specific. It is probably more appropriate to begin with the observation that we are likely to have different interpretations of what the word *police* means and that *police* means different things to different people. Carl Klockars offers a definition of police that is sufficiently broad yet instructive. Klockars observed that definitions of police that focus on the goals or ins of policing tell us more about the person making the definition than they do about the organization of police. He asserted that the police are the police whether they are actively engaged in maintaining public order. He also suggested that rather than looking at what the police are supposed to do, we should focus on the means of police—that is to say, not what police do but how police do it. Policing is accomplished by coercive force.[5]

The significance of coercive force to the definition of the police was first considered by Egon Bittner. Bittner suggested that the capacity to use coercive force is the heart and soul of the police role in our society. The very reason we have police, and the reasons for which we call them, is based on the belief that force may be necessary. Police are authorized to use force to resolve various forms of social problems. Thus, when one calls the police, one calls for force.[6]

Let's consider an example. The police are generally called to the scene of a burglary. We call them, at least in part, so that an investigation can take place whereby we may be enabled to collect insurance money for our losses. So why just not call the insurance company directly without notifying the police? It could be said that the answer is that the collective and coarser power of the police is used to validate our claim of victimization. It has more to do with than simple convenience. It has to do with coercion—power.

Thus Klockars concluded, "police are institutions or individuals given the general right to use coercive force by the state within the state's domestic territory."[7] This definition of police is perhaps the best available and the most commonly used. Defining the police in this manner allows us to consider both police organizations and individual police officers. It allows us to consider federal, state, county, municipal, private, and special jurisdiction agencies and their officers. It also allows us to focus our attention on the process of policing and enables us to go beyond looking at only the goals of the police.

THE ROLE OF POLICE IN GOVERNMENT

Policing systems operate within the realm of government. Government structure helps shape the character of the police. As a rule, police systems today closely mirror the form of government under which they operate. For example, we know that policing systems that operate in dictatorial countries are much different from those operating in democracies. Because governments are institutions for creating and carrying out public policy, the manner in which this is done shapes the character of a society and its social institutions alike.

Of course, government is another institution whose role is to address social problems. In doing so, it provides a forum for debating solutions to problems as well as creating a system of "social control." Additionally, government is but one institution that controls human behavior and possibly the most formidable institution with such a charge. Other types of institutions, such as the family, church, and educational institutions, also endeavor to shape behavior in society, but in comparison, these institutions are considerably less formal than those operating as part of the government. In theory, it is through the political process that government determines what behaviors are acceptable and provides the means by which violations of acceptable behaviors are punished. And it is the police who are charged with detecting and controlling crime through the functions of arrest and prosecution.

POLICE IN A DEMOCRATIC SOCIETY

It has been said that the police are both an aberration and a necessity of modern society. This is because members of law enforcement agencies are granted powers that are greater than powers held by nonpolice persons. These powers include the authority to detain, search, use deadly force when required, and place persons under arrest, resulting in the deprivation of the arrestees' personal freedoms. Ironically, this authority is delegated to individuals who not only occupy a management capacity in the police organization but also represent the lowest rung of the police bureaucracy.[8]

Despite criticism often directed toward the police, it is evident that a free and democratic society cannot function without them. Indeed, the police are agents of the general population and have the job of preventing people from victimizing each other in our communities. Policing is a relatively modern function of society, having emerged as a formalized institution less than 150 years ago. However, as we discuss in Chapter 2, the historical beginnings of policing appeared hundreds of years earlier, originating with many different European cultures.

For those of us who were fortunate to be born in a democratic society like that of the United States, it might be difficult to imagine what it would be like to live in a society that functions under a repressive system of government. Under totalitarian regimes, power is exercised by the dictator and his cohorts, and the government exists for the purpose of maintaining power rather than to serve the populace. Historic examples of totalitarian governments are abundant and include those that have existed under Germany's Adolph Hitler, the USSR's Joseph Stalin, and Italy's Benito Mussolini. Today, we have seen such regimes prevail in numerous countries around the world, including China, Indonesia, Panama, Cuba, Libya, Iran, and Iraq. Essentially, the dictatorship style of government places little to no value on the personal freedoms of people but enacts laws designed to benefit only those in power.

In comparison, democratic governments are based on the philosophy that people should have a voice in the manner in which they are governed. For example, people living in democratic societies have the right to elect their governmental leaders as well as to participate in passing laws that govern criminal behavior.

Majority Rule and Minority Rights

Democratic societies are committed to two core principles: the doctrine of **majority rule** and the protection of **minority rights**. Under the doctrine of majority rule, those in power determine the manner in which resources will be used to achieve social ends such as national security, transportation, medical care, and crime control. General safeguards are in place, however, to protect the rights of the people, regardless of who is in power, and to ensure that a government does not become too powerful and evolve into a despotic dictatorship. In the United States people are protected by a number of legal mechanisms, of which the most important are the U.S. Constitution and the Bill of Rights. In fact, in most democratic countries, constitutions exist that delineate the rights of the people in the society and the guidelines under which the government may exercise its power.

Such constitutions are typically derived from the traditions of their society or as a result of governmental practices of another society, such as English common law. In the United States, governmental authority is based on the rule of law rather than by the whims of influential individuals or powerful organizations such as the police. This means, at least in theory, that laws generated by a democratic process are likely to be fairer and responsive to more people than are those that might be created by only a select few persons. Such a system, as idealistic as it sounds, does not develop overnight but rather through generations of trial and error. The ultimate goal, of course, is for the law in a democratic society to be as free from tyrannical influence as possible. Accordingly, "control" of such abuses is presumed under the rule of law, resulting in all governmental leaders being held responsible for their actions.

American Policing under Fire

When a Killer Can't Be Found: The JonBenét Ramsey Case

When should police stop seeking the murderer of a child? Some would say that only when all evidence is in. Each year, hundreds of children age six and under are murdered and the killers are almost always a parent, family member, or family acquaintance—and the crimes are often solved. Still, dozens of child killings go unsolved, and, in each case, a nagging question lingers: When do you quit? In other words, when is solving a child's murder worth less than the cost of investigating it?

In October 1999, those whispers grew to a roar in the stimulating case of JonBenét Ramsey, who was found dead in the basement of her family's mansion in Boulder, Colorado, on December 26, 1996. The six-year-old beauty pageant contestant was found beaten and strangled in the basement of her home. Despite taking 13 months to consider over 30,000 pieces of evidence, including DNA samples taken from her undergarments and a ransom note written in a hand that resembled her mother's, an eight-woman, four-man grand jury adjourned without returning an indictment.

In most cases, that would have effectively ended the matter. But the Ramsey murder has too many lurid aspects to simply ignore. There are endless videos of JonBenét prancing across the stage in a junior showgirl outfit, a hand on her hip and a disturbing promise in her eyes. There are the well-documented errors by the investigators, who allowed the crime scene to be so compromised by potential suspects—including her parents—that forensic experts have declared most of the evidence worthless. For example:

- The authorship of a 2½-page ransom note could never be conclusively tied to any suspect—including the victim's mother, Patsy Ramsey, who submitted five handwriting samples.
- Some DNA evidence didn't match any suspects.
- The crime scene was hopelessly compromised when the victim's father, Jon Ramsey, picked up and moved his daughter's body from the storeroom where he found her.
- Police, believing the case was a kidnapping instead of a murder, initially failed to search the house for JonBenét's body or any other evidence.

Then there is the infighting between the prosecutor and police department. And, of course, there were the sensationalist media—TV, print, radio—fueling the melodrama. The result has been intense public engagement and interest.

In the minds of many people, JonBenét's murder became a substitute for all of the other unsolved child killings, which, in turn, has made the inability to find her killer all the more anguishing. Indeed, the pressure was so great that the day after the grand jury adjourned, prosecutors held a news conference to say they would continue investigating. By that time, Colorado Governor Bill Owens had already announced he was considering whether to appoint a prosecutor of his own.

The search to find a solution to the JonBenét Ramsey case is certainly normal, but it can also be dangerous. History is rich with instances in which the clamor for conviction has produced gross injustice. The infamous 1954 conviction of Sam Shepard for the murder of his wife is one example. The string of wrongful murder convictions uncovered in Illinois in 1998 and 1999 is yet another.

Timeline of the JonBenét Ramsey Case

At the same time, the decision to defocus the $2 million JonBenét investigation likely would ensure that her killer goes free. It would heighten public cynicism about police work, and it would state as a painful fact that even a child's life has only so much meaning in our fast-paced world.

The outcry for justice in the Ramsey murder case was rekindled once again in April 2000 when a former police detective on the case, Steve Thomas, published a book titled *JonBenét: Inside the Ramsey Murder Investigation,* where he suggested that the victim's mother, Patsy, was responsible for the crime.[9]

As a follow-up, in 2003 a federal judge in Atlanta concluded that the weight of the evidence was more consistent with the intruder theory than with the theory that Patsy Ramsey killed JonBenét. In 2006, following the death of Patsy Ramsey, who died of ovarian cancer, teacher Mark Karr was arrested in Thailand after stating that he was with JonBenét when she died and insisting that he sexually assaulted and strangled her. But after Karr's DNA failed to place him at the crime scene, charges against him were dropped. Finally, in July 2008, prosecutors publicly stated that new DNA tests cleared the Ramsey family in her 1996 slaying.

No one tracks the rate at which police departments manage to charge suspects in child killings. But in 2006, a third of all homicides went unsolved. So a calculation must plainly be made. When do the police put a murder investigation aside, to be reopened only when time permits or a new clue surfaces? In other words, when should the police quit?

THEMATIC QUESTION To what extent should the police and/or prosecutor be blamed for the justice system's inability to bring JonBenét's killer to justice or, for that matter, should blame be assigned to anyone at all? Is it possible that there actually are horrific crimes such as this that will go unpunished, or is it to even suggest so, selling out the rights of the victim? What do you think is the public responsibility of police, prosecutors, and grand juries as they relate to cases such as this?

THE IMPOSSIBLE MANDATE

The values and norms of society are often reflected in the public's response to incidents involving police behavior. It is widely believed that the police are supposed to operate within the framework of community values and in doing so perpetuate the ideals of a free and democratic society. It is also the responsibility of the police to adapt to changing social needs and expectations. This expectation has been termed the **impossible mandate**, meaning that police must serve many masters: the public, prosecutors, politicians, criminals, victims, judges, and so on.[10]

Reinforcing this mandate are the print and electronic media, which often paint an idealized illusion of modern policing. In such cases, especially in movies and books, police work is often associated with its most exciting aspects—similar to other professions, such as medicine and law, where dramatic emergency room or courtroom scenes are depicted. The reality of police work is less exciting, however. Experts estimate that only 20% of a patrol officer's time is spent in arrest and apprehension activities, with the remaining 80% relegated to less glamorous tasks, such as report writing and routine patrolling.

SEPARATION OF POWERS

One of the most important axioms of governmental rule in a democracy is that of separation of powers. In a democratic society, government must not only make and interpret laws but also have the ability to enforce them. To that end, three levels of government exist to provide the necessary system of checks and balances to safeguard against potential abuses of governmental power:

- The *legislative branch* consists of elected officials who represent their constituency in making laws (e.g., city council members, state legislators, members of Congress).
- The *judicial branch* is made up of judges, both elected and appointed, who interpret the laws as they apply to social problems in a diverse society. Judges operate in virtually all levels of government, including municipal, state, and federal.
- The *executive branch* represents both elected and appointed officials on all levels of government whose job is to enforce the laws (e.g., city managers, police officers, sheriffs, and prosecutors).

It is impossible for any branch to operate as a separate entity; rather each must operate in concert with the others. Each branch is designed to interface closely with the others and, in doing so, protect against total autonomy, which could result in the abuse of power. During the O. J. Simpson trial, for example, the suggestion of police abuse of power (executive branch) was offset by the jury verdict (judicial branch).

THE JUSTICE SYSTEM FIT

In addition to making up part of the executive branch of government, police agencies also operate as part of the criminal justice system. Discussed in detail in Chapter 3, the criminal justice system consists of the police, the courts, the juvenile justice system, and the corrections system, which includes jails, prisons, probation, and parole. It is the police, however, that usually begin the criminal justice process by identifying persons thought to have violated the law and placing them under arrest. Many activities contribute to this objective and include various types of patrol and criminal investigation techniques.

Police agencies operate at all levels of government, with each serving a distinct purpose and objective. Accordingly, powers enjoyed by police agencies at each of these levels may vary according to the laws in each jurisdiction. For example, municipal police officers generally have the power to obtain and serve search warrants, while in some states highway patrol agencies are not afforded this authority under law, as it is contrary to their mission statement and jurisdiction. Indeed, it is often the jurisdiction of a police agency that determines the extent of police authority granted to it.

The word *jurisdiction* refers to the geographical area designated as part of a police agency's territory as well as the type of crimes that agency is authorized to enforce. An example could be the authority vested in municipal (city) police officers, which is generally quite broad in nature. However, if investigative leads in a criminal case require police officers to go out of town for, say, an interview, they would no longer have jurisdiction in the town being visited. To continue investigating the case, arrangements should be made to work with the police agency in the second jurisdiction. That agency may then choose to deputize the visiting officers while they are working with officers from the outside jurisdiction. It is also common for more than one police agency to have jurisdiction over a particular type of crime. For example, both the Drug Enforcement Administration (DEA) and the Federal Bureau of Investigation (FBI) have concurrent jurisdiction over drug trafficking at the federal level. In the event that agents from both agencies focus on the same drug trafficker, a cooperative agreement is needed so that only one agency continues the investigation or both work together, sharing mutual resources. Such working relationships are common.

PUBLIC TRUST AND THE POLICE

Sometimes, law enforcement officers act in accordance with what they perceive as being in the public's best interest, but their actions result in social ramifications of immense proportions. Two high-visibility crimes can be used as brief case studies to demonstrate the importance of these social ramifications. As we review these crimes and the policing issues resulting from them, let us also consider how they illustrate a need for balance between ensuring public safety and fair and prudent treatment of citizens.

The Killing of Amadou Diallo

The incident unfolded just after midnight when four white police officers belonging to the street crimes unit were searching for a rape suspect in a Bronx, New York, neighborhood. They discovered West African immigrant Diallo standing in the doorway of his apartment building. While the accounts of what happened next vary from one source to the next, lawyers for the officers told reporters that Diallo resembled the suspect they were looking for. When the officers shouted "Freeze," Diallo apparently did not comply but instead reached into his pocket. The officers then fired on Diallo because they thought he was reaching for a gun. Diallo, struck by 19 of the 41 bullets, died at the scene. Friends of Diallo, however, later said that he spoke little English and may have been reaching for identification.[11]

The Diallo incident became one of the most visible stories of alleged abuse perpetrated by the NYPD (New York Police Department), and what seemed to many to be an excessive use of firepower resulted in charges of second-degree murder being filed against the four officers involved. Although all four officers were acquitted, the public still looks skeptically at the police and questions the integrity of those entrusted with enforcing and upholding the law.

Cases such as these are instructive in that they illustrate several inherent problems facing the police. It is clear that when a heinous crime is committed, the public has great expectations and demands of the police. They are expected to act swiftly to apprehend the perpetrator of the crime while carefully observing individual rights and practices of public safety. On the other hand, when the police do respond to public pressure and move quickly to make an arrest, such actions may prove premature, as methods for identifying suspects may border on the unconstitutional or individuals may be charged with crimes they didn't commit.

No area of criminal justice is more thought provoking and controversial than that of policing, and each day events involving our nation's police claim their place on the front page of newspapers around the country. Police work is dynamic, embracing many academic disciplines, such as history, sociology, political science, and psychology, all wrapped into one of the world's most charismatic professions. Dynamic as it may be, it is not without its problems. Indeed, year after year new stories emerge about the improprieties of some police officers. Whether it is brutality, greed, or prejudice, many people resent the police and view them as a necessary evil, questioning their role in a democratic society.

THE POLICE DILEMMA

This book's theme focuses on the necessity of balancing the public's fear of crime and resulting demands for security with a fair application of the law. As we learn of new crimes unfolding, we must consider to what extent citizens should empower the police in their local communities. For some, too much police presence may infringe on the civil rights of citizens, but others argue that inadequate policing may enable criminals to more freely victimize our neighborhoods.

Let's take an opportunity to consider when a given amount of police protection is enough. For example, chances are that if we have been victimized or are fearful of being victimized by crime, we can more easily justify the adding of more police officers to the local police force. But if we feel safe in our homes and at work, we might be more quick to reject the notion of additional police because not only it is costly but we also fear that our constitutional right to freedom from government harassment might be in jeopardy.

Let's look at the issue from another angle. Suppose that the downtown section of your city is considered a high-crime area and the police department has assigned additional police officers to patrol it at night. Also assume that you don't live in this area of town—would you be supportive of an aggressive patrol policy such as this? Now suppose that you do live in the downtown area—what are your feelings about increased police presence at night? Would more police make you feel more oppressed by their watchful presence or safer from criminals? This is precisely the point. When we complain that crime is out of hand and demand that the police do something, we must also consider what their increased presence will do to our individual freedoms and which individuals will be protected. These are key issues in U.S. policing.

PLAYING BY THE RULES

The U.S. Constitution, as the most significant foundation of modern policing, has as one of its essential purposes to control the government's ability to intervene in the personal matters of its people. Resulting from a long and heated debate by the Constitutional Convention in Philadelphia in 1787, the Constitution serves today as the final authority in virtually all questions affecting the rights of individuals, the limits of power afforded to police and governmental authorities, and the limits of punishments imposed for violations of the law. Of the many important provisions of the Constitution, Articles I and III and four of ten amendments to the Bill of Rights are the most influential in addressing the rights of the accused and of those convicted of crimes. Of particular importance in protecting individual rights are the Fourth, Fifth, and Fourteenth Amendments, which include prohibitions against unreasonable searches and seizures, forced self-incrimination, and violations of procedural due process.

The framers of the Constitution were acutely aware that tyrannical governments had often used accusations of crime to rid themselves of political dissidents. They also recognized that, in punishing crime, the state intervenes to take the life, liberty, or property of its citizens. Hence, respect for the rights of even the most despicable criminals has been a cornerstone of U.S. criminal justice—at least in theory, if not always in practice. As a result, when new technology or scientific knowledge is introduced into the service of policing, it is appropriate to inquire about the possible effects on constitutional safeguards.

Although it is important to afford police legal authority to pursue criminals effectively, society must also be cautious about the ramifications of a too-powerful police system. Some people believe that instead of expanding the powers of police agencies, police should focus on the use of existing laws and methods that have proven successful in the past.

Highlights in Policing

Your Crime-Prevention Key

Just because you visit or work in a high-crime area doesn't mean that you have to become a crime target. You can take several steps to protect yourself. For example, most experts agree that carrying a deadly weapon is not a good idea unless you have been trained as an expert in self-defense. Rather, three protective measures that don't involve deadly force should be considered:

- *Carry a pocket-sized alarm.* Once activated, these $20 to $30 devices emit an ear-splitting racket that alerts everyone nearby that you need help. Muggers sometimes flee, and in other cases the intended victims escape in the confusion.

- *Pack a defensive spray.* A number of manufacturers make $10 to $35 aerosol sprays, some not much larger than a lipstick tube, that can disable an attacker. The pepper formula sprays seem to be more effective than tear-gas sprays. Some sprays even emit an invisible fluorescent dye that can mark crooks for positive identification later by police.
- *Take a self-defense course.* Instead of martial arts, which can take years to master, consider a basic three-hour course on commonsense ways to stay out of trouble. The crime-prevention unit of your police department can recommend a class.

THE NEED FOR BALANCE

Through societies' examination of crime, the public's perception of crime, and problems resulting from the misuse of police authority, we see a clear need for balance. The public clearly relies on the police to keep them safe from crime while expecting fair and impartial enforcement of laws designed to curb crime. But police often find themselves abandoned by the very public they serve when high-profile incidents of police wrongdoing emerge.

Society is quick to point fingers at police for being too quick to rush to judgment, too lax in their response to crime, uncaring, brutal, and dishonest. The list goes on. It is true that one of our highest priorities as a democratic society should be to avoid any semblance of a police state. But if crime is on the rise, to what extent should we empower police to reduce it? Are we prepared to live with our decision, whatever it may be?

A police force that is both efficient and effective is one in which administrative priorities focus on sound recruitment, selection, and training policies. Also, understanding the origins of policing systems and the basis for police authority plays a role not only in formulating a workable public policy regarding policing but also in helping the general public understand who the police are and why they do what they must do. Furthermore, to prevent opportunities for police wrongdoing, administrative mechanisms must firmly be in place on the departmental level to detect and minimize problems within the rank and file. It is true that corruption and abuse of police authority will continue to plague some departments for some time in the future, but one should not assume that such types of behaviors are without remedy. The concept of community policing, for example, has held much promise to rid both citizens and police of harmful stereotypes, resulting in a closer working relationship between the two groups.

IMAGE VERSUS REALITY

Law & Order, *Cold Case*, *Criminal Minds*, *CSI Miami*, and similar television shows represent policing as a series of adventures and struggles between good and evil. Good cops (and sometimes bad cops) pursue this behavior relentlessly until decency and morality triumph. But does this accurately reflect the profession of police work? Are the adventures of Detective Lennie Briscoe or the sage advice of Lieutenant Anita Van Buren of TV's *Law & Order* typical in contemporary policing? And then there are the Fox Television series *COPS* and *World's Scariest Police Chases*. Are these images of police on the prowl a representation of what happens every day to American law enforcement

FIGURE 1.1 The popular television show *CSI* has sparked increasing interest in policing methods and practices. Pictured here are actors William L. Petersen and Marg Helgenberger portraying forensic scientists.

officers? Or, as experience has shown, is police work for the most part "downtime," or extended periods of inactivity?

The image of the police officer poses some additional consequences. According to Samuel Walker, "The public suffers because of unrealistic expectations about the ability of the police to prevent crime and catch criminals."[12] The entertainment industry gives the public the impression that the police are generally successful in solving crimes, when in reality less than one-fourth of all index crimes reported to the police are solved. As a result, because of the overemphasis on the crime-fighting role, both the general public and elected politicians cannot intelligently evaluate the effectiveness of their police. Among other considerations, this makes it difficult to appropriate new budgets or appoint/promote new police managers.

Public Expectations of Police

Shattering glass, splitting brick, shredding human flesh—the explosion engulfed the New Woman All Women Health Care clinic in Birmingham, Alabama, on January 29, 1998. In an instant, an off-duty police officer lay dead and a nurse was severely injured. With a crude but lethal mix of dynamite and nails, the mysterious antiabortion clinic terrorist had struck again. But this time, witnesses spotted a truck near the clinic and had the presence of mind to get the license number. Police quickly identified the owner—Eric Rudolph, a 32-year-old (at the time of his arrest) former U.S. Army demolitions man who lived in a remote area at the western end of the state.

Rudolph's bombs had a signature in the nails he used. That signature, along with other clues, allowed authorities to tie Rudolph to several bombings in the Atlanta area, including the knapsack bomb detonated in the midst of the 1996 Olympics in Atlanta's Centennial Olympic Park.

However, by the time the police were able to formally charge Rudolph with the Olympic bombing and other bombings in the Atlanta area, he had disappeared into North Carolina's

FIGURE 1.2 Eric Rudolph was arrested on May 31, 2003, for the Centennial Olympic Park bombing in Atlanta in 1996. Rudolph eluded law enforcement officers for over seven years.

Nantahala Mountains. For more than seven years, federal and state agents interviewed hikers, local hunters, and campers and conducted extensive searches of the terrain in and around North Carolina, searching for Rudolph, but with no success.

Finally, in May 2003, despite thousands of hours spent by experienced federal and state investigators, rookie police officer Jeffrey Postell spotted Rudolph rummaging through a dumpster near a grocery store in Murphy, North Carolina. At last, Eric Robert Rudolph was in custody and the search for him was over. But the arrest by Jeffrey Postell illustrates the important role of local police and how police patrol officers remain the backbone of law enforcement in America.

Because of the varied images people have about police, their expectations of them also vary. Opinions of the police are generally formed out of personal contacts they have with the citizenry. An important study of police–citizen interactions examined over 5,000 observations that took place in areas that were racially diverse and had different crime rates. Reiss discovered that approximately 86% of the encounters were **reactive** in nature, or originating from citizen complaints.[13]

Only about 14% were **proactive**, initiated by police action. Furthermore, police injuries were greater in number during proactive encounters than in reactive encounters, and those encounters where the police were not summoned tended to be more troublesome than were those when the police were called. This study suggested that the majority of police–citizen interactions originated from the citizenry and not from the police officers.

★ GOALS OF POLICING

A wide variety of tasks and activities are required of the police. Although the obvious function is to arrest lawbreakers, most police departments are responsible for an array of other nonenforcement tasks. These include watching homes of citizens who may be out of town, helping to locate a lost child, unlocking a locked car, or serving as animal control officers. Often, the size of the police department will play a role in the specific duties officers are required to perform in the community. Five primary goals of local police can be identified:

1. Law enforcement
2. Peacekeeping and order maintenance

3. Crime prevention

4. Protecting civil rights

5. Delivery of services[14]

These goals often overlap. For example, officers intervening in a bar fight may not only enforce the law by arresting the aggressor for assault but also maintain order; prevent others from becoming involved in the altercation; protect the civil rights and civil liberties of the arrested person, the victim, and any bystanders; as well as provide emergency services to any injured persons.

Whether an officer is successful in meeting each of these goals impacts the success of carrying out the other goals. While the five goals normally established by police are listed, the fact is that policing is a single role comprised of numerous responsibilities. Furthermore, any discussion regarding the goals of police must address the many differences between small and large agencies, as well as between rural, suburban, and urban departments. For example, smaller agencies, often located in rural or suburban areas, are considerably less specialized, maintain a closer relationship with the citizens being served, and may have considerably less diversity among those citizens. On the other hand, larger agencies, often located in urban areas, are likely to be more specialized, have a more distant relationship to the citizens being served, and have much greater diversity among those citizens.

Law Enforcement

It has been the historic responsibility of the police to enforce the laws, hence the term *law enforcement officer*. It is this capacity that is most often associated with police work. In conjunction with this duty, the police officer is expressly authorized to enforce criminal law and, by offering testimony regarding the offense, must assist in the prosecution of those arrested. It is here that the traditional role of crime fighter is often depicted. In the fulfillment of these duties, officers assume many different roles, requiring them to conduct various tasks. These include enforcing traffic codes, conducting criminal investigations, protecting dignitaries, collecting evidence, interviewing witnesses and victims, interrogating suspects, making arrests, conducting covert surveillance, working in an undercover capacity, and patrolling neighborhoods.

The law enforcement function is one of the police officer's principal mandates. To achieve their enforcement objective, police officers are specifically trained and have been given broad powers of public inquiry and arrest. It is widely held that one of the most basic measures of police effectiveness is the crime rate. In reality, however, police officers spend a very small percentage of their time actually enforcing the law. Rather, a majority of their time is spent on service-related assignments while awaiting circumstances that require their crime-fighting abilities.

A basic tenet of our system of policing is that officers should attempt to promote compliance under the law and resort to arrest only when necessary. The dynamics of this principle are most apparent when considering the task of police patrol, a fundamental police duty requiring officers to resolve an array of conflict situations from quieting a barking dog to apprehending a house burglar. Although police officers are sworn to enforce all laws in their jurisdiction, in reality this cannot be accomplished. From a practical standpoint, the literal interpretation and enforcement by police of all laws on the books could mimic the liking of a totalitarian state. Imagine, if every time a motorist exceeded the posted speed limit, a police officer would show up and write a citation.

Formally, both the law and police policy require **full enforcement**, that is, complete enforcement of all laws in conjunction with constitutional standards. In reality, however, the basis for most law enforcement action lies with discretionary judgment and not an arbitrary application of rules. Only about one-fourth of all victimizations for serious crimes ever result in arrest. Reasons include legal requirements of probable cause to effect an arrest and the officer's personal set of values and

FIGURE 1.3   One of the line-level responsibilities of patrol officers is writing citations for motor vehicle violations.

norms, as well as community standards and expectations.[15] The police don't attempt to make the futile effort to enforce every law on the books.

Nevertheless, legislatures often pass criminal laws to address a number of problems, reflecting the attitude "there oughta be a law." Informally, the police practice **selective enforcement,** whereby they enforce some of the laws some of the time against some people. Crackdowns on drunk driving, prostitution, and speeding reflect some instances of selective enforcement. Because the level and use of police discretion actually increases from the police chief down to a patrol officer, officers must rely on their own judgment as they interpret vague standards when deciding whether and how to intervene. Selective enforcement does not mean that officers can act as they please in choosing when, how, and on whom to enforce criminal laws.

The actions of the police are governed by federal and state constitutions along with state and city laws regulating police conduct. Individual officers are also influenced by the desire to avoid hassles or to save their energies for other more "worthy" police pursuits. Although most police officers aggressively fight street crimes such as muggings, assaults, thefts, drug deals, and robberies, they do not target all crimes equally. For example, a highway patrol trooper once told the writer that he preferred not to write traffic citations; rather, a better use of his time was to profile drug couriers on the highway.

Peacekeeping and Order Maintenance

The functions of modern policing include much more than the task of law enforcement. The need for officers to assume the role of peace officer is more appropriate for this function. For instance, one study showed that the majority of calls received by law enforcement agencies were more related to the resolution of personal problems than the actual enforcement of laws.[16]

The mandate to keep the peace and maintain order is a broad one that attempts to prevent behaviors that threaten the public order. A distinction can be made between the terms *peacekeeping* and *order maintenance.* The peacekeeping function varies in application but includes responding to complaints of loud music in the middle of the night or forcing a panhandler or vagrant to vacate the area. On the other hand, order maintenance requires officers to interpret the law and make decisions as to the principles of proper conduct and the assignment of blame. Examples are breaking up a bar fight, intervening in a domestic disturbance, and quelling a riot.[17]

Officers operating in the patrol capacity are most commonly confronted with the order maintenance situation. In a variety of situations, they are required to confront segments of the public in ambiguous situations while practicing a broad range of discretionary powers to intervene or not. Many such situations call on the officer to make decisions that can result in the taking of another human life. As they conduct their patrol functions on foot or in motor vehicles, officers may be

American Policing under Fire

Are African-Americans Wrongfully Targeted by Police Officers?

In many African-American households, informal survival lessons are routinely passed along to children of driving age, and the training begins with a simple premise that the police are dangerous. The warnings, dispensed at kitchen tables and from the pulpit, go something like this: When the cops stop you (and they will), don't smile, don't stare, don't express emotion, and whatever you do, keep both hands on the steering wheel. In short, don't give the police any excuse to lock you up or worse.

There are no reliable national statistics on the practice of racial profiling by police. But it is widely accepted that African-Americans are disproportionately targeted by police in so many parts of the country that families in communities such as Grand Rapids, Michigan, feel compelled to prepare their children for the experience.

Here's what some African-Americans are doing around the country:

1. In St. Paul, Minnesota, the local civil liberties union has been distributing "green cards" to African-American motorists since 1996 to instruct them on traffic stop etiquette. "Be polite and stay calm," the instruction cards state. "It is your right to remain silent. However, if you refuse to answer questions, it could make the police suspicious of you."
2. In Atlanta, Georgia, Gloria Watts bought her son, Jared Jordan, an innocuous sedan, so he could avoid the police suspicion a shiny jeep might bring while commuting to and from school. The Chrysler Neon is not the most comfortable ride for the 260-pound young man, but Watts states, "I wanted him to be able to drive without having a problem. And I could direct you to ten other people in my neighborhood who have the same concern."
3. In Prince George's County, Maryland, police corporal Danon Ashton shares similar stories every time he speaks to a high school class. "When you are stopped by police as

a black man," says Raven Mason, a community advocate in Minneapolis, "you have to adopt a subservient attitude just for protection." Critics say that in traffic stops, police are far more likely to abuse, arrest, and even shoot motorists who are African-American. Ashton, Mason, and others say a recent string of lawsuits settled in favor of African-American motorists who allege they were disproportionately stopped by police in Pennsylvania and Maryland is evidence that law enforcement is in need of urgent reform.

The issue has consumed law enforcement officials in recent years, and former attorney general Janet Reno found herself potentially at odds with police chiefs. Reno favored some kind of legislation that would enable the Justice Department to document racial patterns in police stops. Police chiefs say requiring law enforcement to collect race-related data from motorists would only inflame an already tense situation.

The issue was also at the core of legislation introduced in the spring of 1999 by Rep. John Conyers of Michigan. Conyers' bill required the Justice Department to collect information about the race and ethnicity of motorists stopped by local police officers. The Justice Department supported similar legislation in 1998, but the proposal died in the Senate. In a powerful lobby, however, the International Association of Chiefs of Police (IACP) has publicly stated it will oppose any attempt to force police departments to collect race-related data. They argue that it is impossible to legislate this problem.

During the summer of 1999, in California, the American Civil Liberties Union launched a media campaign on the issue. Part of that effort included billboards showing African-American men along with the message: "If I had a dollar for every time I'd been pulled over . . ." According to African-American leaders, the real challenge for police is to present a "human face" inside the uniform.[18] (See Chapter 9 for more on racial profiling.)

called upon to intervene in crowd situations, come to the aid of someone in trouble and in need of help, or to assist people who might be incapable of helping themselves.

Domestic disturbances present a different and emotionally charged situation that officers must manage. After responding to such a situation, which might involve a family argument, the officers might be forced to determine whether one of the family members should be arrested and removed from the premises. In all these situations, officers are given the freedom to arrest or not. Where discretion is concerned, external control of the police officers is virtually nonexistent. Complicating the situation is the fact that officers are simply expected to deal with the situation rather than to literally enforce the law.

Crime Prevention

Preventing crime is closely related to the law enforcement and order maintenance functions in that if the peace is maintained, crime has probably been prevented. Crime prevention differs from peacekeeping and law enforcement in that it attempts to eliminate potentially dangerous or criminal situations. In other words, rather than being reactive, it is proactive. For example, officers on routine patrol may not only encounter a crime in progress but also prevent crimes from being committed at the same time. Many people believe that if the local police in any given community maintain a high visibility, crimes may be prevented. This notion is extremely difficult to prove, however, because it is not known what crimes might have been committed if the police were not present.

Just as police officers cannot be expected to enforce all laws all the time, they cannot be expected to prevent all crimes from occurring either. Carl Klockars suggests that the war on crime is a war in which police not only cannot win but also cannot in any real sense fight. They cannot win it because it is simply not within their power to change those things such as unemployment, age distribution in a community, moral education, freedom, civil liberties, individual ambition, and the social and economic opportunities to make them become a reality.[19] He further notes that the police cannot control economic conditions; poverty; inequality; occupational opportunity; moral, religious, family, or secular education; or dramatic social, cultural, or political change.[20] These are the primary determining factors in the amount and distribution of crime.

FIGURE 1.4 Neighborhood watch signs such as this one are commonplace throughout America and encourage citizens to provide information regarding suspected crimes in their neighborhood to police.

This is where the concept of community policing was born—the need for police and the people within the community to work together as "co-producers of crime prevention."[21] Citizens are keenly aware what the community's problems are and how they might be solved. They are on the front lines and know the pain of victimization.

Crime-prevention activities frequently undertaken by police departments include working with juveniles, cooperating with probation and parole personnel, educating the public, organizing operation identification programs, and providing visible evidence of police authority (deterrence).

Protecting Civil Rights

In addition to enforcing laws, preventing crime, and providing services, police departments are expected to observe the U.S. Constitution and the Bill of Rights in the performance of their duties.

Many citizens become angry when they learn that a suspect's rights prevent the prosecution of a criminal case. They may even grow skeptical of the criminal justice system in general. However, should the same individuals find themselves accused of a crime, they would expect and even demand their rights be fully protected. Therefore, agents of the U.S. government must guarantee all citizens, that even those perceived as unworthy of such protection, their constitutional rights, to safeguard against the specter of a police state.

The authority, goals, and methods of police must promote individual liberty, public safety, and social justice. The protection of civil rights and individual liberties is perceived by some as the single most important goal of policing.

Delivery of Services

The service function for the police is one that closely aligns with order maintenance, in the sense that officers are often called upon to provide assistance. Citizens should feel free to call the police in a variety of circumstances, not only for emergencies but also for a number of nonemergency situations that may arise. For example, officers are often called on to give directions to lost citizens, aid mentally ill persons, assist the elderly, rescue animals, and render first aid at scenes of accidents or medical emergencies.

Imagine that you have just attended a baseball game and upon returning to your car you discover that you inadvertently have locked your keys in the car. What would you do? Although you could call a locksmith, it might be faster and less expensive to call the police, for they may have the necessary tools to enter your car without damaging it. Similarly, what if you are getting ready to take a one-week trip out of state and you are afraid that your house might be burglarized? What would you do? You could call the police and ask for any crime-prevention tips they might have, or you could ask them to come by your house each day that you are gone to check locks, doors, and windows.

No study of the police is complete without considering their service-related role in the community. One of the most comprehensive studies of police–citizen interaction reported that out of 5,000 interactions the police made only 225 arrests (less than 5%).[22] While half of those arrested openly challenged police, their challenges were mainly verbal. Only 2% involved any type of physical or nonlethal force, and none involved the use of deadly force. This research suggests that police–citizen interactions are more frequently the result of citizen requests for intervention than police-initiated activities. Interestingly, studies show that an estimated 80% of police calls were matters unrelated to crime. In fact, most calls were requests for information.[23] Victims of crimes and persons seeking directions or information also frequently contact the local law enforcement agency for assistance and service. Despite the noncriminal nature of such services, many police administrators feel that the community service component has a positive effect on crime control. In performing these functions, officers not only gain a feel for the location of trouble spots in their jurisdictions but also earn the respect of the citizens whom they

A Closer Look

The American Bar Foundation Recommendations for Police Departments

1. To identify criminal offenders and criminal activity and, where appropriate, to apprehend offenders and participate in subsequent court proceedings
2. To reduce opportunities for the commission of some crime through preventive patrol and other measures
3. To aid people who are in danger of physical harm
4. To protect constitutional guarantees
5. To facilitate the movement of people and vehicles
6. To assist those who cannot care for themselves
7. To resolve conflict
8. To identify problems that are potentially serious law enforcement or governmental problems
9. To create and maintain a feeling of security in the community
10. To promote and preserve civil order
11. To provide other services on an emergency basis

serve as well. When considering how and why a function of the government acquired such a broad scope of responsibilities, one should note that police are required to be available 24 hours a day, 7 days per week. In addition, their training and structure best suit them for investigation of the foregoing tasks.

The police have always had a broad range of responsibilities, but those that they have today differ considerably from those of their predecessors. During the earliest years of policing, most of the public felt that the police were doing their job simply by investigating crime and making arrests. The idea of prevention was not even considered, nor was the notion of police intervention in domestic disputes or problems relating to juvenile delinquents. The police themselves even thought of themselves as "crime fighters" rather than "service providers." Clearly, today, there is a role conflict within the ranks of the police as they are called upon to control the public while serving them as well. In fact, so strong are the traditions of past policing that current-day police officers are often resentful when confronted with modern social expectations of them.

There is some disagreement about the number and type of services that the police should perform. For example, some people have recommended that the police narrow their focus to concentrate only on serious crime. To do so would entail transferring some traditional police duties, such as traffic enforcement, to other agencies.[24] Police functions do not fall into neatly organized categories. Rather, many police interactions, such as those with public drunks, drug addicts, mentally ill persons, and people involved in domestic disturbances, often overlap to a degree. As Wilson explains, "Though the law enforcement, order maintenance, and service functions can be analytically distinguished, concretely they are thoroughly intermixed. Even in a routine law enforcement situation, like in arresting a purse snatcher, how the officers deal with the victim and onlookers at the scene is often as important as how the suspect is handled."[25]

It has also been suggested that the crime-fighting image lends effectiveness to peacekeeping and community service. For example, effectiveness often relies on respect for police authority, in particular the authority to use force if necessary. A wife batterer will probably be less confrontational in the presence of an officer who is more of a crime fighter than a service-oriented officer.

In Retrospect

As we have seen in this chapter, the role and functions of police are varied in U.S. society. What the police do is determined by a number of variables, which include politics and ideology, expectations of the public, and past experience in policing. How the police work is guided by criminal and constitutional law as well as by the dynamics of individual police officer behavior and how individual officers perceive the citizenry, the law, and their role as the police. In carrying out their role, officers must always be aware of the overriding need to balance public safety with a safeguarding of individual rights.

Five primary functions exist with regard to police services: law enforcement, peacekeeping and order maintenance, crime prevention, protecting civil rights, and delivery of services. These functions encompass the majority of duties required of police officers. The functions of police officers are closely related to the development of the police subculture. Although this culture represents a close-knit bond between officers, this bond begins to develop almost immediately upon acceptance to the police academy. Once an officer is on the street for a while, he or she develops a working style. Cases that represent the manner in which officers exercise their duties and perceive themselves in their role as police officers are discussed in the chapter.

Improve Your Professional Vocabulary

enforcement	majority rule	reactive
full enforcement	minority rights	selective
impossible mandate	proactive	

Discussion Questions

1. In what ways do you think political ideologies influence the role of the police in our society?
2. Discuss the police role and the rule of law and how laws aid or impede the effectiveness of police officers.
3. Explain what is meant by the terms *majority rule* and *minority rights*.
4. Describe the meaning of the term *impossible mandate*.
5. How do you think the stereotypical image of police as portrayed by movies and books aids or hinders the effectiveness of the police?
6. What are the five goals of policing?
7. Which of the functions of police contribute best to crime control and positive community relations?
8. Distinguish between *full* and *selective* enforcement.
9. Discuss the manner in which police officer working styles interact with the functions of police.
10. List and discuss the types of services provided by the police.

Notes

1. Gaines, L., V. Kappeler, & J. B. Vaughn. (1997). *The police in America*, 2nd ed. Cincinnati: Anderson Publishing.
2. Ibid.
3. Ibid.
4. Sherman, L., D. C. Gottfredson, D. MacKenzie, J. Eck, P. Reuter, & S. D. Bushway. (1998, July). *Preventing crime: What works, what doesn't, what's promising.* National Institute of Justice. Research in Brief.
5. Klockars, C. B. (1985). *The idea of police.* Beverly Hills, CA: Sage.
6. Bittner, E. (1976). Community relations, in A. W. Cohn and E. C. Viano, eds., *Police community relations: Images, roles and realities.* Philadelphia: J. B. Lippincott.
7. Klockars, C. B. (1985). *The idea of police.* Beverly Hills, CA: Sage.
8. Goldstein, H. (1977). *Policing a free society.* Cambridge, MA: Ballinger.
9. O'Driscoll, P. (2000, April.11). A new take on JonBenét. *USA Today,* p. 3A.
10. Manning, P. K., & J. Van Maanen. (1978). *Policing: A view from the street.* Santa Monica, CA: Goodyear.
11. Reaves, J. (2000, March 6). Black and blue. *Time,* pp. 3–4.
12. Walker, S. (1992). *The police in America.* New York: McGraw-Hill.
13. Reiss, A. J., Jr. (1967). *The police and the public.* New Haven, CT: Yale University Press.
14. Wilson, J. Q. (1968). *Varieties of police behavior.* Cambridge, MA: Harvard University Press.
15. Forst, B., et al. (1977). What happens after arrest? *BJS Report to the Nation,* 62. Washington, DC: National Institute of Law Enforcement and Criminal Justice, p. 17.
16. Cumming, E., I. M. Cumming, & L. Edell. (1965). Policeman as philosopher, guide and friend. *Social Problems,* 12, pp. 267–286.

17. Gains, L. K., V. E. Kappler, & J. B. Vaughn. (1994). *Policing in America*. Cincinnati, OH: Anderson.

18. Johnson, K. (1999, April 20). Blacks speak out about fear of police officers: Parents teach children to deal with traffic stops. *USA Today,* p. 3A.

19. Klockars, C. (1991). *The rhetoric or community policing.* In J. R. Green & S. D. Mastrofski, eds., *Community policing: Rhetoric or reality?* New York: Praeger Publications.

20. Ibid.

21. Ibid.

22. Reiss, A. J., Jr. (1967). *The police and the public.* New Haven, CT: Yale University Press.

23. Ibid.

24. Morris, N., & G. Hawkins. (1967). *The honest politician's guide to crime control.* Chicago: University of Chicago Press.

25. Wilson, J. Q. (1975). *Thinking about crime.* New York: Basic Books.

CHAPTER 2

Historical Foundations of Policing

This chapter will enable you to:

- Identify notable persons throughout history who made valuable contributions to modern policing in the United States.

- Recognize the old Peelian philosophies in current public mandates for police behavior.

- Identify significant differences in the formulation of police systems in Colonial America and the established police system in England.

- Describe the stages of police development in the United States.

- Understand how technology and public reform contributed to the alienation of the police from the citizenry.

New York City experienced soaring rates of crime during the 1980s. This was followed by great reductions in the crime rate during the tenure of Mayor Rudolph Giuliani in the 1990s. One reason for the change in direction was that Giuliani, a former federal prosecutor, advocated the use of aggressive policing that strictly enforced the law and combated public disorder.

Compelling evidence suggests that the tougher policing methods resulted in safer streets in New York. During Giuliani's tenure, public disorder crimes—such as graffiti, turnstile jumping, and open-air drug sales—declined significantly. More serious crimes also decreased: for example, gun homicides declined by 75%. Law enforcement officers became more efficient, as evidenced by a 25% reduction in officer use of firearms, 67% reduction in shootings per officer, and 150% increase in arrests.

These improvements were not lost on New Yorkers. At the end of Giuliani's time in office, nearly 85% of the city's residents held favorable views of the police. Some of the many questions that are raised by this fascinating phenomenon are: To what extent should police be encouraged to use aggressive policing tactics in fighting crime? And, to what extent are politicians responsible, or to what extent should they take credit for reductions in crime? These and other questions come into play as we consider the historical developments of policing in the United States.

Police officers are a product of their history. To fully understand the structure and functions of the police, it is first necessary to examine them in their historical context. Studying police history provides valuable insights into modern police agencies and procedures. Knowledge of how and why changes in policing occurred can help guide police in the future as they encounter new demands and challenges. Accordingly, familiarity with police history informs modern police problems, such as the use of force and corruption, and provides assistance in dealing with these issues.

All societies maintain order somehow, and whether they do so with the police is a matter of definition. In today's society the word *police* generally refers to persons employed by the government who are authorized to use physical force to maintain public safety and order. Police officers are the most visible component of a government in society. Whether they are local police officers, county deputies, state highway patrol troopers, or federal agents, the almost 870,000 law enforcement officers on U.S. streets play a crucial role in every community. Much responsibility is entrusted to the police as citizens expect them to perform a number of functions and services. Unfortunately, it is not always clear just exactly what those functions and services are or should be.

The police are usually identified by uniform clothing, which is distinctive to the profession, as is their right to carry firearms and make arrests. However, the history of police is infinitely expandable since one of the duties of the police, maintaining order in society, may also be accomplished through interactions with persons in nongovernmental roles, such as teachers, judges, legislators, and members of clergy. Even when the term *police* refers to the dominant modern form, there are many ambiguities in application, both contemporarily and historically. For example, many governmental officials may be authorized to employ force when necessary, but doing so may not be required in many police-related operations, such as searching for lost children or directing traffic. In addition, it is not always clear when a person may be regarded as a government official. The medieval constable, although an officer of the common law, was paid privately by people who wanted to escape the obligatory civic duty of police service. The same is true of the U.S. posse, a deputized unpaid group of citizens. On the other hand, the English sheriff, whose office was created about the same time as the constable, was both appointed and paid by the crown.

So there can be both public and private police, and the distinction between the two is not always clear to members of the general citizenry. Thus, the boundaries of the history of police are both ambiguous and arbitrary, depending on the definition of the word *police*. Understanding the history of police does little in clarifying police functions because the roles of police over time have often been contradictory in nature. For example, are the police social service agents or law enforcers? Should the police serve the people in a community or the government in that community?

The subject of law and order has been a concern since the beginning of recorded history. In thirteenth-century England, the Magna Carta placed limitations on constables and bailiffs, possibly to control police abuse of power and to ensure the maintenance of order. Even then, remedies for police-related problems were better selection and recruitment to ensure that order maintenance was in accordance with the rule of law.

ANCIENT POLICE SYSTEMS

In the ancient empires, law enforcement was primarily a function of the military. Armies were responsible for protecting emperors from outside invaders, and in many cases special units operating as part of the army would be charged with protecting rulers from internal threats. Thus the actions of the protectors were often guided by whims of emperors rather than by the rule of law. Unfortunately, much of what we know about early police systems is restricted to major historical events, and little specific information is available. When studying the formulation of early criminal codes, we know that one of the oldest is the Code of Hammurabi, developed by the king of Babylonia around 2100 B.C.[1] The early Egyptians established laws and courts and a rudimentary rule of law. They later organized marine patrols and custom houses to protect commerce.

Police Development in Ancient Greece

Ancient Greeks also established their own crude system of policing and justice. Rather than a formal police force, they relied on an informal system of "kin police," whereby the victim's family would be empowered to serve as the police and bring the wrongdoer before the magistrate. This system was inadequate at best and soon resulted in widespread lawlessness. The need for police was identified, and a large security force of bodyguards acting as police was established. Bodyguards were widely used as police throughout much of the early history of Greece.

Police Development in Ancient Rome

The development of Roman law resulted from a general political movement toward centralized authority. As a rule, traditional Roman society was organized along strong kinship lines where rigid distinctions were made between domestic and civil responsibilities. Roman families were patriarchal, headed by *pater familias*, or the father, who was the head of the family. Each father had absolute authority over his family and all property associated with the family. Each Roman owed his first allegiance to the family, and the government would not interfere in family matters. Even if a Roman was convicted of a crime, it would be the family who would impose the punishment, not the government.[2]

Changes came with the reign of Augustus, who in 27 B.C. began a movement that continued for some 500 years in which the state, through the Emperor, came to dominate all aspects of Roman life. Over time the power of the family was reduced and that of the government increased. By breaking the bonds of kinship, the Roman emperors created a monopoly on power in Rome. Augustus, among other things, created the Praetorian Guard, which consisted of about 7,000 soldiers within the city of Rome itself. The guard watched the outer perimeters of the city for criminals and invading armies. Hence, the concept of a dedicated "police" force had its beginnings. In addition, other officials, such as *quaestores*, worked for magistrates and had arrest authority. *Vigiles* also served as watchmen and were responsible for both police and firefighting duties. Gradually, the maintenance of public order became the charge of the police in Rome, which took control over the management of public disputes.

The Middle Ages

After over four thousand years of legal development, the centralized style of government required for successful maintenance of law and order ended with the fall of the Roman Empire, an era known as the Middle Ages. Indeed, the historical legal groundwork laid by the Greeks and Romans was all but forgotten. As a means to restore social order from the chaos, the feudal system soon developed. Under feudalism, a social structure was built on the premise of mutual social responsibility. As a rule, however, feudal lords administered justice to those under their control as they deemed necessary. During this period, the church also played a role in determining what constituted a criminal violation as well as how the infraction was to be arbitrated. Interestingly, neither the feudal lords nor the churches answered to a central authority. This period was also characterized by a centuries-long struggle between the power of the crown to consolidate control of the administration of justice and the persistence of the feudal lords and the church to preserve their independent judicial power.[3]

As the twelfth and thirteenth centuries unfolded, kings began to assume responsibility for administration of law and to maintain officials for that purpose. In thirteenth-century Paris, Louis IX created a provost who, assisted by investigating commissioners and sergeants, directed the night watch and commanded a mounted guard. This was the beginning of the *Maréchausée*, which became the *Gendarmerie* that today polices areas outside major towns. In the early fourteenth century, highways were made safe by mounted military patrols. In twelfth-century Scandinavia, the *gjaldkere* was given administrative responsibility of towns, which included responsibility of law and order. Their counterparts, the *lensman*, enforced the law and collected taxes.

POLICE DEVELOPMENT IN ENGLAND

U.S. law enforcement can be traced back to the English experience in fighting crime in densely populated urban areas. Before the Norman Conquest, there was no typical English police force. At the lowest enforcement level, citizens grouped when trouble erupted and the townsman was to make a **hue and cry**, a summon for help.

Then in the twelfth century in England, sheriffs were appointed to levy fines and ensure that the **frankpledge system** worked. This system has existed for centuries and was based on an organization of **tithings**, collectives of ten families, and hundreds (ten tithings). Eventually, these hundreds became known as *parishes*, and several hundreds became known as a *shire*. The area made up of several hundreds was similar to a modern-day county and was supervised by reeves or shire-reeves, later called *sheriffs*.

In this system, men over the age of 15 formed a *posse comitatus*, a group called out to pursue fleeing felons. In 1285 the **Statute of Winchester** mandated that every hundred men be appointed to constables to assist the sheriff. By the fourteenth century, law was administered by magistrates who were appointed by the king, sheriffs, and constables.

In 1326 the office of *Justice of the Peace* was created in England. The individual holding this position assisted the sheriff in policing the county. During this time, the constable's role also became increasingly important. The constable became an assistant to the justice of the peace; constables also conducted investigations, served summons and warrants, took charge of prisoners, and supervised the "night watch." Furthermore, the sheriff continued to play an important role. This established foundations for a system of law enforcement that was to stay in place until the 1800s.

However, much of the work of these individuals (with the exception of the sheriff) was voluntary and not particularly popular, so the work of paying for substitutes became commonplace. In many cases, the same person was paid year after year due to the work of those who were appointed to the position but did not wish to serve. Often the substitutes were inadequately paid, elderly, poorly educated, and inefficient. Of course, this did nothing for the image of policing in the community.

At the end of the 1700s families by the thousands began to travel to factory towns to find work. Patterns of lives were disrupted, and unprecedented social disorder ensued. Existing systems of law enforcement, primarily the justice of the peace and the constable, were inadequate to respond to the problems associated with these changes.

In the justice-constable **night watch** system, the constables, who were appointed by the local justices, patrolled their parishes during the day. The constable had limited power, and when he tried to obtain citizen assistance by raising a hue and cry to capture a fleeing criminal, he was more likely to be ridiculed than assisted by citizens. At night, men of the watch were charged with patrolling deserted streets and maintaining street lamps. However, these individuals were more likely to be found sleeping or causing problems than performing these duties.

The Bow Street Runners

In London, criminals had little to fear from the system of law enforcement, and they moved freely about the city streets. Victims of crime, if well-to-do, were protected by servants and retainers (a bodyguard, or type of private police). However, poorer citizens had no such protection. When property crimes were committed, the usual procedure was to employ a **thief-taker**, or "thief catcher." This person, usually an inexperienced constable familiar with the criminal underworld, would attempt, for a fee, to secure a return of all or part of the stolen property. Often the thief-taker would supplement his fee by keeping part of the stolen property for himself. Thief-takers were not interested in apprehending and prosecuting criminals, but only in getting paid and returning all or part of the stolen property.

Henry Fielding, best known for his eighteenth-century novel *Tom Jones*, is credited by some as establishing the groundwork for the first modern police force. In the mid-eighteenth century and in the wake of London's industrialization, Fielding was appointed magistrate in Westminster. It was there, on Bow Street, that the first English police squadron was born. During the early eighteenth century, a large criminal fencing organization led by Jonathan Wild employed a loosely organized group of thieves and robbers who would turn their spoils over to Wild. He would then negotiate with the rightful owners of the property for a ransom of their possessions. Police response was generally slow, due to corruption and apathy. However, Henry Fielding and his investigators set out to change things. As a first step, he established working relationships with local pawnbrokers and gave them lists and descriptions of newly stolen property. He subsequently requested them to alert him if the property showed up at their shops.

Fielding then placed an advertisement in the London and Westminster newspapers, requesting descriptions of known thieves and robbers in the communities. Fielding's idea was an original concept, as people were not used to sharing information of thefts with authorities. Within the first year, Fielding's efforts were joined by several other constables, who helped form one of the first (unofficial) investigative squads in England, the Bow Street Runners. The Runners were not official police and therefore were not entitled to regular pay. However, upon capture of criminals, they were still entitled to the standard thief-takers' rewards. After a short period of time, Fielding's venture was acknowledged by the government, which offered a small financial subsidy for the continuation of his efforts.

The Runners continued to operate in an unofficial capacity, for had it been known that they were supported with public funds, such a practice would have most likely been publicly condemned as an instrument of oppression. Four years following Fielding's appointment as magistrate, his health declined, restricting him to a wheelchair. After some persuasion, Fielding's half-brother John, the "Blind Beak," was appointed to share his judgeship. The successes of the Bow Street Runners continued until the gradual formation of a horse patrol in 1804. The patrol employed over 50 men, whose uniform consisted of red vests, blue jackets, and blue trousers. This was considered by many to be England's first uniformed police force.

PROFESSIONALIZATION AND THE ENGLISH POLICE

Prompted by an increasing concern with safety and security in a rapidly growing London, six parliamentary commissions studied the problem of policing between 1770 and 1828. Prime Minister William Pitt attempted to create a metropolitan police force in 1785, but the attempt floundered on the opposition of commercial interests. Scottish-born merchant Patrick Colquhoun authored the *Treatise on the Police of the Metropolis*, which estimated the extent and cost of crime and suggested that due to the extent of criminality in England, British law enforcement follow the model of the French police, widely considered a subversive and oppressive organization.

Colquhoun rationalized that a complex and interdependent city relying on commerce for its livelihood cannot tolerate extensive criminal activity.[4] As a result of Colquhoun's *Treatise*, the Thames Police Act (1800) was passed. This statute authorized the establishment of a separate police jurisdiction designed to safeguard the Thames River and adjacent land areas from thieves, who exhibited considerable innovation in their craft. The establishment of the river police was responsible, at least in part, for paving the way for the police reforms promoted by Robert Peel in the coming years.

The London Metropolitan Police

The great watershed in police development occurred in 1829 with the establishment of the London Metropolitan Police Department. For years, Sir Robert Peel, England's home secretary, advocated the use of full-time professional police officers to patrol London. Although Peel drew many of his ideas from centuries of English tradition, his new system of policing was notably different than those in generations gone by. In his book *The Police and the Community*, Radelet pointed out, "In the Anglo-Saxon England of a thousand years ago, every able-bodied free man was a police officer. Every male from 15 to 60 maintained such arms as he could afford. When the hue and cry was raised, every man within earshot dropped whatever he was doing and joined in pursuit of the transgressor. Not to do so was serious neglect of duty."[5]

As advocates of community policing freely concede, the concept is not new. Rather, it represents a return to the principles of policing laid down by Sir Robert Peel, the nineteenth-century

FIGURE 2.1   An English police officer or "Bobby" in uniform with his tall domed helmet that carries the police insignia.

British statesman, when he helped establish the London Metropolitan Police Department in 1829. In Peel's view, these were the main tenets of modern policing.

Despite considerable opposition, the Metropolitan Police Act was finally passed by Parliament, authorizing a police force of 1,000 unarmed officers known as **bobbies,** named for Peel. The new force, replacing the inept and unprofessional constables of the myriad parishes, was led by two magistrates, who later were given the title of commissioner. The police department was structured along military lines. London's first commissioners were career military officer Colonel Charles Rowan and attorney Richard Mayne. Rowan, whom Peel first met in Ireland while Rowan was serving as a police magistrate, believed that the police and the citizenry must have mutual respect in order for the new policing system to be effective. As a result, bobbies

A Closer Look

Sir Robert Peel (1778–1850)

As one of the most influential pioneers in modern policing, Sir Robert Peel paved the way to professionalizing police work during his tenure as the home secretary of England in 1822. Initially, he set out to reform criminal law by rewriting all offenses and postulated that legal reform can only be accomplished with the aid of improved crime-prevention techniques. In 1829, despite much opposition, Peel successfully convinced Parliament to pass the Metropolitan Police Act, which established the first full-time professional police force in the greater London area.

This resulted in abolition of the fragmented and unprofessional private law enforcement system that was prevalent at that time. A committed bureaucrat, Peel's goal was to reduce governmental waste through an efficient and effective civil service that could be trusted to serve the state rather than special interests. In addition to advocating full-time careers for police officers, he advocated compliance with the law through the use of deterrence in enforcement efforts. He believed that the fundamental function of the police was preventive patrol by officers who did not carry guns but who were visually present in the community. Peel's officers were dubbed "**bobbies**," a nickname that has endured to the present.

The new police system in England created standards and efficiency that generated considerable local demand for its services. In fact, it was considered such a great success that outlying rural areas began to summon London's police for law enforcement assistance. A subsequent act passed by Parliament soon permitted justices of the peace to establish local police battalions in their jurisdictions. By 1856, all counties in England were compelled to organize their own police forces, most of which were modeled after London's force. Thus modern-day law enforcement finally became a reality.

would give the impression of professionalism through wearing distinctive uniforms and meeting strict standards of height, weight, character, and literacy. Training was afforded along the lines of a close-order drill. Manning suggests that during the early part of the nineteenth century, English police had a four-part mandate:

1. To prevent local disturbances without the use of repressive force and to avoid intervention by the military
2. To control public order nonviolently, using force to gain compliance only as a last resort
3. To reduce conflict between the public and the police
4. To demonstrate efficiency through the absence of crime and disorder rather than by visible evidence of oppressive police action[6]

By 1842, the Metropolitan Police established its first detective unit, with specially selected and assigned officers. While maintaining a close association with the patrol division, investigators were guaranteed cooperation and sources of information while providing the bobbies on the beat an incentive for polishing their policing skills.

As a result of the English model of policing, three characteristics of U.S. law enforcement have evolved: (1) local control, (2) limited authority, and (3) organizational fragmentation. Like our English counterparts, there is no national police force in the United States but, rather, local community control. Accordingly, law enforcement is fragmented, with many different agencies representing different levels of government and various jurisdictions. These agencies include the Federal Bureau of Investigation (FBI), Drug Enforcement Administration (DEA), state highway patrols, county sheriffs, and city police departments. Our current system of law enforcement, however, was slow in its evolution.

Highlights in Policing

Peel's Principles of Professional Policing

1. The basic mission for which police exist is to prevent crime and disorder as an alternative to the repression of crime and disorder by military force and lessen the severity of legal punishment.
2. The ability of the police to perform their duties is dependent on public approval of police existence, actions, behavior, and the ability of the police to secure and maintain public respect.
3. The police must secure the willing cooperation of the public in voluntary observance of the law to be able to secure and maintain public respect.
4. The degree of cooperation of the public that can be secured diminishes, proportionately, the necessity for the use of physical force and compulsion in achieving police objectives.
5. The police seek and preserve public favor, not by catering to public opinion, but by constantly demonstrating absolutely impartial service to the law, in complete independence of policy, and without regard to the justice or injustice of the substance of individual laws; by ready offering of individual service and friendship to all members of society without regard to their race or social standing; by ready exercise of

courtesy and a friendly good humor; and by ready offering of individual sacrifice in protecting and preserving life.
6. The police should use physical force to the extent necessary to secure observance of the law or to restore order only when the exercise of persuasion, advice, and warning is found to be insufficient to achieve police objectives; police should use only the minimum degree of physical force necessary on any particular occasion for achieving a police objective.
7. The police should at all times maintain a relationship with the public that gives reality to the historic tradition that the police are the public and the public are the police; the police are the only members of the public who give full-time attention to duties that are incumbent on every citizen in the interest of the community welfare.
8. The police should always direct their actions toward their functions and never appear to usurp the powers of the judiciary by avenging individuals or the state, or authoritatively judging guilt or punishing the guilty.
9. The test of police efficiency is the absence of crime and disorder, not the visible evidence of police action in dealing with them.[7]

FIGURE 2.2   A New York City police officer around 1910.

EARLY AMERICAN POLICING (1600–1860)

People tend to perceive police departments as highly structured, salaried bureaucracies, where most members wear uniforms. Such organizations began in the United States in the generation before 1860. From the beginning, the police department has been a multipurpose agency of the municipal government, not just a component of the criminal justice system. New York police officers in the 1850s, for example, spent more time locating stray horses and lost children than they did solving burglaries, just as their counterparts a century later labored to keep traffic moving and filled out paperwork on fender benders. Understanding the origins of U.S. police therefore requires attention to the general context of urban government, as well as official responses to crime and disorder.

The earliest inhabitants of colonial cities in the seventeenth century still had at least one foot in the Middle Ages. Their worldview was dominated by scarcity. The Government's most important task was to regulate economic life so that strangers did not usurp work rightfully belonging to residents, wandering poor gained the right to local relief, or greedy entrepreneurs did not take undue advantage of consumers. Public officials did not think of the government as a provider of services financed through the collection of taxes. The government did encourage private interests to undertake necessary projects, such as streets and wharves, for which the public purse was inadequate. In New York City one mechanism to achieve such goals was to transfer public land to private ownership in return for specific commitments to the construction of public facilities.

In the late eighteenth and early nineteenth centuries, a new worldview came to prevail, at least among the elite, one characterized by the prospect of growth and perhaps even of abundance rather than scarcity. Adam Smith's *Wealth of Nations*, published in 1776, gave a convincing theoretical statement of how the pursuit of individual interests could lead to general economic growth if the market were free of government-granted monopolies or private combinations in restraint of trade. In this intellectual climate, government would be more a promoter of growth than a regulator of scarcity by helping provide what modern economists know as social overhead capital and what the nineteenth century called improvements.

Thus, government now paid for new wharves and streets, built canals, and promoted the development of railways. Tax-supported schools, at least in theory, produced a disciplined and literate labor force; gas lamps made night a little less gloomy and fearful; and publicly equipped, although not yet paid, fire companies provided some protection against this major urban hazard. By 1860, 12 of the 16 largest cities had public water systems to aid in firefighting and to give residents something to drink other than alcohol or possibly fouled well water.

Urban Growth and the Need for Police

Between 1820 and 1860, U.S. cities attracted unprecedented numbers of migrants, whether from rural America, Ireland, or Germany. Growth was the reality as well as a theoretical possibility. Whereas only one of twenty Americans lived in an urban settlement in 1790, the ratio was one in five in 1860. New York and Brooklyn together accounted for more than 1 million people; Philadelphia more than 500,000; and Chicago, not incorporated until 1833, had more than 100,000 residents in 1860. By the early 1870s, the city of Chicago was spending in a day what had sufficed for an entire year in the late 1840s.

When municipal governments examined growth and its consequences, they were both exhilarated and fearful. Historian Edward Pessen has demonstrated that the business elite exercised disproportionate influence on urban government throughout the so-called "age of the common man." When city councils became less patrician and more plebeian in the late 1840s and 1850s, they also lost many of their former functions. Independent boards and commissions replaced council committees as the overseers of public services, while the mayor, almost invariably a leading business or professional man, became a more powerful figure.

The council, usually elected by wards, more often reacted to external initiatives than proposing measures of its own, at least for anything that went beyond the neighborhood level. Most members of the elite liked growth; their businesses and real-estate holdings appreciated in value with more people and higher levels of economic activity. They did not like some of the negative consequences, such as larger numbers of strangers, non-English-speaking immigrants bringing with them new customs and religions who often failed to recognize the cultural superiority and natural righteousness of old-stock American Protestants. Some members of the elite were also troubled by the visible increase in the number of poor and dependent people who neither benefited from the city's growth nor seemed able to cope with its complexity.

Riots, often with specific political targets and goals, were common in preindustrial urban life. Rioters rarely took life, although they often destroyed considerable property. The most famous riots were those associated with the American Revolution, such as the protests over the Stamp Act of 1765, the protest over the Boston Massacre of 1770, and the Boston Tea Party of 1773. The decades before the revolutionary agitation also experienced periodic urban disorders. The most savage reprisals were directed at slaves thought to be plotting against whites, such as in New York City in 1712 and 1741. In most instances rioters seemed content to disperse once they had made their point, whether it was antipopery or a protest against body snatching by doctors and medical students. But by the 1820s, middle- and upper-class urbanites no longer seemed willing to accept levels of unseemly behavior in public places previously thought unavoidable.

From the early eighteenth century onward, urbanites such as Benjamin Franklin organized voluntary societies to achieve desirable social goals. The pace of this activity accelerated in the generation after 1815, especially under the auspices of religious groups who wished to spread the good news of salvation through the publication and distribution of bibles and tracts, to reach children in Sunday schools, to uplift the poor, and to reform juvenile delinquents and fallen women. Whenever families failed in their tasks of nurturing and disciplining their members, other institutions had to step in to remedy the deficiencies. A case in point is New York's House of Refuge, founded by the privately established Society for the Reformation of Juvenile Delinquents in 1825, which received state support for this purpose.

Urban Conditions

Cities created police departments during a period of U.S. history characterized by massive social change brought about by industrialization, immigration, and urbanization. Between 1860 and 1910 the modern U.S. city emerged, as the total population of the country tripled to 92 million. The number of people living in cities grew from a low of 5% in the early nineteenth century to over 45% by 1910. The largest cities—Boston, New York, and Philadelphia—had fewer than 100,000 people in the early nineteenth century and more than 1 million by 1890.[8] This growth did not occur just on the eastern seaboard. Midwestern cities such as St. Louis, Cleveland, and Detroit ranked fourth, sixth, and ninth, respectively, by 1910. Chicago, which was eighth in 1860 with a population of 100,000, moved to second place by 1910 with a population of over 2 million.

Population shifts and immigration rates increased during prosperity and decreased during economic recessions. The resultant strains produced by these economic and population shifts created new challenges for cities that had been organized and operated on a model more appropriate to the pre-urban period of the eighteenth century. One of the new challenges was the need to address the problem of maintaining order in the cities. Cities such as New York, Boston, and Philadelphia created their uniformed police organizations during a period of great social and political turmoil. Some cities experienced riots, others saw rising property crimes, still others had social problems with immigrants and a mobile population. Each of these problems varied in intensity and importance from city to city. But all cities experienced the effects of industrialization and urbanization in some form. Population growth mushroomed and the demands on urban government for services increased dramatically.

Certainly, there was a need for an effective order-maintenance institution. The constable and watch systems of the eighteenth century did not contribute to a sense of security for the community and were not designed to address a preventive role. The constable was attached to the courts and did not serve as an official of city government. The constable-watch system did not act to prevent crime but operated on a reactive basis. For a fee, constables would investigate a crime after the fact and report to the victim who was paying the reward. This form of entrepreneurial policing, although beneficial to some, simply could not address the changing levels of disorder and crime.[9]

The Rise of U.S. Urban Police Departments

The model of the London police prompted U.S. urban leaders to think about establishing police institutions structured similarly, especially since their own cities were undergoing considerable social change. In New York, the city's population had grown almost fourfold between 1790 and 1820—between 1820 and 1860 the growth was more than sevenfold. Before the mid-1820s, city officials considered their problems of crime and disorder to be manageable, but by the mid-1830s they were concerned about spreading instances of street violence. Indeed, 1834 was long remembered in the city's history as the year of riots.

When the great fire struck a year later, authorities could neither fight the fire effectively nor control looting without calling out the militia. Sensational murder cases went undetected and largely uninvestigated unless someone put up substantial reward money. Periodic economic panic and crises meant that thousands of unemployed men and women on the margins of subsistence would fall below it without some form of assistance. Boston and Philadelphia also experienced conflict among religious, ethnic, and class rivals, while cities with substantial slave populations were concerned, above all else, with controlling their blacks.

The New York City Police Department

After a decade of debate, it became clear that a logical response to the growing problem of urban violence was to establish a police department. Finally, state lawmakers adopted legislation in 1844 creating the police department and setting forth its powers and structure in detail. The law required municipal approval before it became effective. This approval was granted in 1845. Increasingly, both legal theorists and municipal officials took the position that any extension of municipal powers required direct action by the state legislature. For the remainder of the nineteenth century, state legislatures sometimes exercised their prerogative to intervene in urban police departments in a heavy-handed fashion.

The city made the police responsible for a wide range of services, from inspecting hacks and stages to lighting the gas lamps in the evening. Over time, many of these functions were transferred to other agencies, but the point is that the police were never thought of exclusively as a crime-fighting and order-maintenance group. The police did have some important responsibilities in keeping the peace and dealing with criminals. In the colonial period, order maintenance and crime fighting were more the responsibility of citizens and communities than of a bureaucratic agency. The colonists brought with them such traditional English institutions as elected constables and the night watch. In theory, constables had extensive legal responsibilities and powers, although rarely did their prestige and authority match their legal position. The watch, often made up of reluctant citizens, kept a lookout for fire as well as crime and disorder. In the case of crime, the aggrieved party bore the burden of initiating the processes of apprehension and prosecution.

By the early nineteenth century, New York had more than 100 persons with police powers, either as elected constables or as appointed mayor's marshals. These officers spent much of their time in the service of civil processes, although they were available for hire by victims of theft. They made a specialty of returning stolen property in exchange for a bounty, usually consisting of a portion of the recovery. Early nineteenth-century police officers were thus fee-for-service professionals rather than salaried bureaucrats.

A Different Structure

The New York Police Department was a salaried bureaucracy differing in significant ways from the London police, even though its first set of rules and regulations was largely copied from London's. The New York police were not uniformed, although members did carry a star-shaped badge for identification. Originally, the term of office was one year, raised to two in 1846 and four in 1849. The alderman of the particular ward had the most to say about who should serve as police officers. If an alderman was voted out of office, most of the police officers he appointed also lost their jobs. The force was decentralized in that each ward constituted a patrol district with little central supervision.

In 1853 a new law made major changes in the organization and administration of the police. It established a board of police commissioners, consisting of the mayor, the city judge, and the recorder (a judicial official), thus reducing the aldermen's role in appointments and administration. Police officers now could be removed only for cause, thus making police work a career. The practice of naming people to senior positions without prior police experience died out, and the standard became entry at the bottom and promotion from within. The new commissioners put the police into uniforms, an innovation resisted without success by some men who cherished their anonymity.

Although the New York police now looked like their London counterparts, there were still substantial differences between the two departments. London's administrators stressed careful control of the use of police powers and tried to keep the police from having to perform unpopular tasks such as closing drinking places on Sunday. In New York, ultimate authority over the police lay in the hands of locally elected officials who, along with New York's judges, were more prone to let the police take a tougher approach than their counterparts in London. Historian Wilbur Miller, Jr., has documented how the New York police were more inclined to use force and make arrests on suspicion than were London's. Despite police rhetoric about judicial intervention or not being backed up, they were rarely disciplined for such actions or discouraged from using such tactics. London's police were generally more circumspect in their dealings with citizens because their superiors wanted them to embody the moral authority of the state, with the uniform accepted as its legitimate symbol.

An obvious and very important difference was the unarmed police of London compared with the armed police of New York. Throughout the nineteenth and most of the twentieth centuries, English police officers were not armed; in recent years a rising volume of violent crime has led to serious questioning of this policy. In New York the police were not armed early in their history. Officers began to carry weapons without legal authorization to do so because they perceived their working environment as dangerously unpredictable. Samuel Colt's technological innovations made handguns cheaper and more readily available in the 1850s. New York newspapers complained in the mid-1850s that the streets of New York were more dangerous than the plains of Kansas, while historians Roger Lane and David Johnson have noted the prevalence of violent crime in Philadelphia during these years. The arming of U.S. police, begun by officers without legal authorization, soon became enshrined in custom. Unlike their British counterparts, U.S. public authorities took the position that the tough, armed cop was the best response to the pervasive problem of crime and disorder within their cities.

Police departments joined other public institutions, such as school systems, as instruments of order, stability, and upliftment to cope with an explosively growing and often disorderly urban environment. Within the ranks, station house socialization passed the norms of the veterans along to the rookies, norms that had less to do with law enforcement than with maintenance of group solidarity and respect. Don't talk about police business to outsiders and don't take any guff from civilians were more important than the statute books or the rules and regulations set forth by the department in such minute details. At top levels, such as among board members and commissioners, political winds could blow harshly.

In 1857 the New York state legislature abolished the municipal police and substituted it with a new department, the Metropolitan Police, with responsibilities for an enlarged district. New York City still had to pay for the officers assigned within its boundaries. This arrangement lasted for 13 years. In other states as well, legislatures stepped in and replaced persons holding senior administrative positions. These interventions were usually related to some hope of partisan advantage or distaste for the way city police were or were not enforcing liquor and vice laws. One branch not always provided for in the first stages of a bureaucratic policy was the detectives. If a preventive police were fully effective, there would be no need for detectives. Establishing a detective squad was an admission that the police had not lived up to expectations. And there was the old fear that detectives and criminals were much too close. Roger Lane has shown how slow Philadelphia was in assigning police officers to work as homicide specialists.

Marxist scholars treat U.S. police within a conceptual framework of class analysis. Historians such as Sidney Harring and Sean Wilentz look at the police as an instrument created by the owners of the means of production to control workers' behavior. The most obvious instances of such control came in strikes, where the police aided owners who wished to keep operating despite turnouts of their workforce. In such situations, say these scholars, the naked realities could not be disguised under such formulas as enforcing the law or protecting life and property. One does not have to be a Marxist to acknowledge that in large cities, at least, local police departments were seldom neutral in labor disputes.

The Trend Continued

Just as London provided the model for New York, Boston, and Philadelphia, these eastern cities served as models for other U.S. communities. Historian Eric Monkkonen cites the establishment of bureaucratic police departments as an innovation beginning in the older and larger cities and then diffusing surprisingly quickly out of and down the urban hierarchy. According to Monkkonen, 15 cities had adopted uniforms as key indicators of a bureaucratic police by 1860 while another 24 joined them in the following decade. Evidently, the salaried, bureaucratic police was an idea whose time had come between 1840 and 1870. Later decades were to see the maturation and expansion of the patterns established during these formative years. A general consensus exists regarding the historical periods of development for modern policing in the United States: the political era (1840–1920), the reform era (1920–1970), and the community policing era (1970–present). These periods have been criticized for describing policing only in urban areas and not taking into account the complexities of police development in the southern and western territories.[10] Even so, examining the stages of police development provides a framework for understanding not just the evolution of modern policing but also how social values have contributed to the formation of our current system of law and order.

THE POLITICAL ERA (1840–1920)

As cities grew, so did instances of public disorder, drunkenness, and violent conduct by citizens. Peacekeepers were unable to maintain law and order adequately, and in many cases, lawmen were corrupt and remiss in their duties. Despite such hardships, urban America had to rely on this system of policing until the mid-nineteenth century. Although many cities enlarged their police forces, the growing incidence of lawlessness, disorder, and public corruption eventually resulted in the formation of formal police forces. Sadly, law enforcement officers of the nineteenth century were grossly disliked, yet were granted broad powers of arrest, search, and seizure.

The political era is labeled as such because of the close association between police and political leaders. In many cases police were viewed as extensions of local politicians whose primary concern was not law and order but getting reelected. This was a reciprocal arrangement as the political machines recruited and maintained the police, while police officers worked on behalf of politicians by rallying votes. Corruption flourished during the political era, as the policeman's first allegiance was not to the public he served but to the local politician who controlled city hall.

THE EMERGENCE OF THE SHERIFF

The county sheriff was the first formal law enforcement officer to appear in the new territories, a position closely modeled after his English counterpart. His charge was not that of a proactive officer of the law but rather one who responded to crimes that had already occurred. Sheriffs were paid on the fee system, incurring a fixed amount for each arrest made. In time the authority of the U.S. sheriff expanded to include the managing of public elections and county tax collection as well as enforcement duties. In addition to the county sheriff, municipalities appointed town marshals who were sometimes aided by night watchmen, constables, and justices.

The Posse Comitatus Act

The staff of a U.S. sheriff seldom included a full-time paid squad of deputies. Often, it relied on the power of **posse comitatus** (Latin for "power of the country"), that is, authority to coordinate the activities of all other police agencies. The sheriff used posse comitatus powers to summon able-bodied young men in the community to assist in tracking and capturing fugitives, a power that would literally place the resources of the entire community at the sheriff's disposal. Even today, 33 states consider the sheriff as a constitutional officer regarded as the chief law enforcement officer of the county.

Southern Justice

During the pre–Civil War era in the South, police administration and policy were greatly influenced by slave trade. While urban areas were carefully readied for control of the masses of enslaved blacks, rural areas employed the use of **slave patrols,** charged with tracking and apprehending slaves who had escaped from plantations and farms. Those slaves found away from their plantation were taken before a special court of magistrates and freeholders, which usually consisted of one local justice of the peace and several landholders. These courts were granted plenary jurisdiction over all matters concerning criminal activity by slaves. Jurisdiction was broad. A typical sentence for "being abroad without a pass" was a flogging, but in some cases capital punishment was imposed.

Plantation owners were legally authorized to punish their own slaves. Such sanctions resulted from a variety of infractions: assaults, thefts, and even antisocial mannerisms. Punishments typically consisted of statutorily defined floggings, but in some cases such discipline resulted in the death of the offender. In other cases, starvation of the servant occurred as a punitive measure. However, due to the financial investment of the plantation owner, the majority of punishments were dispensed in a more humane fashion. Excessive punishments by plantation owners resulting in the willful killing of a slave would sometimes cause the intervention of a justice of the peace and in some cases would result in execution of the slave owner.[11] In general, however, the white society of the South was willing to allow individualized justice to flourish.

Vigilante Justice

While areas such as the East and Midwest easily adopted the British-style police system, other less developed areas adopted a system of justice at the point of a gun. Indeed, in many western territories the practice of offering rewards for the capture of outlaws was common. Some communities would organize a "town vigilance" committee to hunt down offenders and impose on-the-spot justice. Such vigilante justice was often arbitrary and swift, designed to intimidate would-be cattle and horse rustlers.

Among those who became known for their role in vigilante justice was Charles Lynch, a Virginia farmer of the late eighteenth century, after whom the term *lynching* was coined. Lynch and his associates became well known for tracking and punishing offenders, often according to the well-known dictates of the so-called Lynch law. During the settlement of the frontier, vigilante groups and citizen posses were the only law available to the settlers. Other frontiersmen who occasionally took the law into their own hands were Judge Roy Bean, Wild Bill Hickock, Wyatt Earp, Bat Masterson, and Pat Garrett, each of whom acted in both official and unofficial capacities as judge and jury. As urban areas continued to grow, however, such ad hoc groups became increasingly difficult to organize and control.

State Police Agencies

Western settlements also included the organization of regional law enforcement organizations. Although several states had created state-level law enforcement agencies during the nineteenth century, they were not important institutions.[12] Pioneers in state policing organizations were the Texas Rangers, who became well known in history. Originally equipped in 1823 by Stephen Austin to protect settlements against Indian attacks, the Rangers were called upon during the Texas revolution in 1835. Soon after, the Rangers were hailed as a law enforcement agency. (Although for over 170 years the Texas Rangers acted as an exclusively male-dominated organization, in August 1993 the first two female Rangers were inducted into the organization.) Modeled after the Texas Rangers, the Arizona Rangers were organized in 1901, followed by the New Mexico Mounted Police in 1905. Both ranger squads in Arizona and New Mexico served as border patrol units but were soon disbanded. The Pennsylvania Constabulary was also established in 1905 and focused most of its efforts on controlling strikes. In time, many other states established their own agencies, generally consisting of two categories: highway patrols with limited police power and state police that possessed broader investigative powers (see Chapter 3).

The First Police Forces

Modern police forces were formed out of increasing instances of mob violence in urban areas. Boston has been credited with establishing the country's first formal police department in 1838, but its night watch was established as far back as 1801. Subsequent to some initial changes, the Boston model included the construction of station houses that were connected by telegraph lines. This system enabled officers to transmit information quickly and to respond in numbers to emergency situations and with

FIGURE 2.3   The Texas Rangers in the late 1800s.

greater efficiency. Police boxes were soon added, whereby an officer could turn a key in a box and his location would automatically be registered at headquarters—hence the term *turnkey*. By the mid-nineteenth century, the Boston police had added the first detective bureau to the department, a change that ended the practice of thief-taking by bounty hunters hired by victims of crimes.

In 1844, as a result of the rising fear of urban crime, New York established the first police force offering citizens 24-hour protection. Indeed, the demographics of New York had changed dramatically during the 50 years prior to the establishment of the new police force. For example, Rosenwaike writes that the population of the city had increased 1000% from 33,131 in 1790 to 371,223 in 1845.[13]

Because the majority of the new immigrants were of foreign birth, a labyrinth of subcommunities developed, each separated from the other by language, cultural, racial, and ethnic differences. New York's system was closely modeled after the British constabulary but with some differences. For example, New York policemen initially did not wear uniforms due to indifference of the general populace. In 1853, pursuant to pressure from police commissioners and commanders, the police uniform was adopted department-wide. As a symbol of authority, the police department adopted a single copper badge that was mounted on a leather circle. From this they acquired the nickname "copper." Although initially the department only issued officers a truncheon, the killing of numerous officers by armed criminals soon resulted in the departmental issuance of firearms. Philadelphia followed in 1854, within a decade of the establishment of New York's police force. These departments replaced the old system of the night watch and entrusted the sheriff with keeping law and order outside the city limits as well as maintaining the county jail.

One prevailing characteristic of America's new-style police was the prevalence of politics in hiring, promotion, and enforcement priorities. For example, poorly qualified individuals might be appointed to the force, provided they had the appropriate political "connections." In actuality, the police did little to prevent crime or enforce laws. Rather, they assumed the subjective role of pawns for local politicians. Consequently, appointments were sometimes limited to the period of time the officer's sponsoring politician remained in office. As the end of the nineteenth century approached, the position of police officer was highly desired because of the relatively high salary paid to patrolmen, a salary notably higher than that of the average blue-collar worker. For instance, factory workers in the 1880s earned $450 per year, whereas police were paid twice that salary. Immigrants with enough social or political influence to be appointed would consider such employment a significant step up the social ladder.[14] With few technological aids available to assist the officer, the mechanics of early police work were crude at best. Most patrolled on foot without the benefit of radios or police computers or the luxury of backup. Training was also minimal during the early years of law enforcement, but most officers worked under little supervision. Today's public scrutiny stems from the behavior of early officers who were, for the most part, unprofessional and harsh in their administration of justice.

EARLY TWENTIETH-CENTURY CHANGE

Change and reform in policing have historically been slow and laboring processes. Policing at the turn of the century was greatly influenced by the progressive movement. Progressives were generally upper-middle-class Americans concerned with obtaining two goals: operating an efficient government and providing governmental services to the less fortunate. They also wished to rid the government of political control of the police. In essence, progressives called for the creation of more professional police services. Progressive efforts resulted in several sweeping reforms in the criminal justice system. These included the centralization of law enforcement agencies, an improvement in police training for officers, and the restriction of the police role to the enforcement of criminal law. Staufenberger suggests that with professionalization, police services took on several new characteristics:

- Expert officers formally educated and trained
- Police departments free of political influence
- Department formulated and implemented policies
- Efficiency in police administration
- Impartial enforcement of the law[15]

Changes in policing during the end of the nineteenth century and the early part of the twentieth century reflected other changes occurring in the United States. During this period the nation became increasingly industrialized and urbanized. One notable result of urbanization was the creation of the urban middle class, which consisted of those who managed stores and factories. Gradually, these middle-class Americans grew more and more dissatisfied with local politics and the police in particular. Business leaders realized that because of the decentralized nature of urban politics, such leaders in the community had little say in big city politics. Indeed, local political-machine bosses were not concerned with the middle class, but only with the voting constituency of ethnic neighborhoods.

THE REFORM ERA (1920–1970)

Because of their ties and role with city politics, police organizations have always been at the center of political controversy.[16] For the most part, partisan politics were the main influence on the police and contributed greatly to the police's role in corruption, brutality, and political manipulation. As a result, the ultimate goal of reformers was to remove politics from policing. However, these efforts were in essence replacing one form of politics with another. To accomplish this, reformers attempted to redefine the role and function of the police.

Those who were the most emphatic about police reform were the urban upper class and a few "new breed" police administrators. Although these two groups were often in disagreement with each other, they shared a similar vision of police work. The elites were interested in breaking the political stranglehold on the police by crooked politicians, while police administrators sought independence from city hall so that policing could develop into a separate, autonomous, and highly respected field. Gaining independence from politicians meant that the police could operate freely without political interference or corruption. Reformers were appalled by the notion that illegal operations run by political bosses could operate freely without fear of police intervention. In contrast, the police were often employed by unscrupulous politicians to curb "dangerous" behavior such as drinking and gambling among the working class.

Redefining the police role from that of order maintenance and peacekeeping to crime control and law enforcement helped clarify the police function. Instead of meeting a broad social service function, which was used to get votes by local politicians, the police gradually concentrated on more crime-related matters. As a result, police services such as locating lost children and dealing with homeless persons declined during the early part of the twentieth century.[17] External pressure for reform was not sufficient to cause change. What was needed were internal pressures as well, which required police administrators themselves to generate police reform. Early attempts by citizens to "reform" the police were simply efforts by lower-class citizens to exert control and thereby weaken the established political machines.

Police reform was initially an extension of general reform efforts to improve cities and city governments.[18] Cities were ravaged by crime, population growth, and corruption in politics, and policing was only one of many other problems in an expanding urban United States. The major source of the problems was the existence of the political machine—a problem that needed to be eliminated. To do so, urbanites had to seize control of the police from political bosses, a task that was initially unsuccessful because of the power and influence of the machines.

Simply put, the middle class did not possess sufficient power to accomplish the task. As a result, for several decades during the reform era, reformers in a number of cities attempted to control local police through state government. For example, the Boston police were created in part by urban elites to enforce liquor laws.[19] Many reformers wanted to use the police to control immigrant behavior and help "shape" them into their image of moral Americans. Thus police officers were often required to enforce unpopular laws that were focused on immigrants by the elite reformers.

Police Administrators and Reform

In addition to elites pushing for reform, police administrators also sought reform in policing. They wanted to break away from local political control of police and gain professionalism in their field. One of the first goals of reform centered on police personnel. Controlling police officers was to

FIGURE 2.4 Three police officers taking away a civil rights protester during race riots in Newark, New Jersey, during the late 1960s.

make police departments more efficient, but doing so was difficult because of the entrenched political influence over the police. To accomplish reform, police autonomy was needed along with an effort to improve the quality of police personnel. The best way to accomplish this was to separate the police from the rule of the political machine. The result was a more effective and efficient system of law enforcement and order maintenance.

Another kind of reform was reorganization. Toward the latter part of the nineteenth century, the typical U.S. police chief was, at best, a figurehead.[20] Rank-and-file officers owed their allegiance to political bosses rather than to the police chief or the police profession itself. For the most part, command was decentralized to the precinct level, where local precinct commanders made most administrative and command decisions. Perhaps this could have been tolerable if it were not for frequent clashes between citizens and the police. Most conflicts stemmed from confusion about the role of the police. For example, in many cities the people wanted police officers to enforce the law and arrest criminals, whereas in other communities citizens wanted the police to play more of a social service role. For example, in 1834, police in Boston removed 1,500 loads of dirt, emptied privies, and visited every house to check for cholera.[21] In addition, even for those people who wanted police to act as law enforcers, there were still some laws that they didn't wish the police to enforce or at least preferred that the police would only enforce them in certain neighborhoods. As a result, the police chief was the focal point of such conflicts.

Just prior to the reform era, it was typical for the police chief to be directly accountable to either a police commission or an elected official such as the mayor or city manager. The role of the chief was that of a liaison between the commission and the police captains. Although the police chief had little control over individual police officers and their captains, he was still responsible for their actions.[22] The struggle between political factions resulted in gradual change in the administrative structure of police departments.[23] However, police chiefs remained under the control of some partisan group and most control of police officers remained at the neighborhood level, so actual changes in structure had little effect on police practices. The reformers' job of translating ideals into reality had proven to be a nearly impossible task, as they lacked both ideological rationale and a means of controlling police rank and file.[24]

Professionalizing the Police

Throughout the years much has been said about professionalizing the police in our communities. Professionalism is that state of mind, that standard of behavior, that image of competency that one equates with the finest persons who follow a calling, who practice the art and science of a vocation, and who perform the function of a job.[25] As reform efforts slowly gained momentum at the turn of the twentieth century and the local politician wielded less influence on the police, police work gradually became thought of as a profession. By 1920 the reform era was in full bloom, and police administrators struggled to establish members of their field as "professionals" rather than simply as persons working at a job. Among other considerations, the concept of a profession includes the presumption that those who have membership in it will have special skills and training, a high level of commitment, a strict code of conduct, and the understanding that members will enjoy a degree of autonomy and independence in governing their activities. Thus police officers should be appointed because they have a commitment to the profession, not because of political patronage.

Professional organizations soon emerged. For example, as far back as 1893, the International Association of Chiefs of Police (IACP) was formed. The IACP's first president, Washington, D.C. Police Chief Richard Sylvester, preached professionalism around the United States—in particular with regard to technological innovations in criminal investigation and in prevention strategies for controlling crime. For about 20 years, the IACP established itself as the principal organization for police reform, calling for sweeping changes in the civil service system and supporting reformers in the elimination of politics from police work. One such recommendation was to centralize the structure of police departments and maintain records in one location, thereby reducing the amount of

Highlights in Policing

A History of Modern Policing

- The nineteenth century—Modern policing gets its start in Britain and migrates across the Atlantic in somewhat different forms. Police corruption emerges as a problem in the United States.
- 1829—In persuading Parliament to approve legislation establishing the London Metropolitan Police, the world's first modern police force, Sir Robert Peel stresses the need for cooperation between law enforcement officers and the community. In Peel's honor, the police are called "bobbies."
- 1844—The first modern U.S. police force is established in New York. Officers are identifiable only by their star-shaped copper badges, giving rise to the nickname "copper," later shortened to "cop."
- 1894—A special committee of the New York State Senate investigating complaints of corruption in the New York City's Police Department learns that officers regularly obtain appointments and win promotions through political influence and cash payments.
- The early twentieth century—Increasing police corruption results in gradual successful reform efforts by politicians and government officials. These, along with the introduction of the civil service system, place the police on the road to professionalization.
- The 1960s—Increasing crime, racial strife, and antiwar agitation call attention to a widening rift between police officers and many residents of the communities in which they work.
- 1967—The President's Commission on Law Enforcement and the Administration of Justice declares in its report, *The Challenge of Crime in a Free Society*, that "improving [police] community relations involves not only instituting programs and changing procedures and practices, but also re-examining fundamental attitudes."

- 1969—The Law Enforcement Assistance Administration (LEAA) was created by Congress and was charged with combating crime by expending large amounts of money. Between 1969 and 1982 it had expended $8 billion, before Congress discontinued its funding.
- The 1970s—Time-honored concepts of professional policing come under increasingly hostile scrutiny in law enforcement circles.
- 1974—In a year-long experiment to gauge the effectiveness of routine police patrols in marked cars, the Kansas City Police Department finds no significant difference in crime levels when patrols are reduced to 40% below normal or increased to 200% above normal (see Chapter 4).
- The 1980s—Community policing gets its first major tests of effectiveness in two of the country's largest cities, Houston and New York.
- 1983—Under the leadership of new Police Chief Lee P. Brown, Houston's community policing program, the first in a major U.S. city, gets under way.
- 1984—The New York Police Department implements its Community Patrol Officer Program (CPOP), a new and innovative venture in community policing.
- The 1990s—Community policing spreads, despite tight municipal budgets.
- 1994—The Violent Crime Control and Law Enforcement Act provided new research and evaluation initiatives, as well as funding the deployment of thousands of additional police officers while supporting community policing programs across the nation. The act also provides for improving programs dealing with violence against women as well as the funding of drug courts and the establishment of boot camps.

Source: National Institute of Justice Journal, February 1996; *Congressional Quarterly Researcher*, February 5, 1993.

political power enjoyed by police precinct captains. In essence, the professionalization component of the reform era was marked by four important developments:

- The changing role of the police
- The adoption of the bureaucratic model
- The introduction of science and technology
- The introduction of civil service

The Changing Role of the Police

For obvious reasons, the political era emphasized the service role of the police. It wasn't until the 1920s that the police began to adopt more of a law enforcement or crime-control role.[26] As a result of various reform efforts, the police began to move toward a professional model. With the passing of the Eighteenth Amendment in 1920 (Prohibition) and the onset of the Great Depression in 1929, the police were under a new public mandate for crime control and public safety.

Prohibition was an emotionally charged issue that, upon its passing, prohibited the manufacture, sale, and transportation of alcoholic beverages. The police were thrust into an adversarial role that resulted in officers allowing public opinion to dictate police enforcement practices regarding vice and victimless crimes.[27] Enforcement of liquor laws was sporadic at best, with a considerable amount of pressure on the police to act in a proactive role rather than in reactive manner to which they had grown accustomed. As a result, the police were often torn between maintaining positive relations with citizens and jeopardizing public relations with crime-control efforts.

A similar effect was seen with the onset of the Great Depression. The Depression was a desperate time for Americans, marked by widespread unemployment, bank failures, foreclosures on farms, and homelessness. To survive, many people felt they had to commit crime. Well-known criminals also emerged from the Depression Era, including John Dillinger, Pretty Boy Floyd, Baby Face Nelson, and Bonnie and Clyde (Bonnie Parker and Clyde Barrow). Crime sprees by these and many other criminals of the era resulted in the crime wave of the 1930s. To many people, these criminals represented antiestablishment folk heroes, while banks and other institutions profiting from other people's misfortune were viewed as villains. Police officials and politicians alike realized that to ignore this type of criminal behavior would only result in more people breaking the law. Consequently, police agencies on local and federal levels alike adopted a hard-line stance against crime, leaving the service model of police as a distant secondary consideration.

One outcome of the new law and order stance against crime was the establishment of President Hoover's National Commission on Law Observance and Law Enforcement. The Commission, which later became known as the Wickersham Commission, was charged with studying the rising crime rate and the inability of police to enforce laws successfully. The commission, headed by George W. Wickersham, made a detailed analysis of the criminal justice system and disclosed the labyrinth of rules and regulations in the system along with some of the problems inherent in the administration of justice. In 1931, the newly released findings of the commission were so damaging to the image of the criminal justice system that debate over how to remedy the problems ensued for some time. For example, the commission pointed to a lack of effective, honest patrolmen.

The police supervisor's term of office was too brief, and there was no current attempt to educate and train prospective recruits or dismiss those considered unfit. Furthermore, the commission held that police forces in cities with populations of 300,000 or more had inadequate communications systems and equipment too inferior to enforce the laws effectively. In addition, it stated that there was too much responsibility placed on the average policeman.[28] Essentially, the commission held that police officers should adopt less of a service role and more of a crime-fighting role. One of the commission's strongest recommendations was the development of a comprehensive plan for a complete body of statistics covering crime, criminals, criminal justice, and correctional treatment at federal, state, and local levels with the responsibility of the program being entrusted to one single federal agency.[29]

The Adoption of the Bureaucratic Model

The peak of police professionalization came about around 1950. By then there had been many changes adopted by police departments around the nation. It was widely felt that professionalism played a large part in organizational efficiency in police work. Efficiency meant greater control of police officers and a more effective application of police services. The ideal of police professionalism probably owed as much to the bureaucratic organization as it did to reform efforts by progressives. The bureaucratic organization stemmed from the centralization of administrative power and the creation of special bureaus within departments.

Formation of the bureaucracy included a narrowing of focus for the police, the development of rules and norms, and the development of a formal organizational structure. Under this paramilitary model, police officer behavior could be monitored and supervised more closely. In an effort to respond more quickly to calls and to respond to a greater number of calls, most police departments abandoned foot patrols in favor of motorized patrols. In addition, functions were consolidated, and command functions emanated from a central headquarter.[30]

The Introduction of Science and Technology

As technological advances became more prevalent, police officials became intrigued. Many believed that to be truly considered a profession, police work would have to take full advantage of new technology. In time, human aspects of crime detection were replaced with science. On virtually all fronts, technological innovations were pursued. These included record-keeping systems, fingerprint technology, serology, toxicology, ballistics, evidence collection, and communications. The use of physical evidence became paramount in solving cases and obtaining convictions.

Another technological innovation, which revolutionized policing, occurred in the area of transportation. By 1913, police departments in the east were making use of the motorcycle—introduced by the Detroit police in 1867. In Ohio, the Akron Police Department first used automobiles in 1910, and the Cincinnati Police Department implemented police wagons in 1912. In addition to the advent of motor vehicles, the telephone was also developed, allowing the public the capability to report crime to the station house immediately. Under the old horse patrol system, officers had to carry or drag prisoners back to the station house after arrest. With the use of the call box, however, officers could summon a horse-drawn patrol wagon (known as a paddy wagon) to assist in the transportation of prisoners.

The technological revolution also held negative components. Although efficiency and effectiveness were increasing in police work, public relations became strained due to the impersonal nature of the new techno police. Police officers were also discouraged from getting too close to the public, to avoid the opportunity and appearance of breeding corruption. Many police administrators felt that solving crimes was far more important than solving problems, and that human relations skills gave the appearance of being unprofessional. Although technology played an important part in professionalizing the police, it also served to alienate and isolate them from the very public they served.

FIGURE 2.5 A Michigan State Police forensic scientist searching for potential evidence from a suspect's clothing. The application of forensic science to crime solving is based on the theory that anyone who has contact with a person or crime scene inadvertently takes something with them when they leave and leaves something of themselves behind.

The Introduction of Civil Service

Another important step toward the professionalization of policing was the institution of civil service procedures for police officer selection and promotion. Still in use today, the civil service system selects police officer applicants based on their civil service rankings, whereby officer selection is based on what applicants know rather than whom they know. The important implications of civil service are that police officers are committed to public service and police work in general rather than to a particular politician. By the end of World War I, civil service appointments of police officers were the norm, especially in larger cities.[31]

For years, civil service was a primary goal of progressives who wanted a more effective and responsive government. One way to accomplish this, they argued, was by the removal of the partisan allegiance between police officers and politicians. Although civil service was not without its problems, it did serve to weaken the stranglehold by politicians on the police while strengthening the ability of police administrators to control their police officers more effectively. Also, for the first time, civil service created an occupational identity for police officers, paving the way for them to view themselves as a distinct professional group.

Thus, by 1920, police officers were on the brink of professionalization. Indeed, the groundwork laid by progressives, reformers, and police administrators appeared to have paid off. Police organizations were beginning to gain prominence and influence, and entry into the profession was no longer restricted by politics. Most important, police chiefs had finally gained sufficient authority to command and control officers in their departments.

THE EMERGENCE OF THE PROFESSIONAL POLICE OFFICER

A second generation of police administrators led the way toward increasing professionalization in policing. Many newly selected police executives of the reform era were chosen because of their demonstrated effectiveness and leadership ability. Of these, August Vollmer, police chief of Berkeley, California, from 1905 to 1952, earned the reputation as the father of scientific police investigation by establishing the first police training school in 1908. Vollmer was a true innovator. He contributed to the professionalization of police work by adopting fully mechanized patrol systems that enabled officers to cover more distance in a shorter period of time.

The police department added two-way radios for more efficient communication, and the lie detector was employed for use in criminal investigations. Vollmer supported the hiring of college-educated officers and established a police school in his department. Later, in 1939, Vollmer helped organize the first academic criminology curriculum in the United States. The School of Criminology was housed within the Department of Political Science at the University of California, where he later worked as a university professor of police science. In 1951, graduate degrees in criminology were established at the university.

Civil Rights and Police Professionalization

The 1960s set the stage for considerable unrest in the arena of civil rights. College students staged protests on campuses and sit-ins to protest segregation and discrimination. Throughout the country, housing and employment practices were challenged by black activists. In addition, police practices were scrutinized by civil rights advocates. The tension between blacks and the police steadily grew and climaxed during the mid- to late-1960s with riots occurring in most major U.S. cities. Many police departments responded by establishing police–community relations programs (PCRs). Police officers assigned to the PCR unit made speeches at schools and community centers in an effort to bridge the gap between police and the citizenry. In addition, ride-along programs were implemented, as were police store fronts located in high-crime areas, all in an effort to allow the public to view the police from the officer's perspective.

FIGURE 2.6 Criminologist August Vollmer.

Professionalizing Police Organizations

A positive outgrowth of the reform era was an increase in the development and application of standard operating procedures (SOPs) for police officers. These procedures have become an essential part of all police organizations and represent a collection of rules and regulations that police officers are required to follow. Since the professional era, efforts to continue to professionalize police have taken place. One such effort was the establishment of state police standards organizations. These organizations, also called police officer standards and training (POST) organizations, strive to formalize and standardize police training, procedures, and hiring practices. Still another advancement in police professionalization pertains to police accreditation for law enforcement agencies.

Police Accreditation

As we enter the twenty-first century, more and more police agencies are looking toward accreditation as a means to ensure professionalization. Although accreditation has many benefits, the avoidance of lawsuits is one of the more prominent. Accreditation should reduce the likelihood of liability because

A Closer Look

O. W. Wilson (1900–1972)

Criminologist and police administrator Orlando Winfield Wilson was born in Veblen, South Dakota, the son of an attorney. After taking up residence in Berkeley, California, he soon began to study criminology at the University of California, where he completed his degree in criminology in 1924. During the course of his schooling, Wilson became a police officer with the Berkeley Police Department under the supervision of August Vollmer, a professor of criminology at the university. Upon Vollmer's recommendation, Wilson launched his police career by becoming police chief of Fullerton, California.

In 1928, Wilson was hired as the police chief of Wichita, Kansas, where he received national attention by reorganizing the department and implementing innovative ideas,

such as the distinct marking of police vehicles and the use of mobile crime laboratories and polygraphs. From 1939 to 1960 he served as a professor of police administration at Berkeley, where he developed a theory of how law enforcement relates to crime control. Wilson believed that the police were unable to control crime because they had no control over socially related issues such as neglect and poverty. However, he postulated that the police could successfully deter criminals through preventive patrol. Wilson produced the following books: *Police Records* (1942) and *Police Administration* (1957). Finally, in 1960, Wilson assumed the position of superintendent of police in Chicago, where he saw corruption stemming from poor organization and confused lines of command.

accredited departments' policies and procedures will have met stringent national standards, a frequent argument of defense attorneys.[32] In addition, agencies that are accredited receive a discount on their liability insurance premium. Rachlin quotes Levine, the CALEA associate director: "Accredited departments are subject to fewer lawsuits and citizen complaints . . . and they are in a better position to address lawsuits and complaints."[33] The Commission on Accreditation for Law Enforcement Agencies (CALEA) was created in 1979 as a result of efforts by the International Association of Chiefs of Police (IACP), the National Sheriff's Association (NSA), and the Police Executive Research Forum (PERF). Before a police department can gain accreditation, it must meet stringent standards. Many police executives believe that being accredited gives the police agency prestige and respect, and that if accredited, funding for higher salaries, superior equipment, and improved resources can be more readily realized. Although the argument can easily be made for accreditation as a means of professionalizing the department, in actuality, only a few departments have done so.

By the end of 1991, less than 2% or 195 police departments were accredited. It should also be noted that there is no clear-cut evidence that accreditation actually improves the effectiveness or efficiency of police services in a community. Police executives are in agreement, however, that accreditation has boosted the morale of officers, has reduced police liability suits, and has resulted in lower insurance premiums for the department.[34] Many of the assumptions of the professional model were challenged during the 1960s in the wake of urban riots, civil rights and antiwar unrest, and a continual rise in the nation's crime rate.

Professional Organizations

One mark of a professional group is the existence of an organization or association that represents its members in a professional manner. Examples are the American Medical Association (AMA) and the American Bar Association (ABA). Sadly, no such singular group represents the police profession. Probably the organization that comes closest to doing so is the International Association of Chiefs of Police (IACP), which was established in 1893. Since then it has grown from a loose-knit fraternity of law enforcement administrators to a broad-based practitioner-oriented international organization.

The academic community has also made important contributions to police professionalization by the establishment of two major organizations: the American Society of Criminology (ASC), founded in 1941, and the Academy of Criminal Justice Sciences (ACJS), formed in 1970. Both of these organizations promote research and debate in the study of some of the nation's most critical criminal justice issues. Membership is open to all, but its primary membership consists of professors and students of criminal justice and sociology.

THE COMMUNITY POLICING ERA (1970–PRESENT)

With widespread incidents of civil disorder during the 1960s, the professional reforms of the 1950s became endangered. Civil rights unrest created a feeling of anxiety and uneasiness in the impoverished urban slums. Tension between the citizenry and the government stemmed from involvement in the Vietnam War, which often provoked demonstrations and civil disobedience on college campuses across the nation. Drug abuse also gained momentum during the 1960s and has been linked to the antiestablishment sentiments of the decade. As with Prohibition, police were under new pressures to control drug abuse and related crime. Many such efforts were proactive in nature and resulted in considerable animosity between the citizenry and the police. It became evident that the police were ill-prepared to deal effectively with civil disorder during the 1960s. In an effort to bolster police resources, the 1968 Omnibus Crime Control and Safe Streets Act was passed. This act increased funding for another organization which became known as the Law Enforcement Assistance Administration (LEAA). From the late 1960s through the 1970s, hundreds of millions of dollars were invested to improve the criminal justice system. The most important impact on the police was the large number of research studies that produced new knowledge about police methods, behavior, and effectiveness. In addition, LEAA contributed to the growth of academic programs because grants and loans were made available to encourage individuals to pursue higher education. In service, law enforcement officers were given grants to return to college. Prospective law enforcement officers—that is, college students who thought they might become police officers—were given loans to help with college expenses. These loans were forgivable at the rate of 25% per year if the student worked as a law enforcement officer.

During this period, public interest in crime and criminal justice increased substantially. This was the result of a perception of rising crime rates, numerous civil disorders, and the national commissions. The money available from the federal government provided an incentive for colleges and universities to establish criminal justice programs; consequently, the number of programs increased dramatically. And with this growth came more college and university faculty members who also contributed to the growing body of knowledge about the criminal justice system.

In the early 1980s, the LEAA became the National Institute of Justice (NIJ), which still sponsors research projects in criminal justice, although the funding has been reduced considerably. Prior to its demise, the LEAA created the type of analytic climate that had a major impact on changing policing in the United States.

The body of knowledge that existed to change the police during the legalistic era was based largely on the experience of police practitioners such as August Vollmer and O. W. Wilson. By the 1970s, this body of knowledge was being challenged and gradually replaced by knowledge that was derived from empirical research. Many of the ideas produced by this research were controversial because they called into question almost all established ideas and concepts about policing. However, what was not questioned was the importance of professionalizing the activities and behavior of the police. Critics, while challenging many old established methods in policing, did not argue with the idea that officers should be efficient, fair-minded, and dedicated.

Also, beginning in the 1970s was a movement away from the crime-fighting focus toward a community-oriented approach to policing. It was believed that in their pursuit of professionalism through technology and the regiments of the bureaucratic model, the police had lost touch with the citizenry they were sworn to protect. This was especially true because of the newly adopted motorized patrol, which reduced regular citizen contacts with police. Major police studies were also published during the 1960s showing the complexities of police work and how reality clashed with the ideals of the old professional model. Research questioned the ability of police to catch and deter criminals by adding more police units to neighborhoods and increasing police response time. Both of these were major principles of the crime-fighting model.

The new emphasis on police–community relations had several effects on police organizational thoughts and procedures. For example, there was a return to decentralization, where the authority to develop new programs was delegated to police officers. Finally, during the 1980s, the police–community relations model of policing emerged, as crime became a pervasive public issue. Advocates of the community policing approach place a greater emphasis on foot patrol in order for the officer to become better acquainted with citizens, a philosophy that will hopefully result in improved public attitudes toward police.

After his election in 1980, President Ronald Reagan launched an unprecedented attack on the nation's drug problem and corresponding violent crime rate. Police strategies became more responsive by targeting specific aspects of the crime problem through crime analysis. The overall police philosophy focused on providing better public service by dealing more effectively with local crime issues. Stemming from the police–community relations model was the development of innovative concepts such as community-oriented policing (COP) and problem-oriented policing (POP), which became more popular toward the end of the 1980s (see Chapter 9). Under the problem-oriented approach, police are trained to better handle troublesome situations in their districts: runaway children, battered spouses, noisy teenagers, and so on. The police then identify the problem and look for its underlying causes.

These programs, still used by many law enforcement agencies, enable the police to analyze crime more thoroughly by customizing solutions for each specific problem, a contrast with the old-style policing where the police simply responded to calls rather than addressed the cause of the problem that generated the call. In essence, problem solving was viewed by administrators as a way to reduce future crime problems so that police units would not have to return to take additional actions.

In Retrospect

Our English heritage has played an important role in the development and establishment of police systems in the United States. The creation of the urban police during the nineteenth century was testimony to the fact that they were essential to the well-being of cities with growing diverse populations and varying political processes. This role, although somewhat clouded, is still vital today. The lessons learned from 1860 to 1920 are crucial to understanding pressures on our police today. The reliance on individual authority, combined with the U.S. citizen's unwillingness to accept governmental power without question, places the police in the unique position of having to justify their actions in virtually all police–citizen encounters. This climate tends to increase community tensions and confrontations with government figures. Consequently, over time the police have learned to exercise a prudent use of discretionary powers to avoid that tension.

The close link between the police and local politicians places the police in a position to choose between political and public-interest groups. As history shows, however, U.S. urban police emerged as an extension of the political majority and have always sided with that majority. It is the challenge of today's professionalism movement to institute high standards for police as a profession and to remind police administrators and policymakers of the dubious historical record of the police so that the mistakes of the past are not repeated in the future.

Improve Your Professional Vocabulary

bobbies
constable
frankpledge system
hue and cry
night watch
posse comitatus
slave patrols
Statute of Winchester
thief-taker
tithings

Discussion Questions

1. Discuss why the police are both an aberration and a necessity of modern society.
2. Explain Henry Fielding's contribution to the English system of policing.
3. In what ways were the Bow Street Runners similar to modern-day criminal investigators?
4. List the ways in which Sir Robert Peel's early principles of policing affect our current system of policing.
5. Discuss the main reasons for the rise of police professionalism beginning late in the nineteenth century.
6. Discuss the circumstances that led up to the formation of America's first full-time police departments.
7. Discuss August Vollmer's and O. W. Wilson's primary contributions to police professionalization.
8. What events identify the "reform era" as such?
9. Compare and contrast the different eras of policing, and discuss what was learned about policing during each era.
10. What events led to the development of the "community policing era"?

Notes

1. Chambliss, R. (1979). *Social thought.* New York: Irvington.
2. Nisbet, R. (1973). Kinship and political power in first century Rome. In D. Black & M. Mileski, eds., *The social organization of law.* New York: Seminar Press.
3. Gilchrist, J. P. (1948). *A history of the middle ages.* London: Oxford University Press.
4. Johnson, H. A. (1988). *The history of criminal justice.* Cincinnati, OH: Anderson.

5. Radelet, L. A. (1986). *The police and the community.* New York: McGraw-Hill.
6. Manning, P. (1977). *Police work.* Cambridge, MA: MIT Press.
7. Lee, W. L. M. (1901). *A history of police in England.* London: Oxford University Press.
8. Johnson, D. R. (1981). *American law enforcement: A history.* St. Louis, MO: Forum Press; Lane, R. (1975). *Policing the city of Boston, 1822–1885.* New York: Atheneum.
9. Lane, R. (1975). *Policing the city of Boston, 1822–1885.* New York: Atheneum; Richardson, J. F. (1978). *Urban police in the United States.* Port Washington, NY: Kennikat Press.
10. Williams, H., & P. Murphy. (1990). The evolving strategy of police: A minority view. *Perspectives on Policing, 13.* Washington, DC: National Institute of Justice and Harvard University, January.
11. Johnson, H. A. (1988). *The history of criminal justice.* Cincinnati, OH: Anderson.
12. Walker, S. (1992). *The police in America.* New York: McGraw-Hill.
13. Rosenwaike, I. (1972). *Population history of New York City.* Syracuse, NY: Syracuse University Press.
14. Walker, S. (1980). *Popular justice.* New York: Oxford University Press.
15. Staufenberger, R. A. (1980). *Progress in policing: Essays on change.* Cambridge, MA: Ballinger.
16. Johnson, D. R. (1981). *American law enforcement: A history.* St. Louis, MO: Forum Press.
17. Monkonnen, E. H. (1981). *Police in urban America, 1860–1920.* Cambridge: Cambridge University Press.
18. Johnson, D. R. (1981). *American law enforcement: A history.* St. Louis, MO: Forum Press.
19. Ibid.
20. Langworthy, R. H., & L. F. Travis III. (1994). *Policing in America: A balance of forces.* New York: Macmillan.
21. Gains, L. K., V. E. Kappler, & J. B. Vaughn. (1994). *Policing in America.* Cincinnati, OH: Anderson.
22. Fogelson, R. M. (1977). *Big-city police.* Cambridge, MA: Harvard University Press.
23. Walker, S. (1977). *A critical history of police reform: The emergence of police professionalism.* Lexington, MA: Lexington Books.
24. Langworthy, R. H., & L. F. Travis III. (1994). *Policing in America: A balance of forces.* New York: Macmillan.
25. Farris, E. (1985). *A new vista for sheriffs, New Mexico,* 3rd ed. Las Cruces, NM: New Mexico State University Cooperative Extension Service.
26. Moore, M. (1978). The police in search of direction. In L. Gains & T. Ricks, eds., *Managing the police organization.* St. Paul, MN: West.
27. Gains, L. K., V. E. Kappler, & J. B. Vaughn. (1994). Policing in America. Cincinnati, OH: Anderson.
28. National Commission on Law Observance and Enforcement. (1931). *Report on the police.* Washington, DC: U.S. Government Printing Office.
29. Ibid.
30. Uchida, C. (1989). The development of the American police: An historical overview. In R. Dunham & G. Alpert, eds., *Critical issues in policing: Contemporary readings.* Prospect Heights, IL: Waveland Press; Sherman, L. (1974). The sociology and social reform of the American police: 1950–1973. *Journal of Police Science and Administration, 2*(3), 255–262.
31. Johnson, D. R. (1981). *American law enforcement: A history.* St. Louis, MO: Forum Press.
32. Fulton, R. (1994, October). The state of accreditation. *Law Enforcement Technology,* 58–62.
33. Rachlin, H. (1996, January). Accreditation: The complete story. *Law and Order,* 312–317.
34. McCallister, B. (1987, March 17). Spurred in dynamic rise in lawsuits, police agencies warm to accreditation. *Washington Post,* p. A7.

CHAPTER 3

Police Jurisdiction

This chapter will enable you to:

- Understand the operational roles of various police agencies.
- Learn the different types of line and staff services provided by police agencies.
- Learn the new structure of federal law enforcement agencies.
- Understand the new priorities of federal law enforcement.

- Understand the specific duties of officers working as municipal, county, and state police.
- Distinguish between the various agencies operating at the federal level.
- Determine how private policing differs/interacts with public-sector policing.

After Hurricane Katrina swept through New Orleans, Louisiana, in late August 2005, the city needed a hero. Captain Timothy Bayard was just the officer for the job. While much of the New Orleans Police Department (NOPD) seemed ill-prepared to meet the storm's challenges, Bayard turned his narcotics vice squad into a floating rescue unit. The 45 officers commandeered all the boats they could find and spread out through the inundated city. Bayard, who coordinated the effort from a casino parking lot, estimates that the men and women under his command retrieved 10,000 people from the floodwaters.

Barely a year later, Bayard was reassigned to sit behind a desk, his career jeopardized because of what he called a "boneheaded move." In July 2006, Bayard authorized an undercover operation against Bangkok Spa, a downtown New Orleans massage parlor suspected of providing sex for its clients. During a raid that followed, his officers arrested two spa employees who happened to be witnesses in a federal corruption case against two ex-NOPD police officers. Under the circumstances, it appeared as though Bayard was trying to intimidate the witnesses to keep them from testifying against his former colleagues.

A subsequent joint investigation by the NOPD and the Federal Bureau of Investigation (FBI) cleared Bayard of unlawful intent regarding the arrest. However, New Orleans Police Superintendent Warren Riley relieved Bayard of his command and transferred him to a job where his main task is reviewing reports of arrests, not making them. Bayard's friends on the force have no doubt that Riley was using the Bangkok Spa incident to punish him for perceived disloyalty. In January, Bayard had appeared before the U.S. Senate and harshly criticized the NOPD's reaction to Hurricane Katrina. "Taking a man of Timothy Bayard's talent and experience off the street and putting him behind a desk. . . is a total disservice to all the citizens of this city," complained one retired police detective.

For those who lived in New Orleans, Bayard's suspicious demotion was just another example of their police department's ineptitude. Frustrated by a frightening post-Katrina rise in the city's murder rate, 3,000 citizens took to the streets in January 2007. Superintendent Riley, in particular, was a target of the crowd's rage. "You have really let us down," one protester told Riley and other city officials. "You have failed us."[1]

The acrimony directed at New Orleans' finest comes as no surprise. Law enforcement agencies received much of the credit when the news concerning crime in this country is good, and the lion's share of the blame when it is bad. Police officers are the most visible representatives of our criminal justice system; indeed, they symbolize the system for many Americans who may never see the inside of a courtroom or a prison cell. The police are entrusted with immense power to serve and protect the public good: the power to use weapons and the power to arrest. But that same power alarms many citizens, who fear that it may be turned arbitrarily against them. The role of the police is constantly debated as well. Is their primary mission to fight crime, or should they also be concerned with social conditions that presumably lead to crime?

Bayard's story not only illustrates the need for police but the need for them to be resourceful in their endeavors. Hurricane Katrina pushed the limits of police work and made it clear that public safety must sometimes be a joint effort to be shared by many law enforcement officers.

To the outsider, today's system of policing in the United States might appear to be a confusing conglomeration of bureaucratic red tape characterized by turfism and duplication of efforts. In an effort to protect the concept of a democracy and separation of powers, a vast array of police organizations now operates. Thus, when we discuss the police, we must be specific in identifying which police organization we are referring to. Police agencies in the United States exist at all levels of government but are unlike those in other parts of the world, where national police forces are common. In addition, U.S. policing exists in a system of checks and balances, operating in the executive branch of government.

The framers of our Constitution believed that to ensure fair treatment under the law, certain guiding principles should govern police work in a modern society. For example, there is a fundamental assumption that a police organization and the community it serves should agree on the values that guide police policy and crime control. Accordingly, those values must recognize constitutional guarantees while acknowledging the need for protecting life and maintaining order and stability in the community. To be successful in accomplishing this goal, the police executive must be cognizant of the dynamics of both the police culture and the community culture. Although the police culture has remained basically stable over the past few decades, the culture of the community is anything but predictable, with dramatic demographic changes occurring constantly.

THE NUMBER OF POLICE

As we attempt to better understand our police, it is important to understand that police work is the "multilayer ring" of law enforcement. For example, a wide network of local, state, and federal law enforcement agencies was involved in the extensive hunt for Richard Lee McNair after he escaped from a Pollock, Louisiana prison in 2006. McNair had made his way out of the maximum-security facility by hiding in the mailbag. Taking part in the search were hundreds of law enforcement agents including local police and sheriff's departments in the Pollock area, the Louisiana State police, the FBI, and the U.S. Marshals Service.

The manhunt illustrates how many agencies can become involved in a single incident. There are over 14,330 law enforcement agencies in the United States employing nearly 990,000 people.[2] The various agencies include:

- 3,088 sheriff's departments
- 1,332 special police agencies, limited to policing parks, schools, airports, and other areas
- 49 state police departments, with Hawaii being the one exception
- 70 federal law enforcement agencies

Each level has its own set of responsibilities, which we shall discuss starting with local police departments.

Although this book deals with many aspects of policing, any comparison of police agencies should be prefaced with the knowledge that because of the variations of size, community expectations, geographical differences, and managerial differences, only broad generalizations can be made. However, some similarities can be observed. For example, police chiefs are typically appointed to their positions, whereas sheriffs are elected. As a result, sheriffs are very sensitive about enforcement practices that might jeopardize their tenure in office. Thus, rigid enforcement of nonserious violations such as liquor laws, traffic laws, and automobile safety stickers might generate public criticism.

Although most police **sworn personnel** are classified as full-time, many have part-time employee status. Ninety-three percent of police officers are full-time, with the remaining 7% classified as part-time. It should be noted that in addition to sworn officers, many nonsworn or civilian personnel positions exist in police agencies. Since civilian personnel are not technically police officers, they have no statutory power to make arrests or perform other special police functions. As a rule, civilian personnel perform secondary police duties of more of a support or staff function (discussed later in the chapter). Civilian personnel also are not as highly trained or as highly paid as their sworn counterparts, but they still make up an important segment of the police function. This is especially true in light of the growing use of computer technology by police departments in analyzing and solving crime.

Police agencies are unique in size, operation, and mission. A great degree of autonomy is enjoyed by each separate police organization in which administrative and functional decisions are all made in-house. Aside from differences between many police agencies, similarities exist as well. Each operates within the framework of a larger bureaucratic structure. For example, the FBI is located within the Department of Justice, which exists within the framework of the federal government. Other similarities can be observed, in particular with regard to local police organizations, which all share a common function within our neighborhoods (e.g., crime prevention, public service, enforcement of state law as well as municipal codes). In all cases most police agencies enjoy broad powers of discretion. Accordingly, each police agency is afforded a **mission**, which guides its function and helps to establish its enforcement priorities. Because the law does not prescribe enforcement priorities, decisions regarding the types of crimes to enforce and to what extent are made by each police agency. Although such decisions are often based on public consensus, departments will usually focus their enforcement efforts on controlling crimes and situations posing the greatest concern to the community.

THE EXPANSION OF FEDERAL LAW ENFORCEMENT

Since the 1960s, the federal government has expanded its role in dealing with crime, a policy area that has traditionally been the responsibility of state and local governments. The 1967 Report of the U.S. President's Commission on Law Enforcement and Administration of Justice emphasized the need for greater federal involvement in local crime control and urged that federal grants be directed to the states to support criminal justice initiatives. Since that time, Congress has allocated billions of dollars for crime-control efforts and passed legislation, national in scope, to deal with street crime, the "war on drugs," violent crime, terrorism, and juvenile delinquency. Although most law enforcement expenditures and personnel are found at the local level, over the past 40 years the federal government has increased its role in fighting street crime.[3]

Because many crimes span state borders (and are often transnational in scope), we no longer think of crimes as being committed at a single location within a single state. For example, organized crime groups and youth gangs deal with drugs, pornography, and gambling on a national level. Consequently, Congress has expanded the powers of the FBI and other federal law-enforcement agencies to pursue criminal activities that were formerly the responsibility of the states.

Congress has also passed laws designed to allow the FBI to investigate situations in which local police forces are likely to be less effective. For example, under the National Stolen Property Act, the FBI may investigate thefts of more than $5,000 in value when the stolen property is likely to have been transported across state lines. As a federal agency, the FBI is better able than any state or local agency to pursue criminal investigations across state borders.

Disputes over jurisdiction may occur when an offense violates both state and federal laws. If the FBI and local agencies do not cooperate, they may each be pursuing the same criminals. This can have major implications if the court to which the case is brought is determined by the agency that makes the arrest. Usually, however, law enforcement officials at all levels of government seek to cooperate and to coordinate their efforts.

After the September 11 attacks on the World Trade Center and the Pentagon, the FBI and other law enforcement agencies focused their resources and efforts on investigating and preventing terrorist threats against the United States, including tightening security at airports and national borders. This resulted in a major shift in the role of the FBI as a law enforcement agency. One month after the attacks, 4,000 of the agency's 11,500 agents were reassigned to investigations relating to the September 11 terrorist attack. So many FBI agents were switched from their traditional law enforcement activities to antiterrorist initiatives that some observers claimed that other federal crimes were no longer being vigorously investigated. Some fear that the federal government's response to potential threats to national security may ultimately diminish traditional federal law enforcement and thereby effectively transfer responsibility for many criminal investigations back to state and local officials.

The reorientation of the FBI's priorities is just one aspect of changes in federal government agencies as they address the threat of terrorism. Congress and President Bush sought to increase the government's effectiveness by creating a new federal agency. The Transportation Security Administration (TSA), a new agency within the Department of Transportation, assumed responsibility for protecting travelers and interstate commerce. Most importantly, the TSA assumed responsibility for screening passengers and their luggage at airports throughout the country. In light of the ease with which the September 11 hijackers brought "box cutters" on board commercial airliners, there were grave concerns that private security agencies were not adequately trained or sufficiently vigilant to protect the traveling public.

The biggest change in criminal justice occurred in November 2002, when Congress enacted legislation to create a new Department of Homeland Security (DHS). This department was created in order to centralize the administration and coordination of many existing agencies that were previously scattered throughout various departments. The Secretary of Homeland Security is responsible for overseeing the Coast Guard, Immigration and Naturalization Service (INS), Border Patrol, Secret Service, Federal Emergency Management Agency (FEMA), and other agencies (including the new TSA) concerned with protecting the food supply, nuclear power facilities, and other potential terrorism targets. The DHS will take charge of training emergency first responders, coordinating federal agencies' actions with those of state and local agencies, and analyzing domestic intelligence information obtained by the CIA, the FBI, and other sources.

The Secretary of Homeland Security faces an enormous challenge in seeking to integrate departments that previously operated separately. It remains to be seen how long it will take for the new department to handle its duties efficiently. There will, undoubtedly, be unanticipated problems as the combined federal agencies, as well as state and local agencies, begin to develop new working relationships.

FEDERAL LAW ENFORCEMENT AGENCIES

Statistically, employees of federal agencies do not make up a large part of the nation's law enforcement population. In fact, the NYPD has nearly half as many employees as the entire federal law enforcement system combined. The influence of these federal agencies, however, is substantial.

Unlike local police departments, which must deal with all forms of crime, federal agencies have been authorized, typically by Congress, to enforce specific laws or attend to specific situations. The U.S. Coast Guard, for example, patrols the nation's waterways, whereas U.S. postal inspectors investigate and prosecute crimes perpetrated through the use of the U.S. Postal Service. Accordingly, the Federal Controlled Substances Act is enforced primarily by the Drug Enforcement Administration (DEA), and the Criminal Investigation Division of the Internal Revenue Service (IRS) enforces laws against federal tax code violations. In response to terrorist attacks on September 11, 2001, the Federal Aviation Administration has resurrected a program that places law enforcement agents on passenger aircraft. Like local police officers, federal agents possess full police powers, carry guns and badges, make arrests, collect evidence, and testify in criminal court proceedings.

The federal government maintains about 50 agencies that play a role in law enforcement. We will look at the most important ones here, according to the federal department or bureau to which they report.

Although the U.S. Constitution did not specifically establish federal police agencies, Congress created them for the enforcement of specific federal acts. For example, counterfeiting is investigated by the Secret Service, while counterterrorism investigations are the responsibility of the FBI. Accordingly, the Federal Controlled Substances Act is enforced primarily by the DEA, and the Criminal Investigation Division of the IRS enforces laws against federal tax code violations. Because federal agents possess full police powers, carry guns and badges, make arrests, collect evidence, and testify in criminal court proceedings, it is easy to become confused about the authority of federal law enforcement agencies. While the goals of federal agencies differ and their authority covers broad geographical areas, the scope of most agencies is very specific and limited. For example, federal agencies are authorized to enforce only federal statutes enacted by Congress. In other words, federal officers may not enforce state or local laws any more than local officers can enforce federal laws. In many circumstances, however, a particular criminal act will violate both state and federal laws—for example, drug trafficking. In these cases, investigations and arrests may be facilitated by both jurisdictions working together.

Specialization and a relatively narrow focus of authority also characterize federal law enforcement agencies. Indeed, they are a result of how these agencies have developed over the years as well as of the reluctance of Congress to empower any one agency with too much federal enforcement authority, thus preventing a "national police." However, in a practical sense, the effectiveness of such an organization would probably be marginal due to the massive number of federal laws. The federal arm of law enforcement has two related objectives:

1. To enforce the federal criminal code
2. To give officers specialized training to aid them in their enforcement role

ADDRESSING THE TERRORISM THREAT

In the aftermath of the September 11, 2001 attacks, it became obvious that the nation was not prepared to deal adequately with the threat of terrorism. One reason is the very nature of American society. Because we live in a free and open nation, it is extremely difficult to seal the borders and prevent the entry of terrorist groups. For example, even with the assistance of new high-tech sensors, it takes five customs inspectors three hours to conduct a thorough physical examination of a loaded 40-foot container or an 18-wheeler truck. Every day, nearly 5,000 trucks enter the United States on the Ambassador Bridge between Detroit, Michigan, and Windsor, Ontario. With eight primary inspection lanes and a parking lot that can hold only 90 trailers at a time, U.S. Customs officers must average no more than two minutes per truck. If they fall behind, the parking lot fills, trucks back up onto the bridge, and chaos ensues on the roadways throughout metropolitan Windsor and Detroit.

Sensing this problem, law enforcement agencies around the country began to realign their resources to combat future terrorist attacks. In some cases, proposed changes are in the planning or approval stage, whereas for others, change has already been implemented.

THE DEPARTMENT OF HOMELAND SECURITY

On November 19, 2002, Congress passed legislation authorizing the creation of a new cabinet-level Department of Homeland Security (DHS) "providing for intelligence analysis and infrastructure protection, strengthening our borders, improving the use of science and technology to counter weapons of mass destruction, and creating a comprehensive response and recovery division." The creation of the DHS represents one of the major transformations of the U.S. government since 1947, when Harry S. Truman merged the various branches of the U.S. Armed Forces into the Department of Defense to better coordinate the nation's defense against military threats. DHS represents a similar consolidation.

Under the legislation signed by President Bush on November 25, 2002, the office folded existing agencies within its framework to create a super-agency with four divisions.

Border and Transportation Security

The DHS is responsible for securing our nation's borders and transportation systems, which include 350 ports of entry. The department manages who and what enters the United States and works to prevent the entry of terrorists and the instruments of terrorism, while simultaneously ensuring the speedy flow of legitimate traffic. The border security mission incorporates the Customs Service (formerly part of the Department of the Treasury), the INS and Border Patrol (formerly with the Department of Justice), the Animal and Plant Health Inspection Service (Department of Agriculture), and the TSA (formerly with the Department of Transportation). The department also incorporates the Federal Protective Service (formerly with the General Services Administration [GSA]) to perform the additional function of protecting government buildings, a task closely related to the department's infrastructure protection responsibilities. In order to secure territorial waters, including ports and waterways, the department assumes authority over the U.S. Coast Guard.

Emergency Preparedness and Response

The DHS ensures the preparedness of emergency response professionals, provides the federal government's response, and aids America's recovery from terrorist attacks and natural disasters. To fulfill these missions, the department incorporates FEMA within its structure. The department will be responsible for reducing the loss of life and property and protecting institutions from all types of hazards through an emergency-management program of preparedness, mitigation, response, and recovery. It will lead our national response to a biological attack; direct the Nuclear Emergency Search Teams, Radiological Emergency Response Team, Radiological Assistance Program, Domestic Emergency Support Team, National Pharmaceutical Stockpile, and the National Disaster Medical System; and manage the Metropolitan Medical Response System. The department will also coordinate the involvement of other federal response assets such as the National Guard in the event of a major incident.

Science and Technology

The DHS leads the federal government's efforts in preparing for and responding to the full range of terrorist threats involving weapons of mass destruction. To do this, the department sets national policy and establishes guidelines for state and local governments. Its mission includes directing exercises and drills for federal, state, and local chemical, biological, radiological, and nuclear (CBRN) response teams and plans. The department also works to prevent the importation of nuclear weapons and material. It focuses on better detection of illicit nuclear material transport on the open seas, at U.S. ports of entry, and throughout the national transportation system. It also develops, deploys, manages, and maintains a national system for detecting the use of biological agents within the United States. This system consists of a national public-health data-surveillance system to monitor public and private databases for indications that a terrorist attack has occurred, as well as a sensor network to detect and report the release of bioterrorist pathogens in densely populated areas.

Information Analysis and Infrastructure Protection

The department analyzes legally accessible information from multiple available sources, including, for instance, intelligence, the CIA, FBI, the National Security Agency, and local law enforcement. By obtaining and analyzing this information, the department has the ability to review comprehensively the dangers facing the nation, to ensure that the president is briefed on relevant information, and to take necessary protective action. The DHS complements the FBI's enhanced emphasis on counterterrorism law enforcement by ensuring that information from the FBI is analyzed along with all other intelligence. In addition to analyzing law enforcement and intelligence information, the DHS protects the nation's cyberinfrastructure from terrorist attacks by unifying and focusing the key cybersecurity activities performed by the Critical Infrastructure Assurance Office (formerly part of the Department of Commerce) and the National Infrastructure Protection Center (under the FBI). The department augments those capabilities with the response functions of the Federal Computer Incident Response Center (formerly housed under the GSA).[4]

Customs and Border Protection

The transition to cbp.gov is a work in progress. References to the predecessor agencies will be replaced with Customs and Border Protection (CBP) and material from all aspects of the agency will be represented. Look to cbp.gov for the latest mission success stories and program updates within CBP.

The priority mission of CBP is to prevent terrorists and terrorist weapons from entering the United States. This important mission calls for improved security at America's borders and ports of entry as well as for extending our zone of security beyond our physical borders—so that American borders are the last line of defense, not the first.

CBP also is responsible for apprehending individuals attempting to enter the United States illegally; stemming the flow of illegal drugs and other contraband; protecting our agricultural and economic interests from harmful pests and diseases; protecting American businesses from theft of their intellectual property; and regulating and facilitating international trade, collecting import duties, and enforcing U.S. trade laws.

To accomplish its missions, CBP has a workforce of more than 40,000 dedicated employees. In those ranks are inspectors, canine enforcement officers, border patrol agents, trade specialists, and mission support staff. For the first time in our nation's history, people and goods arriving at American ports of entry are greeted by one single agency with one unified goal: to facilitate legitimate trade and travel while utilizing all the resources at our disposal to protect and defend the United States from those who would do Americans harm.

CBP became an official agency of the DHS on March 1, 2003, combining employees from the Department of Agriculture, the INS, the Border Patrol, and the U.S. Customs Service. Unifying the border agencies—a good government reform advocated by many studies over the past 30 years—will improve the way the U.S. government manages the border. The United States is combining its skills and resources to make sure that the country will be far more effective and efficient than when border responsibilities were fragmented into four agencies in three different departments of government.

FIGURE 3.1   The sight of armed National Guard personnel in U.S. airports became common in the aftermath of the terrorist bombings of September 11, 2001.

The Bureau of Immigration and Customs Enforcement

On March 1, 2003, functions of several border and security agencies, including the former INS, were transferred into the *Directorate of Border and Transportation Security* within the DHS. As part of this transition, these agency functions were reorganized into the *Bureau of Immigration and Customs Enforcement* (ICE).

The ICE consists of approximately 14,000 federal employees who focus on the enforcement of immigration and customs laws within the United States, the protection of specified federal buildings, and air and marine enforcement. The bureau is led by an assistant secretary, who reports directly to the Undersecretary for Border and Transportation Security.

The ICE comprises the following primary program areas:

- *Immigration Investigations.* Responsible for investigating violations of the criminal and administrative provisions of the Immigration and Nationality Act (INA) and other related provisions of the U.S. code
- *Customs Investigations.* Responsible for investigating a range of issues, including terrorist financing, export enforcement, money laundering, smuggling, and fraud—including intellectual property rights violations and cybercrimes
- *Customs Air and Marine Interdiction.* Responsible for protecting the nation's borders and the American people from the smuggling of narcotics, other contraband, and terrorist activity with an integrated and coordinated air and marine interdiction force
- *Federal Protective Service.* Responsible for providing a safe environment in which federal agencies can conduct their business by reducing threats posed against the more than 8,800 GSA–controlled facilities nationwide

- ***Detention and Removal.*** Responsible for promoting the public safety and national security by ensuring the departure from the United States of all removable aliens through the fair enforcement of the nation's immigration laws
- ***Immigration Intelligence.*** Responsible for the collection, analysis, and dissemination of intelligence to immigration staff at all levels to aid in making day-to-day, midterm, and long-term operational decisions; acquiring and allocating resources; and determining policy
- ***Customs Intelligence.*** Responsible for the collection, analysis, and dissemination of strategic and tactical intelligence data for use by the operational elements of customs enforcement

The Department of Justice

The U.S. Department of Justice plays an important role in controlling crime through police practices, prosecution, crime prevention, and rehabilitation of offenders. Within the Department of Justice are the FBI, the DEA, and the U.S. Marshal's Service.

The terrorist attacks of 2001 necessitated some degree of reorganization within the Department of Justice. For example, the INS was transferred to the DHS and the Bureau of Alcohol, Tobacco, and Firearms was transferred to the Department of Justice and became the Bureau of Alcohol, Tobacco, Firearms, and Explosives (ATF). Currently, of the 65 components of the Department of Justice, those organizations having the greatest responsibility for law enforcement are the FBI, DEA, ATF, the U.S. Marshal's Service, and related agencies such as the U.S. Attorney's Offices.

Federal Bureau of Investigation

No police agency has had such a profound impact on U.S. policing nor has been more controversial than the FBI. Originally established in 1908 under the Justice Department, the Bureau of Investigation (BOI) was initially active in countering German espionage during World War I. During this period, a young law school graduate named J. Edgar Hoover began his career as a law clerk with the Department of Justice. In 1918 he was promoted to a position in the General Criminal Investigation Division and pursued communist espionage agents.

American Policing under Fire

Policing Our Borders

In the wake of the September 11 attacks and the deaths of more than 3,000 people, Americans felt increasingly vulnerable to terrorists and the threat of violence. Shortly after the terrorist attacks of 9/11, it was discovered that 19 Arab men with terrorist ties had entered the United States prior to the attacks. The attacks put the nation on high alert. Airports shut down; ships with potentially dangerous cargo, such as liquefied natural gas, were blocked from ports; National Guardsmen patrolled power plants, reservoirs, borders, airports, and major bridges. Then, without warning, anthrax-tainted letters began arriving at government and news organization offices around the country, eventually killing two postal workers.

Soon afterward, more sweeping responses were ordered. President George W. Bush formed a new Department of Homeland Security to find answers and coordinate a response to terrorism. Legislators met with legal experts from key agencies and quickly passed legislation giving law enforcement more power to fight terrorism. At the same time, a greater focus was placed on border-security agencies.

The debate on how best to reduce threats to the nation's security continues. In addition to controlling the nation's 7,500-mile-long borders with Mexico and Canada, federal agents must monitor the 11 million trucks and 2.2 million railcars that enter the United States every year, plus 7,500 foreign flagships that make 51,000 calls in U.S. ports.

Included in the responsibility are more than 31 million noncitizens who enter the country each year and who are supposed to notify immigration officials when their visas expire or when they change addresses, jobs, or schools.

Efforts for increased border security include:

- Improved intelligence gathering on visa applicants
- Increased data sharing among federal agencies
- Closer scrutiny of incoming cargo
- Stronger security measures at the borders
- Computer tracking of immigrants and visa holders after they've arrived in the United States

After a short period of time, Hoover became well known as an expert on the U.S. Communist Party and its domestic maneuvers. Like many police organizations operating during this era, the FBI was inundated with political appointees. In 1921, Hoover was named assistant director of the FBI under newly appointed William J. Burns. During his early tenure as assistant director, Hoover focused on tracking, investigating, and prosecuting the Ku Klux Klan in the South.

The Teapot Dome scandal was almost solely the reason for Hoover's progression to director of the bureau in 1924. The scandal involved high-ranking officials under President Harding, who conspired to sell costly oil leases on government-owned land in return for sizable bribes from oil drilling companies. The FBI was not implicated in the scandal, but bureau agents had been in collusion with Director Burns in a scheme to discredit Senator Burton K. Wheeler of Montana. Wheeler was acting as chairman of the Senate committee charged with the investigation of Teapot Dome, and the attempt to embarrass the senator led to public outrage.

During the 1930s, the FBI gained considerable notoriety in its relentless pursuit of well-known criminals who had made the bureau's famous ten-most-wanted list, including Machine Gun Kelly, Baby Face Nelson, Pretty Boy Floyd, Bonnie Parker and Clyde Barrow, "Ma" Barker, and John Dillinger. Media coverage of these investigations gave rise to the term **G-men**, which became closely associated with the bureau's scrupulous image. In 1935, the bureau changed its name to the FBI. Today, the FBI employs over 21,000 people—9,000 of whom are special agents—and operates 59 field offices. Its jurisdiction extends to some 200 crimes. FBI special agents are required to complete a 16-week training program at the FBI National Academy in Quantico, Virginia. In addition, they are authorized to perform investigative duties in a number of fields, which include gathering and reporting facts pertaining to suspected criminal activity, locating witnesses, gathering evidence on violations of federal law, and offering testimony in federal court. The bureau concentrates on white-collar and organized crime but often investigates crimes relating to civil rights violations, violations under the Racketeer Influenced and Corrupt Organizations (RICO) Act, foreign espionage, and drug offenses.

A Closer Look

J. Edgar Hoover (1895–1972)

J. Edgar Hoover began his lengthy career in the U.S. Justice Department in 1917, just after receiving a law degree from George Washington University. In 1924, he was appointed director of the ill-regarded bureau of Investigation (which became the FBI in 1935) and vowed immediately to improve professionalism within the bureau's ranks by rigorously recruiting college students, lawyers, and accountants. During his 48 years as director, Hoover made the FBI into a large, efficient, and internationally famous police agency. He ended political preferment and raised recruiting standards.

Furthermore, Hoover made the bureau the national center of law enforcement activities with its fingerprint files and ability to compile crime statistics. In addition, the FBI maintains a national crime laboratory and training academy. Because of these innovations, the FBI was able to increase its effectiveness and service to state and local police agencies. Displaying a keen sense of public relations, Hoover focused the bureau's activities on areas of public concern. For example, during the 1930s, FBI agents pursued and arrested notorious gangsters. During World War II, the FBI focused on foreign enemy agents, and during the postwar period it concentrated on anticommunism efforts. These activities were widely publicized by Hoover in his own books and articles, while he gave strong support to radio and television dramas that portrayed the FBI in a positive light. Soon Hoover became one of the most powerful figures in Washington—all but immune from control by his nominal superiors, the attorney general, and the president.

Hoover accepted the appointment to director under the condition that he be free from political influence and that he have complete authority to regulate discipline within the bureau. Hoover remained in his position until his death on May 1, 1972. Under Hoover's reign, a plan to increase professionalism among agents was implemented immediately. Only college graduates were considered as possible new recruits. Of these, law school graduates and people with accounting degrees were preferred. Training was extensive, and new agents were required to accept assignments anywhere in the nation.

Among its many divisions, the FBI is famous for its immense Identification Division, which operates the bureau's automated fingerprint service. This information consists of thousands of fingerprint records, which are received daily and maintained on an estimated 200 million persons. Another major division is the bureau's Intelligence Division, which gathers and analyzes data on the composition and movement of terrorists and organized criminal organizations. The FBI National Academy trains over 1,000 local and state police officers per year.

One of the most significant proposals to fight the problem of terrorism has been a realignment of the FBI. By early 2002, the FBI announced a reaffirmation of its priorities, making protecting the United States from terrorist attacks its top commitment.

To carry out its newly formulated mission, the FBI expanded its force of agents, hiring approximately 1,000 additional agents before 2004. In addition to recruiting candidates with a traditional background in law enforcement, law, and accounting, the bureau is concentrating on hiring agents with scientific and technological skills as well as foreign language proficiency in priority languages such as Arabic, Farsi, Pashtun, Urdu, all dialects of Chinese, Japanese, Korean, Russian, Spanish, and Vietnamese and with other priority backgrounds such as foreign counterintelligence, counterterrorism, and military intelligence. Besides helping in counterterrorism activities, these agents staff the new cyberdivision, which was created in 2001 to coordinate, oversee, and facilitate FBI investigations in which the Internet, online services, and computer systems and networks are the principal instruments or targets of terrorists.

Drug Enforcement Administration

The DEA had its beginnings with the passing of the 1914 Harrison Narcotics Act. The Harrison Act was passed under the administration of President Woodrow Wilson and was viewed by many as a rational way to limit addiction and drug abuse through taxation and regulation.[5] One measure of the act, however, called for criminal penalties for "non-registered" personnel who possessed heroin, cocaine, opium, morphine, or any derivatives of these drugs. Hence agents in the Bureau of Internal Revenue's "Miscellaneous Division" were charged with enforcement of the act. As a result of rigorous enforcement of the act, the bureau's agents made enforcement history through a literal interpretation of the law.

FIGURE 3.2 Drug Enforcement Administration agent with automatic weapon guarding a large seizure of multiple kilos of cocaine in Miami, Florida.

For example, most of the arrests and convictions occurring in the first year of its enactment were of physicians who were attempting to treat addicts. Crime in the 1920s required strict enforcement enterprises focusing on Chinese organized crime figures who were suspected of trafficking most of the opium and heroin entering the United States. In fact, San Francisco's famed Chinatown was the site of many drug raids, which resulted in the deportation of hundreds of Chinese thought to be involved in opium importation.

The 1919 Volstead Act was enacted to enforce the Eighteenth Amendment. An immense prohibition unit was formed and operated under the Revenue Bureau. A smaller unit, the narcotics division, also operated within the bureau. This division, headed by former pharmacist Levi G. Nutt, employed 170 agents who worked out of 13 offices around the country. On July 1, 1930, the narcotics division became the Federal Bureau of Narcotics (FBN), headed by Harry Anslinger, a Herbert Hoover appointee. The bureau expanded quickly under the leadership of Anslinger. Indeed, he proved to be a formidable leader in drug-control policy. Some experts attributed Anslinger's effectiveness to being "successful in cultivating and sustaining solid political ties with key members of both parties and gain[ing] support of hundreds of interest groups and lobbies making him virtually immune to opposition within or outside federal government."[6]

In the 1930s, marijuana, which was not covered in the Harrison Act, was deemed to be a major problem in many communities. Under considerable public pressure, Congress passed the 1937 Marijuana Tax Act, requiring a fine of $100 for each ounce of possession of nontaxed marijuana. Some families of the Mafia attempted to capitalize on a segment of the market during the 1930s. For example, Louis "Lepke" Buchalter, an associate of famed crime boss "Lucky" Luciano, allegedly smuggled an estimated 650 kilograms of pure heroin into the United States from Shanghai. The passing of the 1951 Boggs Act made it illegal for heroin to be distributed in any fashion, which included prescriptions. The 1960s saw an increase in drug trafficking and abuse. As synthetic drugs became a major problem in most cities, a massive reorganization of federal enforcement led to the creation in 1968 of the Bureau of Narcotics and Dangerous Drugs (BNDD).

A Closer Look

FBI Director Robert Mueller (September 4, 2001–Present)

Robert Mueller was nominated by President George W. Bush and became the sixth director of the FBI on September 4, 2001. Born on August 7, 1944, in New York City, Mueller grew up outside of Philadelphia. He graduated from Princeton University in 1966 and earned a master's degree in international relations from New York University in 1967. He then joined the United States Marine Corps, where he served as an officer for three years, leading a rifle platoon of the Third Marine Division in Vietnam. He received the Bronze Star, two Navy Commendation Medals, the Purple Heart, and the Vietnamese Cross of Gallantry. Following his military service, Mueller earned a law degree from the University of Virginia Law School in 1973 and served on the *Law Review*. After completing his education, Mueller worked as a litigator in San Francisco until 1976. He then served for 12 years in the U.S. Attorney's Offices, first in the Northern District of California in San Francisco, where he rose to be chief of its criminal division. In 1982, he moved to Boston as an Assistant U.S. Attorney, where he investigated and prosecuted major financial fraud, terrorist, and public corruption cases, as well as narcotics conspiracies and international money launderers.

After serving as a partner at the Boston law firm of Hill and Barlow, Mueller was again called to public service. In 1989 he served in the United States Department of Justice as an assistant to Attorney General Richard L. Thornburgh. The following year he took charge of its Criminal Division. During his tenure, he oversaw several prosecutions, including the conviction of Panama leader Manuel Noriega, the Lockerbie Pan Am 103 bombing case, and the John Gotti mobster prosecution. In 1991, he was elected Fellow of the American College of Trial Lawyers.

In 1993, Mueller became a partner at Boston's Hale and Dorr, specializing in complex white-collar-crime litigation. He returned to public service in 1995 as senior litigator in the Homicide Section of the District of Columbia United States Attorney's Office. In 1998, Mueller was named United States Attorney in San Francisco and held that position until 2001. He then served as Acting Deputy Attorney General of the U.S. Department of Justice for several months before becoming FBI Director.

During the late 1960s, the popularity of drugs such as cocaine, LSD, and PCP increased. In recourse, Congress passed the Comprehensive Drug Abuse Prevention and Control Act of 1970. This new law updated all previous federal legislation and was the basis for all federal enforcement initiatives. In addition, it established five schedules, which classify substances according to their potential for abuse. In 1973, the old BNDD was merged with other federal drug control agencies, and the Drug Enforcement Administration (DEA) was originated and placed under the Department of Justice. Today the DEA is one of the fastest-growing federal law enforcement agencies. Indeed, drug manufacturing, trafficking, and wholesale and retail sales of illegal drugs have become one of today's top public-safety priorities.

The DEA's charge is to focus on the "most significant individuals and organizations involved in drug trafficking both domestically and internationally."[7] Accordingly, investigations may entail both foreign and domestic criminal operations. The DEA maintains offices throughout the United States as well as foreign offices in drug-source countries. One hundred and twenty domestic and 43 foreign offices employ an estimated 250 agents. The DEA has also adopted a "floating" enforcement strategy, which shifts to meet the demands of traffickers who are always changing their trafficking methods. In recent years the Mexican border and South Florida have been prioritized as major concentration points for increased enforcement personnel.

TREASURY DEPARTMENT DUTIES AND FUNCTIONS

The law enforcement function of the U.S. Treasury also underwent considerable reorganization in the 2002–2003 realignment of the federal government. The U.S. Treasury's enforcement functions currently focus on counterterrorist financing, counterterrorism, money laundering and other financial crimes, counterfeiting, violent crime, tariff and trade enforcement, and economic sanctions.

On the Street

The DEA in Action: The Indictment of Arellano-Felix Organization (12 Key Members Charged)

On July 8, 2003, two federal indictments charged 12 individuals who represent the top hierarchy of the Arellano-Felix Organization (AFO). Long reputed to be one of the most notorious multinational drug-trafficking organizations ever, the AFO controlled the flow of cocaine, marijuana, and other drugs through the Mexican border cities of Tijuana and Mexicali into the United States. Its operations also extended into southern Mexico as well as Colombia.

The first indictment against 11 individuals charged an overarching racketeering conspiracy running from 1986 to the present and was the culmination of a decade-long investigation of the AFO led by the DEA in conjunction with the FBI, the IRS, the Bureau of ICE, and the California Bureau of Narcotics Enforcement (BNE). The indictment alleges that, beginning in the mid-1980s and continuing to the present, the AFO was responsible for the importation and distribution in the United States of hundreds of tons of cocaine and marijuana.

Among those arrested were Alberto Benjamin Arellano-Felix, Eduardo Ramon Arellano-Felix, and Francisco Javier Arellano-Felix, all key players in the organization. The indictment charged the suspects with conducting the affairs of an illegal enterprise through a pattern of racketeering activity

(RICO), conspiracy to import and distribute cocaine and marijuana, as well as money laundering. The leadership of the AFO is alleged to have negotiated directly with Colombian cocaine-trafficking organizations, including a Colombian guerilla organization, for the purchase of multiton shipments of cocaine. They allegedly received those shipments by sea and by air in Mexico and then arranged for the smuggling of the cocaine into the United States, where it was distributed. The proceeds of the AFO's drug trafficking, estimated by law enforcement to be in the hundreds of millions of dollars, are alleged to have been smuggled back into Mexico.

The AFO is also alleged to have recruited, trained, and armed groups of bodyguards and assassins who were responsible for protecting the leaders of the organization and also for conducting assassinations of rival drug traffickers, suspected cooperators, uncooperative Mexican law enforcement and military personnel, and members of the Mexican news media who printed stories unfavorable toward the AFO. Law enforcement officials estimate that the AFO was responsible for more than one hundred drug-related murders, both in Mexico and in the United States. The indictment specifically alleges 20 murders in the United States and Mexico that were carried out by the AFO.

The undersecretary is responsible for coordinating all Treasury Department law enforcement matters, including the formulation of policies for all Treasury Department enforcement activities and coordinating law enforcement matters with other federal agencies.

Changes in Treasury Department Organization

As with the Department of Justice, the Treasury Department has undergone some realignment of its agencies. For example, effective March 1, 2003, the Federal Law Enforcement Training Center, the United States Secret Service, and the United States Customs Service were moved to the DHS and no longer were bureaus of the Department of the Treasury. In addition, effective January 24, 2003, the Law Enforcement functions of the Bureau of Alcohol, Tobacco, and Firearms (now called the Bureau of Alcohol, Tobacco, Firearms, and Explosives) was transferred to the Department of Justice. At the same time, theAlcohol Tax and Trade Bureau was created to enforce and administer the laws covering the production, use, and distribution of alcohol and tobacco products.

Financial Crimes Enforcement Network

As reflected in its name, the Financial Crimes Enforcement Network (FinCEN) is a network, a means of bringing people and information together to fight the problem of money laundering. Since its creation in 1990, FinCEN has facilitated information sharing among law enforcement agencies and other organizations in the regulatory and financial communities. Working together is critical in succeeding against today's criminals.

FinCEN is a relatively small federal bureau with approximately 200 employees. The majority of the staff is made up of permanent FinCEN personnel, mostly intelligence professionals, as well as specialists from the financial industry and computer experts. In addition, about 40 long-term "detailees" are assigned to FinCEN from 21 different regulatory and law enforcement agencies.

Today, FinCEN is one of Treasury's primary agencies for the prevention and detection of money laundering. This is accomplished in two ways. First, FinCEN uses counter–money laundering laws (such as the Bank Secrecy Act, or BSA) to require reporting and record keeping by banks and other financial institutions. This record keeping preserves a financial trail for investigators to follow as they track criminals and their assets. The BSA also requires reporting suspicious currency transactions that could trigger investigations. FinCEN establishes these policies and regulations to deter and detect money laundering in partnership with the financial community.

Second, FinCEN provides intelligence and analytic support to law enforcement. FinCEN's work is concentrated on combining information reported under the BSA with other government and public information. This information is then disclosed to FinCEN's customers in the law enforcement community in the form of intelligence reports. These reports help them build investigations and plan new strategies to combat money laundering.

STATE-LEVEL POLICE AGENCIES

The most visible state law enforcement agency is the state police or highway patrol agency. Historically, state police agencies were created for four reasons:

- To assist local police agencies, which often do not have adequate resources or training to handle their law enforcement tasks
- To investigate criminals or committees that cross jurisdictional boundaries (e.g., one bank robber commits a crime and flees to another county in the state)
- To provide law enforcement in rural and other areas that do not have local or county police agencies
- To break strikes and control labor movements

The first statewide police organization was the Texas Rangers. When this organization was initially created in 1835, the Rangers' primary purpose was to patrol the border with Mexico as scouts for the Republic of Texas army. The Rangers evolved into a more general-purpose law enforcement agency, and in 1874 they were commissioned as police officers and given law enforcement duties. The Arizona Rangers (created in 1901) and the New Mexico mounted police (1905) were formed in a similar manner.

Differences between state police and highway patrols. Today there are 23 state police agencies and 26 highway patrols in the United States. State police agencies have statewide jurisdiction and are authorized to perform a wide variety of law enforcement tasks. They provide the same services as city or county police departments and are limited only by the boundaries of the state. In contrast, highway patrols have limited authority. They are limited either by their jurisdiction or by specific types of offenses they have the authority to control. As their name suggests, most highway patrols concentrate primarily on regulating traffic: Specifically, they enforce traffic laws and investigate traffic accidents. Furthermore, they usually limit their activity to patrolling state and federal highways.

Trying to determine what state agency has which duties can be confusing. The Washington State Highway Patrol, despite its name, also has state police powers. In addition, 35 states have investigative agencies that are independent of the state police or Highway Patrol. Such agencies are usually found in states with highway patrols, and they have the primary responsibility of investigating criminal activities. For example, in addition to its Highway Patrol, Oklahoma runs a State Bureau of Investigation and the state BNDD. Each state has its own methods of determining the jurisdictions of these various organizations.

For the most part, state police are complementary to law enforcement agencies. They maintain crime labs to assist in local investigations and also keep statewide intelligence files. State officers in some jurisdictions also provide training to local police and will assist local forces when needed.

In addition to regular police responsibilities, state police officers patrol state parks, offer protection for state legislative personnel and properties, conduct motor vehicle license examinations,

Highlights in Policing

State Police

- *State police officer.* State police provide police services to the public by patrolling state and interstate highways, turnpikes, and freeways and by enforcing motor vehicle and criminal laws. Powers of state police vary greatly from state to state. Some have full police powers throughout the state, while others are restricted to highway patrol and traffic regulation. In most cases, state police units are organized into posts or troops within specific geographical areas. Each troop has a communications center, barracks, lockup, crime laboratory, and pistol range. The vast majority of state police officers use motor vehicles, but a few use motorcycles or aircraft in performing their assignments. In many cases, state police officers provide help to victims of fires, floods, or other disasters and act to control traffic during such situations. In many states, state police officers have powers similar to those of municipal police forces. In such

cases duties include the investigation of burglaries, robberies, homicides, drug offenses, and liquor violations.
- *State police sergeant.* State police sergeants perform many of the duties of state police officers but are also involved in supervising and coordinating the work of those officers. Each workday, they report to their assigned troop where they take command of their designated group of officers at the start of the work shift. At this point, sergeants typically take roll call, prepare attendance records, and inspect other officers' appearance and equipment for adherence to agency regulations. Next, they assign officers to their posts. Because of the nature of state police work, sergeants cannot directly supervise their subordinates. They do, however, maintain radio contact with each other and periodically drive through officers' districts to observe and evaluate individual work performance.

enforce fish and wildlife laws, and evaluate permits for pistols. During special emergencies, such as civil disturbances, state police are commonly brought in for support. Highway patrol organizations are charged with enforcing state motor vehicle codes and related laws dealing with the operation of motor vehicles on highways. In some jurisdictions, highway patrol organizations may employ investigators to probe certain types of criminal activity, such as organized crime, vice, drug violations, fraud, and gambling.

In addition to state police agencies, most states support a crime laboratory and a computerized clearinghouse for criminal information. The state crime lab provides forensic services to police jurisdictions that cannot afford their own laboratory facilities. Laboratory personnel examine evidence and scenes of crimes, identify and compare evidence, and testify in criminal court proceedings on behalf of the prosecution. State clearinghouses for criminal information keep fingerprint files, gather and analyze crime data, and provide information to police organizations on all levels of government.

In addition, most states employ officers to enforce public safety and health codes. For example, the state fire marshal's office has varied responsibilities, which include enforcing statewide fire and safety regulations and developing fire prevention programs. Its efforts are closely coordinated with local fire departments in carrying out their enforcement responsibilities. State public-health officials enforce codes pertaining to public sanitation, pollution, communicable diseases, health facility licenses, and food and drug standards. To aid them in the enforcement of these laws, officers work closely with local and federal agencies.

Finally, it should be mentioned that many other examples of state-level enforcement agencies exist. When examining a chart of state organizational structure, one can observe a variety of bureaus, divisions, and agencies using investigative personnel to some extent: agriculture, which includes dairy and livestock; produce markets; weights and measures; liquor and racing authorities; insurance; commerce; finance; mental hygiene; housing and industrial safety; civil service or merit system commissions; and vocational standards for licensing professionals.

THE COUNTY SHERIFF

A vestige of the English Shire Reeve discussed in Chapter 2, the sheriff is still an important figure in American law enforcement. Almost every one of the more than 3,000 counties in the United States (except those in Alaska) has a sheriff. In every state except Rhode Island and Hawaii, sheriffs are elected by members of the community for two- or four-year terms and are paid a salary set by the state legislature or county board. As elected officials who do not necessarily need a background in law enforcement, modern sheriffs resemble their counterparts from the political era of policing in many ways. Simply put, the sheriff is also a politician. When a new sheriff is elected, he or she will sometimes repay political debts by appointing new deputies or promoting those who have given him or her support. This high degree of instability and personnel turnover in many states is seen as one of the weaknesses of county law enforcement.[8]

Like municipal police forces, sheriffs' departments vary in size. The largest is the Los Angeles County Sheriff's Department with more than 8,600 full-time employees. Of the 3,061 sheriffs departments in the country, 13 employ more than 1,000 officers while 19 have only one.[9]

Over the years, the function of the county sheriff has become infused with local politics, a situation that has resulted in high turnover rates in personnel as well as in low training standards and faulty personnel selection practices. However, some exceptions to these allegations do exist. For example, Dade County, Florida, and Los Angeles County, California, both enjoy a reputation for professionalism and high standards. One suggestion has been to abolish the constitutional authority of the sheriff and empower the office with statutory powers only.

The goal is to replace the plural executive organization of county government with a centralized county administration or a board of police commissioners. This would entail replacement of

Highlights in Policing

County Policing

- *Deputy sheriff.* Deputies are uniformed county law enforcement officers who patrol assigned districts within their jurisdictions to enforce federal, state, and local laws; investigate crimes; and maintain the peace. While patrolling assigned areas, they observe persons and conditions for evidence of suspicious or criminal behavior and investigate such activities. Deputies may also transport suspects between courtrooms, jails, or medical facilities. Investigating, assuming control at scenes of accidents, administering first aid to the injured, and radioing for emergency vehicles are also part of the job. Deputies working as detectives work in plain clothes and investigate crimes of vice, drugs, murder, theft, juvenile offenses, assaults, and missing persons.
- *Sergeant, sheriff's department.* Sergeants in sheriffs' departments supervise and coordinate the work of deputy sheriffs who patrol assigned districts within their jurisdictions. In addition, they supervise activities of deputies who perform certain duties in jails and court facilities. Sergeants also help to direct the deployment of squad members in cases of riots, hostage situations, or natural disasters. In addition, they take part in field duties and perform many of the same duties of deputy sheriffs, enforcing vehicle codes, taking charge at accident scenes, assisting with criminal investigations, and apprehending, criminal suspects at the site of incidents—using physical force if necessary.
- *Chief deputy.* The duties of chief deputies depend on the size and nature of the sheriff's department. In general, they are responsible for all personnel under their command, including supervisory staff. They also develop work schedules and assignments for subordinates, devise new or revised procedures to serve as guidelines for proper conduct of police activities, evaluate the effectiveness of their policies by reviewing reports, and meet with supervisory personnel to gauge the effectiveness of activities such as patrol, traffic, criminal investigations, and jail operations.

the sheriff's department with a police organization that would assume responsibility for countywide police services under the direction of a county board of commissioners. Under this plan, county law enforcement would operate free of political influence. With the sheriff in total control, however, it is virtually impossible for the county to maintain accountability by the sheriff's department.

Finally, besides countywide police and sheriffs' departments, other local police personnel operate within counties. Designated as constables, marshals, or police officers, these people enforce the law in similar communities, such as villages, townships, and boroughs. The continued presence of the local police official in smaller communities is evidence of the citizen's preference for local control of police services. In some jurisdictions, other special police units operate. These police units, although often limited in jurisdiction, patrol parks, tunnels, bridges, freeways, and harbors and provide important services to the general public.

THE MUNICIPAL POLICE FUNCTION

According to the FBI, there are 2.4 state and local police officers for every 1,000 citizens in the United States.[10] This average somewhat masks the discrepancies between the police forces in urban and rural America. The vast majority of all police officers work in small and medium-size police departments. While the NYPD has more than 37,000 sworn officers, some 560 small towns have only one police officer.[11]

Of the three levels of law enforcement, those in fiscal agencies have the broadest authority to apprehend criminal suspects, maintain order, and provide services to the community. Whether the local officer is part of a large force or the only law enforcement officer in the community, he or she is usually responsible for a wide spectrum of duties, from responding to noise complaints to investigating homicides. Much of the criticism of local police departments is based on the belief that local police are too underpaid or poorly trained to handle these various responsibilities. Reformers have suggested that residents of small American towns would benefit from greater statewide coordination of local police departments.[12]

City police derive their authority from the state constitution, and their administrative operations are defined by each municipal government. City police officers enjoy the full range of police powers. The city police department has undergone considerable reform since its inception in the early nineteenth century. Today's city police structure includes the following characteristics:

- The adoption of a civil service system
- Nomination by petition
- Initiative, recall, and referendum
- The short ballot
- The council-manager form of government
- Nonpartisan elections

Police activities can be divided into two basic functions: line and staff. Line functions involve activities that result in directly meeting police service goals. These include patrol, investigation, vice, traffic, juvenile, and crime prevention. In comparison, staff functions help administrators organize and manage the police agency.

LIMITED PURPOSE POLICING AGENCIES   Even with the agencies just discussed, a number of states have found that certain law enforcement areas need more specific attention. As a result, a wide variety of limited purpose policing agencies have sprung up in each of the 50 states. For example, most states have an Alcoholic Beverage Control Commission (ABC), or a similarly named organization, monitors the sale and distribution of alcoholic beverages. The ABC monitors alcohol distributors to assure that all taxes are paid on the beverages and is responsible for revoking or suspending the liquor licenses of establishments that have broken relevant laws.

Many states have fishing game warden organizations that enforce all laws relating to hunting and fishing. Motor Vehicle Compliance (MVC) agencies monitor interstate carriers or trucks to make sure they are in compliance with state and federal laws. MVC officers generally operate the weigh stations that are commonly found on interstate highways. Other limited purpose policing agencies deal with white-collar and computer crime, regulate nursing homes, and provide training to local police departments.

POLICE LINE FUNCTIONS

For the sake of illustration, the following examples of police line functions will focus on those of a municipal police department. It is likely that these functions will be seen in other police agencies as well: county sheriffs' departments, state police agencies, transit authority, water patrol, and park police.

Patrol

At the center of police activities is patrol (see Chapter 5). It involves deployment of uniformed police personnel on foot or in vehicles in designated areas or districts. In a majority of police departments, more than half of the sworn personnel work in this capacity. The many duties performed by patrol officers include making arrests, interviewing witnesses, victims, and suspects, controlling crowds, intervening in family disturbances and public disputes, and providing many services to the general public.

Investigation

When patrol officers are unable to prevent crime or arrest a suspect in the act of committing a crime, the investigation function comes into play. Specialists in criminal investigation, also called detectives, help to solve crime by skillfully questioning witnesses and suspects, gathering evidence at crime scenes, and tracing stolen property. Detectives investigate a number of violations, including crimes against persons (murder, robbery, assault, etc.) and crimes against property (burglary, auto theft, arson, etc.).

Vice Operations

Vice operations are aimed at illegal activities that destroy the physical, mental, and moral health of the public. Generally, vice operations focus on such activities as gambling, drug and liquor violations, pornography, and prostitution. Also, vice detectives often become involved in organized crime investigations because most organized crime organizations are involved in vice enterprises. Many vice investigations are coordinated in conjunction with the patrol division, which is a key supplier of information on persons suspected of wrongdoing.

Traffic Enforcement

The traffic enforcement division of the municipal police department seeks voluntary citizen compliance with traffic regulations to provide maximum movement of traffic with a minimum amount of interruption. An important relationship exists between the traffic enforcement division and other police services in that stopping a motorist for a routine vehicle check will often result in an arrest for a nontraffic offense, such as possession of firearms or illegal drugs.

Juvenile Delinquency

Because laws dealing with juvenile delinquents are quite different than those dealing with adults, some police departments employ specially trained full-time officers knowledgeable in juvenile matters. However, the manner in which departments deal with juveniles may vary. For example, some departments may simply rely on traditional police techniques for juvenile matters. In addition, police efforts also focus on identifying children who are neglected or abused.

Crime Prevention

Crime prevention is the last major line function within the municipal police department. The crime prevention unit is designed to bridge public relations between the public and the police in an effort to preserve law and order in the community. The philosophy of the crime-prevention function is

FIGURE 3.3 A motorist receives a traffic citation from a police officer.

Highlights in Policing

Municipal Police

- *Police officer.* After basic training, most police officers are assigned to patrol duty, where their duties are numerous and varied. Unlike the specialist, patrol officers are generalists who must perform well in a variety of tasks. Police officers have two basic responsibilities: to prevent criminal activities and to furnish day-to-day police service to the community. Situations that require swift, yet sound decisions are frequently faced. For example, they must decide whether to take no action in an incident, to offer advice, to warn, or to make an arrest. Sometimes the use of physical or deadly force is required.
- *Police sergeant.* Police sergeants supervise and coordinate the work of uniformed police officers, whose duty it is to protect the public, interpret and enforce the law, control traffic, and perform preliminary investigations. Sergeants begin their work shifts at police stations, where they assume command of a squad of police officers. Sergeants patrol assigned sectors to observe officers at work, evaluate performance, and ensure adherence with police procedures and standards. They issue orders directly or by radio and provide assistance when problems arise.
- *Police lieutenant.* Police lieutenants are second-line supervisors who oversee activities of designated groups of officers or police sergeants. In addition, lieutenants examine and evaluate police log books, crime reports, special orders, and any information pertinent to police operations. Based on this information, they determine duty assignments and dispatch squads to patrol designated areas determined by work priorities. In some instances, lieutenants discipline officers for violations of rules, regulations, and orders. Where improper conduct is observed or reported through citizen complaints, they investigate to gather facts, take disciplinary action, or dismiss charges when evidence is insufficient.
- *Police detective.* The police detective conducts investigations to prevent crime, protect life and property, and solve criminal cases that range from misdemeanors to homicides. As a rule, police detectives take over criminal investigations after patrol officers have been called to a crime scene to apprehend suspects, question witnesses, and preserve evidence. Working in plain clothes, detectives assigned to the case report to the scene, where possible, and determine the nature of the incident, exact locations and time of the occurrence, and probable reason for the crime. They obtain reports from patrol officers; question witnesses, victims, and suspects; arrange for official statements to be given at a police station; and testify in court proceedings.

that crime is both a social and a police problem and that members of the community must become involved in the detection of crime in neighborhoods. Crime-prevention efforts often result in homeowners notifying police of suspicious circumstances observed in their neighborhoods and the installation of security-related devices in their homes. The open dialogue between the police and members of the community, hopefully, will provide the impetus to settle differences about law enforcement and police services in communities.

POLICE STAFF FUNCTIONS

Staff functions are those designed to aid administrators in organizing and managing the police department. Examples of staff functions include personnel recruitment, selection, and training; budgeting; employee services; and public relations. A police organization is only as effective as its personnel; therefore, the staff function may be the most valuable resource committed to the policing process.

Personnel Recruitment, Selection, and Training

To varying degrees, all police agencies are involved in selecting and training personnel. In doing so, methods for instituting officer qualifications, recruiting and screening procedures, as well as testing and placing personnel in training facilities must be established. The police department also reviews the performance of officers who are on probation and establishes salary schedules and promotion procedures as well. Ongoing (also called in-service) training is also provided by the staff function. It is the responsibility of the training component to keep officers up-to-date on the latest developments in police work. All these factors are important because the quality of personnel determines the character of police performance and ultimately the quality of police leadership in the community.

Budgeting

Maintaining the department's budget is another important aspect of staff functions. The duties of budget officers include fiscal planning and preparation of cost estimates for personnel, facilities, equipment, and programs essential for meeting the goals and objectives of the police organization.

Employee Services

The staff must also provide services to police employees. They must explain benefits and help employees understand the ones to which they are entitled. Health care insurance, sick leave, and death benefits typically are offered to employees.

Public Relations

Public relations is also a vital responsibility of every police organization. Basically, this function involves acquainting the community with the practices and programs of the police department in order to gain public support. To achieve this goal, officers furnish information to the media and work with educational and business organizations.

Auxiliary Staff Services

A number of important police functions are also considered services provided by staff personnel. These include the crime laboratory, property and detention, transportation, communications, and police information systems. The crime laboratory is of great value to the police department because solutions to many crimes are found through application of the physical and biological sciences. Investigators will collect evidence from crime scenes, which is then properly preserved and delivered to the laboratory for analysis. After reaching the laboratory, evidence undergoes qualitative, quantitative, and interpretive analysis by laboratory personnel. Forensic personnel are responsible for fingerprint operations, ballistics, polygraph tests, tests on body fluids, and alcohol and drug tests. Because not all police agencies have crime laboratories, regional crime laboratories have been established in most states to serve police agencies from different jurisdictions.

Police agencies are also responsible for evidence, personal property, and articles of value that are confiscated during the course of an investigation. All property must be safeguarded and stored by authorized police personnel. Accordingly, police personnel must also inspect, inventory, replace, and maintain departmental property and facilities. In addition, police departments are charged with the responsibility of maintaining detention facilities for arrested persons who are awaiting investigation, trial, or imprisonment in county or state correctional facilities. Typical detention activities include booking, searching, fingerprinting, photographing, and feeding prisoners. The mobility of police officers is critical in performing required police duties in the community. Transportation activities focus on the acquisition, use, maintenance, cost, and safety of a number of police vehicles. These vehicles include automobiles, motorcycles, trucks, motorized scooters, aircraft, and all-terrain and four-wheel-drive vehicles. Another critical auxiliary staff function is communications. The communications center is the lifeline of the police organization. In general, police communication systems consist of three parts: the telephone system, command and control operations, and radio communications. The manner in which police systems operate might differ from one organization to another but will probably operate as follows:

- *Telephone Communications Systems.* These systems aim to reduce crime through rapid communication between the public and the police—particularly in an emergency situation. This is of critical importance because the response time of police officers to certain calls may mean the difference between life and death of victims or the capture or escape of suspects.
- *Command and Control.* This component coordinates information between field patrol units and communication centers. In its simplest form, it receives, processes, and dispatches information received by telephone to field patrol officers for action, a function that is vital to ensure the safety of the community. As the use of automated command control equipment increases, this function becomes more complex.
- *Radio Communications.* This function of communications involves the use of radio frequencies by command control officers to both receive and transmit information. Because frequencies are often limited, the effectiveness of the range of radio communication is also limited. Where possible, departments furnish officers with specialized equipment such as miniature transceivers and walkie-talkies to allow officers constant communication with other officers, supervisors, and command and control personnel.

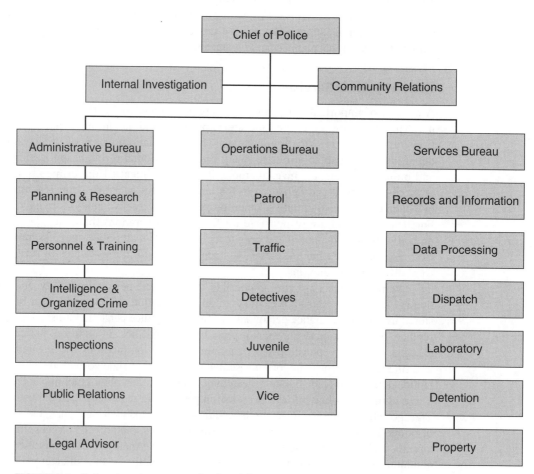

FIGURE 3.4 Police department organizational chart.

Police information systems are another auxiliary staff function that can greatly reduce crime. Such systems generally are made up of three components: reporting, collecting, and recording of crime data, and storing and retrieving information. The reporting phase is thorough documentation of all crimes that come to the department's attention. Included are field interviews, telephone contacts, field investigation reports, and warrant information received from judicial agencies. Collecting and recording of crime data are used to evaluate crime conditions and the effectiveness of police operations. Data are retrieved from sources such as police field activity logs, incident files, accident reports, and investigation reports. The third part of police information systems, information storage and retrieval, supports officers working in the field by providing quick and accurate information on request. For example, field officers have access to arrest records, criminal histories, outstanding warrants, and information about identifiable stolen property.

THE PROBLEM OF FRAGMENTATION

The 1967 President's crime commission concluded, "a fundamental problem confronting law enforcement today is that of fragmented crime repression efforts resulting from the large number of uncoordinated local governments and law enforcement agencies."[13] As a result, the commission published a map of the Detroit metropolitan area indicating the 85 agencies in the area. Almost half of those agencies had 20 or fewer officers.

According to the critics, the *first* problem is a lack of coordination between agencies in the same geographic area. Criminals do not respect political boundaries, and in a large metropolitan area criminals may commit crimes in several different communities, each having its own police force. For example, auto-theft rings are often multistate operations. Investigators in one police department may have information that would help solve a number of crimes in a nearby jurisdiction. In some cases, agencies compete rather than cooperate with one another on such investigations.

Second, fragmentation of responsibility can also lead to crime displacement, especially with regard to vice crimes. For example, one community may adopt a policy of strict enforcement of laws against gambling or prostitution, which has the effect of driving vice activities to a nearby jurisdiction where a different community standard exists.

Third, a number of experts believe that there's a serious problem of duplication of services, with the resulting increase in costs. An example of this would be a municipal police department and the local sheriff's department who may operate their own 9-1-1 telephone systems and their own training academies. Several agencies in the same area may operate their own crime laboratories as well.

Next, fragmentation leads to inconsistent standards for police. Law enforcement agencies in the same area may have different recruitment standards, training programs, retirement programs, and salary scales.

Samuel Walker points out that in countries with a single national police force, uniform standards are established at the national level. In England, for example, which has a tradition of local control of the police, minimum national standards are achieved through a process of inspection and financial incentives. Each of the 45 local police constabularies is inspected annually by the home office.[14]

Merely identifying the problem of police fragmentation does not easily present any solutions. The autonomy of local governments is deeply entrenched in U.S. history. The principle of local control, not just of the police but of schools and other government services as well, is deeply rooted in U.S. political culture. Additionally, there has always been a very strong fear of a national police force in the United States and suspicion of federal control of schools and police. However, Walker offers two major remedies for fragmentation:[15]

1. *Consolidation.* Some experts argue that small agencies should be consolidated into larger ones. The national advisory commission on criminal justice standards and goals recommends the consolidation of all agencies with ten or fewer sworn officers. In some urban areas, the city police and sheriff's department have been merged. For example, the Charlotte,

North Carolina, and the Mecklenburg County Sheriff's departments were merged in the early 1990s. Some cities, meanwhile have combined police and fire departments into a single agency to create a local department of public safety. The consolidation of police and sheriffs' departments has made little progress however. Both are large bureaucracies that do not want to give up their independence. Furthermore, there are practical problems related to merging different interest requirements, salary schedules, and retirement systems.

2. ***Contracting.*** As a second alternative to fragmentation, small agencies could contract with larger agencies for specific services. Approximately 50% of all cities and counties contract with other government units for various services. These contracts cover everything from sewage disposal to tax assessment and water supply. The most common criminal justice services include jails in detention facilities and fire-police communication systems. In many cases, the county sheriff maintains the 9-1-1 service for small towns in the area. In other cases, small towns contract with a sheriff for all police services. An example of this would be the Los Angeles County Sheriff's department, which contracts with about 40 separate towns in the metropolitan area. Some researchers believe that fragmentation is not as serious a problem as others have portrayed it. In the 1970s, the police services study (PSS) conducted research on the issue examining the activities of 1,827 law enforcement agencies in 80 medium-size metropolitan areas. Contrary to the traditional image of fragmentation, the study found that "informal interagency assistance is common" and "strict duplication of services is almost nonexistent in the production of direct police services."[16]

More importantly, the PSS concluded that small police departments were not necessarily less efficient than larger ones. In fact, small departments put a higher percentage of their officers on the street, performing direct police services. In comparison, larger departments did not necessarily achieve any advantage of scale.[17] Furthermore, larger agencies had more complex bureaucratic structures, with a result that a smaller percentage of officers were available for direct police services. Experts go on to argue that the emphasis on decentralized policing, under the community policing philosophy, suggests that local law enforcement agencies might be preferable to larger consolidated agencies for accomplishing the goals of community policing.[18]

PRIVATE POLICE

Until recently, private police—typically called private security—called to mind the image of security guards, individuals with questionable qualifications for other occupations who ended up accepting minimal wages to stand guard outside banks, factories, and businesses. This image reflected a long history of private employment of individuals who served limited police patrol functions. Remember, however, that before the formation of public police forces, private policing was common in Europe and the United States. For example, Chapter 2 pointed out that Henry Fielding's Bow Street Runners in England were forerunners of today's modern and professional police forces. Recall that in the late nineteenth century, the Pinkerton National Detective Agency provided industrial spies and strikebreakers to thwart labor union activities, and Wells Fargo & Co., was formed to provide security for banks and other businesses. These two organizations are discussed later in this chapter as well.

By contrast, in recent years private-sector activities related to policing functions have become more complex and important. Today, if one speaks of people employed in "private security," it is more accurate to envision a variety of occupations, ranging from traditional security guards to computer security experts and high-ranking corporate vice presidents responsible for planning and overseeing safety and security at the company's industrial plants and office complexes around the world. The aftermath of the September 11 attack on the World Trade Center in New York City has led to a heightened awareness of the importance of security management and private-sector employees in handling police functions.

Retail and industrial firms spend nearly as much for private protection as all localities spend for police protection. Many government entities hire private companies to provide security at specific office buildings or other facilities. Furthermore, private groups, such as residents of wealthy suburbs, have hired private police to patrol their neighborhoods. Research has shown that, an estimated 60,000 private agencies employed more than 1.9 million people in security operations.[19] Each year businesses, organizations, and individuals together spend about $90 billion on private security. There are now three times as many officers hired by private security companies as there are public police.

Private security agencies have gained success for several reasons. Private companies recognize the need to be conscientious about protecting their assets, including buildings, financial resources, and personnel. In addition, they must be prepared for fires and other emergencies as well as for criminal activity. Many threats have spurred an expansion in security management and private policing; these include:

- An increase in crimes in the workplace
- An increase in fear (real or perceived) of crime
- The fiscal crises of the states, which have limited public police protection
- Increased public and business awareness and use of more cost-effective private security services.[20]

Functions of Private Police

High-ranking security managers have a range of responsibilities, requiring them to fulfill multiple roles that would be handled by separate individuals in the public sector. For their companies, they simultaneously function as police chiefs, fire chiefs, emergency-management administrators, and computer-security experts. Furthermore, they hire, train, and supervise personnel to protect corporate computer systems that may contain credit card numbers, trade secrets, confidential corporate financial information, and other data sought by hackers intent on causing destruction or stealing money. Such persons regularly combat cybercriminals who are attacking their computer resources from overseas and are beyond the reach of American law enforcement. They also plan security systems and fire- and other disaster-response plans for buildings. Such plans include provisions for evacuating large buildings and coordinating their efforts with local police and fire departments in a variety of locales. In addition, they develop security systems to prevent employee theft, which may involve sophisticated schemes to use company computer systems to transfer financial assets illegally. Due to the fact that so many American companies now own manufacturing plants and office buildings overseas, modern-day security companies must often implement their services in diverse countries around the globe.

At lower levels, specific occupations in private security are more directly comparable to those of police officers. Many security personnel are the equivalent of private-sector detectives. They must investigate "attacks" on company computer systems or any activity that threatens company assets. For example, credit card companies have large security departments that use computers to monitor unusual activity on individual customers' credit cards, which may be a sign that the credit card has been stolen and is being used by a thief. Private-sector detectives must also investigate employee theft. Because this criminal activity extends beyond simple crimes such as stealing money from the store's cash register, investigations might consider whether people are making false reports on expense accounts, using company computers to run private businesses, or misspending company money.

Other activities are more directly comparable to those of police officers, especially for security officers who must guard specific buildings, apartments, or stores. The activities of these private security personnel vary greatly: Some act merely as guards and call the police at the first sign of trouble, whereas others have the power to carry out patrol and investigative duties similar to those of police officers. Still others rely on their presence and the ability to make a "citizen's arrest" to deter lawbreakers. In most cases, citizens are authorized by law to make an arrest only when a felony has been committed in their presence. Thus private security companies risk being held liable for false arrest and violation of civil rights.

Some states have passed laws that give civil immunity to store personnel who reasonably but mistakenly detained people suspected of shoplifting. More ambiguous is the search of the person or property of a suspect by a private guard. The suspect may resist the search and file a civil suit against the guard. If such a search yields evidence of a crime, the evidence might not be admitted in court. Yet the Supreme Court has not applied the Miranda ruling to private police.

Security managers are often willing to accept responsibility for minor criminal incidents that occur on their employer's premises. Included in such tasks are responding to burglar alarms, investigating misdemeanors, and carrying out preliminary investigations of other crimes. Some law enforcement administrators have indicated that they might be willing to transfer some of these tasks to private security firms. They cite several police tasks—such as providing security in public buildings and enforcing parking regulations—that the security might perform more efficiently than the police.

There are an estimated three times as many private police as public. Americans are spending $90 billion a year on private security, compared to $40 billion in taxes for public police.[21] In California, even though the crime rate is at its lowest level in more than 30 years, the number of private security guards grew by 22% from 1996 to 2000.[22]

The Pinkerton National Detective Agency

Nearly 75 years after the formation of England's Bow Street Runners, the concept of private security developed slowly in the United States. The Pinkerton National Detective Agency was one of the earliest private security organizations providing an array of security-related services, such as presidential security, now performed by the U.S. Secret Service. In fact, Pinkerton agents first gained considerable renown for a number of accomplishments:

- Foiling an assassination attempt on Abraham Lincoln in the 1850s
- Relentlessly pursuing famous outlaws, such as members of the Younger brothers' and Jesse James' gangs as well as the famed Butch Cassidy (Leroy Parker) and the Sundance Kid (Harry Longbaugh)
- Tracking members of the famous gang the "Wild Bunch" from Robbers Roost as well as the legendary train robber Sam Bass

The founder of the Pinkerton agency, Alan Pinkerton, also became well known for his **rogues gallery**. The gallery was a forerunner of today's police "mug book" and consisted of detailed descriptions of known criminals and their hideouts. Descriptions included physical characteristics of suspects and their associates. It was the Pinkerton agency that coined the term *private eye* and its slogan "We never sleep." Other private police agencies in the American West included the Rocky Mountain Detective Association, founded by David Cook, a former major general of the Colorado Militia. Like the Pinkerton agency, Cook's operatives combed the United States in search of train and express office robbers, thieves, and murderers who plundered the many small mining towns throughout middle and western United States.

During the frontier move west, railroads became victim to a number of train robbers. Private organizations sought to capture such bandits, but some railroads elected to hire specialists on horseback to pursue the bandits. In some cases, baggage cars were equipped with fast horses ridden by sharpshooters who would exit the train on a moment's notice and pursue would-be bandits. In other cases, strategically placed railroad agents would ride the trains unobtrusively while looking for potential troublemakers, or trains would be accompanied by fast-moving single locomotives that would quickly transport armed railroad agents.

Wells Fargo

One company that employed such specialists operating east of the Missouri River was Wells Fargo & Co., founded in 1852 by Henry Wells and William G. Fargo. It originated as a mail-carrying service, banking institution, and stagecoach line with over 100 offices operating in mining areas in the west. Because Wells Fargo carried millions of dollars in gold dust in areas plagued with desperados, it was forced to develop its own elaborate security system. Armed guards protected treasure boxes from bandits. Outlaws targeting Wells Fargo carriers were relentlessly hunted down by agents who were specially equipped and trained.[23]

The Hallcrest Report

Hallcrest Systems, Inc., concluded a 30-month study in conjunction with the National Institute of Justice to better understand the extent of private security efforts in the United States. While conducted in 1980, the study still has important implications today. The findings of the study were based on interviews with more than 400 people in law enforcement and all areas of proprietary and contractual security, state regulatory agencies governing private security organizations, and over 1,600 security and police managers. The study was conducted in Baltimore County, Maryland, and Multnomah County, Oregon. Results of the study revealed that personnel and expenditures of private security exceed that of the police and that business and industry together spend more than $20 billion on security measures for their organizations. It was the consensus of both police and security managers that private security functions should focus on minor criminal incidents occurring on property it protects, and that the nonpolice-related responsibilities should be contracted out to the private-sector security companies. Currently, there is little interaction and cooperation between the police and private security companies in crime prevention and public safety.

The report expressed the following:

> Citizen fear of crime and awareness that criminal justice resources alone cannot effectively control crime have led to a growing use of individual and corporate protective measures, including private security products and services and neighborhood-based crime prevention programs . . . Law enforcement resources have stabilized and in some areas are declining. This mandates greater cooperation with the private sector and its private security resources to forge a partnership on an equal basis for crime prevention and reduction. Law enforcement can ill afford to continue isolating and, in some cases, ignoring this important resource . . . The creative use of private security, human resources, and technology may be one viable option left to control crime in our communities. . . . Law enforcement officials maintain that they should bear the primary burden for protection of the community; then creative alternative solutions will be limited in the midst of dwindling public resources.[24]

Police-security relations are also hampered by two major problems: off-duty police moonlighting in private-sector security jobs and resentment by the police regarding the excessive number of false burglary alarms to which they must respond. Beginning in the mid-1980s, laws and standards for training of private security were implemented across the country. It is too soon, however, to measure how these regulations may affect the role of the private security officer's relationship to public-sector law enforcement.

PROBLEMS WITH PRIVATIZATION

The idea of privatization of the police has been discussed, and even tried in some cases, as a cost-effective alternative to municipal police services. The concept of privatization of public services is nothing new, as in many cities services that have traditionally been the realm of the public sector have now become privatized. For example, garbage collection, food preparation in public schools, collection of delinquent parking violation penalties, and even vouchers for public education are services that were once strictly public but are now private. But how realistic is the notion of private police to safeguard the public? In an article appearing in the September 1994 edition of the *FBI Law Enforcement Bulletin* such an experience is described.

In a 1992 drug scandal that culminated in the indictment of the police chief and one other officer, the city's police department was taken over by the Sussex County, New Jersey, prosecutor's office for a period of several months. Because the statutory mission of the prosecutor's office was limited only to county jurisdiction, municipal police protection was not possible, and as a result, political leaders voted to abolish the police department and rely on the state police to provide police protection to citizens. But due to a limited number of state police officers and slow response time, the city decided to hire a private security company to provide a more visible, uniformed police presence.

While the security company's mission was simply to supplement the state police, it began to behave like a fully independent police department, stopping vehicles, writing summonses, and detaining and arresting citizens. In many cases incidents were mishandled, such as when the officers returned a knife to a person suspected of assault. As the Sussex County Prosecutor Dennis O'Leary writes: "While the arrangement was designed to 'depoliticize' the administration of law enforcement, it completely circumvented this goal because the security company was responsible only to the entity that awarded its contract."[25] The Sussex County experiment shows that private police may not simply create a police force that is undertrained and unprofessional, but one that is highly political as well.

The Problem of Integrity

Despite the proliferation of private security, many questions remain about this largely unregulated industry. Several years ago, four security guards accidentally suffocated Peter James Lawrence to death outside a nightclub in Las Vegas, Nevada. The security guards were trying to subdue Lawrence, who reacted violently when he was asked to stop bothering his ex-girlfriend.[26] In Nevada, to be a security guard, there are four hours of training required.

Other despite the proliferation of private security, many questions remain about this largely unregulated industry. Other problems impacting private security include low pay. As a rule, few guards earn more than $8 an hour. In addition, training is minimal. For example, Georgia requires only 12 hours of training for a guard to carry a gun. The examination found several incidents of security guards who have gone awry:

- At the Republican National Convention in San Diego in 1996 where the security was tight, a guard stole 16 television sets from NBC. The guard, Lorenzo Littlejohn, was wanted by police in another burglary before he was hired.
- In Rochester, New York, a 24-year-old security guard was charged with murdering a four-year-old girl in 1994 and hiding her body. At the time of the original investigation, he passed a polygraph test.

- A security guard watching Sylvester Stallone's $8 million mansion in Miami was wounded in July 1996 by a fellow guard while apparently trying to break into the actor's home.
- Three security guards were arrested in August 1996 at Simon Fraser University in Vancouver, Canada, for stealing athletic clothing and computers.
- In August 1996, the Whitney Museum of Art in New York became embroiled in a lawsuit because a security guard wrote "I love you Tushee" and "Love, buns" on a borrowed painting worth more than $1.5 million.
- A female executive of Saks Fifth Avenue is suing the company for $50 million. She was raped in 1994 by a store security guard. A preemployment background check on the guard failed to turn up his 1989 conviction for sexual assault of an 11-year-old in Kentucky.

There has been a steady growth of private security companies since the 9/11 terrorist attacks in September 2001. Much of the growth is driven by insurance companies, which have to settle lawsuits against companies for providing inadequate protection. In comparison, the number of police officers has risen 17%, to 700,000, barely keeping pace with the rise in population.[27] In the year 2000, spending for private security was approximately $103 billion versus $44 billion on public law enforcement. Larger companies such as General Motors and IBM will pay a premium for well-trained guards with clean records, but those will probably be the exception rather than the rule.

Recommendations for Private Security

It is difficult to estimate the extent that private security will affect public policing in the future. The determining factor rests on whether the police and private security officials learn to form a closer working relationship. If such a partnership becomes a reality, a number of actions and strategies should be considered. The Hallcrest study makes several recommendations.

- *Upgrade Private Security.* Both police and security managers cite the quality of security personnel as being the most needed change affecting the quality of security services. Statewide regulatory agencies should be established for contract security services. In addition, police background checks and minimum training should be carried out along with the establishment of a private security code of ethics.
- *Increase Police Knowledge of Private Security.* Seminars and training materials should be developed along with the designation of liaison officers to work more closely with local police departments.
- *Expand Interaction.* Specialized investigative resources should be identified to complement police investigations. In addition, joint police–security task forces for investigation of major losses should be created.
- *Experiment with the Transfer of Police Functions.* Research to see which police activities do not require police authority should be conducted. Furthermore, the use of security personnel to adopt these functions should be considered. Special attention should be given to contracting burglar alarm response to the private sector. Of special interest is whether the deterrent value of response time rises from police authority or merely from attention that is quick, uniformed, and armed.

Nontraditional approaches will be required if the police are to be relieved from their large workload of minor and noncriminal calls. Creative use of private security may prove to be a feasible option for conservation of scarce police resources and strengthening the protection of the community. For the most part, experts predict that security will remain as a "rent-a-cop" service, with problems similar to those experienced today. It is likely that the only thing that will serve to professionalize private security is a congressional initiative, which will speed up background checks of security guard applicants. Such checks currently take as long as 18 months.

In Retrospect

Police agencies represent a complex organizational function in our society, and, because of our system of democracy, the police agencies are decentralized and somewhat fragmented. Each police agency in existence today has its own mission, jurisdiction, and resources. Police agencies operate with both line and staff personnel, each representing an important component to the overall effectiveness of the organization. Sworn personnel are assigned ranks and are organizationally structured in a paramilitary-style fashion. As officers prove their worth in each rank, they are eligible for promotion to the next higher rank. Police agencies are also separated according to the level of government in which they operate.

Municipal police represent incorporated cities, while county sheriffs' deputies provide police services to a broader rural area. State and federal organizations are often charged with assisting smaller police agencies who lack resources for patrol, investigation, and crime prevention. These agencies have broader police powers but are limited in mission and scope. Finally, the use of private police agencies to safeguard individual and corporate property continues to increase into the twenty-first century. Some studies suggest that private security may be more efficient and effective than police in the public sector. Although problems with private-sector police often focus on issues of professionalism and competency, it is likely that their role in augmenting future police efforts will continue to expand.

Improve Your Professional Vocabulary

espionage	mission	sworn personnel
G-men	rogues gallery	

Discussion Questions

1. Compare and contrast the commonalties and differences existing among the various levels of police agencies.
2. Explain the purpose of a police agency's mission statement.
3. What are the differences in the various ranks most commonly held by police officers?
4. Explain how municipal and county police agencies differ in function and authority.
5. Discuss the ways in which the creation of the DHS has re-organized federal law enforcement agencies.
6. Explain how the role of the FBI has changed with the new concern over terrorism.
7. Compare and contrast the differing roles, goals, and objectives of the FBI and the DEA.
8. Explain to what extent private security augments the role of the police in society.
9. Explain the influence that Pinkerton's Detective Agency had on U.S. policing.
10. Discuss the problem of police fragmentation.

Notes

1. Quoted in Laura Maggi and Glenn Filosa, Enough! Thousands march to protest these alarming murder rate, *New Orleans Times-Picayune* (January 12, 2007), 1.
2. Federal Bureau of investigation, crime in the United States, 2006 (Washington, DC: US Department of Justice, 2007), at www.FBI.gov.
3. Oliver, W. M. (2002, September–October). 9–11, Federal crime control policy and unintended consequences. *ACJS Today, 22,* 1–6.
4. The section on homeland security relies heavily on "The Department of Homeland Security," *www.whitehouse.gov/deptofhomeland/.*
5. Lyman, M. D., & G. W. Potter. (1991). *Drugs in society: Causes, concepts and control.* Cincinnati, OH: Anderson.
6. Williams, H. (1988). *The evolving strategy of police: A minority view.* Washington, DC: The Police Foundation.

7. U.S. Drug Enforcement Administration. (n.d.). *Manual for special agent applicants.* Washington, DC: U.S. Government Printing Office.

8. Vernon L. Foley. (1980). *American law enforcement* Boston: Allyn and Bacon, 228.

9. Bureau of Justice Statistics, Sheriff's Offices, 2003 (Washington, DC: US Department of Justice, May 2006), 2.

10. Federal Bureau of investigation, crime in the United States, 2006 (Washington, DC: US Department of Justice, 2007), at www.FBI.gov.

11. Bureau of Justice Statistics, Local Police Departments, 2003 (Washington, DC: US Department of Justice, May 2006), 2.

12. G. Robert Blakely, "Federal Criminal Law," *Hastings Law Journal,* 46 (April 1995), 1175.

13. President's. Commission on Law Enforcement and the Administration of Justice. (n.d.). *Task force report: The police.* Washington, DC: U.S. Government Printing Office, p. 68.

14. Walker, S. (1999). *The police in America,* 3rd ed. Boston: McGraw-Hill, p. 58.

15. Ibid.

16. Ostrom, E., R. Parks, & G. P. Whitaker. (1978). *Patterns of metropolitan policing.* Cambridge MA: Bellinger.

17. Ibid.

18. Weishiet, R., D. N. Falcon, & E. L. Wells. (1995). *Crime and policing into rural and small town America: An overview of the issues.* Washington, DC: U.S. Government Printing Office, pp. 69–73.

19. Carlson, T. (1995, Summer). "Safety, Inc." *Policy Review,* 67–73.

20. Cuningham, W. C., J. J. Strauchs, & C. W. VanMeter. (1990). *Private security trends, 1972–2000.* Boson: Butterworth-Heinemann.

21. Welcome to the new world of private security. *The Economist* (1997, April 19).

22. Teri Sforza (2000, April 3). Firm's private canine patrols. *Orange County Register,* p. B1.

23. Hungerford, E. (1949). *Wells Fargo: Advancing the American frontier.* New York: Bonanza.

24. Cunningham, W. C., & T. H. Taylor. (1984). *The growing role of private security.* Washington, DC: U.S. Department of Justice. Information based on the findings of the Hallcrest Systems, Inc., study of McLean, Virginia.

25. O'Leary, D. (1994, September). Reflections on police privatization. *FBI Law Enforcement Bulletin,* 21–25.

26. Security guards won't face criminal charges in death outside strip nightclub, *Las Vegas Review-Journal* (January 24, 2005), 2B.

27. Jones, D. (1996, September 12). On guard: Bad guys behind badge of honor. *USA Today,* p. 1B.

PART 2

Police Work
as a Profession

CHAPTER 4

Becoming a Police Officer

This chapter will enable you to:

- Recognize problems associated with recruitment of minorities and women.
- Consider problems associated with the police selection process.
- List the various stages of the officer selection process.
- Think about the importance and significance of higher education in police work.

- Understand the role and development of the police officer subculture.
- Learn how officer cynicism develops and ultimately affects police performance.
- Think about the various police officer working styles.
- Explain the importance of minorities and women as police officers.

Over the course of a 12-year career in law enforcement, New York City police detective Michael Oliver had never fired a round in the line of duty. He certainly had no expectation that his history could be broken on the night of November 25, 2006, when he and the other members of the squad staked out the club Kalua in Jamaica, Queens.

The early hours of the assignment were spent trying to uncover a sex-for-money trade among the topless dancers, but things got more serious around 4 A.M. when Detective Gescard Isnora, one of Oliver's colleagues, heard a patron say, "Yo, go get my gun." Isnora watched as the speaker and two other men got in a Nissan Altima; he then approached the car, flashing his badge. The car swerved and hit Isnora, and he and the other officers on the scene responded by pouring 50 shots into the car—31 of them coming from Oliver's Sig Sauer pistol. When the shooting stopped, Sean Bell, the driver, was dead, and his two passengers were seriously wounded. No firearms were found on them or in the automobile.

The incident attracted attention for two reasons. First, though Bell was to be married that evening he had been at the nightclub for his bachelor party. Second, the three men in the car were African-American. Minority deaths, of Amadou Diallo, a West African immigrant, in 1999 and Ousmane Zongo, also from West Africa, in 2004 at the hands of the New York police remained a fresh memory in the minds of many, and charges of racism were again leveled at the police department.

A community is in trouble when people start comparing the actions of law enforcement to the mayhem in Iraq. Following Sean Bell's death, New York Mayor Michael Bloomberg called the force used against him "excessive." Resulting from this incident, detectives Michael Oliver and Gescard Isnora were charged with first- and second-degree manslaughter. Accusations of racial motivations for the shootings were somewhat blunted by the fact that two of the four officers who fired into the car were themselves African-American. Because of past incidents, however, many of the city's African-American residents were unwilling to give the police department the benefit of the doubt.

For decades the role of the police has stimulated the interest of a large segment of the population. Much of this concern stems from recent events where police have been documented as abusing their governmental authority in one fashion or another. Egon Bittner notes: "The staffing of an organization is the pivotal process that puts in place the individuals who will carry out the organization's missions and plans. This process is generally regulated by law and is further influenced by the presence of labor union activity."[1]

Although more and more Americans are concerned with the effectiveness, efficiency, and quality of police services, and despite problems occasionally associated with policing, public attitudes toward the police are generally favorable. For example, one national survey showed that 60% of all Americans believe that the police basically do a good job.[2] Despite this, crime rates remain a concern, and efforts are being made by many members of our communities to fight crime through the use of private security forces, ad hoc groups, and even random acts of vigilantism. One of the tenets of this book is that police work is demanding and difficult, requiring that much responsibility be delegated to those who choose this profession. Accordingly, it is a difficult task for police administrators to select the proper people to assume these responsibilities and to become effective police officers in our communities. Administrative concerns often hinge on the following questions:

- Does a college degree contribute to the effectiveness of a police officer?
- How relevant is a previous criminal record for police applicants?
- How significant is physical dexterity and size as they relate to performing specific tasks in police work?
- How important is it that the police department's ethnic and gender makeup reflect that of the community it serves?

This chapter focuses on a number of issues and developmental stages that contribute to the making of a police officer. Included in the discussion are the processes under which decisions are made to join the police force, issues and concerns related to the recruitment and selection of officers, the screening process for officer recruits, issues involving education and training, and some important observations about police behavior.

AN OUNCE OF PREVENTION

As we learned in Chapter 3, proper time taken to "hire well" is critical because of vicarious liability. This is the legal responsibility that one person assumes for the actions of another and is often applied to police work because of the damage that a "bad hire" can do. Remember, the law states that any person who, under color of state law, violates another person's constitutional rights can be sued.

Today, it is generally accepted that the local government be responsible for the wrongdoing of a subordinate enforcing a local ordinance, regulation, or policy. In those cases where police managers directed, ordered, or participated in the acts, they too are liable. Furthermore, in the event that upper-level managers are negligent in hiring, assigning, training, retaining, directing, or entrusting, they may also be liable even though they were not present for the misdeed. Consider it a sign of the times, but police departments are now being held to a higher standard of performance and accountability than ever before in history.

POLICE WORK AS A CAREER

The role of the police is being examined and reevaluated by police administrators as well as by members of the general public. Most of the concern relates to the professionalizing of the police and is correlated with the manner in which police officers treat members of the community as well as to the quality of the performance of their duties. As it relates to the professionalizing of police officers, questions have been posed: Does a separate informal group operate within the rank and file of police organizations? If such a subculture exists, to what extent does it aid or hinder the formalized structure of command and the organizational goals and objectives of the police organization? Answers to these questions might be found in looking at the basis for the informal structure of the police profession and how officers view themselves as individuals, other members of their profession, members of the police command structure, and the public they serve.

Standards of Admittance

As with most occupations that are considered professional, some characteristics will distinguish one from another. For example, someone desiring to be an attorney must compete for entry into law school by taking the Law School Admittance Test (LSAT). Once admitted, law students will spend three or more years in school before graduation, study to pass the bar exam, which permits them to practice law in their chosen state, and finally, observe a code of professional conduct. Physicians also undergo a rigorous selection process for entry into medical school as well as endure many years of uncompromising study. Furthermore, they are obligated to honor the Hippocratic oath and will usually belong to a professional association such as the American Medical Association (AMA).

When considering the rigors of entry and acceptance into these professions, police work is no exception. As we will learn later in this chapter, people desiring a police career realize very early, during the application process, that such positions are difficult to obtain, and if successful, their occupation becomes in part a badge of social identity. Before consideration for appointment, candidates must compete in a labyrinth of tests. In addition, candidates must undergo physical and psychological exams as well as rigid background investigations, any of which can disqualify officers' consideration. Once appointed, the new recruit realizes that he or she is somewhat exceptional to have competed successfully against so many other candidates (sometimes hundreds), and it is likely that this process is what gives birth to the "police personality" and its concomitant, the police subculture.

Although the image of being a law enforcement officer is alluring, after becoming one many find that the reality of being a "cop" is less than attractive and no longer conforms with their career goals. Indeed, the reality of working the street differs greatly from the stereotypical portrayal of police officers by novels and Hollywood movies. When asked why she left her position as a patrol officer in an affluent suburb, a 29-year-old former police officer replied: "I just got tired of riding around waiting for something to happen. I felt like I was wasting my life away." Stereotypes of police officers work both ways as well. To many law-abiding people, police officers are viewed as necessary evils and are not looked at in a positive light. Such impressions might be formed as a result of being the previous recipient of a traffic ticket or knowing someone who might have been treated less than fairly by a police officer somewhere. One 24-year-old police officer tells a story of how his 12-year friendship with his best friend slowly dissolved after the police department hired him and feelings of alienation gradually came between the officer and his friend.

In addition to pressures of inactivity, disillusionment about the job, and stereotypes, police work requires decisive, split-second decisions to be made on the street in order to be accepted by fellow officers. As any officer will admit, there is nothing more demoralizing and discouraging than not being accepted by one's fellow officers. So, to gain acceptance, officers make inordinate attempts to act like, think like, and be like a police officer—at least in the eyes of their peers. Thus the police subculture is developed.

CHOOSING POLICE WORK AS A CAREER

Career decisions to enter police work are made in a variety of ways. In many cases, college students choose to enter criminal justice programs designed to give a perspective of the theoretical, ethical, and practical aspects of police work. When the degree is completed, police agencies are more apt to hire criminal justice graduates, as they have demonstrated an interest in the area. Police work attracts candidates from virtually all fields of endeavor—persons who feel they are working in dead-end jobs, or who desire a change of pace, or who are intrigued by the notion of crime fighting and criminal investigation and a fast-paced, action-oriented career.

The police recruiter should have a feel for what attracts recruits to the profession, as people from literally all walks of life are likely to apply. It is important to learn of such factors as the wrong motivation for wanting to become a police officer, which may result in the newly recruited officer realizing that his or her original perception of the job was based on myth, hype, or misinformation. It is also likely that most people who enter police work decide to do so before they actually seek application. Studies have shown that over half of the police recruits studied made the decision to enter police work five or more years prior to applying for a police officer position. In addition, the study revealed that the most prevalent reasons for wanting to become a police officer included variety, responsibility, public service, and adventure.

The author spent three years as a generalist police academy instructor, during which time police recruits were regularly asked why they chose police work as a profession. The replies varied but included (1) to help people, (2) for the excitement, or (3) to fight crime. Some even cited job security as a major motivator for seeking law enforcement as a career. These personal observations, while anecdotal, have been somewhat supported by empirical studies that consider the same question. For example, two important studies have considered reasons why people are initially attracted to the police profession. The first of these, conducted by Meagher and Yentes, looked at reasons for both men and women aspiring to enter police work.[3] They discovered a high degree of consensus between the two groups, which included reasons such as helping people and job security. Other observations included fighting crime, prestige, excitement, and lifetime interest. Based on their study, it would be safe to say that both men and women enter police work for basically the same reasons.

Research findings over the past 30 years concur that police recruits believe that the police profession is both responsible and exciting. A critical aspect to the recruitment component is that police departments attempt to educate and inform potential police officers about the realities of police work. Failure to do so can result in disenchantment and frustration with the job, which may result in a higher attrition rate for departments. Once a person decides to enter the realm of police work, the candidate is presented with an array of hiring obstacles, including exams and interviews.

CONCEPTS OF POLICE PERSONNEL MANAGEMENT

Before we discuss police officer recruitment, some managerial concepts unique to most organizations should be understood. These concepts included division of labor; chain of command; span of control; delegation of responsibility and authority; unity of command; and rules, regulations, and discipline.

Division of Labor

Clearly, the myriad tasks and duties that must be performed by an organization cannot be performed by one, two, or even all of the members of the organization. Those tasks and duties an organization must perform should be divided among its members according to some logical plan.

In police departments, the tasks of the organization are divided according to personnel, area, time, and functional purpose. Work assignments must be designed so that similar tasks, functions, and activities are given to a particular group for completion. In a police department, control functions are separate from detective functions, which are separate from crime-prevention functions. Geographic and time distinctions are also established, with specific officers working certain times and areas. The division of labor must be reflected in an organizational chart. This is a graphic rendering of reporting relationships in an organization. An accurate organizational chart is a glimpse of the organization. Workers can see exactly where they stand in the organization, what functions they perform, and to whom they report.

Chain of Command

The chain of command, also called the hierarchy of authority, involves the superior/subordinate or supervisor/worker relationship throughout the department. As such, the chain of command as pictured in the organizational chart demonstrates to all workers which supervisor they report to. Accordingly, the chain of command also shows supervisors to whom they are accountable and for whom they are responsible. Each member of the organization should follow the chain of command. For example, each line officer must report to his or her immediate sergeant as opposed to going to the top of the administrative ladder and reporting to a captain or a major. Likewise, a captain should send his or her orders through the chain of command downward to the lieutenant, who disseminates directions to the sergeants, who then disseminate information to the rank-and-file police officers working under them. While it is generally acceptable to violate chain of command in emergency situations, doing so otherwise could jeopardize the police officer's good standing with the department.

Span of Control

The span of control is the number of officers or subordinates that a supervisor can effectively supervise. While no one can say exactly how many officers a sergeant can supervise or how many sergeants a lieutenant can supervise, most police management experts claimed the chain of command should be one supervisor to every six to ten officers at a lower rank. In any case, it is best to keep the span of control as limited as possible so that the supervisor can more effectively maintain control of his or her subordinates. The number of workers a supervisor can effectively supervise is affected by many factors, which include distance, time, knowledge, personality, and the level of difficulty of the work to be performed.

Delegation of Responsibility and Authority

Still another managerial concept in police management is delegation of responsibility and authority. Duties, tasks, and responsibilities are assigned to subordinates, along with the power or authority to control, command, make decisions, or otherwise act in order to complete the tasks that have been delegated or assigned to them.

Unity of Command

The term *unity of command* simply means that each individual in the organization is directly accountable to only one supervisor. This concept is important because no one person can effectively take orders from two supervisors at one time. As with chain of command, unity of command may be violated in emergency situations.

Rules, Regulations, and Discipline

All law enforcement organizations maintain a complicated system of rules and regulations designed to control and direct the behaviors of their officers. Those departments have operations manuals or rules and procedures designed to show officers what they must do in a number of situations they encounter on the street. Such documents are often complex and detailed. Police departments have disciplinary standards that are similar to, but less stringent than those of the military. Violation of department standards with regard to dress, appearance, and conduct can lead to punishments against officers, which include reprimands, fines, suspensions, or even termination from the department.

POLICE OFFICER RECRUITMENT

Perhaps one of the most critical phases of establishing a professional and effective police force is the recruitment and selection process for officer candidates. Many methods exist to allow police agencies to seek out the best candidate for the job. These methods include initiatives such as career fairs on college and university campuses and advertisements through local newspapers and publications. Although each method can boast a degree of success, they are not as effective as one may think. Surprisingly, a study by the Los Angeles Police Department found that the most effective source of police recruitment is word of mouth through the associates, friends, and relatives of police.[4] Although not necessarily by design, such people tend to act as recruitment ambassadors who share, almost firsthand, the exploits of officers in the field as well as stories about the close camaraderie enjoyed by members of the law enforcement profession.

In addition to the problem of generating interest in the police field, other problems present themselves in police officer recruitment and selection. According to the U.S. Commission on Civil Rights, current standards for recruiting and selecting officers not only fail to reflect the qualities needed for job performance but may also reflect discrimination against minorities and women. The commission suggests that to correct unfair and biased hiring practices, departments should closely scrutinize those hiring criteria that tend to result in the disqualification of most minorities and women.

Many police departments receive applications from minority candidates who are citizens of foreign countries. It is legal and common for police departments to hire such individuals, providing they have a work permit issued by the Immigration and Naturalization Service (INS). These documents include an Alien Registration Card (Green Card) or an Employment Authorization Document.

Back in the fall of 2000, and in a tight labor market, police agencies across the nation were confronted with a new recruitment problem—recruits who were more likely than ever to have used drugs, to be out of shape, or to have lied on their application.

This has led to unprecedented recruit washout rates at a time when police agencies were attempting to take advantage of the Clinton administration's six-year, $8 billion grant program aimed at putting 100,000 more police officers on the street. That program fell short of its December 2000 goal largely because of problems in recruiting a sufficient number of qualified officers. As of June 2000, about 68,000 officers had been hired or reassigned to patrol duty under the initiative. As of the fall of 2000, the federal government extended the grant program for an additional two years—hence, police agencies will continue to feel pressure to recruit.[5]

A large percentage of police candidates—30% in Chicago to nearly 80% in Baltimore, for example—fail to become officers because they admit to recent drug use or are caught lying about their former drug use. In Chicago and Baltimore, literally hundreds of applicants have been eliminated each year because of such issues.[6]

While many police departments immediately disqualify candidates who report drug use, most now have policies that acknowledge the impact of the drug culture and tolerate limited marijuana use if it took place several years before a candidate applied. As a rule, recruits who have used harder drugs are more likely to be rejected automatically.

A large number of the failures on mandatory polygraph exams stem from questions about past ongoing drug use. Failure rates are estimated from 30 to 50%. In Chicago, only an estimated one in ten candidates successfully makes it through the recruiting process. In addition to losing candidates for past drug abuse, a large number are also disqualified because of basic physical agility requirements.[7]

In some cases police administrators have attempted to increase the talent pool of recruits by lowering admission standards that were raised several years ago in an effort to improve the quality of officers. For example, New York City's 37,000-officer police department recently dropped its minimum age for recruits from 22 to 21 years of age. The department is also allowing some recruits to substitute work experience for the previously required two years of college. Of course, experts are concerned that such changes in admission requirements might be sacrificing quality in pursuit of filling police officer positions.

Hiring qualified police recruits has become much more difficult since 9/11 because the expansion of federal law enforcement has created more options for people interested in the field. In addition, the wars in Iraq and Afghanistan have siphoned off public service–minded people to the military.[8] Yet other contributors to the reduction in qualified applicants may be the negative publicity over high-profile incidents of police misconduct and excessive use of force.

For police agencies around the country, much is at stake in recruiting qualified officers. Experts warn that recruiting decisions being made today will most likely determine the quality of police work for years to come.

Recruiting Women and Minorities

Whetstone et al. contend, "Police agencies across the United States are dealing with enormous challenges in finding and hiring qualified applicants, especially among minority and female populations."[9] To attract more diverse recruits, agencies have started to advertise in a different manner, portraying the many aspects of police work such as participating in community policing events, assisting those with special needs, and working with youth in schools.[10] To gain the community's general confidence and trust, police departments seek personnel to represent the community. An integrated department helps fight stereotyping and prejudice. Minority officers also provide the department insight into minority groups, their languages, and their subcultures. For example, a police officer who speaks Spanish can help prevent conflicts between the police and Spanish-speaking members of the community.

Recruitment of females has its problems as well. Despite the many benefits female officers bring to police work, they still are not accepted in many departments. Jones suggests, "To successfully increase the number of women in policing, law enforcement agencies should develop a specific plan of action that targets women in the recruiting process and emphasizes the agency's desire to significantly increase the number of women in their ranks."[11]

Without doubt, women and minorities, who have been traditionally underrepresented in the criminal justice work force can anticipate being actively recruited by all levels of the law enforcement field. High-level police managers have come to realize that an integrated police force is better suited to deal with the many conflicts that emerge in our communities. In addition, a diverse police department will be better able to diffuse feelings of hostility and resentment that have developed toward the police.

Over the course of history, police agencies have recruited few minorities as officers. Although many major metropolitan areas are now populated largely by African-Americans and Hispanics, most police departments still predominantly employ white male officers. In fact, in none of the 20 largest cities does the number of nonwhite police officers equal the proportion of nonwhites in the community. This trend is illustrated in Washington, DC, and Atlanta, whose black populations are about 70% but comprise only 41% and 56%, respectively, of the police forces in those cities.[12]

Female Police Officers

In 1910, Alice Stebbens Wells became the world's first policewoman, serving with the Los Angeles Police Department. Before Wells' time women worked in policing only as jailers and police matrons. Wells gained a name for herself as an outspoken advocate of women as police officers, and as a result, many police departments around the country began female officer recruitment. By 1915 the U.S. Census Department reported women police officers in 25 cities across the country. Three years later, in 1918, Ellen O'Grady achieved the nation's first high-ranking position in a U.S. police department when she was appointed police commissioner of New York City. Today it is not uncommon for female police officers to occupy virtually all ranks within the police hierarchy. Despite this, they are dramatically underrepresented in today's police work force. In 2005, only 12–13% of the nation's sworn police officers were women.[13]

A Closer Look

Becoming a Police Officer

What do police officers do? Police officers maintain law and order, collect evidence, and conduct criminal investigations.

- *Urban police officers.* These officers have general law enforcement duties, including maintaining regular patrols and responding to calls for service. Many are assigned to patrol a specific area, such as a business district or residential neighborhood.
- *Sheriffs and deputy sheriffs.* Sheriffs enforce the law on the county level. They are elected to their posts and perform duties similar to those of a local or county police chief. A deputy sheriff in a large agency has duties similar to those of officers in urban police departments.
- *Detectives.* These officers gather facts and collect evidence for criminal cases. They conduct interviews, examine records, observe the activities of suspects, and participate in raids or arrests.
- *State police officers.* State police officers, also known as highway patrol officers, arrest criminals statewide and patrol highways to enforce motor vehicle laws and regulations. At the scene of accidents, they may direct traffic, give first aid, and call for emergency equipment.

What Prerequisites Must I Meet to Become a Police Officer?

As a minimum, you need to be a U.S. citizen over 20 years old, not be a convicted felon, have a GED or high school diploma, and pass several competitive written and physical examinations. Federal and state law enforcement agencies require a college degree.

What Kind of Police Training Will I Need?

Many law enforcement agencies encourage applicants to complete either a two-year associate's program or a four-year bachelor's program in a criminal justice–related area. Knowledge of a foreign language and being physically fit will also help you secure a career in law enforcement.

Once you're accepted by a law enforcement agency, you receive 12 to 14 weeks of training in a police academy. Training includes classroom instruction in constitutional law and civil rights, state laws and local ordinances, and accident investigation. Recruits also receive training in patrol, traffic control, firearms usage, self-defense, first aid, and emergency response.

Continuing education is a necessary requirement for police officers and detectives. Many agencies pay all or part of the tuition for officers to earn a degree in criminal justice, justice administration, or public administration and pay higher salaries to those who earn such a degree.

What Career Opportunities Will I Have as a Police Officer?

In a large department, officers may be promoted to detective or to a specialty area of police work, such as juvenile justice administration. Promotions to corporal, sergeant, lieutenant, and captain usually are made according to a candidate's position on a promotion list, depending on on-the-job performance and examination scores. Many officers retire with a pension after only 20 or 25 years of service and pursue a second career while still in their forties.

What is the Salary Range for Police Officers?

According to the Bureau of Labor Statistics, police and sheriff's patrol officers had median annual earnings of $39,790 in 2000. Police chiefs, deputy chiefs, captains, lieutenants, and sergeants earned between $52,000 and $78,600 per year. In 2000, detectives and criminal investigators earned between $37,240 and $61,750 per year. Competition is keen for the higher-paying jobs with state and federal agencies and police departments in more affluent areas.

NATIONAL DISCRIMINATION COMMISSIONS

Beginning in the 1960s and into the 1970s, the federal government recognized the myriad problems caused by the lack of minority representation in policing. As a result, a number of national commissions were established to study and provide recommendations toward improving the criminal justice system. One such commission, the *National Advisory Commission on Civil Disorders*, observed that discriminatory police employment practices helped contribute to the race riots of the 1960s. It observed that in every city affected by the riots, the percentage of minority group officers was substantially lower than the percentage of minorities in the community.

Established about the same period of time was the *President's Commission on Law Enforcement and Administration of Justice*. This high-visibility commission observed a low percentage of minorities in police departments and stated that police departments must hire and promote minority officers in order to maintain a good standing within the minority community.

Yet another group, the *National Advisory Commission on Criminal Justice Standards and Goals* recognized the need for recruitment of more minorities into police departments across the nation. This commission was formed to study the criminal justice system and issued standards to which police agencies should adhere in order to reduce job discrimination. The standards included the employment of women and minority recruitment. On the subject of female police officer recruitment, the commission stated the following:

> Every police agency should immediately ensure that there exists no agency policy that discourages qualified women from seeking employment as sworn or civilian personnel or prevents them from realizing their full employment.

On the subject of minority recruiting, the commission observed the following:

> Every police agency immediately should ensure that it presents no artificial or arbitrary barriers (cultural or institutional) to discourage qualified individuals from seeking employment or from being employed as police officers. Every police agency should engage in positive efforts to employ ethnic minority group members. When a substantial ethnic minority population resides within the jurisdiction, the police agency should take affirmative action to achieve a ratio of minority group employees in approximate proportion to the makeup of the population.

But in spite of recommendations from national commissions, women and minorities were forced to take their cases to court in an attempt to achieve equality with their white male counterparts in U.S. police departments. For the most part, such cases look to the Fourteenth Amendment as the primary instrument governing employment equality. This amendment, passed in 1868, guarantees "equal protection of the law" to all citizens of the United States.

However, additional legislation was clearly needed to offset job discrimination in policing. Hence, the pathway to equality has roots in not only the Fourteenth Amendment, but also in the **Civil Rights Act of 1964, Title VII** of the same law, the **Equal Employment Opportunity Act of 1972** (EEOA), federal court cases ruling on discrimination, and government-mandated affirmative action programs.

The Civil Rights Act of 1964

In the shadow of the Fourteenth Amendment, discrimination by U.S. government agencies persisted. In an effort to ensure equality, the Civil Rights Act of 1964 was passed by Congress and signed into law by then President Lyndon B. Johnson. Title VII of this law was designed to prohibit all job discrimination based on race, color, religion, sex, or national origin. It covered all employment practices, including hiring, promotion, compensation, dismissal, and all other terms and conditions of employment.

Equal Employment Opportunity Act of 1972

The EEOA extended the 1964 Civil Rights Act and made its provisions, including Title VII, applicable to state and local governments. The EEOA expanded the jurisdiction and strengthened the powers of the federal Equal Opportunity Employment Commission. It also permitted employees of state and local governments to file employment discrimination lawsuits with the EEOC, strengthened the commission's investigatory powers by allowing it to document allegations of discrimination more accurately, and permitted the U.S. Department of Justice to sue state and local governments for violations of Title VII. The EEOA stated that all procedures regarding entry and promotion in police agencies—including application forms, written tests, probation ratings, and physical ability tests—are subject to EEOC guidelines and review, in order to determine whether there has been any unlawful act of discrimination.

Affirmative Action

Perhaps the most controversial method of ending job discrimination was the introduction of **affirmative action**. In 1965, President Lyndon Johnson required all federal contractors and subcontractors to develop affirmative action programs. Subsequent orders have amended and expanded the original executive order. Generally speaking, the concept of affirmative action means that employers must take active steps to ensure equal employment opportunity and to redress past discriminatory practices. Affirmative action must be results oriented. That is, it must focus on the result of employment practices. It is not enough for an agency to merely stop discriminating; the agency must take steps to correct past discrimination and give jobs to those it has discriminated against. Essentially, affirmative action is designed to make up for, or to undo, past discrimination.

Indeed, many police agencies have gone to great lengths to recruit minority officers through extensive recruitment campaigns. In many cases, however, such efforts have failed. Three reasons can be cited for this:

1. Police departments failed to make their searches extensive enough to attract the best-qualified candidates for the job.
2. Many African-Americans don't possess the minimum education qualifications for employment consideration.
3. Many African-Americans have a negative impression of police work.

The efforts of police recruiters to comply with affirmative action hiring practices can also have a down side, as was seen in Miami in the early to mid-1980s. During this time, police and city officials recognized that the demographic makeup of the Miami Police Department was almost exclusively white male. In an effort to create a more racially diverse police force, the city instituted an affirmative action program requiring 80% of all new hires to be African-Americans, Hispanics, or women. The program was restricted, however, to hiring only from within the city of Miami rather than from a national hiring base.

Consequently, many minority members who had criminal records were hired. Many had been convicted of theft and drug abuse. Within three years of the hiring blitz, over 75 officers had either been fired, arrested, or placed under indictment for criminal violations—most officers being new minority hires. In one case, 14 officers were arrested and charged with the heist of 400 kilos (worth $16 million) of cocaine that had been stolen from drug traffickers in a Miami boatyard.

Robert Sheehan and Gary W. Cordner provide an exceptional summation of the efforts of women and minorities to gain equal employment through the courts and affirmative action:

> Such decisions have thrown the police service into some turmoil and have angered many white male police officers, who charge reverse discrimination . . . That police administrators have been forced to hire and promote minority group members rather than attempting to do this on their own it is, in our opinion, a sad reflection on the administrators' real commitment to justice. The personnel task has been obligated significantly by this turn of events.[14]

The plight of African-American police officers has, in many cases, resulted in the formation of separate organizations. For example, the *Afro-American Police (AAP) of New York* and the *Afro-American Patrolman's League (AAPL) of Chicago* have urged courts to rule on such issues as minority recruitment, seniority, and practices of discrimination. The issue of hiring minority police officers is critical for many reasons. First, it is a fundamental matter of equal access to highly desirable government positions, but perhaps more important, it is a matter of more effective policing. Experience has demonstrated that members of the community who feel underrepresented by the police not only feel alienated but also consider themselves victims of prejudice and oppression by police.

Over the years, a number of lawsuits involving affirmative action were filed on behalf of women and minorities. The outcomes of such actions did much to ease the way for women and minorities into U.S. police departments. However, as more police jobs and promotions went to women and minorities, fewer white males received these jobs and promotions. Stories abound about white males who were passed over for entrance and promotional examinations by female and minority candidates—some of whom actually received lower testing scores. Consequently, anger and turmoil stemming from white males has resulted and counter lawsuits have followed.

Those who criticize affirmative action programs have argued that the selection of police officers based on their race or gender actually violates the 1964 Civil Rights Act and is discriminatory on its face. They have also argued that the selection of officers who have scored lower on civil service exams lowers the personal standards of the police department and may result in poor performance by the department (and possibly a higher degree of civil liability). The ongoing need for affirmative action programs continues to be under challenge from its critics who contend that original goals of ending discrimination against minorities and providing parity with white males have been achieved.

Discrimination and the Police Subculture

Studies have shown that police often feel a sense of social isolation from the rest of society, creating a unique **police subculture**. It is not uncommon for certain outgroups to be regarded as inferior or even dangerous. Since most police departments are comprised of white males, persons who are nonwhite are often perceived in this manner. It has been suggested that nonwhites, especially African-Americans, are less likely to receive efficient police services, are often arrested, and are sometimes beaten by police. Events during the 1990s have illustrated this notion in cities such as Miami, Los Angeles, and New Orleans, where riots have erupted over police mistreatment of suspects. One common reason why riots developed was because of nonprosecution of those officers responsible.

While social and political dynamics have provided some jobs for nonwhites in police organizations, Rafky shows that intentional and unintentional barriers contribute to the problem of discrimination.[15] He has labeled these as individual, organizational, and societal. Some individual barriers for nonwhite candidates for police work include lack of interest due to negative past encounters with police or the notion that one can do better than becoming a police officer in terms of pay and social status. Unintentional barriers include inadequate educational or physical qualifications. On the organizational level, the police department may dissuade or deliberately exclude nonwhites from consideration. The first barriers can occur during the selection process. Before the 1964 Civil Rights Act it was easy to get rid of undesirable candidates through a process termed sophisticated patronage. Biases in written tests and subjective decisions made it possible for police administrators to prevent nonwhites from competing successfully in the selection process.

Reverse Discrimination and Quotas

The language and intent of the Title VII legislation did not include preferred treatment of nonwhite and women over white police candidates. Since 1964, however, federal and state case law along with Equal Employment Opportunity Commission (EEOC) rulings have determined that statistical imbalances between the number of nonwhites in the police organization and the determined labor pool constitutes prima facie discrimination. To counter imbalances, policies of quotas and preferred treatment of nonwhites and women have been adopted by some organizations.

Despite immense legal and political criticism by private and public-sector labor, these measures have been deemed constitutional. For example, in 1979 *United Steel Workers* v. *Weber*, the use of voluntary quota system was upheld in the selection of an African-American candidate for a training program over the objections of a white candidate who claimed that he was a victim of discrimination. Discrimination is prohibited under the EEOC guidelines, and there exists no acknowledged theory of **reverse discrimination**. Yet problems arise when courts mandate that employers practice preferential hiring and promotional opportunities for minorities to counter past inequities in employment practices. Some white males have viewed this preferential treatment as reverse discrimination and claim that this is contrary to the spirit of merit system principles.

One of the offshoots of trying to overcome past years of blatant discrimination is the tension between white police officers and minorities who are often promoted or who otherwise receive special treatment because of the need to comply with a court mandate. Despite the compelling need to correct past indiscretions in hiring and promoting minorities, such a concept is often difficult for the average police officer to support. Many feel that the "rules of the game" have been changed unfairly in the favor of persons who may not be the most qualified candidates for the job. As a result, they argue that public safety is being put at risk due to the placement of less than qualified police personnel.

Despite concerns by civil rights leaders that affirmative action policies might alienate majority officers and consequently lessen support for their movement, two major U.S. Supreme Court decisions in 1989 addressed the issue and might, according to some, have turned back the clock on the civil rights initiative. In *Wards Cove Packing* v. *Antonio*, the Court ruled that minorities could not be favored in hiring decisions and that plaintiffs must disprove the claims of the employer—in this case a salmon cannery—that the adverse impact on minority hiring was based on genuine neutral factors. In another case, *Martin* v. *Wilks*, the Court decided that white employees employed at the Birmingham, Alabama, Fire Department could challenge a consent decree because they had not been parties to the negotiations that had the effect of violating their rights. In sum, these decisions have made it more difficult for minorities to challenge employment decisions and practices.

Homosexuals in Police Work

Recently, controversy has stemmed from hiring homosexuals as police officers. Departments who choose to exempt a person from employment based solely on his or her private lifestyle will be hard-pressed to show that such a lifestyle would prevent effective performance on the job. In 1969 the International Association of Chiefs of Police (IACP) rescinded its policy of opposing the hiring of homosexual police officers. In fact, *Law Enforcement News* reported in 1990 that an estimated 20% of the Sheriff's Department in San Francisco and 10% of the Los Angeles Police Department are gay or lesbian. The complaint most often levied by gays is that, like female police officers, they feel a lack of acceptance by other officers on the force. As stated by Sergeant Charlie Cochrane of the New York Police Department's Gay Officer's Association: "There is no conflict in being a cop and being gay. . . . My goal, although it may not be fully realized in my lifetime, is to erase this stigma."[16]

THE OFFICER SELECTION PROCESS

Once the applicant has expressed his or her intent to join the force, it is the job of the police agency to select the most qualified candidate for the job. This task is one of the most important, time-consuming, and expensive aspects of police administration. One reason for this is that there are so many applicants for every police officer position. In fact, typically, there are 100 applicants for every police officer position. In many police agencies, this ratio is much higher. For example, in larger cities, announcements for police officer positions may generate thousands of applications.

One of the many quandaries that present themselves during the selection process is that many personal traits considered important in police work are difficult, if not impossible, to measure. For example, it could be argued that cynicism might be a coping mechanism in police officers, but it is unclear whether it is a character trait in some applicants or whether it develops after officers have been on the job for a period of time. In any case, police agencies are duty-bound to test and determine to the best of their ability the individual traits in people who seek a career in police work, searching for the appropriate working personality.

The Americans with Disabilities Act

There are no hard-and-fast rules regarding the exact steps to be followed in selecting the best police officer candidate. Although it could be argued that hiring steps should be arranged from the least expensive to the most, often this is not the case. One of the most important developments in altering traditional selection methods is the 1990 Americans with Disabilities Act (ADA). The ADA, which became effective in July 1992, was enacted by Congress for the purpose of eliminating barriers for persons with disabilities in a number of areas, including employment, transportation, telecommunications, public accommodations, and access to state and local government facilities. In addition to private business (with 15 or more employees), the ADA applies to state and local law enforcement agencies (the FBI is exempt from ADA regulations). Title I addresses employment issues. This section explicitly states that state and local governments are included as covered entities. Furthermore, while private employers with fewer than 15 employees are not covered, there is no minimum employee requirement for the state and local governments under Title II.

Title II of the act requires that state and local governmental entities, regardless of size, provide equal access for persons with disabilities to programs, services, and activities of the entity.[17] Under the ADA, criminal justice agencies may not discriminate against qualified individuals with disabilities. This antidiscrimination mandate applies to an agency's recruitment, hiring, and promotional practices.[18] It has been hailed as "the most significant piece of legislation affecting law enforcement since the Civil Rights Act."[19]

While it is true that the passing of the ADA seriously increases the amount of bureaucracy and red tape for police administrators, it is of vital importance for millions of Americans. Rubin states that "the goal is to provide the estimated 43 million persons with disabilities access to employment, to government programs, services, and activities, and to public accommodations such as restaurants, hotels, theaters, and shopping centers."[20] Police departments are affected directly by the ADA because it guarantees access to employment and government programs, and services to persons with disabilities. The act prohibits employers from discriminating against a qualified individual with a disability (QID) in all areas of employment, including hiring, training, promotion, termination, and compensation.

The Police Application

A civil service type of application is probably the most commonly utilized application process for police recruits. Typically, it includes basic information, such as the applicant's name, address, and background information, which includes questions about education and experience. Some applications ask the applicant for criminal history information and any convictions of a criminal nature. Although lying about one's criminal history will probably result in the disqualification of the applicant from consideration, a positive response may not preclude the applicant from consideration. In addition, the applicant may be asked to provide a list of references who can attest to the applicant's reliability, honesty, and other personal traits.

Also included on the application are a series of questions of a voluntary nature that inquire about the applicant's age, race, or disabilities. The application should state, however, that such information, although not mandatory, will aid the law enforcement agency in the effectiveness of the selection process. At the conclusion of the application process, the applicant will be asked to sign the application to verify that the stated information is accurate.

Initial Testing Procedures

Depending on the venue of the police position being sought, it is common for the police applicant to be required to take a civil service (sometimes called merit system) exam prior to applying directly to the police organization. The civil service exam is designed to aid police personnel officers in the selection process. First, it is designed to weed out candidates who do not possess the most basic of qualifications, such as reading and writing skills. It is estimated that this basic skills

A Closer Look

Hiring Processes for Local Police

As of June 2000, local police departments had an estimated 565,915 full-time employees, including 441,000 sworn personnel. Nearly all officers worked for departments that used the following to screen applicants:

1. Criminal record checks (99%)
2. Background investigations (98%)
3. Driving record checks (98%)
4. Medical exams (97%)
5. Psychological tests (91%)
6. Aptitude tests (84%)
7. Physical agility tests (78%)[21]

test will eliminate over one-half of those who seek police positions. Second, it is designed to establish a list of eligibles from which the police department can choose its candidates.

More and more police agencies are requiring recruits to undergo a battery of tests to determine if they are physically and mentally fit for the rigors of police work. Personnel officers must take care to conduct such tests without permitting any bias to favor one person over another. A 1971 case, *Griggs* v. *Duke Power Company,* addressed the issue of pre-employment or promotion testing. In this case, Griggs, an African-American employee, argued that a high school diploma and a requirement to pass two aptitude tests discriminated against him. The court ruled that any tests used in promotion or hiring must be job-related.

Physical Ability

Regardless of one's gender or race, what is known about the successful police officer is that an array of distinct personality traits must be possessed. These include maturity, intelligence, the ability to think independently, an understanding of different cultures, and the recognition of the consequences of abusing police authority. Despite safeguards in the recruitment and selection of officers, many police departments throughout the country are held liable in civil actions resulting from misconduct by police officers in their employ, another important reason to ensure hiring of the right person for the job.

The physical agility test is administered to determine if the candidate can physically master the job. This test may consist of a physical agility course (e.g., dragging a dummy or climbing in and out an open window), running an eight-minute mile or equivalent, and a grip-strength and trigger-pull test. Physical traits are considered an important aspect to basic police qualifications, and employment criteria for police departments dictate that all tests and criteria be job-related. Any criteria for disqualifying job candidates that are not considered job-related can be construed as discrimination.

Highlights in Policing

Standard Minimum Requirements for Police Officers

Those who desire to become a police officer must meet what is called the "minimum standards" of the job. These standards are the minimum acceptable criteria that candidates must meet, otherwise they will not be considered for employment in police work. The following are examples of what many police departments require as minimum standards for employment as a police officer:

- Must be a resident of the United States
- Must be 21 years of age
- Must not have a felony conviction
- Must have at least a high school diploma
- Weight must be proportionate to height
- Vision must be no less than 20/100 uncorrected, correctable to 20/30
- Must reside within the position's jurisdiction by the time of appointment
- Must possess a valid driver's license issued by the state of residence

Job-related tasks can be illustrated by the ability to drive a patrol car. Since this is fundamental in the performance of the patrol officer's duties, it becomes a valid criterion in the selection process. In comparison, minimum height requirements have not proven to affect one's ability to perform the job of police officer. In years gone by, many departments maintained a minimum height requirement of five feet eight inches, which has now been deemed "not job-related."

The Oral Interview

A meaningful part of the selection process is the oral interview. The interview is performed by the police review board, which generally consists of four to six sworn officers accompanied by the department personnel officer and possibly a representative of the community. Officers sitting on the board typically hold all ranks within the force, so a fair representation of personalities is present. Officers will each have a chance to review the application and any letters of reference prior to interviewing the applicant and will then question the applicant, usually from a standardized set of questions, regarding his or her reasons and motivations for wanting to become a police officer. Other questions will be asked regarding the applicant's willingness to adjust to the working environment of police work, such as shift changes and overtime work. In many cases the interview board will ask candidates questions about hypothetical situations that enable them to judge the candidate's exercise of discretion. For example, suppose that you observe someone running a red light, and after stopping him, you discover that it is a police chief from a neighboring city—what will you do?

Candidates should begin the interview with a handshake and a smile, generally building a positive rapport with the board members. Candidates should remember not to become too friendly with board members and to keep small talk to a minimum. Listening skills are essential during the interview, and candidates must remember to pay attention to exactly what is being asked of them. After all, it is what the candidate says to the board that will determine how he or she is judged for acceptability.

Job applicants should also remember that the oral interview is a two-way street, allowing for information to be shared by the officers conducting the interview as well as by the applicant. It has been said that an applicant's job during the interview is to both tell and sell—to convey to the interviewers that he or she is a good candidate for the job as well as to sell the board on the premise that although others are also qualified for the position, he or she is the best choice. After the interview, candidates are notified if they have or have not passed the initial phases of the selection process. It is here that a job offer might typically be extended by the police agency. If so, successful candidates will be given dates and times of the next phase of the selection process, physical and psychological testing.

Many departments use the oral interview to rank candidates on their eligibility. Often, this is used to increase the consideration of women and minorities. The greatest departmental disadvantage of the oral interview is that it is subjective, and as a result the outcome of the interview may be affected by the personal characteristics of those on the interview board. In addition, although the use of the oral interview is almost universal in the police selection process, recent research has shown that it is not a valid predictor of the future performance of the candidate.[22]

The Polygraph Exam

Although the federal Employee Protection Act (EPA) of 1988 prohibits use of a **polygraph** (also known as a lie detector) in most private-sector employment screening, all government bodies are exempt from this constraint. Even though courts in many states have restricted the employment of the polygraph in pre-employment screening, over half of all police agencies still use it to screen applicants. In the polygraph system, instrumental responses are recorded on a roll of paper. These responses include primarily three physiological reactions breathing patterns, blood pressure, and perspiration on the surface of the skin. The police don't use the polygraph to disqualify applicants but to identify problem areas in statements made by the applicant that might deserve additional investigation.

Although the polygraph may be an effective investigative tool, it is not a reliable device to determine the truth or innocence of an applicant's statements. Rather, a polygraph is employed to

American Policing under Fire

Is the Polygraph Junk Science?

While the courts still call it "junk science," the lie detector or polygraph continues to be widely used by criminal justice agencies as a tool for determining the truth. In 1998 the U.S. Supreme Court ruled against the use of polygraph evidence in criminal court. But police agencies rely heavily on the polygraph exam every day to make critical personnel decisions from hiring to firing. In recent years, the percentage of police agencies using the technique to screen new employees has increased from 16% in 1962 to 62% in 1999, according to a study conducted by Michigan State's School of Criminal Justice. The same surveys show that police are confident of exam results–more than three-fourths believe that polygraphs are 86 to 100% reliable.

At the FBI, which employs over 11,000 agents, senior officials have requested permission to administer up to 225 polygraphs per year in investigations of suspected employee misconduct. That figure is in addition to the 3,000 tests given each year to new agents, and witnesses, and informants in major criminal investigations. The CIA, National Security Agency, Defense Department, Treasury Department, and many large police departments across the nation also depend on the polygraph.

Failing a polygraph, as in the case of scientist Wen Ho Lee at Los Alamos National Laboratory in New Mexico, can end a career just as quickly as a guilty verdict. Lee was fired after he failed an FBI-administered polygraph in March 1999 and refused to cooperate with the government's investigation of Chinese espionage at the facility—which is the nation's premier weapons facility.

A polygraph examiner attaches a probe to a person's chest and fingers to record heart rate, respiration, and sweat gland activity during the course of questioning. Responses to questions are automatically charted, and with responses to innocuous questions and relevant questions, the examiner can determine if the person is being deceptive.

Fearing unwarranted invasions of individual privacy, Congress passed the Employee Polygraph Protection Act of 1988 to curb what had been a growing use of polygraph tests in private business. In 1998 the U.S. Supreme Court expressed concerns about the reliability of polygraphs when it upheld the military's ban on their use in criminal trials. Yet government agencies still consider polygraphs a valuable personnel tool.[23]

verify the accuracy of background information and to discover any inappropriate behavior—past or present. Essentially, it can convince the applicant that it's a better idea to confess any wrongdoing out of fear that the polygraph will discover the "truth" during the course of the examination. It is not known, of course, how many applicants have the ability to fool the polygraph and how many do not. Traditionally, a polygraph test has been administered early in the screening process, but requirements of the ADA might dictate its administration later in the hiring process.

The Background Investigation

The character or background investigation may be the single most important determinant of an applicant's suitability for the position of police officer. The main thrust of the background investigation is to review and verify information stated or written by the police applicant with past behavior to determine the candidate's general suitability for police work. Areas examined include an extensive personal history of the applicant to determine factors such as honesty and reliability. Other variables examined in the investigation include education, employment history, military service, and criminal record. It is important for investigators charged with this task to verify facts constantly and not make assumptions that might result in negligent hirings.

As a component to the background investigation, many police agencies have also begun interviewing spouses of applicants to be certain they understand the basics of the job that their husband or wife is seeking. Such interviews help minimize misunderstandings about shift work, danger, or other aspects of the police job.

The Medical Exam

Police applicants are also typically asked to submit to a medical exam, which may only be a general physical exam given by the police agency's designated physician or a physician of the candidate's choice. In virtually all police departments, the medical exam is a mandatory component of the selection process. In some agencies the medical exam is very specific and attempts to verify that the applicant has no physical or medical impairments that might inhibit his or her performance on the job, such as heart, back, or knee conditions. If unchecked, health problems may result in considerable expense through long-term disability payments and inconvenience for the police department after the applicant has accepted employment. In addition, such shortcomings might make candidates more vulnerable to performance failures that could ultimately jeopardize their own lives or those of fellow officers.

Psychological Testing

A final component of the hiring process is the psychological testing procedure, which is designed to determine the emotional stability and maturity of the applicant. Although tests may be in oral format, the majority are administered in writing. The most widely used tests are the *Minnesota Multiphasic Personality Inventory* (*MMPI*) and the *California Psychological Inventory* (*CPI*). These tests are administered and then reviewed and rated by a licensed psychologist or psychiatrist. Psychological personnel critically review the examinations for indicators of personality flaws that might disqualify a candidate who might not make an effective police officer. Many officer candidates are disqualified following this phase of the selection process. Obviously, it is difficult to predict which officers will or will not be good police officers, as the criteria adopted by the department may differ from those determined by the psychologist. In addition, whatever the criteria adopted by the department, it is questionable whether they can be successful in determining whether a given candidate will be an effective police officer.

Problems have also been identified regarding the methodology used by police departments in administering psychological tests in that most tests fail to distinguish between good and poorly performing officers. Consequently, the psychological exam should be used in conjunction with other selection criteria in identifying and ferreting out people with mental problems or psychological disorders. Finally, as with the polygraph examination, psychological tests are subject to a broad range of interpretation by the psychologist. To help standardize the interpretation of test results, some researchers have suggested that guidelines be developed to help ensure equitable and fair application of test results.[24] Other critics have suggested that this phase of the selection process be eliminated entirely, and instead, administrators focus more on the candidate's past behavior as the best indicator of his or her future behavior.

POLICE ACADEMY TRAINING

When considering the many important variables in the selection of officers, the basic police training component to police officer readiness is a vital consideration. The police academy is the first step in the preparation of the recruit for police work. The importance of adequate basic police training, particularly in small police departments, was one of the considerations cited in 1967 by the President's Commission on Law Enforcement and the Administration of Justice. In addition, the commission concluded that although police training teaches officer recruits the mechanics of police operations, it fails to prepare them to understand the community, the police role, the prudent use of discretion, or any flaws within the criminal justice system. It also noted that police recruits should be trained in understanding the strengths of the criminal justice system and what it can and cannot do.

In addition to the foregoing recommendations, the commission also recommended a minimum of 400 hours of certified police training spread over a four- to six-month period, so that it can be carefully fused with supervised field training. Accordingly, **in-service training** should be offered at least once a year in addition to financial and career incentives for officers to continue their education. In a related report addressing the state of police training, the National Advisory Commission on Criminal Justice Standards and Goals abruptly declared that "perhaps no other profession has such lax standards or is allowed to operate without firm controls and without licensing."[25] Indeed, in many states the professional licensing and certification requirements for professions such as real estate and cosmetology are much more stringent than for police work.

Police training is usually determined by a state training standards organization, commonly referred to as Peace Officer Standards and Training (POST). Smaller police agencies will usually send recruits to regional academies, while larger ones often maintain their own in-house training programs. Although many states allow officers to be employed as a police officer up to one year prior to attending the academy, this is changing. The current trend is that before a recruit is allowed to work the street as a police officer, he or she must first complete the basic police academy training.

Police training trends have undergone considerable change since the 1950s, when there was little or no mandated training. What training existed during that time was offered by only a few colleges and universities as part of their degree programs in police science or by cities and counties on an individual basis. As far back as 1967, the President's Commission on Law Enforcement and the Administration of Justice made strong recommendations for encouraging state-mandated police training. In doing so, it recommended increased hours and improved curricula to help ensure the professionalization of new police officers.

In addition to traditional classroom lecture techniques and firearms proficiency at the shooting range, modern-day police training is also characterized by the use of multimedia and role-playing scenarios. For example, in the late 1980s the Firearms Training System (FATS) was introduced for police academy use. This system employs a laser disc format in which police officers are issued actual handguns that are altered to show the officer's response time and accuracy when fired. In practice, the officer faces a large video screen that portrays a lifelike police encounter scenario, such as a car stop,

FIGURE 4.1 Police managers conducting a background investigation on a police candidate.

robbery, or drug deal. Once the officer determines that it is necessary to draw and fire his or her weapon, reactions are registered by computer for instant evaluation and critique by instructors.

In 1981, the Commission on Civil Rights expressed concern about the effectiveness of formal police training and how it prepares officers for understanding the interaction between the police force and community human services. The commission also specified that firearms training in many jurisdictions was lax in that it failed to train officers adequately in the use of deadly force. As a result, it recommended that shoot–don't shoot scenario training, such as the FATS system, be implemented by police departments. In addition to multimedia, role-playing scenarios were practiced, which included felony car stops, building searches, and surveillance problems that would place officers in realistic situations where academy instructors can judge their discretion.

A Closer Look

Los Angeles Police Department Police Officer Minimum Requirements

IT IS IMPORTANT THAT YOU CAREFULLY READ THESE REQUIREMENTS

Failure to meet any of these requirements will result in your disqualification from the Police Officer Examination.

Age

You must be 21 years of age at the time of hire. If you are not yet 21, you may take the written test if you are 20-½ on the written test date. The maximum age for a Police Officer is 35. Candidates cannot be 35 years of age at the time of the interview date.

Education

Graduation from a U.S. high school, G.E.D. or equivalent from a U.S. institution, or a California High School Proficiency Examination (CHSPE) certificate. A two- or four-year college degree from an accredited U.S. or foreign institution may be substituted for the high school requirement.

Citizenship (Revised 8/19/98)

The city of Los Angeles requires that a Police Officer candidate be a United States citizen, or that a noncitizen be a permanent resident alien who, in accordance with the requirements of the INS, is eligible and has applied for citizenship. During the selection process, each noncitizen will be required to prove that his or her application for citizenship was accepted by INS prior to the date of application for employment. California State law requires that citizenship be granted within three years after the employment application date. For information regarding citizenship requirements, please contact the Immigration and Naturalization Service (INS) of the federal government.

Background

You must have no felony convictions or any misdemeanor conviction that would prevent your carrying a gun. You must not have a history of criminal or improper conduct, or a poor employment, military, or driving record that would affect your suitability for law enforcement work. You must also have a responsible financial history and a pattern of respect and honesty in your dealings with individuals and organizations. A valid California driver's license is required prior to appointment.

Health

You must be in excellent health with no conditions that would restrict your ability to safely complete academy training and to perform all aspects of police work.

Vision

Your vision must be no worse than 20/40 uncorrected, unless you wear soft contact lenses. Persons who have had refractive surgery are deferred for at least six months after surgery. Normal color vision is required and you must be free of other visual impairments that would restrict your ability to perform law enforcement duties.

Height/Weight (Revised March 1997)

There is no longer a height requirement. Your weight must be appropriate for your height and build.

Hearing

You must have normal ability to understand speech in noisy areas, understand whispered speech, and be able to localize sounds.

If you meet the minimum requirements listed, you may begin the selection process by taking the qualifying written tests. The written tests are offered four times each week and every weekend. Testing is conducted on a walk-in basis and no application is required to take the tests.

Source: Los Angeles Police Department Recruitment Brochure, December 2000.

The traditional police academy has been structured around the stress or paramilitary model, demanding strict discipline on the part of recruits. Such programs often have a strong physical education component, which often requires that recruits engage in rigorous physical workouts, jogging, and maintaining a minimum level of physical competency. Research has shown, however, that this style of police academy may not necessarily be the best way to train recruits.[26] In fact, studies have shown that police academies that adopt a nonstressful approach to training tend to produce officers who are more satisfied with their jobs, receive higher evaluations, and get along better with the general public.[27]

The academy's structure should also be task oriented. That is, the subject matter taught in police academies should prepare officers for performing their duties on the job. It is also important for academy instructors and the curriculum to reflect a realistic image of police work. Failure to do so can result in police officers becoming complacent or disenchanted with their job. For example, if the projected image of police work reflects a career full of car chases, shootouts, and intense interrogations with high-level crime figures, once the officer realizes that a majority of the job is service related, adjustment to the job may be more difficult. Instead, officers should be taught the realities of the job—both the pros and cons.

An important aspect of police academy training is the influence of the informal organizational culture of the officers attending the academy, which may tend to perpetuate a glamorous and sensational image of the job despite formal academy training. This informal image will promote the "macho" orientation of the police role, possibly negating efforts made by the police academy to orient new police recruits properly.

FIELD TRAINING

We have learned how becoming a police officer may be a difficult task, because many openings may have as many as 100 applicants. But once the recruiting and selection process is completed and the recruit completes the police academy training, there is still another training component that must be completed before recruits are allowed to patrol on their own—field training. Various departments may approach this differently from one another, and because of this, field training may take several forms.

Rotation is one method of field training where the recruit spends a period of time in a number of chosen areas within the police department. This "total-person" approach enables the new recruit to acquire a feeling for how the different components of the department operate and interact. Coaching or counseling represents a one-on-one approach to field training and usually takes place on the job. Coaching is accomplished through the use of a specially trained field-training officer (FTO). The FTO program is probably the best-known type of recruit officer field training. Rookies are assigned an FTO whose job it is to teach them "the ropes." The program is advantageous for both parties. Recruits benefit because of the FTO's training and experience. Tasks can be observed and practiced under supervision, and corrections can be made on the spot. FTOs benefit because of their ability to assess the performance of the recruit and identify problems and shortcomings early. This is why it important for the FTO to be selected carefully and trained thoroughly.

FTOs bear the responsibility of teaching recruits skills needed for safe, effective solo duty. Because of this responsibility, FTOs must be selected and trained carefully. But it is also important for them to be given guidelines for recruit evaluations as well as being adequately compensated for their efforts.

In-Service Training

Another common form of police officer training is in-service training. These sessions occur periodically during a police officer's career and address every conceivable topic in policing. The purpose of in-service training is to keep officers current in their fields: patrol, investigation, crime prevention, juveniles, and so on. In many states, in-service training is conducted at the police academy by state-certified trainers. Often, however, outside trainers are contracted to come to the department

A Closer Look

The Los Angeles Police Department Police Officer Selection Process

The selection process consists of seven steps, all of which must be successfully completed before a candidate may be considered for appointment as a Police Officer. Generally, candidates must complete each step before being scheduled for the next. Successful candidates may expect to make four to five visits to various city testing sites during the process.

PLEASE NOTE: The period for which test results are valid varies according to the test. It is the candidate's responsibility to make sure all his or her test results are kept current. Most successful candidates complete the Police Officer testing process in five months to one year. There is also an "Out of Town" expedited testing program and schedule.

Written Test

The qualifying written test consists of two parts: The multiple choice test measures reading comprehension and English usage; the essay determines written communication skills. You are usually notified if you have passed the multiple choice test on the same day, and scheduled for your interview. The essay is scored at a later date. The tests are pass/fail and you must pass both tests to go forward in the process. If you fail either or both tests, you may retake them after six months. A passing score on the written test is valid indefinitely.

Interview

The interview is a behavior-based review of your personal history, providing evaluation of your problem-solving abilities, respect for diversity, community service orientation, role adaptability, communications ability, and motivation. Passing the interview requires a score of 70% or higher. The score you receive will determine your rank on a hiring list. You may take the interview only once every six months. The interview score is valid for a minimum of one year; however, always verify the expiration date of your test.

Medical Examination/Written Psychological Test

The medical examination and written psychological tests are scheduled for candidates who pass the interview with a referable score (the score based on the number of candidates in the process at the current hiring activity of the Police Department). Both tests are administered on the same day and require approximately five to six hours to complete. The medical exam, conducted by a city physician, is thorough and it is essential that candidates be in excellent health with no conditions that would restrict their ability to safely do police work. Medical exam results are valid for up to two years, at the discretion of the city's medical staff. The written psychological test consists of several personality and life history questionnaires. The results are evaluated by staff psychologists in preparation for the oral psychological evaluation.

Physical Abilities Test (PAT)

The Physical Abilities Test (PAT) consists of events designed to measure your strength, agility, endurance, and balance. The PAT is a pass/fail qualifying test. Click here for a description of the current test. One will also be provided when you are scheduled for the test. Testing is normally given twice monthly and you may take this test as often as is necessary to pass. The PAT results are valid for one year.

Background Investigation

The Background Investigation includes fingerprinting, photos, and a background interview, all of which take place on the same day. The investigative phase of the background process includes a thorough check of police records, personal, military and employment histories, as well as reference checks. You are evaluated on your respect for the law; honesty; mature judgment; respect for others; employment and military record, financial record, driving record, and use of drugs and intoxicants. You must submit comprehensive biographical information for this investigation. Investigation results are valid for one year.

Psychological Interview

The Psychological Interview is conducted it if appears that you will be successful in the background investigation. You are interviewed and evaluated by a city psychologist on factors related to successful performance in the difficult and stressful job of Police Officer. The information evaluated includes the previous written psychological tests as well as the background findings.

Certification and Appointment

Certification and Appointment are the final steps in the selection process. To be considered you must have successfully completed steps one through six in the process. Certification of a candidate's name to the Police Department does not guarantee appointment to the Police Academy. More names are provided to the Police Department than there are vacancies so that the Department can select those best qualified for appointment. Appointments to the Police Academy are made by the Police Department from the civil service eligible list in accordance with the score on the eligible list and provisions of the Consent Decree.

Pre-Employment Substance Screening

Additionally, a pre-employment substance screening for drugs and alcohol may be required prior to appointment because this class has been designated as Safety Sensitive, in accordance with City Policy.

Source: Los Angeles Police Department (www.lapdonline.org).

FIGURE 4.2 Basic police academy recruit training, such as this in Philadelphia, PA, is required of all police officers as part of their basic, state-mandated police certification.

and provide training. In-service training differs from basic police training in that it is not certified by the state, and virtually anyone can be contracted to conduct a training seminar. Expense is the primary reason why outside consultants are not used for training more often then they are.

In-service training may accommodate a class of 10 or 100 officers, depending on the cost and interest in the subject matter. Contractors make use of visual aids, handout material, practical simulations, and other training techniques that give the program an impact that would not be possible if done with in-house personnel.[28]

Roll Call

The beginning of each shift is a good opportunity for short training modules. It is not only popular but economical as well, especially with the advent and availability of brief video training tapes. Konkler states that since officers spend an average of 60 hours per year in roll calls, they could receive a full week and a half of training during roll call alone.[29] Since most roll calls last only ten to fifteen minutes, training must be done in brief bursts but will probably be more effective than an extended training session in certain subjects. The best subject matter for roll-call training are subjects of immediate interest to the on-line officer.

HIGHER EDUCATION IN POLICING

For the past couple of decades, law enforcement administrators have been weighing the advantages and disadvantages of a formal college education versus police vocational training and asking themselves which better prepares people for a career in police work. Such conversations among administrators frequently result in the education versus commonsense debate, with an abundance of case examples to be offered on both sides of the issue. It could be argued, however, that a formal college education does tend to raise the level of professionalism in law enforcement, which in turn generates community support, making it more likely for a police department to obtain departmental resources such as higher salaries and improved working conditions. The educational component to police officer recruitment and selection remains a major consideration for police managers. Many departments require only a high school diploma or an equivalency, but many others mandate some amount of college or a bachelors degree.

Over the years, strides have been made in requiring police candidates to have a certain amount of college education to be eligible for appointment. For example, in 1998 the Bureau of Justice Statistics reported that 14% of local police departments and 11% of sheriffs' departments had some type of college education requirement for new officers. One percent of the departments required a four-year degree. The typical new officer recruit was required to complete 1,100 hours of training in local police departments and 900 hours in sheriffs' departments during 1997.[30]

Higher education for the candidates first received attention in 1917, when August Vollmer recruited police officers from student applicants at the University of California. Although Vollmer espoused the importance of formal education in police work, few police agencies followed his lead in their hiring practices. Since then, three national commissions (the Wickersham Commission in 1931, the President's Commission on Law Enforcement and the Administration of Justice in 1967, and the National Advisory Commission on Criminal Justice Standards in 1973) have supported the position that a high school diploma alone is insufficient as a minimal level of education for police officers.

Indeed, the relevance of a college education for police officers has been questioned over the years. During the late 1960s, when few police officers had a college education, the President's Commission on Law Enforcement and the Administration of Justice suggested that "the ultimate goal of all police departments should be that personnel with general enforcement powers have baccalaureate degrees."[31] Shortly thereafter, government programs offered support and financial incentives for the continuance of higher education among police officers. By 1989, after a decade of rigorous governmental budget and funding cuts, it was estimated that 55% had some degree of college education but that the average level of education of all police had risen to only 14 years.

Early research focused on how the attitudes of police officers with a college education differed from that of their counterparts with no college degree. One study revealed that officers with college degrees tended to be less authoritarian than those without.[32] Similarly, police officers who were seniors in college were less authoritarian than those who were freshmen, which indicates that the more formal education people have, the more understanding and open-minded they might be. Other research has suggested that college-educated officers tend to be more flexible and aware of social and ethnic problems in their jurisdictions. Furthermore, they tend to be more accepting of minorities and express a stronger commitment to police professionalism.[33]

Today, however, some evidence indicates that the rate of increase in educational levels for police is flattening out. Several reasons can be cited for this presumption. First, many police administrators believe that in requiring an arbitrary level of education for entry-level police positions, many minority applicants might be discriminated against. Second, educational requirements tend to reduce the size of the applicant pool. Third, the raising of educational requirements has received opposition by some police unions throughout the country.[34] In addition, it can be argued that in smaller jurisdictions, a college degree is not all that important for officers whose main daily tasks are traffic enforcement, parking control, and other clerical tasks that don't require a postsecondary education. Furthermore, in such jurisdictions a highly educated person might become bored with such menial duties and as a result become complacent, ineffective, or even a malcontent.

Another area of concern is the structure of criminal justice programs at colleges and universities. Specifically, many argue that too often such programs focus on the technical aspects of police work rather than offering a broad educational background. In fact, the National Advisory Commission on Higher Education for Police Officers was critical of higher education programs that tended merely to "service the status quo" rather than providing a broadening experience that would give officers more of an ability to deal with their professional problems.

In defense of a stronger educational component in policing is the Police Executive Research Forum, who in 1989 released a study of police education in which the advantages and disadvantages of higher education for police were discussed. After reviewing the literature of the subject, the authors concluded that overall, college-educated officers are more responsible and are better decision makers than are their less educated counterparts. The former are not only more effective in performing their jobs but are also more efficient, in that costs associated with lost personnel time are lower.

Many states are now responding to the educational issue in professional policing. For example, the 1991 Minnesota state legislature approved a pilot project at the Metropolitan State University in St. Paul. Called the School of Law Enforcement, it provides curriculums for a four-year degree, graduate studies, continuing education, and clinical skills training. Students can go straight through the academic and skills program or transfer from a two-year school with full acceptance of credits.[35] The school also supports research, a much-needed area in policing and one usually required to make an academic law enforcement program a professional discipline.

Minnesota's policies are based on studies, which indicate that a better educated police officer makes a better officer. Although many important police skills are learned at the vocational level, studies have suggested that many police activities require officers to have a more educationally diverse background. Such activities are those requiring the officer to become one of many different social and behavioral science experts, such as a counselor, social worker, legal adviser, crime analyst, clergy member, community leader, mediator, and psychologist. Some would argue, how else can an officer acquire such skills?

Florida is another state that has addressed the controversial issue of higher education for police officers. The need for a stronger educational component to police work became apparent after authorities realized that:

1. Many criminal cases were being lost in court because of incomplete, badly written, or illegible police reports.
2. Budget cuts and low salaries were resulting in a higher turnover rate for police officers.

As a result, state and local police agencies originated a broad-based review process to examine these problems, which evolved into the Enhanced Criminal Justice Training and Education Delivery System, also known as the **enhanced system**. The goals of the enhanced system are to encourage higher education among peace officers, to lower training costs to police agencies, to increase local involvement in the delivery system, to increase the labor pool, and to avoid duplication of recruitment training.[36]

Under this program a considerable amount of flexibility is offered by allowing students to enroll in either a two- or four-year degree program to receive both academic and vocational skills training. Since only schools with Florida Department of Law Enforcement–certified curriculums bestow degrees, they satisfy minimum state standards, and graduates can go to work anywhere within the state. In addition, traditional police academies give college credit value to their courses so that if an academy-trained recruit enrolls in a college degree program, the credit can be applied. Although pursuing a college degree places a considerable financial burden on the student, most police managers agree that a college education makes that student more marketable. Especially appealing to recent high school graduates who are too young to be recruited for police academy training are two-year degree programs. Students entering such programs can continue their education while preparing for a career in police work.

As mentioned above, a number of studies have attempted to measure the degree of successful performance by college-educated officers as opposed to that of their counterparts who have only a high school diploma. Cohen and Chaiken report that officers in the New York City Police Department with at least one year of college proved to be good performers and had fewer citizen complaints than average.[37] Officers who had four-year college degrees performed even better than others who did not. Similar to the findings in the New York study were the results of a study involving the Chicago Police Department, which found that the highest-rated group of tenured officers were those with significantly higher educational backgrounds.[38]

Another school of thought is that by adhering to strict educational requirements, otherwise good police officers will be disqualified. Some argue that experience in another law enforcement agency should be considered in lieu of education. To what extent experience should substitute for education, however, is unclear. The best choice, of course, is a candidate who has both a formal education and police experience. In some instances, college-educated officers experience some difficulties that relate to their being college educated. These include:

- Being rejected by officers who themselves don't have college degrees
- Not being placed in positions where their college education could be the most advantageous to the department
- Having few or no rewards for the attainment of a college degree

Furthermore, the lack of a promotional system to recognize or give credit to those with a college education can lower the morale of those officers.

Degree requirements for police officers can hardly be considered as widespread. Yet more and more police administrators are addressing this topic around the country, for a number of reasons. It could be argued that police work is undergoing a gradual educational revolution, which probably won't change police work itself but could augment trends in the profession. If nothing else, the educational component adds a degree of professionalism to aid the administration of justice in a changing society.

POLICE UNIONS

The development of police unions throughout the nation has a long and spirited history. The earliest police employee organizations were developed as fraternal associations to provide fellowship for officers, as well as welfare benefits such as death and insurance benefits. In some departments, labor unions begin to organize the police for the purpose of **collective bargaining** and, by 1919, the American Federation of Labor (AFL) had chartered 37 locals. In 1919, the Boston Police strike was triggered by the refusal of the city of Boston to recognize the AFL-affiliated union. As a result, Calvin Coolidge, then the governor of Massachusetts, fired all the striking police officers—which amounted to almost the entire police department. Because of the police strike in Boston, the police union movement stalled until the 1960s at which time it reemerged.

Today, nearly 75% of all U.S. police officers are members of labor unions. About two-thirds of all the states have collective bargaining laws for public employees. In those states, the police union bargains with the locality over wages and other conditions of employment. In those states that did not have collective bargaining agreements, police unions serve a less formal role.

For the most part, police unions are local organizations that bargain and communicate with the local police department and the mayor's or chief executive's office. Local unions often join into federations on a state or federal level to lobby state and federal legislative bodies. Some of the major federations of local police unions are the International Union of Police Associations (IUPA), the Fraternal Order of Police (FOP), the International Conference of Police Associations (ICPA), and the International Brotherhood of Police Officers (IBPO). Some officers are also members of national federations of civil service workers, such as the American Federation of State, County, and Municipal Employees (AFSCME).

Unions exist in order to harness the individual power of each worker into one group, the union, which can then speak with one collective voice for all of the members. The ultimate bargaining tool of the union has traditionally been the strike. Members of many organizations, such as autoworkers, teachers, factory workers, and so on, strike to win labor concessions from their employees. The appropriateness of police officers going on strike, however, has been widely debated for decades. In fact, most states have laws that specifically prohibit strikes by public employees. Despite such laws, there have been strikes by police employees. For example, in 1970, members of the New York City Police Department waged a wildcat strike, for which all officers were fined two days' pay for each day they participated in the strike. Police strikes have also been staged in Baltimore, San Francisco, and New Orleans.

In an effort to avoid penalties involved in a formal police strike, police union members occasionally engage in informal job actions to protest working conditions or other grievances. Such job actions include the so-called **blue flu** where police officers call in sick.

Other police affiliations, in addition to unions, also exist. The two most common types of affiliations are fraternal and professional. Fraternal organizations generally focus on national origin, ethnic, or gender identification. In addition, two major professional organizations for police officers have been developed as a forum to exchange professional information and provide training. These are the International Association of Chiefs of Police (IACP) and the Police Executive Research Forum (PERF), a research-based organization.

In Retrospect

The development of human resources is the single most important objective of police departments. Police officer selection is based on carefully specified criteria, which usually include making an application, taking a series of tests, passing a background check and interview process, and passing a medical and psychological exam. The selection process is governed by laws that relate to equal opportunity, affirmative action, and labor unions. Title VII of the Civil Rights Act of 1964 prohibits discrimination based on race, color, religion, sex, or national origin for private employers with 15 or more employees, governments, unions, and employment agencies. The Equal Employment Opportunity Commission (EEOC) enforces laws prohibiting job discrimination. An affirmative action program is a written plan to ensure fair recruitment, hiring, and promotion practices.

Included in human resource development is the promotion of both training and education. *Training* refers to a more vocational, task-oriented process that takes place on the job. *Education* refers to an academic setting that takes place at a college, university, or seminar-type facility external to the police department.

Improve Your Professional Vocabulary

affirmative action
blue flu
Civil Rights Act of 1964
collective bargaining

enhanced system
Equal Employment Opportunity
    Act of 1972
in-service training

police subculture
polygraph
reverse discrimination
Title VII

Discussion Questions

1. List and discuss the various aspects of police work that are attractive to potential job applicants.
2. List and discuss the different phases of the police hiring process.
3. List and discuss the various concepts of police personnel management.
4. Discuss some important issues that relate to a police officer's basic academy training.
5. Explain what role higher education plays in selection of the "best" police officer candidates.
6. Explain how police work can be characterized as a profession.
7. Explain what is meant by the term *police subculture*.
8. In what ways does police academy training differ from field training?
9. Discuss what is meant by the police officer's "working personality."
10. Discuss the importance of minorities and women in police work.

Notes

1. Bittner, E. (1989). *The McGraw-Hill 36-hour management course.* New York: McGraw-Hill.
2. U.S. Department of Justice, Bureau of Justice Statistics. (1987, July). Census of state and local law enforcement agencies. Washington, DC: U.S. Government Printing Office.
3. Meagher, M. S., & N. A. Yentes. (1986). Choosing a career in policing: A comparison of male and female perceptions. *Journal of Police Science and Administration, 14,* 320.
4. Slater, H. R., & M. Reiser. (1988). A comparative study of factors influencing police recruitment. *Journal of Police Science and Administration, 16,* 168.
5. Johnson, K. (2000, November 21). Police struggle to find next generation. *USA Today,* p. 1A.
6. Ibid.
7. Ibid.
8. Woska, William J. (2006). Police Officer Recruitment: A Public Sector Crisis. *The Police Chief,* October, p. 54.
9. Whetstone, Thomas, John C. Reed, & Turner Phillip C. (2006). Recruiting: A Comparative Study of the Recruiting Practices of State Police Agencies. *International Journal of Police Science and Management,* August. pp. 52–66.
10. Martinez, Mary, Bruce, Kubu & Bruce, Taylor (2006). *Dealing with a Cop Crunch? Tips for Better Recruitment.* Subject to Debate. August. pp. 1; 4–5.
11. Jones, Robin (2004). Recruiting Women. *The Police Chief,* April, pp. 165–166.
12. Ibid.
13. Ibid.
14. Sheehan, R., & G. W. Cordner. (1989). *Introduction to police administration,* 2nd ed. Cincinnati, OH: Anderson, p. 135.
15. Rafky, D. M. (1975, July). Racial discrimination in urban police departments. *Crime and Delinquency,* pp. 233–242.
16. Mitteage, J. (1984, February). NYPD's gay cops. *National Centurion, 2*(1), 33–36.
17. U.S. Department of Justice, National Institute of Justice. (1994, July). *The Americans with Disabilities Act and criminal justice: Providing inmate services. Research in action.* Washington, DC: U.S. Government Printing Office.
18. Ibid.
19. Schneid, T. D., & L. K. Gaines. (1991). The Americans with Disabilities Act: Implications for police administrators. *American Journal of Police, 10*(1), 47–58.
20. Rubin, P. N. (1993, September). *The Americans with Disabilities Act: An overview. Research in action.* Washington, DC: National Institute of Justice.
21. Bureau of Justice Statistics. (2003). *Local Police Departments, 2000.* Washington, DC: U.S. Justice Department, NCJ 196002.
22. Burbeck, E., & A. Furnham. (1985). Police officer selection: A critical review of the literature. *Journal of Police Science and Administration, 13,* 58–69.
23. Johnson, K. (1999, April 6). Government agencies see truth in polygraphs. *USA Today,* p. 11A.
24. Inwald, R. (1985). Administrative legal and ethical practices in psychological testing of law enforcement officers. *Journal of Criminal Justice, 13,* 367.
25. National Advisory Commission on Criminal Justice Standards and Goals. (1973). *A national strategy to reduce crime.* Washington, DC: U.S. Government Printing Office.
26. Berg, B. L. (1990). First day at the police academy: Stress-reaction training as a screening technique. *Journal of Contemporary Criminal Justice, 6,* 89–101.
27. Earle, H. H. (1973). *Police recruit training: Stress vs. nonstress.* Springfield, IL: Charles C. Thomas.
28. Dees, T. (1990, March). Getting the most from the training budget. *Law and Order,* 48–50.
29. Konkler, G. (1988, November). In-service training in economically distressed times. *FBI Law Enforcement Bulletin,* 1–4.
30. Bureau of Justice Statistics. (1998). *Local Police Departments, 1997.* Washington, DC: U.S. Justice Department.
31. President's Commission on Law Enforcement and the Administration of Justice. (1967). *Task force report: The police.* Washington, DC: U.S. Government Printing Office.
32. Smith, A., B. Lock, & W. Walker. (1968). Authoritarianism in police college students and non-police college students. *Journal of Criminal Law, Criminology and Police Science, 50,* 440–453.
33. Miller, J., & L. J. Fry. (1978). Some evidence on the impact of higher education for law enforcement personnel. *Police Chief Magazine, 45,* 30–38.
34. Carter, D., et al. (1989). *The state of police education: Police direction for the 21st century.* Washington, DC: U.S. Government Printing Office.
35. Benson, K. (1993, July). Who makes the best officer? Merging education and experience. *Police,* pp. 38–39.
36. Ibid.
37. Cohen, B., & J. Chaiken. (1976). *Police background characteristics and performance: Summary.* New York: Rand Institute.
38. Baehr, E. M., J. E. Furcon, & E. C. Froemel. (1968, November). *Psychological assessment of patrolmen qualifications in relation to field performance.* Washington, DC: U.S. Government Printing Office.

CHAPTER 5

Police Operations: Patrol

This chapter will enable you to:

- Understand the role of the police patrol officer.
- Explain the importance of identifying "hot spots" and the assignment of patrol units.
- Distinguish between line and staff police functions.

- Comprehend the principles behind the allocation of patrol units.
- Understand contemporary studies addressing the relevance of police response time.
- Understand the effectiveness of nontraditional police patrol operations.

On her nationally acclaimed television show, Oprah Winfrey asked 15-year-old Sean Hornbeck, "How often did you think about your family?" He replied, "Every day." In autumn of 2002, Hornbeck, then 11 years old, had disappeared while riding his bicycle in Richwoods, Missouri. On January 12, 2007, while searching for another missing child, police stumbled on Hornbeck in an apartment complex in Kirkwood, Missouri, a suburb of St. Louis. Hornbeck had been kidnapped and held captive by a man named Michael Devlin, and his rescue set off a firestorm of media attention, including the appearance on the Oprah Winfrey show.

"Did you ever write or try to call them?" Winfrey inquired, gently. "No," said Hornbeck. This four-year silence was one aspect of the case that fascinated the public. Another was how Hornbeck and Devlin's Kirkwood neighbors failed to notice something suspicious about the pair's strange relationship. Speculation on these matters clogged the nation's airwaves and newspapers. Newscasters and columnists offered helpful hints on "how to keep this from happening to your child," and, for the most part, succeeded in scaring America's parents out of their wits.

Lost in the commotion was one significant detail: Child abductions such as Sean Hornbeck's experienced were exceedingly rare. Just how rare, however, is a bit of a mystery. Even though such cases dominate the headlines whenever they occur, the federal government has not classified child abduction or kidnapping as a major criminal offense. Consequently, no authoritative national statistics on these crimes exist.

Among the many issues that present themselves in the Hornbeck case, one clear message is the important role played by law enforcement officers in detecting the presence of Sean Hornbeck in a suburban Missouri community.

In this chapter we address the operations aspect of police work, but police officers must be cognizant of the fact that the actual operations are only part of the job. Police officers, regardless of their assignment, must always remember the context in which they work: the citizens in the community and criminal justice colleagues with whom they work. The police officer is an integral part of this context, not a separate entity working in a vacuum.

Police officers must make good use of communication skills, which include active listening, report writing, and clear communication techniques. Police officers' actions must not only be legal but also ethical. And they must develop the ability to protect themselves in what could be life-threatening situations. Once officers accept these foundational prerequisites, they can focus on the actual operations police officers perform. Of the many functions performed by contemporary police departments, field operations are the most prominent. These include two basic functions: patrol operations and criminal investigations. In this chapter we examine the dynamics of patrol and investigative operations and how these important functions relate to effective policing.

THE PATROL FUNCTION

After graduation from the police academy, a new recruit's first assignment is generally the uniformed patrol division, a foundational assignment for all subsequent police experiences. The patrol component of police organizations is generally associated with state and local law enforcement and represents the largest organizational unit within those departments. The patrol division is an extremely high-visibility component of the police department, and most sworn officers are assigned to patrol. Estimates are that anywhere from 50% to 70% of a police department's sworn personnel comprise the patrol function, but in actuality, it is often higher than that.[1]

In theory, patrol officers are the most valuable people in the police department. To a certain extent, all activity stems from the uniformed patrol officer. Ironically, this concept is not supported by such measures as salary, working conditions, and degree of authority. As a rule, the most burdensome and dangerous aspects of police work are performed by the uniformed patrol officer. Such work is often performed in an emotionally charged atmosphere of hostility, an environment that fosters distrust and anger. Those situations typically require patrol officers to wear many "hats," such as clergy, psychologist, therapist, lawyer, and even street fighter. Patrol officers are expected to be all things to all people.

Because of their high visibility, the public image of police officers in general is derived from activities and impressions propagated by uniformed officers on patrol. In addition, many citizens tend to view the police as the government rather than as people working on behalf of the community. Critics have even argued that the patrol officers are the main component of the criminal justice system, often acting as the judge and jury in most conflict situations. Hence, it is common for members of the general public to form personal opinions about the police and the criminal justice system based on headlines in print media or by learning of various incidents through radio, television, and casual conversation. Many players are involved in the criminal justice process, including the police officer, prosecutor, defense attorney, and judge. These persons all contribute in one way or another to the administration of criminal justice and the disposition of criminal cases. In reality, the patrol officer is simply one of many persons in the criminal justice system.

With the many public perceptions surrounding patrol officers, one could ask whether there is any operational model depicting the "typical" police patrol operation. For many, patrol is best portrayed by large, high-profile police organizations such as the Los Angeles, Chicago, or New York police departments. In actuality, however, no single police agency in the United States is ideal, nor is there a unique patrol strategy that works well for all departments. Instead, a huge variance exists in the types of police agencies operating in the United States, from small to large, urban to rural, township to federal.

As Gary Cordner points out, the police patrol function is ambiguous and multifaceted, and developing clear and reliable task categories is difficult. In fact, he states that contrary to the popular belief of the past two decades, patrol functions far exceed those of just service-related activities.[2] It is also important to note that the patrol function varies in nature from small to large departments. In smaller departments, for example, most officers are members of the patrol division and assume more of a generalist role. These departments typically require officers who respond to calls to conduct investigations if necessary. In comparison, midsized to large police departments compartmentalize officers into specialist roles. For some, special units are sometimes developed within the patrol division. In addition to patrol, police specialists may be assigned to investigative, juvenile, or prevention divisions within the police department.

Much of what we know about policing stems from research conducted in large police departments. For example, according to one estimate, 80% of all U.S. law enforcement agencies maintain 20 or fewer officers, most of whom are assigned to patrol duties.[3] In fact, even when considering that other units, such as detectives, crime prevention, and records, also comprise players in the police organization, patrol officers still make up over two-thirds of all sworn officers. Hence it has been said that patrol operations represent the backbone of policing. Several reasons can be offered to explain this.

For example, the majority of sworn police officers occupy this role and deliver most of the police services to the community and comprise the highest visibility unit within the department. Clearly, the marked patrol vehicle with its distinctive lights, paint, and ambience clearly announces the presence of the "peacekeeper" in any neighborhood. To what extent this provides a deterrence for crime is discussed later in the chapter. It is ironic that although many administrators espouse the patrol function as being the backbone of the law enforcement agency, the same administrators typically transfer the best and brightest officers from patrol to other assignments within the police organization, such as the investigation bureau, the training division, and so on. This custom can generate problems and confusion within the ranks of officers and may result in the "backbone" of the police organization being comprised of inexperienced officers with minimal training and motivation. The degree of discretion enjoyed by the patrol officer also characterizes his or her role in the community (see Chapter 6). It is the use of this discretion that results in the majority of arrests.

Wilson points out that police departments are unique in that discretion increases as one moves down the organizational hierarchy.[4] Indeed, it is the newest members of the police force who will typically begin in patrol positions demanding the greatest degree of discretion, maturity, knowledge, and self-control. Also, the patrol officer is generally the first one summoned to respond to calls and thus is the most likely candidate for injury on duty. Occupational hazards associated with patrol operations include a considerable amount of danger because uniformed officers are operating on the "front lines" and a substantial amount of public and judicial scrutiny is focused on its members.

Time-on-task or officer "street smarts" are considered very important within the informal culture of the department and contribute greatly to the development of the police social climate. In fact, it is common for some officers to believe that the only officers who really understand law enforcement and the street are those who have worked in the uniformed patrol capacity. These officers are often characterized as those who have earned their "bones" or paid their dues. Despite these observations, members of the patrol division are sometimes viewed by both the general public and other officers alike as occupying the lowest status of the police community. This is primarily because patrol is an entry-level assignment, the lowest-paid sworn position, and officers must work irregular hours, such as weekends, holidays, and night shifts. Officers who aspire to move beyond the patrol function often seek promotion to the position of detective, a much more desirable position within the ranks of the police.

The average working day for the patrol officer is unlike those officers commonly portrayed by the media. Indeed, it is not always filled with exciting crime-fighting activities, but rather, performing noncriminal public activities. It should be noted, however, that the patrol officer's day-to-day duties are also some of the most unpredictable and dangerous in law enforcement. In fact, it is the patrol officer who is first summoned to crimes in progress or crimes that have just been committed. These situations increase the likelihood that the officer will arrive at a crime scene where the criminal is still present and might possibly be prepared for a violent encounter. Patrol officers will spend much of their day dealing with the dregs of society and in situations that often include the following:

1. Drunks who might have urinated on themselves but who must be searched before being transported to jail
2. Prostitutes and their pimps
3. Street thugs who are ready to fight
4. Gang members who daily threaten officers
5. Murderers and sex offenders whose crimes might leave a lasting impression in the minds of the officers

In addition to this list, patrol officers are often required to intercede in domestic disputes (discussed later in this chapter), where not only is the well-being of the officer in constant jeopardy, but it is also difficult to determine which of the participants is in violation of the law.

As we have observed, it is difficult to list exactly the specific duties of patrol officers, because they are called upon to deal with so many different types of situations. In general, however, the patrol function has three components: answering telephone calls for assistance, providing a deterrent for crime through maintaining a high-visibility presence in neighborhoods, and investigating suspicious circumstances. When considering these differences, a distinction should be made between line and staff functions. Line functions directly involve operational activities of the agency, while staff functions support the line.

Included in staff functions are administrative offices such as that of the chief or sheriff. A delicate balance must be maintained between line and staff functions so that they create an effective crime-control organization. It should be noted that the balance between line and staff functions will vary greatly from one law enforcement organization to another. The allocation of personnel to any division, however, should not be viewed as an index of importance because functions within any police agency and the number and type of people needed in those positions will vary.

A Closer Look

Police Dogs—Helper or Threat?

While the police department will tell you police dogs or K9s as many of us call them, are intensely trained animals to help the police in certain situations, a lot of people if asked, will tell you they think police dogs are mean and are trained to attack on command. Is being held by a police dog a form of brutality? If the human officer cannot bite a suspect then why should a dog be allowed to inflict such bodily injury?

German Shepherds are most widely known as being police dogs, but a few other breeds are also used. Most police dogs are trained to intimidate, find, chase, and hold suspects who are either running or hiding from the Police. Police state that the dog's objective is not to bite a fleeing suspect but to find, grab and hold on until the dog's handler gives the release command. While a suspect is being "held" by the dog, he may get bitten even if he's not fighting or trying to get the dog off. Often times the officer will not call the dog off until the suspect has put his hands out to his sides and is laying down on his or her stomach. All the while the suspect is being bitten by the police dog.

How hard would it be for the average person to lay still while having their arm or leg chewed on by a large animal? In many states, attacking a police dog is a felony. So, if you try to defend yourself while a police dog has your leg in its mouth and is biting you, you may find yourself in even more trouble if you accidentally harm the dog while trying to get it off you. In many states, the police dogs now have the same rights as a human officer. If one is killed, the suspect can then be prosecuted the same as if he killed a human officer in the line of duty.

Dogs are also used in other parts of Law Enforcement. Dogs can be trained to sniff out drugs, bombs, explosives, and chemicals, and they can be used in airports to sniff baggage for things that aren't supposed to be there.

HISTORICAL DEVELOPMENTS IN PATROL

Today, the patrol function is generally characterized by a uniformed officer in a marked police vehicle who is designated to safeguard an assigned district or precinct. As we will see, prior to the beginning of this century, patrol work was conducted mainly on foot and to a lesser extent on bicycle or horseback. Shifts would consist of 12-hour watches with officers basically working alone. The role of the patrol officer has undergone extensive changes over the last century. As discussed in the beginning of this book, during the late nineteenth and early twentieth centuries, most police appointments were based on political patronage and the stigma of being a police officer was closely associated with corruption and brutality. Today, virtually all modern police and sheriffs departments have a patrol division, and appointments are generally based on a number of criteria, including civil service exam scores, oral interviews, and extensive background investigations of candidates.

The evolution of policing has taken several significant turns over a period of time. For example, under the night watch system, the citizen served his community, acting as a volunteer to watch over towns and boroughs. Evolving from the night watch system was the watchman system, in which citizens were paid for protective services. Then, in the nineteenth century, the professional, uniformed police officer emerged and formed the basis for the development of the political model of policing. The political model was characterized by the "beat cop," who was well acquainted with his assigned neighborhood and those who resided in it. The degree of closeness experienced between the beat policeman and his community was based on the order-maintenance model of policing, which stressed swift attention to local crime problems. In this regard, the police officer was thought of highly by many members of the community.

Unfortunately, much historical evidence supports the notion of policing during the period as being ineffective, corrupt, and unprofessional. This dark side of policing eventually produced a public image of the patrol officer as inefficient and unresponsive to the needs of the public.

The overwhelming need for change in police practices prompted an era of professionalization. This was characterized by the legalistic model, which replaced the political model and ultimately portrayed policing as more of a profession than merely a job. Police officers operating under this model were a sharp contrast to those in the political model as the professionalization of police work became the focus of administrators and police policy. Professionalization required police officers to conduct their day-to-day operations more "by the book" than before, which had the unforeseen consequence of depersonalizing the police from the public they served. Although many variables could be linked to the downfall of police–community relations, two developments in particular helped contribute to the depersonalization process: the automobile and the adoption of the Uniform Crime Reports (UCR).

Until the invention of automobiles, most of the nation's beat officers would maintain a clear physical presence while walking their beats. When motorized patrol became common, officers were no longer required to walk beats and interact with citizens in the manner to which they had been accustomed. Rather, their new charge was to patrol in automobiles and respond arbitrarily to calls. Consequently, officers on motor patrol observed citizens but were unable to place faces with names as they were in earlier days. Accordingly, citizens, who once knew the names of the local beat officers, now only saw police cars going by from time to time with no direct contact or personal interaction.

The advent of two-way radios not only enhanced the effectiveness of law enforcement response by enabling communication between officers and their headquarters, but it also contributed to depersonalization between police officers and the citizens of the communities. Officers were forced to behave in a more reactive mode than in the proactive mode to which they were accustomed. In addition to radios, the telephone and its modern-day 9-1-1 capability helped provide greater police service for communities. On the one hand, the 9-1-1 system contributed to more communication between police departments as it enabled more direct access to police services and response time.

However, social contact and positive interactions between police and the general citizenry became less frequent. Patrol officers also became less personally involved with the citizenry after the development of the uniform crime reporting system in 1930. Because many police departments chose to adopt the UCR as a means to evaluate their performance (e.g., through clearing Part I and Part II crimes), administrators stressed the crime-fighting aspect of patrol work and abandoned activities emphasizing the public relations component of policing. In short, technology has served to enhance the efficiency of patrol, but in some cases has done little to strengthen the effectiveness of police services.

ALLOCATION OF RESOURCES

Even though police patrol has come a long way since the days of its early development, police administrators still grapple with questions of how best to deploy patrol units. Since the early days, several methods have been developed to help determine the proper number of patrol units to be assigned during a given shift. These methods sometimes include the use of intuition by the police administrator, who can basically use his or her "gut feeling" regarding the deployment of patrol cars. This method may or may not be the best method for making such determinations, as much has to do with the degree of police experience associated with the administrator.

Traditionally, it has been assumed that patrol units should be assigned to locations in the community where it is most likely that trouble might occur. Unfortunately, there are no precise guidelines for the police administrator to determine where to send officers. It is also likely that pressure from certain segments of society can influence the distribution of police resources. For example, pressure from downtown merchants can sometimes influence the police department to concentrate on street crimes that might be "bad for business." In addition, other public interest groups such as Mothers Against Drunk Drivers (MADD) might convince the police department of the importance of concentrating on enforcing drunk driving laws in a particular area of town.

The general philosophy of the police agency will most often dictate the allocation of patrol units in the community. For example, some police administrators may prefer to assign rookie officers to high-crime areas to hasten their experience with the street and problem situations. On the other hand, administrators might choose to assign their new officers to areas within the community that have a low incidence of crime, thus allowing them to accrue experience in situations where they will be less likely to jeopardize their personal safety or place the department in legal difficulties.

Citizens who have been victimized near their homes often feel that crime is randomly distributed and there are no safe places to hide. Research has indicated, however, that pockets or "hot spots" of crime can form in cities. For example, Cohen suggests that predator criminal acts may occur when three elements converge: (1) motivated offenders, (2) suitable targets, and (3) the absence of capable guardians against the violation.[5] A supporting study in Minneapolis showed that a relatively few "hot spots" were responsible for generating a majority of calls to the patrol division. These hot spots most typically corresponded to a specific address or location of town. By analyzing locations of calls, police were able to identify the places most likely to generate crime and determine that criminal offenses were concentrated by the type of offense and not distributed throughout the city. This study has important implications for police allocation and policy implementation and development.[6]

POLICE SERVICES

Research dealing directly with the service functions in the police is relatively scarce. For the most part, the literature mentions police service activities with relation to how little patrol officer time is spent solving crime. According to Whitaker et al., "despite their importance for performance measurement and planning, police activities receive little attention and are not known in any systematic way by public officials . . . or the public at large."[7]

The lack of available and detailed data on police service activities demonstrates the low priority given to such efforts by the police and the public. In particular, during the past few decades, the role of the police has increasingly been defined as that of crime control and law enforcement rather than the provision of services. Consequently, the importance of police service delivery has been measured not in terms of how much of it the police accomplish, but in terms of how such services interfere with law enforcement efforts. However, some data are available on the prevalence and types of police service delivery.

The Police Services Study

During the period 1976 through 1978, the Police Services Study (PSS) closely examined police patrol service in a sample of 60 neighborhoods within 24 jurisdictions in Rochester, New York; St. Louis, Missouri; and Tampa–St. Petersburg, Florida, metropolitan areas.[8] The research involved observing the activities of patrol officers for 900 shifts of patrol work (15 shifts in each of the 60 neighborhoods). The results of this research indicated the types of services police patrol officers provided to their communities.

For the 60 neighborhoods studied, 38% of policing encounters with citizens involved criminal matters and another 22% were traffic-related. The remaining 40% of policing encounters were concerned with what the researchers termed *service* (18%) and *disorder* (22%) calls. Service encounters included medical assistance, provision of information, dealing with dependent persons, and other general assistance. Disorder assignments included dealing with interpersonal violence and disturbance encounters such as noise disturbances, domestic arguments, and juvenile problems. In resolving these problems, officers made arrests in only 14% of cases. Aside from information-gathering activities such as interrogation or search, the most common officer encounters with citizens were to "lecture or threaten" the citizen, followed by "giving information."

The results of the PSS indicated that police officers intervene in as many noncriminal situations as criminal or possibly criminal ones. Even in many criminal matters, the most common mode of officer intervention is to warn citizens or give them information rather than to apply legal sanctions. Much of what officers do, regardless of how they come to intervene with the citizen, is designed to resolve a problem without legal recourse. As such, the PSS indicated that police officers render service to citizens a great deal of the time. Whitaker and his colleagues observed the following:

> We have seen that in most neighborhoods, police patrols spend substantial portions of their time dealing with situations that do not involve crime. Often the majority of their time is spent on non-crime matters. Moreover, in most places police institute formal legal proceedings in only a small fraction of the encounters they have with citizens. Much of this activity concerns traffic violations or disorders rather than crime.[9]

Studies of police calls for service and patrol officer activities reported similar results. The police devoted one-half or more of their time to interactions with citizens in matters not involving crimes in those studies. Furthermore, making an arrest or even giving citation was relatively rare. Rather, the police typically admonished, counseled, or advised citizens in an effort to resolve the problems that led to their intervention.

Traditional Deployment of Patrol Units

As a rule, patrol resources have been allocated equally over a 24-hour period of three eight-hour shifts. Typically, the day shift extends from 8 A.M. to 4 P.M.; the evening or "swing" shift goes from 4 P.M. to midnight; and the "graveyard" shift extends from midnight to 8 A.M. During the course of these 8-hour shifts, officers patrol geographic areas of roughly equal workloads. However, this allocation method fails to take into account the fact that police calls vary based on time of day, day of the week, area within the community, and even the time of year. For example, in most jurisdictions, the swing shift has the heaviest workload with regard to calls for police service. In comparison, the graveyard shift often has a heavy workload for the first several hours (generally from 2:00 A.M. to 3:00 A.M.) and then activity is reduced to almost zero. Officers working the day shift experience a mix of the two—while day shift officers are often busy, their calls are typically of a minor nature.

Due to the disparity in workload across time periods, days, or patrol districts, it is obvious that equal allocation of police patrol units would mean that some officers were being overworked while others were underutilized. This arrangement presents a number of operational problems not only in attempting to respond to calls for service but also in not being able to perform directed or preventive patrol duties. Frequently, underutilized officers become bored and unmotivated and tend to perform poorly over time. To deal with these problems, professionalized police departments have established allocation plans based on need rather than equalization.

These plans address the two most important variables in determining allocation: *location* and *time*. Being aware of the location of problems helps departments divide up a community into geographic **beats** or **sectors** of approximately equal workload. Time of occurrences is critical because it determines how officers will be grouped into working time periods, or "shifts." For the most part, the greater the number of problems, the smaller the size of the beat, and hence the more concentrated the resources. The amount of time it takes to respond to a call is also important because the resource being allocated is a professional officer's time, which needs to be managed in the most effective way possible.

Once data have been collected and analyzed with regard to these variables, beat boundaries, the number of officers, and shift times are identified. Due to population shift and demands for service, it is imperative that departments evaluate their patrol boundaries and personnel assignments on a continuous basis.

In some cases, in an effort to overcome problems in the equal allocation of resources, a number of medium- to large-size police departments have adopted a 4/10 scheduling plan. In this plan, officers work four days a week, ten hours a day, with three days off in a row. For the most part, officers like such a plan because it allows for increased leisure time, and the department gains increased coverage due to overlapping shifts, otherwise assigned during peak workload periods. Another way that patrol coverage can be increased is by creating an additional permanent shift or squad. This fourth squad is then assigned as an overlapping shift during high workload periods—for example, 7 P.M. to 3 A.M. or 8 P.M. to 4 A.M. While such methods provide significant advantages to the resource allocation plan based on need, they are sometimes difficult to implement because of personnel who typically want day shifts with weekends off. Opponents of such methods argue, however, that various accommodations can be made by devising a fair and equitable rotational system.

RESPONDING TO CRIME

Just before noon on April 20, 1999, Patti Nielsen, a teacher at Columbine High School in Littleton, Colorado, made a frantic call to Jefferson County 9-1-1. She was trapped in the school library and had been wounded by glass fragments after a student named Eric Harris had shattered a window with a shotgun blast. "He's outside this hall!" Nielsen told the dispatcher, speaking of Harris. "He's outside the door!" she added, before being interrupted by the sound of gunfire. "Oh my God," Nielsen continued, "that was really close!"[10]

Nielsen was one of hundreds of Littleton residents, both inside and outside the school, who used 9-1-1 to report the disaster being wrought by Harris and fellow student Dylan Klebold. Almost 70 dispatchers worked the local 9-1-1 lines for more than 24 hours following the first reports of the shooting. One dispatcher began asking all callers, "Jefferson County 9-1-1, are you reporting the incident at Columbine High School?" That an entire community reacted in such a similar manner is not necessarily surprising. The reflex to call 9-1-1 emergency is so deeply ingrained in our national consciousness that Americans have been socialized to "call the cops" at the first sign of trouble.[11]

Rapid response to 9-1-1 calls was indeed a benchmark of police reform in the period of the 1960s to the 1980s. The system is far from infallible, however. Miscommunication between personnel

FIGURE 5.1 Sheriff's deputy dealing with emotionally distraught citizens in the aftermath of the school shooting in Columbine, Colorado, in April 1999.

answering 9-1-1 calls and law enforcement officers can occasionally occur. At Columbine, for example, where 12 students and one teacher were killed, the heavy volume of calls caused a great deal of confusion and contributed to the failure of law enforcement agents to enter the school until more than an hour after the first gunshots. Furthermore, 9-1-1 systems are being clogged by crank calls and summonses from citizens who do not understand that the services are for emergencies only. Some cities, such as Baltimore, Maryland, have implemented 3-1-1 systems to divert noncritical calls.[12] Others, such as Dayton, Ohio, are making misuse of 9-1-1 a misdemeanor, subject to a $100 fine and, after multiple infractions, jail time.[13]

Many observers are critical of the reliance on 9-1-1 for theoretical as well as practical reasons. Focusing on calls for service reflects a reactive rather than proactive philosophy of policing and may not be the most effective way to control crime.

Although 9-1-1 systems remain a concern, studies have shown that most crime is not reported to the police. In fact, according to the Bureau of Justice Statistics, only about one-third of all crimes are reported to law enforcement authorities.[14] Those that are reported are generally the most serious in nature with regard to injuries and economic loss. For the most part, however, crimes are brought to the attention of the criminal justice system by either a citizen or a law enforcement officer on patrol. Of these, victims or their families report the majority of crimes, leaving only about 3% of personal crimes and 2% of property crimes reported by police officers.[15]

The Shortcomings of 9-1-1

Early on, the concept of 9-1-1 as an easy-to-remember emergency telephone number seemed like a good idea, and for the most part, it still works as efficiently as originally designed. But because of frivolous 9-1-1 calls, many legitimate emergencies fail to get the attention they need. In many cities the sheer volume of 9-1-1 calls is overwhelming, with some desperate callers getting recordings or being put on hold. It is safe to say that the majority of 9-1-1 calls throughout the country are handled efficiently and courteously, but an increasing number of horror stories are emerging.

In addition, the public has chosen to make use of the 9-1-1 system for tens of thousands of nonemergency calls, resulting in the police having little time left for crime prevention and analyzing incidents of crime. Like so many other problems, 9-1-1 began as a solution. In 1967, the President's Commission on Law Enforcement and Administration of Justice recommended that "a single number should be established" nationwide for reporting emergencies. AT&T soon announced its choice of 9-1-1, and the first 9-1-1 call was made in Haleyville, Alabama, in February 1968. The number of 9-1-1 calls started to grow in the 1970s and has mushroomed to an estimated 268,000 a day. Although also used by ambulance and fire departments, an estimated 80% to 85% of 9-1-1 calls summon the police. The quick fix would be more operators and more lines, but that is an expensive proposition. While customer surcharges fund basic 9-1-1 phone networks, answering centers are funded mostly by local governments that are on tight budgets. In 1992, Los Angeles voters approved a $235 million bond issue for a massive 9-1-1 upgrade, a system that was not completed until the year 2000.[16]

Cell phones add to the confusion. Each year there are an estimated 18 million additional calls from cell phones. Calls from cell phones don't provide operators with the location of the call as conventional telephones do. Panicked callers often fail to give their location, and hang-up calls can't be traced. However, in 1997 a new agreement was drawn up between trade groups and the Cellular Telecommunications Industry Association to phase in cellular technology allowing 9-1-1 operators to locate callers. Soon the system will provide the caller's exact location within a radius of 125 meters.

A study conducted in Kansas City (discussed later in this chapter), and later replicated in other cities, attempted to measure the impact of police response time and the ability of officers to thwart a crime in progress. The research shows that police were successful in only 29 of 1,000 cases and it made little difference whether they arrived in two or twenty minutes. The crucial factor was the speed with which the citizens called the police.[17] Critics argue that if citizens delay in calling the police, the value of the automobile's range and speed is lost. Lawrence Sherman suggests that officers in patrol cars are not attentive to their beats, as they are isolated in their cars and away from direct public contact.[18]

This has created a situation of officers "waiting to respond to crime" opposed to "watching to prevent crime" as was the case before the development of the patrol car. So what accounts for delays in citizens calling the police? Three reasons can be cited for this phenomenon:

1. Some find the situation ambiguous.
2. Others are involved in coping strategies (e.g., helping the victim).
3. Some may avoid making the decision or may ask someone else's advice before making the call.[19]

In addition, logistical problems may arise. For example, a telephone might not be readily available, the person might not have a cellular phone or he or she may not know the number for the police. Because research shows that response time is not a significant variable in crime control, some law enforcement agencies have adopted other differential response strategies.

These strategies assume that it is not always beneficial to rush a police car out to a scene after a call is taken. In fact, in an effort to streamline the efficiency and effectiveness of police service, a number of differential response strategies have been adopted to deal with various types of calls for service. Selection of the alternative depends on factors such as whether the crime is still in progress, has recently occurred, or whether anyone has been injured. Although police officers may be sent, the call may also be responded to in the following manner.[20]

- Telephone report units that take the crime report over the phone. In many departments, over one-third of calls for service are dealt with in this fashion.
- Delayed response if the situation does not dictate immediate police response and if officers can handle the situation once they arrive. Most departments will state a maximum delay time such as 30 or 45 minutes, after which time the closest unit will respond.
- Civilian personnel who are specially trained to take reports. These persons can include evidence technicians, community service aides, animal control officers, or parking enforcement personnel.

A Closer Look

Anatomy of a SWAT Team

During the 2007 campus shooting at Virginia Tech, fully equipped Special Weapons and Assault Teams (SWAT) were on the scene, carrying sophisticated equipment. Such units—highly trained local and state police officers called in for dangerous situations that require special equipment or firepower—have become standard crime-fighting tools in even the smallest cities.

SWAT officers are trained to deal with all types of emergencies—civil disturbances, natural disasters, hostage situations, and bomb scares—but their most frequent assignments are serving "no-knock" search warrants, during which they seize drugs or other contraband. And in places where there isn't much door kicking to do, they find ways to make themselves useful. For example, in Greenwich, Connecticut, the SWAT team performs animal containment when the circus comes to town and crowd control when lottery jackpots top $1 million.

Police departments in nine out of ten U.S. cities with populations above 50,000 maintain their own SWAT teams, resulting in a nationwide force of about 60,000. Funding SWAT teams is costly. For example, a full-time, 18-member unit costs approximately $13 million a year in salaries and benefits, and training could reach $100,000 annually. Equipment maintenance and practice ammo cost $30,000 a year. Federal drug-war outlays cover some of the expenses, and the Pentagon has given local police forces more than a million pieces of military hardware in recent years, including 73 grenade launchers and 112 armored personnel carriers.

Full-time tactical units spend considerable time training—one day is recommended for every three spent in the field. This training is often conducted by the FBI, major weapons manufacturers, and retired Navy Seals.

With the incidence of violent crime down, many communities are becoming outraged by the many incidents of excessive force and wrongful arrests that SWAT teams have been linked to. Other problems have also been identified with such units. For example, during the Littleton, Colorado, siege, SWAT members experienced problems with their communications equipment and fell under criticism for their methodological methods of advancing the target. Still, in the wake of that tragedy, SWAT teams are now employing bomb experts and receiving enhanced explosives training. Some experts have even predicted that biological terrorism will be a concern of tomorrow's SWAT teams.

- Referrals to other criminal justice agencies, such as the fire department, juvenile authorities, or other social service agencies.
- Requests for walk-in reports, whereby the citizen can come to the police department and fill out the necessary report.

Studies have shown that in many cases, such responses are just as effective as a hurried one, and callers are equally satisfied as long as they are advised on what to expect. The outcome of differential response strategies is that valuable police resources are saved, as police units are not tied up on nonemergency calls.

ACTIVITIES OF THE PATROL DIVISION

In Chapter 3 we examined the many roles of the police in the United States. As mentioned, these roles include the specific duties of peacekeeping, maintaining law and order, and detecting and arresting law violators. The word *patrol* stems from the French word *patrouiller*, meaning "to tramp about in the mud." This definition implies that patrol work may be tiresome, difficult, and performed under the worst of circumstances. Let's now examine some of the most typical varieties of patrol that are employed by modern-day police agencies.

Types of Patrol

As the twentieth century developed, the scope and function of police became more narrowly defined. In many departments, police became specialists in areas such as investigation, traffic, crime prevention, and patrol operations. In fact, the patrol function soon became a form of crime prevention in and of itself, whereby local and state law enforcement agencies began analyzing crime patterns and occurrences and responding by assigning patrol officers to the highest-crime areas. Thus several innovative and effective types of police patrol evolved: preventive, saturation, directed, aggressive, and foot patrol.

Preventive Patrol

Probably one of the most widely adopted types of patrol is **preventive patrol**, also known as routine or random patrol. Basically, it involves driving in a designated area or district on a random basis so that the patterns of the police cannot be predicted. This technique is regularly practiced by officers when they are "in service" or not responding to radio calls. Depending on the size of the area to be patrolled as well as other variables, the amount of time that officers can devote to preventive patrol varies. In addition, even the time of day can have an effect on the ability of the officer to patrol in this fashion, depending on how busy he or she is responding to calls. Research shows, however, that an estimated 50% of a patrol officer's time is available for patrol duties.[22]

It is also evident that what patrol officers do with their time while patrolling varies greatly from one department to the next. The area to be patrolled often dictates the manner in which the officer will operate. Such differences are characterized by areas that are high-crime, recreational, residential, or commercial, to name only a few. Intervention is typically accomplished by stopping moving vehicles, approaching people who are on foot, or responding to businesses and residences where personal contact results. Experience has also shown that some patrol officers spend much of their idle time in an inactive status or in tending to personal matters.

Hot Spots

In the past, patrols were organized by "beats." It was assumed that crime can happen anywhere, so the entire beat must be patrolled at all times. Research shows, however, that crime is not spread evenly over all times and places. Rather, direct-contact predatory crimes, such as muggings and

FIGURE 5.2 In-car computers have become commonplace in patrol work and make crime control considerably more efficient.

robberies, occur when three elements converge: motivated offenders, suitable targets, and the absence of anyone who could prevent the violation. This means that resources should be focused on **hot spots**, places where crimes are likely to occur.[23]

In a study of crime in Minneapolis, researchers found that a small number of hot spots—3% of streets and intersections—produced 50% of calls to the police. By analyzing the places from which the calls were made, administrators could identify those who produced the most crime.[24]

With this knowledge, officers can be assigned to directed patrol—a proactive strategy designed to direct resources to known high-crime areas. However, the extra police pressure may simply cause lawbreakers to move to another neighborhood. The premise of this argument is that "there are only so many criminals seeking outlets for the fixed number of crimes they're predestined to commit."[25] Although some public drug markets may participate in this shifting of the "action," it does not happen for all crime or even all vice crimes, such as prostitution.[26]

Police administrators know that the amount of crime varies by season and time. Rates of predatory crimes such as robbery and rape increase in the summer months, when people are outdoors. In comparison, domestic violence is more frequent in winter, when people spend more time indoors in close proximity to each other.

There are also "hot times," generally between 7:00 P.M. and 3:00 A.M. A one-year study done in Minneapolis found that 51.9% of crime calls to the police came during this period, whereas the fewest calls were made between 3:00 A.M. and 11:00 A.M. With this knowledge, the department increased patrol presence in hot spots and at hot times. Although this strategy resulted in less crime, many officers disliked the new tactics. Being a "presence" in a hot spot might deter criminals, but the officers became bored. Preventing crime is not as glamorous as catching criminals.[27]

THE KANSAS CITY PREVENTIVE PATROL EXPERIMENT

For years, the effectiveness of preventive patrol measures was largely unevaluated. Those studies that were conducted on the effectiveness of patrol dealt primarily with foot patrol but not specifically preventive patrol. A yearlong experiment was conducted by the Kansas City, Missouri, Police Department and the Police Foundation between 1972 and 1973 to examine the impact of preventive patrol. The Kansas City Preventive Patrol Experiment looked at 15 districts: five with normal levels of preventive patrol, five with proactive patrol assignments that included two to three times the normal levels of preventive patrol, and five districts with no preventive patrol activity.

Patrol units would be allowed to enter the reactive districts temporarily if their assistance was requested and then exit when no longer needed. During the course of the experiment, a number of indicators were studied to determine the effectiveness of patrol efforts. These included arrests, traffic accidents, victimizations, fear of crime, and citizen satisfaction. Answers to two basic questions were sought in the experiment: (1) What are the effects of preventive patrol compared to that of no patrol? and (2) Is it more effective to increase the levels of patrol?

Findings of the Kansas City Study

Researchers in the Kansas City study made some instructive observations. They found that "decreasing or increasing routine preventive patrol within the range tested in the experiment had no impact on crime, citizen fear of crime, community attitudes toward the police on the delivery of police services, police response time, or traffic accidents."[28] In brief, the study demonstrated that adding or taking away police patrols from an area made no difference within the community. Upon the conclusion of the experiment, no one in the community had any idea that an experiment regarding policing had been underway.

The findings of the Kansas City study shed new light on stereotypes regarding police patrol. Until the time of the study, many people believed that putting more officers on patrol would result in a decrease in crime and, taking away police officers would result in increasing crime rates.

Critiquing the Kansas City Study

James Q. Wilson, in his evaluation of the Kansas City study, cautioned that the result should not be misinterpreted or overgeneralized. "The experiment does not show that the police make no difference and it does not show that adding more police is useless in controlling crime. All it shows is that change in the amount of random preventive patrol in marked cars does not, by itself, seem to affect over one year's time in Kansas City, how much crime occurs or how safe citizens feel."[29] Wilson even suggested that the results of the study might have been considerably different if changes had been made in how the police were utilized and not merely in the number of marked patrol cars placed in one area.[30] In fact, other critics have suggested that the one important thing the experiment failed to show is that a visible presence of police can have no impact on crime in selected circumstances. The director of the Kansas City study, George Kelling, said it would be a mistake to conclude that patrol was completely unnecessary or that police departments could manage with fewer resources. He defended the study by arguing, "the experiment has demonstrated that the time and staff resources exist within police departments to test solutions to the many complex and interrelated problems of police service."[31]

In other words, the police can actually experiment with ways to do more effective police work. Other researchers identified flaws in the research design of the experiment. For example, Richard C. Larson noted that when police cars in the reactive beats entered the area in response to calls, they made a visible presence. In the eyes of citizens and potential criminals, this was the same as routine patrol.[32] Larson also pointed out that police vehicles from other specialized units (not part of the experiment) operated in the reactive beats, thereby creating a visible police presence. Other differences in the reactive beats were also identified by Larson. For example, officers undertook a higher rate of self-initiated activities, such as vehicle stops, using sirens and lights more often in responding to calls. In addition, there was a higher incidence of two or more cars responding to a call for service.[33]

Lessons from the Kansas City Study

Experts have argued that the value of the Kansas City study is not in that it resulted in the elimination of preventive or random routine patrol but rather, in that it set the stage for further experimentation with alternative patrol strategies and tactics. As a direct result of the study, police executives realized that they could try alternative patrol tactics without fearing that reduced random routine patrol would result in increased incidences of crime.

In conclusion, the Kansas City study indicated that traditional methods of policing might not be the most effective way to do police work. Experts agree that the Kansas City study set the stage for the academic study of policing, which in turn has resulted in different ways of thinking about policing.

Styles of Patrol

The actual amount of police work undertaken depends on the work style of the officer. Some officers initiate more activity than others. Officer-initiated sanctions include stopping, questioning, and frisking suspicious subjects; making informal contacts with law-abiding citizens; stopping vehicles for possible violations; writing traffic tickets; checking suspicious events; and making arrests. Patrol officers generally initiate very little contact with citizens. Reiss found that only 14% of all citizen contacts were officer-initiated.[34]

In citizen-initiated calls for service, some officers take a more active role in handling the situation than others. Bayley and Garofalo found that some officers were likely to simply observe the situation and leave; others took control over the situation, asking probing questions, and had citizens explain themselves. According to National Crime Victimization Survey (NCVS) data, police officers only "looked around" in 20% of all reported property crimes and took a report in only about half of all property crimes.[35]

Muir argues that the style of policing reflects the attitudes of different officers toward law enforcement. Cox and Frank, however, argue that individual officers vary their style depending on the type of situation and the type of neighborhood where the incident occurs.[36]

TYPES OF PATROL

Studies such as the Kansas City study generated considerable interest in patrol alternatives. The following have been adopted as viable patrol options.

Saturation Patrol

Although the results of the Kansas City experiment have been hailed as decisive, less-known studies also offer useful information regarding the effectiveness of patrol. These studies are termed **saturation patrol** and have been conducted under numerous situations and circumstances. For example, a study in New York in which foot patrol was doubled seemed to have a positive effect in reducing crime.[37] In comparison, a study in England where foot patrol was increased showed that there was virtually no effect on crime.[38] On the other hand, nighttime patrols in the subways of New York decreased crime substantially while the incidence of crime increased dramatically during the daytime.[39]

Directed Patrol

As an alternative to random patrol operations, the concept of **directed patrol** requires officers to spend an allotted amount of their time in a specific area, usually one that is considered a high-crime area. It is the responsibility of these officers to watch for certain types of activity or offenses. Decisions to implement the directed patrol technique are typically based on crime-analysis information. Not all police departments use this method of patrolling, but the evidence suggests that it can significantly reduce the incidence of crime involving such offenses as automobile larcenies and street robberies.[40] It is not known, however, whether directed patrol is more effective than other types of patrol or whether it actually reduces crime or merely displaces it to another area of the community.

Aggressive Patrol

Another patrol strategy is the aggressive patrol technique, which consists of a high degree of patrol within a given area, including traffic stops and field interviews (also called field interrogations, or FIs) designed to reduce street crime. In San Diego a study was conducted that eliminated the use of FI in specified areas. As a result, the incidence of crime increased. After reimplementing the FI technique, a reduction of crime was reported.[41] A residual negative effect of aggressive patrol is that it can severely inhibit citizen satisfaction with the department. Arbitrary interventions by the police are often looked upon with disdain by citizens who might be stopped or delayed for a period of time. On the other hand, if the police are successful in pinpointing law breakers, public opinion can easily be swayed to convince the public that the practice is effective.

Aggressive patrol policies have often been dubbed as crackdowns by the media and are frequently associated with crimes such as prostitution, street drug sales, and driving under the influence. Evidence exists, however, to support the deterrence value of aggressive patrol in that it seems to have an immediate effect on localized crime. Cordner and Trojanowicz found that the possibility of a residual deterrence suggests that if police become adept at timing their crackdowns, they could "leave behind" some deterrent effects as they move on to the next problem location or target offense.[42]

Foot Patrol

As we have observed in the previous discussions, many limitations are inherent in preventive, saturation, directed, and aggressive patrol. The discouraging results of the Kansas City patrol experiment also offer little encouragement for the future success of police patrol. Although many police executives are supportive of the practice of police patrol, there are still many concerns about the downtime or inactive time squandered by patrolmen between service calls. As a result, some researchers have concluded that **foot patrol** (a form of community policing) can reduce the fear of crime, increase citizen satisfaction, and even reduce the incidence of crime itself. From a research perspective, it becomes clear that studies of foot patrol offer a striking need for evidence of just exactly what happens at the officer level.

The effectiveness of foot patrol continues to fall under scrutiny. A research study in Newark, New Jersey, however, produced some of the most engrossing results. In this study, three beats were examined: (1) those that already had foot patrol and maintained it, (2) those from which foot patrol was eliminated, and (3) those that had no foot patrol but added it for the purposes of the study.

As with the Kansas City study, reported crime in the New Jersey project was measured by examining arrests, traffic accidents, victimization, fear of crime, or citizen satisfaction—all before and after the examination period. Also consistent with the results of the Kansas City experiment, foot patrol was found not to have any significant effect on the incidence of crime. Despite the insight gleaned from the original Newark study, there was no analysis to indicate how foot patrol activities differed from motorized patrol activities. Interestingly, a second foot patrol study in Newark did obtain foot officers' activity reports. Although foot officers were expected to engage in a wide variety of nonenforcement as well as enforcement activities, the study indicated that little effort was given to the latter. Officers engaged in only 1.5 enforcement activities per 8 person-hours (or three activities per shift for each two-officer team). About half of these actions were summonses.[43]

A study of foot patrol was also conducted in Flint, Michigan, at about the same time as the Newark study. Although there is some dispute about the findings of this study, the focus of the study was to determine systematically what police did on foot patrol and how these activities differed from motorized patrol. By examining officers' daily report forms, researchers found that compared with motorized officers, foot officers reported many more self-initiated activities, which included home and business visits as well as security checks. Much higher levels of productivity were reported for foot officers, which included arrests, investigations, stopping suspicious persons, writing parking citations, and increased recovered property.[44] In fact, the only category in which motorized officers excelled over foot officers was in providing miscellaneous services to citizens. In general, the foot officers had a much lower rate of adversarial public contacts than their motorized counterparts, who were frequently required to respond to complaints.

Staffing Patrol Beats

Adequately staffing a single patrol beat takes almost five (4.8) police officers staffed around the clock, seven days a week.[45] The regularly assigned officers must be supplemented because of normal days off, vacations, illnesses, and injuries.

In practice, police departments have a difficult time maintaining full patrol staffing. Retirements, resignations, vacations, and illnesses create frequent shortages. The Newark foot patrol experiment found that an average of 19% of all beat assignments were not covered during the course of a year. Coverage ranged from a low of 64% to a high of 91%.[46]

The Edmonton, Alberta Foot Patrol Study

Other observations can be derived from a study conducted in Edmonton, Alberta, some of which offer an interesting counterpoint to the Flint study. In this study, foot constables handled considerably fewer calls than motorized officers and spent much less time on the street. The majority of their time was spent in citizens' homes, schools, and police offices. In addition, they spent considerable time with other police officers, business merchants, and professionals within the community. Probably the most glaring finding from the Edmonton study was that unlike findings in the Flint study, foot officers were more likely than motorized officers to have contacts with white-collar workers.

In summation, it should be noted that foot patrol is only one of many ways in which police departments can strengthen their ties with the community. Other community-oriented initiatives may include door-to-door surveys of residents and businesses, permanent beat assignments, park-and-walk patrol, neighborhood police substations, and police involvement with citizen groups. However, important aspects of problem-oriented policing, such as how much time officers devote to problem solving, how they do it, with whom, and for whom, are yet to be determined.

Nontraditional Patrol Operations

One recurring theme in this book is the changing roles of police to meet the changing times and needs of our communities. For some 30 years, patrol work was conducted from a patrol vehicle. Although the squad car has enhanced the patrol officer's ability to cover a larger area in less time, many believe that police–community relations have suffered. It is true that face-to-face contact between police and the public has lessened over the years, and in many departments, officers receiving a radio call will respond to it as soon as possible, only to return to their cars to go "back into service." This leaves little (if any) time for positive interaction between police and the citizenry. In addition, officers limit their opportunity to learn what events transpired before their arrival at the scene. To combat this problem, many departments have implemented different methods of enhancing the patrol function. Each of these methods should be considered for use under special circumstances and with different community needs in mind.

- *Horse Patrol.* In many departments, horses have been purchased for use in special geographic conditions and circumstances such as parades and outdoor festivals. Horse patrol officers are highly visible and can offer the department an important public relations tool.
- *Park and Walk.* This program required officers to park their patrol cars and continue the rest of their patrolling on foot. This practice can be implemented several times a day in a number of locations within the officer's assigned district.
- *Bicycle Patrol.* More and more law enforcement agencies have implemented the use of the bicycle in patrol situations. Like the horse patrol officer, officers on bicycle patrol can present an excellent opportunity for public relations. In addition, they can patrol areas of the community that are otherwise difficult to access.
- *Storefront Police Offices.* Many larger cities have established police storefront substations that are typically located in or near community centers in lower-income housing complexes. Decentralization of command within the district permits patrol officers who are assigned to these areas to staff the storefronts as needed. Storefronts are typically manned by officers during day and early-evening hours in addition to the use of 24-hour answering machines.

The greatest benefit in assigning foot patrol officers to special geographic areas is their ability to improve community relations through direct, positive interaction with citizens.

Response Time and Efficiency

Although police do not like to think of themselves as being at "the beck and call" of citizens, that is essentially the method of operation for many law enforcement officers. All departments practice **incident-driven policing**, in which calls for service are the primary instigators of action. More than 85% of police activity is the result of 9-1-1 calls or other citizen requests, which mean that a relatively small percentage of activity is initiated by a police officer in the field.[47]

The speed at which the police respond to calls for service has traditionally been seen as a crucial aspect of crime fighting and crime prevention. The ideal scenario in incident-driven policing is as follows: A citizen sees a person committing a crime and calls 9-1-1; the police arrive quickly and catch the perpetrator in the act. Or, a citizen who is the victim of a crime, such as a mugging, calls 9-1-1 as soon as possible, and the police arrive to catch the mugger before he or she can flee the immediate area of the crime. Although, as we shall see, such scenarios are quite rare in real life. **Response time**, or the time elapsed between the instant a call for services is received and the instant the police officer arrives on the scene, has become a benchmark for police efficiency.

In 1973, the U.S. national advisory commission on criminal justice standards and calls recommended that response time in urban areas, under "normal circumstances," not exceed three minutes for emergency calls and twenty minutes for nonemergency calls. The commission saw a direct correlation between response time and crime rates, stating that "when the time is cut to two minutes, it can have a dramatic effect" on crime rates.[48] The same year, the national commission on productivity optimistically stated that a rapid police response would accomplish three objectives:

1. Rapid response would serve as a deterrent to criminal activity because potential offenders would know that the police would arrive quickly at the scene.
2. A quicker response time would increase the apprehension rate, that, in turn, would serve as a deterrent.
3. A rapid response would increase citizen confidence in law enforcement; each would result in increased reporting and crime-prevention activities.[49]

TOTAL RESPONSE TIME More recent research has shown that these early assumptions did not fully appreciate the complexity of determining total response time—the time from the moment the crime is committed to the moment the first police officer arrives on the scene. In essence, total response time involves three components:

1. The time between the commission of the crime and the moment the victim or witness called the police
2. The time required for the police to answer the call, gather information from the caller, and dispatch a patrol car
3. The time between the moment the patrol car receives a call from the dispatcher and the moment the car arrives on the scene[50]

The problem, these later studies found, with police performance based on response time lies in the first component: Citizens often wait several minutes before calling the police after a crime. This delay can be attributed to a number of factors. Often, victims of a crime are frightened, ashamed, or disoriented after the incident. Victims may call parents, friends, or even the family physician before the police. Another common reason for delay in calling 9-1-1 is even more basic: Once the crime took place, the victim or witness did not have a phone available to call the police. On average, between five and ten minutes elapse from the moment a serious crime is committed to the moment the police are called.[51] Under such circumstances, an emphasis on rapid response time is unlikely to have the intended effect on crime rates or give an accurate reflection of a police department's efficiency.

DIFFERENTIAL RESPONSE Many police departments have come to realize that overall response time is not as critical as response time for the most important calls. In Dallas, Texas, the overall response time rose from 10 minutes in 1986 to 23 minutes in 1996, drawing criticism from local politicians. The Dallas Police Department, however, pointed out that the response time for calls involving shootings, knifings, and robberies had actually dropped—from 9.7 minutes in 1986 to 7.3 minutes in 1996.[52]

The Dallas police had instituted a **differential response** strategy, in which the department distinguishes between different calls for service so that it can respond more quickly to the most serious incidents. For example, suppose that a police department receives two calls for service at the same time. The first caller reports that her house is in the process of being burglarized, and the second says that he has returned home to find his automobile missing. If the department has instituted a differential response strategy, the burglary in progress—a "hot" crime—will receive immediate attention. The missing automobile—a "cold" crime that could have been committed several hours earlier—will receive attention "as time permits," and the caller may even be asked to make an appointment to come to the station.

Several forms of differential response have evolved over time. For example, many departments take reports over the telephone rather than in person. Other departments, rather than immediately dispatching an officer to take a report, make an appointment with a citizen to take any information at a later time. In this manner, the police department is able to reschedule victim interviews for periods where the level of calls for service is not quite as heavy.

In a way, differential response is a balancing act between improving the management of the police workload and satisfying citizens who call for service with the expectation that the police response will be timely, no matter what the nature of the incident they are reporting. Different tests have shown that both these goals can be met. Several departments have diverted up to 50% of their calls to alternative responses without any noticeable drop-off in citizen satisfaction.[53]

ARREST RATES AND EFFICIENCY   The other measure of police efficiency, arrest rates, also seems logical. The more arrests a police department makes, the fewer criminals there should be on the streets of a community.

Once again, practice does not necessarily follow theory. We have already learned that the amount of crime is not a function of arrest rates; a self-reported survey showed that many, if not most, criminal acts do not lead to arrests. To make a generalization, police will never be able to make an arrest for every crime that is committed. Researchers have offered other, more specific reasons for a possible disconnect between arrest rates and crime rates. One explanation is, given the amount of paperwork each arrest forces upon a police officer, more arrests mean less time for crime prevention; perhaps arrest rates and crime rates would prove more consistent if all arrests were made for serious crimes. However, as we have discussed, this is not the case. Most arrests are for misdemeanors, not felonies. Furthermore, arrests are poor predictors of incarceration: One study found that nearly 60 times more Americans are arrested than are sent to prison each year.

Perhaps a more meaningful indicator of the job a police officer is doing is the *clearance rate*, or the percentage of crimes solved over any given time. This measurement allows statisticians to differentiate between types of crime. The clearance rate for violent crimes, in which the victims tend to know their assailants, is generally much higher (around 45%) than that for burglaries (around 17%), which generally are committed by strangers. Low clearance rates for a certain type of crime, as compared to a national average or past performance, can indicate that police response to that crime is deficient.

Processing Calls for Service

Telephone operators, 9-1-1 dispatchers, and patrol officers serve as "information brokers," processing citizen calls and translating them into official police responses. The operator obtains information from the caller and then makes a decision about the appropriate response. If he or she decides that the call requires a police response, the call is communicated to the police dispatcher.

Peter K. Manning provides the most vivid and detailed description of 9-1-1 communications at work. He describes one call reporting an alleged kidnapping. The operator had available four different kidnapping-related codes, but "there are no rules given to determine selection among these options." The operators have a 300-page procedure manual, but it "is virtually never used" because it is too large and there is no room for it on the operators' consoles.[54]

All incoming calls for service do not result in the dispatch of a police officer. In the PSS, only 50% of the 28,052 incoming calls resulted in a dispatch (the figure was 53% in Manning's study). In 17% of the cases, the caller was referred to another agency; the operator took information from the citizen in 16% of the calls and gave information to the citizen in 9%. In the remaining 14% of the calls, the citizen was told that the police could not handle the call, or the call was transferred, or some other response was given.[55]

Obtaining the necessary information from the citizen caller is often difficult, because callers frequently provide vague, incomplete, or inaccurate information. Many are confused or frightened, and some are intoxicated or even mentally disturbed. A situation that a caller describes as a "disturbance" could range from a party with loud noise to an armed or mentally disordered person. The information is often incorrect. Bayley and Garofalo for example, found that a weapon was actually present in only 25% of the reported "weapon present" calls.[56]

Gilsinan observed that 9-1-1 operators of a large Midwestern city handled 265 calls over one 24-hour period. He found that operators interpreted incoming information from callers and translated them into a category that fit an established bureaucratic response. Operators interacted with callers in a problem-solving process, especially in asking for more details, to reach the final determination of what to do.[57]

The dispatcher must also make important decisions. Manning found that dispatchers can ignore the formal coded classification they receive about a call and "act as if the event has another priority informally," including adding his or her own comments when communicating with patrol officers. The most important is deciding whether the situation is an emergency and requires an emergency response. Reiss found that 18% of dispatches received an urgent response.[58]

The dispatcher must also decide which patrol unit to dispatch. The unit assigned to a particular beat is often not available, either because it is out of service handling another call or not on duty at all that day. Consequently, officers are routinely assigned to calls outside their beat.[59]

Manning points out that patrol officers also interpret the information they receive. They frequently "un-found" citizen-reported crimes. In most departments, patrol officers are not required to provide detailed records of how they handle calls. Reports are often limited to "service rendered" or "no police action required."[60]

Because the information processed through the communication systems is often incomplete and inaccurate, patrol officers respond to their calls with considerable uncertainty. They're dependent upon the information as given by the caller, interpreted by the operator, indicated to the dispatcher, communicated to the patrol officer, and interpreted by the patrol officer.

POLICE–COMMUNITY RELATIONS

The concept of foot patrol leads us into a discussion of the importance and effectiveness of community relations (discussed in greater detail in Chapter 9). Beginning in the 1960s, the customary style of legalistic policing began to fade and a newer service-oriented style was adopted. Clearly, this decade was one of social unrest characterized by demonstrations, marches, and riots orchestrated by students and other nonconformists. Most of the violent activity observed during the 1960s centered around protests against the escalating war in Vietnam and civil rights issues. An outgrowth of the riots and marches were new police practices and techniques for crowd control. Police officers, most of whom were inexperienced at crowd containment procedures, were placed in violent situations where their lives were endangered. In the eyes of many, police officers epitomized "the establishment" and were, therefore, targets of violence by the citizenry.

The Police–Community Relations Program

As social unrest flourished, many police departments sought ways to deal with the problem. The most typical of these was the creation of a police–community relations (PCR) program. The PCR program in most departments is characterized by the appointment of a public-relations officer who provides an array of services to the community. These include crime prevention, neighborhood watch, Drug Abuse Resistance Education (DARE), and project ID. PCR programs today, however, seem to fail in bridging the communication gap between police and the community. This can be explained, in part, by the fact that most groups who take advantage of PCR programs are already satisfied with local police services. Conversely, efforts to reach dissatisfied groups within the community are often met with criticism and disdain and frequently alienate officers assigned to PCR duties.[61]

Team Policing

The concept of community policing originated during the 1960s and 1970s and was based on a policing concept from Aberdeen, Scotland. This concept quickly became a logical continuance of the PCR movement. Although it was considered by some to be a way to personalize police services in communities, others argue that it was nothing more than a return to a century-old style of policing first used by the earliest police departments. The program of team policing assigned police officers to specific neighborhoods where they would supposedly become acquainted with that neighborhood's citizens and their unique problems. Team policing officers were granted considerable flexibility in the ability to process complaints coming to their attention. Most crimes were investigated from beginning to conclusion by the officers, who called for specialists only if their own resources were considered insufficient.

Crime Prevention

Crime prevention has emerged over the past decade or so as an alternative to responding to crime after the fact. Crime prevention is designed to foster public relations between the public and the police in an effort to preserve law and order in the community. The philosophy of the crime-prevention function is that crime is both a social and a police problem, and that members of the community must be involved in the detection of crime in neighborhoods. Crime-prevention efforts often result in homeowners installing security-related devices in their homes and notifying police of suspicious circumstances observed in their neighborhoods. The open dialogue between the police and members of the community hopefully will provide the impetus to settle differences about law enforcement and police services in communities. As a public policing concept, the idea of crime prevention is not new. In actuality, Sir Robert Peel of the famed London Metropolitan Police Department identified crime prevention as one of the department's basic roles. However, today's concept of crime prevention is one that can be traced to the establishment of the 1971 National Crime Prevention Institute at the University of Louisville.

ROUTINE ASSIGNMENTS

Idealistically, the patrol officer should have an operational plan for all situations that he or she may encounter. In reality this is not always practical, as every situation requiring police intervention may offer somewhat different aspects. Training in how to deal with numerous types of patrol situations begins in the police academy, where a broad base of information is given to recruits to prepare them in how to deal with a variety of circumstances. Once out of the academy and on the street, the patrol officer is given considerable informal information from fellow officers on how best to deal with different circumstances. Ultimately, each officer must rely on his or her own decision-making ability and draw upon training, education, experience, and personal judgment.

American Policing under Fire

How Reliable Is Eyewitness Testimony?

One August night in Altoona, Iowa, the local McDonald's was filled with customers when a man with a gun in his pocket walked in, looking for cash. He slipped a note to the night manager, who led him to the office, opened the safe, pulled out money, and gave it to him. Before police came, the gunman fled through a rear door, commandeered a car from a drive-through lane, ordered the driver out at gunpoint, and sped away.

Initial descriptions were contradictory, the defense lawyer would later say, but with the help of McDonald's employees, the artist drew a composite drawing, which led to a photographic lineup, and eventually to the arrest of Terry Eugene Schutz. Several eyewitnesses said he was the one, and Schutz was convicted and sentenced to 25 years in prison—based solely on eyewitness testimony. Powerful, indeed. No physical evidence tied Schutz to the crime, and his girlfriend insisted he'd been with her at the time. But how accurate are eyewitness identifications?

Some experts say "not very." Now there's mounting evidence through DNA science and innocent people have been convicted because of faulty identifications. DNA evidence already has freed scores of convicts, and more could be in line if recommendations proposed in September 1999 by the National Commission on the Future of DNA Evidence becomes a reality. The commission has come forth with suggestions on ways to make it easier for prisoners who are convicted before DNA science was available to seek exoneration even after deadlines for appeals have passed. It's difficult to estimate just how many cases of mistaken identity occur, but a 1996 Justice Department study alleged that of 28 men convicted of sexual assault and then freed because of DNA evidence, 24 had been identified as the culprit by eyewitnesses.

Even witnesses who are absolutely certain they fingered the right person are sometimes simply mistaken. A woman in Georgia was very confident that the stranger who'd broken in the apartment door and raped her one night was Calvin Johnson, Jr. So was a neighbor who had been raped two nights earlier. So were two more women who chased away a menacing stranger from their nearby apartments that same week. On the basis of their testimony, a suburban Atlanta, Georgia, jury convicted Johnson of rape in 1983, and a judge sentenced him to life in prison. Now, DNA evidence says the semen in the rape victims was not Johnson's, so he was released during the summer of 1999 after 16 years behind bars. DNA evidence came too late to help Johnson avoid prison.

So did another legal trend: letting juries hear about research into human memory. Increasingly, courts are allowing experts to tell juries that eyewitness identifications are sometimes more convincing than they are reliable, and that juries should be especially wary when certain problematic factors exist. Mistakes are more likely, for example, when the witness and suspect are of different races, especially when the witness is white and the suspect is African-American. We also now know that extreme stress, especially when violence or the threat of violence exists, interferes with recall.

Another problem researchers found is that viewing a composite drawing or lineup can change the witness's memory of the event. That is to say, a witness viewing a photo array may pick out a photo that resembles the culprit, but isn't. But from that point on, the photo becomes part of the witness's memory of the culprit. It is difficult, if not impossible, to quantify the overall reliability of stranger-to-stranger identifications, say experts. In some cases, experts estimate that the chance of faulty identification can rise to 20%.

In the Georgia rape case, the defendant was African-American and witnesses, white. Although the women were frightened or terrified when they encountered the stranger, they believed it was Johnson. Some had difficulty picking him out of a set of photos or a live lineup. Although studies about the unreliability of eyewitness identification had been mounting when Johnson was tried in 1983, few judges then allowed experts to testify about them. But in 1983, Arizona's Supreme Court became the first of many state appellate courts to create a new precedent, set aside a conviction, and order a new trial on the grounds that memory experts should have been allowed to give such testimony to a jury. California did the same the next year, followed in the years since by other state and federal appellate courts. The trend continues.

In April 1999, the New Jersey Supreme Court ruled that the judge in a cross-racial rape case should have told the jury that cross-racial identifications may be less reliable than same-race ones. The Georgia Supreme Court is considering changing the precedent there as well. In September 1999, a public defender asked the court to set aside the robbery conviction of her client because the trial judge, relying on longstanding case law, refused to allow an expert to testify about the unreliability of eyewitness identification. The lawyer asked the justices to give a trial judge discretion to allow such testimony, at least in cases where there's no corroborated evidence and where there's reason to fear a faulty identification. On the other side, a senior district attorney warned that to do so would upset 150 years of statutory and case law grounded in the established principle that it is up to the jury, not an expert, to assess a witness's credibility. As for Terry Schutz and his case in the McDonald's robbery, in 1998 it became the vehicle for the Iowa Supreme Court to reverse its own precedent. Citing the wealth of new research into memory, the court reversed his conviction and said that Schutz should be allowed to present such evidence at retrial. Even at retrial, even with new expert testimony, the defense would still have to overcome several eyewitnesses.

Schutz, who already had spent two years in prison, didn't want to risk more. He pleaded guilty to lesser charges and received a probated sentence. But other Iowa defendants have used the experts the Schutz case made possible. Des Moines, Iowa, prosecutors, however, claimed they saw little difference in trial outcomes.[62]

THEMATIC QUESTION
What can the criminal justice system do to prevent false eyewitness testimony while encouraging witnesses to come forward with information about crime?

Some assignments, however, regularly call on the services of the patrol officer and may employ a "routine" response. Becoming routinized is one of the most dangerous habits to which an officer can fall victim. Once officers perceive the outcome of a situation as the same as previous situations, they become extremely vulnerable targets. So the term *routine* will be used in this chapter only with these observations in mind.

As mentioned, of the many routine assignments encountered by the patrol division, some are regarded as the most common: searching for missing persons, driving while intoxicated (DWI) and alcohol cases, rescue incidents, traffic enforcement, and public courtesy services. In addition to these, one of the most dangerous patrol functions is responding to a domestic disturbance.

Special Populations

Over the past several years, social and economic changes in America have increased the workload of police agencies with regard to their dealing with categories of people such as the homeless, mentally ill, and juveniles. Regardless of the reason, citizens have traditionally called the police to handle problem persons in their communities.[63] The movement in the mental health field, for example, to deinstitutionalized treatment of the mentally ill has resulted in larger numbers of mentally ill people present in communities. Accordingly, economic changes have resulted in large numbers of homeless persons throughout the nation.

According to Peter Finn and Monique Sullivan, "the public repeatedly calls on law enforcement officers for systems with people who are mentally ill, drunk in public, and homeless."[64] Additionally, requests for these services from police agencies have increased. At the same time, the options open to police officers when handling troubled and troublesome persons have been limited.

In 1967, the President's Commission on Law Enforcement and the Administration of Justice described the problem of public intoxication as leading to "2 million unnecessary arrests" each year.[65] The commission noted that police were frequently called to deal with people who were drunk in public, and that although officers often used alternative dispositions, arrests of the intoxicated person was a common occurrence. The commission recommended the decriminalization of public intoxication and the creation of detoxification centers throughout the nation. Rather than arresting offenders and using the criminal justice process, they urged, medical solutions should be applied to what they defined as a medical problem.

In fact, many communities did develop detoxification centers, but police use of the centers was limited for a number of reasons. For example, force of habit, familiarity with the use of arrest, or informal orders to "move along!" led to many police officers continuing their past practices. In many communities, adequate resources for the population of intoxicated persons did not exist. Yet in others, stringent admission standards prevented the police from using the centers for those found drunk in public.[66]

The mentally ill are another problem population with whom the police come into contact. The police service study found that fewer lesser than 1% of police encounters involved mentally ill or disturbed individuals, but other studies and conventional wisdom suggest that the problem, at least in urban areas, is more widespread.

Beginning in the 1960s, mental health professionals initiated a policy of community treatment and deinstitutionalization of psychiatric patients.[67] In the same time period, the rights of the mentally ill were strengthened as courts increasingly restricted the circumstances under which persons could be civilly committed against their will. The result was an increase in the number of persons with mental illness or other psychological/psychiatric troubles who were in the general population. A related fact is that it became more difficult for police to respond to these individuals, as the number of institutions was decreasing, and procedures for commitment more cumbersome. Telpin observed that persons with symptoms of mental illness are at higher risk of arrest than those not showing such symptoms. She suggests that this might be the evidence of a "criminalization" of mental illness. That is, faced with limited options, the police might resolve problems involving the mentally ill by defining their behavior as criminal and making arrests.[68]

In contrast, Engle and Silver examined the police handling of mentally disordered suspects and concluded that the police tended toward "informal" resolutions by ignoring, counseling, or otherwise calming and controlling the suspects without resort to physical force or arrest.[69] Kelvin observed that experienced officers "often . . . know just how to soothe the emotionally disturbed person, to act as a 'street corner psychiatrist.' In this way, they help to maintain many mentally ill people within the community and make deinstitutionalization a more viable public policy."

Homeless persons are not, unfortunately, a new phenomenon. Rather, concern about the homeless and the numbers of homeless people who are estimated to exist in the population has grown tremendously in the past several years. Some experts estimate that as many as 3 million Americans are homeless. These homeless persons are a police concern for a number of reasons, including the fact that they might commit crimes. Perhaps more importantly, the homeless are also potential crime victims.

Although the contemporary concern about both the homeless and the problem this population poses for the police has increased recently, homeless persons have traditionally been a police problem. From the earliest days of the American police, when police departments provided lodging to the socially disenfranchised, until the present, the homeless person has been a police target. Dilworth notes that concern about what to do with tramps and hobos was a key topic at meetings of American police leaders in the late 1890s and early 1900s. The discussions continued through the Great Depression as thousands of unemployed people again took to wandering the streets.

It is important to note that today's homeless population appears to be different from those of earlier years. For example, many more women and children—and even intact families—find themselves within the homeless population. Problems posed by this new population of homeless are, however, essentially the same as before. Such people are obviously suffering "problems in living" and are in need of basic services at a minimum. Furthermore, they are potential criminals and potential criminal victims as a result of their precarious social and economic situation. Yet, the ability of the police to intervene has been limited.

Taken together, the mentally ill, public drunks, and homeless constitute what are called **street people.** As Finn points out, "even the most docile street people generate fear among many residents, shoppers, and commuters. The prospect of being accosted by a drunken, disoriented, or hostile panhandler can be as frightening for many people as the prospect of meeting an actual robber."

Avoidance of places where one is likely to encounter street people, in turn, has negative consequences. Businesses suffer a loss of customers, and citizens suffer a loss of security and freedom. Usually, there are too few shelters and treatment facilities to handle the full population of street people. Additionally, many of these persons do not seek admission to such facilities. Finally, the police are typically called to deal with troublesome street people—the type of clients that most shelters do not wish to admit. There is an unwillingness to accept police referrals at many of the existing shelters and treatment facilities.

In response to the growing problem of street people, police agencies across the nation are developing policies for the needs of this population. Such programs involve police agencies forming networks with social service agencies to respond to the problem of the street person population. The majority of these programs involved an agreement between the police and mental health professionals to deal with mentally ill persons coming to the attention of the police. One-third of the programs included arrangements for the handling of intoxicated persons, and one-sixth were designed to help with the homeless. The goals of these programs were to relieve police officials from the responsibility of dealing with persons whose problems were primarily psychiatric, medical, or economic. The programs also sought to prevent further criminal justice system attention being paid to the special population and to ensure that the police would refer these populations to the appropriate facilities involved. This way, it was hoped that these networks would benefit all concerned—street people, service facilities, and the police themselves.

Domestic Violence

Responding to a domestic disturbance is considered one of the most hazardous duties of the patrol officer. Statistics showing the incidence of domestic violence are instructive. In 1994, the NCVS reported that of the 621,015 reported rapes, robberies, and assaults between intimates in 1992, 51% were attacked by boyfriends or girlfriends, 34% were attacked by spouses, and 15% were attacked by ex-spouses. Most reported cases (81%) were assault.[70]

Violence in the home, or domestic violence, is by far the most prevalent form of violence confronting contemporary society, and patrol officers must frequently respond to such occurrences. Only a small portion of violence is ever reported to legal or policing authorities.[71] Hence, police are involved in only a small percentage of domestic incidents. For example, in Kentucky only 9% of all victims of spouse abuse called the police, and only 17% of victims of severe violence reported the incident. Nonwhite women are twice as likely (18%) to call the police as white women (8%). Low-income people call the police most frequently.[72]

Domestic dispute calls will often address disputes between neighbors or family, tenants and landlords, or dismissed and disgruntled employees. As a rule, one of the participants of the dispute will call the police and request an officer. On occasion, neighbors or witnesses to the incident will make the call. The dispatcher who receives the call for assistance will then relay the intensity and severity of the call to the responding officer. Such information is based on the details received from the calling party, background noise, and the tone of the caller's voice. The dispatcher then determines how many units should respond. After receiving this information from the dispatcher, the officer will have a sense of the seriousness of the situation. Thomas Adams describes the guidelines for police dispatchers to follow when taking the call and deciding the most appropriate response while officers are enroute to the location:

- Find out exactly what is happening, or as nearly as possible. Listen to the background noises as well as to the voice of the calling party.
- Determine if someone has been injured and is in need of immediate medical attention.
- Ascertain if there is an immediate and imminent danger confronting someone who is on the scene.
- If there is danger, determine who or what it is.
- If someone is armed with some sort of weapon, find out what type of weapon, the present whereabouts of the armed subject, and the person's state of emotionalism and/or sobriety.
- Decide if the person is using the weapon for self-defense or to assault another person.
- Find out from the calling party, if possible, and by checking the records (if time permits) if this is a reoccurrence of similar activity that has occurred in the past.
- Keep the caller on the telephone line as long as possible.
- As any new developments arise while you are still talking with the calling party and the assigned officers have been dispatched, keep the officers updated on any information that will assist them in responding to the call.
- Dispatch only those officers who are necessary to handle the situation effectively.[73]

If the situation calls for response from another police agency, such as contiguous jurisdiction, or from an organization or agency that is specifically geared for this particular problem, advise the calling party that another agency should handle the matter. What they may need instead of, or in addition to, the police may be paramedics or the fire department.

Instead of instructing emotionally involved callers to dial another telephone number, either help them transfer the call or take what information you need; then instruct them that you will call the other agency and handle the matter. Do not add to the caller's frustration and/or anger by stating: "Sorry, ma'am, that's not our jurisdiction. Try the sheriff's office. . . . No, I don't know what their number is, but I'm sure they are in the book."

- Send backup cars, if necessary. Consider the specific location of the call, the people involved, experience with the nature of the call and the principals, the neighborhood characteristics—which may be hostility toward the police in general—and the information you receive by phone.
- Call off the units that are no longer needed if there is a change in the circumstances at the scene as reported by the first officer to arrive and other officers.

It is unfortunate, but calls for police assistance in domestic situations will most generally be made after the situation has escalated into a crisis or even violence. In this case the emotions of the parties involved will be at their peak and chances for negotiation will be limited. Responding officers are often viewed as saviors by onlookers and participants alike and will often be expected to work miracles with the situation.

Clearly, officers can only do what they can with limited resources at their disposal. Responsibilities of the responding officer in a domestic situation begin with protecting the participants from harm to one another. If an assault is under way, any continuation must be thwarted and a determination must be made as to any criminal responsibility. In this case, an arrest should then be made based on available evidence. Where the situation appears volatile but there is no ongoing violence, the officer's next responsibility is to attempt to arbitrate the situation and seek a satisfactory solution. At this phase, it is generally good practice to remove any children from what appears to be a hostile environment as well as to separate the parties and discuss the situation one-on-one with them, outside the earshot of the other party.

It is here that the patrol officer's diplomatic skills will be called upon because a biased word or hostile gesture on the officer's part could reignite the situation. The officer will then become part of the problem rather than the solution. It is common that the person calling the police will remind the officer that it was he or she who made the call and therefore should escape any blame for the incident. Again, diplomacy is needed, but objectivity is also required to ensure fairness to all parties. Indeed, parties on both sides of the dispute might encourage the officer to take sides and "punish" the other party by arresting or striking him or her. More than any other in the encounter, this situation demands unbiased mediation.

Special problems, such as with the case of an abused spouse, present very real problems for a patrol officer. The responding officer did not witness the assault and thus cannot act without a signed complaint, so the greatest hurdle to overcome is to convince the battered spouse to file charges against the batterer. In calling the police, battered women have asked that the violence directed toward them be stopped. To do so, police have relied on four basic strategies: talking out the dispute among all parties, threatening to arrest all parties and then leaving, asking one of the parties to leave the premises to "cool off," and making an arrest.[74] In recent times, however, shelters and support groups for victims have made some headway in this regard.

An experiment was conducted by Sherman and Berk in Minneapolis in 1984 to test the effects of different police responses to misdemeanor violence in the home. Officers who participated in the experiment were assigned one of the following strategies: (1) arrest, (2) give some form of advice or attempt to mediate the situation, or (3) separate the participants—the "walk-around-the-block" solution. The effectiveness of each of these responses was examined by researchers in terms of how many of the subjects had at least one repeat incident of violence and how long after arrest the violence developed. The results showed that the police should "probably employ arrest in the majority of cases of minor domestic violence."[75]

As an outcome of the Minneapolis experiment between 1984 and 1986, the percentage of big-city police departments with arrest-preferred policies increased from 10% to 46%.[76] Meanwhile, 20 cities revised their laws affecting police and domestic disturbance calls. Many states have now expanded the extent to which police may exercise arrest procedures in domestic-violence situations once they identify the "primary aggressor" in the situation. In brief, many states may now allow officers to make arrests for misdemeanors not committed in their presence or violations of restraining orders against assailants.

A 1985 telephone survey of police departments in cities with populations over 100,000 revealed that 47% relied on individual officer discretion, while 27% had adopted presumptive arrest policies in cases of domestic violence.[77] Since the Minneapolis study, other researchers have replicated the research to see if the arrest of domestic-violence offenders would have the same effects nationally. One such replication, in Omaha, Nebraska, failed to show significant differences in outcomes related to different police interventions.[78] The study read "arresting suspects had no more effect on deterring future arrests or complaints (involving the same suspects and victims) than did separating and counseling them." What the Minneapolis and Omaha studies illustrate is that whether arrest of aggressors is used, the police play an integral role in the intervention and prevention of domestic violence. These studies also illustrate how the role of the police in society is much more than the arresting of suspects. So the arrest and/or counseling of persons involved in domestic-violence calls are merely two strategies by which this goal may be accomplished.

The Impact of Mandatory Arrest Laws and Policies

The full impact of mandatory arrest laws and policies is still to be seen. One important question is whether officers actually carry out mandatory arrest policies or not. Data on arrest trends suggest—but do not necessarily confirm—that they do. For example, between 1971 and 1994 arrests for aggravated assault increased 140%. During the same time period, arrests for rape increased 33.6%, and those for robbery increased 8.2%, but arrests for burglary declined by 24%. Arrests for misdemeanor assault, meanwhile, also increased at a far higher rate than for other Part II crimes.

Some commentators have warned that mandatory arrest may discourage calls by women who want the police only to calm the immediate situation. Also, mandatory arrest is likely to have a disproportionate impact on lower-class men and poor African-American men in particular. On the other hand, the traditional no-arrest approach had a negative effect, primarily on poor, African-American women, by denying them equal protection of the law.

Highlights in Policing

Dealing with Domestic Violence

- *Arrest.* Arrest incidents stemming from domestic-violence calls ranged from a high of 40% of all incidents to a low of 12%.[79]
- *Mediation.* As one of the most common types of police responses, mediation includes one of several types of verbal actions. Officers may respond in a sympathetic or nonsympathetic way; the officer may or may not ask complainants what they would like done; officers may order the parties to be quiet or might threaten arrest.
- *Separation.* Asking the assailant to leave is another option for officers. Studies have shown that, to a great extent, people comply to requests that they leave.
- *No action.* Another option would be for the officer to take no action at all.
- *Referral.* The mediation process also includes the recommendation that one or all of the parties involved seek professional help. These referrals include marriage counselors, substance abuse counseling, or legal assistance.

The Future of Domestic-Violence Policy

The future of police policy toward domestic disturbances and domestic violence is not clear. Mandatory arrest policies remain extremely popular, but the full impact of these policies is uncertain. In a comprehensive review of domestic-violence policies, Jeffrey Fagan concludes that there is "weak or inconsistent evidence" on the deterrent effect of arrest, prosecution, protection orders, and the treatment of batterers. Lawrence W. Sherman, who directed the original Minneapolis experiment, no longer supports mandatory arrest in all situations.

Traffic Enforcement

Clearly, the popular image of patrol officers is that of crime fighters, but a major part of their function in the community is to deal with vehicular traffic. Probably no other function of law enforcement creates greater ill will between the police and public than the enforcement of traffic codes. Regardless of public-service efforts to rally support of traffic enforcement, the general public has never taken lightly the proposition of getting ticketed for a traffic offense. Public displeasure for enforcement of traffic laws can be evidenced by the occasional highway driver who is seen flashing bright lights to warn oncoming traffic of a traffic officer spotted up ahead. Of course, the speeders are not even known to those flashing their lights but are still perceived as undeserving "victims" of the traffic enforcement officer.

The duties of traffic officer may include parking enforcement, directing traffic, radar operations, and accident reconstruction (investigation). The function of traffic control shares its responsibilities with the patrol division in that it relieves patrol officers from traffic duties, which can be quite time-consuming. The task of traffic enforcement is one of the most pervasive problems confronting law enforcement agencies. The task of traffic enforcement may involve managing thousands of motor vehicles within a given jurisdiction. As a result, most law enforcement agencies employ the practice of selective enforcement to deal with traffic problems. Obviously, it is not practical to assume that all traffic violators will or could be punished. So one primary component of the traffic enforcement function is for the police to act as a deterrent to other would-be violators. Allocation of traffic officers can be based on the number of accidents at a certain intersection or on citizen complaints.

Indeed, traffic control lights alone cannot adequately facilitate all traffic problems. Certainly, officers must ensure that traffic signals are obeyed and that intersections are kept clear of congestion. Wide discretionary powers are commonly practiced in traffic enforcement, permitting many violators to go unchecked. Law enforcement agencies don't expect all violators to be identified or cited for their violations. Often, when a traffic violator is stopped, the arresting officer may choose not to write the driver a citation but to give a verbal or written warning instead. Other officers who are more "by the book" will write tickets for all violations observed.

Many law enforcement agencies employ the use of motorcycle officers for traffic duty. Some even use three-wheeled motorcycles or scooters to facilitate movement in congested traffic areas. Other traffic control duties include enforcing tow-away areas and the removal of traffic obstacles such as stalled or abandoned automobiles. Traffic direction is also needed at the scene of accidents or fires where rerouting traffic might be required to facilitate the continual flow of traffic.

Accident Reconstruction

Accident reconstruction is also a vital function of the traffic control unit. This function requires the literal reconstruction of automobile accidents to determine how and why accidents occurred and the extent to which parties are liable. Accident investigators respond to accident scenes and interview parties to the accident and witnesses. In addition, they collect and evaluate **physical evidence** found at the scene. At times, it is important for the traffic officer to render first aid to injury victims at accident scenes as well as to remove damaged vehicles from the flow of traffic to avert additional traffic hazards for motorists.

Reports generated by accident reconstructionists are a critical part of civil litigation arising from traffic mishaps. In such cases the accident investigator is called to testify as a witness. The intent of traffic accident litigation is to determine civil liability and to allow for financial reimbursement of victims to help offset their damages and/or financial losses.

In Retrospect

The police are the most visible component of the criminal justice system, yet one of the most misunderstood. It is therefore important to understand the day-to-day operations of the police in order to identify problems and solutions to their effectiveness and efficiency. For good reasons the patrol function is considered the backbone of policing. Although many of the traditional duties of patrol officers are still in use, the true value and utility of patrol are debatable, and much research is needed to best determine how to use it.

Although policing is constantly undergoing some form of change in our society, it is clear that the police must be responsive to the public they serve and each official function of the police organization must strive to guarantee public satisfaction.

Improve Your Professional Vocabulary

beats
differential response
directed patrol
foot patrol

hot spots
incident-driven policing
physical evidence
preventive patrol

response time
saturation patrol
sectors
street people

Discussion Questions

1. List and discuss the different aspects that characterize the patrol officer's role in the community.
2. Explain and discuss the various guidelines police administrators should use in determining the allocation of patrol units.
3. What did we learn from the Kansas City patrol experiment?
4. List and discuss the various types of investigations that present themselves to law enforcement officers.
5. Discuss the meaning of the term *hot spots* and how the assignment of patrol units can be impacted by our understanding of them.
6. Explain how the PSS has affected our understanding of the police role in America.

Notes

1. Garmire, B. L. (1977). *Local government, police management.* Washington, DC: International City Management Association.
2. Cordner, G. (1989). The police on patrol. In D. J. Kenney, ed., *Police and policing: Contemporary issues.* New York: Praeger, 60–71.
3. Adams, T. F. (1990). *Police field operations.* Upper Saddle River, NJ: Prentice Hall.
4. Wilson, J. Q. (1973). *Varieties of police behavior,* 2nd ed. New York: Atheneum.
5. Cohen, H. (1986, Summer/Fall). Exploiting police authority. *Criminal Justice Ethics,* 23–31.
6. Sherman, L. (1983). Patrol strategies for the police. In J. Q. Wilson, ed., *Crime and public policy.* San Francisco: ICS Press.
7. Whitaker, G., S. Mastrofski, M. Ostrom, R. Parks, & S. Percy. (1982). *Basic issues in police performance.* Washington, DC: U.S. Department of Justice.
8. Ibid.
9. Ibid.
10. Howard Pankraz, H. (2000, May 12). Columbine 911 calls released to kin. *Denver Post,* p. B1.
11. Kelling, G. L., & M. H. Moore. (1988). From political to reform to community: The evolving strategy of police. In

Community Policing: Rhetoric or Reality. Jack Greene and Stephen Mastrofski, eds. New York: Praeger Publishers, p. 13.

12. Smith, L. (1998, January 28). Manassas wants to ease 911 load. *Washington Post,* p. V3.

13. Bischoff, L. A. (1998, February 18). Abusers of 911 may face jail. *Dayton Daily News,* p. 3B.

14. U.S. Department of Justice, Bureau of Justice Statistics. (1988). *Report to the nation on crime and justice,* 2nd ed. Washington, DC: U.S. Government Printing Office.

15. Ibid.

16. Wilken, G. (1996, June 17). This is 911, please hold. *U.S. News & World Report.*

17. Spelman, W. G., & D. K. Brown. (1984). *Calling the police: Citizen reporting of serious crime.* Washington, DC: Police Executive Research Forum.

18. Sherman, L. (1983). Patrol strategies for the police. In J. Q. Wilson, ed., *Crime and public policy.* San Francisco: ICS Press.

19. Spelman, W. G., & D. K. Brown. (1984). *Calling the police: Citizen reporting of serious crime.* Washington, DC: Police Executive Research Forum.

20. Spelman, W. G., & D. K. Brown. (1984). *Calling the police: Citizen reporting of serious crime.* Washington, DC: Police Executive Research Forum.

21. Mitchell, S. (1999, May 30). Hometown commandos. *New York Times Magazine,* p. 15.

22. Famega, Christine, James Frank, & Lorraine Mazerolle. (2005). Managing patrol time: The role of supervisor directives, *Justice Quarterly*, September, p. 550.

23. Cohen, L. E., & M. Felson. (1979). Social change and crime rates: A routine activity approach. *American Sociological Review,* 44, 588–608.

24. Sherman, W. L., P. R. Gartin, & M. E. Burger. (1989). Hotspots of predatory crime: Routine activities and the criminology of place. *Criminology,* 27, 27–55.

25. Sherman, W. L., & D. A. Weiserburd. (1995, December). General deterrent effects of police, patrol in crime "hot spots": A randomized controlled trial. *Justice Quarterly,* 12, 625–648.

26. Ibid.

27. Ibid.

28. Kelling, G. L. (1974). *The Kansas City preventive patrol experiment: A summary report.* Washington, DC: Police Foundation.

29. Wilson, J. Q. (1975). *Thinking about crime.* New York: Vintage Books, p. 99.

30. Ibid.

31. Ibid.

32. Larson, R. C. (1975). What happened to patrol operations in Kansas City? A review of the Kansas City preventive patrol experiment. *Journal of Criminal Justice, 3,* 267.

33. Ibid.

34. Reiss, A. (1971). *The police and the public.* New Haven: Yale University Press, p. 6.

35. Bureau of Justice Statistics. (1994). *Criminal victimization in the United States.* Washington, DC: U.S. Government Printing Office, p. 100.

36. Cox, S. M., & J. Frank. (1992). The influence of neighborhood context and methods of entry on individual styles of policing. *American Journal of Police II,* 2, 1–22.

37. Wilson, J. Q. (1975). *Thinking about crime.* New York: Basic Books.

38. Bright, J. A. (1969). *Beat patrol experiment.* London: Home Office.

39. Chaiken, L. M., M. W. Lawless, & K. A. Stevenson. (1974). *The impact of police activity on crime: Robberies in the New York subway system.* New York: Rand Institute.

40. Cordner, G. (1989). The police on patrol. In D. J. Kenney, ed., *Police and policing: Contemporary issues.* New York: Praeger, pp. 60–71.

41. Boydstun, J. E. (1975). *San Diego field interrogation: Final report.* Washington, DC: Police Foundation.

42. Cordner, G., & R. Trojanowicz. (1992). Police. In G. W. Cordner & D. C. Hale, eds., *What works in policing: Operations and administration examined.* Cincinnati, OH: Anderson.

43. Pate, A. M., & W. G. Skogan. (1985). *Reducing the signs of crime: The Newark experience.* Technical report. Washington, DC: Police Foundation.

44. Trojanowicz, R. (1982). *An evaluation of the neighborhood foot patrol study in Flint, Michigan.* East Lansing, MI: Michigan State University.

45. Wilson, O. W., & R. C. McLaren. (1977). *Police administration,* 4th ed. New York: McGraw-Hill, p. 320.

46. The Police Foundation. (1981). *The New York foot patrol experiment.* Washington, DC: The Police Foundation, p. 36.

47. Wrobleski, H. M., & K. M. Hess. (1997). *Introduction to law enforcement and criminal justice,* 5th ed. Minneapolis/St. Paul: West Publishing Company, p. 326.

48. U.S. National Advisory Commission on Criminal Justice Standards and Goals. (1973). *Police.* Washington, DC: U.S. Government Printing Office, p. 194.

49. National Commission on Productivity. (1974). *Conference on an Agenda for Economic Research on Productivity.* Washington, DC: U.S. Government Printing Office.

50. Walker, S. (1983). *The police in America: An introduction.* New York: McGraw-Hill, 118.

51. Kansas City Police Department. (1978). *Response time analysis: Executive summary.* Washington, DC: U.S. Government Printing Office; and Spellman, W., & D. K. Brown (1981). *Calling the police: Citizen reporting of serious crime.* Washington, DC: Police Executive Research Forum.

52. Stahl, L., & S. Power. (1998, September 28). Response slows on 911 calls. *Dallas Morning News,* p. 1A.

53. McEwen, J. T., E. F. Connors III, & M. J. Cohen. (1986). *Evaluation of the Differential Police Responses Field Test.* Washington, DC: National Institute of Justice.

54. Manning, P. K. (1992). Information technologies and the police. In M. Tonry and O. Morris, eds. *Modern policing.* Chicago: University of Chicago Press, pp. 349–398.

55. Manning, P. K. (1988, February). *Symbolic communication: Signifying calls and the police response.* Cambridge: MIT Press.

56. Bailey, D. H., & J. Garofalo. The management of violence by police patrol officers. *Criminology, 27,* 1–25.

57. Gilsinan, J. F. (1989, May). They is clowning tough: 911 and the social construction of reality. *Criminology, 27,* 329–344.

58. Reiss, A. (1971). *The police and the public.* New Haven: Yale University Press, 6.

59. Ibid.

60. Manning, P. K. (1992). Information technologies and the police. In M. Tonry & N. Morris, eds., *Modern policing.* Chicago: University of Chicago Press, p. 371.

61. Bittner, E. (1976). Community relations. In A. W. Cohn & E. C. Viano, eds., *Police community relations: Images, roles and realities.* Philadelphia: J. B. Lippincott.

62. Woolner, A. (1999, September 29). Courts eye the problems of eyewitness identifications. *USA Today,* p. 15A.

63. Panzarella, R., & J. Alicea. (1997). Police tactics and incidents with mentally disturbed persons. *Policing: An International Journal of Police Strategies and Management,* 20 (2), 326–338.

64. Finn, P., & A. Sullivan. (1988). *Police response to special populations: Handling the mentally ill, public inebriate, and the homeless.* Washington, DC: U.S. Department of Justice.

65. President's Commision on Law Enforcement and Administration of Justice. (1967). *The challenge of crime in a free society.* Washington, DC: U.S. Government Printing Office.

66. Finn, P., & A. Sullivan. (1988). *Police response to special populations: Handling the mentally ill, public inebriated, and the homeless.* Washington, DC: U.S. Department of Justice.

67. Scull, A. (1977). *The incarceration: Community treatment and the deviant; a radical view.* Upper Saddle River, NJ: Prentice Hall.

68. Telpin, L. (2000, July). Keeping the peace: Police discretion and mentally ill persons. *NIJ Journal,* 8–15.

69. Engle, R., & E. Silver. (2001). Policing mentally disordered suspects: a re-examination of the criminalization hypotheses. *Criminology,* 39 (2), 225–252.

70. U.S. Department of Justice, Bureau of Justice Statistics. (1994, November). *Violence between intimates: National crime victimization survey. Selected findings.* Washington, DC: U.S. Government Printing Office, NCJ-149259.

71. Stanko, E. A. (1992). Domestic violence. In G. W. Cordner & D. C. Hale, eds., *What works in policing: Operations and administration examined.* Cincinnati, OH: Anderson.

72. Schulman, M. A. (1979). *A survey of spousal violence against women in Kentucky.* Washington, DC: U.S. Department of Justice.

73. Adams, T. F. (1990). *Police field operations.* Upper Saddle River, NJ: Prentice Hall.

74. Parnas, R. (1972). The police response to domestic disturbance. In L. Radnowitz & M. E. Wolfgang, eds., *The criminal in the arms of the law.* New York: Basic Books.

75. Sherman, L. W., & R. A. Berk. (1984, April). *Minneapolis domestic violence experiment. Police Foundation Report 1.* Washington, DC: Police Foundation.

76. Walker, S. (1992). *The police in America.* New York: McGraw-Hill.

77. Sherman, L. (1982, Spring/Winter). Learning police ethics. *Criminal Justice Ethics, 1*(1), 10–19.

78. Dunford, F., D. Huizinga, & D. Elliott. (1986). The role of arrest in domestic assault: The Omaha Experiment. *Criminology, 28*(2), 183–206.

79. Schulman, M. A. (1979). *A survey of spousal violence against women in Kentucky.* Washington, DC: U.S. Department of Justice.

CHAPTER 6

Police Operations: Criminal Investigation

This chapter will enable you to:

- Discuss the role of police investigations.
- Understand the different resources available to police investigators.
- Understand the ways in which the police share the responsibility of investigative function with the patrol.

- Identify and explain the goals of criminal investigation.
- List and discuss the various responsibilities of the criminal investigator.
- Discuss the constitutional concerns of the criminal investigator.

A crowd had gathered on the campus of North Carolina Central University (NCCU) in Durham, and they were angry. A month earlier, on March 13, 2006, a captain of the Duke University lacrosse team had called an escort service and hired two "exotic" dancers to perform at a party. Early the next morning, one of the dancers wound up in the emergency room of the local hospital. The woman, a 27-year-old African-American NCCU student, told local police that she had been raped, sodomized, and choked by three white men in a bathroom at the house where the party took place. Why, someone in the crowd asked Durham County District Attorney Michael Nifong, had no charges been filed yet? "My presence here means that this case is not going away," promised Nifong.

Nifong kept his word, eventually charging three Duke lacrosse players—Senior David Evans and sophomores Colin Finnerty and Reade Seligmann—with first-degree rape, sexual assault, and kidnapping. The three defendants, who had been identified from a photo by the alleged victim, were to face 30 years behind bars for each charge. In December 2006, however, Nifong dropped the rape charges against the suspects after the alleged victim changed her story, saying that she could not be certain about exactly what had happened that night. Then, on April 11, 2007, the North Carolina attorney general threw out the entire case, citing the woman's "faulty and unreliable" accusations.

By this time, Nifong himself had, contrary to his promise, "gone away." North Carolina officials removed him from the case after the state bar opened an ethics investigation concerning his prosecutorial strategy. Eventually, he lost his license to practice law. Nifong expressed remorse for "judgments that ultimately prove to be incorrect," but the defendants were having none of it. "You can accept an apology from someone who knows all the facts and simply makes an error," said Reade Seligmann's attorney. "If a person refuses to know all the facts and then makes a judgment, that's far worse—particularly when that judgment destroys lives."

In this chapter we address the operations aspect of police work, but police officers must be cognizant of the fact that the actual operations are only part of the job. Police officers, regardless of their assignment, must always remember the context in which and the people with whom they work: the citizens in the community and criminal justice colleagues. The police officer is an integral part of this context, not a separate entity working in a vacuum.

Police officers must make good use of communication skills, which include active listening, report writing, and clear communication techniques. Police officers' actions must not only be legal but ethical. And police officers must develop the ability to protect themselves in what could be life-threatening situations. Once officers accept these foundational prerequisites, they can focus on the actual operations police officers perform. Of the many functions performed by contemporary police departments, field operations are the most prominent. These include two basic functions: patrol operations and criminal investigations. In this chapter we examine the dynamics of patrol and investigative operations and how these important functions relate to effective policing.

THE INVESTIGATION FUNCTION

While the patrol officer takes on a variety of tasks, the investigator is freed from those responsibilities and allowed to pursue a more narrowly defined role in policing. Poland explains: "In theory, the detective, by virtue of his or her expertise and lack of responsibility for responding to citizen's calls for assistance, will be able to solve the case. The patrol officer, lacking expertise and diverted by demands of patrol, is incapable of devoting the time and attention needed to gather the evidence required to identify the offender and solve the case. Thus the detective is the premier crime fighter among police. Therefore, a position as a detective is often a career aspiration for police officers."[1]

Highlights in Policing

Becoming an FBI Agent (Criminal Investigator)

To become an FBI special agent you must be a U.S. citizen or a citizen of the Northern Mariana Islands. You must be at least 23 years of age, but younger than 37 upon your appointment as a special agent. You must possess a four-year degree from a college or university accredited by one of the regional or national institutional associations recognized by the United States Secretary of Education. You must have at least three years of professional work experience. You must also possess a valid driver's license and be completely available for assignment anywhere in the FBI's jurisdiction.

All applicants for the Special Agent position must first qualify under one of five Special Agent Entry Programs. These programs include:

- Accounting
- Computer Science/Information Technology
- Language
- Law
- Diversified

More details about Special Agent Entry Programs.

After qualifying for one of the five entry programs, applicants will be prioritized in the hiring process based upon certain critical skills for which the FBI is recruiting. The FBI is currently recruiting for special agent candidates with one or more of the following critical skills:

- Accounting
- Finance
- Computer science/Information Technology Expertise
- Engineering expertise
- Foreign language(s) proficiency
- Intelligence experience
- Law experience
- Law enforcement/investigative experience
- Military experience
- Physical sciences (e.g., physics, chemistry, biology, etc.) expertise
- Diversified experience

Candidates with these critical skills will be prioritized in the hiring process.

In addition to effective patrol operations, high-quality investigations are also important to the performance and accountability of any police department. Obviously, it is impossible to solve every crime, but the work of a criminal investigator or detective is critical to solving the most important crimes coming to the agency's attention. The term *criminal investigation* can be defined as simply a method of reconstructing the past, so that the facts and circumstances of a crime can be better understood. Although police detectives investigate crimes, modern police departments also delegate this function to many members of the patrol division as well, such as officers assigned to traffic enforcement or special service uniformed units within the department.

Other police personnel are also included in the task of criminal investigation. For example, records clerks, crime analysts, and communication personnel often take the initiative to search and to provide information to detectives in investigations. So it should be noted that the investigative function includes literally all police personnel.

TYPES OF INVESTIGATIONS

The police perform a number of duties in the community. Of these, three of the most fundamental are protection of life, protection of property, and maintenance of order. In the event that these duties cannot be accomplished, the fourth results—the criminal investigation of offenses and the persons believed to be responsible. Although an array of situations resulting in investigation may arise, some basic types of investigations are most commonly undertaken:

- Violations of the law, which include state laws, city ordinances, and certain traffic offenses, such as traffic accidents
- Personnel investigations into the background of persons to determine their suitability for employment or promotion or as a result of allegations of wrongdoing
- Organized crime investigations, which if left unchecked would result in an increase of vice-type criminal activity and related violence

Criminal investigations are conducted for three basic purposes: first, as a reactive measure to follow up on the occurrence of a crime that has already been committed; second, as a proactive measure to monitor crimes as they occur (these generally include vice crimes such as drug, gambling, and prostitution violations); and finally, as a preventive measure to ensure that certain crimes will not be committed. In the first two instances, it is also the objective of the law enforcement officer to identify, locate, and apprehend the person(s) responsible for the perpetration of the crime.

The Goals of Criminal Investigation

There is more to the criminal investigation than simply identifying and arresting a suspect in a particular crime. In fact, a thorough investigation can accomplish many objectives:

- To ascertain if a crime has been committed
- To determine the jurisdiction of the crime
- To procure evidence in a legal fashion
- To identify the suspect in the crime
- To arrest the suspect
- To recover stolen property
- To identify associates in large criminal organizations
- To identify clients (customers) of large criminal organizations
- To present evidence to prosecutors in an orderly manner
- To testify in court proceedings

The basic premise behind criminal investigation is that people are not perfect and they make mistakes. After committing a crime, investigators believe that all suspects will leave something behind to identify them as the perpetrators.

Patrol Investigations

As we learned in the discussion on patrol operations in this chapter, the role of the uniformed officer has been expanded to include conducting criminal investigations. In many cases, these responsibilities were formerly those of the plainclothes officer. There are several ways that the patrol officer can be responsive to the challenge of criminal investigations. For example, it is the patrol division that will be the first to respond to the scene of a crime in many cases.

Accordingly, patrol officers will generally offer initial assistance to victims of crime and therefore have the first opportunity to learn information about the perpetrator, motive, and other details of the crime. In addition, it is the patrol officer who will first identify witnesses at the crime scene and may even apprehend the suspect if he or she is still on the premises. In the case

A Closer Look

Can Police "Stop-and-Frisk" Programs Curb Gun Violence?

The old pro-gun rights slogan goes, "Guns don't kill people, people kill people." Whether people or their weapons are to blame, research has shown that guns play a major part in recent crime increases and that reducing the number of guns on the street seems to have played a role in New York City's drop in crime rate.

In 2007, the majority of the 56 chiefs and sheriffs surveyed by the Police Executive Research Forum (PERF) cited increased availability of firearms as one of the causes of increase in violent crime in their cities and towns. "We need to talk about national policies with guns, because that's what's killing inner-city youths today," said Garry McCarthy, Previous director of Newark, N.J. Police Department "If the guns weren't available, the shootings wouldn't be occurring at the rates that they're occurring. It's a lot harder to kill somebody with a golf club than it is with a gun."

Police Focus on "Hotspots"

We learned in Chapter 5 how police patrol of "hotspots" can reduce crime. Research shows that monitoring crime hotspots is the most effective approach to reducing violent crime, according to nearly two-thirds of law enforcement agencies polled.

Programs/policies implemented in response to increases in violent crime

Programs/policies	Percentage of agencies implementing policy/program
Hotspots enforcement	63
Community-oriented initiative	44
Problem-solving policing	37
Cooperation with other departments	37
Shifts and police resources	28
Drug enforcement	23
Targeting repeat offenders	22
Hiring/recruiting more officers	20
Federal grant programs (we & see, etc.)	17
Technology (cameras, computer systems, etc.)	15
School resource officers	12
"Zero tolerance" for low-level disorder	12
Juvenile crime programs	10
Creation of antigang unit	9

Source: "Violent Crime in America: A Tale of Two Cities," *Police Executive Research Forum*, November 2007.

McCarthy's comments were made in the aftermath of the August 4 execution-style slaying of three college students in a Newark playground; a fourth student, a young woman, also shot at point-blank range, survived. Using her eyewitness account, fingerprint evidence and other supportive evidence, within weeks police had arrested six people, including three juveniles. All were Latin American immigrants, one of them without legal status. They apparently had planned to rob the victims.

How to keep guns out of the hands of criminals has long ranked as one of the most troublesome issues in U.S. law enforcement. The legal debate over gun laws aside, face the practical question of how to disarm gun-packing criminals. As in other aspects of crime fighting, New York City changed the nature of the debate. In 1994, Mayor Rudolph Giuliani's celebrated previous chief, William J. Bratton, directed the 400-officer Street Crime Unit to aggressively target people suspected of carrying guns. One of their tactics was to stop and search young men—typically members of minority groups—known as "stop and frisk."

The approach was controversial from the beginning. Criticism that the police were overly confrontational was validated by the 1999 shooting of a West African immigrant from Guinea, Amadou Diallo, who turned out to be unarmed. And statistics showed that searches for guns far outnumbered seizures of them—18,023 searches in 1997, for 4,899 guns; and 27,061 searches in 1998, yielding 4,647 firearms.

Giuliani turned to the courts as well. As of the preparation of this test, New York Mayor Michael Bloomberg is pursuing a lawsuit that his predecessor began, seeking tens of millions of dollars from more than a dozen gun manufacturers and distributors, on the grounds that they didn't do enough to keep guns out of criminals' hands.

Some criminologists note that street seizures were especially effective in a city whose strict gun laws made it hard for criminals to buy replacement guns or steal them from lawful owners. There were a lot of guns on the street and none in apartments.

Still, another set of statistics stands out as well. As police in New York focused on guns, gun-related crime dropped drastically. From 1988 to 1998 (the last year of Giuliani's first term), gun homicides dropped from 1,330 to 376.

For some researchers, those ends justify the aggressive means. "Gun carrying in those neighborhoods where violence is endemic provides an incentive for a preemptive strike. If the other guy is going to get you, you're going to get him first," says criminologist Alfred Blumstein, a professor of urban systems and operations research at Carnegie-Mellon University's H. John Heinz III School of Public Policy and Management, in Pittsburgh.

Blumstein acknowledges that the aggressive policing involved in seizing guns endangers civil rights. But, he notes, Nutter won election last year as mayor of Philadelphia based in part on promises to implement a New York-style campaign against gun violence. "My sense, and the election bears it out, is that the public would rather have safety than an avoidance of stop-and-frisk."

Some Philadelphians disagree. "It plays into racial profiling," says Jubilee School founder Falcon, who calls for tougher laws against gun ownership. "As long as guns are so available, you can take the guns away all you want; they're just going to be replaced. I don't think it's the stop-and-frisk that stopped the guns in New York. They have very strict gun laws."

The Diallo shooting gave pause even to some stop-and-frisk advocates. "Bratton did that very well in New York City; then it got out of control," says George L. Kelling, a professor at Rutgers University's School of Criminal Justice in Newark, who advised Bratton when he headed New York's transit. Kelling coauthored "Broken Windows," a 1982 article that still influences policing across the country. (The article argued that if city officials attended to problems and cracked down on minor crimes, such as fixing broken windows and arresting vagrants, more serious crimes would also be reduced.)

Kelling blames the Diallo shooting on inexperience. "That was the first time those guys had worked together; they were relatively inexperienced," he says. If you're going to use special units for gun tactics, you need officers who are highly trained, mature, and who have worked together for a long time."

But Minneapolis Chief Tim Dolan questions the tactic. "I don't think we'd get much support here if we were stopping and frisking without at least reasonable suspicion or some articulable reason," he says.

Dolan does encourage his officers to look for guns. But—unlike in New York—seized guns are easy to replace. Criminals can obtain weapons through middlemen who buy them legally. And purchases at flea markets and the like are unregulated.

Sources: See "Violent Crime in America: 'A Tale of Two Cities,'" *Executive Research Forum*, November, 2007, pp. 6, 22, www.policeforum.org; "Crime in the United States by Volume and Rate per 100,000 Inhabitants, 1987–2006," Department of Justice, FBI, September 2007, www.fbi.gov; Daryl Fears, "City to Take New Tack to Curb Gun Violence," *The Washington Post*, December 23, 2007, p. A3, www.washingtonpost.com; See David C. Anderson, "Crime Stoppers," *The New York Times Magazine*, February 9, 1997, p. 47; See Diane Cardwell, "Bloomberg Begs to Differ With Giuliani on Gun Suit," The *New York Times*, September 25, 2007, p. B2; See James Q. Wilson and George L. Kelling, "Broken Windows," *The Atlantic, March*, 1982, www.theatlantic.com.

of crimes such as burglary and larceny (when the value of property is under a certain amount) and in certain domestic disputes, the patrol officer determines what types of evidence to document. In other cases, smaller law enforcement agencies have entrusted patrol officers with the responsibility of conducting entire criminal investigations. This system seems to work well for general offenses that are as easily investigated by patrol officers as by investigators. Obviously, in cases requiring specialized training, such as in organized crime offenses, a full-time investigator is a requirement.

Undercover Investigations

Criminal investigations can also be **proactive** in nature. Proactive investigations occur when a crime has not yet been committed but the police have reason to believe that it will. The goal of the undercover investigator is to identify criminal suspects and collect evidence of crimes they have committed, are committing, or are planning to commit. Typically, undercover investigations take place with multiple jurisdictions working together to pool resources and manpower. These resources make available resources such as personnel, computer systems, criminal and intelligence records, informants, surveillance equipment, vehicles, and funding.

As a rule, undercover investigations focus on illicit drug investigations, sting operations, gambling, prostitution, and the buying of stolen goods. Decoy operations target robbery, burglary and assault; antiprostitution; and organized crime operations.[2]

Federal undercover operations generally attempt to detect and arrest people involved in official or political corruption, insurance fraud, labor racketeering, and so on. More recently federal investigations have focused on terrorism and identifying **sleeper cells** where terrorists plan their operations.

Because of the covert nature of their assignments, undercover investigators do not wear uniforms. Rather, they dress in a manner that fits in with the persons they are investigating. As such, they drive vehicles that cannot be identified as police vehicles and assume names and fictitious identities to keep from being identified as police. Many larger police departments recruit officers who are recent graduates from police academies because their uniformed presence is not yet known on the streets.

As a rule, undercover assignments are either light cover or deep cover in nature. In this capacity they may pose as a number of persons in the community such as a water and light worker or telephone company employee for the purpose of gaining access to a suspect's residence or place of work. Listening devices are sometimes planted, authorized by court order, to covertly listen to conversations. Light cover assignments are when the officers associate directly with the criminal targets, but for only short periods of time—sometimes even a matter of minutes. Deep cover assignments are when the investigator spends lengthy periods of time with the criminal targets and their associates in order to gain their trust. Deep cover assignments are extremely dangerous as the officer typically works without supervision or surveillance from other officers. Haberman notes, "The very nature of this work can lead to nightmarish situations, because by definition, undercover officers are supposed to melt into their surroundings. Snap decisions—when to back off, when to make arrests, certainty when to shoot—are rarely uncomplicated or without peril."[3]

While undercover investigations are often perceived as exciting and glamorous, they are fraught with danger and psychological pitfalls for the investigator. It is common that family and social relationships suffer because investigators are forbidden from discussing their investigations with others outside the police. Moreover, the long and trying hours required of officers can lead to burnout which can result in complacency where an investigator loses focus and might misread a potentially dangerous situation. For those investigators who have spent long periods of time working in an undercover capacity, they often find it difficult to return to their role as a patrol officer.

THE ROLE OF THE INVESTIGATOR

The criminal investigator plays a significant role in the composition of any law enforcement agency. Investigators specialize in activities related primarily to law enforcement, whereas patrol officers spend much of their time on order maintenance and the provision of general services. Nonetheless, the diversity of tasks performed by investigators is considerable. For example, detectives gather crime information, effect arrests, and prepare cases for prosecution and trial. In addition, they must observe constitutional restraints while conducting their duties and satisfy both the needs of the public and the victim.

Gathering Information

Important tasks performed by investigators include rapid response to crime scenes; searching crime scenes; and identifying, collecting, and preserving **physical evidence**. In addition, in more recent times it is important for the investigator to be familiar with the department's computer and records system for rapid retrieval of criminal history information, photos of suspects, and fingerprint and intelligence information. Once leads are identified, the investigator must be able to follow up on them through various means. These can include visits to pawn shops, suspected drug-trafficking and/or fencing locations, and other places frequented by known criminals. Interviews are often useful in identifying suspects, which may lead to an arrest. The success of the interview will often depend on the verbal communication skills of the detective and the ability to demonstrate sensitivity and perception during the interview process.

Field Operations

The investigator is also called upon to conduct field services such as stakeouts or surveillances. In addition, undercover operations are often used to infiltrate covert activities such as drug-trafficking or fencing operations. These operations typically require that the investigator has knowledge of technical equipment, such as concealed microphones and sophisticated photography equipment.

Case Preparation

Obviously, when the offender is caught in the act, the question of who did it becomes moot. However, when the offender is not identified promptly, the criminal investigation may take a number of directions.

In the case of a suspect whose identity is known, victims and witnesses can provide information that may aid the investigator in his or her apprehension and conviction. Cases involving an unidentified perpetrator present the greatest challenge to the skills and intelligence of the law enforcement investigator. The victim may be one of the most valuable leads for the investigator. In addition to an investigation into the victim's background (discussed later), interviews with victims regarding the commission of the offense may provide information indicating the suspect's motive and opportunity—two fundamental questions in any criminal investigation. Field reports by patrol officers written around the time and place of the crime can also provide significant leads for the investigator. In addition, fingerprints and other trace evidence can show that a certain person has been on the scene. Photographs of persons previously arrested may help identify a criminal and can be viewed by victims and witnesses. When searching for clues in the investigation, the law enforcement investigator should consider four fundamental realms of information about the suspect's incentive to commit the crime:

- The victim's background
- The benefits of the crime

- The opportunity to commit the crime
- Knowledge to commit the crime

Identifying the Method of Operation

In addition to showing the elements of the crime, investigators must identify the person suspected of committing it. In doing so, the suspect's **method of operation** (MO) should be identified in case it is used again. The MO was considered with more weight in years past; in recent years it has become more common for suspects to adopt different methods of operation. In all cases, however, the investigators should at least attempt to identify established methods, as some criminals prefer to stay with techniques that have worked well for them in past crimes. Once the MO is identified, a pattern of victims, locations, and other variables can possibly be recognized. This information could aid the investigator in predicting future crimes.

Crime Scene Responsibilities

The crime scene can be defined as the area in which the suspect(s) and victim(s) maneuver during the commission of the crime. It typically involves only one location, but may well include several sites, as in the case of a struggle between victim and assailant. Law enforcement officers should attempt to define the exact boundaries of the crime scene. Once this is accomplished, the scene should be protected from unauthorized personnel who might inadvertently destroy or alter evidence.

Hence, the crime scene provides an opportunity for the discovery of evidence that, it is hoped, will identify the person responsible. Such evidence can include fingerprints; clothing particles; body fluids such as urine, blood, or saliva; or personal items left by the suspect. In addition to leaving evidence at the crime scene, the suspect may have taken evidence from the scene, such as soil samples or blood. In this case, once the suspect has been identified, the investigator should collect evidence from both the suspect and the crime scene location for comparison.

The Preliminary Investigation

If the suspect was not caught in the act of committing the crime, as is often the case, the first officer to the scene must assume the duties of the preliminary investigation. As mentioned previously, these duties include the following:

- To administer first aid or summon medical help for injured parties
- To broadcast information that might be of immediate importance to field officers, such as the description of the suspects or vehicles driven
- To protect the crime scene from unauthorized entry until the investigation team arrives
- To arrest or detain any persons suspected of committing the crime

In addition to the duties described above, it is also essential for the first officer to make notes regarding the general condition of the crime scene. For example, was the door ajar? Were any windows open? Was any furniture overturned? Were there any odors (e.g., cigarette smoke, perfume, gunpowder)? Such evidence may easily be overlooked in the excitement of the moment, but it could prove to be critical later in the investigation.

Locating Physical Evidence

The hallmark of the criminal investigation process is the identification, collection, and preservation of physical evidence (any evidence having shape, size, or dimension that may be brought to or removed from the crime scene).[4] It can consist of fingerprints, impressions, weapons, blood,

FIGURE 6.1 A crime scene technician searching for trace evidence.

fabric from clothing, cigarette butts, and so on. Such evidence is critical to the identification and prosecution of the suspects. Many large law enforcement organizations today employ squads of evidence technicians who are highly trained in locating and collecting minute fragments of evidence that might otherwise go undetected by the untrained eye. The search of the crime scene should begin with the most logical locations for the particular type of crime in question. In general, the search should include the following areas:

- Escape routes that appear to be most likely for the suspect
- Locations where suspects might be tempted to discard a weapon
- The suspect's point of entry
- The route followed by the suspect once he or she arrived on the crime scene
- Any objects or locations that might have attracted the criminal (e.g., a safe)
- Unusual areas such as the bathroom or the kitchen

Generally, a walk-through by officers will reveal much of how and where the crime occurred. Care should be taken, considering that fingerprints might have to be processed and photographs will need to be taken. Once a complete search of the premises is under way, officers should be certain that it is thorough and comprehensive so that no evidence is missed. The evidence's location must be recorded through photographs and/or sketches before it is moved. This is important, for example, if spent cartridges from a firearm are located that, based on their location and position, might indicate where the shooter was standing at the time of the shooting. Once this information is well documented, the items can be moved for storage and transportation to the crime lab.

Collection and Preservation of Evidence

After evidence has been documented at the crime scene, it must be collected. This is a process that requires the investigator to be mindful of both the roles of the lawyer and scientist and systematically accumulate all evidence separate from all other evidence so as to prevent contamination.

The evidence must be maintained in its original condition and not be altered in any fashion or confused with any other items of evidence. For any item of evidence to be admissible in court, it must be readily identifiable by the officer who collected it at the scene. So the bag of cocaine must be absolutely recognizable by the seizing officer; the spent shell casings must be identified as the very casings seized by the investigators at the specific crime scene in question.

When seized, all evidence should bear the initials of the officer seizing the item as well as the date of the seizure. If possible, the location of the item at the scene of the crime should be indicated. These procedures will ensure an easily identifiable article of evidence once the case goes to court, which could be months after the arrest or crime scene search. Clearly, attempting to compress a lot of detailed information on the item itself may not be practical, but placing the item in an envelope or container that has room for writing is more practical. Evidence tapes can also be used for this purpose and works well.

The Challenge of Electronic Evidence

Modern technology has presented many challenges to modern day criminal investigation. For example, the Internet, computer networks, and automated data systems have afforded many criminals opportunities for criminal activity.[5] Computers and other electronic devices are used increasingly by criminals to perpetuate crimes against people, organizations, and property. Whether the crime involves attacks against computer systems or more traditional offenses such as money laundering, drug trafficking, or fraud, electronic evidence is, increasingly, important.

Electronic evidence can be defined as, "information and data of investigative value that is stored or transmitted by an electronic device."[6] Such evidence is often acquired when physical items like computers, CDs, DVDs, flash drives, personal data assistants, and cellular phones are identified at a crime scene or seized from a suspect.

Electronic evidence is of particular concern to criminal investigators because of its characteristics. For example, it is latent; it can transcend national and state borders quickly and easily; it is fragile and easily altered, damaged, compromised, or even destroyed by improper examination; and, it may be time sensitive. Similar to DNA or fingerprints, electronic evidence is characterized as **latent evidence** because it is not readily visible to the human eye under normal conditions. Special equipment and software are needed to "see" and evaluate electronic evidence. When presented in court, expert testimony may be required to explain how electronic evidence was acquired and the examination process used to interpret it.

In 2002, in recognition of the special challenges posed by electronic evidence, the Computer Crime and Intelligence Property Section (CCIPS) of the Criminal Division of the United States Department of Justice released a how-to manual for law enforcement officers titled *Searching and Seizing Computers and Obtaining Electronic Evidence in Criminal Investigations*.[7] At about the same time, the Technical Working Group for Electronic Crime Scene Investigation (TWGECSI) released a detailed guide for law enforcement officers to use in gathering electronic evidence. TWGECSI guidelines say that law enforcement must take special precautions when documenting, collecting, and preserving electronic evidence to maintain its integrity. The guidelines also note that the first law enforcement officer on the scene should take steps to ensure the safety of everyone at the scene and to protect the integrity of all evidence, both traditional and electronic.

Once digital evidence has been gathered, it must be evaluated. As such, in 2004, the government-sponsored Technical Working Group for the Examination of Digital Evidence (TWGEDE) recommended that digital evidence should be acquired in a manner that protects and preserves the integrity of the original evidence and that examination should be conducted only on a "copy" of the original evidence.[8]

Profiling

From the earliest beginnings of criminal investigation, detectives have focused on relatively super-ficial characteristics to identify suspects. These characteristics include height, weight, race, gender, age, accent, type of vehicle driven, and method of operation. While these identifiers remain valid and are still considered when searching for suspects in a crime, profilers had begun to dig deeper into suspect personalities, psyches, pathologies, and resultant behaviors to develop a more complete picture of serial criminals. These profiles can and often do exist in the absence of any physical descriptors.

Profiling has evolved over the last 30 years with the FBI's increasing understanding of serial murder. Drug courier profiling emerged as a part of the war on drugs during the 1980s and began in airports. It was upheld as a constitutional investigative technique in *United States* v. *Sokolow*. Profiling can be reactive or proactive. Investigators using reactive profiling attempt to solve crimes that have already occurred. Proactive profiling, in comparison, attempts to interdict and stop crime before it happens.

Profiling uses pattern recognition through systemically collecting, organizing, and analyzing information gathered through observation or measurement; drawing conclusions in assessing crim-inal suspicion; and sharing data with others. Although race, sex, and religion are among the most controversial elements of profiling, profilers also use such things as travel patterns, socioeconomic status, geographic locations, and clothing. It is essential to distinguish between racial profiling and psychological profiling and geographic profiling and criminal profiling. The former profilings are crimes in violation of civil rights, while the latter are accepted tools for criminal investigators.

Crimes suitable for profiling include sadistic torture in sexual assaults, postmortem cases of slashing and cutting, motiveless arson, last emulation murders, rapes, occult crimes, child sexual abuse including pedophilia, and bank robberies. According to the FBI, profiling techniques have assisted in 77% of cases, have provided leads for stakeouts involving cases 45% of the time, and have actually helped identify the perpetrator or unidentified suspect in 17% of cases.[9]

A major source of research and development on criminal profiling is the investigative support unit of the National Center for the Analysis of Violent Crime (NCAVC).

In addition to criminal or psychological profiling, departments may use geographic profiling. Like mapping, geographic profiling uses computers to specially analyze crime sites, allowing inves-tigators to determine the most likely areas where offenders live. Because geographic profiling can help investigators zero in on where a suspect lives, the Roanoke, Virginia, Police Department saw the following results after initiating this technique:

- Decreased police response times
- A team policing approach in which officers work together to address crime problems
- Improved delivery of services to residents
- Increased accountability and responsiveness
- Completed management goals and objectives
- Customization of the police response to each citizen concerned[10]

Johnson and Staples conclude, "The geographic policing initiative has instilled a sense of ownership and responsibility in patrol officers and their supervisors... the GPI has been the Department's single most effective strategy to improve quality of life and fight crime."[11]

Identifying the Suspect

One of the greatest challenges to the investigator is to identify the suspect in the crime. Many tech-niques have been refined over the years for this purpose and include the use of surveillance, lineups, neighborhood canvasses, and information provided by informants.

FIGURE 6.2 Plainclothes narcotics detectives often field test suspected illicit drugs to determine probable cause for arrest or search.

SURVEILLANCE The term **surveillance** can be defined as the surreptitious observation of persons, places, or things by law enforcement officers. The surveillance technique is a time-tested method for identifying suspects as well as learning much valuable information about them. Such information can include the locations or hangouts of suspects, vehicles driven, associates, and habits that might be of interest to the criminal investigator. Surveillance can be fixed (stationary), moving, or electronic in nature. Fixed surveillance can either be covert, as with the use of undercover or plainclothes officers, or overt, as with the use of uniformed officers. More often than not, the suspect will be moving about and a moving surveillance will be required. Moving surveillances usually require special vehicles that are unobtrusive in appearance, two-way communication to allow officers to converse, and a clear knowledge of streets and thoroughfares on the part of the officers assigned.

Electronic surveillance includes wiretaps and the use of electronic audiovisual enhancement devices such as concealed voice transmitters, bumper beepers, pen registers, and night-viewing devices. Laws will vary from state to state regarding the use of such devices. In some cases, law enforcement agencies can use such devices at their discretion, whereas in other states a court order may be required. Because the wiretap is considered as the greatest encroachment on one's privacy, it must be conducted pursuant to law (state or federal) and with a court order authorizing its use.

Although surveillance might be thought of as an independent investigative technique, in fact, it is used most effectively in conjunction with other traditional investigative techniques, such as interviewing suspects and witnesses, using informants, and conducting wiretaps. The surveillance operation can be costly, due to the number of officers sometimes required, special equipment, and the amount of overtime needed to maintain long periods of observation. More often than not, however, the technique produces valuable information that might not be available through other means of investigation.

POLICE LINEUPS

Over the years, the Supreme Court has allowed certain forms of nontestimonial evidence for the purpose of identifying suspects in criminal cases. One of the most common is the **police lineup**. In a lineup the suspect is placed together with several other people, and the victim or a witness is allowed to view them and pick out the suspect. Constitutional considerations have generally focused on the fairness of this technique and on the suspect's right to counsel during the procedure. The case of *United States* v. *Wade* (1967) addressed the issue of a suspect's right to counsel during a lineup. In this case, the defendant was shown to witnesses prior to trial at a post-indictment lineup without giving notice of the lineup to the suspect or his attorney and without his attorney present. The court ruled in this case that a person who is subjected to a pretrial lineup is entitled to representation by counsel at the time. An important aspect to the decision was that it applied only to post-indictment lineups and not to those occurring in earlier phases in the criminal justice process.

The Photo Lineup

If the suspect is not in custody, the investigator can conduct a photo lineup to determine identification. Photos of the suspect can be obtained through police files of the suspect if he or she has been arrested previously. If not, surveillance photos can be used. Photo lineups are commonly used and, if administered correctly, will not only identify possible suspects but can also eliminate innocent persons from suspicion. The use of a single photo will taint the identification procedure and jeopardize the case. Rather, to ensure a fair and legal outcome of the photo-lineup procedure, a minimum of five photos should be used, each depicting subjects with similar characteristics and features (e.g., gender, race, build, age). The photos can be mounted on any flat surface, allowing the witness to study them. It should be pointed out to the witness that it is not necessary for an identification to be made.

We should remember that the *Wade* decision pertains only to a suspect participating in a lineup. In other words, in a photo lineup the suspect does not have a constitutional right to counsel (*United States* v. *Ash Jr.*, 1973). In all situations, it is a good idea for police to videotape the lineup process in anticipation of future charges of inappropriate behavior on the part of the police.

Informants

In July 1997, the FBI began using its Internet home page to encourage current or past employees of tobacco companies to become "whistle-blowers" in its criminal probe of the industry. Agents were investigating claims that tobacco executives lied to Congress and the Food and Drug Administration about manipulating nicotine levels in cigarettes. This is only one of many examples of how police rely, to a great extent, on information from citizens in the investigation and prosecution of criminal suspects. Although the term *informant* has undergone many interpretations over the years, it can be defined as anyone offering information to law enforcement. Although problematic at times, informants have proven to be an invaluable investigative tool. They can aid the investigation in many ways:

- Prevent crimes that have been devised but not yet acted out
- Help locate suspects in crimes
- Help locate stolen property
- Create dissension within criminal groups by providing information resulting in arrests

The manner in which informants can best be utilized rests with the timely identification of their motivations. In general, there are informants who offer information out of a sense of civic duty, those who are money motivated, and those who harbor other motivations (fear, revenge, and competition). The informant may also be anonymous, offering his or her information over the telephone or

A Closer Look

CSI and the Real World

Crime Scene Investigation (*CSI*) was a surprise television hit. Rather than relying on shootouts and car chases, it depicts a dedicated team of forensic scientists who work for the Las Vegas, Nevada, Police Department and use their forensic skills to trap the most wily criminal offenders. Rather than using their brawn, the *CSI* investigators rely on their wits and scientific training.

The team is led by the level-three head *CSI* investigator Gil Grissom, played by character actor William Petersen. Grissom is a trained scientist whose specialty is forensic entomology, the study of insects found on or near a crime scene. He uses his expertise to search for clues within victims' bodies, outside of their bodies, or in any other way that can provide evidence to identify the suspect or solve the crime. For example, he tests the waste products from an insect found on the body of a deceased to determine the time of death, whether the body has been moved, and so on. Rather than a hard-drinking, two-fisted crime fighter, Grissom is a shy quiet guy who, when not working, can be found doing crossword puzzles.

Although not all *CSI* members are trained scientists, most have the skills and education to make them formidable forensic specialists. For example, Sara Sidle, played by Jorja Fox, holds a B.S. degree in physics from Harvard; she was brought in specifically by Grissom. She is completely dedicated to her work and seems to spend her free time studying forensics.

Each show revolves around a seemingly unsolvable crime. In some instances, a leading suspect is exonerated when the team uses its skills to show that, despite appearances, the person could not have committed the crime. For example, in one episode—"Sex, Lies, and Larvae"—which first aired on December 22, 2000, the team investigated the shooting death of a young woman whose bloodied and bug-infested body was found on a nearby mountain. At first glance, it seemed that the woman's abusive husband was the killer. But the analysis of the bugs found on the woman's body indicated that the victim was killed three days earlier, a time when the husband was out of town. The *CSI* series has proven so popular that a second version, set in Miami, premiered in 2002.

The *CSI* series draws attention to the developing field of forensics and police work. Forensics is defined as "pertaining to the law," and forensic scientists perform comprehensive chemical and physical analysis on evidence submitted by law enforcement agencies. Although most forensic scientists focus on criminal cases (they are sometimes referred to as criminalists), others work in the civil justice system—for example, performing handwriting comparisons to determine the validity of a signature on a will. When working on crimes, their analysis involves a variety of sciences, mathematical principles, and problem-solving methods, including use of complex instruments and chemical, physical, and microscopic examining techniques. In addition to analyzing crime scene investigations, forensic scientists provide testimony in a court of law when the cases are brought to trial. Although some forensic scientists are generalists, others—like Gil Grissom—specialize in a particular scientific area. The specialties include the following:

Controlled substances and toxicology. Crime lab professionals specializing in this area examine blood and other body fluids and tissues for the presence of alcohol, drugs, and poisons.

Biology. Crime lab professionals compare body fluids and hair for typing factors, including DNA analysis. Analysis of hair found at a crime scene can determine factors such as whether the hair belongs to a human or animal, the body area the hair came from, if the person or animal had a disease, and, sometimes, race.

Chemistry. Forensic scientists analyze physical trace evidence such as blood spatters, paint, soil, and glass. For example, blood spatters help reconstruct the crime scene: the pattern of spatters and the shape of blood droplets tell how the crime was committed.

Document examination. Document examination includes many areas of expertise, including forgery, document dating, and analysis of handwriting, typewriting, computer printing, and photocopying.

Firearms and tool-mark identification. Firearms examination involves matching identifying characteristics between a firearm and a projectile and between a projectile and a target. Typically, this includes matching bullets to the gun that fired them. Tool-mark verification involves matching some of the identifying characteristics of a tool, such as a pry bar, to the object on which it was used, such as a doorframe. It also includes explosives and imprint evidence.

Source: Information on forensics used here comes from Dillon, H. (1999). Forensics scientists: A career in the crime lab, *Occupational Outlook Quarterly,* 4(43), 2–5.

through a "crime stoppers" program where they are not identified. Some function only in a one-time situation, while others regularly work for specific officers.

Informants should be assigned to one control officer, with a second officer as a backup. All contacts during the course of the investigation should be made with the primary control officer. The backup officer can become acquainted with the informant by attending occasional meetings with the primary officer. Dealing with informants can be laden with problems; therefore, one major responsibility of the primary officer is to continually evaluate the reliability of the informant. This is accomplished by regularly checking information provided by the informant against other sources of information. This practice is extremely important because the motives of the informant may change during the course of the investigation.

THE SECRET INFORMANT   In court, the informant's information is considered as hearsay and will be evaluated for reliability. If the information is deemed to be reliable and credible, it can be accepted under certain conditions. Conversely, if the court is doubtful about the informant's reliability, the information may be rejected. The source of the information is the primary question. In other words, who is the informer? If he or she is a reputable citizen, public officer, or an informant with an established track record of reliability, the information will carry more weight than information from an anonymous phone call.

When working with an informant, control officers should be careful about promising to keep the identity of the informant secret. Investigators must ask themselves: "Is this a promise I can keep or might I be compelled later on to disclose the informant's identity?" In many states, as well as in the federal government, if the identity of the informant cannot be kept secret, the prosecution has a choice either to disclose the informant's identity or to dismiss the case against the defendant in which the informant's information was used. All potential informants should be made aware of this possibility.

On the other hand, if the informant's role in the crime is basically that of a bystander and if the investigators develop independent evidence to support prosecution of the case, the informant's identity is not relevant. Other occasions may present themselves in which an informant may provide information to officers but may not be available to testify in court (hearsay). A number of Supreme Court cases address this issue. In *Draper* v. *United States,* informant hearsay information to make a warrantless arrest was approved by the courts.

In *Aguilar* v. *Texas,* the court reaffirmed previous decisions that the affidavit for an arrest warrant need not include the personal or direct observation of the affiant and that it can be based on hearsay information from a secret informant. A few years later, *Spinelli* v. *United States* resulted in a two-prong test for informants to determine when an unnamed informant's information could be used to show probable cause. These prongs were (1) that the informant be reliable, and (2) that the informant's information be reliable. After 15 years, the two-pronged test was abandoned in *Illinois* v. *Gates* (1983). In this case the Bloomingdale, Illinois, Police Department received an anonymous letter containing the following statements: that Gates and his wife were involved in selling drugs, that the wife would drive her car to Florida on a designated date to be loaded with drugs, that Gates would fly down and drive the car back to Illinois, that the trunk would be loaded with drugs, and that Gates had more than $100,000 worth of drugs in his basement. Acting on the tip, a police officer acquired Gates' address and learned that he had made reservations for a flight to Florida. Arrangements for surveillance of the flight were made with the DEA. Surveillance officers learned that Gates took the flight, stayed overnight in a hotel room registered in his wife's name, and left the following morning with a woman, driving northbound in a car bearing Illinois license plates.

A search warrant was obtained for Gates' house and car based on the information from the informant's letter and the surveillance. When Gates arrived home, the police served the warrant and searched for drugs. A quantity of marijuana was recovered, Gates was charged, and he was subsequently convicted. The issue in this case is whether the affidavit and anonymous letter provided sufficient probable cause for the issuance of the warrant. The Supreme Court ruled yes, and in doing so, abandoned the old standard two-prong test of *Aguilar* and *Spinelli* in favor of a "totality-of-the-circumstances" approach.

An old adage says, "An investigator is only as good as his informant." It is therefore important for the investigator to remember that the informant's job is only to provide information, not to run the investigation. Many legal pitfalls can emerge when investigators do not keep this principle in mind, and cases may ultimately be lost in court if departmental guidelines are not followed when interviewing, handling, and paying informants (see also Chapters 6 and 11).

In Retrospect

The police are the most visible component of the criminal justice system, yet one of the most misunderstood. It is therefore important to understand the day-to-day operations of the police in order to identify problems and solutions to their effectiveness and efficiency. The investigative function is a dynamic component of the modern police organization, although it is comprised of a comparatively small number of sworn personnel.

Investigations can be either proactive or reactive in nature and must be conducted in accordance with strict rules of procedure to ensure a prosecutable case. Although policing is constantly undergoing some form of change in American society, it is clear that the police must be responsive to the public they serve and each official function of the police organization must strive to guarantee public satisfaction.

Improve Your Professional Vocabulary

electronic evidence
latent evidence
method of operation

physical evidence
police lineup
proactive

sleeper cells
surveillance

Discussion Questions

1. List and discuss the various types of investigations that present themselves to law enforcement officers.
2. What is the difference between reactive and proactive investigations?
3. To what extent does the preliminary investigation play a role in the overall investigative process?
4. Explain and discuss various problems associated with the use of informants in a criminal investigation.
5. List and discuss the four "fundamental realms of information" that help identify a suspect's incentive to commit a crime.
6. Discuss the measures a professional criminal investigator should observe during a police lineup to protect the constitutional rights of suspects.
7. Identify the ways in which criminal investigation differs from that portrayed by television.
8. Discuss the ways in which patrol investigations can be utilized by a police department.
9. List and discuss the ways in which undercover operations are dangerous to the investigator.
10. Identify the various types of surveillance commonly used in criminal investigations.

Notes

1. Poland, J. (1989). Detectives. In W. G. Bailey, ed., *Encyclopedia of police science.* New York: Garland, 142–145.

2. Dempsey, John & Linda Forst (2005). *An introduction to policing*, 3rd ed. Belmont, CA: Wadsworth Publishing Company.

3. Haberman, Clyde (2007). Plain clothes, perilous choices. *Subject to Debate*, January, pp. 1–5.

4. Lyman, M. D. (2008). *Criminal investigation: The art and the science*, 5th ed. Upper Saddle River, NJ: Prentice Hall.

5. Technical Working Group for Electronic Crime Scene Investigation, Electronic Crime Scene Investigation: A Guide for First Responders (Washington, DC: National Institute of Justice, 2001), from which much of the information in this section has been taken.

6. Ibid.

7. Computer Crime and Intellectual Property Section, US Department of Justice, Searching and Seizing Computers and Obtaining Electronic Evidence in Criminal Investigations (Washington DC, US Department of Justice, 2002), http://www.USDOJ.gov.

8. Technical Working Group for Electronic Crime Scene Investigation, Electronic Crime Scene Investigation: A Guide for First Responders (Washington, DC: National Institute of Justice, 2001).

9. FBI website (www.fbi.gov); Accessed April, 2006.

10. Johnson, Aisha & Greg Staples. (2006). Geographic policing initiative in Roanoke. The *Police Chief*, 78–79.

11. Ibid.

CHAPTER 7

Police Culture

This chapter will enable you to:

- Define the police culture.
- Consider departmental and supervisory variables associated with the police subculture.
- List the various components of the police subculture.
- Think about how the police subculture impacts police decision making.

- Understand the role and development of the police officer subculture.
- Learn how officer cynicism develops and ultimately affects police performance.
- Identify the cultural variables that contribute to police use of force.
- Identify the cultural variables relating to police use of force.

O n December 28, 2006, in Santa Ana, California, police officers were conducting surveillance on a career criminal, Oscar Gabriel Gallegos, who was wanted for the attempted murder of two Long Beach police officers. An illegal alien with prior deportations to Mexico, Gallegos had extensive criminal history that included arrests for assault, weapons violations, making terrorist threats, and narcotics possession. After being pulled over for routine traffic stop, Gallegos jumped out of his vehicle and shot at the two law enforcement officers. Luckily, both officers survived. Six days later, when the surveillance team located Gallegos in a strip mall, the fugitive opened fire again. The officers returned fire and killed him.

This case illustrates one of the most difficult aspects of law enforcement—the decision to use deadly force and accepting responsibilities that go with doing so. With these considerations in mind, questions arise, including which aspects of police organization and culture led to the use of lethal force in this case? And, what does this incident show about police culture?

WHAT IS THE POLICE CULTURE?

Over the years, academic studies have suggested that the nature of the police profession along with the experiences of officers caused them to group together into their own subculture, which is commonly referred in the police literature as *the police culture*, or the police subculture. The subculture can be readily recognized. For example, if someone who is not a police officer enters a nightclub late at night and hears a group of men and women engaged in conversation using words such as snitches, pops, and collars, he or she may not understand what is being said. If the same person, however, were an off-duty police officer having a few drinks with fellow officers, each word would have a specific meaning and make perfect sense.

In a general sense, the word *culture* refers to patterns of human activity or the way of life for a society. It includes informal codes or rules addressing manners, language, dress, behavior, rituals, and systems of belief. The key components of culture are values, norms, and institutions. In this context, values comprise ideas about what in life seems important. These tend to guide the rest of the culture. Norms are made up of expectations of how people will behave in various situations. Moreover, each culture has ways of enforcing its norms. Finally, institutions are the structures of the society within which values and norms are transmitted.[1]

Subcultures are pervasive and large societies or groups of people with distinct sets of values, attitudes, behavior, and beliefs that separate them from a larger culture of which they are a part. For example, physicians, lawyers, teachers, and even construction workers have their own unique subcultures. Occupational, religious, or other factors often define subcultures. Researchers have pointed to a separate police culture or subculture. This is not to suggest that the police do not share the same dominant values of the larger culture. The police culture or police subculture is a combination of shared norms, values, career patterns, goals, lifestyles, and occupational structures that differ from the combination held by the rest of society. Like most cultures, the police subculture is characterized by clannishness and secrecy in addition to isolation from those who are not part of the group. Police officers work with other police officers during the course of their workday. Many socialize together after work and on days off, often to the exclusion of others—even "nonpolice" friends and family. Typically, when police officers socialize, they talk about their jobs and experiences.

As with many public service professions, police work involves **shift work**. Shift work typically involves working shifts of duty, as from 4 to 12 (4:00 P.M. to 12 midnight) and weekends and holidays. This makes it difficult for police officers to socialize with the average person who might work a 9-to-5 job.

Many police officers find it difficult to sleep after a tense, busy evening. If they want to socialize or relax after work instead of going home where family members have to get up at 6 to go to their jobs at 6:30 A.M., many officers tend to socialize with their associates from work. As with most shift workers, officers work weekends, and their days off often fall during the workweek.

The spouses of police officers also tend to socialize with other police spouses, and families of police officers typically associate with other police families as well. In time, "the job" is the only world many police officers know.

Research in policing has shown that police officers create their own culture to deal with recurring anxiety and emotional stress that is endemic to policing. For example, Michael Brown, in *Working in the Street*, states that the police subculture is based on the three major principles: honor, loyalty, and individuality.[2]

Officers who engage in dangerous or risky behavior, for example, an officer who is the first one through the door during the service of a high-risk search warrant, earn *honor*. *Loyalty* is a major part of the subculture as well and is considered extremely powerful. The word *backup* is often heard in conversations between police officers. Police officers rely heavily on **backup** by other officers in emergency situations. They also rely on one another's aid when they are challenged, criticized, or facing charges of wrongdoing. Brown states that because of the violence that police must deal with and the resulting bond that occurs, police officers ". . . place the highest value upon the obligation to back up and support a fellow officer."[3]

As such, according to the police subculture, the ideal officer takes risks, is the first on the scene to back up a fellow officer, and is able to handle any situation his or her own way—*individually*.

The constant presence of danger in police work permeates the police subculture and the conversations between officers. Researcher George L. Kirkham discusses the police mistrust of civilians and how police rely on some of their own peer-group support to survive on the streets. In his research on the police subculture he discovered, "as someone who had always regarded policeman as paranoid, I discovered in the daily round of violence which became part of my life that chronic suspiciousness is something that a good cop cultivates in the interest of going home to his family each evening."[4]

Police researcher Egon Bittner states that the esprit de corps develops in police work as a function of the dangerousness and unpleasant tasks police officers are required to do. Police solidarity, a "one for all, and all for one" attitude, Bittner states, is one of the most treasured aspects of the police profession.[5]

Former police officer and police suicide expert, John M. Violanti, conducted research on the police subculture and suicide. He found that entry into law enforcement involves a process of abrupt change from citizen to police officer. This process is very strong in basic training and continues to dominate officers' lives throughout their careers. Police officers can quickly become addicted to excitement and danger, which can decrease their ability to assess the nature of current challenges and interfere with rational decision processes. Through psychological and physiological mechanisms, police officers become ingrained in police work and isolated from other roles such as family, friendships, or community involvement.[6]

Yet another researcher, Eugene A. Paoline III, in his authoritative work, *Rethinking Police Culture: Officers' Occupational Attitudes*, talks about the ways in which police officers perceive and cope with the aspects of their working environments in modern police departments. He notes that the occupational attitudes associated with police culture include distrust and suspiciousness of citizens, assessing people in terms of their potential threat, a "we versus they" attitude toward citizens, and extreme loyalty to the peer group.[7]

Police officers also have their own coping mechanisms. For example, the police personality uses different strategies, including humor and keeping emotional distance between themselves and stressful events, to deal with stress. It has been said that police officers tend to use **gallows humor** or appear disinterested in the suffering of others. Citizens, sometimes wrongly, assume that this attitude of appearing disinterested indicates that the police are uncaring.[8]

In 2003, Paoline produced another study on the police culture. He stated that the unconventional wisdom about police culture hinges on the descriptions of a single occupational phenomenon in which the attitudes, values, and norms of members are homogeneous. However, he believes that as departments continue to diversify and community policing becomes part of the philosophy of policing, there will be more cultural variations. He suggests that researchers should focus their efforts on studying this increased cultural variation of the traditional police culture and how it expresses itself.[9]

An Occupational Subculture

An occupational subculture is made up of a group of specialists recognized by society (and themselves) as having a common culture complete with values, communication, techniques, and related behavior patterns. The law enforcement profession forms a unique occupational subculture through habits their members adopt in their occupation. Studies show that the subculture has a specialized vocabulary, uses esoteric knowledge, makes use of internal sanctions on peers, has a strong sense of unity, and often exercises professional courtesy.

Much has been written about the police subculture and how it forms and operates in our system of justice. In its most basic sense, a subculture develops around a group's perception of the world. Subcultures may be ethnically, racially, occupationally, social class, or gender based. The police subculture is based primarily on the officers' duties, training, the type of people attracted to the profession, and the daily experiences of those in the profession. Subcultures exist in most professional occupations, which include the military, the medical profession, educational fields, and the legal community.

The subculture of a police department is apparent not only in how it responds to community needs but also in the selection and recruitment of officers, training, procedures, and ultimately in the

FIGURE 7.1 The police culture represents one of the closest social and professional relationships. Here Port Authority police embrace at the funeral of a fellow officer.

performance of police officers while engaged in their day-to-day duties. There is little question that all police departments have some form of a police subculture. What remains in question, however, is whether that subculture has been carefully cultivated or whether it has developed on its own without guidance or structure.

For example, there are police organizations in which the use of force is rare, and when an incident involving force arises, the event receives much attention. This type of response reflects the culture of an organization as the use of force is viewed as an uncommon occurrence. As a result, officers working in the department are aware of the type of behavior that is expected of them by fellow officers, police administrators, and the public in general.

The notion of a police subculture was considered first in 1950 by Westley in his study of the Gary, Indiana, Police Department.[10] His objective was to identify "the major social norms governing police conduct and to describe the way they influence police action in specific situations." Westley felt that a distinct subculture existed within the ranks of police, with the norms stressing secrecy and violence. Police were thought to view the general public as adversaries and therefore justified a code of secrecy and deceit to protect themselves from condemnation by citizens. As a result of his research, Westley found that 73% of officers surveyed believed that the public was hostile to the police.

This was generally thought to be so because on a day-to-day basis, police officers rarely met what many people would consider an "average" person. Rather, most police–citizen contacts were with citizens who had broken the law and felt resentment toward the police for being placed under arrest. In addition, police officers also sensed hostility from other components of the community, such as attorneys, social workers, and the media. As a result of this alienation, police officers relied only on themselves in times of crisis and, in doing so, justified the use of force to protect their solidarity.

In accordance with Westley's work, several variables can be considered when determining what contributes to the making of the police culture. As with all things in human nature, mutual experiences contribute to the creation of a bond between individuals. As mentioned earlier, the rigors of application and the acceptance of the police candidate by the organization serve as rights of passage in the profession.

Officers also experience newly formed friendships and acquaintances during the many weeks of intense police academy training. Such relationships endure as a result of the mutual support given each other during academy sessions as well as the social experiences shared by officers after long and tiring days spent in class. Both friendships and professional relationships developed while working as a police officer tend to create a unique brand of socialization. It is generally thought that shared experiences are the greatest contributor to the formation of the police culture, which is often characterized by detachment from society, clannishness, and secrecy (the "blue curtain" of secrecy).

Research has also shown that police officers protect one another from outsiders, often refusing to aid police supervisors or other law enforcement officials in investigating wrongdoing on the part of fellow officers. This protective barrier has been termed the **Blue Wall of Silence**. In addition, the police subculture involves maintaining a tough, macho image and being distrustful of nonpolice persons. Egon Bittner, in his writings about the Blue Wall of Silence, states that "policing is a dangerous occupation and the availability of unquestioned support and loyalty is not something officers could readily do without."[11] The socialization aspect of policing persists throughout most of an officer's career and reinforces the feeling that the profession cuts police off from the rest of society. The socialization process is reinforced by a multitude of instances in the officer's career whereby officers are placed at odds with criminals and their attorneys, certain members of the law-abiding community, the court system, members of the media, police supervisors, and occasionally, other officers. Being placed on the defensive tends, over time, to develop a "macho-type" persona and a feeling of suspiciousness toward all nonpolice persons in the community. In fact, most officers develop an automatic sense of detecting the unusual, from persons who simply "don't fit" to situations that "don't feel right." Much of this is justifiable in that officers must regularly deal with persons who are:

- Under the influence of drugs or alcohol
- Generally hostile toward law enforcement officers
- Considered mentally unstable and dangerous
- Known offenders in the community

These examples illustrate that officers may easily develop a sense of distrust and cynicism toward much of society.

SIX CORE BELIEFS

Other research has shown that the police profession embraces six core beliefs at the heart of the police culture. These include:

1. Police are the only real crime fighters; the public wants an officer to fight crime; other agencies, both public and private, only play at crime fighting.
2. No one else understands the real nature of police work. Lawyers, academics, politicians, and the general public have little concept of what it means to be a police officer.
3. Loyalty to colleagues counts above everything else. Police officers have to stick together because everyone is out to get the police and make the job more difficult.
4. The war against crime cannot be won without bending the rules. Courts have awarded criminal defendants too many civil rights.
5. Members of the public are basically uncooperative and unreasonably demanding. People are quick to criticize police unless they need police help themselves.
6. Patrol work is the pits. Detective work is glamorous and exciting.[10]

For the most part, the forces that support a police culture develop out of on-the-job experiences. The majority of officers who join the police force do so because they want to help people; fight crime; and have an exciting, interesting, and prestigious career with a high degree of job security.[11] Recruits often find that the social reality of police work is not the same as their original career goals. For the most part, they are unprepared for the emotional turmoil and conflict that accompany police work today.

Membership in the police culture is one-way; recruits adjust to the practices of police work according to those officers who have seniority and influence in the organization.[12] The culture encourages decisiveness in the face of uncertainty and the ability to make split-second decisions that might later be subject to extreme criticism by supervisors and the courts. Officers who view themselves as crime fighters are the ones most likely to value solidarity and depend on the support and camaraderie of their fellow officers.[13] The police subculture encourages its members to draw a sharp distinction between good and evil. Officers, more than mere enforcers of the law, are warriors in the age-old battle between right and wrong.[14] In contrast, criminals are referred as *terrorists* and *predators*, terms that convey the fact that they are evil individuals ready to prey upon the poor and vulnerable. Because the predators represent a real danger, the police culture demands that its members be both competent and concerned for the safety of their peers and partners. Confidence is also translated into respect and authority, and citizens must obey or risk payback.[15]

In summary, the police culture has developed in response to the insulated, dangerous work life of police officers. Policing is a hazardous occupation, and the availability of the unquestioned support and loyalty of their peers is not something officers should readily do without.[16] Nonetheless, some experts fear that the subculture will divide police officers from the people they serve and create an "us against the world" mentality.[17]

STAGES OF INITIATION

Van Maanen, who attended a police academy and then became a police officer in California for a short period of time, published a study on police behavior in 1973. He reported on his experience and observed that four stages of initiation exist when recruits are becoming police officers:

- *Stage 1: Pre-entry choice.* This is the initial decision to join the police force. Van Maanen suggests that those who do so believe that they are entering an elite fraternity and may even know something about the job before making application. Generally, the applicant's original goals are to do something to help society.
- *Stage 2: Admittance.* Once hired, the recruit is required to go through the police academy, where both formal training and informal socialization take place. Van Maanen observed that the police academy was extremely military in structure, with strict rules and regulations governing recruit behavior. One common theme shared in the police academy is that officers must be committed to assisting, protecting, and backing up each other on the job.
- *Stage 3: Change-encounter.* Once completing the police academy, new officers must work with a more experienced officer in a **field-training program**. It is during this on-the-job training that they are more receptive to attitude change than at any other time in their career. Field training quickly teaches the recruit that things are different on the street than they are portrayed in the police academy. In doing so, innovative alternatives to crime problems are suggested, many of which are in violation of police policy and procedure. It is also during this phase that recruits are judged as to whether they have the "right stuff" for police work. They are scrutinized for their knowledge of criminal law and procedure, technical equipment, tactical ability, and possession of good common sense.
- *Stage 4: Continuance-metamorphosis.* Here the recruit is forced to adjust to the realities of police work. Included is the realization that police work operates within a bureaucratic environment and requires considerable paperwork. Through assignments and experiences, officers deal with the emotional aspects of policing. This can include working auto accidents with fatalities, being involved in a shooting or skirmish, getting hurt on the job, and so on. All of these cause officers to reevaluate their career choice and examine their own personal philosophy of crime control, and force officers to become closer to other officers who have had similar experiences.

Van Maanen's research in the four previously discussed stages resulted in his additional research in the area of how and why police officers categorize persons. He asserts that the most common category used by police officers is the "asshole." While it is true that the lingo used by police from one jurisdiction to another will differ somewhat, Van Maanen suggests that the derogatory term *asshole* is one of the most prevalent and usually refers to anyone who challenges the authority of the police or those who victimize others (e.g., drug dealers and assaultive people).[18]

It is true that many police have little tolerance for those who show no respect for the law and for those who are vested with enforcing it; as a result, derogatory labels for those people are adopted by officers. When officers categorize people as "asshole," "scumbag," or "turd," those persons are then viewed as fair game for harsher treatment by the police. Such treatment may include the simple issuance of a citation, verbal abuse, or even harsh physical contact and arrest. Accordingly, those persons who are viewed as deserving harsher treatment by police are also viewed as less deserving of civil treatment as well.

ENVIRONMENTAL "STREET" FACTORS

The street is by far the most important environment in which police officers operate. This is the environment by which themes of territoriality, force, and uncertainty are played out. Officers are assigned to a particular area and become responsible for crime control in that area. In this environment, police behavior reflects the interaction of their personal temperament, the circumstances of the encounter, and the attitudes of the individuals involved in the encounter. The way in which a police–citizen encounter is resolved is an aesthetic through which officers play out their roles as police. For the street officer, this environment can be separated into two types of activity, citizen-invoked interactions and traffic stops.

CITIZEN-INVOKED INTERACTIONS   These interactions occur when a citizen telephones a police department or an alarm is sound and a patrol car responds to the source of the call. This type of interaction accounts for the majority of police–citizen contacts. It is a reactive style of policing and is powerfully shaped by police–citizen relations. For calls involving property crimes, police can do little more than take a report. The likelihood of solving a property crime is distant, and citizens are aware of this. Accordingly, the police officer is often the verbal target of a citizen's frustration and the police become frustrated in their reactive role, locked into dealing with the problems caused by crime without being able to actually do anything about it. As a result, these encounters tend to be dispiriting for police and citizens alike; they tend to be perfunctory and ceremonial, satisfying the record-keeping requirements of crime reporting and the needs of insurance companies.[18]

The level of frustration police officers deal with in property crime is also experienced in their dealings with violent crime. Typically, violent crimes are felonies and about half of felonies are assaults, depending on the specific offense category. Of course, a higher clearance rate is associated with those crimes when the victim is also a witness to the crime. In spite of Hollywood glamour, dealing with violent crimes is not particularly satisfying. They involve rough, ordinary crimes of impulsive violence between friends and acquaintances.[19] Instead of providing police with a satisfactory sense of work accomplished, they often reveal the seedy, coarse, and destructive side of ordinary human relations. Moreover, such crimes tend to be repetitive, involving assailants and victims the police have been in contact with previously and who are involved in crimes that police can do little about. In addition to failing to provide the police officer with a sense of satisfaction, these contacts tend to breed cynicism and disillusionment.[20] As with property crimes, very little can be done by police to prevent violent crimes.

TRAFFIC STOPS   Patrol officers also routinely come into contact with the citizenry through traffic stops. Perhaps because stops are so mundane in the scope of police activity, observers of the police have paid them little attention. However, traffic stops are integral to the patrol task. Through formal and informal quotas, traffic stops are semi-articulated—officers aren't assigned particular stops, but they often face departmental expectations that they will issue a certain number of citations. Public response to citations is less than friendly. Even in the rarest of traffic stops, when a citizen responds to the news of his or her violation and impending ticket with "you're absolutely right, officer. I deserve the ticket and I will be more than careful in the future," cops know the citizens are giving a better shot at appearing apologetic in the hopes that they will be forgiven.

In spite of the seeming autonomy and low visibility of police attributed by many authors to contemporary patrol practices, police–citizen interactions are increasingly modulated through the organization. As a result, much of the police subculture stems from this extraordinary task ambiguity and the way in which administrators seek to control line officer–citizen encounters by controlling inputs and outputs through communications and dispatch.

"US VERSUS THEM"

A number of years ago, Richard Herzog, a King County (Washington) sheriff's deputy was killed trying to restrain a man who had been running naked in traffic. The man, Ronald Matthews, turned and attacked Herzog who pulled out his pepper spray instead of his firearm. Matthews knocked Herzog to the ground and grabbed his holstered gun and shot him several times. In the days following his death, the question on the minds of the law enforcement community in Seattle was, "why didn't Herzog draw his gun?" For many, the answer came down to racial politics. County executive Ron Sims, the highest-ranking African-American in the city, had no doubt that Herzog had been inhibited using his weapon because he was white and Matthews was African-American. Several killings of African-American suspects by white police officers in the months before Herzog's death—and the ensuing criticism—Sims said, made police officers afraid to protect themselves in situations involving African-Americans.

Racial tension is one of the many on-the-job issues that makes law enforcement such a challenging and often difficult career: When faced with these issues, sometimes police officers make the right decisions, and sometimes they make the wrong ones. In the worst-case scenario, as with Deputy Herzog, even a seemingly "right" decision may have an unexpected outcome.

DEPARTMENTAL FACTORS

Yet another environment in which police officers exist is that of the organizational administration.[21] As a general rule, **line officers** are expected to be in the street performing their duties on a day-to-day basis. For the most part, they are physically present at the police station twice each day—prior to and at the end of their regular shift. Pogrebin and Poole (1988) described both the beginning and the end of shift work as follows.[22]

ROLL CALL   Before the beginning of each shift, officers arrive at the police station and go to their locker room to change into their uniforms. They then go to a briefing room for assignments and roll call. As a rule, the briefing session will last anywhere from 15 to 20 minutes, during which officers receive information on the activities of the previous shift or the focus of the current shift and any new policy or procedures that have been adopted. Shift sergeants, who often conduct a roll call, identify specific dangers the officers may face during the course of their shift and acknowledge those officers who have done a good job in dealing with past issues.

The roll call session may also contain mild criticisms of officers. A number of other things can also occur during the course of a roll call. For example, some officers may be singled out for unpleasant duty or may be assigned partners with whom they would rather not work. Jocular humor provides a way in which officers maintained face when subjected to criticism during roll call.[23] During the periods of time before and after roll call, when officers are on their way to or from their police units, they talk and exchange information. Much of this information is exchanged outside the presence of supervisors. In fact, it could be argued that some of the most important information of the day is sometimes shared among officers on their way to their cars, away from superior officers but not in their cars, where their conversation can be monitored by the police dispatcher.

SHIFT END   When the shift is over, officers return to the briefing room to complete paperwork. Typically, the reports are reviewed by their sergeants and time is spent in briefing. As Pogrebin and Poole note, officers often spend more time than necessary here, relaxing and exchanging stories about shift activities. Shift end is consequently an environment for the types of interaction and storytelling that contribute to the creation of local cultural knowledge. The end of the shift can also extend to the local tavern or to officers' residences, furthering interaction and storytelling—what some observers call "bullshit sessions."

SUPERVISION BY SERGEANTS   Sergeant supervision is relatively informal, occurring prior to and during patrol activity. Sergeants are the first to link in the chain of command above that of a line officer. They are responsible for the supervision of the line officers during patrol. Many people believe that the Sergeant is one of the most influential persons over the day-to-day activities of officers, but there is evidence that sergeants exercise little control over line personnel.[24] Alan Maxfield (1983), studying arrest, citation, and warrant behavior of officers, discovered that sergeants had no substantive attacks on officers line activities, and only in a few cases did supervisors' emphasis on work quantity affect officers total output. Interestingly, even the perception that they worked under arrest quotas had scant impact on arrest practices. The implications were clear:

> The influence of first-line supervisors in directing the behavior of officers is seriously limited. Even though supervisors emphasize a particular performance criterion or suggest that a certain level of performance be met, officers under their command do not seem to respond positively to these cues.[25]

Stated differently, sergeants themselves appear to be loosely associated with the police culture.

INTERNAL EVALUATION   Officers are articulated to the organization through internal evaluation procedures. Rule violation may be mandatory, for example, when an officer fires a service weapon, or may occur under subpoena, when an officer is being investigated for misconduct or is a witness to other wrongdoing. This is a process that is most feared by officers.[26] Ideally, internal evaluation will penetrate police culture and curb its excesses. However, internal evaluation is often perceived by line officers as an arbitrary tactic used by management to "hang officers out to dry" rather than as a tool for the uncovering of wrongdoing. Observers of police reform have consistently failed to realize that the internal review and evaluation process is a primary source of the development of the police culture.

STANDARD OPERATING PROCEDURE (SOP)   The rules with which officers must conform are known as standard operating procedures (SOP), which are intended to guide police encounters in specific circumstances. They are written by department administrators and reflect state and municipal influences over police conduct. SOP is typically a thick manual that defines the enormous collection of rules and regulations that tell officers what they can and cannot do in various circumstances. Representing the rules by which the organization seeks to coordinate its functions, the SOP provides little insight into the creative process officers use to deal with their most uncompromising concerns—unpredictable police–citizen interactions. Police officers instinctively recognize that SOP is a tool used punitively, always in retrospect, by managers who seek to protect themselves from line-level mistakes. For many line officers, SOP represents the systemic formalization of department "bullshit."

Police officers are in contact with people on a regular basis. They function under a set of rules and procedures that are established by the institution for which they work. For example, police officers interact with courtroom personnel at the courthouse and occasionally in the station house. The police interact with the public primarily on the streets in particular traffic stops or in the homes of citizens when responding to calls for service. They may also be called back to the station to be held accountable for actions that are not in compliance with departmental policies or norms. These environments tend to be replicated in a similar fashion across municipal districts. Furthermore, the work and the organization of squads is influenced by radio, television, movies, newspapers, and other media that carry notions of police values and behavior.

The institutional environment in which police officers work can be complicated. For example, patrol officers are not presented with a single environment in which they conduct their work, but instead they are confronted by a series of environments, each with its own particular expectation of the police. These expectations can't vary across different groups in any particular jurisdiction, and line officers have to present themselves appropriately to these different audiences.

POLICE CULTURE AND THE COURTS

Once an arrest has been made by a police officer, the police are then connected with another component of the criminal justice system—the courts. There are several components to this relationship. First, police are connected with the courts through the service of warrants. If the police suspect that a crime has occurred and that evidence for the crime exists, they must seek a warrant, unless there is a warrantless basis to obtain information or evidence. Doing so can be a frustrating process.

A number of additional circumstances connect the police with the courts. If an officer has made a felony arrest, for example, he or she will have to appear at a preliminary hearing. An officer may face cross-examination and direct examination. Even more frustrating to a line officer is that the case may be postponed, and the officer will have to reappear multiple times during this and subsequent proceedings. An officer's work, time off, and, even vacation may be disrupted at the whim of the court.

During the course of the pretrial activities, the defense has the right of discovery, to find out about all evidence that may be used against the defendant at trial. The trial itself may demand precious off-duty time. All testimony is recorded and available for reference by the defense for future use. An officer's legitimacy will be measured by the police report, the transcripts of earlier proceedings, the interview with the district attorney, and the quality of the evidence brought by the officer.

The extent to which police officers are considered credible in the courtroom is based on the legality of their behavior. During the course of patrol, officers can rely on the presence of a wide variety of subtle clues in deciding where and how to intervene in the affairs of the citizen. **Instinct**, such as the presence of probable cause, may guide their behavior. And arrest may represent a desire to bring to justice some "asshole" rather than a calculated estimate of the presence of probable cause.[27] While on patrol, officers learn how to use personal authority to handle situations. In the courtroom, credibility involves the quality of the evidence and demeanor in front of the judge; officers must express obedience to the judge.

Opposed to the common belief that criminals rarely beat the law because of liberal due process protections, courts operate basically as most people would like them to operate. Samuel Walker notes that, of the cases brought from the police to the courts, approximately 30% of all cases are rejected by the prosecutor during the pretrial period. This should not be surprising: Arrests have a lower evidentiary standard and noble cause (that the crime in fact occurred and the person did it) than do courts (beyond a reasonable doubt, or a moral certainty of will). This lower standard and the even lower standard for an initial intervention into citizens' affairs—reasonable suspicion—enable the police to conduct their work unhampered by the substantial rigors of proof beyond a reasonable doubt needed for conviction.[28]

Of the cases that are accepted for prosecution, about 95% result in a conviction of some type of penalty. When prosecutors don't carry cases forward, it's for obvious reasons of lack of evidence or witnesses. Due process issues are simply irrelevant to the day-to-day activity of the court. In fact, it is extraordinarily rare that a case of murder, robbery, or rape is rejected for due process reasons: Statistically, less than 1% of such cases are rejected for due process reasons.[29]

THE MEDIA

The next area of articulation is with members of the media, who frequently interact with the police. Newspaper reporters are social control agents whose influence can both negatively and positively affect the police. The police are aware of this and seek their sanction through co-op strategies. For example, Ericson has observed,

> . . . the police try to incorporate the news media as part of the policing apparatus. They do so by giving journalists physical space within police headquarters and by making them part of the everyday social and cultural practices in the police organization.[30]

Some news reporters, especially those in the "inner circle," frequently carry scanners so that they, like the police, can arrive at the scene of breaking crime events. These are often the individuals who support the police and may have worked with them for a number of years. For the most part, their values are same to those of the police culture. At the scene of criminal activity, the police try to steer the flow of information to friendly reporters and avoid the release to others who might also look at the conduct of the police.

Police manage the release of friendly information through the inner circle whenever possible. They seek to otherwise tightly control release of information that might ideologically cast a negative light on the department. The careful use of secrecy and silence enables the police to control information to nonfriendly press, while inner circle reporters will censor themselves.[31]

In brief: The relationship between line officers and these groups helps define police subculture. The values, stories, metaphors, and meanings that give each police culture its unique identity stem from police officers' relations with these groups in one way or another. Because culture is grounded in the relations of line officers with these groups, culture has an immediacy and practicality often overlooked by students of culture. The manner in which police deal with these groups and share knowledge with recruits is what the police culture is all about.

EXERTING AUTHORITY

Yet another revealing study was done by Muir, who conducted interviews with 28 police officers in Oakland, California, in the late 1970s.[32] He observed not only that many officers are comfortable in exercising their authority, but also that many officers respond differently when doing so. He considered two variables in distinguishing between officer styles: (1) The degree of compassion shown by officers while they exercise their authority and (2) how comfortable officers were while exercising their authority. As a result, Muir identified four distinct types of police officer behavior:

1. The *professional* officer is comfortable with his or her role but compassionate in the use of it. Coercion is sometimes employed if it is viewed as serving a worthwhile purpose.
2. The *reciprocator* is not comfortable in exercising his or her authority but may be compassionate. This officer attempts to persuade suspects to cooperate while not relying on coercion.
3. The *enforcer*, although comfortable exercising his or her authority, is not compassionate. Generally, coercion is employed too often and with little hesitation, as enforcers believe that they have many enemies.
4. The *avoider* is neither compassionate nor comfortable with his or her vested authority. As the term implies, the *avoider* will often dodge certain police responsibilities to avoid making ripples with police managers and supervisors.

"Stop-Snitching" Street Code Hampers Police in Chicago

"If someone did something to your mother and you tell on them, is that snitching?" Ronald Moten asks young people in Washington, D.C.'s toughest neighborhoods. They shake their heads "no." But, "If a white man came to your community and did a drive-by [shooting], would you tell?" The typical response: "Hell yeah!"

Moten, a co-founder of the anti violence group Peaceoholics, has a simple, but controversial message: "Stop snitching" may sound like righteous street conduct, but there are built-in exceptions. In fact, he explains, it's only criminals who traditionally are discouraged from ratting out a crime buddy. He says, "The code is not supposed to apply to law-abiding citizens, which is what most people are."

But even young people who admit that talking to the police isn't always bad still need persuading that providing tips about crimes is a good thing, even when the victims aren't their mothers. "They've been brainwashed that there's something wrong with being a good citizen," Moten says. In recent years, police and prosecutors in D.C. and other cities around the country have been running into stone walls because of uncooperative witnesses in inner-city neighborhoods.

In Chicago, police blame their inability to solve some two-thirds of local murders on a "no-snitching" code fueled by an underground media campaign using all the tools of modern marketing. During the summer of 2007, a man wearing a T-shirt bearing the image of a tombstone and the words "RIP Snitches" was ejected from a Chicago courthouse. That same year the police solved only 36% of the city's 443 murders, roughly the same percentage as the year before. According to Chicago Police Department's Chief of Detectives Maria Maher, "A lot of people will not cooperate with the police because it is not the thing to do."

The year before, in Pittsburgh, the alleged victim of an attempted murder was wearing a "stop-snitching" T-shirt as he was about to take the witness stand. When prosecutor Lisa Pellegrini told him to reverse the shirt, he refused and walked out of the courthouse. The judge threw out the case.

Baltimore produced one of the most notorious examples of "no-snitch" propaganda—a rough-hewn 2004 video that's still circulating on DVD. "Stop Snitching" featured a gun-toting man who raps: "They're giving evidence to the pigs. I'll . . . destroy your house like you had 100 elephants in your crib." The makers of the DVD knew whereof they spoke. Cameraman Akiba M. Matthews was later convicted and sent to prison for his intent to distribute heroin. Police in Baltimore acknowledged

that the DVD got them interested in Matthews—a sign of how much the video infuriated Maryland law-enforcement officials. "Think how bold criminals must be to make a DVD," Baltimore Circuit Judge John M. Glynn said. "It shows that threatening snitches has become mainstream—so much so that they make a DVD joking about it."

Indeed, Rodney Bethea, the independent Baltimore-based producer behind the video, reportedly has made a sequel, set for release this year. According to the *Baltimore Sun*, the new video features a small boy exclaiming, "We don't know who snitches are, but when we find out, we gonna bust a cap," or shoot the snitches.

Word of the "stop snitching" code didn't remain in the underground media. In 2007, rap star Cam'ron told interviewer Anderson Cooper on CBS' "60 Minutes" that he wouldn't tell police even if he knew a serial killer was living next door. After a furor erupted, Cam'ron added fuel to the fire by saying that tipping police to a crime would hurt his business. The rapper then proclaimed a change of heart, saying he understood that earlier comments might offend crime victims.

Some hip-hoppers, however, took a strong anti crime line from the beginning. A founding father of the genre, Chuck D of Public Enemy, has denounced the "stop snitching" campaign. Writing on the group's Web site, he condemns "violent drug thug crime dogs, who've sacrificed the black community's women and children."

But Moten adds that another motive not to snitch often comes into play, one that is understandable. "They feel that something might happen to them—which is a good reason not to tell." One of the most notorious cases of retaliation against witnesses occurred in Baltimore in 2002, when seven members of a family died in an arson fire at their home after they reported neighborhood drug dealing to police.

Police have to take those fears into account, Moten wrote in the *Washington Post* last year. "Showing up in uniform and knocking on someone's door could get an innocent person killed. If police are clumsy in their investigations and let word out about who is cooperating, that can also lead to more bloodshed."

But making people feel secure if they do the right thing is not easy, he says. "Me and you both know that if a person in [affluent] Georgetown is a witness, they're not about to have to sell their house [to leave the neighborhood]. But we also know that in Georgetown, 50 people will talk. In our communities, you only get one or two people who want to speak. The culture can intimidate people."

Sources: Annie Sweeney, "Police blame 'no snitching' for unsolved murders," *Chicago Sun-Times*, January 22, 2008, p. A13; Rick Hampson, "Anti-snitch campaign riles police, prosecutors," *USA Today*, March 29, 2006, p. A1; Julie Bykowicz, "Another weapon in war on witnesses," *Baltimore Sun*, December 12, 2004, p. A1; Julie Bykowicz, "Thug life—the sequel," The *Baltimore Sun*, December 23, 2007, p. B1; Lynn Anderson, "'Stop Snitching' cameraman arrested," *Baltimore Sun*, March 3, 2005, p. B1; Ryan Davis, "Homemade DVDs about informing gave police clues," *Baltimore Sun*, December 4, 2004, p. A1; Ronald Moten, "The real meaning of 'snitching,'" *Washington Post*, August 19, 2007, p. B2.

As with other researchers in the area of police behavior, Muir's work aids us in understanding why police officers do what they do and behave in the manner in which they do. Regardless of how police officers acquire their individual behaviors, they will favor a distinct police officer working style.

Police Culture and Force

To a great extent, the use of force is at the heart of police work. In the United States, democratic principles fuel our belief in law over order and the police are expected to behave objectively and fairly in the performance of their duties. We seek laws that are just and dispassionately enforced. We want police to use force when necessary, but to avoid its use unless absolutely necessary. It could be said that our distrust of force is so strong that we encircle the police with due process laws, internal review, education, training, and professional standards, and threaten them with civil litigation, public disclosure, and loss of employment in even the most minor misapplication of force against a citizen.

After doing so, we turn around and ask our cops to deal with our most profound social problems and to use whatever force is necessary to protect us from the criminal and the uncivilized. When police don't quickly resolve problems, we complain bitterly. It is a contradictory and impossible responsibility. When police show too much passion, do their work too well, display too much aggression, or exceed some bureaucratic guideline, we seek their punishment. We shake our heads in horror, failing to comprehend that they have done precisely what we expected them to do. Police culture provides a barrier of protection behind which they can hide so that they can do whatever we want them to do, at the same time without incurring our chastisement. In fact, in many regards, police culture protects us as much as it does them.

Fictional media portrayals of the police frequently focus on their capacity for force. From positive portrayals of the police in productions such as *Miami Vice*, a popular television series of the 1980s, to *Prince of the City*, a movie about entrenched police corruption in New York, the capacity to use force makes the police a powerful source of media inspiration. We are simultaneously interested and terrified by the social presence of force and its destructive implications. The police indeed have power, and the media know what sells.

What does not sell, however, and what we don't see, are the police living ordinary lives, facing the same daily petty problems experienced by the rest of us. As thoughtful, ordinary people, the police are invisible and we don't see them; they are known to us only through their evocative and sometimes controversial symbols: centurion and blue, sunglasses, nightstick, badge, and gun. We don't see their pain, their celebrations, and their humanity. We don't see the culture in which they, like all groups, engulf themselves.

Force is central to the literature on policing. The idea that force is central to the work of the police is common among academic studies of the police. Writers, seeking to understand the unique characteristics of police work and culture, almost always focus on some aspect of the use of force. The use of **coercive force**, more than any other idea about the police, seems to capture the unique role that the police play in contemporary American society.

Westley and the Use of Police Force

Westley (1970) was among the first of police scholars to recognize the importance of force to the police and the paradox that implied in a democratic society.[32] He argued that, as a nation, the United States is committed to the virtues of peace—virtues embodied in the law of the Constitution. So ingrained is the notion of peace to our social sensibilities that we not only seek peace in our social relationships, but we believe that social relationships be maintained only through peaceful means. Accordingly, we limit as much as possible the use of force by citizens to solve their problems.[33]

In order to eliminate violence as an acceptable way to conduct our affairs, society creates a "core institution whose special competence and defining characteristic is its monopoly on a general right to use coercion or force."[34] The police stand out: Their occupation is inherently offensive to democratic process, yet they and they alone can act as protectors of society.

How are we then to reconcile the offensive nature of routine violence in a democratic society committed to peace? Bittner argued that we must conceal what the police do.[35] The history of the police, he noted, was marked by a tradition of themes that serve to hide the role of a police force and surround the police with harmful themes more acceptable to peaceful citizens.

Bittner, Klockars, and the Mystification of Force

Bittner (1970) contended that police use of force became comprehensible in specific situations, when it was used to resolve particular problems. He called this "situationally justified force."[36] Regardless of the activities police officers were involved, in the common thread that tied them together was the use of coercion to rectify some immediate problems. Police alone had a legitimate use of coercion at their disposal. This use of coercion uniquely marked the police as agents of the state, and set them apart from the public often uncomfortable with the use of force. The inherent contradictions of **situationally justified force** and a democratic society, particularly because coercion is acted out in concrete everyday circumstances of coercive problem-solving, irrevocably separated the police from the public.

Klockars (1991) extended Bittner's ideas to the contemporary community policing movement. Klockars argued that the community policing movement was simply another of the history of "circumlocutions" used by the police to skew what they did—use force to deal with citizens' problems.[37]

Community policing gave police a new legitimacy when the police professionalism movement lost its credibility as a justification for police behavior. As both Klockars and Crank (1994) noted, community policing gained a great deal of headway with a compelling argument that traditional police practices didn't work.[38] However, there was no evidence that tenants of community policing worked either—it gained momentum on a blind faith in the ability of the police to act benignly and favorably on behalf of local communities and neighborhoods. This, Klockars suggested, was simply another mystification of police work. The centrality of coercion to the police, hidden behind a smokescreen of police professionalism and community policing rhetoric, "circumlocuted" the true police role and made coercive encounters more socially palatable.

In the long run, the public uses the police for one reason: So they can deal with situations where "something ought not to be happening about which something should be done now" (Klockars, 1985:16–17). The first part, *something ought not to be happening*, refers to a legal act, but also includes a wide variety of order maintenance situations such as controlling crowd, removing disabled vehicles on the roadway, and calling on an elderly man who hears a suspicious noise at night. The second part, *about which something should be done now*, means that the police deal with situations that need immediate resolution.[39] This is where coercive authority comes in. Klockars notes that, "despite resistance or protest by participants or observers...the general right to use coercive force gives police the right to overcome any and all opposition immediately." From this, Klockars concludes that coercion is at the core of the police role: In response to the question, "Why do we have the police," he responds, "We have them to deal with all those problems in which coercive force may have to be used."[40]

Wilson and the Emotional Content of Force

The idea that police used force is mystified behind ideas of peace is also embedded in the notion that police can act without showing emotions in order to enforce the law in an evenhanded manner. The notion is nonsense. Wilson (1968) was the first to note that police work was carried out in a context that is frequently emotional, and that the police had to get personally involved in order to do their job. Wilson recognized that the dynamics of police work were sensible only in the immediacy of day-to-day interactions with citizens. To understand what police do, one had to recognize the actual circumstances of their interactions with the public.[41] This, not a set of formal policies or job description handed down by department superiors, determines what police officers did in specific encounters.

Police, Wilson observed, were far more likely to deal with order maintenance situations—a family dispute, a loud stereo, a rowdy teenager—than with actual violations of the criminal law. Police–citizen interactions in these kinds of encounters, he argued, were predictable in a way that had disproportionate effect on officers. Police lacked clear guidelines to deal with order maintenance. Where, he asked, did one draw the line between order and disorder? Officers thus approached order maintenance situations from the view of "playing it by ear" or "handling the situation" rather than in terms of "enforcing the law."[42]

The lack of clear legal guidelines in order maintenance situations meant that officers had to use personal authority. They had to get involved, to become emotionally engaged. Rubenstein (1973), citing an officer in his survey, noted "you wear a uniform and a badge, you got a gun, stick . . .—whose gonna give you any trouble? Who would want to fight with you? You learn quick."[43] As he and many others have noted, reliance on formal police authority is rarely enough to deal with problems—indeed, often the presence of the police uniform heightens hostilities. Officers thus become emotionally involved: They cannot do otherwise.[44]

Wilson recognized that emotions were an inevitable part of police–citizen encounters. Many police–citizen encounters, he noted, looked at the character of contests, in which each tested the other to see who would control the situation. The uniform and authority that the police had were not sufficient to gain citizen acquiescence: Personal involvement was necessary.

Wilson's way of looking at police authority is helpful in understanding police–citizen interactions when citizens refuse to do what a police officer tells them to do. It utterly fails to explain police use of force in situations when suspects are citizens who have come under police custody. Yet, such circumstances are disturbingly frequent and repeatedly cited throughout the history of research on the police.[45]

Street-citizen encounters are marked by a powerful and sometimes destructive emotional energy. To understand these energies we must look at how force links with other themes of police work. Officers are motivated by a need to maintain respect; this need is not always acknowledged and is often challenged by citizens. When a citizen fails to acknowledge the personal authority of the police, an encounter takes on a visceral life of its own, and the officer's efforts to reassert control override all other aspects of the encounter. Themes of machismo also bear on citizen encounters. An officer's self-image is brought into question, and it must be accounted for when a citizen fails to acknowledge the officer's authority in any police–citizen encounter.

In Retrospect

The culture of a police organization has distinct rules and loyalties that impact the everyday decisions made by its officers. Research in the police subculture has determined that many police officers develop distinct personality traits that embrace cynicism and authoritarianism.

Police officers also develop their own working style that greatly impacts their decisions on the street.

The sense of police solidarity and unity is one of the strongest components to the police subculture. This has proven to be both a blessing and a curse as it unifies the goals and functions of police while creating an atmosphere of secrecy within.

Improve Your Professional Vocabulary

backup
Blue Wall of Silence
coercive force

field-training program
gallows humor
instinct

line officers
shift work
situationally justified force

Discussion Questions

1. Do you think police officers working on the street will develop a cynical personality and distrust of civilians?
2. Would you like to live in a society in which the police department has abolished police discretion in officers' decision-making processes? Why or why not?
3. Discuss the ways in which the existence of the police culture is advantageous in a democratic society.
4. In what ways does the police subculture impede the effectiveness of a professional police force?

Notes

1. Hoult, Thomas Ford. (1969). *Dictionary of modern sociology.* Totowa, NJ: Littlefield, Adams, 93.
2. Brown, Michael. (1981). *Working in the Street.* New York: Russell Sage Foundation, 82.
3. Ibid.
4. Kirkham, George L. (1981). A professor's street lessons. In R. Culbertson & M. Tezak, eds., *Order under law.* Prospect Heights, IL: Waveland Press, 81.
5. Bittner, Egon. (1979). *The functions of police in modern society.* Cambridge, MA: Oelgeschlager.
6. Violanti, John M. (2003). Suicide and the police culture. In Dell P. Hackett & John M. Violanti, eds., *Police suicide: Tactics for prevention.* Springfield, IL: Charles C. Thomas, 81.
7. Paoline, Eugene A., III. (2001). *Rethinking police culture: officers' occupational attitudes.* New York: LFB Scholarly.
8. Violanti, John M. (2003). Suicide and the police culture. In Dell P. Hackett & John M. Violanti, eds., *Police suicide: Tactics for prevention.* Springfield, IL: Charles C. Thomas, 81.
9. Paoline, Eugene A., III. (2003, May/June). Taking stock: toward a richer understanding of police culture. *Journal of Criminal Justice, 31*(3), 199–214.
10. Sparrow, Malcolm, Mark Moore, & David Kennedy. (1990). *Beyond 911: A new era for policing.* New York: Basic Books, 51.
11. Meagher, M. Stephen, & Nancy Yentes. (1986). Choosing a career in policing: A comparison of male and female perceptions. *Journal of Police Science and Administration, 16,* 320–327.
12. Brown, Michael K. (1981). *Working in the street.* New York: Russell Sage Foundation, 82.
13. Shurnock, Stan. (1988). An empirical examination of the relationship between police solidarity and community orientation. *Journal of Police Science and Administration, 18,* 182–198.
14. Ibid.
15. Ibid.
16. Bittner, Egon. (1980). *The functions of police in modern society.* Cambridge, MA: Oelgeschlager, Gunn, and Hain, 63.
17. Garcia, Vanessa. (2005). Constructing the "other" within the police culture: An analysis of the deviant unit within the police organization. *Police Practice and Research, 6,* 65–80.
18. Van Maanen, John. (1973). Observations in the making of policemen. *Human Organization, 32,* 407–418.
19. Felson, Marcus. (1994). *Crime and everyday life.* Thousand Oaks, CA: Pine Forge Press.
20. Niederhoffer, Arthur. (1967). *Behind the shield.* Garden City, NY: Doubleday.
21. Reuss-Ianni, E. (1983). *Two cultures of policing: Street cops and management.* New Brunswick, NJ: Transaction Books.
22. Pogrebin, & Poole. (1998). Humor in the briefing room. *Journal of Contemporary Ethnography, 17*(2), 183–210.
23. Ibid.
24. See for example: Trojanawicz, R. C. (1980). *The environment of the first-line supervisor.* Englewood Cliffs, NJ: Prentice Hall; Rubenstein, Jonathan, (1973). *City police.* New York, NY: Farrar, Straus, and Girox.
25. Maxfield, Alan. (1983), 82.
26. Perez, Douglas W. (1994). *Common sense about police review.* Philadelphia, PA: Temple University Press.
27. Van Maanaen, John. (1978). The asshole. In P. K. Manning & J. Van Manning, eds., *Policing: A view from the street.* Santa Monica, CA: Goodyear Publishing, 221–238.
28. Walker, S. (1977). *A critical history of police reform.* Lexington, MA: Lexington Books.
29. Walker, S. (1994). *Sense and nonsense about crime and drugs: A policy guide.* 3rd ed. New York, NY: McGraw-Hill.
30. Ericson, Richard B. (1989). Patrolling the facts: Secrecy and publicity in police work. *British Journal of Sociology, 40,* 205–226.
31. Ibid.
32. Westley, W. (1970). *Violence and the police.* Cambridge, MA: The MIT Press.
33. Bittner, Egon. (1970). *The functions of police in modern society.* Washington, DC: National Institute of Mental Health.
34. Klockars, Carl B. (1991). The rhetoric of community policing. In C. Klockars & S. Mastrofski, eds., *Thinking*

about police, 2nd ed. New York, NY: McGraw-Hill, 530–542.

35. Bittner, Egon. (1970). *The functions of police in a modern society.* Washington, DC: National Institute of Mental Health.

36. Ibid., 39.

37. Klockars, Carl B. (1991). The rhetoric of community policing. In C. Klockars & S. Mastrofski, eds., *Thinking about police.* 2nd ed. New York, NY: McGraw-Hill, 530–542.

38. Ibid; Crank, John P. (1994). Watchmen and community: A study of myths and institutionalization in policing. *Law and Society Review, 28*(2).

39. Klockars, Carl B. (1985). The idea of police. *Law and criminal justice studies,* Volume 3. Beverly Hills, CA: Sage.

40. Ibid., 74.

41. Wilson, James Q. (1968). *Varieties of police behavior: The management of law and order in eight communities.* Cambridge, MA: Harvard University Press.

42. Ibid., 32.

43. Rubenstein, Jonathan. (1973). *City police.* New York, NY: Farrar, Straus, and Girox.

44. Wilson, James Q. (1968). *Varieties of police behavior: The management of law and order in eight communities.* Cambridge, MA: Harvard University Press, 33.

45. Van Maanaen, John. (1978). The asshole. In P. K. Manning & J. Van Manning, eds., Policing: *A view from the street,* Santa Monica, CA: Goodyear Publishing, 221–238; Skolnick, J., & J. Fyfe. (1993). *Above the law: Police and excessive use of force.* New York: Free Press, 111–112; National Institute of Ethics. Police code of ethics facts revealed. (International Association of Chiefs of Police [NAACP], 2000 conference, 2000), 1993.

PART 3

Understanding and Managing Police Authority

CHAPTER 8

Police Authority

This chapter will enable you to:

- Learn the processes leading to the arrest decision.
- Understand the role of probable cause in arrest and search and seizure.
- Distinguish between the various types of police discretion.
- Learn how the use of force can be lawfully applied by police.

- Explain how police authority is delegated.
- Appreciate the role of search and seizure in police work.
- Distinguish between legal searches with and without warrants.

Janet Randolph was furious with her husband, Scott. Months of marital tension had reached a boiling point, and he had just disappeared from the family home in Americas, Georgia, with their young son. Janet promptly called the police. A few minutes after two officers arrived at the house, Scott returned home and explained that he had left his son at the neighbor's because he was concerned that his wife would take the boy to Canada. Janet insisted that Scott used drugs and that "items of drug evidence" could be found in the house. The officers asked for permission to search the home. Janet said "yes." Scott said "no."

Eventually, Janet led the police to her husband's bedroom, where they found a straw covered with a powdery substance that turned out to be cocaine. This discovery led to Scott's eventual arrest and indictment for possession of a banned substance. His lawyers claimed that the cocaine could not be used as evidence. According to the U.S. Supreme Court, unless police have an order from a judge called a warrant, the police cannot search a home without the consent of the occupant or unless certain special circumstances exist. In this case, argued Scott's attorneys, the police did not have a warrant, so the search was improper. Prosecutors countered that Janet's consent made the search legal, and she was occupying the home at the time of the incident.

In 2006, the Supreme Court agreed with Scott and held that the search warrant was invalid. "We have, after all, lived our whole national history with an understanding of the ancient adage that a man's home is his castle," wrote Justice David H. Souter. "Disputed permission is thus no match for the central value" of the Constitution.

The Supreme Court's decision, however, was not unanimous. Three justices thought that the search of Scott Randolph's bedroom was reasonable, with Chief Justice John G. Roberts, Jr., arguing that because Scott had agreed to "share" his "castle" with his wife, both have the ability to consent to a police search against the wishes of the other. In effect, each member of the Court had the task of weighing Scott's personal freedom against the ability of Georgia law enforcement to combat illegal drugs.

Police officers in the United States are vested with considerable authority to perform their duties. For example, police officers are given authority to **stop and frisk** persons suspected of criminal involvement, to arrest persons thought to have committed a crime, and to search homes and vehicles where contraband is thought to be located. For officers to perform any of the preceding tasks, adequate probable cause must be present. It is true that as citizens of a democracy, we all must give up some freedom in order to coexist with fellow citizens, but to control crime the police are also expected to operate within the framework of the law. That is, they must conform to the law as it is stated in the Constitution and the Bill of Rights and in federal and state statutes. In short, in today's game of cops and robbers, it is more important to focus on the means by which crime is controlled rather than the end result. As discussed in Chapter 2, the word *democracy* would have little meaning in a society where the police were allowed to stop, search, and arrest any citizen at will and with no just cause. Of the many important provisions of the Constitution, the Fourth, Fifth, and Sixth Amendments are the most important, as they restrict how the government deals with individuals. When police recruits are sworn in as officers, they become agents of the government; therefore, their actions are restricted and subject to the provisions of the law. In this chapter we address the power domain of the police.

DELEGATION OF AUTHORITY

Delegation of authority is a critical component in the chain of command, especially in larger departments. The chief of police delegates authority to division chiefs, who delegate authority to commanders, and so on down through the organization. This structure creates a situation in which every member of a police department is directly accountable to his or her superior. As was the original goal of police reformers, these links encourage discipline and control and lessen the possibility that any individual police employee will have the unsupervised freedom to abuse his or her position. In keeping with the need to delegate authority, police departments and large cities divide their jurisdiction into *precincts*. The precinct commander is held responsible by his or her superiors at police headquarters for the performance of the officers in the precinct.

Police departments also control their officers through the use of written guidelines. These guidelines, which can be found in nearly every law enforcement organization in the country, attempt to standardize police behavior by defining what is acceptable and what is unacceptable. Written guidelines often try to limit the use of discretion by a police officer in any dangerous or stressful situation. Many departments have written policies concerning high-speed automobile pursuits that are designed to ensure that the pursuing officer will not sacrifice public safety in the effort to catch a suspect. Guidelines may also set out a specific procedure that must be followed under certain circumstances. When an officer handcuffs a violent suspect when standing behind his or her back, for example, the officer places the suspect in danger of **positional asphyxia**, a phenomenon that occurs when a person's body position interferes with his or her ability to breathe. To avoid positional asphyxia, some departments have procedural guidelines requiring officers to:

- Roll suspects on their backs immediately after they have been handcuffed
- Ask suspects if they have recently ingested any drugs or have a history of respiratory problems
- Monitor suspects carefully and have medical treatment available
- Be trained to recognize serious breathing difficulties or loss of consciousness[1]

Following these procedures not only will reduce the risk of *positional asphyxia*, but they may also protect the police department against a civil lawsuit should a death occur following an officer's failure to take the precautions.

POLICE DISCRETION

As we begin our discussion of police discretion, let's ask a couple of thought-provoking questions. When a police officer observes a violation, is he or she required to make an arrest? If not, who does get arrested and who is allowed to go free? The most important aspects of police authority are the field officer's powers to make arrests, conduct searches and interrogations of suspects, and even use deadly force if necessary. In performing these functions, an officer's personal discretion plays an important role, since the decision to stop or arrest someone is usually made on an individual basis by the officer. The subject of police discretion has long been a topic of interest to social scientists.

If and how an officer intervenes in any given situation is a product of discretion. In some cases the choice is easy—arresting a robbery suspect in a jewelry store heist. Other times, it is unclear just what to do, such as intervening in a feud between neighbors. The application of discretion is influenced by many different factors, which include the law, department policy, individual characteristics of the suspect, and characteristics of the alleged offense. Furthermore, it can be affected by the influence that other members of the police department have on the officer, such as supervisors and chief executives, who may mandate officers to act (to arrest or not) on offenses they have observed.

Although we encourage police to be vigilant in arresting lawbreakers, it is not realistic for the public to expect the police to enforce each law fully. It could even be argued that a full-enforcement or a "no tolerance" police policy would place the essentials of a free democracy in peril. Courts would be backlogged for months, jails would be even more overcrowded than they already are, and large sections of the public would be reacting against the police. As a result, the police are forced to adopt a policy of selective enforcement, to be used in conjunction with the prudent application of discretion. The police decision-making process takes effect when the police officer makes the decision to arrest one particular suspect over another or to issue a verbal or written warning, to arrest, or to dole out harsh treatment to the violator—all of which are discretionary acts. In brief, the discretion process entails three fundamental decisions on the part of the officer:

1. Whether to get involved in the incident
2. The manner in which to become involved in the incident
3. Selecting options to solve the problem

There are times when a police officer may choose to do nothing, even after a violation has been observed. Generally, for offenses of a less serious nature, as with the case of most traffic offenses and misdemeanors, this is the officer's prerogative. On the other hand, it is usually the policy of police agencies to require officers to make an arrest when a felony offense is involved.

The discretionary decisions made daily by police officers are usually free of examination by superiors. In fact, with the exception of a police action involving the alleged violation of a suspect's constitutional rights, most police officers operate on a daily basis free of much, if any, on-the-spot scrutiny. As a result, freedom to make individual discretionary decisions may sometimes deteriorate into blatant discrimination based on personal bias. So the question can be posed: To what extent are an officer's powers of discretion affected by external variables? Further, what variables tend to influence the officer's discretionary powers? Although many factors can be identified, several have been recognized as being most influential.

Defining Discretion

A number of theorists have attempted to define police discretion. In his writings on discretionary justice, Kenneth Culp Davis wrote, "a police officer has discretion whenever the limits on his power leave him free to make a choice among possible courses of action or inaction."[2] According to this definition, a police officer exercises **discretion** whenever he or she has a choice as to the outcome of the encounter. This means that police officers, especially those operating in a patrol capacity, almost always exercise discretion.

Herman Goldstein categorized police discretion with regard to the application of criminal law into two classes: *invocation discretion* and *noninvocation discretion*. As the labels imply, **invocation discretion** refers to situations in which a officer chooses to invoke or use criminal law and thus issues a citation or makes an arrest. In comparison, **noninvocation discretion** covers those circumstances where the officer could employ the law but elects not to do so.[3] Of these two categories of discretion, Herman Goldstein expressed concern about noninvocation choices as they were "low visibility" options for the law enforcement officer. In other words, if the officer on the street chooses not to cite or arrest, this decision will never be scrutinized by a higher authority. Conversely, if the officer arrests or cites a suspected violator, this choice will be reviewed by a police supervisor, the prosecutor, and probably a court. Noninvocation decisions are problematic because of their low visibility.

In a subsequent work, Davis argued that by virtue of their ability to choose which laws to enforce, when and against whom, the police effectively act as policy makers. It is the police, not the legislature, who decide what behaviors should be controlled by the criminal law and what behaviors can be tolerated. Davis asserts that this power of the police should be recognized by both the police and the legislature and that the police administration devise rules and regulations that will give guidance and structure to the discretionary decisions of police officers.[4]

Goldstein concurred with Davis when he also called for the structuring of police officer discretion through the development of rules and regulations.[5] For example, rulemaking can be observed in the recent trend toward zero tolerance limits for traffic enforcement. A number of police agencies have devised policies to guide officers and their traffic enforcement duties. Implementation of such a policy, for example, might instruct the officer generally to ignore or at least not issue citations in situations where the motorist is not exceeding the posted speed limit by at least ten miles per hour. Consequently, the agency has a ten-miles-per-hour tolerance limit because officers are expected to tolerate a certain degree of speeding as long as it does not exceed the ten-miles-per-hour limit. This tolerance is based on an expectation that motorists may bend the law a little and the fact that speedometers are not always accurate or standardized based on the age of the car, the size and quality of the tires, and other factors.

Officer Perception

Discretion decisions, especially as they relate to order-maintenance situations, are affected strongly by the personal perceptions of the officer. Pepinsky points out that police responses to crime can be categorized as either universalistic or particularistic.[6] In a universalistic response, the officer bases decisions on the characteristics of the situation itself. This would include bank robberies and domestic disputes.

Particularistic responses, on the other hand, are based on the characteristics of the participants. Examples are citizens showing disrespect for the police or dealing with known offenders. Pepinsky suggests that universalistic approaches take time to develop and, because of this, are more widely used by veteran officers. These responses are situation-based and are designed to meet the public's expectations of the officer (as perceived by the officer). For example, the officer may believe that social drinking at public parks is acceptable, but not when people become drunk and disorderly in public.

Approaches that are particularistic are more closely tied to the current situation in which the officer is involved. Whereas universalistic methods serve to reinforce community norms as they are perceived by the officer, particularistic ones support the officer's claims to legitimacy. The officer can establish his or her power and authority when criminal law is invoked against a disrespectful citizen. When conflicts arise between citizens of different status, police support for the higher-status party identifies the police with the higher-, rather than the lower-status group.[7]

The point is that the officer's definition of the situation as being one that warrants formal law enforcement intervention is a discretionary decision. In many situations, particularly those involving order maintenance, the officer is faced with ambiguous information from conflicting sources. In most cases, all parties to a dispute are of the opinion that they are right and that their opponents are wrong. The responding officer seeks to resolve the dispute and restore order, but to do so, an arrest is not the officer's primary goal—controlling the situation is. The ambiguous nature of order-maintenance situations, coupled with the goal of maintaining order, gives rise to the exercise of discretion by police officers.

Departmental Influences

One must remember that in addition to the necessity for an officer to comply strictly with laws affecting his or her jurisdiction, other influences, such as the application of local customs, traditions, and police procedures, also play a role in the decision-making process. These variables vary from one department to the next and rely greatly on the department's chief officer and others in command positions within the organization.

Herman Goldstein expressed his support for controlling police officer discretion through the development of departmental rules and regulations.[8] An example would be establishing tolerance limits for speed enforcement. Many police departments have policies that guide officers in their traffic enforcement efforts. These policies might instruct the officer generally to ignore, or at least not issue traffic citations, in situations where the motorist is not exceeding the posted speed limit by at least five miles per hour. This would mean that the department has a tolerance limit of five miles per hour, or, stated differently, officers are expected to tolerate instances of minor speeding provided that it does not exceed the five-miles-per hour limit. Through such policies police administrators are able to control the discretionary behavior of their officers. Of course, doing so does not guarantee absolute control over police officer behavior, but the policies do encourage consistent and uniform decisions by the police.

American Policing under Fire

The FBI's National DNA Database

In the annals of police work, Colin Pitchfork occupies a special place. It was in 1987 that Pitchfork, a 27-year-old baker in Leicestershire, England, was turned in, so to speak, by the cells of his own body. Three years earlier, researchers at a nearby Leicester University had invented a technique for recording segments of DNA in a pattern resembling a grocery barcode. Police investigating the rapes and murders of two teenage girls took blood samples from more than 5,000 people—every man between 13 and 30, in three villages—and it was Pitchfork's genetic material that matched semen recovered from the bodies. Convicted and given a life sentence, he became the first murderer to be caught just by his DNA. But his story is incomplete without mentioning Rodney Bacon, the 17-year-old boy who was originally suspected of one of the murders and, therefore, was the first person in history to be cleared of a crime based on DNA evidence.

Since then, thousands of people have been convicted by DNA's ability to identify suspects across space and time.

But, hundreds of innocent people have also been freed, often after years behind bars, and in some cases, just short of the death chamber. In fact, since its introduction in U.S. courts in 1987 and through 1999, DNA was used to exonerate 62 wrongfully convicted men.

Since its earliest days, DNA-based investigations have reached back into history to implicate Thomas Jefferson in an extramarital affair with Sally Hemings—a slave; and to suggest that Dr. Sam Sheppard, convicted in 1954 of killing his wife, was innocent. It has also been used to help identify the remains of the last Russian czar and his family. More recently, the nation watched as DNA evidence became central to the 1995 murder case against O. J. Simpson, which fell apart when defense attorney Berry Scheck showed how the police mishandled the crucial blood drops. Finally, in 1998, it was DNA that was used in the case against President William Jefferson Clinton to identify the source of the stain found on the dress owned by Monica Lewinsky. Indeed, the utility of DNA evidence continues to increase as time goes by.

(continued)

American Policing under Fire

The FBI's National DNA Database (continued)

FIGURE 8.1 A San Antonio police officer prepares booking paperwork for an arrestee.

On October 13, 1998, the U.S. Federal Bureau of Investigation (FBI) announced the establishment of a national DNA database. The database was designed to promote significant crime prevention benefits as the program can identify offenders who might otherwise escape detection for their repeat crimes. The FBI states that this exciting technology is designed to solve violent crimes through nationwide information sharing.

Though the FBI has operated state and local DNA databases in 41 states and the District of Columbia since 1991, the National DNA Index System (NIS) serves as a repository for hundreds of thousands of DNA profiles of convicted criminals in all 50 states. And NIS profiles are accessible by police and law enforcement laboratories across the country, allowing speedy tracking of individuals convicted of felony sex offenses and other violent crimes, as well as the crime-scene evidence such as blood, semen stains, or hair.

So far, the U.S. system and a more advanced version in Great Britain have helped solve an impressive number of crimes by linking crime scenes and identifying criminals, even in cases in which no suspects had otherwise been identified. In the United States, state and local FBI databases have already produced more than 400 such matches. As of the preparation of this text, states have collected over 600,000 DNA samples and analyzed, or profiled, more than 250,000. But the FBI, by its own admission, is not sure what the full potential of the new database is, or even how long it will take to become fully operational. One reason is simple enough: The enabling federal legislation, the DNA Identification Act of 1994, sharply circumscribes its lawful uses. To accommodate strict constitutional guidelines for privacy, confidentiality, and lawful search and seizure, the FBI index can collect genetic information only on convicted criminals, crime scenes, and unidentified human remains. Theoretically at least, that means the FBI cannot keep the DNA samples or profile from a person unless that person is convicted of a crime. It also means that police or federal agents cannot collect DNA samples from suspects, not even from indicted, not-yet-convicted, felons—including terrorists—for investigative purposes. What's more, DNA law also sharply limits DNA identification technology to 13 basic probes that can isolate genetic characteristics, but that are unable to provide fuller details of identity, such as hair, eye, or skin color.

While FBI officials are reluctant to admit it, it is likely that as U.S. law enforcement officers gain experience with DNA fingerprinting, monitor arrest records of less constitutionally constrained police abroad, and track the inevitable advance in DNA identification technology, the 1994 law will rapidly become outdated and need amending. Some experts suggest that any future adjusting of the law will significantly expand the segment of the population from whom DNA samples may be collected and will bring to bear increasingly sophisticated DNA identification technology. But because of staffing shortfalls in state and local crime laboratories, the massive backlog of offenders' samples that must be analyzed and profiled, not to mention the new biological evidence that arrives every day, the development of a full-blown National DNA database is likely to take several years before it is fully operational.

However, in March 1999, U.S. Attorney General Janet Reno established a federal panel, the National Commission on the Future of DNA Evidence, which consisted of judges, defense lawyers, police officers, prosecutors, and scientists. Their charge was to conduct a feasibility study of the subject. Driving Reno's request was a recent Louisiana law as well as proposals in North Carolina and New York City to permit widespread DNA testing. But in July 1999, in an official report, the panel expressed to the attorney general its opposition to use DNA testing on everyone charged with a crime, claiming that it would overtax the criminal justice system.

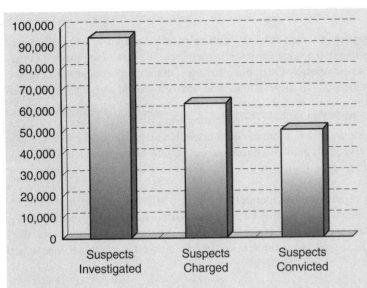

FIGURE 8.2 In 1999, the National Commission of Police Evidence reported that collecting genetic information from everyone arrested would snare data on a large number of innocent people, as a sizable portion of arrestees don't end up convicted of any crime. *Source:* Bureau of Justice Statistics, 1998.

Perhaps it's natural for law enforcement officials to advocate wider latitude in applying DNA identification technology; however, legal watchdogs caution about possible problems presented by the gathering, storing, and utilizing the genetic data on criminals. In response, the FBI formed an in-house DNA advisory group to oversee establishment of the new database. As of the writing of this text, legal challenges were undertaken in 13 states and aimed at laws establishing DNA databases, mostly on Fourth Amendment grounds—but these initiatives were defeated in all states but one. But the ethical question still prevails: How can a government ask citizens to give up bodily tissues that may ultimately incriminate them?

Already, FBI guidelines on the scope of genetic testing have been broadened to include a separate category for juvenile offenders—along with violent felons, burglars, and convicted criminals on parole or probation. The question has been posed: Why are juveniles singled out? The FBI responded by arguing that because juvenile crime is increasingly violent, genetic testing might catch juvenile offenders before they become adult offenders. In fact, police argue that experience so far has shown that DNA testing has worked well to curb youth crime.

But the issues of privacy and confidentiality are likely to continue to plague the stockpiling of genetic data and tissue samples. In fairness, the FBI's national database will store only limited genetic profiles, not samples. But before the system is fully operational, simple genetic analysis of that huge backlog of biological samples—which will only increase as time passes—will require storehousing samples in crime laboratories across the country. Though the use of tissue samples for other purposes is prohibited in most states, ethicists point out that pressure not to destroy samples may be considerable, especially from scientific researchers. In fact, researchers complain that destruction of such a well-defined body of biological samples would be a tremendous waste.

Still, what does happen to samples or data in cases where juvenile records are erased, as happens in many states? For that matter, what happens when genetic material from a deceased person is requested for an unanticipated purpose, such as genetic research? How can researchers be expected to isolate genes indicating a predisposition to criminal behavior without the best available data?

By law, of course, none of this is supposed to happen. Today, the federal law enforcement community has taken the lead toward the establishment of a national DNA database that identifies criminals and matches them to their crimes. The question, of course, is whether such a national network will be able to deflect pressures in the future to abuse this harmful new tool in the name of expanding DNA-based law enforcement strategies.[9]

Officer peer pressure may also play a role in the application of discretion and illustrates yet another dynamic of departmental influence. As discussed in Chapter 10, police officers tend to experience a degree of social isolation and pressure from the citizenry. Because of this experience, they have a strong urge to be accepted by their coworkers. For example, the individual officer may be influenced by peers who dictate the "best" way to respond to disturbances in the community. Failure to act differently than coworkers prescribe may result in the officer being labeled as a "cowboy" or one who doesn't want to be a team player. So pressure exists to conform to other officers' behavior, and such conformity may affect discretionary decision making on the job.

Environmental Factors

An officer's living and working environment may play an important role in influencing discretion. For example, if police officers live in the same community they serve, their thinking processes may greatly affect the application of discretion by the mutual sharing of community concerns and values. The parks, schools, and neighborhoods in the community all take on special significance and personal importance to the resident officer. In fact, in recent years many police departments have offered financial incentives for officers who move their families into crime-ridden inner-city areas. These incentives include pay raises and low-interest-rate home loans. However, for officers who live in the communities they serve, their ability to remain objective may be hampered, and the overall effectiveness and reputation of the police in that area may actually be impeded rather than enhanced.

An officer's perception of community alternatives can also affect his or her discretionary powers. For example, officers may choose to arrest a person for public drunkenness or drug addiction if no other community outlet is available. Conversely, if many different community alternatives such as social service agencies are available to the officer, the formal arrest might be avoided in lieu of treatment.

Extralegal Factors

One critical issue that often emerges with regard to the use of police discretion is whether people—because of their race, sex, or other **extralegal factors**—either receive preferential treatment by police or become the targets of police intervention. According to recent research, arguments can be made for both positions. For example, one study showed that racial bias was a major consideration in the handling of juvenile offenders by some officers, and in a different study, it was shown that females who failed to behave in a stereotypical role were more likely to be arrested than those displaying conventional behavior.[10] In a related study, Smith and Visher discovered that although the race and demeanor of suspected law violators affect police discretion, police officers are equally likely to arrest males as females.[11]

Not all studies have supported the premise that minorities are more likely to be arrested by police than are nonminorities. In fact, many studies suggest that such decisions are not affected by racial bias at all. However, one school of thought has supported the assumption that the victim's race may play a more important role in determining who is arrested than does the race of the suspect. Specifically, when the victim is white, some police officers are more likely to pursue formal criminal action than if the victim is a minority member.[13]

This hypothesis was supported through the work of Willis and Ward who suggested that in child abuse cases, those involving white victims are more likely to be reported to police than are instances involving minority victims.[14] It becomes apparent that such studies show a clear need to consider both the perpetrators and victims of crimes when examining how police discretion is applied. In addition to these observations, it must be noted that not all police agencies or officers abuse their powers of discretion. Abuse of power is usually seen on a fragmented basis and varies considerably.

USE OF FORCE

Police are granted the specific legal authority to use force under certain conditions. But the authority of officers to use force is limited. Penalties for abuse of authority can be severe, so police officers must be clear on what they can and cannot do. The management of force by police officers is a constant challenge facing law enforcement managers. Balancing issues of a violent society with the safety concerns of police personnel creates many obstacles and concerns in developing departmental policies and procedures. The prevailing police perspective is based on a serious concern for the

A Closer Look

Extralegal Factors Affecting Police Discretion

1. *The officer's background.* Because like persons in other occupations, police officers bring their personal life experiences with them to the job, it is logical that, at times, personal values and biases may contribute to the decision to arrest (or not to arrest).

2. *Suspect's characteristics.* Stories appearing in newspapers and magazines have alerted us to the sad reality that at times some police officers treat persons differently, possibly due to the suspect's gender or race. Research has shown that other suspect's characteristics may also tend to improperly influence an officer's decision. These characteristics can include the suspect's mannerisms, type of clothing, or personal grooming. For example, it is likely that an officer who stops a belligerent and uncooperative traffic violator may be unduly influenced to write a traffic citation rather than simply to give the person a verbal warning.

3. *Community interest.* The contemporary attitudes of the community at large will also affect the officer's willingness to arrest. For example, crimes such as child abuse, spouse abuse, and other types of domestic violence may be at the forefront of community concern and can therefore create pressure for the police to focus on those types of criminal behavior.

4. *Department policy.* Even though police discretion is usually an individual decision made by individual officers, departmental standard operating procedure (SOP) may also dictate certain circumstances under which arrests will be made. Such directives can include a general order to arrest for certain traffic offenses, vice offenses, or other offenses that pose a particular concern to the departmental mission or stem from public cries for police action.

5. *Victim pressure.* Crimes such as spouse abuse and child abuse have gained much attention in recent years, and the victims or their advocates have exerted increasing pressure on police departments to pursue arrests and prosecutions of perpetrators.

6. *Individual officer practices.* Although police officers should enforce the law objectively, some police officers may view certain law violations as being more serious than others. For example, for those officers who view themselves as being in more of a crime-fighter role, traffic violations may be thought of as "busy work" or unworthy of their time. Accordingly, they may feel that pursuing felons is a more effective and appropriate use of their time.

7. *Personal disagreement with the law.* Some laws, such as vice laws, lack unanimous support among police officers. For example, some officers may view prostitution or gambling as victimless crimes, feeling that because all parties are in agreement, there is no wrongdoing. Subjective law enforcement such as this or in any form should be seriously discouraged by police managers, as it tends to set the stage for discrimination.

8. *Community alternatives.* Depending on the community, a police officer's decision to arrest may also be affected by other available resources in the community. For example, rather than arresting a drug addict or drunk, the police officer may choose to refer him or her to a local treatment facility. In doing so, an arrest is avoided and the offender is given a second chance through other programs in the community.

welfare of officers who must cope with the constant threat of a violent society.[15] In contrast, citizens are fearful that police officers may exceed their legal bounds and use force as a means of punishment rather than control.

Serious cases of abuse of police authority often stimulate intense public debate. For example, a videotape of Rodney King being beaten by Los Angeles police officers or reports of the torture of Abner Louima by New York City police capture the public's attention and raise troubling questions regarding the limits of legitimate police authority in a free society. Such cases raise important questions:

- Are such events isolated occurrences in particular police departments or extreme examples of a more general problem plaguing police departments across the nation?
- Does the fact that such abuses often involve minority victims reveal important disparities in the way the law enforcement officers treat members of certain racial, socioeconomic, or cultural groups?
- What measures can be taken to constrain police abuse, and which are likely to be most effective?

Although such questions have been raised and debated in the media by politicians and by police scholars and by administrators, little is known about how and why these issues arise. In our earlier discussion, recall that the most obvious function that separates private citizens from the police is peacekeeping. It is this role that permits the lawful use of force in urgent circumstances that require it. After all, police work is dangerous, and many facets of it are unpredictable.

Police officers deal every day with persons who are violent, under the influence of drugs or alcohol, mentally deranged, or who are just desperate to avoid arrest. To cope, officers are granted specific legal authority to use force under constitutional law and the laws of most states. However, the authority of officers to use force is limited. Those limitations may be enforced through the use of criminal prosecution, civil lawsuits, and disciplinary actions. Our society recognizes three legitimate and responsive forms of force: the right of self-defense, including the valid taking of another person's life in order to protect oneself from harm; the power to control those for whom some responsibility for care and custody is granted an authority figure, such as prison guard; and the institution of a police group that has relatively unrestricted authority to use force as required.[16]

The extent of improper use of force gives us insight about police officer attitudes. For example, in his reexamination of Albert Reiss's 1967 data, Robert Friedrich found that excessive force was used in approximately 35% of cases where police used force.[17] In comparison, in 1996 Robert Worden replicated a previous Police Foundation study by conducting telephone surveys of a representative sample of more than 900 U.S. police officers. As with Friedrich's study, Worden revealed that improper force was used in 38% of encounters that involved force.[18] While these studies provide suggestive findings about police attitudes on the abuse of authority, any conclusions that may be drawn from them may be limited because of recent advancements in police hiring and training practices.

The federal standard for police use of force was established by the Supreme Court in *Graham* v. *Connor* (1989). In that case the Court recognized that the police officer's duty to make arrests and to conduct searches and investigatory stops carries with it the authority to reasonably use or threaten the use of force. The *Graham* decision allows officers to use force only for two reasons: defense and control—not for punishment. One must remember that the Fourth Amendment protects the "right of the people to be secure in their persons . . . against unreasonable searches and seizures and shall not be violated. . . ." Because a police officer's use of force constitutes a seizure, using excessive force is a violation of a citizen's rights under the Fourth Amendment. Based on the totality of the circumstances, three key factors can be used to evaluate the extent of the officer's use of force:

1. The severity of the crime committed
2. Whether the suspect posed an immediate threat to the safety of the officers or others
3. Whether the suspect actively resisted arrest or attempted to evade arrest

When police are compelled to use force, the Court use the following standards to determine whether such force was reasonable. First, the officer's conduct will be compared to that of a "reasonable officer" confronted by similar circumstances. Second, when the judge and jury evaluate the officer's actions, they must do so from the "standing in your shoes" standard. This means that they can make use only of the information the officer had at the time that he or she exerted force. So 20/20 hindsight cannot be considered for this analysis.

One of the confusing aspects about the use of force is that there are no clear-cut answers regarding how it is applied. Worse yet, there are many severe penalties for police officers who take the wrong course of action on the street. We know that numerous dangerous situations confront police officers every day. From time to time officers are required to use force—it's inevitable. After the police officer makes the decision to use force, his or her department and the courts will take considerable time scrutinizing the situation to determine if such actions were appropriate.

Remember, the modern-day police officer must not only know how to use force techniques, such as the swinging of a baton, but also when to apply those techniques. The use of force by police officers stems from the premise that in a modern democratic society citizens are discouraged by law from employing force to solve personal disputes. Instead, they are expected to rely on the justice system to arbitrate and resolve conflicts. With few exceptions, such as cases involving self-defense, this restriction applies to most situations.

Defining Use of Force

Police officers are taught that the penalties for abusing their authority to use force can be severe. To avoid harsh penalties, police officers must be aware of the rules that govern the use of force. Such rules are included in state law, federal law, and department policy. So just how can force be defined so that we can understand it better? Bittner suggests that force is "the distribution of nonnegotiable coercive remedies."[19] He also makes the following observations regarding force:

> The duty of police intervention in matters of social disorder means above all making use of the capacity and authority to overpower resistance to an attempted solution in the native habitat of the problem. There can be no doubt that this feature of police work is uppermost in the minds of people who solicit police aid. Every conceivable police intervention projects the message that force may . . . have to be used to achieve a desired objective. It does not matter whether the persons who seek police help are private citizens or other government officials, nor does it matter whether the problem at hand involves some aspect of law enforcement or is totally unconnected with it.[20]

The authority to use force carries with it awesome responsibilities. The fear of criticism can cause officers to second-guess themselves and hesitate, which could be dangerous. People have different ideas about just what constitutes force and police brutality. Earlier, we considered Bittner's definition of the use of force, but let us now consider an operational definition as well.

Police officers, in particular, have specific ideas of what justifies the use of force. As a rule, force is defined through the concepts of assault and battery. **Battery** (a term not used in all states) is generally defined as intentional, nonconsensual bodily contact that a reasonable person would consider harmful. Certainly, if we hit someone with our fists or with a baton or even shoot someone, these actions would be considered offensive, harmful, and forceful by a reasonable person. However, battery also includes any intentional, nonconsensual contact associated with the body. For the most part, battery and assault are often used in the same language. However, under most criminal statutes, there is a significant difference between battery and assault.

Assault is intent to put someone in fear of immediate battery or to threaten someone while having the apparent ability to carry out that threat. So although battery requires actual contact, the legal concept of assault doesn't necessarily include actual bodily contact at all. It's wrong to think that an officer uses force only when striking someone. In other words, an officer who displays his or her weapon while shouting "Stop or I'll shoot!" fits the definition of assault. So even though the officer doesn't fire in that situation, force was still used. Acting in any manner that implies a threat, such as raising fists, mace, weapons, or batons, constitutes the use of force.

Understanding Reasonableness

Under the *Graham* decision, the Court identified three key factors based on the totality of the circumstances to use in evaluating the "reasonableness" of the officer's use of force: (1) the severity of the crime committed, (2) whether the suspect posed an immediate threat to the safety of the officers or others, and (3) whether the suspect actively resisted arrest or attempted to evade arrest by flight. According to the *Graham* decision, active resistance to arrest includes any physical actions by the suspect that make the arrest physically more difficult to accomplish. Active resistance to arrest includes pushes and shoves as well as more obscure actions, such as holding on to the steering wheel while being removed from a car.

An interesting finding of the *Graham* decision was an explanation of the standards under which officers' conduct should be judged by the jury and the trial judge. First, the actions of the officer(s) will be compared to actions of a "reasonable officer" involved in a similar situation. Second, the Court said that when the judge and jury evaluate the officer from within the "shoes" of the officer under review, they must make their decision based on the information the officer had at the time he or she took action. So hindsight cannot be used to consider the behavior of the officers in question.

The Misuse of Force

In general, the use of physical force by law enforcement personnel is very rare, occurring in only about 1% of police–public encounters.[21] Still the Department of Justice estimates that law enforcement officers threaten to use force or use force in encounters with about 665,000 Americans a year.[22] Of course, police officers are often justified in using force to protect themselves or other citizens. At the same time, few observers would be naive enough to believe that police are always justified in the use of force. How, then, is "misuse" of force to be defined?

One attempt to qualify excessive force that has been lauded by legal scholars, if not necessarily by police officers, was offered by the Christopher Commission. Established in Los Angeles in 1991 after the beating of African-American motorist Rodney King, the commission advised that "an officer may resort to force only where he or she faces a credible threat and then may only use the minimum amount necessary to control the subject."[23]

The Phoenix Study

Terms such as *credible* and *necessary* are, of course, quite subjective, rendering these definitions too vague to be practical. To better understand the subject, the Phoenix (Arizona) Police Department, while working with Rutgers University and Arizona State University, conducted a study to measure how often police officers use force. The results showed that police use some form of "physical force"—defined as any "weaponless tactic" (such as kicking or shoving) or the threatened or actual use of any weapon—in 22% of the surveyed arrests.[24] The study also examined the predictors of force; that is, the factors that were present in the situations in which force was used. As one might expect, the study found that the best predictor of police use of force was the subject's use of force.[25]

Types of Force

To comply with the various, and not always consistent, laws concerning the use of force, a police officer must understand there are two kinds of force: nondeadly force and deadly force. Most force used by law enforcement is nondeadly force. In most states, the use of nondeadly force is regulated by the concept of reasonable force, which allows the use of nondeadly force when a reasonable person would assume that such force was necessary. Conversely, deadly force is force that an objective police officer realizes will place the subject in direct threat of serious injury or death.

Less-Lethal Weapons

In recent years police administrators and public policy planners have been searching for ways to reduce the incidence of police use of deadly force. The goal is to find effective, nondeadly alternatives to the use of conventional firearms. Ideally, if the police can identify an effective alternative to deadly force or the use of firearms, numerous lives would be saved and police departments would avoid a substantial amount of negative criticism from the media and the community.

Over the past 20 years, police departments have adopted various less-lethal weapons. The term *less lethal* is somewhat misleading because almost any use of force can result in fatal consequences. A more appropriate way of understanding the concept is to note that less-lethal force is any force that is not "intended" or "likely" to lead to death or serious physical injury. The most common examples are water cannons or 37 mm pistols that fire wood, rubber, bean bags, or polyurethane bullets.

These control tools were initially adopted by the European police departments and more recently by American police departments. Other forms of less-lethal technology include tear gas, which has been used by American police departments since the 1960s and concussion grenades, which have been used more recently. Typically, concussion grenades are used to deal with barricade of suspects. As a rule, none of the weapons are useful when officers are confronted with deadly force situations on the street.

In recent times, police across the United States have begun to use pepper spray and stun guns to reduce the frequency of deadly force. Researchers have examined the effects of less-lethal technology on the police use of deadly force. For example, Bailey found that although the idea of less-lethal technology theoretically had promise, it did not have a significant impact on the number of deaths. Furthermore, he found that race was not a factor with the implementation of less-than-lethal force alternatives. Consequently, there were no reductions or increases in force against white or African-American citizens. In short, Bailey's findings suggest that law enforcement has not identified a less-lethal technology that effectively meets law enforcement's needs. For the technology to be effective, it must be issued and available to officers when they encounter deadly situations and it must work better (safer for officers and citizens when deployed). An example of such a weapon that has gained national acceptance is pepper spray.

"OC" OR PEPPER SPRAY   An estimated 99% of local police departments authorize the use of force in Oleoresin Capsicum, or "OC pepper spray."[26] An organic substance that combines the ingredients such as resin and cayenne pepper, OC causes a sensation "similar to having sand or needles" in the eyes when sprayed into a suspect's face.

There is some concern that pepper spray is not as effective as the manufacturers tend to indicate. There is some evidence that pepper spray is not effective in dealing with all suspects, particularly those who are intoxicated, violent, goal oriented, or mentally ill attackers. Some have projected effectiveness rates at about 85% (ACLU of Southern California, 1995).

ELECTRONIC CONTROL DEVICES (ECDS)   One of the most popular "less-lethal" weapons used by police is the electronic control device, often referred to as a *stun gun* or *Taser*. "Taser" is an acronym for the Thomas A. Swift Electric Rifle. Swift was a character in a series of science fiction books published in the 1930s.

In modern times, however, the Taser has gained popularity as a handheld weapon shaped like a handgun that delivers an instantly incapacitating 50,000-volt shock to its target. The Taser is designed to interfere with the body's neuromuscular system; under most circumstances, its force drops its target to the ground almost instantly. The device can be operated in two modes—as a projectile device or as a contact "drive stun" device. As a projectile device, it fires two barbs resembling straightened fish hooks that are attached to copper coils. The projectiles are designed to travel a distance of up to 21 feet. The barbs attach to the clothing or skin of the target and the coils deliver a high-voltage, low-amperage, five-second electroshock. The deploying officer can lengthen the duration of the shock or repeated bursts of electricity can be delivered. The darts are designed to attach to or penetrate the clothing of the target. Advanced Taser models have laser sights and replaceable cartridges. In stun mode, the weapon is used by making direct contact with the suspect's skin. In this mode, the weapon is often used as a pain compliance technique.

The Taser is becoming very popular with law enforcement, correctional, and military agencies. Worldwide, it is reported that they are used by law enforcement in over 50 countries and they have been used in the Iraq war. While estimates vary, it is thought that about 8,000 law enforcement agencies are currently using the weapon. And literally hundreds of departments are either adopting or planning to adopt the weapon as an alternative to the use of deadly force. The device, however, is

FIGURE 8.3(a)   The Advanced Taser, manufactured by Taser International, shoots two fishhook-like barbs at a distance of up to 21 feet. Once in place, the barbs deliver a 50,000-volt charge to the subject.

not without controversy. While the available research and reports on these weapons is relatively scarce, the question has been raised regarding a number of important concerns.

For example, it has been determined that since 2001, at least 150 people in the United States have died after being shocked by these devices. During 2005 alone, more than 60 people died after being struck by police Tasers, raising concerns about the safety of the weapon. While in many cases deaths are attributed to factors other than the Taser, such as so-called excited delirium associated with drug intoxication or violent struggle, in 23 cases coroners have listed the use of these weapons as a cause or a contributory factor in death. In three cases in 2005, the Taser was listed as the "primary cause of death."

Also, while the Taser is touted as an effective alternative to the use of deadly force by police, and in some cases it is described as a "last resort" weapon, there is growing evidence that in the

FIGURE 8.3(b)   An Air Taser stun gun manufactured by Taser International.

majority of police applications, these weapons are not used as an alternative to deadly force or as a weapon of last resort. Rather, an examination of 74 Taser-involved deaths found that "most of those who died were unarmed men who, while displaying disturbed or combative behavior, did not appear to present a serious threat to the lives or safety of others."

Furthermore, there is growing concern about police use of Tasers on vulnerable populations. These devices have been used against schoolchildren, "unarmed mentally disturbed or intoxicated individuals, suspects fleeing minor crime scenes and people who argue with police or fail to comply immediately with a command." Examples of such cases include using the Taser on a 15-year-old Florida schoolgirl following a dispute on a bus, and on a 13-year-old Arizona girl who threw a book in a public library.

With these considerations in mind, there is serious concern as to whether these devices have reduced the police "need" to use force, or merely permitted the police to use force on a greater number of citizens in a greater number of situations. Because of the dangers and abuses involved with these weapons, some departments have developed policies that either prohibit or restrict their use. For example, the Las Vegas Metropolitan Police Department policy limits the use of Tasers as follows:

The Taser will not be used:

1. When the officer knows the suspect has come in contact with flammable liquids or is in a flammable atmosphere;
2. When the subject is in a position where a fall may cause substantial injury or death;
3. Punitively for the purposes of coercion, or an unjustified manner;
4. When the prisoner is handcuffed;
5. To escort or jab individuals;
6. To awaken unconscious or intoxicated individuals; or
7. When the subject is visibly pregnant, unless the deadly force is the only other option.

Police Attitudes and the Use of Force

While public attitudes toward the police are important, responses from the police themselves about the use of force also provide valuable information about the mindset of the police. Results of a 2000 study conducted by David Weisburd and his colleagues published by the National Institute of Justice (NIJ) provided some instructive insights.[27] For example, the study suggested that police officers have contradictory attitudes toward the abuse of authority and that police officers are not in agreement about how acceptable it is to use more force than legally necessary—even to control someone who physically assaults them.

Interestingly, the study also showed that a vast majority of responding officers described serious and well-publicized incidents of police abuse (such as the Rodney King and Abner Louima cases) as isolated and very rare occurrences, and indicated that their own departments take a tough stance on police abuse. The survey also suggested that police abuse remains a problem that needs to be addressed by policy makers. Even though most police officers disapprove of the use of excessive force, a substantial minority consider it acceptable sometimes to use more force than permitted by the laws that govern them.[28]

The *code of silence* also remains a troubling issue for U.S. police according to the NIJ study. The following key points were revealed:

1. Approximately one-quarter of police officers surveyed stated that whistle-blowing is not worth it.
2. Two-thirds stated that police officers who report misconduct are likely to receive a "cold shoulder" from fellow officers.
3. Over half reported that it is not unusual for police officers to turn a "blind eye" to improper conduct by other officers.[29]

These findings suggest that the code of silence that has continually plagued the reform of U.S. policing continues.

The Use-of-Force Continuum

One way police departments have attempted to control the level of force used by officers in the street is by adopting a use-of-force continuum. The continuum sets forth the level of force that officers can use in arresting or otherwise subduing a suspect. It is based on the premise that officers should use only the amount of force necessary to effect the arrest or subdue a suspect. The purpose of the continuum is to guide officers so they are less likely to use excessive force. Police officers are expected to use more force than a resisting suspect, but excessive force should not be used. The officer is expected to use that force which minimizes the likelihood of injury to the officer and a suspect. For example, an officer is not expected to use an impact weapon such as a baton on a subject who is merely being verbally uncooperative. On the other hand, if the actions of that same suspect result in the officer being physically attacked, the use of the baton would be justified. Police departments have incorporated the use-of-force continuum in their training and SOPs. For many departments, the use-of-force continuum sets forth the following.

COMMAND PRESENCE   The physical presence of the officer, typically a uniformed officer, is often sufficient to control situations. Most subjects become subdued or cooperative in the presence of a police officer and recognize the officer's authority to intervene in situations.

SOFT-HANDED CONTROL TECHNIQUES   This level of force refers to situations in which an officer physically grabs a subject to control them. As a rule, soft-handed control techniques are used when the subject verbally resists or becomes abusive. They are used to prevent the situation from escalating and brings the officer into direct contact with the subject while increasing the probability that the resisting subject can harm the officer.

"OC" OR PEPPER SPRAY   Considered a step up the continuum from soft-handed control techniques, the use of "OC" or pepper spray is another control technique. As a rule, pepper spray is placed somewhere between the passive and assaultive stages of suspect resistance. Pepper spray is considered a lower level of force because it is less likely to inflict physical injury on the suspect.

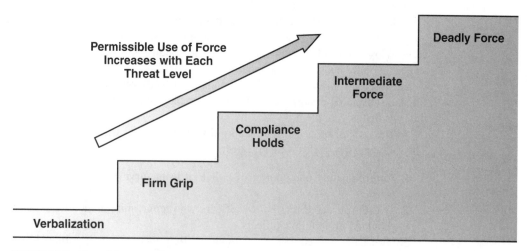

FIGURE 8.4 Use-of-force continuum.

HARD-HANDED CONTROL TECHNIQUES   This level of control technique is generally used when an officer fights with the suspect. Fighting can include pushing, hitting, or other physical action to subdue the suspect. Police trainers teach officers that they should be aware of hard-handed combat with the suspect because it places the officer in greater danger because of his or her immediate proximity to the suspect.

IMPACT WEAPONS   For the most part, the impact weapon is the police baton. Some departments authorize the use of a metal flashlight as an impact weapon. The baton increases the likelihood that there will be physical injury to the suspect and should be used only when the suspect cannot be overcome by using the previous stages, identified, in the continuum. Officers are carefully trained to use impact weapons by striking many areas of the suspect's body. Strikes to the head from impact weapons may result in substantial physical injury and are generally considered deadly force.

THREAT OF DEADLY FORCE   If the officer is unable to control the suspect with a baton or by other physical means, the officer can threaten the use of deadly force by firing his or her firearm. The desired effect of doing so is to cause the suspect to conform to the officer's commands and to allow the officer to effect an arrest.

DEADLY FORCE   The most common application of the deadly force is when the officer discharges his or her firearm at the suspect. Most police departments have policies prohibiting warning shots and the shooting of suspects for the purpose of wounding them. Rather, officers are taught to shoot to stop. This is accomplished by targeting "center mass," which is defined as the largest available area on the suspect's body. Most state statutes authorize police use of deadly force in instances where the officer believes there is a threat to "great bodily harm" to the officer or another person.

The use-of-force continuum provides officers a guide for the application of force against suspects, but depending on the nature of the confrontation, officers may not necessarily start at the beginning of the continuum. For example, if an officer often encounters armed suspects, the officer would advance to the next-to-last stage in the use-of-force continuum—threat of deadly force. When encountering such a situation, the officer must evaluate it and determine the appropriate level of force, with the guideline being that the level of force should be greater than that being displayed by the suspect. Police officers are not expected to fight on an even level with suspects, but the force level adopted by them must be reasonable.

The use-of-force continuum is based on the premise that law enforcement officers will encounter uncooperative and resistant citizens. Officers may use only the appropriate level of force in response to a citizen's actions. In many situations, the police are active participants in violent encounters and they have the ability to either escalate or de-escalate confrontations. A police officer with a poor attitude can provoke a violent confrontation on almost any tour of duty. Furthermore, the continuum presupposes a one-to-one relationship in the use of force, a single officer using a single level of force that is raised or lowered based on the suspect's actions. In that regard, a properly drafted use-of-force continuum not only identifies levels of force for the police officer but also the corresponding levels of resistance on the part of citizens they encounter.

THE COOPERATIVE SUBJECT   The least critical subject behavior is a cooperative subject who complies with the officer's appropriate nonverbal or verbal direction.

RESISTERS   Resisters are subjects who do not respond to social or verbal control, but whose actions do not rise to the level of an assailant. Resisters are more difficult to control than cooperative subjects. They must be seized and physically compelled to cooperate. Two levels of resisters are generally recognized in police training: the passive resister and the active resister.

The passive resister. Degrees of passive resistance (refusal to move as directed) can be measured by the degree of muscular resistance of the arm to the touch of the officer and, resistance against the officer's attempts to pull, twist, or roll. This category of subject behavior does not include attempts to flee or to create greater distance between the subject and the officer. Rather, the subject simply tries not to be moved. This is sometimes attempted by grasping a fixed object.

The active resister. This subject actively resists in a defensive manner, by attempting to avoid physical control by the officer and create space between the officer's reach and himself or herself. This includes slight evasive movements of the arm that include flailing all the way up to full flight. Active resister behaviors are not harmful but are, merely difficult to control.

THE ASSAILANT   Assailants are grouped into three categories according to the probable harm their actions may cause.

Aggression without a weapon. In this category of subject actions, the subject closes the distance between himself or herself and the officer, limiting the officer's available alternatives, and taking control of the situation from the officer without immediately actually or potentially harming the officer. The subject attempts to make physical contact with the officer.

The specific actions of this subject will probably not cause immediate physical injury to the officer but may create a situation in which the officer may have neither the time nor resources to react properly in defense of self or others.

The officer may be under the physical control of the subject so that he or she may not be able to control his or her own body positioning reliably. By his or her actions, even without causing injury, the subject places the officer in fear of diminishing or losing all force alternatives.

Fighting without a weapon. This is when a suspect attacks the officer or someone else. Because of the mode of attack, the injury will be less than "serious" physical injury. Probable physical injury may include minor broken bones, sprains, scrapes, contusions, cuts to the skin, or damage to the teeth or hair. This type of injury is usually found in weaponless fights.

Fighting with a weapon. This is when a suspect's actions will probably result in death or serious physical injury to the officer or someone else. The specific way in which the subject may cause death or serious physical injury is immaterial except as it affects the timeliness of the officer's reactions or as it lessens the officer's alternatives in producing a reaction. For a subject to be placed in this category, he or she could be using a firearm, bomb, acid, vehicle, or brick, as long as the mode and weapon are capable of causing immediate serious physical injury. This type of force is termed _lethal force_.

Deadly Force

In 1967 the President's Commission on Law Enforcement and the Administration of Justice noted that most police departments had no policy to guide them in the use of **deadly force**. At that time, most state laws were extremely broad in defining the circumstances under which officers could employ deadly force. In its most commonly used parlance, the term _deadly force_ refers to actions of police officers that result in the killing of a person. As mentioned earlier, police officers are legally authorized to use deadly force under certain circumstances.

As a rule, such actions result from situations where persons are fleeing the police, assaulting someone, or attempting to use lethal force against another person (including a police officer). If deadly force is used improperly or illegally, the officers responsible may be criminally liable, and both the officers and the police department may be sued in a civil action. Most rules regarding the use of deadly force come from federal statutes and case law and as a rule are concerned with the police use of deadly force to arrest fleeing felons engaged in nonviolent felonies. These cases are different from those pertaining to suspects committing violent felonies, such as murder, as to assault, rape, robbery, or other types of behavior that represent a substantial risk of bodily harm or death.

The Fleeing-Felon Rule

Until the mid-1980s, the shooting of a suspect by police was tolerated by many police agencies. Although this is currently not the case, it was prevalent in the early development of policing when most felonies were punishable by death and there was an assumption that all felons would avoid arrest at any cost. Therefore, the **fleeing-felon rule** was developed during a time when apprehension of felons was considered more dangerous than today. Police officers in those early days often worked alone and lacked sophisticated communications technology with which to track suspects who were wanted by police. The concern was that felons would escape arrest and retreat to another community where they could begin a new life of crime.[30] As time went by and more efficient means were developed for apprehension, arrests became easier for law enforcement officials. For a period of time, police still relied on the ability to use deadly force even though some felons were not considered dangerous and posed no particular threat to the officer or the community. Prior to 1985 police officers were legally authorized by most states to employ the use of deadly force in apprehending fleeing felons.

Over the years, many states had modified the fleeing-felon rule, but some still allowed rather broad discretion about when to use deadly force. In a watershed decision by the U.S. Supreme Court in March 1985, it was determined that Tennessee's fleeing-felon law was unconstitutional. *Tennessee* v. *Garner* (1985) involved the police shooting and subsequent killing of an unarmed boy as the youth fled from an unoccupied house. In this case the officer could see that the suspect was a youth and that he was unarmed. The officer argued, however, that if the youngster was able to leap a fence, he would be able to escape. The state statute in Tennessee at the time permitted officers to shoot fleeing felons to prevent escape. Pursuant to *Garner*, the Court ruled that the employment of deadly force by police must be "reasonable" in order to be lawful. Reasonable deadly force is authorized under three circumstances:

1. To prevent an escape when the suspect has threatened the officer with a weapon
2. When there is a threat of death or serious physical injury to the officer or others
3. If there is probable cause to believe that the suspect has committed a crime involving the infliction or threatened infliction of serious physical injury and, when practical, some warning has been given by the officer

In some instances, the Tennessee statute allowing an officer to shoot a fleeing felon may be constitutional, but the special circumstances in the *Garner* case, in which the suspect was an unarmed juvenile involved in a nonviolent crime, made the shooting both unreasonable and unlawful. The use of force by police is necessary and appropriate but only when used properly. Otherwise, it violates the rights of others and can result in serious injury or death as well as a loss of confidence in the police department. It is not known exactly how much abuse of police power occurs, but research indicates that, overall, it is minimal.[31]

PERSONS KILLED BY POLICE

Currently, no uniform reporting system exists for determining the exact number of police-caused homicides in the United States. The two most commonly cited sources of statistical data for determining police-caused homicides are the FBI's supplementary homicide reports and the National Center for Health Statistics' (NCHS) monthly vital statistics report, but even these sources are considered less than reliable. The FBI estimates that about 250 persons each year are killed by police, while the NCHS report suggests that the number may range from 265 to as many as 400 per year.

According to another well-known survey, which examined 57 of the nation's largest cities, approximately 260 citizens are killed by police each year.[32] Research indicates that the incidence of police killings is on the decline. Several reasons can be cited for this: overall increased scrutiny of police departments, increased police training, a rise in civil litigation, and implementation of policies and administrative controls to regulate such activity.[33]

It is possible, however, that figures cited by official reports and surveys may not accurately reflect the actual number of killings by police. For example, Sherman and Langworthy suggest that some killings might actually be hidden from official records.[34] This could be accomplished by medical examiners and coroners who might underreport killings by police either intentionally or accidentally. In addition, research suggests that the rate of police-caused homicides varies greatly from one police agency to the next. For example, Sherman and Cohn report that citizens in Atlanta were killed by police at a rate 44 times greater than in Oklahoma City.[35] This is attributed not so much to the high crime rate in Atlanta but rather to individual differences in police policy as it relates to the use of deadly force by officers.

Citizen killings represent a rare circumstance in a police officer's career, even in large cities with high-crime rates. Sherman and Cohn note that on the average, a police officer in Jacksonville, Florida, would have to be on the job 139 years before killing a citizen.[36] In comparison, a Honolulu police officer would have to work 7,692 years before being required to take the life of a citizen.

However, that is not the perception of many persons, in particular minorities, who have expressed anger and frustration over occurrences such as the acquittal of the police officers involved in the Rodney King beating in Los Angeles. At best, it is difficult to regulate and judge the use of deadly force by police, although most police departments have determined, at least in part, what types of force work best in certain situations. Rodney King was struck 51 times by Los Angeles police officers after leading them on a high-speed chase. This case presents the issue of whether the amount of force used by police was excessive and unlawful. Several of the key officers involved in the case were subsequently brought up on state criminal charges and tried. Although many were outraged by the Rodney King beating episode, the state jury acquitted the officers in a highly publicized trial that resulted in three days of rioting and looting in South-Central Los Angeles. In a subsequent federal trial, however, several officers were convicted and sent to prison.

RACE AND DEADLY FORCE

The Amadou Diallo shooting incident in New York City illustrates how race and deadly force by the police can often become a serious social issue (see Chapter 9). Diallo was shot 41 times while standing in front of his apartment just after midnight. Police mistook his reaching for his wallet as him reaching for a gun. Diallo allegedly resembled the criminal suspect the police were searching for.[37]

Probably no other issue in the use of police officer deadly force generates more concern than that of racial discrimination—and the shootings of African-Americans in particular. Such incidents were the impetus for many urban race riots during the 1960s. Since then, similar incidents have been observed that have fostered mistrust and resentment between minorities and the police. Cities such as Los Angeles, Houston, Atlanta, New York, Miami, and Detroit have all experienced controversial incidents that have fueled dissent between the police and the public they serve. The results of these incidents have prompted a substantial body of research focusing on police shootings of African-Americans. Such research indicates that, in fact, a disproportionate number of police killings, approaching 80%, involve minority citizens.[38]

The use of force is a relatively rare occurrence in U.S. policing. The previous studies suggest that when it does occur, it may often escalate to the level of excessive force. In an NIJ report issued in May 2000, some constructive findings were identified regarding police abuse of authority. For example, the study revealed that most police officers disapprove the use of excessive force. Nonetheless, a substantial minority believed that officers should be permitted to use more force than the law currently permits and found it acceptable sometimes to use more force than permitted by the laws that governed them. While a substantial minority of officers expressed the view that the police should be permitted to use more force, the overwhelming majority did not believe that officers regularly engaged in the excessive use of force. A mere 4.1% thought that police officers regularly use more physical force than necessary when making arrests compared to 97.1% who agreed that the serious cases of misconduct (like that in the Rodney King and Abner Louima cases) were "extremely rare" in their departments. However, almost 22% strongly agreed that officers in their departments sometimes use more force than necessary.

One of the most glaring questions is whether the use of deadly force by police is based on discrimination. Research by Fyfe examined police shootings in New York over a five-year period.[39] He discovered that police officers are most likely to shoot people who are armed and pose a threat to the officers. But Conner explains that 84% of assaults against police officers during an arrest situation are committed by suspects using feet, hands, and fists.[40]

Once certain factors were considered, such as the displaying of a weapon or a person attacking a police officer, racial differences in the police use of force were no longer significant factors. In fact, Fyfe discovered that African-American officers were almost twice as likely as white officers to shoot citizens. Several reasons were given to explain this. African-American officers might be assigned to high-crime areas more frequently than are white officers. In addition, more African-American officers tend to hold line-level positions than their white counterparts, who occupy more administrative positions in the department.

The Code of Silence

Recent research has disclosed that some of the strongest opinions expressed by police officers centered on the difficult question of whether officers should report misconduct by fellow officers. Interestingly, the research shows a large gap between attitudes and behavior. That is, even though police officers do not believe in protecting wrongdoers, they probably won't turn them in.

In a May 2000 survey on police attitudes toward abuse of authority sponsored by the NIJ, more than 80% of police surveyed reported that they do not accept the "code of silence" (i.e., keeping quiet in the face of misconduct by others) as an essential part of the mutual trust necessary to good policing. However, about one-quarter (24.9%) of the sample agreed or strongly agreed that whistle-blowing is not worth it, with more than two-thirds (67.4%) reporting that police officers who report incidents of misconduct are likely to be given a "cold shoulder" by fellow officers. Furthermore, over half of the officers (52.4%) surveyed agreed that it is common for police officers to "turn a blind eye" to other officers' improper conduct.[41]

In summary, it would be fair to say that as long as the police function includes that of law enforcement, many contacts made by the police will require the application of force as a tool to overcome resistance, prevent escape, take suspects into custody, or defend themselves or others. If the use of force is viewed as a tool to be used in a reasonable and necessary manner, officers should not fear legal or disciplinary repercussions from their actions. In addition, the public will have more confidence in police departments that are both professional and responsible.

CONSIDERATIONS FOR USE OF FORCE POLICY

The use-of-force continuum, as discussed in this chapter, represents only one part of a police agency's policy regarding the use of force. Many departments have attempted to develop a comprehensive policy providing guidance for officer discretion when using force. For example, police accrediting bodies have established that departments should have use-of-force standards.

The Commission on Accreditation for Law Enforcement Agencies (*CALEA*) is the organization that oversees the national accreditation of police agencies. One of its standards, standard 1.3 Use of Force, contains 13 different standards dealing with lethal and less-than-lethal force. Police agencies have substantial discretion in meeting these standards, which basically require that the topics be addressed and departmental policies be implemented. For example, the firing of warning shots is addressed in standard 1.33. For the most part, police departments that forbid warning shots at others may be willing to authorize them under certain circumstances such as when deadly force can be used. The CALEA standards serve to provide guidelines on what a police department should address in its policies. As such, it is recognized nationally that departments should adopt standards regarding the use of force.

MECHANISMS FOR DEALING WITH PROBLEM OFFICERS

Many police departments employ some problem officers. The actions of these officers come to light when civil lawsuits are filed or there is a questionable death of a suspect or multiple citizen complaints about the officer's behavior on the force. Concern about problem officers gained national attention in 1991 after the issuance of a report by the independent commission on the Los Angeles Police Department (Christopher Commission). The commission found that some officers were overrepresented in the use-of-force statistics. The Los Angeles Police Department database contained 44 officers who had an inordinate number of complaints. The commission found,

> Of approximately 1,800 officers against whom an allegation of excessive force or improper tactics was made from 1986 to 1990, more than 1,400 had only one or two allegations. But 183 officers had four or more allegations, 44 had six or more, 16 had eight or more, and one had 16 such allegations.
>
> But nearly 6,000 officers identified as involving use of force reports from January 1987 to March 1991, more than 4,000 had fewer than five reports each. But 63 officers had 20 or more reports each. The top 5% of the officers (ranked by number of reports) accounted for more than 20% of all reports.

The commission took note that the discrepancies could be accounted for by the fact that these officers may have been assigned to high-crime or high-activity areas. However, the commission also noticed that if this was the case there were an ample number of officers working in such areas who did not generate the kinds of complaint activity as those officers identified as receiving the most complaints or using the most force.

Research in police use of force has identified that chronic deviants are a significant part of the use-of-force problems for many police departments. Toch found that chronic deviants are those officers who repeatedly use excessive force, are abusive, and disrespectful. He argues that police agencies should identify and target these chronic deviants before their behavior gets out of hand. One way of accomplishing this task is to implement "early warning systems" (EWS) for problem police officers. An EWS is designed to identify officers who, as a result of their performance, may exhibit behavioral problems in using force and dealing with citizens. The benefit of having such a system in place is that it could reduce the number of civil lawsuits against a department, reduce the incidence of excessive force and abuse, and ultimately foster better police–community relations.

One of the first EWS was developed by the Miami Police Department. Miami's EWS system included the following performance criteria:

1. *Complaints.* An officer receiving five or more sustained or inconclusive complaints in a two-year period.
2. *Use of force.* An officer involved as a principal in five or more use-of-force incidents in a two-year period.

3. *Reprimands.* An officer receiving five or more reprimands in a two-year period.
4. *Discharge of firearms.* An officer who has three or more discharges in a five-year period.

Under this system, once an officer hit one of the thresholds mentioned earlier, supervisors would review his or her file that contains all complaints, reports, and investigative materials relating to the officers actions. The supervisor would then meet with the officer for the purpose of reducing the number of incidents. The supervisor had a number of corrective options, including additional training, transfer, counseling, and disciplinary action. Once the supervisor made a recommendation, the commander of the internal affairs unit reviewed it. Over time, the Miami EWS contributed to a reduction in the rate of complaints lodged against the department. While improving officers' performances, it reduced the number of civil suits against the department and saved the careers of some officers.

In Retrospect

The principles of individual freedom and social justice are at the heart of the U.S. way of life. In principle, the role of the criminal justice system is to ensure justice while safeguarding liberty. From the most mundane duties of the police to the highly complex renderings of the U.S. Supreme Court, the issue of liberty–justice is the thread that sews the justice system together. The dilemma rings clear—how can we empower our police to adequately protect society, while at the same time safeguard our constitutional freedoms from the possibility of police tyranny and oppression? While there is no simple answer to that question, we must accept that liberty is a double-edged sword carrying with it both obligations and rights. For the actions of the police to be "just," they must recognize the individual rights of citizens while holding them accountable for their social obligations under law.

Improve Your Professional Vocabulary

assault
battery
deadly force
discretion

extralegal factors
fleeing-felon rule
invocation discretion
noninvocation discretion

positional asphyxia
probable cause
stop and frisk
totality of the circumstances

Discussion Questions

1. Discuss the concept of probable cause and how it relates to police authority and power.
2. Compare and contrast the concepts of probable cause and discretion as they relate to the application of police authority.
3. Discuss the manner in which police authority is delegated.
4. List and discuss the various types of extralegal influences that might affect police discretion and the decision to arrest.
5. Discuss how the 1985 *Tennessee* v. *Garner* case has affected the fleeing-felon rule.
6. Discuss the concept of search and seizure as it relates to police authority and power.
7. Explain the distinctions that exist between searches with and without a warrant.
8. Explain how a "stop and frisk" differs from an arrest.
9. List and discuss the various types of abuses that can occur during a custodial interrogation.

Notes

1. San Diego Police Department. (1992, June). *Final Report of the Custody Death Task Force* (unpublished).
2. Davis, K. C. (1969). *Discretionary justice.* Baton Rouge: Louisiana State University Press.
3. Goldstein, H. (1977). *Policing a free society.* Cambridge, MA: Ballinger.
4. Davis, K. C. (1975). *Police discretion.* St. Paul, MN: West.
5. Goldstein, H. (1977). *Policing a free society.* Cambridge, MA: Ballinger.
6. Pepinsky, H. (1975). Police decision making. In D. Gottfredson, ed., *Decision making in the criminal justice system: Reviews and essays.* Washington, DC: National Institute of Health, 21–52.
7. Ibid.
8. Goldstein, H. (1977). *Policing a free society.* Cambridge, MA: Ballinger.
9. Hoyle, R. (1998, November). The FBI's national database. *Nature Biotechnology, 16,* 987; Klaidman, D., et al. (1998, November 6). The DNA detectives. *Newsweek,* pp. 66–71; Willing, R. (1998, October 12). FBI activates 50-state DNA database Tuesday. *USA Today,* p. 1A; Willing, R. (1999, March 1). Commission would consider sampling everyone arrested. *USA Today,* p. 1A; Willing, R. (1999, July 6). Panel to oppose mass DNA testing. *USA Today,* p. 1A; Willing, R., & K. Johnson. (1999, September 28). DNA tests cast doubt on justice system, panel finds. *USA Today,* p. 3A.
10. Dannefer, D., & R. Schutt. (1982). Race and juvenile processing in court and police agencies. *American Journal of Sociology, 87,* 1113–1132; Visher, C. (1983). Arrest decisions and notions of chivalry. *Criminology, 21,* 5–28.
11. Smith, D., & C. Visher. (1981). Street-level justice: Situational determinants of police arrest decisions. *Social Problems, 29,* 267–277.
12. Krohn, M., J. Curry, & S. Nelson-Kilger. (1983). Is chivalry dead? An analysis of changes in police dispositions of males and females. *Criminology, 21,* 417–437.
13. Smith, D., C. Visher, & L. Davidson. (1984). Equity and discretionary justice: The influence of race on police arrest decisions. *Journal of Criminal Law and Criminology, 75,* 234–249.
14. Willis, C., & R. Ward (1988). The police and child abuse: An analysis of police decisions to report illegal behavior. *Criminology, 26,* 695–716.
15. Buchanan, G. W. (1993, August). Managing police use of force. *Police Chief,* p. 20.
16. Peak, K. J. (1993). *Policing America: Methods, issues and challenges.* Upper Saddle River, NJ: Prentice Hall.
17. Friedrich, R. E. (1980). Police use of force: Individuals, situations, and organizations. *The Annals of the American Academy of Political and Social Science, 452,* 82–97.
18. Worden, R. (1996). The causes of police brutality: Theory and evidence on police use of force. In W. A. Geller & H. Toch, eds., *Police violence: Understanding and controlling police abuse of force.* New Haven, CT: Yale University Press.
19. Bittner, E. (1978). The functions of the police in modern society. In P. K. Manning & J. Van Maanen, eds., *Policing: A view from the street.* Santa Monica, CA: Goodyear, 32–50.
20. Ibid.
21. Bureau of Justice Statistics. (2006 June). Citizens complaints about police use of force. Washington, DC: U.S. Department of Justice, 6.
22. Bureau of Justice Statistics. (2005 February). Contacts between police and the public. Washington, DC: U.S. Department of Justice, v.
23. Independent Commission on the Los Angeles Police Department. (1991). *Report of the independent commission on the Los Angeles Police Department,* ix.
24. Garner, Joel, et al. (1996, November). Research in Brief: *Understanding the use of force by and against the police.* Washington, DC: Office of Justice Programs, 5.
25. Ibid., 1.
26. Bureau of Justice Statistics. (2006, May). *Local Police Departments, 2003.* Washington, DC: U.S. Department of Justice, 8.
27. Weisburd, D., et al. (2000, May). *Police attitudes toward abuse of authority: Findings from a national study.* National Institute of Justice, Research in Brief, Office of Justice Programs.
28. Ibid.
29. Ibid.
30. Sherman, L. (1980, January). Execution without trial: Police homicide and the Constitution. *Vanderbilt Law Review, 33,* 74–75.
31. Federal Bureau of Investigation. (1992, September). *Killed in the line of duty: A study of selected felonious killings of law enforcement officers.* Washington, DC: U.S. Government Printing Office.
32. Matulia, K. (1985). *A balance of forces,* 2nd ed. Gaithersburg, MD: International Association of Chiefs of Police.
33. Geller, W. (1982). Deadly force: What we know. *Journal of Police Science and Administration, 10,* 151–177.
34. Sherman, L., & R. Langworthy. (1979). Measuring homicide by police officers. *Journal of Criminal Law and Criminology, 4,* 546–560.
35. Sherman, L. W., & E. G. Cohn. (1986). *Citizens killed by big city police, 1970–1984.* Washington, DC: Crime Control Institute.

36. Ibid.

37. Reaves, J. (2000, March 6). Black and blue. *Time*.

38. Blumberg, M. (1981). Race and police shootings: An analysis in two cities. In J. Fyfe, ed., *Contemporary issues in law enforcement*. Thousand Oaks, CA: Sage.

39. Fyfe, J. (1978). *Shots fired*. Ph.D. dissertation, State University of New York, Albany, NY.

40. Conner, G. (1989, September). Cover cuffing. *Law and Order,* pp. 98–99.

41. Weisburd, D., et al. (2000, May). *Police attitudes toward abuse of authority: Findings from a national study*. National Institute of Justice, Office of Justice Programs.

CHAPTER 9

Ethics and Deviance

This chapter will enable you to:

- Understand the development of contemporary police ethics.
- Learn the meaning underlying law enforcement code of ethics.
- Understand the link between police behavior and the police subculture.

- Consider the implications of police discretion and ethical behavior.
- Distinguish between police misconduct and corruption.

The Rampart Police Station is an eight-square-mile area located near downtown Los Angeles, in the middle of one of the city's toughest neighborhoods. The area is a densely populated mix of Latino immigrants, Korean shopkeepers, drug addicts, and gangs—lots of gangs. The area is said to be the home to 30 different youth gangs, with thousands of members among them, each fighting one another for turf.

During the 1990s, in an effort to win back the area, the Los Angeles Police Department (LAPD) established a special antigang unit, Community Resources Against Street Hoodlums, or CRASH. In addition to their weapons and bravado, CRASH officers were armed with a special legal tool—an antigang injunction that gave them free rein to intervene in what they perceived as suspected gang members' behavior. Among the offenses the injunction covered were blocking sidewalks and carrying pagers.

Within their jurisdiction, Rampart's CRASH officers ruled. During the 1990s, the CRASH unit lived up to its name, with a confrontational style of policing that aggressively took back the streets. It seemed to be getting results—in the 1960s, the area had 170 murders a year whereas in 1999 there were only 33.[1]

However, there were long-time complaints that Rampart police officers were corrupt. Included were allegations that the police took drugs from suspects and then let them go, and that drugs were even planted on suspects in order to arrest them. But for the most part, these complaints were unsubstantiated and were ignored because the majority of them came from gang members themselves.

However, all that changed when one of CRASH's own officers testified against the unit. Rafael Perez says he was part of a tight-knit group of CRASH officers who played by bending the rules. He claimed that the antigang unit acted much like a gang itself. When a new recruit joined the unit, CRASH members allegedly circled around and beat him—an initiation ritual of the criminal gangs called "jumping in." Perez recounted a stunning array of such illegal acts, many as bizarre as they were disturbing. He told of one officer whose car tires were slashed by a suspected gang member. The officer and his partner tracked down the gang member they believed was responsible and dropped him off—naked—in a rival gang's turf. In another story, Perez told of another CRASH officer who shot a suspect repeatedly with a beanbag shotgun—a nonlethal weapon designed to knock a suspect to the ground—for the fun of it. However, other malfeasances were even more lethal. Perez's most incendiary story concerned the 1996 shooting of admitted gang member Javier Francisco Ovando. Ovando was a 19-year-old whom Perez and his partner shot on a drug raid and then, according to Perez, planted a rifle on him to make it look as if Ovando had attacked them. Ovando was paralyzed. But, at the trial, the judge supported the officers and harshly scolded Ovando (who had to be wheeled into court on a gurney) for endangering the lives of two hero police officers. Ovando was sentenced to 23 years in prison. However, in September 1999, the scandal broke and Ovando was released after serving two years and 11 months.[2]

When the case finally went to trial in the fall of 2000, three Rampart officers were found guilty of corruption. Soon after, however, the credibility of Perez's testimony came into question, and the guilty verdicts were overturned. The scandal ultimately resulted in the dismissal of more than 100 criminal cases on the basis of tainted and falsified evidence, as well as civil rights damage claims ranging from $100 million to $300 million.

To many, the officers' behavior in this scandal represented a clear misuse of police authority and brought back into question issues involving possible racism and brutality on the part of the LAPD.

While most people recognize that law enforcement officers are for the most part professional and dedicated public servants, such stories continue to shock and anger citizens. More than ever, police today are faced with considerably more scrutiny than ever before. Stories such as those mentioned earlier remind people that the police are as vulnerable to temptation and misconduct as anyone, and as a result, the question of police ethics is a constant in any discussion about them. Within the context of police behavior, three forms of behavior can be identified: ethical, organizational/political, and legal.

Those standards outlining ethical behavior are reflected in the law enforcement code of ethics and codes of professional conduct. Differing from ethical standards are organizational and political standards. These include those established by individual police departments as well as by state and national commissions. Recommendations made by the latter may or may not be adopted by the profession at large. Organizational standards often emerge from the informal as well as formal organization and are closely related to ethical standards. Legal standards result from procedural and substantive laws that dictate appropriate police behavior. Of these, ethical standards have most recently come under scrutiny by media and public-interest groups.

In our system of criminal justice, the initial decision makers are the police. In addition to being the enforcers of the law, they have the power to define what constitutes law-breaking. In that regard, police are afforded a great deal of discretionary power. For example, they often have the choice to arrest or not to arrest or to mediate or to charge. Furthermore, they possess the power to decide whether to use deadly force, giving them the power of life and death in some circumstances. No other public figure possesses greater authority over the personal destiny of people. After a lengthy criminal trial and painful deliberation, a jury may find a defendant guilty of murder and recommend the death penalty; the judge may respond by giving the death penalty after more personal deliberation; the state may follow through with the recommended execution many years after lengthy appeals. But the police officer, in one split second, without the benefit of law school or judicial roles or legal appeals, acting as judge, jury, and executioner, may accomplish the same end result.

When police stop people for minor traffic violations, they choose either to write tickets or give warnings. When teenagers are picked up for delinquent acts, they may be brought downtown for formal processing or taken home. After stopping a street fight, police may arrest both parties, or they may allow the combatants to work out their problems. As we learned in Chapter 5, in many day-to-day decisions, police hold a great deal of decision-making power over people's lives, because of their power to decide when to enforce the law.

Although there have been many instances of corrupt behavior on the part of the police over the years, it has been said that 1995 will be remembered for a long time as the year when police misconduct emerged as a major social issue. One of the biggest revelations was during the double-murder trial of O. J. Simpson, when retired detective Mark Fuhrman took the stand. In taped interviews Fuhrman repeatedly used the epithet "nigger" and bragged about suspects he had beaten. "We basically tortured them.... Their faces were just mush," he told a would-be screenwriter.

Fuhrman's remarks were revealing, as people wondered whether this was what police were really like. Although it was unclear whether Fuhrman's stories were anything more than empty boasts or true testimonials, his repeated use of the "N-word" gave newfound credibility to citizen complaints of police misconduct around the country. For example:

- In Philadelphia, more than 50 criminal cases made by six rogue police officers were thrown out of court after the officers were implicated in rousting known felons and committing such crimes as robbery, obstruction of justice, and civil rights violations.
- In Atlanta, seven police officers were arrested in 1995 on charges including stealing money during drug searches and extorting money from citizens in exchange for police protection.
- In New Orleans, dozens of police officers were arrested between 1992 and 1995 on charges that included rape, robbery, drug dealing, auto theft, and murder.
- In New York City, 16 officers, implicated in a scandal that broke in 1994 in Harlem, pleaded guilty to charges including stealing cash from drug dealers, extorting money from suspects, and lying about arrests.

American Policing under Fire

The "Rampart Corruption Incident"

The Los Angeles Police Department's Board of Inquiry Report into the "Rampart Corruption Incident" detailed 108 recommendations for improvements in the department. Here are some of the board's major recommendations:

- *Testing and screening of police officer candidates.* Obtain all publicly available information, including criminal records, on candidates; give polygraph examinations to all candidates prior to background investigations.
- *Personnel practices.* Improve tracking of personal investigations; "restore integrity" to the evaluation system; standardize selection for specialized units; and limit tour of duty in specialized units.
- *Personnel investigations and management of risk.* Expand internal affairs investigations to cover all but most minor complaints; expand sting operations and checks of officers financial records; eliminate city charter provisions setting time limits for administrative investigations.

- *Corruption investigations.* Expand the anticorruption unit within internal affairs section; improve consultation with the city attorney and district attorney; allow anticorruption investigations to be conducted from noncity facilities to ensure confidentiality.
- *Operational controls.* Increase the number of field sergeants to improve supervision; improve oversight of specialized units; establish uniform rules on use of informants; strengthen the security of the property division and disposition of evidence; improve review of the use of force to detect patterns involving individual officers.
- *Anticorruption and inspection audits.* Improve audits of investigations.
- *Ethics and integrity training.* "Greatly increase" ethics and integrity training for all employees.
- *Job-specific training.* Improve training for supervisors and watch commanders in particular; develop comprehensive training on cultivating and managing informants.

Source: www.lapdonline.com, 2001.

Historically, police corruption has been associated with bribery, where officers accept cash payments from criminals in exchange for overlooking their offenses. But many of today's corruption cases tend to involve the abuse of criminals rather than collusion with them. Of course, drugs present yet another variable in the police corruption problem. With so much cash money being available to officers, temptations are prevalent. But experts tend to look at the root cause of police corruption as the department's failure to set high standards in hiring, training, and supervision.[3]

In this chapter, police ethics and misconduct are at issue, and we see how the vested authority of the police can be abused. Police officers occupy a high-visibility position in our society, and thus they are often criticized for things the public feels they should be doing or perhaps what they have done. Often, police feel singled out and, therefore, defensive. Perhaps we do tend to critique police activities with the benefit of hindsight, yet the scrutiny is warranted if one understands that police represent government's interface with the lives and freedoms of individuals. Many people expect police to be perfect, both on and off duty, probably because they are the guardians of society, the role models of what is good and right.

Of course, the police aren't any more perfect than anyone else, for news stories abound citing flagrant misapplications of their authority and judgment. But in this chapter we discuss unethical behavior in police organizations and mechanisms that lend support to such behavior. We are also concerned with the individual police officer and personal decision-making processes when confronted with ethical dilemmas.

FOUNDATIONS OF POLICE ETHICS

The belief that police officers should be expected to exhibit a higher standard of behavior than nonsworn citizens should be based on a philosophical foundation. The idea that police officers must display a higher standard of behavior than that of the "average citizen" was originated by enlightenment philosopher Jean-Jacques Rousseau in *The Social Contract* (1762), John Locke in *Two Treatises on Civil Government* (1690), and Thomas Hobbes in *Leviathan* (1651). Based on the concept of the social contract, Rousseau writes: "Each of us puts his person and all his power in common under the supreme direction of the general will, and in our corporate capacity, we receive each member as an indivisible part of the whole."

Under this philosophy, to have an orderly society, the public relinquishes some of its freedoms to the government in exchange for control mechanisms that contribute to the maintenance of order. The government collectively represents the society as a whole and appoints agents (the police) to enforce these control mechanisms. Privileges granted to the government include permission by the people to develop strictly limited processes and procedures.

For example, the government has the right to deprive people of their freedom in specific circumstances or to use force if necessary to protect the rights of the greater society. In exchange for this relinquishment of freedoms, society expects that the government will protect citizens, respect the rights of citizens, and appoint agents who have the integrity to protect citizens and adhere to the conditions of the social contract.

Based on this philosophy, a society can expect the highest standards of behavior and ethical conduct in persons afforded that power to deprive others of their basic liberties. In other words, the public expects the police to behave at the highest levels of integrity and to obey the rules and laws of society clearly in order for a social contract to remain a valid principle. Accordingly, it should be noted that the principles of law in both criminal and civil justice systems are rooted in these values. The expectation of integrity and rule obeyance for police is stamped clearly in our social history.

Formal Ethics

Police take their role of protector very seriously. This role and that of crime fighter form the self-definition of a police officer. Both the formal and informal value systems of any police department promote these definitions and encourage officers to live up to high standards of behavior consistent with them. Most police departments have adopted official, formalized ethical codes. Even departments where large-scale corruption has been found have had well-documented ethical codes with which all the officers must have been familiar. Ethical standards are more prevalent today than they have been in the past. In 1957, the International Association of Chiefs of Police (IACP) promulgated the Law Enforcement Code of Ethics and the Canons of Ethics for Police Officers. Even though these codes are widely adopted, academics have questioned their relevance to individual police officers, arguing that officers should be more concerned with identifying the moral and ethical issues in police decision making than arbitrarily following a code of ethical standards.[4] One academic perspective suggests that police ethics must find their foundation within the values that provide society's foundation.[5]

The police officer code of ethics sets forth ethical expectations for professional police officers and is fairly specific. Principles of justice or fairness are the single most dominant themes. Police officers learn that they must uphold the law regardless of who the offender is and not single out special groups. They cannot use their position to take advantage of people, and they must avoid gratuities, which could give the appearance of special treatment.

Another theme in the police code of ethics is the importance of the law. Police are thought of as tools of the Constitution and are mandated not to go beyond it or supplant rules of their own. Because the law is so important, police must not only be concerned with lawbreakers, but their own behavior must be within the bounds of the law. In all they do, investigation through arrest, their behavior must conform to the dictates of law and policy.

Finally, the theme of behavior is emphasized in the police code of ethics. Police officers must at all times maintain a high standard of behavior consistent with the position as a public servant. To accomplish this, they must practice a higher standard of living in both their public and private lives than other people in society.

Why, then, are ethics so important to the police? The answer could be that ethics play an important part of the internal image of the police, as well as how they are perceived by the citizenry. In theory, the police are supposed to make their decisions in a lawful, fair, and humane manner. Ethical requirements also help to ensure self-respect in individual officers and mutual respect among them. So agreement regarding methods and means is important. As with many professions, an agreed-upon code of ethics can help unify a profession and define it as a professional occupational endeavor.

Ethics and Integrity

Ethical principles are founded in philosophies that are moral, legal, and social in character. They are the embodiment of philosophical principles that apply to the application of one's duties, and are acceptable to society as a whole. As noted sociologist Emile Durkheim observed, "There is no form of social activity which can do without the appropriate moral discipline."[6] Lawyers, physicians, engineers, psychologists, and the clergy all have fundamental ethical principles they rely upon in making everyday decisions that in some way relate to their vocation. Accordingly, police also have important ethical responsibilities that relate to their duties.

Professional misconduct and corruption, by their very nature, violate the spirit of the code of law enforcement officers. Indeed, in any professional organization or profession, the establishment of a code of professional ethics is essential to govern the conduct of any profession's members. The IACP's Law Enforcement Code of Ethics and the Canons of Ethics for Police Officers act as guides of police behavior and decision making.

Similarly, the Canons of Police Ethics places significant responsibilities on officers with specific attention to their off-duty behavior. Notably, Article 6—"Private Conduct" of the Canons states, in part: "The law enforcement officer shall be mindful of his or her special identification by the public as an upholder of the law. Laxity of conduct or manner in private life . . . cannot but reflect upon the police officer and the police service. The community and the service require the law

A Closer Look

The Law Enforcement Code of Ethics

As a law enforcement officer, my fundamental duty is to serve the community; to safeguard lives and property; to protect the innocent against deception, the weak against oppression or intimidation, and the peaceful against violence or disorder; and to respect the constitutional rights of all to liberty, equality, and justice.

- I will keep my private life unsullied as an example to all and will behave in a manner that does not bring discredit to me or to my agency. I will maintain courage and calm in the face of danger, scorn, or ridicule; develop self-restraint; and be constantly mindful of the welfare of others. Honest in thought and deed both in my personal and official life, I will be exemplary in obeying the law and regulations of my department. Whatever I see or hear of a confidential nature or that is confided to me in the performance of my official capacity will be kept ever secret unless revelation is necessary in the performance of my duty.
- I will never act officiously or permit personal feelings, prejudices, political beliefs, aspirations, animosities, or friendships to influence my decisions. With no compromise for crime and with relentless prosecution of criminals, I will enforce the law courteously and appropriately without fear or favor, malice or ill will, never employing unnecessary force or violence and never accepting gratuities.
- I recognize the badge of my office as a symbol of public faith, and I accept it as a public trust to be held so long as I am true to the ethics of police service. I will never engage in acts of corruption or bribery, nor will I condone such acts by other police officers. I will cooperate with all legally authorized agencies and their representatives in the pursuit of justice.
- I know that I alone am responsible for my own standard of professional performance and will take every reasonable opportunity to enhance and improve my level of knowledge and competence. I will constantly strive to achieve these objectives and ideals, dedicating myself before God to my chosen profession . . . law enforcement.[7]

enforcement officer to lead the life of a decent and honorable person. . . . The officer will also conduct his or her private life so that the public will regard him or her as an example of stability, fidelity, and morality."

These standards have been part of the underlying philosophy of police behavior for over 25 years. As one can see, both the Code and the Canons clearly articulate expectations of police officers both on and off duty, but the influence of these writings on actual police behavior is difficult if not impossible to measure. Perhaps one method to help ensure compliance with prescribed ethical practices and avoid corrupt practices is to incorporate the expectations of both the Code and the Canons of Ethics into formalized police procedures and administrative mandates.

THE POLICE SUBCULTURE AND ETHICS

Probably one of the most resistant forces to the acceptance of a formal code of ethics is the police subculture. The police subculture lies at the heart of police work and represents a kind of support system for its officers. To understand how the police subculture relates to police ethics, let's consider some other professions that also have a subculture.

One characteristic of most professions is a dual set of standards—certain behaviors may be considered acceptable for a member of the profession to perform even though the behavior would be wrong if performed by anyone else. For instance, doctors justify certain life-or-death decisions; lawyers withhold information regarding lawbreaking; and politicians often withhold information from the public on the basis of national security. The police are no exception. They too have justifications for certain actions that would be wrong if engaged in by anyone else. Professional ethics should guide these special privileges, but often the occupational subculture endorses less than ethical standards of performance.

The Police Value System

Much research has been conducted to describe the police and the police subculture and through these sources an image of police and the police value system emerges. Some elements of the police value system are inconsistent with the high ideals of the Canons or Codes just described. For example, Sherman describes some common themes running through police attitudes: First, loyalty to colleagues is essential; and second, the public, with few exceptions, is the enemy.[8] Further, he explains that the values of police officers include the use of force and discretion, and a protective use of the truth.

Other writers have also discussed the theme of loyalty. Brown describes police loyalties arising from a fundamental distrust of superiors and bureaucratic administration.[9] Muir explains loyalty by reference to the complicity that develops when police engage in individual rule breaking; once a police officer has violated a standard or rule, he or she is bound to remain silent regarding others' violations, even if they are more serious.[10] Scheingold emphasizes the dominant characteristics of the police subculture: cynicism, use of force, and the police as victims.[11]

Cynicism

Police view all citizens with suspicion. Everyone is a possible problem, but especially those who fit a type. Recruits learn this way of looking at others from older officers if they have not come to the job already holding these perceptions. Cynicism spills over to their relations with other people, since they have found that friends expect favors and special treatment, and since police routinely witness negative behavior even from the most upstanding of people. As a result, their work life leads them to the conclusion that all people are weak, corrupt, and dangerous.

The Use of Force

The police subculture embraces force for all situations wherein a threat is perceived. Threats may be interpreted as acts or statements "against the officer's authority" rather than those against the officer's physical person. So anyone with an "attitude problem" deserves a lesson in humility. Force is both expressive and instrumental. It is a clear symbol of the police officer's perceived authority and legitimate dominance in any interaction with the public, and it is also believed to be the most effective method of control. In other words, everyone understands a club; it cuts across all social and economic barriers and is the most effective tool for keeping people in line and getting them to do what is required without argument.

The Police as Victims

This concept is based on the idea that the police are victims of public misunderstanding and scorn, of low wages and self-serving administrators. This feeling of victimization sets police apart from others and rationalizes a different set of rules for them as opposed to other members of society.[12] There are several factors that lead to the extreme nature of the police subculture:

- The police typically form a homogeneous social group.
- They have a uniquely stressful work environment.
- They participate in a basically closed social system.

Historically, police in the United States have always come from the white middle and lower classes; they are similar racially, culturally, and economically. Because of these similarities, police feel themselves to be more similar to each other than the groups they interact with as part of their job. Homogeneous social groups lead people to think that everyone agrees with the group value or belief because to do otherwise would ostracize the person. Police are set apart further by their work life.

The job of a police officer entails a great deal of stress caused by potential danger and generally unpleasant experiences. Again, this results in the feeling that police are special and different from everyone else. Finally, because of erratic working hours and social stigmatism, their social life tends to be totally centered around other police officers. This results in closed viewpoints and legitimization of subculture values.[13]

The New Subculture

The subculture and the values discussed in Chapter 7 might be breaking down among police departments today. Several factors contribute to the possible weakening of the traditional police subculture. The increasing diversity of police recruits has eliminated the social homogeneity of the workforce. Many diverse groups are now represented in police departments, including African-Americans, Hispanics, women, and the college-educated, even if only in token numbers. These different groups bring elements of their own cultural backgrounds and value systems into the police environment.

Also, the rising power of police unions formalizes relationships between the line staff and the administration, and subcultural methods for coping with perceived administrative unfairness are becoming more formal than informal. Increasingly, individual officers, especially those who come from other backgrounds and are not tied in as strongly to police tradition, may challenge the informal system rather than ignoring or going along with obvious misconduct or corruption. Finally, civil litigation of police misconduct has heightened the risk of covering for another officer. Although police officers may have lied to internal affairs personnel or even on a witness stand to save a fellow officer from sanctions, they are less likely to do so when large money damages may be leveled against them because of negligence and perjury. Yet, it is still safe to say that like any occupational group, the police maintain a value system that guides and provides a rationale for decision making. This value system is more important in influencing behavior than the police standard operating procedures book and code of ethics.

It is apparent that the formal ethical standards of police are quite different from their subcultural values. Violations of formal ethical standards, such as in the use of force, the acceptance of preferential or discriminatory treatment, use of illegal investigation tactics, and differential enforcement of laws, are all supported by the subculture. The police subculture has ethical codes of its own. Muir describes some elements of the informal police code: "You cover your men: don't let any officer take a job alone," "keep a cool head," and "don't backdoor it," a prohibition against certain gratuities.[14] The reason these differences exist may be related to the mixed goals under which police are forced to operate. On the one hand, they are given the task of protecting society and catching criminals, but this would sometimes be impossible to do if they followed all legal guidelines.

For some crimes it seems that one must act like a criminal to catch a criminal. To investigate prostitutes or drug dealers usually involves undercover work, which in turn involves methods that may violate established court guidelines. Very few criminal cases would be solved if police depended on observation and chase alone to catch criminals. Innovation is often required. Yet the most expedient methods to uncover crime may also directly violate ethical and legal standards.

Ethical dilemmas may differ depending on police function. Patrol officers are the most visible members of the police force and have a duty to patrol, detect, and intervene in matters of reported crime and conflict within the community. In comparison, detectives are concerned primarily with discovering wrongdoing and collecting evidence to be used in court, for purposes of securing a conviction. The ethical decisions these two units encounter often differ.

Patrol officers may have to make ethical decisions relevant to their decision-making power in defining crime and initiating the formal legal process. In doing so they are subject to the temptations

Highlights in Policing

Police Values

Discretion A. Decisions about whether to enforce the law, in any but the most serious cases, should be guided by both what the law says and who the suspect is. Attitude, demeanor, cooperativeness, and even race, age, and social class are all important considerations in deciding how to treat people.

Discretion B. Disrespect for police authority is a serious offense that should always be punished with an arrest or the use of force. The number one "offense," known as "contempt of cop" or P.O.P.O. (pissing off a police officer), cannot be ignored. Even when the party has committed no violation of the law, a police officer should find a safe way to impose punishment, including an arrest on fake charges.

Force. Police officers should never hesitate to use physical or deadly force against people who "deserve it," or where it can be an effective way of solving a crime. Only potential punishment by superior officers, civil litigation, citizen complaints, and so on, should limit the use of force when the situation calls for it. When you can get away with it, use all the force that society should use on people like that—force and punishment that bleeding-heart judges are too soft to impose.

Due process. Due process is only a means of protecting criminals at the expense of the law-abiding citizen, and should be ignored whenever it is safe to do so. Illegal searches and wiretaps, interrogation without advising suspects of their *Miranda* rights, and if need be (as in the much admired movie, "Dirty Harry"), even physical pain to coerce a confession are all acceptable methods for accomplishing the goal the public wants the police to accomplish: fighting crime. The rules against doing those things merely handcuff the police, making it more difficult for them to do their job.

Truth. Lying and deception are an essential part of the police job, and even perjury should be used if it is necessary to protect yourself or get a conviction on a "bad guy." Violations of due process cannot be admitted to prosecutors or in court, so perjury (in the 5% of cases that ever go to trial) is necessary and therefore proper. Lying to drug pushers about wanting to buy drugs, to prostitutes about wanting to buy sex, or to members of Congress about wanting to buy influence is the only

way, and therefore a proper way, to investigate these crimes without victims. Deceiving muggers into thinking that you are an easy mark and deceiving burglars into thinking you are a fence are proper because there are not many other ways of catching predatory criminals in the act.

Time. You cannot go fast enough to chase a car thief or catch a violator, nor slow enough to get to a "garbage" call; and when there are no calls for service, your time is your own. Hot pursuits are necessary; anyone who tries to escape from the police is challenging police authority, no matter how trivial the initial offense. But calls to nonserious or social work problems such as domestic disputes or kids making noise are unimportant, so you can stop to get coffee on the way or even stop at the cleaner's if you like. When there are no calls, you can sleep, visit friends, study, or do anything else you can get away with, especially on the midnight shift, when you can get away with a lot.

Rewards. Police do very dangerous work for low wages, so it is proper to take any extra rewards the public wants to give them, such as free meals, Christmas gifts, or even regular monthly payments (in some cities) for special treatment. The general rule is: Take any reward that doesn't change what you would do anyway, such as eating a meal, but don't take money that would affect your job, such as not giving traffic tickets. In many cities, however, especially in the recent past, the rule has been to take even those rewards that do affect your decisions, as long as they are related only to minor offenses: traffic, gambling, prostitution, and so on, but not murder.

Loyalty. The paramount duty is to protect your fellow officers at all costs, as they would protect you, even though you may have to risk your own career or your own life to do it. If your colleagues make a mistake, take a bribe, seriously hurt somebody illegally, or get into other kinds of trouble, you should do everything you can to protect them in the ensuing investigation. If your colleagues are routinely breaking rules, you should never tell supervisors, reporters, or outside investigators about it. If you don't like it, quit or get transferred to the police academy. But never, ever, blow the whistle.

Source: Learning police ethics, by L. Sherman, *Criminal Justice Ethics, 1*(1), 10–19 (1982). Copyright 1982 by the John Jay College of Criminal Justice. Reprinted by permission.

of gratuities. On the other hand, by the nature of their work, undercover officers are not under the same scrutiny as their patrol counterparts, since they work with minimal supervision. As a result, they are removed from formal ethical guidelines because the nature of their work emphasizes the end of conviction rather than the means of how one goes about collecting evidence.

Another reason that subcultural values are not consistent with ethical standards is related to the social isolation and feeling of victimization characteristic of the police subculture. When a group feels that it is special for any reason, very often different rules are perceived to apply only to them. These rules may also involve different ethical standards created to justify the rules. This is true for other professions as well; for instance, business professionals often justify leaving work early because they work evenings and weekends as opposed to hourly staff, who punch a clock regardless of tasks yet to be completed.

Representatives and senators in Congress may find it appropriate to take trips and receive services at the public expense because they could earn more money in private business than their government salary. In similar ways, police are able to justify behavior that would be wrong if engaged in by others because of their unique position. For instance, police may feel that the use of force to exact revenge is acceptable because they are often the victims. Police may feel justified in accepting gratuities because their pay is less than they feel they deserve, and they risk their lives every day.

Police also hear mixed messages from the public regarding certain types of crime. They are asked to enforce crimes against gambling, pornography, and prostitution, but not too stringently. They are expected to enforce crimes against DWI but also to be tolerant of individuals who "really didn't mean any harm." They are expected to uphold laws regarding assault, unless it is a family or interpersonal dispute that is being settled privately. In other words, we want the police to enforce the law unless they enforce it against "us."

The police role as enforcer in a pluralistic society can be problematic. The justification for police power is that police represent the public: "The police officer can only validly use coercive force when he or she in fact represents the body politic."[15] But if they do not represent all groups, their power is defined as extreme and oppressive. It should be no surprise that the police were seen as an invading army in the south central ghetto of Los Angeles in the early 1990s after the officers accused of beating Rodney King were acquitted by an all-white jury. They were not seen as representatives of the people who were the target of their force. Even now, police encounter resistance from groups that feel threatened and thus are unwilling to accept police power on an individual level. Some police officers may themselves have personal difficulties enforcing laws against the interests of certain groups.

Police feel that it is appropriate and acceptable to the public to use a great deal of discretion in their enforcement of the law. Discretion is a good thing and it is a necessary element in the law, but it also leads to a greater dependence on individual ethical standards in place of rules and laws. It is in these areas that police sometimes face ethical dilemmas. For police officers, these ethical dilemmas are part of the job. Muir describes the moral dilemmas of the police officer as frequent and unavoidable; not academic; always unpopular with some groups; usually made quickly; dealt with alone; and involving complex criteria.[16]

DISCRETION AND ETHICS

As we have seen so far in this book, police possess a great deal of discretion in defining criminal behavior and their reaction to it. Discretion gives the police officer the latitude to make either a formal or informal contact with a lawbreaker: the freedom to follow through with a full-blown arrest or simply warn violators. In one study it was found that police do not make arrests in 43% of all felony cases and 52% of all misdemeanor cases.[17] The amount of discretion depends on the style of the policing characteristic of a certain area. For instance, the legalistic style of policing is described as the least amenable to discretionary policing, since full enforcement and established procedures are emphasized.

The watchman and the caretaker styles, however, are characterized by discretionary enforcement. In the watchman style, police have the power to decide whether situations are threatening or serious, depending on the groups or individuals involved, and to act accordingly. The caretaker style treats citizens differentially depending on their relative power and position in society.[18]

The new "professional police" are said to be increasingly bureaucratic in their decision making. However, old values die hard, and even in departments that emphasize a professional orientation, one finds individual adaptations. For instance, Brown describes four types: the "old-style crime fighter," who is only concerned with action that might be considered crime control; the "clean beat officer," who seeks to control all behavior in his or her jurisdiction; the "service style," which emphasizes public order and peace officer tasks; and the "professional style," which is the epitome of bureaucratic, by-the-book policing.[19]

Muir describes the following types: the professional, who balances coercion with compassion; the reciprocating officer, who allows citizens to solve problems and may engage in deals to keep the peace; the enforcer, who uses coercion exclusively; and the avoider, who either cannot handle the power that he or she must use or fears it and so avoids situations where he or she may be challenged.[20]

The very nature of policing necessarily involves some amount of discretion. Gaines and colleagues write that discretion is at the heart and soul of policing and is an inescapable part of our justice process.[21] But discretion opens the door, however, for decision making outside the confines of legality. Unethical police behavior often arises directly from the power of discretion. Because police officers have the power to select and entrap suspects, they can also make that decision unethically, such as by taking a bribe in return for letting a suspect go. Since they have the power to decide how best to conduct an investigation, they may decide to use this power to entrap and select suspects in a biased or otherwise unfair manner rather than by probable cause. They also may resort to extralegal means to control behavior. Selective enforcement, for instance, may not necessarily be crime control but rather, harassment designed to make an undesired person leave an area.[22]

Discretion is by no means limited to law enforcement. As we observed in earlier chapters, discretion is an important element in the criminal justice practitioner's role and plays a part in the creation of numerous ethical dilemmas. Discretion in criminal justice has been attacked as contributing to injustice. An argument could be made that solutions to discretion are unsatisfactory, since the suggested rules and standards either limit decision making to mechanistic applications of given rules or provide only rhetorical ideals with little or no enforcement capability.

POLICE MISCONDUCT

On July 30, 1996, just hours after chatting with Katie Couric on the set of NBC's *Today show*, Richard Jewell found himself on a very different kind of studio set. FBI headquarters in Atlanta was a frenzied place three days after the Centennial Olympic Park bombing, and Jewell was under the impression that he had been invited to a fourth-floor conference room to help agents make a training film on interrogating witnesses. What Jewell didn't know was that at the very minute he was obligingly answering the FBI's questions on videotape and waiving his rights to a lawyer, newspaper vendors on the streets just outside were selling special editions identifying him as the prime suspect in the July 27 bombing.

That early evening encounter soon became the focus of an internal Justice Department investigation of tactics the FBI used to interrogate Jewell, who three months later was exonerated of the crime. But more than that, the meeting provided a rare window on the nation's premier law enforcement agency and what some believe are controversial techniques commonly used to pry information from suspects or witnesses in high-profile criminal investigations. Some have argued that the Jewell interrogation technique was an innovative lawful ploy, while others have condemned the technique, saying it was a blatant abuse of Jewell's constitutional right to counsel. The question in the Jewell case is whether this technique constitutes corruption; but more importantly, the broader question is: While pursuing dangerous criminals, to what extent may police bend the rules?

Over the years, high-level investigations have revealed large numbers of police misconduct cases in a number of U.S. cities. Among them are Los Angeles, New York, Detroit, Philadelphia, Washington, DC, and Miami. In 1997, the *Law Enforcement News* reported some revealing statistics regarding the number of police misconduct cases in Florida.[23] A report issued by the Florida Department of Law Enforcement and internal affairs reports that in 15 south Florida police departments, from 1977 to 1989, the state investigated 2,047 offenses. But from 1990 through 1996, there were 5,136 cases investigated—more than twice as many in less than half the time. One should consider that certain forms of improper police conduct may not lend themselves to some definitions of corruption, per se. For example, on August 27, 1996, Indianapolis Police Chief Donald Christ sponsored a special night out for officers of his elite tactical team as a reward for a job well done. What was supposed to be an all-American night out turned into an ugly downtown street brawl after the officers were confronted by two men who, after some racial slurs were exchanged, were then beaten and arrested on minor charges. As a result, two officers were fired, two suspended, and three demoted. Chief Christ resigned one month later under severe public criticism of the incident.

To some, a "boy's night out" might be an excuse for some civilians on a rowdy night out, but in this case the behavior of the officers was clearly unacceptable. It might not have constituted what many would consider "corrupt behavior," but such behavior was clearly unacceptable according to the city's standards of professional conduct. On the other hand, since it was done purposely and under "color of law," some might argue that the incident could be considered corrupt in nature.

The available research and literature on police deviance offers little with regard to police misconduct. It is likely that many instances of misconduct are handled informally within the police department without much public notoriety, thus resulting in such cases being difficult to discover and study. Barker and Carter suggest that police deviance can take one of several forms: criminality, corruption, and ethical and work norm violations. They also suggest that each of these violates at

FIGURE 9.1   A provocatively dressed prostitute leans over the side of a New York City cruiser.

least one of three normative standards: (1) criminal laws, (2) departmental standards, and (3) ethical police standards.[24] So police misconduct can vary from flagrant violations of criminal law to a breach of prescribed ethical standards.

Sex on Duty

The job of policing requires officers to come into contact with members of the opposite sex on a daily basis. Such contacts include both criminal and civilian encounters, complainants, victims, informants, and so on. Many such encounters pave the way for familiarization between the officer and the subject. For example, a male investigator might cultivate a female informant with whom he is required to work closely over a long period. In addition, patrol officers responding to crimes of violence may be perceived by victims as "heroes," and personal relationships may develop. Police officers typically work late shifts and are often under minimal direct supervision. Patrol officers also have the opportunity to stop women driving home after drinking with friends. These conditions make it opportune for officers, if so inclined, to meet and engage in sexual activity during their shifts. Such activity may occur while on duty and sometimes in official police vehicles or at the residences of their paramours.

Sleeping on Duty

As with all occupations in which supervision is minimal and the occupational environment is slow, as with nighttime work, sleeping can be construed as misconduct. Police work, in particular, poses special concerns for administrators because the public trusts that the police are conducting their rounds in the community rather than sleeping. The most important consideration regarding officers sleeping on duty is that police work is a 24-hour occupation and that most of society functions during daylight hours. The criminal justice system, in particular, court proceedings, also operates primarily during the daytime hours, Officers who are subpoenaed for court must often report during their sleeping time or days off, creating a sleep deficit. As mentioned, when supervision is lax, according to recent research, sleeping on duty becomes more prevalent. So when the officer's official duties require him or her to go without sleep and when little supervision is employed, the likelihood for sleeping on duty increases.

Drinking on Duty

As with other occupations, police officers are prohibited from consuming alcohol while on duty. This prohibition is set forth by departmental policy and procedure. For obvious reasons, the police officer who drinks while on duty poses unique dangers to the department and the public citizenry. Police officers carry guns, possess powers of arrest, and are relied upon by the general public to be alert and able at all times in the event they are needed.

Officers who drink on duty also place in jeopardy the well-being of officers whom they are required to back up. Alcohol may make officers overreact to situations and it will slow down officers' responses when dealing with violent persons or when operating their police vehicle. The problem of drinking by police officers may be construed as a symptom of a problem in addition to being a problem in its own right. For example, the officers may be experiencing family problems at home, problems with coworkers or supervisors, boredom with their job, or may simply be experiencing a drinking problem, which requires professional treatment.

SEXUAL HARASSMENT

While the abuse of power is the focus of this chapter, another type of abuse of power should also be discussed—sexual harassment. Sexual harassment is nothing new, nor are the legal remedies against it. It has been recognized for over 20 years as a form of sex discrimination under the Civil Rights

Act of 1964. However, allegations of improper behavior in all branches of government have become more commonplace in today's society. As one might guess, these cases have resulted in a heightened awareness about sexual harassment. In recent years, members of the police profession have seen their share of claims in this area.

The **Civil Rights Act of 1964** makes it illegal to discriminate on the basis of race, color, age, religion, national origin, and sex. **Title VII** of the act prohibits employers from, among other things, discriminating on the basis of sex with respect to compensation, terms, conditions, or privileges of employment.[25] Sexual harassment is simply one of several forms of sexual discrimination. Sexual harassment is defined as unwanted sexual advances, requests for sexual favors, and other verbal or physical conduct that enters into employment decisions or that reasonably interferes with a person's work performance. Two types of sexual harassment are at issue since they are the most likely to occur in a work environment: quid pro quo and hostile work environment harassment.

Quid Pro Quo Harassment

Loosely translated, *quid pro quo* means "something for something." This type of harassment occurs when an employee is required to choose between submitting to sexual advances or losing a tangible job benefit. An essential part of quid pro quo harassment is the harasser's power to control the employee's employment benefits. Typically, this type of harassment occurs between supervisor and subordinate. Criteria for quid pro quo harassment include:

- The harassment must be based on sex.
- The claimant was subjected to unwelcome sexual advances.
- A tangible economic benefit of the job was conditional on the claimant's submission to the unwelcome sexual advances.

In quid pro quo cases, harassment consists of unwelcome sexual advances, requests for sexual favors, and other verbal or physical conduct of a sexual nature. However, there is no requirement that these requests be express demands for sexual favors. Advances may be implied by the circumstances and actions: for example, inviting a claimant out for drinks or offering a claimant sexually explicit magazines. The hallmark of sexual harassment (either type) is that the advances are unwelcome. "Unwelcome" means that the person did not invite or solicit the advances. This is determined by an objective standard and not by the claimant's subjective feelings.

Hostile Work Environment Harassment

Hostile work environment harassment is unwelcome conduct that is so severe or pervasive as to change the conditions of the claimant's employment and create an intimidating, hostile, or offensive work environment. In the landmark case of *Meritor Savings Bank* v. *Vinson* (1986), the U.S. Supreme Court found that a hostile work environment amounts to unlawful sex discrimination even in the absence of the loss of a tangible job benefit. Allowing supervisory personnel to date or cohabit with subordinates poses considerable risk for police departments. This is because under quid pro quo liability, the supervisor engaged in the relationship may be considered to be acting on behalf of, or as an agent of, the employer. So if the romantic relationship is determined to be unwelcome, the employer is automatically held accountable for sexual harassment by the supervisor, even if the supervisor may believe that the relationship is consensual.

Even before a dating relationship develops, flirting and romantic pursuits between coworkers may be viewed as sexual harassment, as illustrated in *Ellison* v. *Brady*. In that case, Ellison, a female Internal Revenue Service (IRS) Agent was approached by a coworker who attempted to strike up a relationship. The female agent did go to lunch with the male agent, but thereafter, she expressed no interest in a dating relationship. The male agent continued to pester and write notes to the female agent, and the IRS interceded by transferring the male agent temporarily. Eventually, however, the male agent was transferred back to the same office as that of the female agent, and she sued, alleging a hostile work environment. The court reviewed the case and agreed that the hostile working environment did constitute a valid sexual harassment claim.

Because of the threat of sexual harassment claims, some argue that dating relationships be discouraged between coworkers. However, constitutional rights to privacy and association do not support such an across-the-board prohibition.[26] The right-to-privacy cases, however, generally do not support attempts by police managers to restrict off-duty relationships between employee and a nonemployee, and few police cases discuss the constitutionality of restricting dating and cohabitation between coworkers of equal stature in the workplace. Those involving superior–subordinate relationships, however, are supported by case law.

POLICE CORRUPTION

As history attests, policing is an occupation that is rife with opportunities for misconduct. Policing is a highly discretionary, coercive activity that routinely takes place in private settings, out of the sight of supervisors, and in the presence of witnesses who are often regarded as unreliable. Corruption—the abuse of police authority for gain—is one type of misconduct that has been particularly problematic. Klockars and colleagues note that the difficulties of controlling corruption can be traced to several factors:[27]

1. The reluctance of police officers to report corrupt activities by their fellow officers (a.k.a. "The code," "The code of silence," or "The Blue Curtain")
2. The reluctance of police administrators to acknowledge the existence of corruption in their agencies
3. The benefits of the typical corrupt transaction to the parties involved
4. The lack of immediate victims willing to report corruption

Police corruption erodes communities and the governments that oversee them. Where official corruption exists, erosion of public service, falloff of confidence in government competency, and an overall lack of public trust and credibility result.

While the LAPD Rampart investigation (Chapter 1) was one of the largest police corruption investigations in history, it illustrates a growing concern throughout the nation. The statistics speak for themselves: Between 1994 and 1998, over 500 officers in 47 cities were convicted of various

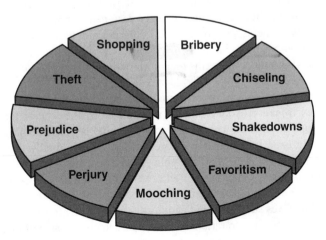

FIGURE 9.2 Types of police corruption.
Source: From Stoddard, 1968.

federal crimes. Local and state authorities in 32 other jurisdictions were also engaged in active investigations or prosecutions of police corruption.[28] Consider the following cases:

- In Detroit, federal agents arrested three city police officers in early 1997 who were planning a "home invasion" in the suburb of Southfield, Michigan, with the intent to steal $1 million in cash.
- In March 1998, Starr County, Texas Sheriff Eugenio Falcon resigned from office after pleading guilty to conspiracy to commit burglary. The investigation revealed that Falcon and other officers referred prisoners to a local bail bond business in exchange for kickback payments. On some occasions, payments were made directly to the sheriff's department.
- In New Jersey, nine current or former West New York police officers were charged in a 69-count federal indictment with taking part in a $600,000 bribery and kickback scheme.

Such cases differ somewhat from those of earlier generations of police officers, when officers were simply paid to look the other way while prostitution or gambling rings prospered. But it is becoming increasingly clear that many police officers are choosing to cross the line and become active participants in crime.

As we consider the many issues involving ethics and corruption, a distinction should be made between misconduct and corruption, and that distinction could be the difference between a lapse of good judgment and criminal wrongdoing. Police corruption takes place when an officer receives or is promised significant advantage or reward for any of the following four behaviors:

1. Doing something that he or she is under duty to do anyway
2. Doing something that he or she is under duty not to do
3. Exercising a legitimate discretion for improper reasons
4. Employing illegal means to achieve approved goals[29]

Use of this definition provides clarification of a number of issues that have surrounded discussions of police corruption. For example, the reward may be personal (money, gifts, access to power) or organizational (promotion, peer support, approval of superiors).

The reward may also be other than material; it may consist, for example, of professional preferment resulting from advancing the agency's goals through illicit means. At the same time, it distinguishes corruption from other forms of police misconduct. These include brutality that is not in furtherance of the organization's goals, "cooping" (sleeping on the job), performing private errands during one's shift, "landing a cushy detail" (e.g., getting a comfortable assignment, or pilfering), absenteeism, and cutting administrative corners. Corruption, as opposed to other forms of misconduct, always involves a benefit for the police officer in exchange for an abuse of the officer's power.

Herman Goldstein attempts to clarify the issue by offering his own definition: "[Corruption is] the misuse of authority by a police officer in a manner designed to produce personal gain for the officer or others." Two key elements should be noted in this definition: misuse of authority and personal gain.[30] In comparison, Sherman defines corruption as "an illegal use of organizational power for personal gain." In this definition, the terms *illegal use*, *organizational power*, and *personal gain* are emphasized.[31]

We must consider that corruption comes in many forms and may be a matter of perception. To accept protection money from a prostitute may be rationalized by the relative lack of concern the public shows for this type of violator. The same argument could be made about gambling or even drugs. We often, formally, expect the police to enforce laws while, informally, encouraging them to ignore the same laws. Would we even want the police to enforce every law fully? Many laws are outdated and exist only on paper. Other laws, if enforced against the general populace, would lead to ridiculous scenarios: for example, laws restricting certain sexual behaviors or other private matters. As long as the public gives such clear indications that it is willing to overlook many crimes, it is no surprise that the police are able to rationalize nonenforcement of some of those crimes.

Police routinely deal with the seamier side of society, not only drug addicts and muggers, but middle-class people who are involved in dishonesty and corruption. The constant displays of lying, hiding, cheating, and theft create cynicism and threaten even the strongest code of ethics, especially when judges, prosecutors, supervisors, and politicians carry out these behaviors. The following are some rationales that might easily be used by police to justify behavior.[32]

- "The public thinks that every cop is a crook, so why try to be honest? The money is out there—if I don't take it, someone else will."
- "I'm only taking what's rightfully mine; if the city paid me a decent wage, I wouldn't have to get it on my own."
- "I can use it—it's for a good cause—my son needs an operation, or dental work, or tuition for medical school, or a new bicycle...."

Given constant exposure to others' misdeeds, peer pressure to conform, and previously vague or nonexistent ideas about right and wrong, the question is not why some officers engage in corrupt practices but rather, why more don't. Although research indicates the lack of an affinity argument for police corruption, one belief is that deviant individuals are attracted to police work. Affiliation theory is persuasive, arguing that police learn from each other. Many police develop along what Lawrence Sherman calls a **moral career**.[33] People pass through various stages of rationalization to more serious misdeeds in a graduated and systematic way. Once a person is able to get past the first moral crisis, it becomes less difficult to rationalize new and more unethical behaviors. The previous behaviors serve as an underpinning to a different ethical standard, since one must explain and justify one's own behavior for psychological well-being.[34]

Books such as *Serpico* and *Prince of the City* detail the pervasiveness of this type of behavior in some departments and the relative ease with which individual officers may develop rationales to justify greater and greater infractions. For instance, the main character in *Prince of the City* progressed from relatively minor rule infractions to fairly serious unethical conduct, such as supplying drugs to an addicted informant, without having to make major decisions regarding his morality. It was only when the totality of his actions became apparent that he realized the extent of his deviance. Bribes from prostitutes may lead to bribes from drug pushers and organized crime figures. Justifying taking a few things from a store burglary and adding them to the list of stolen goods may lead to greater and more blatant theft.

When lines are drawn between gradations of behavior, they can more easily be moved farther and farther away from an absolute standard of morality. Many believe that gratuities are only the first step in a spiral downward. In Sherman's discussion of the moral career of a police officer, the first decision to engage in unethical behavior makes subsequent decisions easier. Other authors are more pessimistic: "For police, the passage from free coffee at the all-night diner and Christmas gifts to participation in drug dealing and organized burglary is normally a slow if steady one."[35] Malloy describes a passage from "perks" to "shopping" (taking items from a burglary scene before the victim arrives) to premeditated theft.[36]

Police misdeeds are only marginally different from the unethical behaviors of members of other occupations: for instance, doctors who prescribe unneeded surgery or experiment with unknown drugs, businesspeople who cheat on their expense accounts or overcharge clients, and contract bidders and purchase agents who offer and accept bribes. It is an unfortunate fact of life that people in any profession or occupation will find ways to exploit their positions for personal gain. This is not to excuse these actions but rather to show that police are probably no more deviant than other professional groups.

HISTORICAL IMPLICATIONS

America's experience with police corruption and the response to it has been unique, and the history of corruption in the United States has influenced the character of U.S. law enforcement in a number of ways. Historically, urban U.S. police officers bought their jobs, their assignments, and their promotions; they expected to recoup the costs and make a tidy profit from graft. The vice laws—those regulating alcohol, gambling, and prostitution—were the most common source of such graft, which were supplemented by violators of regulations pertaining to traffic, health, building codes, and Sabbath closings. Less common but not unknown were shakedowns, extortion, sale of information and protection to criminals, armed robbery, auto theft, and looting. A series of postwar scandals did not eliminate corruption, and in 1979 a federal prosecutor indicted the entire Philadelphia police force for its methods and its unwillingness to cooperate in the investigation of corruption.

The Knapp Commission

Perhaps the most publicized scandal in the past 30 years, and the one with the farthest-reaching impact was the Knapp Commission investigation of the New York City Police Department. By televising its hearings, the commission focused national and international attention on the widespread and highly organized corruption it uncovered, corruption that reached into the upper ranks and was commonly accepted by police officers. It also revealed how the traditional distinction between "clean" and "dirty" money had become blurred in practice with the introduction of the buying, selling, and stealing of narcotics. Finally, the Knapp Commission introduced the memorable terms **grass eater** and **meat eater** to describe officers who, respectively, simply accepted whatever corrupt money came their way and those who actively sought out corruption opportunities.

The Christopher and Kolts Commissions

In response to the 1991 Rodney King incident, Mayor Tom Bradley of Los Angeles assembled a commission to conduct an internal investigation into the infrastructure and ethos of the LAPD. Warren Christopher chaired the Independent Commission on the LAPD; thus the Christopher Commission evolved as the name of the report. At the same time, the Los Angeles County Sheriff's Department (LASD) was experiencing similar difficulties with chronic incidents of excessive force followed by citizen complaints. Sheriff Sherman Block of Los Angeles County responded to the events surrounding his own deputies, the King incident, and the formation of the Christopher Commission by creating an internal commission to examine the operations of the LASD. Block named Judge James G. Kolts to act as chair and special counsel on this internal commission. Together, these commission reports painted a grim picture of pervasive tolerance by both the LAPD and the LASD of chronic misconduct by a core group of officers.

Soon after the King incident, the Christopher Commission began an internal investigation of the LAPD. In July 1991, it published its findings and recommendations. One year later, in July 1992, the Kolts Commission released its findings. Although the two commissions were not collaborative, the Kolts Commission indicated that its investigation of the LASD was influenced by the Christopher Commission. Furthermore, although the two commissions investigated different agencies—LAPD and LASD—the departments had many elements in common: such factors as indigenous residential populations, similar agency practices, adjacent and overlapping police jurisdictions, operational collaboration between agencies, and police subcultural customs being the most obvious. Initial impressions of the Rodney King incident suggested that police use of excessive force might be an aberration or isolated event. Members of the Christopher and Kolts commissions, Mayor Bradley, and law enforcement advocacy groups nationwide hoped that the King incident was indeed an anomaly of police behavior. However, many Los Angeles city and county residents held different views about the incident and described the agencies as callous, unresponsive, and often abusive.[37]

The Christopher Commission was openly critical of the LAPD's failure to control brutal officers as the "heart of the problem." The commission, a blue-ribbon panel appointed in the wake of the Rodney King incident, issued over 100 recommendations, ranging from tighter supervision and better screening of job applicants to racial sensitivity training. Studies have also shown that a few officers tend to be responsible for a high proportion of shootings, citizens' lawsuits, or complaints of brutality. The commission found that from 1986 to 1990, 10% of LAPD officers accounted for 28% of the complaints of excessive force or improper tactics. Out of the 8,000-member police force, citizen complaints of excessive force were filed against 1,800 officers. Over 1,400 had only one or two complaints against them. But 183 officers had four or more allegations. The 44 officers singled out by the commission as "problem officers" had six or more complaints. As Walker and colleagues observed, "the commission found evidence of a subculture that tolerated racist statements and failed to discipline officers guilty of misconduct."[38]

The Mollen Commission

In 1993, another large-scale corruption case was revealed in New York City by the Mollen Commission. The commission's star witness, police officer Michael Dowd, testified how his so-called losers club of rogue police officers extorted protection money from drug dealers and sold stolen cocaine to suburban Long Island teenagers. Dowd further testified that beating up drug dealer suspects in the presence of other officers became a test of officers' tolerance for further acts of corruption. Dowd testified, "You kick some punk down the stairs in front of 10 cops and you have 10 friends.... Young officers tested one another: How much bad could you be entrusted to see before you ratted on another cop?" The Mollen Commission found that police officers who engaged in the most egregious corruption, such as pocketing drug money, had started out by abusing and beating defendants. Experience has shown that once minor offenses have been committed, officers are more likely to graduate up to more serious offenses.[39]

Types of Police Corruption

Corruption is not limited to its most conspicuous form: the acceptance of cash in exchange for an official favor. A number of researchers have made contributions to the literature of police corruption in attempting to explain its phenomenon. For example, Johnston identifies different varieties of police corruption and cites four major corruption categories:[40]

1. *Internal corruption.* This includes acts among police officers themselves and involves behaviors from the bending of rules to the outright commission of illegal acts. For example, in October 1996, the FBI Chief E. Michael Kahoe was charged with obstructing justice by destroying all traces of an after-action internal critique of FBI operations during the siege of white separatist Randy Weaver's mountain home in Ruby Ridge, Idaho. The Ruby Ridge incident resulted in the murder of a federal U.S. marshal and the killing of Weaver's wife and teenage son.

2. *Selective enforcement.* Police officers exploit their officer discretion. For example, a detective who arrests and releases a drug trafficker in exchange for valuable information about the trafficker's organizations is not abusing his or her authority, but one who releases the same trafficker for money is in clear abuse of his or her discretion and authority.

3. *Active criminality.* Police officers participate in serious criminal activity using their positions of power and influence to commit the criminal acts they are entrusted to enforce. An example is the March 4, 1995, robbery and murder of a Vietnamese restaurant owner by Antoinette Frank, a 23-year-old New Orleans police officer. Frank then executed the son and daughter of the restaurant's immigrant owners. Frank exited in a battered Toyota only to return in her police cruiser as though she was responding to the robbery call, which came out on her police radio. But a third sibling was hiding in a nearby walk-in refrigerator and later in court identified Frank as the killer.

4. *Bribery/extortion.* This occurs when police officers use their vested authority to generate a personal source of money. Bribery is initiated by the citizen while extortion is initiated by the officer.

Building on our understanding of corruption, researcher Elwin Stoddard has constructed a list of several specific forms of behavior that he considers corrupt in nature.[41] Note that some categories are more serious in nature than others, suggesting that unacceptable police behavior may be blatant violations under law or simple lapses in professional judgment.

- *Bribery.* The receipt of cash or a "gift" in exchange for past or future assistance in avoidance of prosecution, as by a claim that the officer is unable to make a positive identification of a criminal or by being in the wrong place at a time when a crime is to occur, or by any other action that may be excused as carelessness but not offered as proof of deliberate miscarriage of justice. It is distinguished from mooching (see later in this list) by the higher value of the gift and by the mutual understanding in regard to services to be performed upon the acceptance of the gift.

- *Chiseling.* The demand for price discounts or free admission to places of entertainment regardless of any connection with official police work. This differs from mooching (see later in this list), as it is initiated by the officer, not the business proprietor. In this case, business owners and workers comply out of fear—fear that the police officer will be less than responsive when and if a crime is ever committed on the premises or fear that the officer will look closer for violations committed by the business or its employees if the favor is not granted.

- *Shakedown.* The common practice of holding "street court," where minor traffic tickets can be avoided with a cash payment to the officer and no receipt given. Using the **shakedown**, police have also been known to extort money from tavern owners and other businesses by threatening to enforce city health and zoning codes.

- *Favoritism.* The practice of issuing license tabs, window stickers, or courtesy cards that exempt users from arrest or citation from traffic offenses (frequently extended to family members of officers).

- *Mooching.* The acceptance of free coffee, cigarettes, meals, liquor, or groceries, justified by being in an underpaid profession or for future acts of favoritism for the donor. Many restaurant chains, as well as doughnut and coffee shops, have adopted policies of providing discount meals on a regular basis. This ensures that there will be a continued police presence at the establishment at virtually all times and is justified as being cheaper than hiring a full-time security guard for protection.

- *Perjury.* A willingness to lie under oath to provide an alibi for fellow officers apprehended in unlawful activity.

- *Prejudice.* Treatment of minority groups in a manner less than impartial, neutral, or objective, especially members of such groups who are unlikely to have "influence" in city hall that might cause trouble for the arresting officer.

- *Premeditated theft.* Predatory criminal activity, including planned burglary involving the use of tools, keys, or other devices to gain entry or any prearranged plan to acquire property unlawfully. Unlike some others, this form of corruption is rarely tolerated by police departments.

- *Shopping.* Opportunistic theft, including picking up small items such as cigarettes, candy bars, jewelry, or money at a store that has accidentally been left unlocked at the close of business hours or at the scene of a fire or burglary.[42]

Even seemingly benign actions such as accepting a free cup of coffee or free admittance to the local movie theater may constitute corruption—or at least a predisposition for such behavior. More suggests that although on the surface the acceptance of a free meal or cup of coffee may seem insignificant, there is every reason to believe that it creates an atmosphere conducive to corruption.[43] So, to ensure a police force that can function within the community while being free of compromises, all such behavior should be scrutinized closely. This will protect the citizenry from a police force that gives preferential treatment to businesses that offer gratuities.

A Closer Look

Profiles of Violence-Prone Police Officers

- Young officers: badge-happy, immature, and impulsive
- Those facing serious personal problems such as divorce or death in family
- Suffering from burnout

- Troubled by enduring personality problems, such as abusive or paranoid tendencies
- "Old-school" officers, or "dinosaurs," who use a heavy-handed policing style[44]

Lawrence Sherman suggests that police agencies can be classified according to the amount and type of corruption that exists. Sherman's typology describes corruption as a progressive problem.[45] Police agencies can be classified as one of three types:

1. *Rotten apples and rotten pockets.* A department in which most officers do not condone corruption may nevertheless occasionally produce a **rotten apple**, a uniformed officer who accepts an occasional bribe while on such assignments as traffic patrol. "Rotten pockets are small groups of officers, typically assigned to enforce vice laws, who cooperate in low-level corruption."

2. *Pervasive unorganized corruption.* **Pervasive unorganized corruption** occurs when a large percentage of the department is corrupt, but officers act independently and there is little if any collusion among them.

3. *Pervasive organized corruption.* **Pervasive organized corruption** includes situations in which corruption is not only widespread but in which both police officers and those who corrupt them are organized. This type of corruption may extend into the department's highest ranks and permits the influence of organized crime in law enforcement.

Most people would agree that taking bribes, participating in shakedowns, or "shopping" at a burglary scene are wrong, even illegal. We must remember, however, that police are often tempted with fringe benefits that some may assume are merely poor compensation for the less desirable aspects of the job. One should understand that for the police, life is not always black and white but rather, shades of gray.[46]

CONTEMPORARY RESEARCH ON POLICE CORRUPTION

Until recently, police administrators viewed corruption primarily as a reflection of the moral defects of *individual* police officers. They fought corruption by carefully screening applicants and aggressively pursuing morally defective officers in an attempt to remove them from their positions before their corrupt behavior had spread through the agency. This administrative/individual approach, sometimes called the "bad apple" theory of police corruption, has been subject to severe criticism in recent years.

In 2000, Carl Klockars and his colleagues combined findings from a National Institute of Justice (NIJ) study measuring police integrity in 30 police agencies across the United States with interviews conducted with 3,235 law enforcement officers. Most of the officers responding to the survey were line officers (63%) with an average of ten years of experience in service. The study differs somewhat from previous research on police corruption in that it was based on *organizational/occupational* approach to police corruption.[47]

In the study, researchers asked officers for their opinions about 11 hypothetical cases of police misconduct (listed in the following section) and measured how seriously officers regarded police corruption, how willing they were to support its punishment, and how willing they were to report it. The survey revealed substantial differences in the environments of integrity among the agencies

studied. The more serious the officers considered a behavior to be, the more likely they were to believe that more severe discipline was appropriate, and the more willing they were to report a colleague for engaging in that behavior.[48]

Pioneered by Herman Goldstein, traditional theories of police corruption are based on organizational and occupational dimensions.[49] These are as follows:

Dimension 1: Organizational rules. The first dimension concerns how the organizational
rules that govern corruption are established, communicated, and understood. In the United
States, where police agencies are highly decentralized, police organizations differ vastly in
the types of activities they officially prohibit as corrupt behavior. This is especially true of
marginally corrupt or *mala prohibita* behavior, such as off-duty employment and acceptance
of favors, small gifts, free meals, and discounts. Further complicating the problem is that the
official policy of many agencies formally prohibits such activities while their unofficial policy, supported firmly but silently by supervisors, is to permit and ignore such behaviors so long
as they are limited in scope and conducted discreetly.

Dimension 2: Prevention and control mechanisms. This dimension emphasizes the wide
range of mechanisms that police agencies employ to prevent and control corruption. These include education in ethics, proactive and reactive investigation of corruption, integrity testing,
and corruption deterrents through the discipline of offenders. Goldstein observes that the
extent to which agencies use such organizational anticorruption techniques varies greatly.[50]

Dimension 3: The code. The third dimension of corruption, inherent in the occupational
culture of policing, is "The code" or the "Blue Curtain" that informally prohibits or discourages police officers from reporting the misconduct of their colleagues. The parameters of the
code—precisely what behavior it covers and to whom its benefits are extended—vary among
police agencies. For example, "The code" may apply to only low-level corruption in some
agencies and to the most serious corruption in others. Furthermore, whom and what "The
code" covers can vary substantially not only *among* police agencies but also *within* police
agencies. Particularly in large police agencies, the occupational culture of integrity may differ
substantially among precincts, service areas, task forces, and work groups.

Dimension 4: Public expectations. The fourth dimension of police corruption that varies in
contemporary police emphasizes the influence of the social, economic, and political environments in which police institutions, systems, and agencies operate. For example, some jurisdictions in the United States have long, virtually uninterrupted traditions of police corruption.
Other jurisdictions have equally long traditions of minimal corruption, while still others have
experienced repeated cycles of scandal and reform. Such histories indicate that public expectations about police integrity exert vastly different pressures on police agencies in different
jurisdictions. These experiments also suggest that public pressures to confront and combat
corruption may be successfully resisted.

While a number of theories can be applied to police corruption, the contemporary organization/
occupational culture theory may be more meaningful than the traditional individual "bad apple"
theory because the research is more amenable to systematic, qualitative research.

Corruption is difficult to research in an empirical manner because most corruption is never
reported or officially documented. Even with assurances of confidentiality, police officers are unlikely
to report corrupt-officer behaviors.

The 11 case scenarios in the NIJ study were classified into three categories of perceived
seriousness. The findings were as follows:

- Four cases were not considered very serious by police respondents: case 1, off-duty operation of
a security system business; case 2, receipt of free meals; case 4, receipt of holiday gifts; and case 8,
cover-up of a police accident that involved driving under the influence of alcohol (DUI).

THE 11 NIJ STUDY CASE SCENARIOS

Case 1. A police officer runs his own private business in which he sells and installs security devices, such as alarms, special locks, and so on. He does this work during his off-duty hours.

Case 2. A police officer routinely accepts free meals, cigarettes, and other items of small value from merchants on his beat. He does not solicit these items, and he is careful not to abuse the generosity of those who give gifts to him.

Case 3. A police officer stops a motorist for speeding. The officer agrees to accept a personal gift of half the amount of the fine in exchange for not issuing a citation.

Case 4. A police officer is widely liked in the community, and on holidays local merchants and restaurant and bar owners show their appreciation for her attention by giving her gifts of food and liquor.

Case 5. A police officer discovers a burglary of a jewelry shop. The display cases are smashed, and it is obvious that many items have been taken. While searching the shop, he takes a watch, worth about two days' pay for that officer. He reports that the watch had been stolen during the burglary.

Case 6. A police officer has a private arrangement with a local auto-body shop to refer the owners of cars damaged in accidents to the shop. In exchange for each referral, she receives payment of 5% of the repair bill from the shop owner.

Case 7. A police officer, who happens to be a very good auto mechanic, is scheduled to work during

upcoming holidays. A supervisor offers to give him these days off, if he agrees to tune up his supervisor's personal car. Evaluate the supervisor's behavior.

Case 8. At 2:00 A.M., a police officer, who is on duty, is driving his patrol car on a deserted road. He sees a vehicle that has been driven off the road and is stuck in a ditch. He approaches the vehicle and observes that the driver is not hurt but is obviously intoxicated. He also finds that the driver is a police officer. Instead of reporting this accident and the offense, he transports the driver to his home.

Case 9. A police officer finds a bar on her beat that is still serving drinks half an hour past its legal closing time. Instead of reporting this violation, the police officer agrees to accept a couple of free drinks from the owner.

Case 10. Two police officers on foot patrol surprise a man who is attempting to break into an automobile. The man flees. They chase him for about two blocks before apprehending him by tackling him and wrestling him to the ground. After he is under control, both officers punch him a couple of times in the stomach as punishment for fleeing and resisting.

Case 11. A police officer finds a wallet in a parking lot. It contains an amount of money equivalent to a full day's pay for that officer. He reports the wallet as lost property and keeps the money for himself.[51]

- The majority of police respondents, in fact, reported that the operation of an off-duty security system business (case 1) was not a violation of agency policy. Respondents considered four other areas of misconduct to be at an intermediate level of seriousness: case 10, the use of excessive force on the car thief following a foot pursuit; case 7, a supervisor who offers a subordinate time off during holidays in exchange for tuning up his personal car; case 9, acceptance of free drinks in exchange for ignoring a late bar closing; and case 6, receipt of a kickback.
- Respondents regarded the remaining three cases—those that involve stealing from a found wallet (case 11), accepting a money bribe (case 3), and stealing a watch at a crime scene (case 5)—as very serious offenses.[52]

PERFORMANCE OF DUTY

Another ethical concern in general police practice involves the use of discretion in the performance of duty. It is now clearly established that most police work is order maintenance: Police are called into situations that involve activities other than crime control, often termed *social work calls.* Many police officers do not feel that these are legitimate calls on their time and either give them superficial attention or do not respond at all. Brown calls the skill that police develop in avoiding these calls *engineering*.[53]

Police may be called upon to answer calls outside their formal crime-control responsibilities. For instance, police may respond to a domestic dispute and find a woman bruised, upset, and without money or resources to help herself or her children. The officer may ascertain that departmental policy or law does not dictate any action and the woman is afraid to press charges, so the officer can leave with a clear conscience that official duties have been completed. The officer might, however, take the woman to a shelter or otherwise help her get out of a bad situation. What is the ethical choice? It is difficult to determine the extent of the officer's responsibility in this case.

The formal code of ethics gives no clear guidelines for how much consideration police should give a citizen in distress. The caretaker style of policing found in small cities and suburbs, where police departments are oriented to the community, emphasizes service and encourages police assistance to victims or citizens who need it. Our traditional image of police and fire departments getting cats out of trees had a basis in reality, but only in certain areas with certain types of policing. In major cities, if police spent their time in service roles, they would have precious little left to spend on crime control.

Those officers who become personally involved or commit the resources of the department beyond the necessary requirements are not rewarded but are viewed as troublemakers. Structural support for this ethical action therefore does not exist. Officers who attempt to do what they believe is right often do so on their own, risking formal or informal censure. Yet beyond the departmental policies concerning service actions, what is the individual responsibility of the police officer to a fellow human being in distress?

If a young boy, upset over a lost bicycle, approaches two police officers during their dinner break, what do the strict guidelines of their job dictate? What is the ethical thing to do? Should they interrupt their dinner and go search for the missing bicycle? Should they take a superficial report to make the boy feel better? Should they tell the boy to go away because they've had a hard night and are looking forward to a hot meal? Often, the police encounter travelers who are robbed during their passage through a city. Should they leave such victims on the street to fend for themselves? What do they have to do? What should they do? In all these situations we face three questions: (1) What must police do under job guidelines? (2) What do professional ethics dictate? (3) What do individual ethics dictate? Again, referring back to our ethical frameworks we can find support for either a very altruistic, involved style of interaction, where the police officer would be compelled to help the victims in any way possible, or a more self-protective standard, where the actions mandated would be only those necessary to maintain a self-image consistent with the police role. The answer is not necessarily as simple as it may seem.

If police became personally involved in every case and went out of their way to help all victims, they would probably exhaust their emotional reserves in a very short time. As a matter of survival, police develop an emotional barrier between themselves and the victims they encounter. It is impossible to observe suffering on a consistent basis if one does not protect oneself in such a way. Unfortunately, the result is often perceived as callousness and may even result in unethical behavior toward individual victims.

In summary, the role of the police involves a great deal of discretion in definition and enforcement of criminal behavior. In some cases, discretion leads to unethical behavior of minor (gratuities) or serious (bribes and theft) proportions. Asking why there is unethical behavior among police is like asking why there is unethical behavior among any group of people, since police are neither better nor worse than the general population. What makes them different from others are the role responsibilities associated with the profession and the possibilities this role creates for abuse.

Deception and the Police

Deception often takes a different form in the investigation phase of a case. Several court cases document the use of mental coercion, either through threat or promise. The use of the "father confessor" approach (a sympathetic paternal figure for the defendant to confide in) or good cop–bad cop partners (a "nice guy" and a seemingly brutal officer) are other ways to induce confessions or obtain other information.[54] Some experts have warned that because physical means of coercion are no longer common, the infamous third degree for instance, mental deception is the only means left for police officers to gain information or confessions from suspects.

How does one get a killer to admit where he or she left the murder weapon? If police are imaginative, they may be able to get the defendant to confess by encouraging him or her to think about what would happen if children found the gun. Or police may discover the location of a body by convincing the killer that the victim deserves a "Christian burial." Courts have ruled that police who use these methods are tacitly infringing on the defendant's right to counsel.

Coercion

Another question that one might ask is whether tricking someone into confessing is ethical police behavior. It is certainly much easier to justify deceptive interrogation than physical coercion and intimidation. The justification for physical coercion is the same as that for mental deception: namely, that it is effective and perhaps necessary to get needed information from a resisting subject. Although some countries endorse physical coercion as acceptable police practice, most have refused to accept this justification and formally condemn the practice. It is important to note that where coercion is condoned, the police are often used as means of control by the dominant political power. They operate, therefore, not under the law, as the code of ethics dictates, but above the law. Police coercion may be either psychological or physical in nature. During the 1930s, both types were common. In one study, during the 1930s, the NYPD used some type of physical coercion in 23% of the instances studied.[55] The most frequent method was striking the suspect with a fist to evoke a confession. While this study was conducted over 60 years ago, we know that recent cases of police misconduct suggest that, while probably isolated, instances of coercion still occur.

Many would argue that whatever information is gained from a person tricked or deceived into confessing or giving information is not worth the sacrifice of moral standards. The court is concerned primarily with prohibiting methods that would bring the truth of the confession into question. The original legal proscriptions against torture, in fact, came not from an ethical rationale but from the legal rationale that torture endangers the veracity of the confession. In other words, people under torture may confess to stop their suffering; thus the court would not be getting truthful information. Our concern is with the ethical nature of the action itself. Is it wrong to use physical force or coercion to obtain a confession?

MAKING USE OF THE SUBCULTURE

An alternative way to address ethics and to achieve high ethical standards is to use the subculture to its best advantage: as a socializing tool to promote high ethical standards. The police subculture, as discussed in Chapter 7, may endorse desirable ethical standards, but this may involve a change in police values. It seems impossible since the police value system is so entrenched; however, one example of how this might occur presents an interesting possibility. The police value of force endorses the use of violence and gives only vague guidelines for when force should not be used. The consequence of this is that many police officers view their uniforms as a license to aggress against anyone considered a threat. Police use of unreasonable force is an individual problem, but it is also a value problem, because the police subculture does not condemn but rather protects police officers with aggressive tendencies.

Some could argue that any employee behavior is influenced directly by the behavior of superiors and not by the stated directives or ethics of the organization. An example would be executives who engage in actions such as price fixing and whose employees steal company supplies or time. One cannot espouse ethical ideals, act unethically, and expect employees to act ethically. Thus, regardless of formal ethical codes, police are influenced by the standards of behavior they observe in their superiors. One may note that many cases of large-scale corruption that have been exposed have implicated very high officials. Alternatively, police departments that have remained relatively free of corruption have administrators who emphasize ethics in their behavior on a day-to-day basis.

PREVENTING CORRUPTION

U.S. police have experimented with a number of measures designed to prevent, detect, and punish corruption. Several of these have been identified as being particularly successful.[56]

- *Positive leadership.* The effective chiefs show by example and support, as well as by their statements, that their anticorruption policies are important to them. In departments with a reputation for misconduct, new chiefs have found that it is important to take steps early in their administration and that waiting too long may make it impossible to overcome the hostility that forceful anticorruption methods will produce in those who subscribe to "the code."
- *Political influence.* Politics intrudes upon police administration primarily when politicians ask that certain laws not be enforced, that violations of law be ignored, or that they be allowed to influence the assignment and promotion of police personnel. Since most U.S. police chiefs report to an elected official, it has proven impossible and perhaps undesirable to eliminate politics entirely. Nevertheless, chiefs successful in fighting corruption have observed that when external political influences dictate their decisions, they lose the confidence of their officers and the public, and they have made it clear that responsibility for managing their departments rests with them.
- *Authority and responsibility.* The Knapp Commission recommended that primary responsibility for all but the most serious corruption investigations be vested in the commands concerned, rather than in headquarters. Thus, all members of the department, including first-line supervisors, have the duty to take action against corruption, and failure to do so results in disciplinary action against all officers in the chain of command.
- *Policies and procedures.* Effective anticorruption policies are clear, unambiguous, and systematically disseminated to all members of the department. Careful planning results in a set of procedures that makes it clear which areas of action are handled by supervisors or command officers and which are handled by the internal affairs unit.
- *Internal affairs units.* Most departments with more than a hundred sworn personnel include an internal affairs or inspection unit in their organizational structure. The unit provides an ongoing effort to detect actual or potential problems of police misconduct and investigates the more serious cases. The unit generally reports to the chief or deputy chief; its size is dictated by such factors as the size of the department, the number of complaints received, the number of cases handled, the actual responsibilities of the unit, and the nature of the department's misconduct problems.
- *Field associates programs.* In these programs, selected recruits and veteran police officers are given special responsibility for covertly obtaining and reporting information on corruption or other misconduct. Although the program itself is well publicized internally, the identity of the field associates is kept secret. Such programs are particularly useful in departments where reporting of fellow officers has been rare and is considered an offense against "the code," although the personnel of such departments can be expected to be most hostile toward them.
- *Turning.* "Turning" occurs when an officer who is discovered to be corrupt is promised immunity or some other inducement in exchange for collecting evidence against other corrupt officers; this may involve wearing a recording device. This has often proven to be an effective way of uncovering and prosecuting systemic corruption, although the ethics of encouraging an officer to continue in corrupt activities have been debated.
- *Integrity testing.* This consists of exercises such as leaving wallets full of cash in places where police officers will find them and waiting to see if the officers return the "found"

property; department personnel may or may not be informed that such a program is being carried out. Although departments with corruption problems may find integrity testing worthwhile both as an investigating device and as a deterrent, it is open to both ethical and legal charges of entrapment.

Another solution is to change the social context of policing itself by making police operations more visible and open to public scrutiny and input. All too often, the public finds out about police corruption only when a scandal breaks in the local newspaper. Some have suggested that because vice operations seem to be more prone to fostering police corruption, some of them could be deprioritized or even abandoned. It is likely that some vice offenses could be deferred to social service agencies for intervention.

As a last resort, decriminalization of some vice offenses has even been suggested, an action that would require legislative consideration and debate. In any case, police administrators should strive to identify alternatives to lowering the pressure placed on individual police officers and eliminating their moral dilemmas.

In Retrospect

In this chapter we have examined some basic concepts of police ethics and misbehavior. We considered the influence of the police subculture on ethical behavior and its opposition to formal ethical standards. We also examined the lack of consistency between the two. Various practices of the police were discussed, both in general performance of duty and more specifically in investigation and interrogation, and we emphasized various activities that raise ethical questions. Finally, we considered some possible techniques for changing undesirable aspects of the police subculture.

In the ethical dilemmas described toward the chapter's conclusion, try putting yourself in the place of police officers. What would you do? How would you arrive at your decisions? As with the dilemmas in earlier chapters, decide on your course of action, but take some extra time to try to justify your action using an ethical framework. Or approach it in another way: Use any ethical system and try to solve the dilemma using the principles of the framework, whether or not you agree with them. In either procedure you will find that these dilemmas are not easy to solve.

Improve Your Professional Vocabulary

Civil Rights Act of 1964
grass eater
meat eater

moral career
pervasive organized corruption
pervasive unorganized corruption

rotten apple
shakedown
Title VII

Discussion Questions

1. Explain to what extent ethical values are realistic for police officers.
2. Discuss whether the Law Enforcement Code of Ethics is realistic.
3. How would you explain the police value system? What are its components?
4. To what extent does the police subculture affect police values and unethical conduct?
5. Describe the distinction between police misconduct and corruption. Give examples of each.

6. List and discuss the different typologies of corruption.
7. In what ways does the police subculture foster or discourage police misconduct?
8. List and discuss the behaviors that constitute corruption.
9. What types of police misconduct are more severe than others?
10. Explain the types of official police operations that are most prone to corrupt behavior by police officers.

Notes

1. Cohen, A. (2000, March 6). Gangsta cops. *Time,* pp. 30–33.
2. Ibid.
3. Glazer, S. (1995, November 24). Police corruption: Can brutality and misconduct be rooted out? *CQ Researcher, 5*(44), 1041–1064.
4. Roberg, R., & J. Kuykendall. (1993). *Police and society.* Belmont, CA: Wadsworth.
5. Rhoades, P. W. (1991). Political obligation: Connecting police ethics and democratic values. *American Journal of Police, 10,* 10–19.
6. Durkheim, E. (1958). *Professional ethics and civic morals* (translated by C. Brookfield). New York: Free Press.
7. *Police Chief Magazine.* (1992, January), p. 15.
8. Sherman, L. (1982, Spring/Winter). Learning police ethics. *Criminal Justice Ethics, 1*(1), 10–19.
9. Brown, M. (1981). *Working the street.* New York: Russell Sage Foundation.
10. Muir, W. K. (1977). *Police: Streetcorner politicians.* Chicago: University of Chicago Press.
11. Scheingold, A. (1984). *Understanding police culture.* New York: Moss.
12. Ibid.
13. Ibid.
14. Muir, W. K. (1977). *Police: Streetcorner politicians.* Chicago: University of Chicago Press.
15. Malloy, T. E., & G. Mays. (1984, June). The police stress hypothesis: A critical evaluation. *Criminal Justice and Behavior, 11,* 197–224.
16. Muir, W. K. (1977). *Police: Streetcorner politicians.* Chicago: University of Chicago Press.
17. Williams, H. (1988). *The evolving strategy of police: A minority view.* Washington, DC: The Police Foundation.
18. Wilson, J. Q. (1975). *Thinking about crime.* New York: Basic Books.
19. Brown, M. (1981). *Working the street.* New York: Russell Sage Foundation.
20. Muir, W. K. (1977). *Police: Streetcorner politicians.* Chicago: University of Chicago Press.
21. Gains, L. K., V. E. Kappler, & J. B. Vaughn. (1997). *Policing in America,* 2nd ed. Cincinnati, OH: Anderson.
22. Brown, M. (1981). *Working the street.* New York: Russell Sage Foundation.
23. Anonymous. (1997, May 31). Florida police misconduct soars, penalties lag. *Law Enforcement News,* p. 7.
24. Barker, T., & D. Carter. (1991). *Police deviance,* 2nd ed. Cincinnati, OH: Anderson.
25. U.S. Department of Justice, National Institute of Justice. (1995a, October). *Civil rights and criminal justice: Primer on sexual harassment. Research in action.* Washington, DC: U.S. Government Printing Office.
26. McCormack, W. U. (1995, January). Managing relations between the sexes in a law enforcement organization. *FBI Law Enforcement Bulletin,* 27–32.
27. Klockars, C. (1985). *The idea of police.* Newbury Park, CA: Sage; Klockars, C. B., J. R. Greene, S. Wasserman, & H. Williams. (1988). *An evaluation of resource allocation of the Wilmington Police Department.* Wilmington, DE: Office of the Director of Public Safety.
28. Johnson, K. (1998, January 22). 44 Law officers arrested in sting, Cleveland-area FBI raids hit five agencies. *USA Today,* p. A3.
29. Punch, A. (1985, July 2). Dangerous decisions. *Parade.*
30. Goldstein, H. (1977). *Policing a free society.* Cambridge, MA: Ballinger.
31. Sherman, L. (1974b). *Police corruption: A sociological perspective.* New York: Doubleday.
32. Murphy, P. V., & T. Plate. (1987). *Commissioner: A view from the top of law enforcement.* New York: Simon & Schuster.
33. Sherman, L. (1982, Spring/Winter). Learning police ethics. *Criminal Justice Ethics, 1*(1), 10–19.
34. Ibid.
35. Malloy, T. E., & G. Mays. (1984, June). The police stress hypothesis: A critical evaluation. *Criminal Justice and Behavior, 11,* 197–224.
36. Ibid.
37. Christopher Commission. (1991). *Report on brutality in the Los Angeles Police Department.* City of Los Angeles.
38. Walker, S., et al. (1996). *The colors of justice: Race, ethnicity, and crime in America.* Belmont, CA: Wadsworth.
39. Glazer, S. (1995, November 24). Police corruption: Can brutality and misconduct be rooted out? *CQ Researcher, 5*(44), 1041–1064.
40. Johnston, M. (1982). *Political corruption and public policy in America.* Pacific Grove, CA: Brooks/Cole.
41. Stoddard, E. (1979). Organizational norms and police discretion: An observational study of police work with traffic violators. *Criminology, 17*(2), 159–171.
42. Stoddard, E. L. (1968). The informal code of police deviancy: A group approach to blue-coat crime. *Journal of Criminal Law, Criminology, and Police Science, 20*(3).
43. More, H. W. (1992). *Special topics in policing.* Cincinnati, OH: Anderson.
44. Scrivner, E. (1994). *Controlling police use of excessive force: The role of the police psychologist.* Washington, DC: National Institute of Justice Research.
45. Sherman, L. (1974). The sociology and social reform of the American police: 1950–1973. *Journal of Police Science and Administration, 2*(3), 255–262.
46. Cohen, H. (1986, Summer/Fall). Exploiting police authority. *Criminal Justice Ethics,* 23–31.

47. Klockars, C., et al. (2000, May). *The measurement of police integrity*. National Institute of Justice, Research in Brief. Office of Justice Programs.

48. Ibid.

49. Goldstein, H. (1975). *Police corruption: Perspective on its nature and control*. Washington, DC: Police Foundation; Goldstein, H. (1977). *Policing a free society*. Cambridge, MA: Ballinger.

50. Ibid.

51. Klockars, C., et al. (2000, May). *The measurement of police integrity*. National Institute of Justice, Research in Brief. Office of Justice Programs.

52. Ibid.

53. Brown, M. (1981). *Working the street*. New York: Russell Sage Foundation.

54. Kamisar, C., W. LeFave, & R. Israel. (1980, November 21). The invisible enterprise. *Forbes,* p. 58.

55. Hopkins, E. J. (1931). *Our lawless police*. New York: Viking Press.

56. McCormack, B., & D. Ward. (1979). *Crime control establishment*. Thousand Oaks, CA: Sage.

CHAPTER 10

Controlling Police Behavior

This chapter will enable you to:

- Understand basic issues in police accountability.
- Understand the role and function of internal affairs
- Explain the significance of proper officer recruitment

- Describe the role of civilian complaints and the identification of officer misconduct
- Understand the pros and cons of civilian review boards in addressing police misconduct
- Identify external entities that help control and monitor possible officer misconduct

---

Within a matter of hours after the swearing in of the new Police Chief Richard Pennington in New Orleans on October 13, 1994, one of his officers ordered the execution of a woman who had filed a brutality complaint against him. This came in the midst of the worst crime wave in the city's history. The city had experienced the greatest number of murders in its history and had earned the national reputation of the nation's murder capital. Police corruption was rampant and citizens were reluctant to file complaints because they were afraid the police would tell the criminals or the officers themselves were criminals. Among the good cops on the force, the only thing lower than morale was the pay.

By February 2000, the number of murders was down by more than half, a third of the officers who were on the force when Pennington was sworn in were gone or arrested, and starting salaries were up 53%. In fact, the New Orleans Police Department had become a model of how to fight both crime and a negative public image. So much so that the International Association of Chiefs of Police held its first-ever national conference there in 2000.[1]

At the core of New Orleans's success is a revamped **internal affairs unit**. To regain public trust, Pennington reassigned the officers who had previously been in the unit. He then created the Public Integrity Division to conduct those investigations and staffed it with different personnel, including two FBI agents. Pennington also moved the new unit out of the police headquarters in hope of encouraging citizens to come by and file complaints. Also, the unit began conducting undercover sting and surveillance operations. Statistics tell a large part of the story. In 1994, the "Big Easy" had 425 murders. In 1999, it had 162, a 62% drop. Nationally, murders fell 27% from 1994 to 1998.[2]

Citizen's fear of the police in New Orleans has not been without reason. In 1994, Officer Len Davis was convicted of ordering the execution of 32-year-old Kim Groves after she reported him to the internal affairs unit for allegedly pistol-whipping a teenager. In another case, Officer Antoinette Frank was sentenced to death for her role in the murders of three people when she and an accomplice robbed a restaurant in March 1995. Frank had eaten there less than an hour before the robbery. One of the victims was 25-year-old Ronnie Williams II, who was an off-duty police officer working security. He and Frank were sometimes partners at work. Frank shot Williams in the head after he had been wounded by her accomplice.

The quality of police recruits was a problem as well. When Pennington visited the police training academy, he discovered that 12 of the 17 recruits had arrest or criminal records on charges ranging from drunken driving to rape. Today, people with similar records or other negative marks such as dishonorable discharge from the military, delinquent child-support records, bad driving records, excessive debt, or a history of consorting with criminals cannot join the force. These new rules also applied to existing officers on the force, leading to a mass exodus. Between 1994 and early 2000, 458 of the 1,630 officer force left. That number included 85 who were arrested, 100 who were fired, and 200 who left during or after they were being disciplined.[3] Other departmental changes included:

- Moving all 250 detectives, including those in robbery-homicide, out of headquarters and into eight police districts. District captains command them.
- Using computerized statistics to identify problem areas and the crimes committed there.
- Establishing substations at three of the most crime-ridden public housing complexes in the city and staffing them with a total of 50 officers.
- Limiting the number of off-duty hours that officers can work to 20 hours per week.[4]

While working to reorganize the department, Pennington was working with the business community to raise police salaries and increase the department's budget. Part of the money came from increases in property tax and sales tax collections and the rest came from casino taxes. The result: A beginning police officer in 1994 made $17,000 a year compared to $26,000 in 2000. The salary goes up 15%, to $30,000 after one year.[5]

Not all efforts to clean up corruption in some of the nation's most troubled police departments have been as successful as those in New Orleans. Corruption and misconduct are difficult elements to purge, especially in entrenched, older police departments. Before we can fully understand solutions, we must first consider what some experts consider the hub of police corruption—the police subculture.

BASIC ISSUES IN POLICE ACCOUNTABILITY

The subject of police accountability is an extremely complex one, involving two basic questions. The first question affects substantive issues: For what should the police be held accountable? The second question involves procedural issues: What procedures are necessary for holding the police accountable?

With respect to the substantive issues, the police should be accountable for both what they do and how they do it. David Bailey classifies these issues in terms of effectiveness, efficiency, and rectitude. What police do includes the basic responsibilities of law enforcement, or maintenance, and service. The police should be held accountable for preventing crime, apprehending criminals, reducing public fear of crime, maintaining order, and providing miscellaneous services to the public. These responsibilities can be measured in terms of whether the police perform them in an effective and efficient manner. Effectiveness involves the question of whether, in fact, they accomplish their task (e.g., do the police control crime?). Efficiency involves the question of whether they accomplish their tasks in a cost-effective manner (e.g., how many police officers does it take to control crime?).

At the same time, the police are responsible for how they perform their duties. Bailey refers to these as rectitude issues, including obeying the law, respecting the constitutional rights of citizens, and treating citizens in a respectful and equal manner.

As noted earlier in this text, the police have many different responsibilities, and they often conflict. As Skolnick notes in *Justice without Trial*, certain law enforcement tactics can violate standards of due process and the rights of citizens and can damage police–community relations.[6] One of the major challenges of accountability, therefore, is to maintain effectiveness in one area without doing harm in another.

With respect to the procedural question of how to achieve police accountability, many different officials, agencies, and groups have some control or influence over the police. Government agencies can be classified according to their locus in terms of the three branches of government: legislative, judicial, and executive. Other groups claim important roles in controlling the police. These include the news media, public interest groups such as the National Association for the Advancement of Colored People (NAACP) and the American Civil Liberties Union (ACLU), and police unions.

Civic Accountability

Relations between citizens and the police depend greatly on citizen confidence that officers will behave in accordance with law and with department guidelines. Rapport with the community is enhanced when citizens feel sure that the police will protect their persons and property and protect the rights guaranteed by the Constitution. Making the police responsive to citizen complaints without burdening them with the flood of such complaints is difficult. The main challenge in making the police more accountable is to use citizen input to force police to follow the law and department guidelines without placing too many limits on their ability to carry out their primary functions.

CONTROL MECHANISMS

In addition to compliance with the Constitution, state and federal law, and established policies and procedures, other control mechanisms are in place to ensure responsible police behavior. Included are watchdog organizations such as the ACLU and the NAACP. Both of these organizations are concerned primarily with police mistreatment of minorities and the socially disenfranchised.

INTERNAL AFFAIRS

The effective control of police corruption requires meaningful investigations of suspected corrupt officers by the department itself. As a rule, this is the responsibility of the Internal Affairs Unit (IAU) or Office of Professional Conduct (OPC).

Any anticorruption investigation requires several elements in order to be successful. First, it needs the strong support of the chief executive. According to the International Association of Chiefs of Police (IACP) the unit commander "should report directly to or have regular access to the chief," because that person is ultimately responsible for discipline.[7] However, in 1993, the **Mollen Commission** found that in New York City, command officers sent strong messages to investigators that they should not aggressively pursue certain reports of corruption. The commission's chief witness in that scandal, Michael Dowd, was in fact arrested on drug charges by suburban Suffolk County police, and not by the New York City Police.[8]

Secondly, an IAU needs an adequate number of personnel to handle the investigative workload. In New York City, Patrick V. Murphy increased the size of the internal affairs division (IAD) by bringing the ratio of investigating officers from 1 to 533 line officers to 1 to 64. Lawrence Sherman found investigator-to-officer ratios of 1 to 110 and 1 to 216 in two other departments he reviewed.[9] Murphy also decentralized anticorruption by creating a network of **Field Internal Affairs Units (FIAUs).** Twenty years later, however, the Mollen Commission found that IADs investigated few corruption allegations, and that most cases were delegated to the FIAUs, which were then too overloaded to conduct effective investigations.[10] The problem was not necessarily the structure of the anticorruption effort but the lack of administrative commitment to make it work.

Next, there exists disagreement over whether anticorruption efforts should be centralized or decentralized within the police department. Most departments have centralized management of investigations, with the commander of the IAU reporting directly to the chief. Patrick V. Murphy took a different approach in New York City in the early 1970s, creating a decentralized structure of FIAUs.[11]

Proper staffing of the IAUs can be problematic. As a rule, police officers do not like IAUs, regard internal affairs officers as "snitches," and reject the assignment themselves. Research into current and former internal affairs officers in one southwestern metropolitan area found a number of examples of the stigma attached to internal affairs assignments. One officer was told by a friend, "you're crazy, what the hell you want to work there for?"[12]

According to many officers, internal affairs violates the norms of group solidarity. Furthermore, many officers regard internal affairs investigations as more intrusive than criminal investigations. Finally, many officers believe that internal affairs is biased and out to "get" certain officers.[13]

Depending on the department, because of union contracts, the chief may have no choice over who is assigned to the IAU. It is obvious that an officer who does not want the assignment, or who may have a problematic performance record, is not likely to be a good candidate for an anticorruption investigator. In other departments, the Chief Executive Officer has full control over assignment to the IAU, and it is a preferred assignment that is considered a key to promotion.

THE POLICE CHIEF'S ATTITUDE

To a great extent, controlling police misconduct begins with the attitude of the chief executive officer—the chief. It is the responsibility of the chief to make his or her position on corruption and misconduct clear and that such behavior will not be tolerated. In the early 1990s, the Mollen Commission argued that the "commitment to integrity cannot be just an abstract value. It must be reflected not only in the words, but in the deeds, of the police commissioner, the department's top commanders, and the field supervisors who shape the attitudes of the rank and file."[14]

Taking a strong public stand against corruption can be a difficult position for a police chief. This is because publicly discussing the department's problems is tantamount to admitting the existence of possible wrongdoing within the department and admitting that it has not yet been successfully dealt with. History has shown that many anticorruption mechanisms have failed, in part, because department officials do not want bad publicity. Consequently, cases of alleged misconduct are sometimes not investigated.

POLICIES AND PROCEDURES

Another positive step in maintaining the integrity of a department is to control the actions of police officers; this involves communicating exactly what actions will not be tolerated. The use of written policies, also known as **standard operating procedures,** is one responsible way to control police

FIGURE 10.1   The criminal justice process begins with the arrest of a suspect by police. Arrests must be made legally and in accordance with departmental policy and procedure.

discretion and achieve some degree of police accountability. Research has shown that administrative rules on corruption serve six basic purposes. For example, they: (1) inform officers of expected standards of behavior; (2) inform the community about those standards; (3) establish the basis for consistency and police operations; (4) provide grounds for discipline and counseling of problem officers; (5) provide standards for officer supervision; and (6) give direction for officer training.[15]

In police work, there is little agreement as to where to draw the line on some issues. For example, not all law enforcement officers believe it is necessary or even possible to prohibit free meals or other discounts while on the job. In other cases, police leaders argue that the line must be drawn prohibiting all gratuities. For example, Patrick V. Murphy told his officers, "Except for your paycheck there is no such thing as a clean buck."[16] William Parker of Los Angeles and O. W. Wilson of Chicago believed that even a free cup of coffee compromised the integrity of the police. The argument against all gratuities is based on the belief that this one small favor creates a climate in which increasingly larger steps toward corruption become possible. Of course, other experts argue that anticorruption efforts should focus on serious acts of corruption opposed to seemingly minor infractions.

RECRUITMENT EFFORTS

One of the most important elements in controlling police misconduct is the proper screening of police recruits. As one might guess, it is not always possible to spot potentially corrupt officers at this stage. The Mollen Commission found that some of the most corrupt officers were ideal recruits in terms of their backgrounds at the time they were hired.[17]

History has shown that departments such as Miami, Florida; Washington, DC; and Los Angeles, California have had major corruption scandals as a result of hiring officers with crime and drug-related histories. For the most part, these departments were under political pressure to hire more officers and did not conduct normal background investigations. An example would be the Rampart scandal in Los Angeles where officers were found to have criminal records, financial problems, histories of violent behavior, and drug problems. After further investigation, the department found that these officers were all hired in the late 1980s and early 1990s, a time when the department compromised its hiring protocol in an effort to quickly fill empty positions within the police department.

One of the most essential parts of an effective police force is a proper and thorough background investigation. Experience shows that persons with prior arrest records (even without convictions) and particularly people with prior involvement with drugs are extremely high risk in terms of becoming corrupt if employed as police officers.

There is a considerable amount of disagreement, among police departments over whether applicants should be automatically eliminated on the basis of any prior criminal activity and/or drug involvement. Virtually all agencies refuse to hire anyone with a felony conviction. However, only half automatically reject someone with a misdemeanor conviction. About a third reject applicants with a misdemeanor arrest but no conviction.[18]

Drug usage by police applicants remains a concern. The International Association of Chiefs of Police argues that the ideal standard should be "no prior drug abuse of any kind." However, given the extent of drug abuse in contemporary society, maintaining an absolute standard would screen out a very large percentage of applicants. As a rule, most departments are willing to hire individuals with some prior drug history, making distinctions between experimentation, use, and abuse. Most departments are willing to accept individuals with some minor usage or experimentation, but not recent and/or heavy drug use.

DRUG TESTING OF POLICE OFFICERS

The widespread instance of corrupt behavior generated by the illicit drug business has precipitated the implementation of drug-testing policies by many police departments. In a 1986 survey, the National Institute of Justice contacted 33 large police departments across the nation to determine what measures were used to identify instances of drug abuse by police personnel. The findings were that almost all police departments surveyed had some formal policy in place by which to identify employees who abuse illicit drugs.

Police applicants were being tested by 73% of the departments surveyed, while 21% of them were considering implementing such a policy. In another interesting finding, 21% of all departments surveyed said they would prefer to treat officers confirmed to be involved with drug abuse rather than simply fire them.[19] Drug testing of police officers is a sensitive issue, as many officers claim that results are not accurate and disciplinary action could be based on false-positive test results. Repeated testing and high threshold levels for drugs could eliminate this problem, but the issue of privacy and the protection of individual rights remains an ongoing concern.

DECERTIFICATION

Still another method of controlling police officer abuses is the possible **decertification** of officers. A majority of states throughout the nation have some form of decertification process in place. For example, in Florida, the Criminal Justice Standards and Training Commission is authorized to decertify (or suspend or put on probation) officers for the following:

- Violating the constitutional rights of individuals
- The "negligent deprivations of liberty or property"
- Failing to maintain the required qualifications for the job
- Falsifying or misrepresenting information during the application process
- "Gross insubordination, gross immorality, habitual drunkenness, willful neglect of duty, incompetence, or gross misconduct"

Once a police officer has been decertified, he or she is no longer eligible for employment as a sworn law enforcement officer. Research has shown that in over 20% of decertification cases, the behavior that resulted in the decertification involved criminal conduct.[20]

PUBLIC OPINION

It has been argued that police misconduct and corruption is permitted to flourish in some departments because of local political culture that tolerates it. Accordingly, controlling corruption requires mobilizing public opinion. The media plays a major role in shaping public opinion about corruption and police misconduct. They often expose the existence of police wrongdoing and set in motion the reform process.

For example, *New York Times* reporter David Burnham, was instrumental in exposing corruption in the New York City Police Department in the 1970s. His front-page article on corruption on April 25, 1970, led to the Knapp Commission Investigation.[21] It is noteworthy that the *Times* took up the issue only after both the mayor and high-ranking administrators within the police department refused to follow up on allegations brought to them by officers Frank Serpico and David Durk.

Overreliance on the media, however, can be problematic. For one thing, media-generated scandals tend to be short-lived. Both the media and the public tends to have short attention spans that quickly turn to other more recent crises. Furthermore, the media also tends to cover the most dramatic aspects of the scandal, usually focusing on individuals who become scapegoats. The underlying causes of misconduct and corruption are often complicated and seldom have public appeal. Lastly, scandals tend to produce dramatic responses, such as the removal or transfer of certain officers, which does not necessarily address the underlying problem. Departments often reassign personnel in response to the scandal and in doing so, honest officers as well as those who are problem officers, are affected.

CIVILIAN COMPLAINTS

Police departments exist to serve the public, and in doing so, citizens can be thought of as consumers of police services. As with any business, departments should "aim to please," especially considering that each unsatisfied "customer" will tell at least 11 others about their negative experience, while customers with positive experiences will tell only about six.[22]

Complaints against police can be made by individuals or groups and tend to range from the insignificant to the serious. People who call the police with complaints but who choose not to leave their names are not taken as seriously as those by people who leave their names. This is not to suggest that anonymous complaints should be ignored, but an identified complainant affords investigators a means to verify and substantiate leads in the case. Police should be careful to try to identify the motive for police complaints, as many defendants will attempt to retaliate against an arresting officer, but citizen complaints often yield important leads about problem officers. When officers take citizen complaints, the categories of misconduct should be clearly defined. The Police Executive Research Forum identifies these categories:[23]

- *Crime:* Involvement in illegal behavior such as bribery, theft, perjury, or drug violations
- *Excessive force:* Use or threatened use of force against a person
- *Arrest:* Improper or unjustified restraint of a person's liberty
- *Entry:* Improper entry into a building or onto property and/or excessive force used against property to gain entry
- *Search:* Improper or unjustified search of a person or property, in violation of established law enforcement practices
- *Harassment:* Taking, or failing to take, a method of police action predicated on irrelevant factors such as race, gender, attire, age, or sex
- *Demeanor:* A department member's bearing, gestures, language, or other actions being offensive or of doubtful social propriety or giving the appearance of conflict of interest, misuse of influence, or lack of jurisdiction or authority
- *Serious rule infractions:* Disrespect toward supervisor, drunkenness on duty, sleeping on duty, neglect of duty, false statements, or malingering
- *Minor rule infractions:* Untidiness, tardiness, faulty driving, or failure to follow procedures

The Police Executive Research Forum points out that the best way to reduce the incidence of police misconduct is through **proactive prevention measures.** These include improved recruitment and selection, training, standard operating procedures manual, supervisory responsibility, and community outreach.

CIVILIAN REVIEW BOARDS

The demand for citizen oversight first occurred in the 1950s and 1960s as a result of the civil rights movement and the perception in many quarters that law enforcement responded to racial unrest with excessive force. Many of these early review procedures were short-lived.

Citizen review revived in the early 1970s as urban African-Americans gained more political power and as more white political leaders came to see the need for improved police accountability. Most oversight procedures have come into existence after a high-profile case of alleged police misconduct (usually a shooting or other physical force incident), often involving white officers and minority suspects. Racial or ethnic allegations of discrimination are often at the heart of movements to introduce citizen oversight.

By 2008, citizen review had become more widespread than ever before in the United States. As of early 1998, there were more than 90 citizen review procedures. Almost 80% of the largest cities had some form of citizen review. However, only a small fraction of law enforcement agencies in the country had citizen oversight.

The police need a complaint and disciplinary procedure to ensure that complaints against officers and staff are investigated and dealt with effectively. The theory underlying the concept of civilian review is that civilian investigations of citizen complaints are more independent because they are conducted by people who are not sworn officers. This is not to suggest, however, that civilian review boards are a guaranteed way to monitor police work carefully. But many municipalities are convinced that they are effective. According to *Law Enforcement News,* the public overwhelmingly

System	Type*	Openness to Public Scrutiny	Mediation Option	Subpoena Power	Officer Legal Representation
Berkeley Police Review Commission (PRC)	1	• hearings and commission decisions open to public and media • general PRC meetings available for public to express concerns • full public report, including interview transcripts • city manager makes response public after review of PRC and internal affairs (IA) findings • appeal process • IA's dispositions and discipline not public	dormant	yes	during investigation; during hearing
Flint Office of the Ombudsman	1	• findings distributed to media and city archives • no appeal • chief's finding public, but not discipline	no	yes, but never used	not interviewed in person
Minneapolis Civilian Police Review Authority (CRA)	1	• hearings are private • general public invited to monthly CRA meeting to express concerns • appeal process • complainant told whether complaint was sustained • chief's discipline not public until final disposition	yes	no, but cooperation required under *Garrity* ruling	during investigation, union representative may advise office; during hearing union attorney defends officer
Orange County Citizen Review Board	2	• hearings open to public and media scrutiny • findings and the sheriff's discipline are matters of public record • no appeal	no	yes, but never used	during hearings
Portland Police Internal Investigations Auditing Committee (PIIAC)	3,4	• PIIAC audits open to public and media • citizen advisory subcommittee meetings open to public and media • appeal to city council • PIIAC decisions are public; chief's discipline is not	no	yes	none
Rochester Civilian Review Board	2	• reviews are closed • results are not public • no appeal	yes	no	none
St. Paul Police Civilian Internal Affairs Review Commission	2	• hearings are closed • no appeal • no publicizing of disciplinary recommendations	no	yes, but never used	none
San Francisco Office of Citizen Complaints	1	• chief's hearings are closed • police commission hearings are public • appeal process for officers • complaint histories and findings confidential • chief's discipline not public	yes	yes	during investigation; during hearing
Tucson Independent Police Auditor and Citizen Police Advisory Review Board	2,4	• monitoring is private • appeal process • board holds monthly public meeting at which public may raise concerns	no	no	not applicable

* Type 1: citizens investigate allegations and recommend findings; type 2: police officers investigate allegations and develop findings; citizens review findings; type 3: complainants appeal police findings to citizens; type 4: an auditor investigates the police or sheriff's department's investigation process.

FIGURE 10.2 Types of police oversight systems.
Source: National Institute of Justice. Civilian Review of Police: Approaches and Implementation, Citizen Complaint Process in Berkeley, by Peter Finn, 2001, p. 18.

supports civilian review boards, with 80% of the 1,248 respondents supporting civilian review boards with both police and civilian members.

Historically, police have resisted the establishment of civilian review boards because they feel they can police their own. Police officers often view civilian review boards as "anticop," perceiving citizens as "too prone to bias or ignorant of actual police practices to make sound judgments."[24] Reasons given for police opposition to civilian review boards include:

- They single out police officers from other municipal employees.
- They tend to polarize the police and the public.
- They infringe on the authority of the police chief and may erode police authority in other areas as well.
- They utilize laypeople with little knowledge of police work.

Because of its strong civilian component, many people have unrealistic expectations of the abilities of a civilian review board. As a rule, the way the process has worked is as follows: The process begins with a citizen filing a complaint against a police officer. If the police officer in question denies the charge, the civilian review board takes it on, but usually this review results in no conclusive findings either way. But many have argued that the establishment of a civilian review board may also be a good way to enhance police–community relations. For example, in Indianapolis an initiative to form a civilian review board brought about not only the establishment of the board but an effective coalition between the Indiana ACLU, the local branch of the NAACP, and other community groups that could take future action on other issues. It is clear that strong community advocacy is necessary to overcome resistance at every stage, even after a civilian review board is established.

Types of Civilian Review Boards

Because civilian review systems vary so greatly across the nation, confusion is still common about them. Simply put, some are more "civilian" than others. Three basic models of civilian review are common:

Type I: Independent. Persons who are not sworn officers conduct the initial fact-finding. They submit an investigative report to a nonofficer or a board of nonofficers, requesting a recommendation of discipline or leniency.

Type II: Infused. Sworn officers conduct the initial fact-finding. Once completed, they submit an investigative report to a nonofficer or a board of nonofficers for a recommendation.

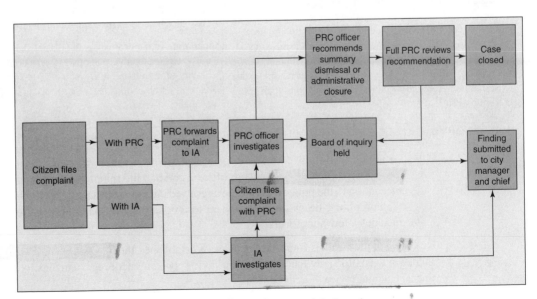

FIGURE 10.3 Possible responses resulting from citizen oversight boards.

A Closer Look

The Berkeley, California, Police Review Commission: A Citizen Board and the Police Department Investigate Complaints Simultaneously

After allegations of police use of excessive force in clearing street people from a local park, Berkeley voters in 1973 approved a ballot initiative that created by ordinance the Police Review Commission (PRC), the oldest continuously operating citizen oversight agency in the nation.

Citizens filed 42 cases with PRC in 1997. The board conducted hearings in 12 cases, which sometimes included multiple allegations (some of which came from the previous year's filings). The board sustained at least 1 allegation in 2 of the 12 hearings, for a total of 4 sustained allegations. The board did not sustain 30 allegations. The board closed another 34 cases without hearings, either because the case lacked merit or the complainant failed to cooperate. For the first half of 1998, in 5 of the 11 hearings held, there was at least 1 sustained allegation.

The review process

Intake

Citizens may file complaints directly with PRC within 90 days of the alleged misconduct. The ordinance requires PRC to forward complaints to the police department's internal affairs bureau within 30 calendar days. Internal Affairs (IA) and PRC then both investigate the case independently. PRC and the police department have 120 days to communicate their findings to the city manager and for the city manager or chief to determine discipline.

Citizens who file a complaint initially with the police department's internal affairs bureau may file the complaint subsequently with PRC within the 90-day limit, after which the parallel PRC and IA investigations occur. The IA investigators give complainants a brochure on the complaint process that mentions PRC, and they tell citizens who express dissatisfaction with the Internal Affairs (IA) investigation about the PRC option. From 1994 through 1998, 53% of complainants registered their complaints initially with IA rather than being referred by PRC.

Investigations

Either the PRC officer or the PRC investigator conducts an investigation of each complaint. Subject officers must appear and answer questions, but they may appear with a union representative or lawyer.

Hearings

To hear each complaint, PRC staff impanel a board of inquiry consisting of three of the nine board members. The three choose a chairperson from among themselves. One week before the hearing, PRC staff provide the members with a packet containing the results of their investigation along with relevant ordinances, statutes, and department policies and procedures. Attard sends a notice to the chief who, according to the ordinance, must order the involved officer(s) to attend. A lieutenant, the duty command officer for the week, is always present to answer questions about police policy, procedures, and training.

As soon as the hearing begins, the chairperson makes clear that the board can offer only recommendations to the city manager and the chief. The hearing then proceeds as follows:

1. The complainant presents the complaint and introduces any witnesses.
2. Board members, and subject officers or their attorneys, may question the complainant and witnesses.
3. Steps 1 and 2 are followed for the subject officer.
4. Each party may make a closing statement.
5. The board deliberates in closed session.
6. The board returns to announce its finding.

According to the ordinance, the parties may present evidence "on which reasonable persons are accustomed to rely in the conduct of serious affairs," including hearsay. The chairperson rules on objections, but other board members can overrule the chair.

Source: Citizen Review of Police. U.S. Department of Justice; Office of Justice Programs: National Institute of Justice, March, 2001.

Type III: Quasi-internal. Sworn officers conduct the initial fact-finding and make a recommendation to the police chief. If the aggrieved citizen is not satisfied with the chief's action on the complaint, he or she may appeal to a board that is made up primarily of officers but includes a few nonofficers.

Civilian review is important because it establishes the **principle of accountability**. Strong evidence exists to show that a complaint review system encourages citizens to act on their grievances. Civilian review boards can:

- Be important sources of information about police misconduct
- Reduce public reluctance to file complaints

- Reduce procedural barriers to file complaints
- Increase the likelihood that police reports will be more complete
- Increase police scrutiny of police policies that lead to citizen complaints

Probably more than any other event, the Rodney King incident fueled debate over the utility of civilian review boards and demonstrated how any show of police force ensures citizen backlash. Often, this backlash comes in the form of protests, demonstrations, and even riots by citizens demanding that police officers responsible be held accountable for their actions. The shock value of the Rodney King (and other) incidents has stimulated renewed interest in civilian review boards and other control mechanisms.

STANDARDS AND ACCREDITATION

One way to increase police accountability is to require that police actions meet nationally recognized standards. The movement to accredit departments that meet such standards has gained momentum during the past decade. It has the support of the Commission on Accreditation for Law Enforcement Agencies (CALEA), a private nonprofit corporation formed by four professional associations: the International Association of Chiefs of Police (IACP), the National Organization of Black Law Enforcement Executives (NOBLE), the National Sheriffs' Association (NSA), and the Police Executive Research Forum (PERF).

The CALEA standards, first published in 1983, have been updated from time to time. The fourth edition, published in 1999, has 439 specific standards. Each standard is a statement, with a brief explanation, that sets forth clear requirements. For example, under "Limits of Authority," standard 12.1 requires "a written directive [governing] the use of discretion by sworn officers." The explanation states, "In many agencies, the exercise of discretion is defined by a combination of written enforcement policies, training, and supervision. The written directive should define the limits of individual discretion and provide guidelines for exercising discretion within those limits."[25] Because police departments have said almost nothing about their use of discretion, this statement represents a major shift. However, the standard still is not specific enough. For example, it does not cover stop-and-frisk actions, handling of intoxicated people, and the use of informants.

Police accreditation is voluntary. Departments contact CALEA, which helps them in their efforts to meet the standards. This process involves some evaluation by department executives, the development of policies that meet the standards, and the training of officers. The CALEA representative acts like a military inspector general, visiting the department, examining its policies, and seeing if the standards are met in its daily operations. Departments that meet the standards receive certification. Administrators can use the standards as a management tool, training officers to know the standards and be accountable for their actions. By 1998, more than 460 agencies had been accredited.

Obviously, the standards do not guarantee that the police officers in an accredited department will not engage in misconduct. However, they are a major step toward providing clearer guidelines to officers about proper behavior. Accreditation can also show the public that the department is committed to making sure officers carry out their duties in an ethical, professional manner.

MEDIA OVERSIGHT

Law enforcement officials probably place second only to politicians in having a difficult time coping with the news media. Police–media communications result in frequent misunderstandings, often because neither party fully appreciates the job the other has to do. This lack of comprehension tends to breed mutual feelings of fear and mistrust. Generally speaking, law enforcement officials tend to look upon news reporters as snoopers poking their noses into things that are none of their concern. A ready quip is that some reporters "never let the facts get in the way of a good story." Moreover, many law enforcement officials believe that reporters are extremely liberal and permissive and actually fight or attempt to impede police investigations.

Traditionally, the media in their role as public watchdogs have zealously sought to expose alleged internal police corruption, selective enforcement, and other types of police misconduct that almost always garner headlines and television attention. This glaring exposure has often resulted in law enforcement agencies becoming wary of media personnel since such news coverage reflects adversely on the agencies.

Part of the problem is that reporters often believe that the police routinely withhold information from them, or worse yet, regularly release inaccurate information. Sometimes this causes a reporter to "dig" for the "real" story when, in fact, there is none. This tends to polarize the police and the media. Also, police executives wary of being misquoted tend to respond in a reticent manner and are thus perceived as uncooperative. Since successful working relationships cannot be founded on mutual mistrust, many police–media interactions deteriorate into an exchange of noncommittal responses, which further exacerbates misunderstandings. When this happens, the reporter after a story might just go ahead and fill in the blanks. This reinforces law enforcement's perception that regardless of what one tells a reporter, the story will reflect that reporter's personal beliefs. So the cycle of mistrust continues.

Freedom-of-information acts have been codified in many states and localities. These statutes were originally enacted to counteract government abuses of power. But as with many well-intentioned legal changes, these soon backfired. Volumes of once-classified information useful to foreign governments and organized crime became readily available to anyone who requested them, including the media. The rift between the police and the media grew that much wider due to the declassification. Now a reporter can confront a law enforcement official with documented evidence of an investigation planned or in progress and request confirmation. The law enforcement official must then deny any knowledge of the investigation, thereby driving an additional wedge between these two groups. When confidentiality is at stake, rules are often skirted.

It is clear that as we delve deeper into the information age, it will be more likely that the media will monitor police operations in some way. Rosenthal suggests that merely asking a reporter to ride along is not enough to bridge the communication gap; a better idea would be for officers to ride along with a TV news crew or spend some time in the newsroom of the local newspaper.[26] Not only will this help the observing officer understand the news business, but valuable, mutual contacts can be made as well.

In Retrospect

Because police corruption remains one of the most serious problems in policing, professional police departments and their administrators must be able to successfully address is important issues. Controlling police misconduct is incredibly difficult. The problem of corruption is not simply the result of a few miscreant officers but is deeply rooted in the nature of American society and the criminal law. Despite these problems, there are affirmative ways in which solutions can be found. A few departments have succeeded in reducing or eliminating corruption through effective control techniques. Police corruption can also be monitored and effectively dealt with through an external means as well. External control mechanisms include civilian review boards, oversight groups, and the media. Each control mechanism places the police on notice that misconduct and corruption will not be tolerated and that police administrators must be held accountable for the actions of the officers in their employ.

Improve Your Professional Vocabulary

certification
decertification
Field Internal Affairs Units

internal affairs unit
Mollen Commission
principle of accountability

proactive prevention measures
rectitude issues
standard operating procedures

Discussion Questions

1. List and discuss the basic issues in police accountability as discussed in this chapter.
2. Describe the way in which the "Internal Affairs" section of a police department functions and how it can rid the department of corruption.
3. When recruiting officers, discuss the best way to identify potential problem officers before they are hired.
4. In what way does the attitude of the police chief affect the ability to fight police corruption in a police department?
5. List and discuss how decertification and drug testing of officers represent viable ways to control police corruption and misconduct.
6. Explain the ways in which the media can influence police corruption both positively and negatively.
7. Discuss the synergy between the civilian complaint process and civilian review boards.
8. Identify and discuss the pros and cons of civilian review boards.
9. Explain the ways in which police policies and procedures help administrators avoid problems with problem officers.
10. Discuss why public opinion can contribute to the continued misconduct and corruption of officers within a police department.

Notes

1. Fields, G. (2000, February 1). New Orleans crime fight started with police. *USA Today,* p. 6A.
2. Ibid.
3. Ibid.
4. Ibid.
5. Ibid.
6. Skolnick, J. (1994). *Justice without trial: Law enforcement in a democratic society,* 3rd ed. New York: Macmillan.
7. International Association of Chiefs of Police. (1989). *Building integrity and reducing drug corruption in police departments.* Washington: Government Printing Office.
8. Mollen Commission to Investigate Allegations of Police Corruption [Mollen Commission]. (1994). *Commission report.* New York: Author.
9. Sherman, L. W. (1974). *Police corruption: A sociological perspective.* Garden City, New York: Anchor Books.
10. Mollen Commission to Investigate Allegations of Police Corruption [Mollen Commission]. (1994). *Commission report.* New York: Author.
11. Sherman, L. W. (1974). *Police corruption: A sociological perspective.* Garden City, New York: Anchor Books.
12. Aogan, M. (1967, April). Headhunter or real cop: Identity in the world of internal affairs officers. *Journal of Contemporary Ethnography, 24,* 99–130.
13. Ibid.
14. Mollen Commission to Investigate Allegations of Police Corruption [Mollen Commission]. (1994). *Commission report.* New York: Author.
15. Carter, David L., & Thomas Barker (1994). Administrative guidance and control of police officer behavior: Policies, procedures, and rules, 2nd ed. In Barker & Carter, eds., *Police deviance,* Cincinnati: Anderson, 22–23.
16. Goldstein, Herman. (1975). *Police corruption: A perspective on its nature and control.* Washington, DC: The Police Foundation, 3.
17. Mollen Commission to Investigate Allegations of Police Corruption [Mollen Commission]. (1994). *Commission report.* New York: Author.
18. Eisenberg, Terry, et al. (1973). Police personnel practices. Washington, DC: The Police Foundation.
19. U.S. Department of Justice, National Institute of Justice. (1986). *Employee drug testing policies in police departments.* Research in Brief. Washington, DC: U.S. Government Printing Office.
20. Goldman, R., & S. Puro. (1987). Decertification of police: An alternative to traditional remedies for police misconduct. *Hastings Constitutional Quarterly, 15,* 50–80.
21. Burnham, David. (1977). *The role of the media in controlling corruption.* New York: John Jay College.
22. Hartman, F., L. Brown, & D. Stephens. (1988). *Community policing: Would you know it if you saw it?* East Lansing, MI: Michigan State University, National Neighborhood Foot Patrol Center.
23. Police Executive Research Forum. (1985). Police agency handling of citizen complaints: A model police statement. In *Police management today.* Washington, DC: International City Managers Association.
24. Tyre, M., & S. Braunstein. (1994, December). Building better civilian review boards. *FBI Law Enforcement Bulletin,* pp. 10–14.
25. Commission on Accreditation for Law Enforcement Agencies (CALEA). (1989). *Standards for law enforcement agencies.* Fairfax, VA.
26. Rosenthal, L. (1997, May). The media and the police. *Law Enforcement News.*

CHAPTER **11**

Police Civil Liability

This chapter will enable you to:

- Learn the processes leading to the arrest decision.
- Understand the role of probable cause in arrest and search and seizure.
- Learn how the use of force can be lawfully applied by police.

- Explain how police authority is delegated.
- Understand the requirements of a Title 42, Section 1983 civil action
- Understand the various state law torts that can be filed against police

ases involving the abduction, rape, and murder of children are among the most horrifying cases to pass to the U.S. criminal justice system. They are precisely the cases that can least afford being weakened by technicalities of law. Yet, in the case of John Couey—the convicted kidnapper, rapist, and murderer of nine-year-old Jessica Lunsford—police misconduct ruined crucial evidence in the case, making a taped confession inadmissible. While being questioned by police detectives, Couey confessed to the crime and directed police to Jessica's body, which was buried in his lawn. But Couey also told police that he wanted to consult with an attorney—an opportunity he was denied. Because his right to counsel was violated, a judge ruled that the initial confession cannot be admitted as evidence. The following year, a second confession by Couey was also ruled inadmissible; police again continued questioning Couey after he requested a lawyer.

In court, Couey pleaded not guilty to charges of first-degree murder, sexual battery, kidnapping, and burglary. Even without the confessions, strong physical evidence linked Couey to the murder, and he was convicted of kidnapping, rape, and murder. On August 24, 2007, John Couey was sentenced to death for his crimes.

In the Jessica Lunsford case, had it not been for the strong physical evidence used against her murderer, it is likely that Couey would have gone free had the case relied on an illegal confession taken by officers. As such, the extent to which law enforcement officers ignore constitutional protections remains a "hot-button" issue in modern policing and will be discussed in this chapter.

Among the many duties of a police officer, apprehending criminals, providing citizens with protection, treating persons in distress, and maintaining the safety of our streets and communities are included. As difficult as these tasks can be, the duties of a police officer are complicated because they are often the targets of lawsuits. Legal actions taken against police officers may present themselves for a number of reasons, some of which are inherent in the nature of the police role and the services they provide to the public.[1] When police officers fail to perform their assigned duties, perform them in a negligent fashion, or even abuse their authority, they face the possibility of civil liability. Lawsuits against the police, however, do not always result from their failure to perform their assigned duties. A disturbing number of police liability cases are filed against police officers claiming misconduct and abuses of authority, ranging from false arrest to allegations of excessive force. These lawsuits often allege intentional violations of constitutional, civil, and statutory rights.

Of course, there are police officers who engage in acts of misconduct and step beyond the scope of their official authority. From time to time such events are spotlighted by the media as they occur and occasionally make headlines across the nation. For example, the beating of motorist Rodney King by Los Angeles police officers following a traffic stop captured the nation's attention in the 1990s. As a result of this beating, attorneys for King filed a civil rights lawsuit against the police asking for a multimillion-dollar compensatory award in damages. The officers who were involved in the beating of King were found criminally liable for the assault, and the city of Los Angeles was found liable for the actions of its police officers. King was awarded more than $3.5 million in damages.

In October 2005, in the aftermath of hurricane Katrina, three New Orleans police officers were captured on video beating 64-year-old Robert Davis. One of the officers "grabbed a news producer, leaned him backward over a car, jammed him in the stomach and unleashed a profanity laced tirade."[2] Countless incidents of police wrongdoing are published in the newspapers or shown on television, and are eventually addressed by the courts and civil lawsuits.

The filing of a liability suit against a police officer, however, does not always mean the officer has engaged in some obvious wrongdoing. Moreover, many perceive the government as having "deep pockets" and the ability to pay either out-of-court settlements or large punitive damage awards. Consequently, some lawyers and citizens are quick to bring litigation against the government and the government's most visible agents—police officers. This, coupled with the recent rise in court findings of police liability, has led some to conclude that no other group of government employees is more exposed to civil lawsuits and liability than are the police. In fact, civil liability is an occupational hazard for many officers and their departments. Some have even maintained saying, "suing public officials has become the second most popular indoor sport in the country."[3]

CIVIL LIABILITY SUITS

Civil lawsuits against police departments for police misconduct can increase civic accountability. But, only recently have citizens been allowed to sue public officials. Title 42 United States Code Section 1983 allows citizens to sue public officials for violations of their civil rights. This right was extended in 1978 when the Supreme Court ruled that individual officers and the agency may be sued when a person's civil rights are violated by the agency's "customs and usages." If an individual can show that employees whose wrongful attacks were the result of these "customs, practices, and policies, including poor training and supervision," then he or she can sue.[4]

Lawsuits charging brutality, false arrest, and negligence have been brought in both state and federal courts. In several states people have received damage awards in the millions of dollars, and police departments have settled some suits out of court. For example, a Michigan court awarded $5.7 million to the heirs of a man who had been mistakenly shot by a Detroit officer, and Boston paid $500,000 to the parents of a teenager who had been shot to death. Over a year, city governments can end up paying quite a lot. In 1997, for example, New York City paid $27.3 million to settle 521 cases of police misconduct.

Civil liability rulings by the courts tend to be simple and severe: Officials are ordered to pay a sum of money, and the courts can enforce that judgment. The potential for costly judgments give police departments an incentive to improve the training and supervision of officers. One study asked a sample of police executives to rank the police issues most likely to be affected by civil liability decisions. The top-ranked issues were the use of force, pursuit driving, and improper arrests. Most departments have liability insurance, and many officers have their own insurance policies.

The courts have ruled that police must follow generally accepted professional practices and standards. The potential for civil suits seems to have led to some changes in policy. Plaintiffs' victories in civil suits have spurred accreditation efforts because police executives believe that liability can be avoided or reduced if they can show that their officers are meeting the highest professional standards.

The Prevalence of Civil Suits

The special vulnerability of the police and a trend toward allowing governmental liability have led to an explosion of lawsuits. Accurate information regarding the actual number and type of lawsuits filed against the police is difficult to obtain. Even so, several trends can be noted from the available information on police liability. First, since the 1960s, there has been a sharp increase in the number of civil suits filed against the nation's police. Second, there has been an increase in civil cases successfully litigated against police officers, police departments, and municipalities.[5] Lastly, while police officers and their departments have a good record in defending themselves from civil lawsuits, there are still a significant number of judgments handed down against the police, and there is a reason to believe that the number of cases the police are losing is growing.

From 1967 to 1971, the number of civil suits filed against the police increased by 124%. In 1976, there were more than 13,400 civil suits filed against law enforcement officers in the United

FIGURE 11.1 The failure on the part of some law enforcement officers to follow accepted police procedure has resulted in the wrongful conviction of over 100 persons. Here, renowned attorneys Barry Scheck and Johnnie Cochran stand with four African-American men who were racially profiled, stopped, and shot by state troopers on the New Jersey Turnpike. The troopers faced charges of attempted murder for the racially based vehicle stop and shooting.

States. This trend continued. Between 1967 and 1976, the yearly number of civil suits brought against law enforcement officers increased by more than 500%.[6] Studies conducted by the International Association of Chiefs of Police (IACP) and other organizations indicate that during a five-year period, 1 in 34 police officers was sued. Studies such as these predicted that by 1980 there would be more than 26,000 civil lawsuits filed against the nation's police.[7] Each year during the 1980s, thousands of civil liability cases were brought before courts claiming police violations of citizens' constitutional rights. Today, it is estimated that there are more than 30,000 civil actions filed against the police each year. While these trends are expected to continue in the years to come, police administrators have taken a guarded view of liability.

The Fear of Litigation

One interesting aspect of police civil litigation is that while police chiefs have taken a guarded view of the liability situation and generally feel that civil liability has yet to reach a point of crisis, the officer on the street is not as confident.[8] This may be because police chiefs are afforded some insulation from personal liability for the actions of their officers. Research shows that many police officers do fear civil litigation. For example, a study of 101 police cadets conducted by Scogin and Brodsky found that 9% of the officers interviewed felt their fear of civil litigation had reached the point of being irrational and excessive.[9] Several of the officers interviewed expressed a very simplistic understanding of prevention measures, as well as a fatalistic sentiment regarding potential litigation. The research noted that, "typical [officer] responses were, for example, 'what seems to be the only word in the English language is sue' and 'we can be sued for anything.'" Other officers expressed their risk management precautions in terms of "treating people fairly" and "going by the book." The researchers concluded, "the percentage of litigaphobic candidates is considerably higher than the 9% self-identified figure."

A survey of 50 police officers from three different law enforcement agencies in Pennsylvania conducted by Garrison (1995) found that 28% of the officers agreed with the statement that, "the idea that a police officer can be sued by others bothers me."[10] A replication of the studies in Kentucky found that 50% of 220 police cadets in another statewide training academy were worried about civil liability, and 31% thought they were worried to excess.[11] Female police officers showed less anxiety over the potential to be sued even when controlling for age, education, years of service, and job assignment. In all, lower-ranking police officers seem more concerned with the potential of civil liability than do their chiefs. More recently, a survey of 658 sworn officers from 21 agencies across the United States found that 51% of the officers ranked civil liability third among the top ten serious challenges they face on the job.[12] A study of police officers in Cincinnati, Ohio, found that 55% of the responding officers thought civil suits were a "barrier to effective law enforcement."[13]

Participants in Police Lawsuits

The civil litigation arena differs considerably from that of the criminal proceeding. In a civil case, jurors are selected from the community in which the offense occurred and decide the outcome of the case. A judge acts as a referee or moderator in the proceeding, instructing the jury on the law of liability in ruling on the motions of attorneys representing the parties involved. The individual who brings the lawsuit against the police is referred to as the *plaintiff*. Plaintiffs can be almost anyone in the community. Typically, they are citizens whose rights have allegedly been violated. From time to time, law enforcement officers themselves are plaintiffs bringing lawsuits against the very departments for which they work. The person or government agency that is being sued, that is alleged to have inflicted damage or injury, is called the *defendant*. In police civil litigation, defendants may include individual officers, their supervisors, high-level administrators, agencies, and the government entity, such as the city or county.

Typically, when a civil lawsuit has been filed against a police officer or police agency, numerous defendants are named. It is common that anyone associated with the injury or damage including the officer, the department, the supervisor, or the chief may be named in the suit. Doing so allows plaintiffs to seek out the person or the agency with the "deepest pocket." This is because while the individual police officer may have limited financial resources, the police agency itself has "deeper pockets" and the ability to pay large damage awards either on an individual basis, by raising taxes, or through its insurance carrier.[14]

It is common for plaintiffs to name unknown officers as "John Doe" defendants in the lawsuit. It is not uncommon for civil action to succeed against police departments and governments even when the plaintiff does not know which officer inflicted the injury.

Because of the enormous costs of police liability as well as the increasing frequency in the number of people whose lives are affected by this type of litigation, it is important to understand the framework of the federal and state law as it relates to police liability in the delivery of public services. One of the best ways for police officers and their departments to insulate themselves from police civil liability is to have a thorough understanding of the framework of liability law. As a rule, there are two legal avenues for litigating police misconduct. First, plaintiffs may file lawsuits in state court claiming the police negligently or intentionally failed to perform their duties in violation of state law. Second, a civil suit can be brought in federal court in which the plaintiff claims of the police violated a constitutional right. These are examined in this chapter.

Civil Liability under State and Federal Tort Laws

Allegations arising from public officials' misuse of authority may be addressed in federal or state court. Negligence claims against criminal justice personnel are based on state tort law. Negligence definitions differ from state to state. These differences may be due to specific categories and definitions allowed under state laws or court decisions.

The standard applied in a negligence tort is whether the officer's act or failure to act created an unreasonable risk of harm to another. Negligence occurs when the person acting unreasonably does not intend to harm another but fails to exercise due care to prevent such harm (*Harris* v. *City of Compton*, 1985). More precisely, negligence can be defined as subjecting a person to an unreasonable risk of injury. When a police officer exercises control over an arrestee, he or she has a duty to exercise reasonable care (*Wager* v. *Hasenkrug*, 1980; *Abraham* v. *Maes*, 1983).[15]

Any person is in custody when he or she is arrested and later transported by the police or confined by detention officers. This means that the police have a legal duty to take reasonable precautions to protect the health and safety of prisoners in their custody, render medical assistance as needed, and treat arrestees humanely. This, however, does not imply that law enforcement officers are the absolute guarantors of the welfare of those in their custody.

Establishing negligence is difficult. In some negligence cases, an agency's own policies and procedures have been used to determine the level of care expected of police personnel when performing their duties. For example, in *Miller* v. *Smith* (1995), the wrongful death by the suicide of an arrestee rose to a level of negligent conduct on the part of the chief. Failing to provide directives and guidelines about handcuffing or otherwise restraining an arrestee at the scene of a drunk-driving arrest prior to the suicide caused liability to attach to the city. In *Clark* v. *District of Columbia* (1997), the violation of the suicide-prevention policy was not negligence per se. The standard of care provided to prisoners in the facility exceeded a national standard, and liability did not attach.

To prove a state tort negligence claim, four elements must be established: (1) legal duty, (2) the breach of that duty, (3) proximate causation, and (4) an actual injury. All these elements must be proved by the plaintiff in order to prevail in a state tort claim of negligence. If any of the four elements is absent, there is no liability.[16]

Duty

Negligence generally stems from common law concepts, and most courts have held that the defendant must have violated duty to the person injured. It may arise from laws, customs, judicial decisions, or agency regulations.

Negligence is based on two concepts: (1) the existence of a duty and (2) fault, or the breach of that duty. Duty, as a matter of law, is to be determined by the court, whereas a jury examines fault from the perspective of a reasonable person.

Police officers perform a variety of duties. The authority to perform these duties does not automatically create a legal duty to perform these functions or a duty to perform them with reasonable care. In *State* v. *Hughes* (1989), however, the court concluded that police officers have a duty to exercise reasonable care in their official dealings with citizens who may be injured by their actions.

In order to require an officer to act in accordance with certain standards or level of care to avoid a risk of harm to another, there must be a legal duty. Determining whether a duty exists at all is essential. Where no duty exists, there is no liability. *Hurely* v. *Eddingfield* (1901) illustrates that our society continues to be reluctant to impose liability for inaction or to create too many duties to act. A classic example is the case of a drowning person. Although there may be a *moral* duty to attempt to rescue, there is no *legal* duty to do so. The law of negligence is preoccupied with the notion that there is no legal duty to act in many situations where a moral duty exists. Although the outcome in *Nelson* v. *Trayer* (1966) might be different today under Section 1983 cases, a deputy was held not negligent in arresting a man for hitchhiking but not his wife, who was later struck and killed by a passing vehicle.[17]

Statutes will frequently stipulate certain actions of a law enforcement officer when performing his or her duties. Legislatures have passed many laws that form the basis of negligence liability. A plaintiff may assert that the defendant officer violated a statute and that the violation caused his or her injury. For example, if a police officer fails to arrest a drunk driver and the driver later causes an accident in which another person is injured or dies, that officer could be liable for failing to arrest the driver. In this example, the statute would require a sobriety test. If the driver fails the test, arrest would be required. The court could possibly conclude that the officer failed to follow the duty of adhering to departmental regulations and state law. Such failure would be construed as creating or causing the later accident, and liability would probably attach.

Breach of Duty

Identifying a **legal duty** owed to the plaintiff is sufficient on its own. The plaintiff must also prove that the officer failed to perform or breached the legal duty owed. Failing to perform a duty is based on the factual situation of the incident. Police have a duty to arrest drunken drivers, but this does not imply that if the police fail to arrest every drunk driver and an accident occurs that causes an injury or death, liability will attach.[18]

Courts have recognized that the police are liable only to specific individuals and not the general public (*Harris* v. *District of Columbia*, 1991). For example, a police officer restrained a violent arrestee who was under the influence of phencyclidine (PCP) and locked him in a police van. Medical care was delayed because the emergency room physician required the officer to fill out certain forms that initially had been completed incorrectly. The arrestee subsequently died. The court determined that the officer did not breach a duty of care, because there was no clearly established obligation to provide general medical services or to provide such services to those not formally committed.

In order to prevail, the plaintiff must show some special knowledge or circumstances that set him or her apart from the general public and show that a relationship exists between the officer and the plaintiff. For example, in *Azure* v. *City of Billings* (1979), officers were held liable for violating a statute requiring police to transport intoxicated arrestees to the treatment facility. The arrestee had sustained injuries prior to the arrest and was noticeably intoxicated. There were some signs that he had been assaulted—he was unsteady in his balance, and his speech was slurred. Rather than transport the arrestee to the medical facility, where his condition could have been treated, officers transported him to the local jail.

Proximate Cause

If the plaintiff is successful in establishing that there was a legal duty and the officer breached that duty, he or she might show that the breach was the proximate cause of the injury. **Proximate cause** is a direct factual link between the act of negligence and the plaintiff's injury.[19] Many courts define proximate cause differently. It may be enough in one court to show that the officer's act or omission rose to a level that caused the plaintiff's injury, whereas other courts may rely on a higher standard of recklessness, wanton conduct, or gross negligence rather than simple negligence.

A close causal link between the officer's negligent conduct and the harm to the plaintiff must be proven. This may be determined by asking, "But for the officer's conduct, would the plaintiff have sustained the injury, harm, or death?" An additional relevant question may be, "Was the officer acting recklessly?" The court in *Carlin* v. *Blanchard* (1988) held that a sheriff's deputy was negligent in the shooting of a fellow officer and was the proximate cause of the officer's injuries, despite the fact that the officer's own conduct contributed to his injuries.[20]

Occurrence of Actual Injury

The final element required in state court actions is that of **actual injury** or damage to the plaintiff. The plaintiff must prove that actual damage occurred as a result of the officer's negligent conduct. If not able to show an actual injury, a plaintiff will not prevail. The injury or damage does not have to be physical. Emotional stress is sufficient for recovery in a tort action. Because the police are part of a public agency and are accountable to the public, they have a duty to report their activities in a reasonable manner.[21] A false message that a prisoner died in custody was actionable on a theory of intentional infliction of emotional distress (*Texas Department of Corrections* v. *Winters*, 1989).

Rather than serving a prison sentence, penalties in civil actions are monetary and address two possible areas. **Compensatory damages** are those designed to restore or compensate a victim for expenses, time off work, and so on. **Punitive damages** are usually considerably more severe and are designed to impose a financial punishment on the defendant. It is not uncommon for both compensatory and punitive damages to be assessed, especially if there are "willful and malicious" aspects to the defendant's behavior in question.

Legal liabilities may apply to all public officers, not just to law enforcement personnel. Probation and parole officers, jailers, prison officials, and other personnel in the criminal justice system are liable under the provisions of state and federal torts. An officer may be liable under any or all of the categories, based on what may essentially be a single act, if the act is serious and all elements that trigger liability are present. The double-jeopardy prohibition of the Fifth Amendment does not apply because double jeopardy arises only in criminal prosecutions for the same offense by the same jurisdiction.

Although various legal remedies are available to the public, plaintiffs are inclined to use two remedies against police officers. In this discussion we focus on those two liability sources—(1) civil liability under state tort law and (2) civil liability under federal law (42 U.S. Code, Section 1983, also known as civil rights cases)—to the exclusion of others.

DEFENDANTS IN CIVIL LIABILITY CASES

Just what constitutes unacceptable behavior is hard to define but can probably best be described as the officer's lack of compliance with criminal law, constitutional law, and the department's policy and procedure manual, sometimes known as the standard operating procedure (SOP) manual.

A secondary issue of great importance is the question of whether supervisors of the agency in which the police officer is employed should also be held accountable for an individual officer's actions.

The extension of civil liability to supervisors is known as the doctrine of respondent superior or **vicarious liability**. The thinking behind this doctrine is based essentially on the assumption that supervisors will be more likely to pay for damages articulated by the courts. As a result, increasing use of Section 1983 (see further explanation later in this chapter) has caused supervisors to reexamine their policies and procedures. To this end, courts have been supportive of a number of negligence theories that apply to police supervision. These include death or injury of innocent bystanders, failure to protect citizens, and negligent police training.[22]

Plaintiffs generally use the "shotgun approach" in liability lawsuits. This means that plaintiffs will include as defending parties everyone who may have any possible connection with a case. For example, while on patrol, a police officer shoots and kills a suspect. The victim's family will probably sue under Section 1983 or state tort law and include as defendants the officer, his or her immediate supervisor, the police chief, and the city or county. The allegation may be that the officer is liable because he or she pulled the trigger; the supervisor, police chief, and the city are also liable because of failure to properly train, direct, supervise, or assign, or because of an unconstitutional policy or practice. The legal theory is that some or all of the defendants had something to do with the killing, hence liability attaches. It is for the court during the trial to sort out culpability and assign fault.

The Individual Officer

The officer is an obvious liability target because he or she allegedly committed the violation. The officer will be a defendant whether he or she acted within or outside the scope of authority. Most state agencies, by law or official policy, provide representation to state law enforcement officers in civil actions. Such representation is usually undertaken by the state attorney general, who is the legal counsel of the state.

The situation is different in local law enforcement agencies. In most counties, cities, towns, or villages, there is no policy that requires the agency to defend public officials in liability lawsuits. Legal representation by the agency is usually decided on a case-by-case basis. This means that the local agency is under no obligation to provide a lawyer should an officer be sued. If the agency provides a lawyer, it will probably be the district attorney, the county attorney, or another lawyer working in some capacity with the government. In some cases the officer is allowed to choose a lawyer, and the lawyer's fees are paid by the agency. This is an ideal arrangement, but unpopular with agencies because of the cost factor.[23]

Supervisors

Although lawsuits against law enforcement officers are usually brought against field officers, a recent trend among plaintiffs is to include supervisory officials as defendants. The theory is that field officers act for the department and therefore what they do reflects departmental policy and practice. There are definite advantages to the plaintiff when supervisors are included in a liability lawsuit. First, lower-level officers may not have the financial resources to satisfy a judgment, nor are they in a position to prevent similar future violations by other officers. Second, chances of financial recovery are enhanced if supervisory personnel are included in the lawsuit. The higher the position of the employee, the closer the plaintiff gets to the "deep pockets" of the county or state agency.[24] Finally, inclusion of the supervisor may create inconsistencies in the legal strategy of the defense, hence strengthening the plaintiff's claim against one or more of the defendants.

If the supervisor does not want to defend the officer, a conflict of interest ensues. In these cases, the agency makes a choice and that choice will probably be to defend the supervisor. There is nothing the officer can do about that choice unless formal policy requires the agency to undertake the officer's defense even in these cases.

Police Agency Liability

Most courts have decided that where supervisory liability extends to the highest ranking person in the department, municipality or agency liability follows. Inclusion of the governmental agency (specifically the city or county) as defendant is also anchored in the deep pockets theory, meaning that while officers and supervisors may have shallow pockets, agencies have deep pockets because they can always raise revenue through taxation. States and state agencies generally cannot be sued under Section 1983, because they enjoy sovereign immunity under the Eleventh Amendment to the Constitution.[25]

This does not mean that state officials are immune from liability. Sovereign immunity extends only to the state and state agencies; state officials may be sued and held liable just like local officials. Although states are generally immune from liability in Section 1983 cases because of the Eleventh Amendment, such protection has largely been terminated for liability purposes in state courts. This means that states may generally be sued under state tort for what their officers do. *Local agencies* (referring to agencies below the state level) enjoyed sovereign immunity in Section 1983 cases until 1978. That year the Court decided that local agencies could be held liable under Section 1983 for what their employees do, thus depriving local governments of the sovereign immunity defense (*Monell* v. *Department of Social Services*, 1978). The court held in *Monnell* that the municipality will be liable if the unconstitutional action taken by the employee was caused by a municipal policy or custom. The Fifth Circuit Court of Appeals defines "policy or custom" as:

1. A policy statement, ordinance, regulation, or decision that is officially adopted and promulgated by the municipality's law-making officers or by an official to whom the lawmakers have delegated policy-making authority, or
2. A persistent widespread practice of city officials or employees which although not authorized by officially adopted and promulgated policy is so common and well settled as to constitute a custom that fairly represents municipal policy (*Webster* v. *City of Houston*, 1984)[26]

There are instances when an officer or a supervisor cannot be held liable for damages but the agency or municipality may be. In *Owen* v. *City of Independence* (1980), the court said that a municipality sued under Section 1983 cannot invoke the good faith defense that is available to its officers and employees if its policies violate constitutional rights. In *Owen*, a police chief was dismissed by the city manager and city council for certain misdoings while in office. The police chief was not given any type of hearing or due process rights because the city charter under which the city manager and city council acted did not give him any rights prior to dismissal. The court held that the city manager and members of the city council acted in good faith because they were authorized by the provisions of the city charter, but that the city could not invoke the good faith defense.

In a 1985 decision, the U.S. Supreme Court ruled that a money judgment against a public officer "in his official capacity" imposes liability on the employing agency regardless of whether the agency was named as a defendant in the suit (*Brandon* v. *Holt*, 1985). In *Brandon*, the plaintiff

A Closer Look

Areas of Supervisor Liability

- Failure to train the officer adequately
- Negligent retention of the officer
- Negligent hiring of the officer
- Failure to supervise the officer adequately
- Failure to intervene

alleged that although the director of the police department had no actual notice of the police officer's violent behavior, administrative policies were such that he should have known. The Court added that although the director could be shielded by qualified immunity, the city could be held liable.[27]

In a 1986 case, the Court decided that municipalities could be held liable in a civil rights case for violating constitutional rights on the basis of a single decision (as opposed to a "pattern of decisions") made by an authorized municipal policy maker (*Pembaur* v. *City of Cincinnati*, 1986). In this case the county prosecutor in effect made official policy and thereby exposed his municipal employer to liability, by instructing law enforcement officers to make a forcible entry, without a search warrant, of an office in order to serve capiases (a form of warrant issued by the judge) on persons thought to be there. The case was brought by a Cincinnati, Ohio, physician based on an incident where law enforcement officers, under advice from the county prosecutor, broke down the door to his office with an axe. The officers were trying to arrest two of the doctor's employees who failed to appear before a grand jury. The Court decided that this violated the Fourth Amendment Rights of the office owners and concluded that the city of Cincinnati could be held liable.

TRADITIONAL STATE LAW TORT

It is within the rights of all citizens to take legal action against persons whom they feel have wronged them. If the action in question is a violation of criminal law, the proper course of action begins with a formal complaint, an arrest, and the suspect's being processed through the criminal justice system. However, if the alleged wrong fails to meet any of the listed elements in criminal law but the aggrieved person still feels that he or she was wronged, a civil tort may be filed. All 50 states have tort laws dealing with practically all variations of civil wrongdoing.

A tort is defined as a civil wrong in which the action of one person causes injury to another person or his or her property, in violation of a legal duty imposed by law.[28] Three general categories of state tort based on a police officer's conduct are (1) intentional tort, (2) negligence tort, and (3) strict liability tort. Of these, only intentional and negligence torts are used in police cases. Strict liability torts are applicable in activities that are abnormally dangerous, such that they cannot be carried out safely even with reasonable care. Police work does not fall under strict liability tort, hence that category is not discussed.

Intentional Tort

Intentional tort occurs when someone intends to cause physical harm or a particular mental effect upon another person. Intent is mental and difficult to establish; however, courts and juries are generally allowed to infer the existence of intent from the facts of the case. We discuss next the kinds of intentional torts often brought against police officers.

FALSE ARREST AND FALSE IMPRISONMENT   In a tort case for false arrest, the plaintiff alleges that the officer made an illegal arrest, usually an arrest without probable cause. False arrest also arises if an officer fails to arrest the "right" person named in the warrant. An officer who makes a warrantless arrest bears the burden of proving that the arrest was in fact based on probable cause and that an arrest warrant was not necessary because the arrest came under one of the exceptions to the warrant rule. If the arrest is made with a warrant, the presumption is that probable cause exists, except if the officer obtained the warrant with malice, knowing that there was no probable cause (*Malley* v. *Briggs*, 1986).[29] Civil liability for false arrest in arrests with warrant is unlikely unless an officer serves a warrant that he or she knows to be illegal or unconstitutional. *Malley* also stated that an officer cannot excuse his or her own default by pointing to the greater incompetence of the magistrate. That is, it is the officer rather than the judge who issued the warrant and is ultimately responsible for establishing the basis for pursuing the arrest or search.

When an officer makes an arrest without probable cause, or when he or she simply impedes a citizen's right to leave a scene without good reason, that officer may be liable for the charge of false arrest. False arrest is often committed by officers who enjoy "throwing their weight around." Since the suit is grounded on the basis of abuse of police authority, supervisors and entire departments can be sued for the actions of just one employee.[30]

The best defense in false arrest and false imprisonment cases is that the arrest or detention was justified and valid. An officer who makes an arrest with probable cause is not liable for false arrest simply because the suspect is later proven innocent, nor does liability exist if the arrest is made by virtue of a law that is later declared unconstitutional. In the words of the U.S. Supreme Court: "We agree that a police officer is not charged with predicting the future course of constitutional law" (*Pierson* v. *Ray*, 1967). In these cases, however, the officer must believe in good faith that the law was constitutional. Also, the fact that the arrested person is not prosecuted or that he or she is prosecuted for a different crime does not make the arrest illegal. What is important is that there should be a valid justification for arrest and detention at the time those took place.

ASSAULT AND BATTERY   Although sometimes used as one term, *assault and battery* represent two separate acts. Assault is usually defined as the intentional causing of an apprehension of harmful or offensive conduct; it is the attempt or threat, accompanied by the ability, to inflict bodily harm on another person. An assault is committed if an officer causes another person to think that he or she will be subjected to harmful or offensive contact. In contrast, battery is the intentional infliction of a harmful or offensive body contact. Given this broad definition, the potential for battery exists every time an officer applies force on a suspect or arrestee. The main difference between assault and battery is that assault is generally menacing conduct that results in a person's fear of imminently receiving a battery, whereas battery involves unlawful, unwarranted, or hostile touching—however slight. In some jurisdictions, assault is attempted battery.

The police are often charged with "brutality" or using "excessive force." In police work, the improper use of force usually constitutes battery. The general rule is that the police in various situations may use non deadly force as long as such force is reasonable.[31] Reasonable force, in turn, is the force that a prudent and cautious person would use if exposed to similar circumstances and is limited to the amount of force that is necessary to achieve valid and proper results. Any force beyond that necessary to achieve valid and proper results is punitive, meaning that it punishes rather than controls.

The defense in assault and battery cases is that the use or threat of the use of force by the police was reasonable under the circumstances; however, what may be reasonable force to one judge or jury may not be reasonable to another. The use of reasonable force includes self-defense or defense of others by the police. The defense is available not only when an officer is actually attacked, but also when the officer reasonably thinks that he or she is in imminent danger of an attack.

WRONGFUL DEATH   The wrongful death tort, usually established by law, arises whenever death occurs as a result of an officer's action or inaction. It is brought by the surviving family, relatives, or legal guardian of the estate of the deceased for pain, suffering, actual expenses (such as expenses for the funeral), and for the loss of life to the family or relatives. In some states, the death of a person resulting from police use of deadly force comes under the tort of misuse of weapons. An officer has a duty to employ not merely ordinary care but a high degree of care in handling a weapon, otherwise he or she becomes liable for wrongful death.

The use of deadly force is governed by departmental policy or, in the absence thereof, by state law that must be strictly followed. The safest rule for any agency to prescribe is that deadly force should be used only in cases of self-defense or when the life of another person is in danger and the use of deadly force is necessary immediately to protect that life. Agency rules or state law, however, may give the officer more leeway in the use of deadly force. These rules are to be followed unless declared unconstitutional.

The use of deadly force to apprehend fleeing felons has been severely limited by the U.S. Supreme Court in *Tennessee* v. *Garner* (1985). In that case the Court said that deadly force is justified only when the officer has probable cause to believe that a suspect poses a threat of serious physical harm either to the officer or to others. Thus, if the suspect threatens the officer with a weapon or there is probable cause to believe that the suspect has committed a crime involving the infliction or threatened infliction of serious physical harm, the officer may use deadly force if necessary to prevent escape, and if, when feasible, some warning has been given. Therefore, fleeing-felon statutes in many states are valid only if their application comports with the requirements of *Tennessee* v. *Garner.* The use of deadly force to prevent the escape of a misdemeanant should not be resorted to except in cases of self-defense or in defense of the life of another person.[32]

INTENTIONAL INFLICTION OF EMOTIONAL DISTRESS Intentional infliction of emotional distress takes place when an officer inflicts severe emotional distress on a person through extreme and outrageous conduct that is intentional or reckless. Physical harm need not follow. What is extreme and outrageous is difficult to determine; moreover, the effect of an act may vary according to the plaintiff's disposition or state of mind. Most state appellate courts that have addressed the issue have held, however, that more than rudeness or isolated incidents is required. There is need for the plaintiff to allege and prove some kind of pattern or practice over a period of time rather than just isolated incidents. The case law on this tort is still developing, but it has already found acceptance in almost every state.

Negligence Tort

For tort purposes, negligence may be defined as the breach of a common law or statutory duty to act reasonably toward those who may foreseeably be harmed by one's conduct. This general definition may be modified or superseded by specific state law that provides for a different type of conduct, usually more restrictive than this definition, in particular acts.

NEGLIGENT OPERATION OF MOTOR VEHICLE High-speed chases are common in many police departments but are a particular source of liability for officers since they may result in injury or death to innocent bystanders. The switching on of one's red or blue emergency lights only "requests" that traffic clears the way. Police department manuals usually provide guidelines on the proper use of motor vehicles in both emergency and nonemergency situations. These guidelines, if valid, constitute the standard by which the actions of police officers are likely to be judged. In some states, departmental policies are admitted in court merely as evidence, while in other states the departmental policy is controlling. An example of negligent behavior is found in *Biscoe* v. *Arlington* (1984), when Alvin Biscoe lost both legs after being struck by an out-of-control police car as he was walking across the street. Biscoe, an innocent bystander, was awarded $5 million.

To some extent, departments may limit their susceptibility to lawsuits through regulations that limit the authority of their personnel. In 1985, for example, a Louisiana police department was exonerated in an accident that occurred during a high-speed chase because of a policy that limits officers from driving more than 20 mph over the posted speed limit. The individual officer, however, who was driving 75 mph in a 40-mph zone, was held liable for damages (*Kaplan* v. *Lloyds Insurance Co.*, 1985). In a related case, *Grandstaff* v. *Borger* (1985), $1.4 million was awarded to the family of a man who police mistook for a fugitive and killed in a barrage of gunfire. In the lawsuit, the official policy issue was based on inadequate training on the part of the officers involved in the shooting.

Highlights in Policing

Illinois Pursuit Driving Study Finds Accidents Result in Four Out of Ten Chases

James H. Auten of the Police Training Institute at the University of Illinois conducted a study of police pursuit driving operations in Illinois. Eighty-three law enforcement agencies participated in the research, which included 286 pursuits that involved police vehicles. Auten's study generally supports similar research conducted elsewhere in the United States; however, his study is especially significant since it involves primarily local and county law enforcement agencies. A general finding of the study was that four out of every ten police pursuits in Illinois resulted in an accident involving the police officer, the suspect driver, or a citizen.

The most common cause of the accident was the suspect losing control of his or her vehicle. Another important finding in the research was that the majority of the pursuits began when the police officer observed a traffic violation rather than as a follow-up to an actual vehicle stop. Only about 10% of the pursuits were initiated when the police officer knew or suspected that the fleeing driver had committed a felony. Of the pursuits that were initiated in terms of the officer's suspicion or knowledge of a felony, 90% of the felony offenses were auto theft. Another significant finding in Auten's research was that approximately 70% of the pursuits ended with the arrest of the suspect driver. The majority of the arrests were for nonfelony violations. A significant new finding in Auten's research, not found in studies in other states, was that approximately 20% of the pursuits ended with the suspect's vehicle being abandoned or crashed by the driver and the suspect fleeing on foot.

Source: Crime Control Digest (1991).

FAILURE TO PROTECT   There is no general civil duty to prevent a crime, even in high-crime areas. This means that police are not liable for failing to protect the victim of a crime. This is in accordance with the public-duty doctrine. The U.S. Supreme Court adopted the doctrine in *South* v. *Maryland* (1896). An individual who was victimized by a mob requested protection from the sheriff's office. The sheriff refused, and the individual was seriously injured and filed a lawsuit against the sheriff. The Court held that the sheriff committed no malfeasance or nonfeasance to the person injured and liability failed to attach. Most states recognize this doctrine, and there is no liability, harm, or injury if the police fail to protect the general public. The public-duty doctrine insulates police from liability when members of the general public are harmed or injured and desire to file a lawsuit against the police for failure to protect. This helps to enhance discretionary decision making on the part of the police and helps in reducing the risk of lawsuits for these types of actions.[33]

Generally, police correctional personnel have a duty to protect those under their control and custody. Numerous lawsuits have emerged from this *special relationship doctrine.* States define a special relationship in varying ways, but the concept basically means that criminal justice personnel will add duty to the particular individual in their custody rather than to the general public. The plaintiff must prove that there was an actual failure to protect and that there were facts and circumstances that made the harm or injury that occurred different from the general public. Factors that create a special relationship include actual knowledge of a dangerous condition or situation (foreseeability) and any statute, rule, or policy that requires officers to perform duties that can be reasonably said to be for the protection of the members of society. Common examples may include failing to respond to a call, failing to arrest in domestic violence situations, failing to protect a witness or informant, failing to obtain medical assistance for an arrestee or prisoner, failing to arrest a drunk driver, responding late to a call, failing to summon assistance, and failing to protect prisoners from themselves and other prisoners.

Liability did not attach in the *City of Hamseed* v. *Brown* (1995) for the stabbing of a woman by her boyfriend. The boyfriend had escaped from an officer who was attempting to arrest him for violating a no-contact domestic violence order. The officer allowed him to go upstairs to get some clothes, and he fled out a window. The boyfriend later found his girlfriend and stabbed her several times. The boyfriend was not under the officer's control. In *State* v. *Powell* (1991), merely receiving a subpoena to testify in court did not create an affirmative duty to provide protection. A woman was subpoenaed to testify against her ex-husband in a child abuse case. He poured gasoline on her and set her on fire. She sued the state, claiming that it had a duty to protect her from him and failed in that duty. The Court concluded that there was no special relationship. Conversely, in *Doe* v. *Calumet* (1994), the Court ruled that police officers' failure to rescue a minor girl being raped resulted in failure-to-protect liability. The mother of the child ran into the street yelling for help while her daughter was being raped. The officer's refusal to intervene constituted a willful and wanton disregard for the safety of the child.

In *Mills* v. *City of Overland Park, Kansas* (1992), officers did not have a duty to take intoxicated person without a jacket into protective custody in winter weather. The person came in contact with police after he was escorted out of a bar where there had been a disturbance. He walked away from the bar and was found frozen to death the next morning in a field near the bar. The state statute that allowed (but did not require) emergency detention of intoxicated persons was also not a basis for liability.

SPECIAL DUTY AND FORESEEABILITY   Courts have established that police may owe a **special duty** when they have reason to believe that an arrestee presents a danger to himself or herself (*Thomas* v. *Williams*, 1962). A special duty of care may arise when a particular arrestee is recognized to have a diminished ability to prevent self-injury or cannot exercise judgment within the same level of caution as an ordinary arrestee. Two types of individuals fall into these categories: (1) the mentally disabled, who have diminished capacity for self-protection; and (2) those who are impaired by drugs or alcohol. When it is evident that a particular arrestee has a diminished capacity or cannot exercise the same level of care as an ordinary person because of mental illness or intoxication, police officers must ensure that reasonable measures are taken to care for that individual while he or she is in their custody.[34]

The concept of special duty lacks precise definition but can be based on two factors: (1) the officer's knowledge of the arrestee's mental state and (2) the extent to which the arrestee's condition renders him or her unable to exercise ordinary care. If it is foreseeable that an arrestee's condition creates a hazard in a given circumstance (if there is a reasonable anticipation that an injury or damage is likely to occur as a result of an act or omission), the general duty of care can be required of the police. A combination of several factors must exist in order to indicate **foreseeability**, such as a level of knowledge of the arrestee's condition by the officer, a condition in the history of the arrestee, known propensities and the arrestee, and so on. As these factors increase in severity, a court may be more likely to hold that a special duty existed. This may lead to liability and a breach of duty.

A special duty stems from a specific mandate (such as statutory) rather than from situational relationships. If an officer possesses sufficient knowledge of an arrestee's mental or intoxicated condition and the prisoner is rendered helpless, a special duty to render care may exist. A special duty of care creates a higher level of responsibility for officers. Other examples of a special duty may include securing accident scenes, protecting witnesses and performance, suicidal prisoners in detention facilities, prisoner-on-prisoner assaults, failing to follow departmental rules, and operating equipment negligently.

MALICIOUS PROSECUTION   Malicious prosecution claims are made by a plaintiff who alleges that he or she was illegally prosecuted and a criminal proceeding was instituted for improper purpose and without probable cause. The plaintiff might show (1) the institution or continuation of original judicial proceedings, either criminal, civil, or administrative by or at the request of the defendant; (2) the termination of such proceedings in the plaintiff's favor; and (3) the suffering of injury or damage as a result of the prosecution. Proximate cause is also critical in malicious prosecution cases if the initiator of a criminal proceeding loses control of it due to the actions of the prosecutor or judge—actions that may be deemed to supersede the original complaint.[35]

Malice is a core element of malicious prosecution and involves an intentional wrongful act done without legal justification. Malice may consist of any proper and wrongful motive for bringing a criminal proceeding and does not require hatred of, or ill-will toward, the plaintiff (*Davis* v. *Muse*,

1992). Further, a lack of probable cause for the institution of the original proceedings must be shown. The Court in *Stitle* v. *the City of New York* (1991) ruled that claim of malicious prosecution can arise only after an arraignment, indictment, or some other evaluation by a neutral body that the changes were warranted. The claim cannot arise from an arrest only.

Malicious prosecution actions are generally not subject to qualified immunity found in many states, particularly where "bad faith," or acting outside the scope of employment, is involved. In *McDaniel* v. *City of Seattle* (1992), prosecutorial immunity was not applicable to immunize the city against malicious prosecution by officers, especially where false representations may have been made to the prosecutor.

NEGLIGENT POLICE TRAINING   One of the more compelling reasons for adequate police training is the fact that police departments can be held liable for the actions of their officers. To this end, negligence in training can create immense problems for police organizations. In a typical scenario, someone sues a police officer under Title 42 U.S.C. Section 1983 for allegedly depriving that person of a federal constitutional right, which can include the excessive use of force, unreasonable search, or other event. Because defendants with deeper pockets and less formidable defenses make more attractive targets, the plaintiff may name the local governmental entity as a defendant for allegedly causing the violation through "inadequate training."

This premise was upheld by the U.S. Supreme Court in 1989 when it was confirmed that inadequate police training can result in civil liability for the municipality under which the police department functions. The Court's position on this subject was made clear in the following excerpt from the case *City of Canton, Ohio* v. *Harris* (1989). "In this case we are asked to determine if a municipality can ever be liable . . . for constitutional violations resulting from its failure to train municipal employees. We hold that under certain circumstances such liability is permitted." [36]

In April 1978, Geraldine Harris was arrested by officers of the Canton Police Department and transported to the police station in a patrol wagon. When the police wagon arrived at the station, Harris was found sitting on the floor of the wagon. When asked if she needed medical attention, she responded with an incoherent remark. After she was brought inside the station for processing, Ms. Harris slumped to the floor on two occasions. Eventually, police officers let Ms. Harris remain on the floor to prevent her from falling again. No medical attention was ever summoned for Ms. Harris. After about an hour Ms. Harris was released from custody and taken by ambulance, which was provided by her own family, to a nearby hospital. There she was diagnosed as suffering from several emotional ailments, and subsequently hospitalized for one week. Ms. Harris received outpatient treatment for one additional year.

After a period of time Ms. Harris initiated this action, alleging many state law and constitutional claims against the city of Canton and its officials. Among these claims was one seeking to hold the city liable for its violation of Ms. Harris's right, under the due process clause of the Fourteenth Amendment, to receive medical attention while in police custody.

> We hold today that the inadequacy of police training may serve as the basis for liability only where the failure to train amounts to deliberate indifference to the rights of persons with whom the police come into contact. . . . [When] a municipality fails to [properly] train its employees, such neglect may demonstrate a "deliberate indifference" to the rights of its inhabitants and therefore can be properly thought of as a city "policy or custom" that is actionable. . . . [37]

Moreover, for liability to attach in this circumstance the identified deficiency in a city's training program must be closely related to the ultimate injury. Thus, in the case at hand, the respondent must still prove that deficiency in training actually caused the police officer's indifference to her medical needs. Would the injury have been avoided had the employee been trained under a program that was not deficient in the identified respect? Predicting how a hypothetically well-trained officer would have acted under the circumstances may not be an easy task for the fact finder, particularly since matters of judgment may be involved, and since officers who are well trained are not free from error and perhaps might react quite like the untrained officer in similar circumstances. But judge and jury, doing their respective jobs, will be adequate to the task.

According to Hall, before being able to sue successfully under the pretense of inadequate training, three links must be established:

1. A constitutional violation
2. A "policy" of inadequate training
3. A causal connection

It is not enough to show that some degree of harm resulted from a police officer's improper performance of his or her duties, but that a clearly defined constitutional right was infringed upon. Accordingly, establishing that an officer committed a constitutional violation is not sufficient to attach liability to the department. Rather, it is necessary to show that the officer's training was deficient and that the deficiency was due to the department's policy or custom.

Finally, even if a plaintiff establishes that an officer violated the plaintiff's constitutional rights and that the violation was caused by a training program of the municipality, it is still necessary to establish a causal connection between the deficient training policy and the constitutional injury. As the Supreme Court explained in *Canton*, "[F]or liability to attach . . . the identified deficiency in a city's training program must be closely related to the ultimate injury." In brief, failure to train is a legitimate cause of action under federal law and affixes liability on local government entities or policy-making officials when it can be shown that the failure to train constituted a policy or practice that resulted in a constitutional violation.[38]

CIVIL LIABILITY UNDER FEDERAL LAW

A significant trend in the area of police misconduct litigation is use of the **1983 action**, which is the most frequently used remedy in the arsenal of legal liability statutes available to plaintiffs. The name is derived from the provisions of Section 1983 of Title 42 of the U.S. Code, which was passed in the aftermath of the Civil War. The law, originally passed by Congress in 1871, was then known as the Ku Klux Klan law, because it sought to control the activities of state officials who were also members of that organization. For a long time, however, the law was given a limited interpretation by the courts and was seldom used. In 1961, the Court adopted a much broader interpretation, thus opening wide the door for liability action in federal courts.

Among the reasons for the popularity of this statute are that Section 1983 cases are usually filed in federal court, where discovery procedures are more liberal and attorney's fees are recoverable by the "prevailing" plaintiff in accordance with the Attorney's Fees Act of 1976. In essence, the law recognizes that city, county, and state police officers take an oath to uphold and enforce the laws of their specific state, and much public confidence is entrusted to them to do so. Consequently, the law prohibits the depravation of life, liberty, or property without due process of law. Section 1983 specifically states: "Every person under color of any statute, ordinance, regulation, custom, or usage of any state or territory, subjects, or causes to be subjected, any citizen of the United States or any other person within the jurisdiction thereof to the depravation of any rights, privileges, or immunities secured by the Constitution and laws, shall be liable to the party injured in an action at law, suit in equity, or other proper proceeding for redress."[39]

After remaining virtually idle for over 90 years, Section 1983 was revived by the U.S. Supreme Court in the 1961 case of *Monroe* v. *Pape*. The Court concluded in this case that when it has been found that a police officer acts improperly, such as in cases of brutality, that officer can be sued in federal court for violations of constitutional protections. A crucial aspect to Section 1983 is that the infraction must have occurred while the officer was acting under **color of state law**. This means that the police officer in question must have been on duty and acting within the scope of his or her employment.

The term *acting under color of state law* is instructive because it means that the misuse of power possessed by virtue of the law and made possible only because the wrongdoer is clothed with the authority of the state cannot be tolerated. The difficulty is that although it is usually easy to identify acts that are wholly within the color of law, such as when an officer makes a search or an arrest while on duty, there are some acts that are not as easy to categorize. Let's consider an example: A police officer works during off-hours as a private security agent in a shopping center. While in that capacity he shoots and kills a fleeing shoplifter. Was he acting under color of law? Or suppose that an officer arrests a felon during off-hours and when not in uniform. Is the officer acting under color of law? The answer usually depends on job expectation.

As a rule, if officers are carrying out police functions, such as making arrests or conducting a search, it can be argued that they are acting under color of state law for purposes of liability.

A number of factors can be considered when making determinations of whether a police officer was acting under color of state law for the purposes of liability. These include:

- Did the police properly identify themselves?
- Were officers conducting an investigation?
- Were police documents properly filed?
- Was an arrest attempted by the police?
- Did the police invoke powers beyond their jurisdiction?
- Did the officer utilize police powers in order to settle a private vendetta?
- Did the police officer display weapons or other police equipment?
- Was the officer acting according to state or city law?
- Does police department policy require officers to be on duty on a 24-hour basis?

Many police departments, by state law, judicial decision, or agency regulation, expect officers to respond as officers 24 hours a day. In these jurisdictions any arrest made on or off duty comes under the requirement of color of law. In the case of police officers who "moonlight," courts have held that their being in police uniform while acting as private security agents, their use of a gun issued by the department, and the knowledge by department authorities that the officer has a second job all indicate that the officer is acting under color of law. On the other hand, acts by an officer that are of a purely private nature are outside the color of state law even if committed while on duty.

The courts have interpreted the term *color of law* broadly to include local laws, ordinances, or agency regulations; moreover, the phrase does not mean that the act was authorized by law. It suffices that the act appeared to be lawful even if it was not in fact authorized; hence an officer acts under color of law even if he or she exceeds lawful authority. Moreover, it includes clearly illegal acts committed by the officer by reason of position or opportunity. There must be a violation of a constitutional or federally protected right. Under this requirement, the right violated must be given by the U.S. Constitution or by federal law. Rights given only by state law are not protected under Section 1983. Example: The right to a lawyer during a police lineup prior to being charged with an offense is not given by the Constitution or by federal law; therefore, if an officer forces a suspect to appear in a lineup without a lawyer, the officer is not liable under Section 1983. If state law gives such right, its violation may be actionable under state law or agency regulation, not under Section 1983.

The Bivens Action

The 1983 action is the most widely used statute against official misconduct by municipal and state officers, but surprisingly, the statute rarely applies to federal officers such as agents of the Federal Bureau of Investigation (FBI), Drug Enforcement Administration (DEA), or U.S. Customs Service. The reason for this is that the statute specifically states that the plaintiff be acting under color of state law. Therefore, federal officers can be sued under one of two complaints: a **Bivens action** against individuals for violations of constitutional rights but not against the United States or its agencies, or a tort against the United States under the Federal Tort Claim Act, or a combination of the two.[40]

The Bivens action is basically a judicially created counterpart to the 1983 action suit, and the Supreme Court has allowed federal officers (not the federal government) to be sued for constitutional violations that would otherwise be the subject of a 1983 suit against a state or local officer. The law stems from the landmark case *Bivens* v. *Six Unknown Federal Narcotics Agents* (1971), where the Supreme Court held that a violation of the Fourth Amendment's protection against unreasonable search and seizure can be cause for legal action.

DEFENSES AND CIVIL LIABILITY CASES

Various legal defenses are available in state tort and Section 1983 cases. Three of the most often used defenses are official immunity, probable cause, and good faith.

Official Immunity Defense

Generally, federal officers have been granted a court-created qualified immunity and have been protected from suits where they were found to have acted in the belief that their action was consistent with federal law. In times gone by, the doctrine of sovereign immunity was a legal premise that held that a governing body could not be sued because it made the law and therefore should not be bound by it. The right to sue police for transgressions of their authority has been the result of slow historical erosion of the doctrine of sovereign immunity. The erosion began during the civil rights era of the 1960s when a provision of the 1871 Civil Rights Act was used by state prisoners in suing officers.

Another development was the 1978 case of *Monnel* v. *New York City Social Services*, a non-criminal justice case, in which a maternity case resulted in the court declaring that under Section 1983, cities and local governments could be sued if the action that is considered unconstitutional results in a policy, ordinance, or practice officially adopted and promulgated by that body's officers. In essence, monetary awards under Section 1983 are based on the premise that constitutional injury was an outgrowth of official policy adopted by the police organization.[41]

The concept of immunity is far more complex today and doesn't carry the same implications as the old doctrine did. For example, in some states, including New York, the legislature has declared that public and private agencies are equally liable for violations of constitutional rights. But other states, including California, have enacted statutory provisions limiting the extent of governmental liability. This seems to be the trend; other states are following along with the adoption of immunity principles such as "good faith" and "reasonable belief," designed to protect officers. Official immunity is composed of three categories.

ABSOLUTE IMMUNITY   This means that the court dismisses a civil liability suit without going into the merits of the plaintiff's claim. Absolute immunity does not apply to police officers; it applies only to judges, prosecutors, and legislators. There is one instance, however, when police officers enjoy absolute immunity from civil liability. In *Briscoe* v. *LaHue* (1983), the Supreme Court held that police officers could not be sued under Section 1983 for giving perjured testimony against a defendant in a state criminal trial. The Court said that under common law, trial participants—including judges, prosecutors, and witnesses—were given absolute immunity for actions connected with the trial process. Therefore, police officers also enjoy absolute immunity when testifying, even if such testimony is perjured. The officer may be criminally prosecuted for perjury.

QUASI-JUDICIAL IMMUNITY   This means that certain officers are immune if performing judicial-type functions but not when performing other functions connected with their office. An example is a probation officer when preparing a presentence investigation report upon order of the judge. Quasi-judicial immunity does not apply to police officers because the functions that officers perform are executive and not judicial in nature.

QUALIFIED IMMUNITY   The qualified immunity doctrine has two related meanings. One is that the immunity defense applies to an official's discretionary (or optional) acts, meaning acts that require personal deliberation and judgment. The second and less complex meaning relates qualified immunity to the good faith defense. Under this concept, a public officer is exempt from liability if he or she can demonstrate that the actions taken were reasonable and performed in good faith within the scope of employment.[42]

In *Malley* v. *Briggs* (1986), the Supreme Court said that a police officer is entitled only to qualified immunity in Section 1983 cases. The *Malley* case is significant in that the Court refused to be swayed by the officer's argument that policy considerations require absolute immunity when a police officer applies for and obtains a warrant, saying that qualified immunity provides sufficient protection for police officers because under current decisions the officer is not liable anyway if he or she acted in an "objectively reasonable manner." The Court has therefore made clear that in the immediate future, absolute immunity will not be available to police officers but only to judges, prosecutors, and legislators.

Probable Cause

Probable cause is a limited defense in that it applies only in cases of false arrest, false imprisonment, and illegal searches and seizures, either under state tort law or under Section 1983. For the purpose of a legal defense in Section 1983 cases, probable cause simply means "a reasonable good faith belief in the legality of the action taken" (*Rodriguez* v. *Jones*, 1973). That expectation is lower than the Fourth Amendment definition of probable cause, which is that probable cause exists "when the facts and circumstances within the officers' knowledge and of which they have reasonably trustworthy information are sufficient in themselves to warrant a man of reasonable caution in the belief that an offense has been or is being committed" (*Brinegar* v. *United States*, 1949).

Good Faith

This is perhaps the defense used most often in Section 1983 cases, although it is not available in some state tort lawsuits. Good faith means that the officer acted with honest intentions under the law (meaning lawfully) and in the absence of fraud, deceit, collusion, or gross negligence. The definition of good faith, however, may vary from one state to another by either judicial decision or legislation. In some cases, state law may provide that officials acting under certain circumstances enjoy good faith immunity. Courts and juries vary in their perception of what is ultimately meant by good faith, but chances are that the good faith defense will be upheld in the following instances:

1. If the officer acted in accordance with agency rules and regulations
2. If the officer acted pursuant to a statute that is believed to be reasonably valid but is later declared unconstitutional
3. If the officer acted in accordance with orders from a superior that are believed to be reasonably valid
4. If the officer acted in accordance with advice from legal counsel, as long as the advice is believed to be reasonably valid

Frivolous Lawsuits

Lawsuits that can be characterized as frivolous represents a small number of suits brought against the police. An examination of published cases decided by the federal district courts indicates that less than one half of a percent of those cases resulted in a judicial sanction because plaintiffs brought forth cases that clearly lacked merit. For example, in one year, the issue of sanctions was brought up only twice in police liability cases published by the federal courts. In one case the court refused to impose sanctions on a plaintiff and in the other case the court refused to impose sanctions against the defendant—the sheriff. Accordingly, of 658 police liability cases decided by the federal circuit courts in 2004, only

6 cases, or less than 1%, contain a claim of frivolous lawsuit against the police. One of the six cases was a frivolous lawsuit brought by a police officer against the Boston Police Department.[43]

It is important to consider the millions of interactions that take place between the police and citizens each and every day and the number of incidents that result in litigation. With approximately 18,000 state and local law enforcement agencies in the United States employing more than 800,000 people, the rate of litigation would seem relatively small compared to its potential. In fact, Novak, Smith, and Frank point out,

> The police have contact with over 43.6 million people annually. Of these contacts, over half of them (56% or over 24.5 million) are with citizens who are suspects of criminal activity . . . if we take these figures at face value, we then must conclude that 1/10 of 1% of all encounters between police and persons suspected of committing a crime could result in civil litigation . . .

The International Association of Chiefs of Police (IACP) conducted a study that concluded that about 40% of the liability cases were brought against the police for officer misconduct, not just technical error or minor rights violations.

There are good reasons for concern over potential civil liability, but such concerns are not founded when they are premised on the notion that citizens file an inordinate number of unjustified claims against the police. The feeling that police officers can be sued and held liable for almost anything is similarly unfounded. The civil litigation process has safeguards to prevent and, if necessary, punish frivolous and unjust claims brought against the police. Unfortunately, civil liability cases serve only to divide the police from citizens and to close minds to understanding the complex issues of police liability and the need for professionalism and accountability.

CAN THE POLICE SUE BACK?

Can the police strike back by suing those who sue them? The answer is yes, and some departments have done just that. The number of civil cases actually brought by the police against the public, however, has remained comparatively small. The reality is that although police officers may file tort lawsuits against arrestees or suspects, doing so can present some difficulties. One is that in a tort case the officer will have to hire his or her own lawyer. This necessitates financial expense that the officer cannot recover from the defendant. In the event the officer files a tort case for damages, it is unlikely that he or she will be able recover any monetary damages as many criminal defendants are too poor to pay such damages.

Moreover, officers often refrain from filing civil cases for damages because it is less expensive and more convenient to get back at the suspect in a criminal case. Almost every state has provisions penalizing such offenses as deadly assault of a peace officer, false report to a police officer, resisting arrest or search, hindering apprehension or prosecution, and aggravated assault. These can be added to the regular criminal offense against the arrested person, thereby increasing the penalty or facilitating prosecution. Finally, many officers feel that the harsh treatment they sometimes get from the public is part of police work and is therefore to be accepted without retaliation. Whatever the attitude, the police do have legal remedies available should they wish to exercise them.

Responses to Police Civil Litigation

Some research suggests that the strategy of suing police departments to achieve general reforms was not successful. Edward Littlejohn's study of police misconduct litigation in Detroit through the 1970s found that suits produced few reforms.[44] A study of 149 police misconduct suits filed in Connecticut between 1970 and 1977 found they had little apparent effect on the police. The study showed that plaintiffs rarely win because juries tended to be sympathetic to the police.[45]

McCoy argues that rising damage awards involving police abuse provoked an insurance crisis in many cities in the late 1970s and caused police departments to take steps to curb misconduct. He suggests that city attorneys need to provide feedback to the police department not just in the few cases where large damages are awarded but in all cases that are filed.[46] The director of the Institute for Liability Management argues that an effective risk management program is to include training for all officers, ensuring that officers have copies of department policies, regular training for supervisors, an atmosphere of accountability in the department, constant monitoring of changes in relevant laws, and good legal advice.[47]

Due to the rising cost of civil suits, some cities have taken proactive steps to reduce the instance of misconduct. For example, the Los Angeles County Board of Supervisors hired an attorney as special counsel to the Los Angeles Sheriff's Department (LASD) for the specific purpose of investigating problems in the department, recommending reforms and reducing the costs of misconduct litigation.[48] The special counsel represents one form of citizen oversight. The attorney, Special Counsel Eric Bob, has investigated virtually every aspect of the department including: recruitment, training, and assignment of officers; the use of deadly force and canines; sexual harassment in the workplace; and other issues. The results have been improvements in several areas. As a result, the docket of excessive force lawsuits against the LASD fell from an average of 300 in fiscal years 1992–1993 and 1993–1994 to about 77 in fiscal years 1997–1998 and 1998–1999.[49]

Consent Decrees: "Pattern or Practice" Lawsuits

In 1997, a **consent decree** against the Pittsburgh Police Department ordered sweeping changes in management and accountability procedures within the department. The police were ordered to begin keeping systematic data on all officer use of force to create an early warning system and to require officers to record the race and ethnicity of all persons they stopped for questioning, including pedestrians and motor vehicle drivers.[50] The consent decree was a result of a suit brought by the civil rights division of the U.S. Department of Justice. Three years later, the justice department negotiated a similar consent decree with the city of Los Angeles as a result of the Rampart scandal in the Los Angeles Police Department.

The justice department suits were brought under a section of the 1994 violent crime-control act that authorizes the justice department to bring civil suits against police departments where there is a "pattern or practice" of abuse of citizen's rights. In addition to Pittsburgh and Los Angeles, the justice department has sued any reached consent decrees with the New Jersey State Police over racial profiling and the Steubenville, Ohio, police over excessive force. In each of these cases, the federal courts have appointed a monitor to ensure compliance with the consent decree.[51]

The "pattern or practice" section of the 1994 law became a powerful tool for achieving police accountability. Instead of the traditional pattern of private lawsuits focusing on individual acts of misconduct, the federal law addresses general patterns. Instead of monetary damages for individual plaintiffs, successful suits result in court-ordered reforms of police management practices. In this respect, suits look to the future and seek to prevent conduct in the years ahead.[52]

Injunctions

In the event police practices systematically violate citizens' rights, civil rights groups have sought injunctions against the police to stop the alleged practice. If, for example, police officers are systematically stomping, questioning, and frisking all African-American males in a community—without regard for individualized suspicion—members of that group can seek an **injunction** ordering the practice stopped. For the most part, however, injunctions have not been an effective remedy for police misconduct.[53] In an important case involving the Philadelphia Police Department (*Rizzo* v. *Goode*, 1976), the U.S. Supreme Court held that the plaintiffs had failed to prove that the police chief and other city officials were directly responsible for the alleged police misconduct and that the plaintiffs themselves were likely to be the targets of misconduct in the future.[54]

In Retrospect

In this chapter, police liability was discussed and the difficulty in performing law enforcement duties in a legally hostile environment was acknowledged. Because of the special role and function that police play in society, police officers are especially vulnerable to civil litigation. There is a general concern among practitioners and scholars alike concerning the growing number of cases filed against the nation's police and increasing costs of these cases to citizens and cities alike. The cost associated with police civil liability goes well beyond the actual damage awards rendered by courts and can have an effect on the operation of police department and municipal governments. The actual costs and liability judgments against the police were considered, and while the police

have had a good record in defending themselves from civil liability, the number of cases the police lose is increasing.

Various reasons that people file lawsuits against police were discussed and the roles of their actions in the civil litigation process were identified. The distinction between crime and torts was made, and three different types of torts were considered. These state actions make up the vast majority of claims filed against the police and state courts. Federal litigation against the police is also a growing area of concern. Federal liability was considered, and elements of a lawsuit under 42 U.S.C. Section 1983 were presented. Section 1983 actions have become the cornerstone of police civil liability at the federal level.

Improve Your Professional Vocabulary

1983 action
actual injury
Bivens action
color of state law
compensatory damages

consent decree
deep pockets
foreseeability
injunction
legal duty

probable cause
proximate cause
punitive damages
special duty
vicarious liability

Discussion Questions

1. Explain the concept of "deep pockets" as it relates to police civil litigation.
2. Compare and contrast the terms *compensatory* and *punitive damages*.
3. Discuss the historic roots of police civil law.
4. Explain the significance of the concepts of existence of a duty and the breach of that duty.
5. List and discuss the areas of police supervisor liability.
6. Discuss the concept of foreseeability as it relates to negligence torts.
7. Explain a police officer's general duty, if any, to prevent crime.
8. What are the three components to a civil action alleging inadequate police training?
9. Considering the 1978 case of *Monnel* v. *New York City Social Services*, explain what elements must be present for a civil action to be successful.
10. Explain the usefulness of a consent decree under police civil law.

Notes

1. Kappeler, V. E. (2006). *Critical issues and police civil liability*, 4th ed. Prospect Heights, Illinois: Waveland press.
2. Out, N. (2006). The police service and liability insurance: responsible policing. *Policing: International Journal of Police Science & Management*, 8(4): 294–314.
3. Del Carmen, R. V. (1981). An overview of civil and criminal liabilities of police officers and departments. *American Journal of Criminal Law*, 9: 33.
4. Kappeler, V. E. (2006). *Critical issues and police civil liability*, 4th ed. Prospect Heights, Illinois: Waveland Press; Ross, D. L., & M. R. Bodapati. (2006). A risk management analysis of claims, litigation and losses of Michigan law enforcement agencies: 1985–1999. *Policing: International Journal of Police Science & Management*, 29(1): 38–57.
5. Kappeler, V. E. (1989). Special issue: police civil liability. *American Journal of Police*, 8(1): i–iii.

6. Americans for Effective Law Enforcement (1974). *Survey of Misconduct Litigation*: 1967–1971, p. 67. San Francisco, California: AELE.

7. Americans for Effective Law Enforcement (1980). *Lawsuits against police skyrocket*, p. 7. San Francisco, California: ATLE.

8. McCoy, C. (1987). Police legal liability is "not a crisis" 99 chiefs say. *Crime Control Digest, 21*: 1.

9. Scogin, F., & S. L. Brodsky. (1991). Fear of litigation among law enforcement officers. *American Journal of police, 10*(1): 41–45.

10. Garrison, A. H. (1995). Law-enforcement civil liability under federal law and attitudes on civil liability: A survey of university, municipal and state police officers. *Police Studies, 18*(3): 19–37.

11. Kappeler, V. E. (2006). *Critical issues and police civil liability*, 4th ed. Prospect Heights, Illinois: Waveland Press.

12. Stevens, D. J. (2000). Civil liabilities and arrest decisions. *Police Journal, 73*: 119–142.

13. Hughes, T. (2001). Police officers and civil liability: The ties that bind. *Policing: An International Journal of Police Strategies & Management, 24*(2): 240–262.

14. Ross, D. (2006). *Civil liability in criminal justice*, 4th ed., LEXIS-NEXIS Publishing, p. 71.

15. Del Carmen, R., & J. Walker (2006). *Briefs of leading cases and law enforcement*; LEXIS-NEXIS Publishing, p. 265.

16. Ross, D. (2006). *Civil liability in criminal justice*, 4th ed., LEXIS-NEXIS Publishing, pp. 281–287.

17. Ibid.

18. Ibid.

19. Ibid.

20. Ibid., pp. 34; 103–312.

21. Adams, T. (2004). *Police field operations*, 6th ed., Prentice-Hall Publishing: a Purcell River, New Jersey.

22. Kappeler, V. E. (1989). Special issue: police civil liability. *American Journal of Police, 8*(1).

23. Walker, S. (2001). *Police accountability: The role of citizen oversight*; Wadsworth Publishing: Belmont, California, pp. 268–269.

24. Ross, D. (2006). *Civil liability in criminal justice*, 4th ed., LEXIS-NEXIS Publishing, pp. 101–103, 183.

25. Del Carmen, R. & J. Walker (2006). *Briefs of leading cases and law enforcement*, LEXIS-NEXIS Publishing, pp. 270–272.

26. U.S. Commission on Civil Rights, *Revisiting who is guarding the guardians*? (2000) Washington, DC: Government printing office.

27. Walker, S. (2001). *Police accountability: The role of citizen oversight*; Wadsworth Publishing: Belmont, California.

28. Ross, D. (2006). *Civil liability in criminal justice*, 4th ed., LEXIS-NEXIS Publishing, pp. 12, 48–49.

29. Del Carmen, R., & J. Walker (2006). *Briefs of leading cases and law enforcement*. LEXIS-NEXIS Publishing, pp. 269–270.

30. Ross, D. (2006). *Civil liability in criminal justice*, 4th ed., LEXIS-NEXIS Publishing, pp. 270–274.

31. Adams, T. (2004). *Police field operations*, 6th ed.: Prentice-Hall publishing. Prentice-Hall publishing: a Purcell River, New Jersey: Prentice-Hall publishing.

32. Ibid.

33. Ross, D. (2006). *Civil liability in criminal justice*, 4th ed., LEXIS-NEXIS Publishing, pp. 8; 13.

34. Ibid.

35. Walker, S. (2001). *Police accountability: The role of citizen oversight*; Wadsworth Publishing: Belmont, California.

36. Del Carmen, R. & J. Walker (2006). *Briefs of leading cases and law enforcement*; LEXIS-NEXIS Publishing, p. 272.

37. Ibid.

38. King, J. K. (October 2005). Legal digest: Deliberate indifference: Liability for failure to train (Legal digest). *FBI Law Enforcement Bulletin, 74*(10).

39. Ross, D. (2006). *Civil liability in criminal justice*, 4th ed., LEXIS-NEXIS Publishing, pp. 27–28.

40. Ibid.

41. Ibid, pp. 48–49.

42. Walker, S. (2001). *Police accountability: The role of citizen oversight*; Wadsworth Publishing: Belmont, California.

43. Ibid.

44. Edward J. Littlejohn. (1981). Civil liability and the police officer: The need for new deterrence to police misconduct. *University of Detroit Journal of Urban Law, 58*: 365–431.

45. Project: Suing the police in federal court. *Yale Law Journal, 88* (1979): 791–824.

46. McCoy, Candace. (January–February 1984). Lawsuits against police: What impact do they really have? *Criminal Law Bulletin, 20*: 53.

47. Cited in Newell, Pollock, & Tweedy, Financial aspects of police liability, p. 8.

48. Special counsel, Los Angeles County Sheriff Department, Sixth Semiannual Report (Los Angeles: Los Angeles County, 1996), 33–39.

49. U.S. Commission on Civil Rights, *Revisiting who is guarding the guardians*? (Washington, DC: Government printing office, 2000).

50. *United States* v. *City of Pittsburgh* (W. D. Pa, 1997).

51. Ibid.

52. *United States* v. *State of New Jersey* (2000).

53. Monrad G. Paulson. (1970). *Securing police compliance with constitutional limitations*. National Commission on the Causes and Prevention of Violence, Law and Order Reconsidered. New York: Bantam books, 402–405.

54. *Rizzo* v. *Goode*, 423 US 362 (1976).

PART 4

The Impact and Challenges of Contemporary Policing

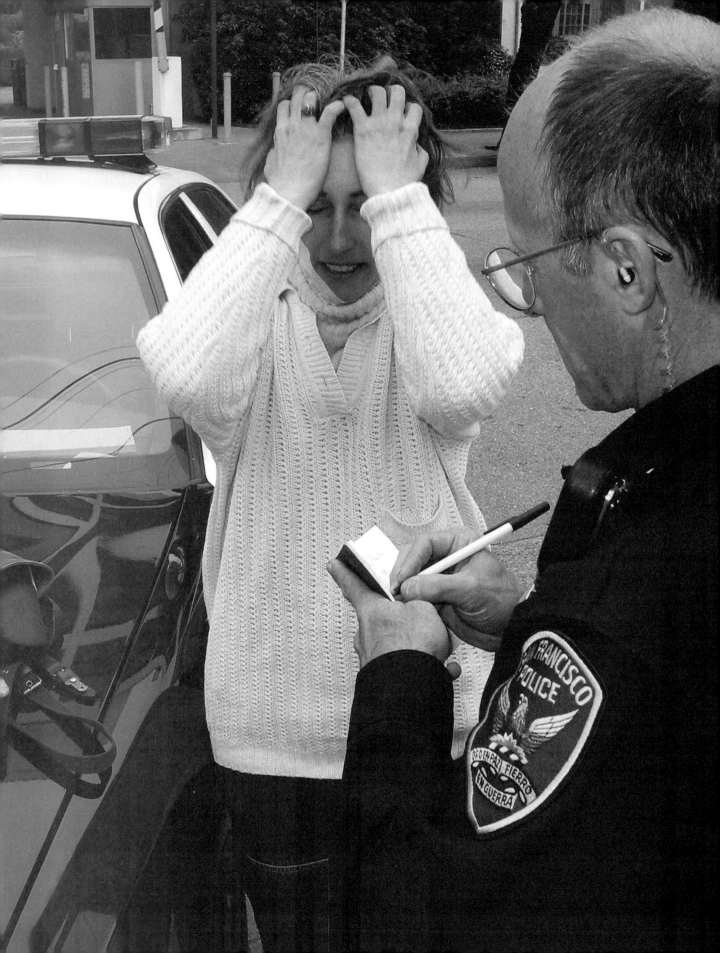

CHAPTER **12**

The Police and the Community

This chapter will enable you to:

- Understand the relationship between citizen attitudes and police–community relations.
- Appreciate how citizen attitudes toward the police affect the development of police policies.
- Realize how stereotypes develop on both sides of the police–community realm.

- Understand the development of current police–community relations.
- Learn how community policing developed.
- Understand the extent to which community policing is effective in reducing crime.

One prevailing theme of this book is that the police cannot perform their functions successfully without interacting with the community they serve. After all, the police are somewhat reliant on the public to perform some of the basic functions of police work. Citizens report crimes and provide important information about them. But from time to time, internal and external influences affect both the police and the citizenry, and such influences have a profound effect on how one views the other. So in our examination of the police, we should also study community dynamics to best understand this important working relationship.

Although it could be argued that the police are unable to control the causes of crime, they are the governmental entity to which people turn when crime is perceived to have reached an unacceptable level. Public scrutiny of the police also reaches peak levels when crimes of an especially gruesome nature remain open. Stated differently, unsolved crimes tend to make the police look incapable and public pressure is placed on the police and on those elected officials who lend a hand in the administration of justice: the city manager, mayor, district attorney, and so on. In December 1996, for example, six-year-old JonBenet Ramsey was found strangled in her upper-class Boulder, Colorado, home, leaving the police with few clues. As the months went by and the case went unsolved, speculation abounded regarding the competency of the police search of the crime scene and the investigation that ensued.

A community must have trust in their police and feel safe by their presence. Incidents of police abuse of authority, incompetence, or unprofessional behavior tend to erode the bond between the public and the police. Often the public can be less than forgiving after a well-publicized incident of police misbehavior. In this chapter we examine the all-important bond between the citizenry and the police and consider what the police are doing to strengthen police–community relations (PCR).

CITIZEN ATTITUDES AND THE POLICE

Studies of PCR have shown that public perceptions of the police differ widely but that for the most part, the general public views the police in a positive way. Certainly, from time to time, problems arise and citizens become resentful of the police. But generalizations are hard to make. Citizens in each community may feel positively or negatively about their police, depending on their personal experiences. The police are extremely interested in how they are perceived by the public since their legal authority, programs, budgets, and crime-reduction initiatives depend heavily on public support.

Background

In the late 1960s, significant attention was given to PCR. A key document was the report in 1967 of the President's Commission on Law Enforcement and Administration of Justice, "The Challenge of Crime in a Free Society." This report viewed tensions between police and community as contributing to rising crime. With even more urgency, the 1968 *Kerner Report* put forth by the National Advisory Commission on Civil Disorders, detailed African-Americans' widespread dissatisfaction with and anger toward police and concluded that these had been important factors in the urban riots that began in 1964.

Concerns over PCR had conflicting connotations that depended on their source. Liberals' concerns were related to the civil rights movement and stressed the need for more principled treatment of citizens at all stages of criminal justice processing. Among other things, this required more control over police behavior. Conservatives, on the other hand, wanted to strengthen police operations to combat rising crime rates and stressed the need for greater economic and moral support for "your local police."

A Closer Look

Highlights from the Police–Public Contact Survey

Prevalence

- An estimated 44.6 million persons (21% of the population age 12 or older) had face-to-face contact with a police officer in 1996.
- Males, whites, and persons in their twenties were the most likely to have face-to-face contacts with the police.
- Hispanics and African-Americans were about 70% as likely as whites to have contacts with the police.
- In 1996, nearly three in ten persons with a contact reported multiple contacts with police during the year.

Reasons

The most common reasons cited for contact with police among residents age 12 or older are as follows:

- An estimated 33% had asked for or provided the police with some type of assistance.
- An estimated 32% had reported a crime, either as a victim or as a witness.

- Receiving traffic tickets and being involved in traffic accidents were also common reasons for police contacts.
- For just under one-third of those with contacts, the police initiated the contact; for most, however, the citizen initiated the contact.
- Teens were most likely to have police-initiated contacts; persons 60 or older were least likely.
- Persons 60 or older were the most likely to have citizen-initiated contacts with police.

Police Actions

- An estimated 1.2 million persons were handcuffed in 1996 (0.6% of the population 12 or older).
- Most of those handcuffed were males, minorities, and persons under the age of 30.
- An estimated 500,000 persons (0.2% of the population age 12 or older) were hit, held, pushed, choked, threatened with a flashlight, restrained by a police dog, threatened or actually sprayed with chemical or pepper spray, threatened with a gun; or experienced some other form of force.

Source: Bureau of Justice Statistics. *Police Use of Force: Collection of National Data.* U.S. Department of Justice, January 6, 1998.

Public Perceptions of the Police

It has been said that America is the "melting pot" of the world. Traditionally and historically the United States has maintained an open immigration policy that has resulted in a diverse and highly multicultural nation. We know that individual cultures teach different views of how society should function. Within this context, a liberal or conservative ideology affects how people perceive the police. Accordingly, cultural attributes such as socioeconomic class and values can affect the nature of people's attitudes toward the police and impact their interactions with the police. Those interactions ultimately have a profound effect on citizen attitudes toward the police.

As a rule, research has shown that the general public perceives the police in a positive light. Of course, problems exist, and in some communities the police are viewed negatively. However, many researchers agree that the overall public perception of the police and what they do is positive. This is important because public perceptions of what the police do and how effective they are affect public participation in crime-reduction programs and political support for the police, police programs, and anticrime legislation. Furthermore, budgetary and other administrative and operational decisions rely, to a great extent, on public support.

Positive relationships between the police and the public result in numerous benefits for both. For example, there's greater cooperation between police and the people of the community; crime rates and delinquency tend to experience a decline when PCR are positive; lines of communication between the police and the public are stronger and problems can be resolved more easily; positive police relations tend to generate greater interest in police careers by a larger cross section of community; finally, positive public relations often result in increased governmental support for the police with regard to increased salaries and expanded resources for new programs.

We should note that when examining attitudes toward the police, it is important to recognize that there are numerous groups of people within each jurisdiction, and these groups may have differing opinions and perceptions of the police and their effectiveness in dealing with community problems. Community dynamics differ from one jurisdiction to the next. For example, many

FIGURE 12.1 The importance of public relations is an ongoing priority for professional police departments. Here, police officers with the Austin, Texas Police Department meet residents at a block party during National Night Out.

communities are surrounded by major highways, mountains, or lakes. Many communities offer theme parks or other attractions to draw people into the community. Furthermore, some communities contain small ethnic communities, such as "Little Italys," "Little Havanas," or "Chinatowns." These respective cultures are also reflected in those who live and work in these areas. These dynamics and public attitudes toward the police will now be examined.

The Police and Public Attitudes

Research has shown that, for the most part, citizens view the police positively. Black, for example, notes that 76% of police activity in Chicago, Boston, and Washington, D.C., was initiated through citizen telephone calls to the police. He theorized that citizens must have a high regard for the police for this large amount of information to be supplied to them.[1] Accordingly, this high level of participation suggests a high level of trust and support for the police.

As previously noted, although general perceptions of the police are positive, a percentage of the citizenry view police officers with skepticism. Decker points out that individual and community variables tend to mold and describe the types and levels of support that exist in a community.[2] The individual-level variables include age, race, gender, and personal experience with the police. In comparison, community variables include socioeconomic status, likelihood of victimization, general attitudes toward the police, and crime rates.

INDIVIDUAL-LEVEL VARIABLES

Many studies regarding police–citizen relations have dealt with demographic characteristics of citizens. As such, these data help us determine how different types of people view the police.

AGE For the most part, older persons tend to view the police more positively than their younger citizen counterparts. But research has shown that after negative interactions with the police, younger citizens were more prone to view the police less positively than older citizens. Persons under the age of 30 were especially critical of the police.

A number of reasons have been cited to explain why younger persons fail to view the police as positively as older persons. For example, younger persons are resistant to authority figures and tend to require more police intervention than do their older counterparts. So, when police officers inquire into their activities or stop them for traffic violations, younger persons tend to see this as an encroachment on their freedom. In addition, younger persons tend to have more negative contacts with the police than older persons, especially with regard to traffic violations and other minor offenses. It is not uncommon to believe that the police target, or "pick on," young people. Yet another explanation is that older people are more vulnerable to crime and victimization and tend to view the police more positively as their protectors.

RACE A substantial amount of research has been generated over the years regarding how minorities view the police. Many people believe that white citizens tend to view the police more positively than do minorities. Hahn confirmed this hypothesis and noted that African-American residents had poor perceptions of the police and that African-Americans tended to believe that the police were more corrupt, more unfair, harsher, tougher, less friendly, and crueler than did whites. Jacob discovered that African-Americans generally were more dissatisfied with police services in comparison with the white population.[3]

The attitudes of Hispanics toward the police were studied, and findings coincided with the research on African-American attitudes toward the police. Overall, Carter found that Hispanics feel less safe concerning crime compared to the general population and do not feel that the police are capable of reducing the incidence of crime. He also found that Hispanics feel they receive less-than-adequate protection from the police relative to the general population.[4] Overall, Hispanics believe that the police did a poor job and that they harbored some prejudice against the Hispanic community.

We should consider, however, that a number of explanations exist for these attitudes. First, the minorities have a higher number of negative contacts (higher representation in arrest statistics) with the police compared to nonminorities. Secondly, minorities tend to be victimized at higher rates relative to nonminorities. Finally, it is possible that generally police officers do in fact treat minority citizens differently than they treat white citizens. White police officers typically do not comprehend or understand other cultures, which may cause them to treat minorities differently. Furthermore, some white police officers, unfortunately, are biased against a minority that often affects how they treat minority suspects or victims of crime.

GENDER   Many people believe that females view police more positively than males. However, the research does not bear this out. In their study of attitudes toward the police, researchers Campbell and Schuman, along with research conducted by Smith and Hawkins, found that gender accounted for fewer variants in citizen attitudes toward the police.[5] Consequently, age and race tend to be the major individual factors that help form an individual's impression of the police.

SOCIOECONOMIC STATUS   Research suggests that persons from a lower socioeconomic background are less likely to view the police positively. In their study, Albrecht and Green found that minorities from poor urban areas held the least favorable attitude toward the police, and persons with the most positive attitudes were urban, middle-class whites. Reasons for the lowered perceptions included lack of concern and attention on the part of the police, ineffectiveness, and perceived injustice. Statistically, lower socioeconomic areas within most jurisdictions have the greatest crime rates and generally contain a higher number of minorities that may help explain socioeconomic differences.

As with gender, some research suggests that socioeconomic status may be less important in determining public attitudes toward the police and other variables. For example, Jacob suggests that socioeconomic class may be less important than race, neighborhood, or cultural orientation.

Citizen Satisfaction

An additional measure of police effectiveness, which has only recently been recognized, is *citizen satisfaction*. As discussed in Chapter 1, fear of crime continues to exist even though violent crime rates have dropped over the past decade. Part of the reason for this may be found in public attitudes toward the police. A recent poll found that one out of every two Americans had little or no confidence that the police would protect them from violent crime. Many police administrators believe that this trend can be reversed if departments begin to treat citizens as "customers" who pay for the services provided by law enforcement agencies. As all business persons know, the customers are the most important people in any service industry (which includes police work), and the greater the effort to listen to customers' concerns, the greater their levels of satisfaction will be. In analyzing the results of a foot patrol experiment in Flint, Michigan, in which the police made a concerted effort to forge bonds and citizens, Robert Trojanowicz of Michigan State University found a significant increase in citizen satisfaction. A number of observers believe that the strategy of increasing police presence in the community is a crucial step toward improving citizen satisfaction with police departments.

In short, it is difficult to measure the effectiveness of the police. Even crime rates are at least partially determined by elements beyond police control, such as the sociological, biological, and psychological factors. Hence, crime rates cannot be relied on as definitive indicators of the job a police department is doing.

THE PROBLEM OF RACIAL PROFILING

In the late 1990s, both print and broadcast media exploded with coverage of the problem of racial profiling illustrating the individual and social costs of racial profiling. Indeed, the allegations have become so commonplace that the community of color labeled the phenomenon with a derisive term "driving while black" or "driving while brown."

Defining Racial Profiling

Before we address the nature of the problem of racial profiling, a suitable definition of the phenomenon should be identified. In a June 2000 publication for the National Institute of Justice, Deborah Ramirez and Jack McDevitt defined racial profiling as

> any police initiated action that relies on the race, ethnicity, or national origin rather than on the behavior of an individual or information that leads the police to a particular individual who has been identified as being, or having been, engaged in criminal activity.[6]

Stemming from this definition are two corollary principles of policing: (1) that police may not use racial or ethnic stereotypes as factors in selecting whom to stop and search and (2) that police may use race or ethnicity to determine whether a person matches a specific description of a particular suspect.

However, developing consensus on whether race can be used when police are addressing a crime committed by a group of individuals who share racial or ethnic characteristics is more complicated. For example, when police know that a particular individual is a member of a criminal organization, officers may legitimately use that information as a factor in the totality of the circumstances that may indicate ongoing criminal activity. As an example, many criminal organizations such as the Sicilian Mafia or the Black Guerilla Family are composed of persons with similar ethnic, racial, or national origin characteristics. Under the definition used in this guide, however, if police use a person's race and ethnicity or national origin in determining whether a specific individual is a member of the criminal organization, they have engaged in racial profiling.

Can Race Be a Legitimate Factor?

As we consider the issue of racial profiling, we must also be able to distinguish a link between the legitimate use of profiling and unlawful racial profiling. Profiles based on officers' training and experience are legitimate tools in police work. For example, the "drug courier profile" has long been recognized as an investigative technique used by narcotics investigators. This drug courier profile has been described as the "collective or distilled experience of narcotics officers concerning characteristics repeatedly seen in drug smugglers." Courts have held that matching a profile alone is not the equivalent of a reasonable suspicion or probable cause necessary to conduct an investigative detention or arrest, but police officers are entitled to assess the totality of circumstances surrounding the subject of their attention in light of their experience and training, which may include "instruction on a drug courier profile." Therefore, profiles, combined with other facts and circumstances, can establish reasonable suspicion or probable cause.[7] On the other hand, if race or color may be a factor to consider during certain police activity, race or color alone is insufficient for making a stop or an arrest.[8]

Nature and Extent of Perceptions of Racial Profiling

Recent national surveys have confirmed that most Americans, regardless of race, believe that racial profiling is a significant social problem. For example, according to a Gallup Poll released in December 1999, more than half of Americans polled believe that police actively engaged in the practice of racial profiling and, more significantly, 81% of them said they disapprove of the practice. In a national sample of adults, 59% said that racial profiling is widespread. When the responses to the survey question were broken down by race, 56% of whites and 77% of African-Americans responded that racial profiling was pervasive. Additionally, the Gallup survey asked respondents how often they perceived having been stopped by the police based on their race alone. Six percent of whites and 42 percent of African-Americans responded that they had been stopped by the police because of their race, and 72% of African-American men between ages 18 and 34 believe they had been stopped because of their race.[9]

Recent survey data also confirm a strong connection between perceptions of race-based stops by police and animosity toward local and state law enforcement agencies. In addition to gathering data on individual perceptions of stops by the police, the 1999 Gallup Poll asked respondents how favorably they viewed the police. Eighty-five percent of white respondents had a favorable response toward local police, and 85% of white respondents had a favorable response to state police. In comparison, African-American respondents, overall, had a less favorable opinion of both state and local police—58% having a favorable opinion of the local police and 64% having a favorable opinion of the state police. Fifty-three percent of African-American men between ages 18 and 34 said they had been treated unfairly by local police.[10]

Similarly, a 12-city survey conducted by the U.S. Department of Justice in 1998 demonstrated that, although most people in the African-American community felt dissatisfied with police services in their neighborhoods, their level of satisfaction was approximately twice that of the white community. This wide schism in all 12 cities surveyed indicates the need for law enforcement agencies to work harder to restore the confidence of communities of color in the critical work done by them. Police departments that fail to address the perception of racially discriminatory policing within minority neighborhoods may find law enforcement efforts undermined.

Evidence of Racial Profiling

Both anecdotal and empirical evidence suggest that racial profiling is a growing problem. To better understand the issues associated with identifying racial profiling and police stops, concerns about police discretion have been broken into two stages: an officer's decision to stop a vehicle or person and the actions of the officer during the stop. The second issue may include a number of questions:

1. Are passengers and drivers ordered to step out of the car?
2. Is the suspect treated with respect?
3. Are police questioning the occupants about subjects unrelated to the traffic stop violation?
4. Were drug-sniffing dogs used on the scene?
5. Did the officer request permission to search the car and its contents?
6. How long did the encounter last?

The answers to these and other questions are critical for understanding the complexities and nuances of racial profiling. Evidence from anecdotal accounts and statistical studies has begun to address these important issues.

Anecdotal Evidence

Personal anecdotes and stories help illustrate the experiences of those who believe they have been stopped because of racial profiling and, in turn, give rise to the set of common concerns about police stop-and-search practices. In a 1999 report by David Harris titled *Driving While Black: Racial Profiling on Our Nation's Highways*, numerous accounts of inappropriate treatment toward minorities by police are cited. The following examples illustrate the emotional impact of such incidents.

INCIDENT 1   The concern that police stop drivers because they or their passengers do not appear to "match" the type of vehicle they occupy is common in racial profiling accounts. This "driving in the wrong car" concern is illustrated by the experiences of Dr. Elmo Randolph, a 42-year-old African-American dentist who commutes from Bergen County to his office near Newark, New Jersey. Since 1991, he has been stopped by the New Jersey troopers more than 50 times. Randolph does not drive at excessive speeds and claims he has never been issued a ticket. Instead, troopers approach his gold BMW, request his license and registration, and ask him if he has any drugs or weapons in his car.

The experience of Randolph and many other minority drivers on New Jersey's highways led to the recent consent decree and settlement between the state of New Jersey and the U.S. Department of Justice. As a result of the settlement, New Jersey state police are collecting data on the race and ethnicity of persons stopped by state troopers and improving their supervision and training.

INCIDENT 2   Another common complaint is that police stop people of color for traveling through predominantly white areas because the police believe that people of color do not "belong" in certain neighborhoods and may be engaged in criminal activity. This type of profiling was reported by Alvin Penn, the former African-American deputy president of the Connecticut State Senate. In 1996, a Trumbull, Connecticut, police officer stopped Penn as he drove his van through this predominantly white suburban town. After reviewing Penn's license and registration, the officer asked him if he knew which town he was in (Bridgeport, the state's largest city, where African-Americans and Latinos comprise 75% of the population, borders Trumbull, which is 98% white). Penn, recalling that he had been turning around on a dead-end street when the officer stopped him, responded by asking why he needed to know which town he was in. The officer told him that he was not required to give Penn a reason for the stop and that, if he made an issue of it, the officer would cite him for speeding. Three years after this incident, Penn sponsored legislation that made Connecticut the second state to begin collecting data on the demographics of individuals stopped by state police.[11]

INCIDENT 3   By far, the most common complaint by members of communities of color is that they are being stopped for petty traffic violations such as underinflated tires, failure to signal properly before switching lanes, vehicle equipment failures, speeding less than ten miles above the speed limit, or having an illegible license plate. One example of this is the account of Robert Wilkins, a Harvard Law School graduate and a public defender in Washington, D.C., who went to a family funeral in Ohio in May 1992. On the return trip, he and his aunt, uncle, and 29-year-old cousin rented a Cadillac for the trip home. His cousin was stopped for speeding in western Maryland while driving 60 miles per hour in a 55-mile-per-hour zone of the interstate. The group was forced to stand on the side of the interstate in the rain for an extended period while officers and drug-sniffing dogs searched their car. Nothing was found. Wilkins, represented by the American Civil Liberties Union (ACLU), filed suit and received a settlement from the State of Maryland.

Although these small samples of anecdotal evidence do not prove that police officers actively engage in racial profiling, they are representative of a large number of personal stories cataloged in newspaper articles, interviews, ACLU commentaries, and courtroom lawsuits.

Empirical Research on Racial Profiling

In addition to a growing body of individual accounts of racial profiling, scholars have begun examining the relationship between police stop-and-search practices and the racial characteristics of individual drivers. The majority of research collected to date has been used in expert testimony accompanying lawsuits. _Wilkins v. Maryland State Police (1993)_ was one of the first cases to introduce empirical evidence of racial profiling into the court record area.

In 1995 and 1996, as a result of Wilkins' settlement with the Maryland State Police (MSP), John Lamberth, a professor of psychology at Temple University, conducted an analysis of police searches along I-95 in Maryland. Using data released by MSP pursuant to the settlement, Lamberth compared the population of people searched and arrested with those violating traffic laws on Maryland highways. He constructed a violators' sample using both stationary and rolling surveys of drivers violating the legal speed limit on a selected portion of the interstate. His violators' survey indicated that 74.7% of speeders were white, while 17.5% were African-Americans. In contrast, according to MSP data, African-Americans constituted 79.2% of the drivers searched.

Lamberth concluded that the data revealed "dramatic and highly statistically significant disparities" between the percentage of African-American I-95 motorists legitimately subject to stop by

Highlights in Policing

Making the FBI's Top 10

Criteria for Making the FBI's Most Wanted List

- The fugitive must be considered particularly dangerous.
- The crime must be particularly heinous.
- There must be reason to believe that publicity will help catch the fugitive.

Criteria for Getting Off the List

- The fugitive has been captured or is dead.
- The charges have been dismissed.
- The fugitive no longer fits the criteria.

Who decides? The Criminal Investigative Division, based on recommendations from the field and from the Office of Public Affairs.

In its earliest stages, when few Americans owned television sets, the list contained bank robbers, burglars, and car thieves—criminals who dominated the crime scene. "Today's Most Wanted list includes cop killers, drug dealers, and international terrorists who aren't even in the country."[12] Skeptics argue that the list has outlived its usefulness because of the age of modern technology: the Internet, electronic billboards, and television. In 1992, the U.S. Post Office discontinued putting top 10 posters on its walls. Perhaps it could be argued that the FBI's list has become ineffective, especially with the advent of so many different high-tech mediums showcasing the nation's fugitives.[13]

the MSP and the percentage of African-American motorists detained and searched by troopers on this roadway.

In the summer of 2000, the U.S. Department of Justice published its findings on racial profiling and made recommendations to states regarding how data collection should be performed by law enforcement agencies across the nation.

THE FUSION OF THE POLICE AND THE COMMUNITY

In 1996, *USA Today* reported that Fort Worth, Texas, a city distinguished by having the worst crime rate in the country, was able to slash the incidence of violent crime by 45% between 1991 and 1996. The reason cited by police was the presence of more police officers and more community involvement.[14]

Beginning in 1991, police commanders, detectives, and officers were sent to field offices scattered throughout the city. Patrol officers were dispatched to the troubled southeast side of the city to work in tandem with neighborhood groups in an effort to mediate disputes before they exploded into violence. While the fusion of police and community leaders has collectively been credited with playing an important role in the drastic reduction in crime, we must be aware that any number of variables could be attributed to the decline in crime in some of our nation's cities. Although frequently cited by public officials, cause-and-effect relationships are often disputed by social scientists.

Kelling and Moore have shown that like all other institutions, the police establishment is subject to change, with the changes often resulting from the reaction of the citizenry to occurrences in the community, which they find to be intolerable.[15] Recall our earlier discussion in Chapter 2: When U.S. police departments were established as public organizations during the 1840s, the police were closely tied to political entities. The police establishment of the "political era" had many of the characteristics of community policing. Included was a decentralized neighborhood-based structure with close personal relationships with the citizens. Programs and techniques were grounded in foot patrol, call boxes, and police performing a variety of functions, including patrol, investigations, and order-maintenance and service activities. Keeping prominent citizens and politicians satisfied was a major goal of the police.

A reform era emerged during the 1930s, but in succeeding decades there was still considerable involvement of the police in politics. By the 1960s, police work had moved to the opposite extreme. The decade was fraught with race riots and student protests. Issues such as the war in

Vietnam, racial equality, and women's rights resulted in large public demonstrations and marches. The police, who found themselves in the center of each controversy, were untrained to deal adequately with crowd control and violent encounters with citizen groups. In the eyes of many, the police became the embodiment of the "establishment," and many a skirmish between the citizenry and the police ensued.

Police–Community Relations

Across the nation, the police searched for ways to best deal with the problem of a disenfranchised and estranged society. As an outgrowth of this, PCR programs were developed. The PCR movement represented a movement away from the practice of apprehension of law breakers to that of more positive citizen interaction. Resulting from the nationwide movement toward PCR, many police innovations were developed. For example, storefront centers cropped up where citizens had better access to police to vent community concerns and interact face to face with police officers.

Other innovations included the appointment of public relations officers, the establishment of neighborhood watch programs, drug-awareness workshops for concerned citizens, and Project ID programs, which make use of police technology to mark valuables for identification in case of theft. As stated by Bittner: "For PCR programs to be truly effective, they need to reach to the grassroots of discontent" where citizen dissatisfaction with police exists.[16] Unfortunately, despite this array of new police programs, PCR failed to achieve its goal of increased community satisfaction with police services because it focused on providing services to groups who were already satisfied with the police.

Team Policing

During the latter part of the 1960s and into the 1970s, communities began to experiment with the idea of **team policing.** Originating in Aberdeen, Scotland, team policing was viewed as the reorganization of conventional patrol strategies into an integrated and adaptable police team assigned to a permanent district. While some have hailed team policing as a new technique designed to deliver total police services to all neighborhoods, others have criticized it as a simple return to the old-style policing of the nineteenth century.[17]

The idea behind team policing is that police officers are assigned to fixed neighborhoods and therefore become personally acquainted with residents and the problems of those residents in those neighborhoods. One of its more distinguishing features is that it gave patrol officers the authority to process complaints and resolve localized crime problems. Crimes that occurred were investigated and closed at the local level, with specialists being called in only when necessary. Thus the movement toward community policing was under way.

It was stimulated by the realization that various segments of the community, in particular youth, poor persons, and minority-group members, were dissatisfied with the performance of the police. In addition, there was dissatisfaction with the services that they provided and the realization that the traditional approaches of dealing with crime, in particular street crimes, were less than acceptable.

Crime Prevention

One of the prevailing goals of the justice system is **crime prevention**, and the police play an important role in initiating this program in the community. The specific goal is to reduce the need to commit crime by providing opportunities for success and achievement. For example, building stronger family units, providing counseling in schools, and developing better environmental conditions are all examples of crime-prevention efforts throughout the country.

While crime rates escalated during the late 1970s and 1980s, public concern and fear about victimization grew as well. Politicians and community leaders became increasingly concerned about drug abuse and related crime, while the public response was to hire additional police and build more prisons. So, rather than the public being concerned about how police treated them, concerns focused on the reduction of crime rates. As a result, PCR programs were supplanted by those focusing on crime prevention.

A localized example of crime-prevention efforts by police is drug abuse–prevention programs such as **Project DARE** (Drug Abuse Resistance Education), which involve specially trained, uniformed officers who visit the classrooms of grade schools. The training focuses on decision-making skills, peer pressure, and alternatives to drug use. Another successful crime-prevention program, Crime Stoppers, encourages citizens to engage in anonymous informing to assist police in developing suspects in crimes or to catch criminals in the act of committing them. Although some people complain that Crime Stoppers makes "snitches" out of law-abiding citizens, others argue that it is simply a system of public responsibility similar to the old days of the "hue and cry," when all citizens assumed responsibility for public order.

In addition to allowing tipsters to call the police anonymously, many receive cash rewards for their cooperation. The amount of the reward depends on the quality of information provided by the citizen, that is, information that results in an arrest. All communication between the police and the citizen is accomplished by the assignment of a number to the caller. That number is used in lieu of a name for the remainder of the citizen–police relationship, negating the need for the police ever to know the true name of the tipster.

One misconception of crime-prevention programs is that the police can control crime. Of course, since police cannot actually control what causes crime (poverty, lack of education, etc.), little can realistically be done about it by the police. But crime prevention poses a different concern, in that it is difficult, if not impossible, to measure what crimes were averted or how many people were spared victimization due to crime-prevention efforts. Crime is a multifaceted problem requiring a multifaceted approach from all segments of the community.

Public Forums for Victims

Along similar lines as Crime Stoppers are efforts by victims of crimes to convince the community to become more involved in identifying known criminals and reporting violators to police. One example of this is the well-known television show *America's Most Wanted*. During its tenure, the show helped track down over 1057 fugitives and 60 missing children.[18] The show twice spotlighted fugitives who shot and killed Newark law enforcement officers. Both men were caught within a week of the segments on them. Following the show's 1996 cancellation, the FBI issued a statement commending it for putting a "human face on crime" and depicting the dangers of law enforcement.[19] Other shows have shown similar promise. These include *Unsolved Mysteries* and *U.S. Customs: Classified*.

Another public forum for locating criminals has been around longer than the television shows discussed earlier—the FBI's Top Ten Most Wanted list. The FBI has maintained its most wanted list since 1950, and although it was once a mainstay of crime fighting, it has all but lost its appeal in today's high-tech age of television, computers, and the Internet. The most wanted list was invented by a wire service reporter and later adopted by the publicity-driven director of the FBI, J. Edgar Hoover. As of 1997, 422 of the 449 fugitives who appeared on the list had been captured, a 94% success rate.[20]

STRATEGIES FOR POLICING

In recent years, the old PCR concept has undergone considerable change. Previously, PCR programs were molded by the concept of police as law enforcers. This program tended to create a police self-image of isolation and, in some cases, one of opposition to the very communities they served. PCR never became the public relations panacea much desired by the public. In comparison, an increasing number of police administrators are abandoning the notion of police as strictly law enforcers and embracing the idea of police as service providers.

It is clear that more and more police departments are being called upon to serve the community in ways other than capturing lawbreakers. Included are searches for lost children, aiding citizens locked out of their vehicles, facilitating new neighborhood watch programs, conducting drug abuse–prevention seminars, and controlling crowds at public events. Resulting from these activities is a referral-type function, which is often used in lieu of arrest. Referrals include Narcotics and Alcoholics Anonymous, state or county family service agencies, and rape and domestic violence shelters. Moore and Trojanowicz suggest that because police departments often function like corporations, three types of "corporate strategies" guide U.S. policing today: strategic policing, problem-oriented policing (POP), and community policing.[21]

Strategic Policing

Held over from the reform era during the mid-twentieth century is **strategic policing**. The concept emphasizes an increased capacity to deal effectively with nontraditional crimes. Offenders of such crimes include serial rapists and killers, domestic terrorists, drug-trafficking organizations, white-collar criminals, and organized crime syndicates. In furtherance of the strategic approach are specialized, often proactive enforcement techniques such as criminal intelligence gathering, undercover operations, reverse stings, wiretaps, and other types of electronic surveillances.

Problem-Oriented Policing

Problem-oriented policing takes the view that underlying social conditions cause crime. To control crime effectively, police must uncover and address the existing social problems that contribute to those crimes. The strength of POP lies in its ability to make use of social resources such as counseling centers and job training facilities. The incorporation of citizens is also an important part of the POP program. It is as important for police departments to respond to specific incidents as it is for them to fulfill their general responsibilities to provide order maintenance, community service, and law enforcement.

As a rule, a specific event is brought to the attention of a police officer when either the officer observes it personally or it is called in to the police dispatcher. Because the police spend their time responding to specific incidents, it is difficult for them to seek the underlying reasons for those incidents. As a variation of community-oriented policing (COP), POP was developed. Its goal is to determine the cause of citizen complaints rather than simply treating the symptom of the problem. Once the problem is identified, local social service agencies can then be employed to resolve the situation. The problem-oriented approach permits the police department to intervene in a number of situations that affect the quality of life in the community—not just crime.

Police departments in Baltimore County, Maryland, and Newport News, Virginia, gained national recognition for their efforts in implementing the POP approach. The specific programs adopted by each department differed somewhat, but both sought to involve police officers and the community in finding the source of complaints to reduce future incidents of crime. Police managers have encouraged their officers to look beyond the police department for information leading to the cause of the crime, thus reducing fear and turmoil in the community.

Specifically, they urged officers to canvass neighborhoods and talk with residents, speak with leaders in the business community, interview offenders, and even to contact public officials—virtually anyone who might have information about a problem. Once the information has been analyzed, a solution is sought. Solutions come in many different forms. For example, perhaps rigid enforcement of closing hours of a local bar or aggressive arrests of streetwalkers is what it takes to solve a problem. In any case, employing agencies other than criminal justice agencies is the key.

In light of the positive response to service-related policing, it appears that some problems may still be inherent with the program. For example, it is likely that some police officers may not yet be ready to accept their new role as public relations experts as opposed to that of law enforcers. Indeed, traditional values in police work are often difficult to change, and the stereotypical image of the cop who always "gets his man" may be jeopardized by any new programs. In addition, not all citizens are ready to accept the new role of police officers becoming more involved in their everyday lives. Communities who have had negative experiences with their police departments in the past may still harbor suspicions about them. The likelihood of community policing becoming a panacea is grim, for some gaps between the public and police may never be bridged.

Community Policing

In 1994, Congress passed a comprehensive crime bill that provided for putting 100,000 police officers on the street and allocating $11 billion to enhance law enforcement programs. Of its many components, it lent support for community policing efforts across the country, and much funding to state and local police departments hinged on their adoption of community policing programs in their jurisdictions. Indeed, many police managers have since endorsed **community policing** as the most promising way to address a number of social problems relating to crime and public disorder.

Community policing extends beyond the bounds of strategic and POP and has found considerable support within the law enforcement community. Recently, the National Institute of Justice (NIJ) sampled 2,000 law enforcement agencies and found that a majority supported the adoption of some type of community policing program.[22] Community policing (often referred to as community-oriented policing) has been given a variety of titles and definitions but remains as one of the most promising public policies to date. Some police professionals and policymakers distinguish COP from POP, while others consider the terms to be interchangeable. We discuss the concept of POP in the coming pages, but first let's take a look at what many feel is today's best approach to fighting crime—community policing.

Before we get under way with our examination of community policing, it would be instructive to identify the meaning of the term. Trojanowicz and Bucqueroux, pioneers in the study of community policing, describe community policing as follows:

> Community policing is a philosophy and an organizational strategy that promotes a new partnership between people and their police. It is based on the premise that both the police and the community must work together to identify, prioritize, and solve contemporary problems such as crime, drugs, fear of crime, social and physical disorder, and overall neighborhood decay, with the goal of improving the overall quality of life in the area.
>
> Community policing requires a department-wide commitment from everyone, civilian and sworn, to the community policing philosophy. It also challenges all personnel to find ways to express this new philosophy in their jobs, thereby balancing the need to maintain an immediate and effective police response to individual crime incidents

Highlights in Policing

The Elements of Community Policing

- Moving the police officer from a position of anonymity in the patrol car to direct engagement with a community gives an officer more immediate information about problems unique to a neighborhood and insights into their solutions.
- Freeing the officer from the emergency response system permits him or her to engage more directly in proactive crime prevention.
- Making operations more visible to the public increases police accountability to the public.
- Decentralizing operations allows officers to develop a greater familiarity with the specific workings and constituencies in the community and adopt procedures to accommodate those needs.
- Encouraging officers to view citizens as partners improves relations between police and the public.
- Moving decision making and discretion downward to the patrol officer places more authority in the hands of the person who best knows the community's problems and expectations.[23]

and emergencies with the goal of exploring new proactive initiatives aimed at solving problems before they occur or escalate. Community policing also rests on establishing community policing officers as decentralized "mini-chiefs" in permanent beats, where they enjoy the freedom and autonomy to operate as community-based problem solvers who work directly with the community—making their neighborhoods better and safer places in which to live and work.[24]

For some, the definition of community policing includes an orientation that permeates all facets of police work and emphasizes police accountability to the community and the organization, management based on stated values, decentralized structure, shared decision making with the community, and officers being empowered to solve problems.

Thus, community policing is characterized by organizational values that stress community involvement and embraces key concepts such as decentralization (neighborhood police having responsibility for handling problems in the neighborhoods), problem solving, and respect for the community being policed.[25]

THEORETICAL BASE FOR COMMUNITY POLICING

Aside from what seems to be a commonsense approach to policing, people often ask whether community policing is based on a credible theory. Three well-known theories—**broken windows theory**, normative sponsorship theory, and critical social theory—attempt to explain.

The Broken Windows Theory

In an article in the March 1982 issue of the *Atlantic Monthly,* political science professor James Q. Wilson and criminologist George Kelling introduced a theory that would have a tremendous influence on law enforcement thinking.[26] They observed that if someone breaks a window in a building and it is not repaired quickly, others will break more windows. Eventually, the broken windows create a sense of disorder. A lack of attention to disorder sends a message that nobody cares about the neighborhood. That sort of environment attracts criminals, who thrive on public apathy and neglect. Ultimately, this results in an ever-increasing spiral of predatory behavior and citizen fear. This idea became known as the *broken windows theory.*

There are two sources of disorder in society: offenders and physical disorder. Both lead people to believe that a neighborhood is run down, triggering the broken windows effect. The central challenge for police is to take the small signs of disorder seriously and deal with them before they can turn into major problems. That could mean dealing with small-time offenders, cleaning up

Highlights in Policing

Goals and Objectives of Community Policing

Goals

- To define and explain the principles and policies of COP
- To strengthen community policing efforts and establish model approaches
- To evaluate community policing strategies and tactics
- To institutionalize community policing within policing agencies

Objectives

- To access community policing efforts
- To provide technical assistance to police
- To develop training guidelines[27]

physical disorder, or a combination of both. The broken windows theory gave police a new way to examine the underlying causes of social problems. It also provided them with a reason to do something about problems such as graffiti, panhandling, and public drunkenness. Previously considered nuisances rather than serious crimes, they began to be seen as early warning signs that had to be addressed before they dragged down an entire neighborhood.

The challenge to the police is to establish and/or maintain the rules in the neighborhood—to see if those broken windows are repaired. This effort at maintaining order pays off when residents see that behavior is controlled and therefore feel safer.[28] The feeling of safety, in theory at least, translates into a willingness to be out in public, which in turn makes it safer.[29] Consequently, the presence of larger numbers of law-abiding citizens on the streets makes these people safer from becoming victimized. So police should focus their efforts toward neighborhoods with a few broken windows to prevent their further decay. By doing so, the police prevent the fear of crime and, in actuality, improve the quality of life for residents.

In his earlier work, Goldstein anticipated the observations of Wilson and Kelling by urging police administrators to distinguish between combating the actual incidence of crime and fighting the fear of crime. Of the two, he suggested that it might be more important for the police to reduce people's fear of crime.[30] In doing so, he suggested that what the police do to reduce the citizen's fear of crime might be different than what is needed to reduce the incidence of crime. "A police agency might put together an entirely different blend of services in dealing with fear, which would contain, in addition to massive efforts to educate the community, variations in the usual form of patrol, increased use of technical surveillance equipment, and a campaign to acquaint citizens with methods for providing themselves with security at their own expense."[31]

Sherman summarized contemporary thinking on the link between order and safety by stating that "both physical and social signs of crime indicate disorder in the neighborhood and convey a sense that things are 'out of control.'"[32] Ultimately, disorder may attract such predatory violent crimes as robbery. "A neighborhood that can't control minor incivilities may advertise itself to potential robbers as a neighborhood that can't control serious crime either."[33]

The Normative Sponsorship Theory

Normative sponsorship theory relates to community policing in that it says that most people are of good will and that they will cooperate with others to facilitate the building of consensus. The more the various groups share common values, beliefs, and goals, the more likely it is that they will agree on common goals when they interact together for the purpose of improving their neighborhoods.

The Critical Social Theory

Critical social theory focuses on how and why people coalesce to correct and overcome social, economic, and political obstacles that prevent them from having their needs met.[34] Critical social theory embraces three basic concepts:

1. ***Enlightenment.*** People must become educated about circumstances before they can lobby for change.
2. ***Empowerment.*** People must take action to improve their condition.
3. ***Emancipation.*** People can achieve liberation through reflection and social action.

Zero Tolerance

One approach utilizing some of these new ideas is known as **zero tolerance**. Rather than being a theory, zero tolerance represents more of a practice. The basic premise is that small crimes must be taken as seriously as big crimes. Not all crimes are major, but they do affect the quality of life. In a zero-tolerance environment, police take the small signs of disorder seriously. This could mean dealing with small-time offenders, cleaning up physical disorder, or a combination of both.

In an article in the journal *Law and Policy,* Bratton explains how he tested the broken windows theory as he and Mayor Rudolph Giuliani cleaned up the New York City subway system when he was commander of the transit police. "Subway disorder and subway crime exploded in the late 1980s. Chronic fare evaders, violators of transit regulations, aggressive panhandlers, homeless substance abusers, and illegal vendors hawking goods on station platforms all contributed to an atmosphere of disorder, even chaos, in the subways. I was convinced that disorder was a key ingredient in the steeply rising robbery rate, as criminals of opportunity, including many youthful offenders, looked upon the subway as a place where they could get away with anything."[35]

Bratton instructed the transit police to enforce quality-of-life laws. He also ordered the removal of the graffiti that had come to symbolize the New York subway system. The New York police discovered that the people who broke the law by jumping turnstiles were often the same people who broke the law by robbing subway riders. The lesson they learned was that it is possible to reduce major offenses by arresting minor offenders.

Despite its apparent successes, zero tolerance may have a downside. This was illustrated by an unfortunate incident that occurred in Brooklyn, New York, during the summer of 1997. On Saturday, August 9, a fight broke out between two women in a bar and the police were called. Haitian immigrant Abner Louima, a 30-year-old bank security guard, was taken into custody in connection with the incident. As Louima was being driven to the station house, he was beaten. Upon arrival, he was strip-searched and sodomized with a wooden stick attached to a toilet plunger. Doctors examining Louima discovered that he suffered a ruptured bladder, a punctured lower intestine, and several broken front teeth.

COMPONENTS OF COMMUNITY POLICING

Before we proceed further into the discussion about community policing, it will be instructive to first define what elements of the community are considered the most influential. Trojanowicz and Bucqueroux identify six components of society, which they call the "Big Six," that can be identified in playing the most important part in achieving community policing goals:

1. *The police department.* Including all personnel, from the chief to the line officer, civilian, and sworn
2. *The community.* Including everyone, from formal and informal community leaders such as presidents of civic groups, ministers, and educators; to community organizers and activists; to average citizens on the street
3. *Elected civic officials.* Including the mayor, city manager, city council, and any county, state, and federal officials whose support can affect the future of community policing
4. *The business community.* Including the full range of businesses, from major corporations to the "mom-and-pop" store on the corner
5. *Other agencies.* Including public agencies (code enforcement, social services, public health, etc.) and nonprofit agencies, ranging from Boys and Girls Clubs to volunteer and charitable groups
6. *The media.* Both electronic and print media[36]

The goals of community policing are generally characterized as controlling crime, reducing the fear of crime, maintaining order, and improving the quality of life in neighborhoods. Although the programs differ in structure and may include such features as foot patrol, neighborhood-based stations, and specialized crime-control units, they share many of the following operational and organizational principles:

• Permanently assigning officers to specific neighborhoods or beats
• Developing a knowledge base about problems, characteristics, and resources in the neighborhood

- Outreaching to businesses and residents, making the police more visible in the neighborhoods
- Involving the community in identifying, understanding, and prioritizing local problems, and in developing and implementing plans to resolve them
- Delegating responsibility to community police for creating solutions to crime and order-maintenance problems
- Providing information to the community on local crime problems and police efforts to solve them
- Opening the flow of information from the community to the police to assist with making arrests and developing information

The theory underlying community policing is well expressed in an article by Wilson and Kelling. In this work, the authors emphasize that the police have a responsibility to protect the community as a whole as well as people residing in that community. Thus, police must take care of order-maintenance problems such as disorderly conduct, vagrancy, drunkenness, youth rowdiness, and vandalism, and they must also work to improve the quality of life for the residents of the community. Police are responsible for reducing crime, since its existence leads citizens to avoid the streets and each other and thus weakens the social controls in a community.[37]

Greene and Taylor suggest that community officers can be more effective in fulfilling the order-maintenance function than regular motorized patrol officers because "these community-based officers are said to be more familiar with local rules and community regulars, have a better idea of what response may be desired because they have spent more time in community contact and are better able to distinguish between regulars and strangers. This enhanced community sensitivity makes a successful resolution of incidents more likely." Community policing should also lower citizens' fear because the daily presence of the officer in the community makes people feel safer.[38]

THE DIFFERENCE BETWEEN COMMUNITY-ORIENTED POLICING AND PROBLEM-ORIENTED POLICING

POP has been viewed by some as an alternative to COP,[39] and by others as a component of COP.[40] Moore views POP and COP as overlapping concepts with a distinctive thrust differentiating them.[41] He describes POP as a situational approach and COP as fostering a working partnership between the police and the community.

A POP approach grounded in the directives of the NIJ requires that the problem-solving system follow five basic principles:

1. Officers of all ranks and from all units should be able to use the system as part of their daily routine.
2. The system must encourage the use of a broad range of information, including but not limited to conventional police data.
3. The system should encourage a broad range of solutions, including but not limited to the criminal justice process.
4. The system should require no additional resources and no special units.
5. Any large police agency must be able to apply it.

One might argue that this is an approach that has always been used in police work and thus does not represent anything new. Others, however, argue that the systematic approach to solving problems has not always been that apparent in police work, particularly when the department is highly centralized, specialized, and reactive. Certainly, POP and COP are compatible. As Cordner and Hale concluded, the combination of COP and POP offers "one of our brightest prospects for improved police effectiveness."[42]

THE EXTENT OF COMMUNITY POLICING

In a survey of large-city police departments conducted by Cardarelli and McDevitte, it was found that of the 25 large city departments that indicated they had a community policing program, 24 were recently started; the newness of these programs was reflected in the confusion of law enforcement administrators on the meaning of community policing. Some equated community policing with foot patrols and periodic meetings with community residents, while others thought of community relations. Only a small number stated that community policing must involve the residents in the decision-making process related to policing policies.[43] Greene and Taylor reported that 35% of the 202 police agencies in Florida listed in the "Directory of Florida Chiefs of Police" had some form of COP. They found that many police departments mentioned utilizing such approaches as neighborhood crime watch, team policing, citizen advisory boards, and bicycle- and foot-patrol approaches to police work falling into the scope of community policing, but they did not interpret these activities as being a form of community policing.[44]

Skolnick and Bayley have identified a number of obstacles to the introduction of community policing into a police department. These include resistance from police administrators, police unions, patrol officers, and the prevailing culture of policing. The resistance of the administration may stem in part from the fact that with community policing, officers have autonomy and have the authority to make decisions.[45]

In some cities the rank-and-file patrol officers have reacted against the media attention given to community-policing programs by exhibiting a lack of willingness to cooperate or to acknowledge the importance of the COP program. In other cases, not fully understanding the essence of community policing, police administrators and patrol officers have characterized COP as a community-relations program and have not regarded it as within the realm of real police work. This attitude is reinforced by the police culture, which mistakenly equates real police work exclusively with law enforcement activity. While voicing full support for community policing when speaking to the

---

Highlights in Policing

Where Community Policing Has Worked

The benefits of community policing aren't limited to big cities. It can work in communities of all sizes. For example:

- *Aurora, Illinois.* For 20 years Kane Street was the most dangerous in this city west of Chicago. Open-air drug markets thrived and there were so many gang shootings that police hated to patrol alone there. In 1992, police decided to take the street back. Two veteran officers assigned to the community walked door to door to gain the confidence of residents. It took time, but eventually residents organized, began meeting, and held marches. The gangs got the message.
- *Georgetown, Texas.* Blue Hole Park holds special memories for men and women who grew up here. But alcohol-related crimes, drownings, fights, and sexual assaults scared families away. After consulting with communities near the park and other government agencies, the police designed a comprehensive plan to control parking and traffic flow and to stop drinking and dangerous behavior. Soon, undesirable partiers were

replaced by families once again strolling along the South San Gabriel River.

- *Kansas City, Missouri.* The middle-income families of the 6100 block of Charlotte Avenue were besieged by drug activity at one house, prostitution at another, and loud parties, gunshots, and burglaries. Police observed the suspect residences after receiving numerous complaints. They trained neighbors to spot and report suspicious activity. Working together, the police, the residents, and other government agencies shut down the drug and prostitution houses and stopped the burglaries.
- *Reno, Nevada.* Friendship Lane, a poorly lighted neighborhood of Hispanic families, became a haven for intimidating gangs. When disorderly conduct and drug use escalated to drive-by shootings, the residents sought help. The police worked with them and local businesses to clean up the neighborhood and remove graffiti. The power company installed new street lights. The city repaved the streets and added speed bumps. A hardware store donated 30 home motion-detector lights.[46]

public or the political establishment, the actions of police administrators may differ when resources become scarce and a decision must be made on what programs to delete.

Some writers perceive community policing as a philosophical approach to police work that must prevail throughout the entire department if it is to be effective. For example, Trojanowicz and Bucqueroux state that community policing is not something to be used periodically; instead, it is a permanent commitment to new community problem solving.[47] Albritton noted that "police organizations have often transformed reform proposal and experiments to fit their own agenda and priorities; rarely have they adopted these proposals in all their theoretical purity."[48] He attributes this phenomenon to the fact that in the final analysis, police administrators still believe that the most efficient way to achieve the demands of effective crime-fighting approaches is through the traditional centralized, highly mechanized, organizational structure employed by most large-city police departments. He states: "Pursuing the traditional crime fighting mandate seems to be the 'one efficient way' for policing to justify its operations and maintain a relative degree of police credibility and support in society."[49] Cordner and Hale concede that "in most departments community policing is not intended to completely substitute for motor patrol but rather to supplement and complement motor patrol's reactive efforts."[50]

DOES COMMUNITY POLICING WORK?

On Monday, March 10, 1997, members of the Los Angeles Police Commission voted to oust Chief Willie Williams. Williams was appointed police chief after his predecessor Daryl Gates was removed following riots resulting from the 1991 Rodney King beating incident. While the commission credited Williams with some achievements, they cited his inability to become an effective leader. Upon his appointment in 1992, Williams vowed to bring community policing to Los Angeles, a city long entrenched with racial strife. While parts of the city were more adaptable to the idea, the South Central area clearly was the most resistant to the idea of working with police officers to fight crime.

In comparison to Los Angeles, in 1997, another of the nation's largest cities, New York City, boasted the lowest crime rates in over a decade. In addition to adopting more of a community-policing approach to public order, the NYPD has professionalized its department by raising the minimum age requirement from 20 to 22 and instituting a minimum of 60 college credits for recruits. This demonstrates how community policing, because of a number of varying conditions, is more likely to work in some communities than others.

In 1994, the sheriff's department in Sacramento, California, attempted to evaluate its community-policing program and chose to use a survey to do it. Over a two-week period, 1,200 residents were polled by about 15 volunteers. Results were instructive. For example, one concern revealed by the survey was that residents thought police response time should be 8 minutes or less, the same as the county ambulance service. While the actual response time was 15.8 minutes, the department decided its options were to improve performance or possibly inform the public about what it can realistically expect.[51]

More recently, the Dallas Police Department set out to assess their community-policing program, which was implemented in 1992. In 1996 the department created a Professional Standards Coordination Bureau to implement a fully automated reporting system for evaluating community policing.[52] Here's how the system works. When a community-policing officer enters an activity, it is automatically assigned a tracking number for future reference. Information is entered about the location, type of activity, complainant, and problem resolution. The officer also has at his or her disposal a narrative field that has room for extensive situation descriptions. To evaluate community-policing activities, a section was added to rate activities from 1 to 5 in the following categories:

- Public-interest value
- Economic development
- Overall effectiveness

As a result, the commander can evaluate activities such as parking violations or drug enforcement to determine how effective they are in particular areas. So when a question arises about a particular activity, activity reports can be generated.[53] But to most people, regardless of why, the litmus test of a law enforcement program is whether it controls crime. But as we learned in earlier chapters, there exist many ways to do that and their results seldom agree. Crime usually is thought to be in check if the number of major offenses—homicide, rape, robbery, aggravated assault, larceny, burglary, and auto theft—declines or remains relatively stable. Locally and nationally, the crime rate is seen as a reliable gauge of police performance. However, some experts argue that tracking crime rates is not the best way to tell whether a community-policing program is accomplishing what it set out to do.

Perhaps the best way to gauge the effectiveness of the police is customer satisfaction. Are the citizens happy with their police? Are they willing to work with them? This is important because when the actual tasks of police are reviewed, the crime rates are not that reliable a factor. Since the police don't control the factors that produce crime, it is unrealistic to use crime rates as a criterion for evaluating police effectiveness. Additionally, the police don't control the other components of the criminal justice system either. They can't force a district attorney to file or dismiss a case, or influence a judge or jury to behave in a given manner, or control an overcrowded prison system deciding who stays incarcerated and who is released early.

It could be argued that keeping a community's residents satisfied over an extended period of time might be a nearly impossible task, especially in light of the negative publicity police received in recent years—for example, the Abner Louima beating, the Amadou Diallo shooting in New York City, and the Rampart scandal in Los Angeles. It could be argued that police officers represent only part of the partnership needed to make community policing a success.

Carl Klockars voices other concerns about the claims made for community policing. First, no one knows exactly what community policing is. Although it is true that most police departments seem to be doing it, general phrases such as "family values" and "doing away with welfare as we know it" are used frequently in association with community policing and tend to contribute to the vagueness of the term.[54] Second, it is unclear just who is doing community policing. Politicians and police administrators are quick to reveal that community-policing officers have been assigned to bike patrol or that a police substation has just been opened, but proclamations notwithstanding, nothing in the community has really changed.[55]

The third concern is that those who are in the community are doing very different things. In some departments the conversion to community policing reflects genuine changes in the department's philosophy, practice, structure, and organization, but specifics in what departments are doing vary radically from one jurisdiction to another—even within the same county, state, and so on. Finally, Klockars suggests that there is no empirical evidence that the reduction in crime is related directly to community-policing efforts. While many police departments involved in community policing efforts point to a reduction in crime, so do those who have not adopted community policing.

The Effectiveness of Community-Oriented Policing

Goldstein notes the many perceived benefits of community policing: decreased tensions between the police and the community, more effective use of police resources in increased quality of police service, increased effectiveness in dealing with community problems, increased job satisfaction for the police participating in the programs, and increased accountability to the community.[56] To implement and assess the effects of community policing, one must establish a framework that considers both the external environment and the internal environment of the police agency in which community policing is employed. External environmental factors such as the socioeconomic conditions of the community (large cities have undergone significant changes in their racial and ethnic makeup as well as a decline of population), legislative mandates and court orders (rights of victims in domestic cases, rights of homeless people), budgetary constraints (budget reductions), and the community

A Closer Look

A Community Police Officer's Day

- Operating neighborhood substations
- Meeting with community groups
- Analyzing and solving neighborhood problems
- Working with citizens on crime-prevention programs
- Conducting door-to-door surveys of residents

- Talking with students in school
- Meeting with local merchants
- Making security checks of businesses
- Dealing with disorderly people[57]

dynamics (residents requesting some control over the decision-making process on matters affecting their quality of life) all affect the type of policing employed.

Internal environmental factors to consider in implementing community policing include the predominant style of policing endorsed by the organizational norms of the department. For example, since community policing requires considerable cooperation between the police and the citizenry in crime prevention and control activities, an administrative philosophy that stresses the service element of community policing is required. The political environment of a department must also be considered. For example, are the political leaders interested in portraying an image of being tough on crime, or are they really interested in improving the quality of life in their city? The matter of whether the upper administrators of the department are willing to decentralize and share decision making with lower-level administrators is also of considerable importance in determining if community policing can be implemented.

Most of the research on community policing has focused on changes in citizens' fear of crime, satisfaction with the police, reduction of crime, and the organizational problems created when trying to incorporate new programs into an existing structure. To date, most of the findings are inconclusive. Many of the administrative concerns, such as appropriate training for community policing and developing an equitable method to reward community policing officers, are currently being debated.

In Retrospect

It could be said that today's emphasis on PCR is an outgrowth of a number of negative citizen–police encounters over the decades. It is the realization that the police are part of our communities and they should act in accordance with what the community wants and needs. It is important for the community to have a sense of trust toward their police department and to feel safe from victimization as well. Therefore, citizen attitudes toward the police are examined early in the chapter. When we study the subject of citizen attitudes toward the police more closely, we see many variables that have a bearing. Demographics such as race, gender, and age of the citizenry all play a role in how the public at large sees its police. In addition, each citizen's personality and personal interactions with the police also play a role in how the police are viewed.

Next, we examined the gradual development of community policing as we know it today, beginning in the 1960s with PCR programs, team policing, and finally an emphasis on unifying police initiatives with the community they serve—community policing. Social science research was the impetus behind community policing, with many scholars contributing to its development and acceptance. Hence community policing's theoretical base is examined and examples of where it has worked best are discussed. As with any policing initiative, community policing has its detractors. So the question of just how effective is community policing is raised. Comments from some well-known scholars are offered in response. Finally, we discussed about how community policing differs from traditional policing.

Although the subject of PCR is still on the table, many police practitioners and scholars are convinced that it is the most promising initiative yet. Crime rates were down in the late 1990s, and many have pointed to good community-policing relations as the major contributing factor. Whether that is truly the case, time will tell.

Improve Your Professional Vocabulary

broken windows theory
community policing
crime prevention

normative sponsorship theory
problem-oriented policing
Project DARE

strategic policing
team policing
zero tolerance

Discussion Questions

1. To what extent are citizen attitudes toward the police important? Explain your response.
2. Explain how the background and attitude of citizens help form their opinion of the police.
3. Describe how race and other demographic variables play a role in the formation of citizen attitudes toward the police.
4. Explain what the term *problem-oriented policing* means.
5. In what ways did the broken windows theory pave the way toward the establishment and development of community policing as we know it today?

6. List and discuss the different phases since the 1960s that contributed to the fusion of the police and the community.
7. Explain to what extent social science research plays a role in positive police–community relations.
8. List and discuss the components of community policing.
9. Describe the effectiveness of community policing.
10. In your opinion, does community policing work?

Notes

1. Black, D. (1970). The production of crime rates. *American Sociological Review, 35,* 733–748.
2. Decker, S. H. (1981). Citizen attitudes toward the police: A review of past findings and suggestions for future policy. *Journal of Police Science and Administration, 9*(1), 80–87.
3. Jacob, H. (1971). Black and white perceptions of justice in the city. *Law and Society Review, 5,* 69–89.
4. Carter, D. (1985). Hispanic perception of police performance: An empirical assessment. *Journal of Criminal Justice, 13,* 487–500.
5. Campbell, A., & H. Schuman. (1973). The comparison of black and white attitudes and experiences in the city. In C. M. Haar, ed., *The end of innocence: A suburban reader.* Glenview, IL.: Scott Foresman.
6. Ramirez, D., & J. McDevitt. (2000, June). *A resource guide on racial profiling data collection systems: Promising practices and lessons learned.* National Institute of Justice. U.S. Justice Department.
7. Schott, R. G. (2001, November). The role of race in law enforcement: Racial profiling or legitimate user? *FBI Law Enforcement Bulletin.* Federal Bureau of Investigation, U.S. Government Printing Office, 24–32.
8. Ibid.
9. Ramirez, D., & J. McDevitt. (2000, June). *A resource guide on racial profiling data collection systems: Promising practices and lessons learned.* National Institute of Justice, U.S. Justice Department.
10. Ibid.

11. Ibid; also see Harris, David A. (1999). Driving While Black; 84 Minnesota Law Review, pp. 265–326.
12. Puente, M. (1997, July 29). A no longer most wanted list. *USA Today,* p. 3A.
13. Ibid.
14. Johnson, K., & G. Fields. (1996, October 14). Fort Worth blazes a crime-busting trail. *USA Today,* p. 9A.
15. Kelling, G. L., & M. H. Moore. (1988). The evolving strategy of policing. In *Perspectives on policing.* Washington, DC: U.S. Department of Justice, National Institute of Justice.
16. Bittner, E. (1976). Community relations. In A. W. Cohn & E. C. Viano, eds., *Police community relations: Images, roles and realities.* Philadelphia: J. B. Lippincott.
17. Hale, C. (1981). *Police patrol: Operations and management.* New York: Wiley.
18. See: http://www.amw.com/about_amw/index.cfm
19. Ibid.
20. Puente, M. (1997, July 29). A no longer most wanted list. *USA Today,* p. 3A.
21. Moore, M. H., & R. C. Trojanowicz. (1988, November). Corporate strategies for policing. *Perspectives on policing, 6.* Washington, DC: U.S. Department of Justice, National Institute of Justice.
22. U.S. Department of Justice, National Institute of Justice. (1995b, November). *Community policing strategies.* Washington, DC: U.S. Government Printing Office.
23. U.S. Department of Justice, NIJ. (1992).

24. Trojanowicz, R., & B. Bucqueroux. (1990). *Community policing: A contemporary perspective.* Cincinnati, OH: Anderson.

25. Hartman, F., L. Brown, & D. Stephens. (1988). *Community policing: Would you know it if you saw it?* East Lansing, MI: Michigan State University, National Neighborhood Foot Patrol Center.

26. Wilson, J. Q., & G. Kelling. (1982, March). Broken windows. *Atlantic Monthly.*

27. U.S. Department of Justice, NIJ. (1992).

28. Moore, M. H., & R. C. Trojanowicz. (1988, November). Corporate strategies for policing. *Perspectives on policing, 6.* Washington, DC: U.S. Department of Justice, National Institute of Justice.

29. Skogan, W. (1986). Fear of crime and neighborhood change. In A. Reiss & M. Tonry, eds., *Communities and crime.* Chicago: University of Chicago Press.

30. Goldstein, H. (1977). *Policing a free society.* Cambridge, MA: Ballinger.

31. Goldstein, H. (1987). Toward community-oriented policing: Potential, basic requirements, and threshold questions. *Crime and Delinquency, 33*(1), 6–30.

32. Sherman, L. (n.d.). *Neighborhood safety.* Washington, DC: U.S. Department of Justice.

33. Ibid.

34. Fay, B. (1984). *Social theory and political practice.* London: George Allen & Unwin Publishers, Ltd.

35. Glazer, S. (1997, April 4). Declining crime rates: Does better policing account for the reduction? *CQ Researcher, 7*(13), 289, 291–308.

36. Trojanowicz, R., & B. Bucqueroux. (1994). *Community policing: How to get started.* Cincinnati, OH: Anderson.

37. Wilson, J. Q., & G. Kelling. (1982, March). Broken windows. *Atlantic Monthly.*

38. Greene, J. R., & R. B. Taylor. (1988). Community-based policing and foot patrol: Issues of theory and evaluation. In J. R. Greene & S. D. Mastrofski, eds., *Community policing: Rhetoric or reality.* New York: Praeger.

39. Eck, J., & W. Spelman. (1987). *Problem-solving: Problem-oriented policing in Newport News.* Washington, DC: Police Executive Research Forum; Goldstein, H. (1987). Toward community-oriented policing: Potential, basic requirements, and threshold questions. *Crime and Delinquency, 33*(1), 6–30.

40. Trojanowicz, R., & B. Bucqueroux. (1994). *Community policing: How to get started.* Cincinnati, OH: Anderson.

41. Moore, H. W. (1992). *Special topics in policing.* Cincinnati, OH: Anderson.

42. Cordner, G., & D. Hale. (1992). *What works in policing: Operations and administration examined.* Cincinnati, OH: Anderson.

43. Cardarelli, A. P., & J. McDevitte. (1993). Toward a conceptual framework for evaluating community policing. In P. C. Kratcoski & D. Dukes, eds., *Issues in community policing.* Cincinnati, OH: Anderson.

44. Greene, J. R., & R. B. Taylor. (1988). Community-based policing and foot patrol: Issues of theory and evaluation. In J. R. Greene & S. D. Mastrofski, eds., *Community policing: Rhetoric or reality?* New York: Praeger.

45. Skolnick, J. H., & D. H. Bayley. (1986). *The new blue line: Police innovation in six American cities.* New York: Free Press.

46. Zhao, J. (2002). Future of policing in a community era. In W. R. Palacios, P. F. Cromwell, & R. G. Dunham, eds., *Crime and justice in America: Present realities and future prospects,* 2nd ed. Upper Saddle River, NJ: Prentice Hall, 191–203.

47. Trojanowicz, R., & B. Bucqueroux. (1994). *Community policing: How to get started.* Cincinnati, OH: Anderson.

48. Albritton, J. S. (1993). *The technique of community-oriented policing: An alternative interpretation.* Unpublished manuscript.

49. Ibid.

50. Cordner, G., & D. Hale. (1992). *What works in policing: Operations and administration examined.* Cincinnati, OH: Anderson.

51. Marquand, B. (1994, December). How are we doing? *Law and Order,* p. 41.

52. Johnson, S. (1997, May/June). Department develops activity management system to track progress. *Community Policing Exchange,* 5.

53. Johnson, K. (1997, July/August). Evaluating community policing. *Community Policing Exchange.*

54. Klockars, C. (1996, January 26). This is just the latest fad. *USA Today,* p. 12A.

55. Ibid.

56. Goldstein, H. (1987). Toward community-oriented policing: Potential, basic requirements, and threshold questions. *Crime and Delinquency, 33*(1), 6–30.

57. Mastrofski, S. D. (1992, August). *What does community policing mean for daily police work?* Washington, DC: U.S. Department of Justice, National Institute of Justice.

CHAPTER **13**

Job-Related Issues

This chapter will enable you to:

- Learn the extent of police killings in the United States.
- Understand the numerous problems created by stress disorders.
- Discuss the extent of police suicides and contributing factors.
- Identify the psychological and physical manifestations of stress.

- Understand the extent of police mortality rates and factors that contribute to them.
- Learn what causes posttraumatic stress disorder in police officers.
- Understand which critical life events law enforcement officers consider the most important.

On Friday, February 28, 1997, two Los Angeles patrol officers were driving by a bank at 9:30 in the morning when one of the officers glanced into a bank window and saw a customer being shoved by someone holding what appeared to be a shotgun. The officers summoned help and one of the biggest shootouts in the city's history ensued. The bank was in fact being robbed and the two gunmen, clad in bulletproof body armor, exited the bank and began unloading hundreds of rounds from fully automatic AK-47 rifles.

The shootout was broadcast live via a news helicopter and America watched in horror as the two robbers, showing little emotion, calmly walked down the street as they emptied and reloaded their weapons over and over again. In a matter of minutes, buildings, police cars, and parked vehicles were permeated with bullet holes. The shootout, which drew almost 300 LA police officers, lasted about 30 minutes and ultimately ended with the death of both robbers. Sixteen bystanders and police officers were wounded in the shootout, but miraculously, no one other than the robbers was killed. In the days that followed the LA shootout, police officers were outraged that their departmentally issued weapons were no match for those used by the robbers. In a national press conference, a number of officers involved in the incident wiped tears from their eyes as they shared their feelings about their brush with death.

The annual statistics for law enforcement officers killed are always disturbing. For example, according to FBI statistics, in 2006, 48 law enforcement officers were feloniously killed. Of those, the average age was 38 years old and the average length of service was 11 years. Forty-five of the 48 officers killed in the line of duty were male. Finally, in the ten-year span of 1997 through 2006, the FBI reported that 562 officers were feloniously killed in the line of duty.[1]

305

	Total	1997	1998	1999	2000	2001	2002	2003	2004	2005	2006
Number of victim officers	562	70	61	42	51	70	56	52	57	55	48

FIGURE 13.1 Law enforcement officers killed, 1997–2006. *Source:* FBI, 2007.

The statistics about the circumstances under which these deaths occurred are instructive. For example, 46 of the 48 officers who died were murdered with firearms. Of these, 36 were slain with handguns. Thirty-two incidents involving firearms occurred when the distance between the offender and the victim was 10 feet or less. Disturbingly, of these, 24 officers were 5 feet or less from their attackers when shot.[2]

It is well known that police work is a hazardous occupation. In 2007, the FBI published its *Law Enforcement Officers Killed and Assaulted Summary*, which contained statistical tables and aggregate data on officers feloniously killed, accidentally killed, or assaulted in the line of duty.[3] The numbers contained in the report serve as a grim reminder that every day, every law enforcement officer runs the risk of becoming the victim of a sociopathic or deranged individual.

The world was shocked on September 11, 2001, when airliners were used as murder weapons against unsuspecting American citizens. Perhaps less astounding, but no less appalling, is that 12 officers died in 2006 as a result of felonious attacks during arrest situations; 10 officers were fatally assaulted when ambushed; 8 officers were killed when responding to disturbance calls (e.g., bar fights, family quarrels), and 8 additional officers were killed while conducting traffic pursuits or stops.

When police officers are killed in the line of duty, there may be a tendency to assume that they died while intervening in felonies, transporting prisoners, or engaging in other police duties that involve them with clearly antagonistic individuals. However, during 2006, at least nine of the victims were coming to the aid of persons whom they perceived to be in danger (for example, from a mentally unstable family member). Three others were intervening to stop an assault. Ten officers were victims of unsuspected violent attacks. In three of these instances, the unwary officer walked into an ambush situation; in seven others, the officer was gunned down for no apparent reason, perhaps just for being a law enforcement officer.

Assignments

Twenty-seven of the victim officers who died in the line of duty in 2006 were on assigned vehicle patrol.

Three of the officers fatally attacked were off-duty but acting in an official capacity.

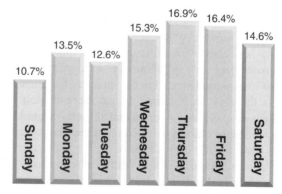

FIGURE 13.2 Law enforcement officers feloniously killed—by day of the week: 1997–2006. *Note:* The 72 deaths that resulted from the events of September 11, 2001, are not included in this table.

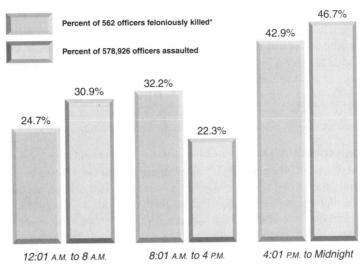

* Time was not reported for 0.2 percent of all law enforcement officers feloniously killed.

FIGURE 13.3 Law enforcement officers killed and assaulted—by time of day: 1997–2006. *Note:* The 72 deaths that resulted from the events of September 11, 2001, are not included in this figure.

Eighteen of the slain officers were assigned to other duties (e.g., special assignments, under-cover) at the time of the incidents.

Twenty-seven of the officers killed were assisted at the time of the attack.

Weapons Used

Forty-six of the 48 officers who died from felonious attacks in 2006 were murdered with firearms. Of these, 36 were slain with handguns.

Two officers were killed with vehicles that were used as weapons.

Eleven officers fired their own weapons during the incidents that led to their deaths; an additional seven officers attempted to use their own weapons.

Thirty-two incidents involving firearms occurred when the distance between the offender and the victim was 10 feet or less. Of these, 24 officers were 5 feet or less from their attackers when shot.

Stories abound within the police subculture about the killing of their own. Not all police killings are high-visibility crimes such as bank robberies. Consider these real-life examples.

NEVADA Assisting in a tactical situation, a patrol officer with the Reno Police Department was mortally wounded about 8:00 A.M. on August 22, 2001. The 17-year law enforcement veteran responded to assist another officer after a vehicle pursuit ended when an injured man drove to his residence and then refused requests to surrender. The man stated that he was armed and threatened to kill officers. As police tried to reason with the man, he apparently fired a shotgun through the door of his residence and forced officers to seek cover. The 35-year-old patrol officer retreated to a delivery van parked nearby and used an open door as a shield. The man reportedly continued to threaten officers verbally and then fired one round from a .30-06 rifle through a window. The armor-piercing round penetrated the engine compartment of the van, traveled over the top of the engine, passed through the dash, and struck the officer as he crouched behind the door. The victim officer sustained wounds to his arms, hands, and pelvic area, and a fatal wound to his front lower torso and stomach. As two officers initiated a rescue plan that required them to cross an exposed area, the suspect fired more than 20 rounds from a rifle in their direction. The victim officer was rushed to a nearby trauma center but did not survive his injuries. The suspect surrendered after SWAT officers fired gas canisters into the residence. The 50-year-old male, who had a previous arrest record and was reportedly intoxicated at the time of the incident, was arrested and charged with murder with a deadly weapon. In the subsequent search of the suspect's residence, officers found three rifles, a shotgun, a handgun, cases of ammunition, a tactical vest, a gas mask, survival literature, and a working video-monitoring system with four remote cameras.

MISSOURI   A 54-year-old veteran police officer with the Independence Police Department was shot and killed on March 17, 2001, at approximately 11:30 P.M. while responding to a family disturbance involving a mentally unstable subject. Two officers accompanied the 32-year veteran officer into the man's residence, where they talked to the homeowner's son through a closed door for more than one hour without success. The officers decided to remove the man from the home and proceeded to break down the door of the room where he was barricaded. As the veteran officer, who had a previous relationship through law enforcement with the man, leaned into the hallway facing the room, he was shot three times in the face and once fatally in the chest at close range with a .22-caliber rifle. Assisting officers removed the victim from the home. Before they were able to return to arrest the man, there was an explosion from the room where he was barricaded. The officers evacuated the suspect's father, mother, and sister as the home erupted into flames. The body of a 34-year-old male was recovered the following day from the charred remains of the home.

VIRGINIA   On September 28, 2001, about 6:00 A.M., a 28-year-old officer with the Norfolk Police Department was shot and killed while handling a mentally deranged person. The officer, with nearly four years of law enforcement experience, and a second officer were dispatched to investigate the report of a man threatening suicide. The officers approached the man's apartment. After announcing their presence and receiving no response from inside, they entered the building through the unlocked front door. The officers searched the apartment and discovered a man lying on an air mattress in the bedroom armed with a handgun. When the officer, who had a prior relationship through law enforcement with the man, ordered him to drop the weapon, the individual reportedly fired several shots with a .45-caliber semiautomatic handgun, striking the victim officer in the head. The assisting officer returned fire, fatally wounding the man. The victim officer was transported to a local hospital, where he died at about 4:00 P.M. A 21-year-old male with a history of mental disorders was pronounced dead at the scene.

These stories represent only a small fraction of similar stories told in police precincts and academies. Although police recruits will often say that the job is attractive because of the action involved, there is always an underlying fear of injury or death. These concerns, along with other job-related pressures, are often at the heart of difficulties experienced by police officers. A once-popular misconception was that premature police deaths were attributable to homicide, and occurred as a result of the dangers of police work.

As we consider later in the chapter, in reality, a large percentage of police officers die prematurely from stress-related disease and other causes. Evidence from research indicates an increased risk of disease and mortality among those in the police profession and suggests that police officers, on the average, die at a much younger age than others in the general population. Research has shown that the overall mean age of death for police officers in the United States is 59.[4] The average death age for the general population is 73 for males and 77 for females.

The Departmental Response

It is incumbent on the department administration to handle the matter of a police officer's death carefully. Compassionate treatment must be afforded the deceased officer's family and the effects of the officer's death on other officers must be considered. Newland recommends psychological counseling for officers involved at the scene of an officer killing. Such assistance benefits officers two to four weeks after the incident and should continue for three to six months.[5] Family members and other significant persons associated with the deceased officer should be afforded counseling as well.

EVIDENCE OF POLICE MORTALITY

Not many major studies have been conducted on police mortality. An FBI study revealed that in spite of the high number of police officer deaths each year, most officers were good-natured and conservative in the use of physical force. They were well-liked by both their departments and the communities they served.[6] The study also revealed that most police officer victims were not wearing protective vests.

But not all of the dangers facing police officers are as forthright as violence and assault. Many dangers are of a more insidious nature, such as bloodborne diseases contracted by dealing with infected accident victims. This is especially common for officers who are "first responders" to accident scenes. Also, officers can accidentally stick or cut themselves on edged weapons or needles that are contaminated with infected blood. Such injuries, previously thought of as minor, are now considered a major priority for police trainers and crime-scene investigators concerned about AIDS, HIV, hepatitis A and B complex, tuberculosis, and other air- and bloodborne diseases.

While the numbers of police officers killed in the line of duty are tragic, we must consider that with an estimated 800,000 state and local police officers, coupled with another 70,000 federal agents, the numbers of those men and women who die in the line of duty are still relatively modest.

Cancer

Police mortality from cancer at specific body parts was significantly higher than expected when compared with the general work population. In particular, cancers of the digestive organs, especially the esophagus and colon, were the highest. The length of police service appeared to have an effect on cancer mortality rates. Overall, elevated mortality rates from cancer were influenced heavily by the increased risk among officers with 10 to 19 years of service and those with over 40 years of service. In the 10- to 19-year-employed group, there was a threefold risk for digestive cancer and a fourfold risk for cancer of the lymphatic and blood-production tissues. In the over-40-year-employed group of officers, there was a fourfold risk for bladder cancer, a twofold risk for cancer of the digestive organs, and a threefold risk for cancer of the lymphatic and blood-production tissues. A statistically significant fourfold risk of brain cancer was found in the 20- to 29-year-employed group of officers.

Heart Disease

Past research on police mortality indicates that heart disease seems to be prevalent among the police population. Early studies show police officers ranked at or near the top of occupations for mortality from heart disease. More recent studies show similar results, demonstrating that heart disease among police generally appears to increase with increasing years of service. For the most part, young police officers have lower heart disease mortality, due to the stringent physical requirements for recruit officers. However, by the time officers complete 40 years of service, the risk increases significantly. Suggestions from research indicate that stress, poor diet, lack of exercise, and carbon monoxide exposure may be contributing factors to this increased risk.

Police Suicide

On March 21, 2008, 38-year-old Norwalk, Connecticut police officer Matthew Morelli was found slumped in a secluded parking lot with an AK-47 rifle. State and local authorities spent two days looking for a suspect, with helicopters and police dogs scouring the neighborhood, where witnesses reported hearing multiple shots. The culprit turned out to be a stealthy if surprisingly familiar cop killer: suicide.

FIGURE 13.4   Law enforcement officers paying respects at the funeral of fallen police officers Jennifer Fettig and Matthew Bowens at Greater Grace Temple in Detroit, Michigan. The officers were killed during a traffic stop on February 16, 2004.

Within one recent week, a 35-year-old New York State trooper fatally shot himself with his service pistol after learning that he might be disciplined for minor misconduct, and a New York City police officer was found dead in her home in Upper Manhattan, propped up in bed with the Glock pistol that delivered the fatal shot in one hand, and a beer can in the other hand.

While line-of-duty deaths grab the public's attention, law enforcement officers more often—perhaps two or three times more often—die by their own hands. Comparing suicide rates within law enforcement with those in the general population is difficult because statistics are kept by different agencies and it is difficult to account for demographics. Also, the general population does not undergo the extensive psychological and physical screening most officers undergo when they are hired, making comparisons questionable. But many who have studied the phenomenon agree that the stress of the job and easy access to weapons can contribute to a higher risk for suicide.

According to the Centers for Disease Control and Prevention, each year more than 32,000 Americans, or about 11 per 100,000 people in the general population, take their own lives. A number of academic studies have estimated the number of law enforcement officers who commit suicide at about 18 per 100,000.[7]

In 2009, the National Police Suicide Foundation reported that most departments lose more officers to suicide than they do to violence in the course of their jobs. Furthermore, the police suicide rate is always higher than that of other working populations. Compounding the problem is the fact that even these high rates for suicide may actually be underestimated. The official causes of police deaths, as listed on death certificates, depend largely on investigation by local police agencies. The fact that the victim is a police officer and the stigma associated with suicide may influence the kind of data eventually recorded. Recent studies have shown that even coroner reports involving police deaths of a suspicious nature are often presented vaguely.[8]

Reasons discussed in the literature for high rates of police suicide are frustration with the police and criminal justice system, reactive depression, demands of the police subculture, and loss of personal control. The majority of police suicides involve use of the officer's own service firearm. Police suicide appears to be an occupation-specific problem and needs to be examined by further research.

When we think of suicide, we may think of a deliberate attempt by a person to end his or her life immediately—the woman on the ledge or the man with a gun placed next to his temple.

However, people can also be self-destructive in the manner in which they act. For example, the diabetic who purposely neglects the taking of insulin, the alcoholic who refuses to seek medical help, or the police officer who ignores policy and procedure and enters into dangerous situations knowing that there is a high probability of death or injury. Such circumstances only serve to complicate the understanding of this enigmatic problem.

Although statistics indicate that both the young and old are generally high-risk groups for suicide, younger police officers aren't as likely to fit into this category as are their older counterparts. Studies have revealed that suicide among officers is typically accompanied by life stressors such as retirement, physical illness, divorce, or other family problems. Warning signs of suicidal officers include:

- A recent loss (family member, friend, etc.)
- Sadness
- Frustration
- Disappointment
- Grief
- Alienation
- Depression
- Loneliness

Of course, the most obvious warning sign is an attempted suicide, and as a rule, the more recent the suicide attempt, the more at risk the police officer is.[9]

Police work is a lifestyle, and older officers are typically involved with their work up until the time they retire. This differs from many other occupations. Retirement represents a drastic departure from their chosen lifestyle, and as a result many become estranged and depressed. Often, they allow their physical health to deteriorate and may even fall into a cycle of drug addiction or alcoholism.

Reasons why police officers are subject to such higher suicide rates include:

- Familiarity with the use and effectiveness of firearms, which are readily available
- Constant exposure to death and misery, which has many negative psychological effects
- Long and irregular work schedules, which strain friendships and break down family ties
- Public criticism and disdain directed toward police officers and law enforcement in general

The frustration and aggressiveness sometimes seen in police officers may stem not from internal problems but from external (societal) sources. It has been suggested that aggression directed inward manifests itself as suicide, and outward aggression manifests itself as homicide (or assault). Therefore, if an officer rejects the notion of outward aggression because of his or her training, upbringing, or personal sense of morality or ethics, the only other alternative may be suicide.

Despite a growing acknowledgment of the problem, the topic of suicide remains taboo among much of law enforcement rank and file. Some psychologists claim that to some extent that is merely a reflection of society as a whole—uncomfortable with the idea of people taking their own lives. But many policing experts argue that those who make their living projecting strength and control are especially reluctant to admit that they need psychological help. They fear that they will be perceived as weak.

Yet another school of thought is that many departments are reticent about the subject of suicide because they are afraid of being held liable if the death is linked to stress on the job, and fearful that all cops will be tarnished if the public learns that an officer took his or her own life. As a result, those who have studied the issue say it is difficult to get an accurate tally of suicides because many departments do not keep official statistics on the problem.

Furthermore, some experts believe questionable incidents, such as reports of officers accidentally killing themselves while cleaning their guns, may actually be efforts to mask suicides. Accordingly, because those who commit suicide are not killed in the line of duty, they are seldom given an official department funeral. Plus, their families also are not entitled to various benefits, such as the $143,943 that the family of an officer slain in the line of duty receives from the justice

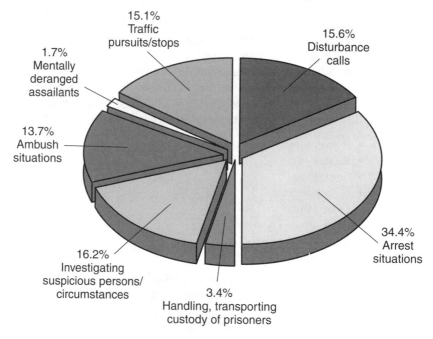

Percent of 643 officers feloniously killed

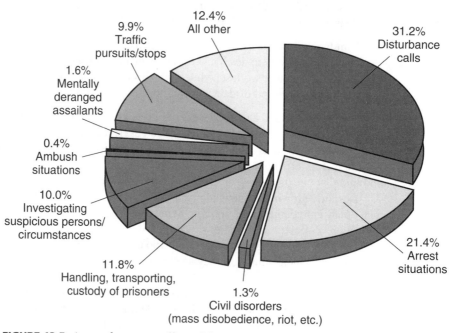

Percent of 597,277 officers assaulted

FIGURE 13.5 Law enforcement officers feloniously killed and assaulted. Circumstances at scene of incident (FBI, 2006).

department. Relatives of suicide victims also complain that they are suddenly ignored by their loved one's colleagues and unceremoniously banished from the law enforcement community.

The pain of police suicide often reaches beyond the family into the department as a whole. The San Diego police officers who killed themselves within two days during 1998 were both undergoing

---

Highlights in Policing

Common Signs and Factors in Police Suicide

Common Factors in Suicide by Police Officers

- *Alcohol.* Coupled with an always-present firearm, drinking and depression are major causes of police officer suicides.
- *The breakup of a relationship or marriage.* Often, the only people an officer trusts outside law enforcement is his or her family. When a relationship ends, an officer loses his or her emotional support base.
- *Stagnated career.*
- *An officer under investigation.*

Common Police Suicide Warning Signs

- An officer who starts having a high number of off-duty accidents
- A rise in citizen complaints against the officer about aggressiveness on the job
- A change in personality in which a sullen officer suddenly becomes talkative or an officer who is normally very social becomes silent and withdrawn
- The officer starts giving away prized possessions or telling friends they will be missed
- The officer suddenly writes a will[10]

---

counseling for emotional problems at the time of their deaths. Captain Lesli Lord was 45 years old, married, a mother of three children, and one of the highest-ranking women in the department. She had been on the police force just under 20 years when she shot herself to death at her home.

The next evening, the body of detective Anthony Castellini was discovered by his girlfriend, dead from a self-inflicted gunshot wound to the head. He was a 12-year department veteran who had been separated from his wife and children for 18 months. In 1989, he had been awarded the department's Medal of Valor for pulling a suspect from a vehicle moments before it burst into flames.

The literature on police suicide states that there is no particular profile of the officer who will attempt suicide. He or she may be a few years out of the academy or at the end of his or her career. Intrapersonal crises run the gamut. Divorce and the breakup of relationships are common problems, but those who killed themselves may also have been suffering from stagnated careers or under investigation for alleged misconduct or for drinking heavily.

It is important to note that there is considerable difficulty in studying police suicide because data is often not collected or departments are reluctant to allow access to such data.[11] In addition, many suicides may be classified routinely as either accidents or undetermined deaths.[12] Because police officers traditionally subscribe to a myth of indestructibility, they tend to view suicide as particularly disgraceful to the victim officer and to the profession alike.

THE POLICE MORTALITY FRAMEWORK

There exists a good probability that high mortality rates for cancer, heart disease, and suicide are related to police occupational factors and accompanying lifestyle habituation. Risk factors evident thus far in the literature include a high-stress work environment, irregular sleeping and eating habits, poor health practices, and lack of sufficient exercise.

Stress

Stress remains as one of the most important factors relating to a police officer's career and home life. Police work has been implicated as one of the most stressful occupations in the world, and stress has been linked to many of the diseases from which police officers die: heart disease, diabetes, high blood pressure, and ulcers. Hans Selye described diseases of adaptation, where stress disrupts the regulatory functions of the body and eventually leads to a breakdown of affected organs.[13] A related condition brought on by stress is suppression of the immune system. This may lead to lowered immunity to disease-producing viruses and cancer-causing agents. The connection between cancer and stress is not yet clear, but future research may confirm this relationship. Related environmental factors thought to be related to job stress are smoking, caffeine use, and alcohol consumption. These factors appear to exacerbate the deleterious health effects that stress has on police officers.

Fatigue

Accounts of tragedies associated with law enforcement fatigue are nothing new. In fact, such stories become more commonplace every year. Clinical studies examining the effects of fatigue are instructive. For example, researchers assessed behavioral functions after 17 hours of wakefulness and reported performance impairment on a range of tasks. Impairments after 20 hours of wakefulness equaled that of an individual with a blood alcohol concentration of 0.10, twice the presumptive level of intoxication in most states. Furthermore, the ability to maintain speed and road position on a driving simulator is significantly reduced when the awake period is prolonged by three hours. Each of these studies indicated that moderate levels of sleeplessness can substantially impair a person's ability to drive safely.

In police work, sleep deprivation has become a serious concern for practical as well as legal reasons. The cumulative work hours for many professionals, such as pilots, locomotive engineers, ship captains, public transportation and commercial truck drivers, firefighters, and emergency room doctors, are standardized and regulated through federal or state regulatory commissions. Unfortunately, no such regulations exist for the majority of federal, state, and local police officers. Police work is one profession in which all practitioners should have adequate and healthful sleep to perform their duties at peak levels.

Fatigue is defined as a "tiredness concerning the inability of disinclination to continue with activity, generally because the activity has been going on for too long" or "a feeling of weariness, tiredness, or lack of energy." Fatigue is a lack of energy and motivation. Over the past 25 years, police work has become increasingly complex from a cognitive perspective. Furthermore, policing the community is creating tasks that require much higher levels of attentiveness than in the past. Long work hours are widely accepted as a major contributing factor to fatigue. As hours of work increase, sleep is reduced with a concomitant elevation in fatigue and reduced levels of alertness.

Research suggests that fatigue-related errors are common well before the point at which an individual is no longer able to stay awake. Inattention may get much of the blame, but fatigue is often the culprit. Research in fatigue shows that it is four times more likely to cause workplace impairment than alcohol and other drugs. Ironically, alcohol and drug use normally are addressed immediately by management. However, lack of sleep, probably the most common condition adversely affecting law enforcement, is often ignored.

Diet

Cancers of the colon and digestive organs have been found to be related to diet. The ingestion of high-fat foods and lack of vegetables, for example, have been associated with increased colon cancer risk. Other foods that increase risk are fried foods, high meat and animal-fat consumption, and bacon. These types of foods are commonly eaten by police officers on duty. Often police rotate shifts and do not have access to proper foods. Many times, officers fit in their meals whenever possible during tours of duty.

Exercise

The majority of police officers in the United States do little or no meaningful exercise. Surveys of police show that approximately 86% report lack of exercise and that 25% are overweight. These may be important antecedents of disease progression among police. Lack of exercise has been pointed out as a risk factor in heart disease, diabetes, and colon cancer.[14]

FIGURE 13.6 Alice Stebbins Wells, the first American woman police officer.

Shift Work

Working different shifts on a rapid rotation basis may have adverse effects on the health of police officers. Shift work is thought to cause an imbalance in many of the body's normal regulatory functions, such as temperature, electrolyte balance, and heart rate. Officers generally experience poor sleeping and eating schedules, a common feeling of dullness, and family problems as a result of shift work. Medical evidence exists that cardiovascular disease is associated with shift work.

Alcohol Use

Cancers of the esophagus and cirrhosis of the liver have been associated with alcohol use. Police officers have an increased mortality risk for both of these diseases. Police officers appear to depend heavily on alcohol as a coping technique to deal with job stress. Besides causing physiological anomalies, alcohol abuse among police may lead to family and job difficulties. This area is discussed in greater detail later in this chapter.

Personality Factors

The type A behavior pattern, characterized by high striving, achievement, time urgency, competition, anger, and hostility, has been associated with an increased risk of heart disease. Police officers tend to be type A.

WOMEN AS POLICE OFFICERS

In Chapter 8, we discussed hiring practices and the importance of having a racially balanced police department. It is equally important for modern police managers to recruit qualified females for the job of police officer, as experience has shown the many advantages of having a diverse force in terms of reducing the crime rate, public relations, and officer morale.

Women have been police officers since Alice Stebbins first joined the LAPD in 1910. It was much later, however, that women were permitted to be on regular patrol, first seen in the Indianapolis, Indiana, Police Department in 1968,[15] the Secret Service in 1971, and the FBI in

1974.[16] Although today, women play a much more significant role in the everyday operations of police agencies across the country, their overall acceptance in the police profession has been sluggish compared to other professions that have traditionally been male dominated. Indeed, Weisheit and Mahan state that in 1985, when half of the new admissions to law school were female, less than 7% of all sworn police officers were women.[17]

Conventional wisdom might suggest that becoming a police officer might bring about a more radical change to a woman's life than that of her male counterpart. Even today police work is a predominantly male occupation and there persists the notion that assertiveness, aggressiveness, physical capability, and emotional toughness are "male" characteristics necessary to perform the job. But when female officers display these qualities they are often perceived as cold, emotionless, and uncaring—a breach in the preordained role prescribed for their gender by society. Daum characterizes the problem in the following fashion:

> For a man, police work is a career option that can be selected without question. To secure the position, he simply must demonstrate his capabilities as they relate to the job requirements. In contrast, a woman desiring to become a police officer may be viewed as unique or unusual. This makes her "different" from other women. So, in order to get the job she must demonstrate that she is as good as any other male officer candidate. Stated differently, she is under pressure to be what she is not—a male.[18]

Another problem facing female officers is not being taken seriously as police officers. Granted, male officers often experience a degree of lack of respect, but it is not uncommon that when a female officer responds to a call, citizens will request a male officer instead. So although legal and formal barriers no longer exist, a female is still subjected to the stereotype of being of the "weaker sex" and perceived as not being as capable as a man.[19] Thus, women must continue to fight an uphill battle to prove their worth as officers.

FIGURE 13.7   A crisis intervention officer talking with another officer in Lewiston, Maine. As of 2003, every officer in the department was issued a copy of the book, *Responding to Emotionally Disturbed Persons* written by Laurie Cyr-Martel.

By the end of 1998, women made up 13% of the total police force in the United States, but recent research has suggested that that number is on the increase. The International Association of Chiefs of Police (IACP) made some interesting observations in 1998 regarding what some researchers have described as one of the most comprehensive analyses of women and policing.[20] Findings revealed that women remained grossly underrepresented in the ranks; they are routine targets of gender bias and sexual harassment; and they have largely been unable to punch through a virtually bulletproof "glass ceiling." The study, which involved a survey of 800 police departments, further revealed the following:

- Nearly 20% of the departments surveyed had no female officers at all. Overall, 12% of the nation's nearly 600,000 police officers are women, a number that has not moved appreciably in nearly a decade—this, despite an unprecedented wave of police hiring since 1994 under a federal grant program designed to put 100,000 new police officers on the nation's streets by the year 2000.
- Ninety-one percent of departments reported having no women in policy-making positions. Of the nation's 17,000 police departments, only 123 have women chiefs.
- Nearly 10% of the departments surveyed listed gender bias among the reasons that women were not promoted. That number has added significance since all of the survey's respondents were police chiefs or top department executives.
- Women have won more than one-third of the lawsuits in which they charge police departments with gender bias or sexual harassment.
- Twenty-five percent of the departments surveyed expressed concerns about the ability of female officers to handle physical conflicts.[21]

Throughout most of the twentieth century, the number of women in policing was insignificant at best with their ranks increasing during periods of war while males were in short supply. Until the 1970s, women primarily served in the capacity of specialists with assignments in juvenile crime, crime prevention, female offenders, and vice. Because they were not assigned to patrol, a necessary step for promotion, their eligibility for advancement within the department was gravely hindered. Horn argues that women during these early years often had college degrees in areas such as social work and nursing but viewed their contribution to policing as being unlike that of male officers.

> These women considered themselves unique and different from their male counterparts. They viewed themselves as social workers rather than "cops," and as such, they brought a philosophy of social work and reform to law enforcement, which emphasized the helping and reform of troubled delinquent women and children.[22]

A 1999 report issued by the National Center for Women and Policing concluded that not only are the nation's law enforcement agencies recruiting women at an alarmingly low rate, but also women in the ranks are not advancing to higher ranks of command at the same pace as their male counterparts. It concluded that:

- Women represent about 14% of law enforcement positions nationwide, up only 3.2% between 1990 and 1999.
- More than one-third of the 176 police departments surveyed have no women in top command ranks and nearly three-fourths have no high-ranking women of color.
- Of the ten big-city police departments with the largest number of female police officers, eight were forced by federal courts to hire more women.[23]

In spite of the low numbers of female officers, ample empirical evidence suggests that female police officers add a positive dimension to police work and that they can be as effective as male officers. To many, the perception of a female officer is that of a more understanding, caring, compassionate, and empathetic law enforcer. Experience has shown that, indeed, women may be more effective in some circumstances than their male counterparts. Female officers, for example, may be more apt to calm a potentially violent dispute or might be a more sensitive respondent to the rape victim or abused child. In addition, evidence suggests that not only are women more energetic and assertive than males, but they are also less authoritarian and dogmatic than male officers.[24]

The police subculture is one of the most unique and influential characteristics of police work. Officers who feel a sense of underappreciation by the general public can often gain a feeling of acceptance through interaction with other police officers. However, because female officers are often rejected from acceptance by many of their male counterparts, a great degree of job dissatisfaction often results. In fact, one study suggests that the negative attitudes of male officers are often the greatest source of stress for female officers.[25]

Researcher Sharon Martin conducted a revealing study on the impact of women entering the predominantly male occupation. Her observations were that females disrupted the solidarity of the group because they often did not share some of the same interests as males: hunting, fishing, sports, and so on. Martin found that "the rules of the game" were altered by the presence of women and that the image of the "macho" officer was no longer necessary. Although seemingly biased, others have argued that if female police officers are not the primary "breadwinners" in their families, they might be less dedicated to the job.

In her study, Martin also categorized the attitudes of male officers toward female officers into three groups: the traditionals, the moderns, and the moderates.

1. *Traditionals* were least willing to accept women into police work; they tended to cling to the image of police work as being dangerous and physically exhilarating work requiring a degree of aggressiveness.
2. *Moderns* accepted and even encouraged the introduction of women into police work by recognizing that police work calls for a variety of people with different talents.
3. *Moderates* were a more ambivalent sort, characterized by the acceptance of women into police work in general but resistant of women serving in a patrol capacity.[26]

By considering these categories, we see how the working personality of the police officer may be much more diversified than some of the earlier studies had indicated. Research has shown that although many women police officers meet some resistance by males in the police academy, the majority of gender-related problems begin when they leave the academy. For example, it is well known that experienced officers often, informally, show rookies the "ropes" of police work, but all too often female officers are excluded from this liturgy. In addition, when female officers are paired with a male partner, it is common for the male officer to dominate the situation, such as by driving the car and dictating watch activities, leaving females to do paperwork or serve as assistants.[27]

Male police officers who resent female officers do so for a number of reasons. After all, according to some male officers, catching criminals is associated with bravery and danger, making it a "man's job," although the daily routine of police work is far less glamorous.[28] Consequently, many male officers believe that female officers cannot protect their male partners in tactical confrontations where physical prowess is required. Others are skeptical about the female's ability to deal psychologically with the many crisis situations commonly encountered on the job. Much of this thinking can be attributed to the stereotyping of women, but it is difficult to know just how much.

However, several studies have indicated that male officers tend to adopt a protective or "big brother" attitude toward their female counterparts.[29] Other males are concerned about "sexually charged" working conditions where male–female partners are involved. In patrol or investigative situations where long hours may be spent with little to no direct supervision, the possibility exists of romantic involvement or unfounded allegations of such involvement.[30]

Yet another concern of male officers is that females may receive preferential treatment in hiring, promotion, and delegation of assignments. This view is supported to some degree by affirmative action programs and equal opportunity concerns of modern police administrations, but it is still viewed as favoritism on the part of more tenured officers. Whether founded or not, such beliefs pave the way to weak morale and organizational disunity and should be addressed in an open, honest way by police managers so that all officers have an understanding of departmental personnel practices.

In summation, from a historical standpoint women have been admitted to police work for only a short time. Although some resistance was still present in the 1990s, it is being overcome with gradual success. However, of all the forces that oppose women in policing, the greatest opposition lies within the ranks of male police officers, many of whom view the female as a status threat to a traditionally male profession. Women police officers must deal with such opposition with intelligence, professionalism, and perseverance. On the other hand, male officers should realize that women sometimes think and behave differently than males, and their performance as police officers may reflect this contrast.

In many cases this could be advantageous. For example, women officers may view themselves as social worker types, while males may consider their role as more of a crime fighter. It could be argued that a combination of philosophies could be healthy for the overall mission of the police, as is evident in many of today's community policing approaches to public safety. In any case, the presence of women in police work has dramatically changed the complexion of the profession and will continue to encourage modern police managers to reevaluate the meaning of what constitutes a "good cop."

The question has also been posed: Does the general public perceive female officers differently than male officers? According to public opinion polls, the answer is no. In fact, citizens report satisfactory service from female officers as well as from males.

AFRICAN-AMERICAN POLICE OFFICERS

The 1960s represented a time of social unrest, which was punctuated by war, campus protests, and civil rights demonstrations. By all accounts, racial tensions were at an all-time high, and police–community relations were deteriorating rapidly. Many people viewed the police as hostile toward minorities, while many police officers felt a sense of alienation from the public. As a means to deal with the problem and to reestablish good community relations, many police departments began hiring more minorities. The philosophy is that African-American officers can establish better rapport with other minority members in the community and are less likely to practice discrimination in making arrests or fulfilling other police duties.

In addition to the goal of improving community relations, the introduction of African-American officers into the ranks of police has also affected the composition of the police subculture. In a study of police officers who were assigned to predominantly minority neighborhoods, Rossi and colleagues found that African-American police officers viewed such neighborhoods in a more positive manner than their white counterparts.[31]

Specifically, African-American officers had a more positive attitude toward their districts than did white officers and were also more likely to live and have friends there as well. What remains questionable, however, is whether the more positive attitude displayed by many African-American officers results in different behavior. In fact, studies have shown that the individual characteristics of a particular neighborhood seem to affect the behavior of police officers more so than do their personal attitudes or their race. As a result, many have concluded that the differences between African-American and white police officers are slight at best.[32]

Minority Leaders in Policing

Over the past three decades, African-Americans have been appointed as police commissioners or chiefs in some of the nation's largest police departments. The list includes William Hart (Detroit), Benjamin Ward (New York City), and Willie Williams (Los Angeles). Smaller jurisdictions are also becoming more open to minority leadership of their police forces, with African-Americans taking control of police departments in Tacoma, Washington; Evansville, Indiana; and Portsmouth, Virginia, in 1998. Other minorities are seeing progress as well. In 1996, Fred Lau became the first Asian-American appointed as police chief in the history of the San Francisco Police Department. In 2000 Raul Martinez became the first Hispanic police chief in Miami. In spite of these successes, however, the problems historically faced by minority officers have not yet been solved. Reasons for this include the fact that programs to recruit minority officers have not been as successful as many observers had first hoped. This has been attributed to a lack of aggressiveness on the part of police recruiters and the continuing negative view of law enforcement in minority communities, which discourages African-Americans and Hispanics from applying for the jobs.[33]

FAMILY PROBLEMS

While at work in the stressful arena of law enforcement, officers hide their emotions to perform their duties effectively. As a non-duty officer, it is necessary to control all situations and to be in full command of both emotions and reactions. When officers return home, however, their role changes to spouse and parent—a role that requires a reversal of their behavior as police officers. At home, officers, just like other married persons, should show their emotions openly, communicate freely, and act as partners instead of authority figures. However, this daily transition from police officer to spouse is not easily made and can create problems both at home and at work.

ADJUSTING TO THE JOB

There is strong evidence that not only does an officer's home life impact job performance, but also the job pressures affect home life. Hence, it is of primary importance that officers learn to handle the special demands that the career places on their home life and simply learn not to bring the stresses of home to the job. With some insight in practice, the negative effects of the job on officers' home life and vice versa can be minimized.

The Individual Officer

Most police officers enter the law enforcement field with much idealism and enthusiasm about serving the public. They are initially dedicated to the profession and committed to doing whatever is necessary to get the job completed. Long and unpredictable hours, rigorous physical demands, lack of public support, and inequities in the criminal justice system usually do not discourage their efforts during the first few years of service.

Unfortunately, after this period, their enthusiasm typically begins to wane. Perhaps the first disillusionment occurs with prosecutorial conditions that previously had been ignored. Frustration often surfaces when the officer personally experiences that arrests are thrown out of court because of technicalities, dangerous criminals plea-bargain for reduced convictions, and juvenile offenders are released without any punishment.

Another area of disillusionment is often the police department itself. The officer may feel that the department is insensitive to personal needs and that the department makes continual demands without regard for the quality of an individual's personal life. Consequently, the officer may become dissatisfied with the job.

The problem now is that many officers become very cold and embittered and either act these feelings out on others inappropriately or become isolated from their families. The danger may develop to the point where the officer may become disheveled in appearance and seek other outlets to ventilate frustrations. As a result, some officers may turn to drinking for superficial relief of this inner conflict.

Frequently during this stage, the officer may begin to experience the early signs of career burnout. Often the officer does not recognize what is happening, or if aware that some changes are occurring, the officer may feel helpless to resolve the problems. At this point, the officer has few options:

- The officer can continue the present lifestyle, feeling dissatisfied but unable to do anything to change;
- The officer can accept the situation and take the necessary steps to adapt and to cope;
- The officer can leave police work altogether.

What is important to realize is that officers in the situation must do something. To do nothing is a particularly dangerous situation since the officer may become a threat to himself, the department, the family, and the community.

Personality Changes

The personality changes that police officers experience are developed as a coping mechanism for dealing with the stresses they confront on the job. Three commonly experienced changes are secretiveness, restrictiveness, and aggressiveness.

SECRETIVENESS   Because an officer must repress emotions while on duty, expressing feelings at home becomes more difficult. To avoid communicating with a spouse, an officer may isolate himself or herself, especially when returning home from work. The officer's seeming lack of interest for the spouse may be interpreted as indifference, but the officer may be "digesting" the day's work problems. For example, the officer may find it difficult to discuss the trauma of a nonduty incident because of the desire to protect the family from the negative aspects of police work. Because the officer has to be patient and understanding in stressful work situations, there may be little tolerance for the demands and requests of the family and the officer may simply want to be alone. The officer's inability to communicate these feelings to the spouse can result in greater pressures at home and further distancing in the relationship.

RESTRICTIVENESS   Officers are often accused by their families as being harsh, restrictive, and authoritative. They may demand to know the whereabouts of family members at all times, prohibit certain activities, and impose limitations somewhat arbitrarily. Family members in turn feel that their freedom is being violated and believe that the officer no longer trusts them. In fact, the officer is showing concern for the safety of loved ones and is trying to protect them. The restrictive demands of the officer are usually the result of experiences on the job. Because the officers involved with the most negative aspects of life on a daily basis, the desire to insulate family members from potential dangers by isolating them is commonplace. The imposition of unreasonable limitations on family members fosters secretiveness on their part, further damaging family life.

AGGRESSIVENESS   Because of the frustrations of the workplace, the officer's tolerance for ambiguity and overall impulse control may be reduced. Often the officer's family becomes a target of feelings of frustration. They officer may become overly punitive with the children, develop a negative and hostile attitude toward others, and become moody and inflexible in attitude and action. At work, the officer's problems may be manifested by overreacting to situations, taking unnecessary chances, or using excessive force.

As with the occupation of a physician, a law enforcement officer's career represents not merely a job but a lifestyle. In addition, it is also a way of life for his or her spouse, children, and family. Police officers are faced routinely with making important decisions that pit the job against the family, and vice versa.

Additionally, police officers have a tendency to bring home problems and frustrations encountered at work and to vent those frustrations on an unsuspecting family. Conversely, officers may also tend to bring family problems with them to work and vent them during the course of their duties. In both scenarios, problems can backfire on the officer. Another problem that commonly develops is when police officers begin to overprotect their families. Because police officers experience such trauma on the job every day, they tend to develop a sense of overprotectiveness for their families. This tends to occur more commonly with male police officers and stems from the officer's on-duty requirement to become suspicious of people and situations as well as becoming sharply observant.

Discord at home can also have an indirect effect on an officer's motivation, professional development, effectiveness, and productivity on the job. The requirement of officers to show emotional restraint while on the job can create great stress on an officer's home life, where he or she might be unable to muster additional self-restraint. Much research addressing problems associated with police stress have reported an unusually high incidence of divorce among police officers, especially younger officers. Research has shown that earlier this century, divorce rates among police officers ranked thirteenth out of 39 categories of professional occupations. Ranking higher than police officers were salespeople, physicians, teachers, and lawyers.[34] Because the police officer represents an authority figure in society, a failure in his or her marriage may have implications affecting the community as well. Certainly, the officers themselves are affected, as are their family and friends as well as the general population. Studies also show that prior to the dissolution of marriage, there exists a long period of poor communication, confrontation, and frustration.[35]

Programs for Police Spouses

Over the years, many programs have been developed to deal with the problem of stress and a police officer's home life. These include the following:

1. *Interviewing spouses of police candidates.* This program has been implemented by most larger police departments and includes an interview with the spouse of the police officer applicant. The interview is conducted as one segment of the candidate's background investigation and provides the spouse with a comprehensive view of the day-to-day operations of the agency as well as the specific duties that will be required of the candidate should he or she be hired. In addition, the interview allows the candidate's spouse a chance to ask pointed questions that the candidate may not be willing or able to ask. The spouse interview permits investigators the opportunity to gauge the willingness of the spouse to accept the hardships commonly encountered in marriages involving law enforcement personnel.

2. *Orientation programs.* Many departments have implemented orientation programs for the spouses of newly hired officers. Unlike a detective's questioning of a police candidate's spouse during the background interview, orientation programs are typically facilitated by top police administrators. They are designed to give the spouse a chance to ask questions regarding the expectations of the department as well as questions about any job-related problems that might be encountered by the officer regarding overtime, promotions, and working conditions.

3. *Ride-along programs.* Many police agencies have organized officer–spouse ride-along programs. This program gives spouses a firsthand opportunity to experience and observe a police officer's occupational role. It is thought that such programs aid officers' home lives by helping officers and their spouses communicate about problems encountered at work.

4. *Firearm familiarization programs.* Because police officers are required to possess a firearm both on and off duty, the very presence of a weapon in the home may contribute to a stressful family environment. One way to deal with this problem is to familiarize the spouse with the mechanics and safety precautions of dealing with a firearm. This program gives spouses an opportunity to fire a service weapon and, hopefully, reduces the chance of an in-home firearm accident.

ALCOHOL AND DRUG ABUSE

For generations, alcohol abuse has remained a public health problem. Excessive alcohol consumption causes more than 100,000 deaths annually in the United States, and although the number shows little sign of declining, the rate per 100,000 population has trended down since the early 1980s.[36] Over the years, alcohol-related problems have stricken society at virtually all levels—accidents, mostly due to drunken driving, accounted for 24% of alcohol-related deaths in 1996, while alcohol-related homicide and suicide accounted for 11% and 8%, respectively.[37]

One of the most important contributors to alcohol-related deaths is a group of 12 ailments wholly caused by alcohol, among which alcoholic cirrhosis of the liver and alcohol dependence syndrome are the most important. These 12 ailments together accounted for 18% of the total alcohol-related deaths in 1996.[38]

Aside from health-related factors, alcoholism is also a costly problem in both government and industry. It is estimated that 6.5% of workers in the United States are alcoholics, which accounts for an estimated $10 billion in lost productivity costs. Informally, police administrators have reported that serious alcohol problems among police officers are as high as 25%.

In police work, problems associated with drinking may manifest themselves in a number of ways, which include high absenteeism, misconduct or citizen complaints, insubordination, intoxication while on duty, and traffic accidents while on and off duty. Research suggests that police work is particularly conducive to alcoholism because police officers must often work in environments where drinking is commonplace. Hence the stress stimulus of the job creates a forum for social drinking, which in turn creates opportunities for problem drinking.

Problem drinkers are generally dealt with through each department's employee assistance program where the officer is permitted to seek treatment that is paid for by departmental insurance and is accomplished during on-duty hours. Departments often experience difficulty in convincing officers that they are problem drinkers and need to seek medical help. However, due to increasing costs, lack of productivity, and potential legal liability for the department, the police administrator cannot afford simply to ignore the problem.

Project Shield

In an effort to learn from past experience, the U.S. Department of Justice's National Institute of Justice conducted research involving one of the major law enforcement agencies in nine states. Through an anonymous survey of the officers in this agency, researchers discovered that apparently, the law enforcement profession had not learned from its history of negative influences of job stress and what that stress does to officers exposed to it. The study, *Project Shield*, provided information about the negative effects of stress and broke these down into categories of psychological, physical, behavioral, and organizational public health.

During this research project, officers admitted anonymously to increased vulnerability to alcohol abuse and anxiety within the first five years. Project Shield also found that officers experienced increased risk of mortality and morbidity from cancer, heart disease, hypertension, acute migraine headaches, reproductive problems, chronic back problems, foot problems, and insomnia.[39]

The study showed that profound emotional effects from stress occurred most often when officers attended a police funeral, were the subject of an internal affairs investigation, experienced a needle stick or exposure to body fluids, made a violent arrest, or personally knew victims. In addition, the study discovered that officers experienced organizational, or job-related, stress most often when making split-second decisions with serious consequences; hearing media reports of police wrongdoing biased against police; having administrators who did not support their officers; putting work ahead of anything, including family; and not having enough time for personal or family responsibilities.[40]

Project Shield demonstrated that whereas only a small percentage of officers in this agency reported these problems, they also were 30% more likely to report health problems than other officers in the agency, three times more likely to abuse their spouses, five times more likely to report alcoholism, five times more likely to have some multiple, recurrent, and long-term physical complaints apparently not due to any physical disorder, six times more likely to have anxiety, ten times more likely to be depressed, and the least likely to seek help.

DISEASE PREVENTION

Whether the aforementioned factors are causally related to police mortality will be determined by future research. At present these factors have been proposed as playing a part in the increased risk of disease. In today's work environment, there is a renewed emphasis on prevention of disease at the workplace. Prevention may best be accomplished in police work through education and organizational policy. Police agencies have been encouraged to initiate exercise and fitness standards; to promote dietary education; to make available medical screening for heart disease, high blood pressure, and certain types of cancers; and to create awareness of the police mortality problem. Improved health among police officers should become an important goal for both the individual officer and the police organization.

STRESS

Only in recent years has there been a growing recognition among law enforcement administrators that real or perceived traumatic incidents by officers while performing their duties may affect both their physical and psychological wellness. In general, administrators in both business and industry have been slow to address problems with stress in the workforce, but due to extensive research in the area, it has now been resolved that a healthy, contented worker is also a much more productive one. In fact, it has also been discovered that employees suffering from stress may also become a serious financial liability to their employers as well.

Sadly, government agencies and the public service sector typically lag behind business and industry in recognizing problems and addressing reform in employee benefits. Lately, however, government agencies are beginning to become more aware of such problems with their employees. From a medical perspective, the problem of stress has received much attention over the years and those who suffer from it are generally viewed as being dysfunctional. Certainly, stress has many consequences, and if unchecked, it can result in an array of physical and psychological disturbances that can lead to many serious organic diseases. Stress can also lead to numerous psychological disorders as well that can result in a myriad of problems in the employee's personal and professional life. In 1936, Hans Selye introduced the **general adaptation syndrome** (GAS), a model used to describe the biological reaction to sustained and unrelenting physical stress. This model has three phases:[41]

1. *Alarm reaction.* The autonomic nervous system is activated to resist the stress. If the stress is too dominant, gastrointestinal ulcers form, the adrenal glands become enlarged, and there is deterioration of the thymus.
2. *Resistance.* The organism adapts to the stress through available coping mechanisms. If the coping mechanisms fail to deal adequately with the stress, the third stage follows quickly.
3. *Exhaustion.* The organism dies or suffers irreversible damage.

So what is the evidence that illness is stress-related? For years it has been known that illness could be produced in laboratory animals exposed to stressful situations. These diseases were typically ulcers and hypertension, but it is now known that certain tumors tend to grow when one is exposed to stress. Although everyone seems to know what stress is, there is little agreement about its precise definition. Stress can be defined as "the body's nonspecific response to any demand placed on it."[42] The term **job-related stress** has been used to describe a condition in which a function or combination of functions at work interact with the worker to upset his or her psychological or physiological equilibrium.[43] For the sake of simplicity, it might be easier to define stress as an occupational pressure or burden that affects workers adversely.

Although the term has many negative connotations, researchers suggest that stress can be either positive or negative. For example, certain sporting events or a college final examination can challenge a person to excel in performance and may even become a source of pleasure.[44]

Stress and Police Work

Courts have ruled that a police officer who suffers a heart attack on duty is entitled to worker's compensation. This should alert police administrators that prevention and early detection of all stress disorders can lessen the impact of liability on any organization. In an effort to understand the problem of stress in policing, one study of 2,300 officers in twenty departments concluded that 37% had serious marital problems, 36% serious health problems, 23% problems with alcohol, 20% problems with their children, and 10% drug problems.[45]

It is logical to assume that in police work, an officer's well-being will be influenced by dealings with persons who are criminals, mentally ill, or highly critical of the police function in the community. In fact, it is one of the few occupations where an employee is asked, and even required, to face physical danger on a daily basis. Even without the element of great danger, whenever police officers are summoned to a location, they can usually expect to encounter various forms of crime, hostility, pain, or suffering—all of which generate confusing and even negative feelings within. In addition to the stressors mentioned earlier, "in-house" circumstances can also affect the wellness of police officers, such as boredom, shift changes, and administrative pressures placed on officers. As a result, police work has been identified as one of the most stressful of all occupations.[46]

The problem of stress in policing poses a twofold threat, jeopardizing both the individual officer and the department as a whole. If unchecked, it can lead to an array of physical disorders. In addition, individual departments can be faced with residual problems such as a shockingly high rate of absenteeism, high insurance rates for disability, and administrative costs relating to early retirement.

Historically, the law enforcement profession has not acknowledged the negative stress related to being an officer. For example, many law enforcement academies throughout the nation have rarely instructed recruits with regard to stress in police work. Numerous cases clearly illustrating the need for addressing stress have been slow in doing it successfully. Today, appropriate methods and programs are needed for identifying stress in police officers. Until recently, many law enforcement agencies did not implement any programs whatsoever to assist officers struggling with stress-related issues.

Case in Point: "The Onion Field"

One example of the need for police departments to have stress programs for their officers is the historic case of the *Onion Field*. In *The Onion Field*, author Joseph Wambaugh described the horrible tale of two Los Angeles police officers' abduction while on duty one night in 1963. Criminals took the officers to an onion field outside of Bakersfield, California, and murdered one officer at the feet of the other. Somehow, miraculously, the second officer escaped and survived, only to experience second-guessing by his colleagues and the criminal justice system and incredible effects of negative stress without any assistance or support.

The surviving officer not only was victimized by watching his partner murdered but was second-guessed by his colleagues because he escaped and survived. The result was a second victimization. However, in 1963, no critical incident stress management debriefings or employee assistance programs existed, so he had no place to turn for support within his agency. His family members could not support him because no family education programs existed to teach them about the job and its negative stressors. He could not communicate with a police chaplain because his agency had no chaplain program. To make matters worse, a main aspect of the police personality dictated that officers, regardless of traumatic experiences, must endure repeated emotional and physical exposure to the incident as if nothing had happened. In such an environment, the surviving officer's agency would not have had meaningful peer discussions or formal peer support programs in place to encourage him to talk about his problems.

The case ultimately went to court. For the next nine years, the surviving officer had to recount the horror of the night over and over again during all of the hearings and appeals of the case. This left an open and infected psychological wound that never properly healed so that he could return to duty as a fully functional officer.[47]

In recounting this true story, Wambaugh described the effects of what has come to be known as posttraumatic stress disorder (PTSD) along with some of the symptoms that someone with PTSD may exhibit (discussed later in this chapter). Tragically, the surviving officer ultimately was lost to PTSD and to the law enforcement profession because he became a thief himself by shoplifting some tools that he could have paid for but did not.

Fortunately, the law enforcement profession has made significant strides since 1963 in the development of programs to treat officers exposed to such horrific incidents. Moreover, the law enforcement community remains duty-bound to remind officers of the negative effects of stress and provide them with the skills to deal with the demands of their profession.

Categories of Stress

In the past, dealing with such problems typically occurred reactively when the conditions presented themselves. A more proactive approach has now been adopted by many police administrators. Kroes and Hurrell have grouped police stressors into four broad categories.

1. *Organizational practices and characteristics (internal stress).* The class of **internal stress** generally includes functional duties, policies, and procedures that have been implemented as a part of a department's standard operating procedure. Stress develops when such policies are implemented without input from officers and when insufficient departmental resources are available to meet the requirements of the policies. Kroes notes that police productivity suffers greatly as a result of officer shift rotations and resulting alterations to body rhythms.[48] The shift from days to nights or the "graveyard" shift not only creates havoc in an officer's personal life but also causes considerable biological change in that officer's chemical makeup. Other stressors in this category are poor supervision, lack of support for officers by administrators, lack of recognition for tasks well done, insufficient training, disciplinary transfers, deficient career ladders, and excessive paperwork.

2. *Criminal justice system practices and characteristics.* Pressures and stress from the criminal justice system stem from several variables. For example, an often-cited source of stress is the scheduling of court testimony at a different time than within the officer's regular work schedule (including on his or her day off). Officers are typically subpoenaed for court hearings and therefore are required under law to be present at the courthouse at the specific time and date designated on the subpoena. The mandatory court appearance tends to interfere with officers'

personal time off, family commitments, and even sleeping schedules. The court appearance itself can also be a great source of pressure for officers who are not comfortable with testifying at hearings and trials. Although many officers enjoy the challenge of courtroom tactics, many find it intimidating and degrading to be under the spotlight with their professional behavior subject to intense public scrutiny. Additional stressors in this category include: (a) the acceptance of court decisions that hinder the daily duties of police officers, (b) the leniency of many courts toward offenders, and (c) interagency competition for case recognition.

3. *Public practices and characteristics (external stress).* The class of **external stress** includes concern about a general lack of public support for law enforcement officers in the community, including social stressors placed on officers both off and on duty. Although this problem is greater in some communities than in others, it can be exacerbated by the negative influence of the media and social service agencies to which police departments must refer persons who come to their attention. Also included in this category is social stress created by the dissimilarity between the officers' own socioeconomic status and that of their constituencies.

4. *Police work itself (operational stress).* **Operational stress** in policing results from police officers confronting the daily tragedies of life on the street. It is logical to assume that dealing with liars, thieves, murderers, drug dealers, and the like on a regular basis tends to make officers cynical about persons not associated with police work. Officers are also often confronted with role conflicts when enforcing laws in the community. Often, their personal sense of values conflicts with those proscribed by law.

As Goolkasian and coworkers report, other police work-related stressors include:[49]

- The constant threat to an officer's health and safety
- Boredom, alternating with the need for sudden alertness and energy
- Responsibility for protecting others' lives
- Continual exposure to people in pain or distress
- The need to control emotions, even when provoked to anger
- The presence of a gun even during off-duty hours
- The fragmented nature of police work, with only rare opportunities to follow a case to conclusion or obtain feedback or follow-up information

Individual Officer Stressors

Personal stressors may also hamper an officer both on and off the job. These can include pressure placed on an officer by the person's peers, to perform, act, and think in conformity with others in the department. In addition, police managers and agency policy can apply additional stress to officers to further their education and training to enable them to compete for promotions. Personal finances may also cause an officer to seek part-time employment just to make ends meet.

The Progressive Career Stages of Stress

Resulting from these categories of stress-related problems, Dietrich suggests that a related five-stage progression in the careers of officers can also be observed:[50]

1. *0–5 Years: Alienation from the nonpolice world.* Young people initiated into the force bring a fresh enthusiasm and energy that is often quickly depleted by the reality of crime, suffering, and death, to the degree that there is usually the following reaction: There is so much evil in the non-police world that it must be unreal; therefore, the only true reality is the police world.

A Closer Look

Stressors in Policing

External Stressors

- Frustration with the U.S. judicial system
- Lack of consideration by the courts in scheduling court appearances for officers
- Lack of support by the general public toward law enforcement
- Negative or distorted media coverage of law enforcement

Internal Stressors

- Policies and procedures that are offensive to officers
- Poor or inadequate training
- Minimal career development opportunities
- Lack of identity or recognition for good performances
- Poor economic benefits and working conditions
- Excessive paperwork
- Inconsistent discipline
- Perceived favoritism

Stressors in Police Work Itself

- The rigors of police work
- Role conflicts between enforcing the law and serving the community
- Frequent exposure to life's miseries and brutalities
- Boredom interrupted by the need for sudden alertness
- Fear and dangers of the job
- Constant responsibility for protecting other people
- Work overload

Individual Officer Stressors

- Fears regarding job competence, individual success, and safety
- Necessity to conform
- Necessity to take a second job or to further education
- Altered social status in the community due to attitude change toward a person because he or she is an officer

This leads to alienation from the nonpolice world. There is a deep hurt in many members arising from the realization that their own resources may be unable to match the trauma they have seen.

2. *5–10 Years: Emotional shutdown.* In the next stage, officers are commonly bothered by early experiences and try to put into perspective the relationship between their reactions to the crime, suffering, and death of police work and their attempts to live normal lives with normal relationships. But slowly, officers who conclude that the police world is the only true reality realize that this also has its drawbacks, thus these officers are confronted with two seriously flawed worlds. Rather than face this, many officers shut out both worlds. Since these feelings are not discussed in most police departments, officers often go through this process alone.

3. *10–15 Years: Emotional unsureness.* At this stage, police officers become unsure of how to start to express their emotions again as they bring with them the alienation and emotional shutdown of their early years on the force and try to look for an administrative outlet so that they can "normalize" their lives. The supervisor often "drifts," realizing that because there is so much that needs to be changed and so many fellow officers in the same situation, it is naive to think that any change is possible.

4. *15–20 Years: Namelessness.* At this stage, a supervisor may find a safe administrative niche and try to do something positive. But the system closes in around him or her, since many good efforts are filtered out and depersonalized and many of his or her fellow supervisors are in the same emotional vacuum. Many of these nameless officers lose their energy for change and retreat emotionally to their own narrow areas of expertise.

5. *20–35 Years: Maintaining the status quo.* At this stage, officers have a stake in "not" changing because (a) there is too much that needs changing; (b) they may not want to admit that they have failed; and (c) they do not want to "let down" the new members coming in with the same enthusiasm they once had. Often, even small changes are opposed because change itself is threatening.

Clearly, the most compelling problem associated with stress is that it has been known to create physiological and/or psychological manifestations that may affect an officer's ability to function both on and off the job. Let's now look more closely at both categories.

Physical Effects of Police Stress

Job stress can affect a person's health, personality, and/or job performance. Research suggests that psychological stress is an important causal agent in such health problems as coronary heart disease, gastrointestinal malfunctions, dermatological problems, severe nervous conditions, and any number of other physical disorders. A study conducted by Jacoby reported the results of psychiatric analysis of 50 disabled police officers in Los Angeles.[51] He reported that a "whole gamut of psychological stress can be generated by police work and later result in organic disease of varying severity." A broad range of physical disorders was listed in the study:

Backaches	Headaches
Cramps	Muscle aches
Asthma	High blood pressure
Hyperventilation	Heartburn
Thyroid disorders	Ulcers

In general, studies addressing the problem of police stress have centered on digestive disorders and heart disease. For example, an early study conducted in 1950 revealed that police officers and sheriffs had a considerably higher rate of heart disease than did those in other occupations.[52] In 1973 it was discovered that 15% of sheriffs and police officers assigned to patrol duty had more than double the recommended cholesterol levels, thus doubling their risk of heart disease.[53] Further findings of the study revealed that over half of the officers were 6 to 20 pounds overweight, while 28% of officers were 21 pounds or more overweight. In summation, in excess of 27% of officers surveyed had a moderate or high risk of heart disease.

In a 1974 study, through an examination of death certificates, it was determined that police officers were admitted to hospitals more frequently than were people in other occupations. Two-thirds of police officers admitted to hospitals had digestive or circulatory problems, compared to less than 50% of people working in other occupations.

Kroes and coworkers conducted interviews with one hundred Cincinnati police officers who reported that their jobs had adversely affected their family lives.[54] Of these, 32% reported digestive disorders and 24% reported headaches, compared to only 14% of the civilian population. In addition, it was learned that more police officers smoke cigarettes than do their general population counterparts, and with greater frequency. Experience has shown that there are also organizational ramifications of the cumulative effects of stress.[55] These include:

- Impaired officer performance and reduced productivity
- Reduced morale
- Public relations problems
- Civil suits stemming from impaired personnel performance
- Tardiness and absenteeism
- Increased turnover

In brief, it is clear that there is a strong link between stress-related activity and serious physical health consequences. Research fails, however, to show exactly how much more likely it is that serious physical disorders will develop in police officers than in other occupational groups. Research is also needed with regard to how various police duties correlate with stress and serious physical disorders.

Posttraumatic Stress Disorder (PTSD)

Posttraumatic stress disorder (PTSD) occurs after a traumatic event such as rape, combat, a natural disaster, serious threat to the safety of loved ones, or seeing another person maimed or killed. It manifests itself in several ways, including difficulties with concentration and memory, an inability to relax, impulsiveness, a tendency to be easily startled, disturbed sleep, anxiety, depression, and most important, psychic numbing.

Those who suffer from PTSD lose interest in activities enjoyed previously and experience a feeling of estrangement from others. If the disorder stems from witnessing the killing of a companion, there is a sense of guilt for having survived. Indeed, flashbacks and nightmares are common and vivid. PTSD may be either acute, chronic, or delayed. It is thought to be more severe and longer-lasting after a trauma caused by people, such as war, physical assault, and torture (as opposed to acts of nature such as an earthquake). The symptoms tend to worsen when the person is exposed to situations similar to those resembling the trauma. For example, a thunderstorm may remind a police officer of a shooting incident that resulted in the death of his or her partner.

Highlights in Policing

Police Stress—An Insider's View

- To most people, death and violence are abstract fears; to a cop, they are daily reality.
- Every cop with even a year or two on the job knows another cop that has been down—if not killed, then badly hurt.
- It's like being an occupation army in a foreign country . . . only your tour of duty is not for a year or two, it's for many years.
- Each day you realize in the back of your mind (although you don't talk about it) that your partner, who has become a closer friend than your wife, may be dead by the end of your tour of duty. That sounds overly dramatic, but it's true.
- To a street cop, there is no release. The soft jobs are all gone to the civilians. To save the city a few bucks, the cops are kept under more stress.
- The people hate you because you interfere with their fun or you're not fast enough or there is too much crime or their wife burned the dinner.
- The politicians hate you because you're not keeping voters happy.
- The brass hate you because you're not satisfying the politicians.

The only friends you seem to have are other cops, a friendly lady, a bottle, or a joint. It builds up. Every year, several cops kill themselves.

- Cops need:
  - More appreciation, more recognition, more money. Cops' pay shouldn't be tied to firefighters' pay. Cops need far more skills than any other city employee, but get laborers' wages.
  - Some paper-shuffling jobs where a man can be out doing some useful work instead of going on sick leave.
  - More time off to get away from the pressure (e.g., a four-day week, periodic extra vacation, something to look forward to).
- The spouses of cops should have some training. It is hard to talk to your wife about work when everything that happens to you probably threatens her security.
- The chaplains in the department should be far more visible and available. No one knows who they are or how to get a hold of them. They are almost perfunctory. There should be more of them. They should not be politically appointed.
- Psychiatric help should be more available—perhaps on a regular basis, so there is no dent in your macho image as a result of going to the "shrink" on your own. Probably some suicides could have been prevented if this had been mandatory.
- The career should be adjusted to provide for earlier retirement or placement in a softer job after so many years. Most cops in their late forties or fifties don't need fights with punks in their twenties. The city doesn't have much to say about retirement times, but it has everything to say about personnel placement.

—Anonymous police officer with posttraumatic stress disorder.

Source: The Police Chief, February 1989, p. 21.

PTSD and the War Connection

In World War I, the term *shell shock* referred to the belief that soldiers' brains suffered chronic concussions through sudden and severe atmospheric pressures caused by nearby explosions. This was ultimately recognized as a cumulative emotional reaction to the strain of war. In World War II and the Korean War the terms *exhaustion* and *combat fatigue* were given to stress evident in soldiers who were startled by the slightest sounds and experienced sleeplessness and an inability to speak. PTSD was seen most commonly following the end of the Vietnam conflict. After military personnel had been home for a few months or years, signs of great distress began to appear. The general public became aware of PTSD after veterans began to take advantage of the free psychological and medical services offered to them through the Veterans Administration.

In an effort to understand the effects of PTSD on veterans, Penk and colleagues studied 87 combat veterans and 120 who had not seen combat.[56] All had sought treatment for substance abuse at a Veterans Administration medical center. The results were that those veterans who experienced combat showed significantly more stress than those who did not see combat. Accordingly, Inciardi reports that a number of Vietnam veterans suffering from PTSD have argued successfully that the intense reliving of their war experiences has destroyed their ability to distinguish right from wrong.[57] A 1987 study showed that PTSD occurs in 1% of the general population, 3.5% of civilians exposed to physical attack and Vietnam veterans who were not wounded, and 20% of wounded Vietnam veterans.[58]

Police Officers and PTSD

Research suggests that police officers who are exposed to traumatic or crisis events may suffer from some form of posttraumatic stress disorder. Solomon suggests that, when involved in a shooting incident in which someone is killed, an estimated one-third of all police officers have mild PTSD reactions, another third have moderate reactions, and the remaining third have severe reactions.[59] In fact, on-duty shooting incidents have been called "the most dangerous and traumatic experience that officers can face during their police careers."[60] Even in the absence of personal injury, the psychological stress created by such events can be devastating. There are currently no systematic studies to show the short- and long-term effects of shooting experiences on police officers.

One recent study examined the emotional reactions of the San Ysidro massacre on police officers. In this case, 21 persons were murdered and 19 others were wounded in a McDonald's restaurant after being terrorized by a lone killer. Findings were that in less than six months after the incident over half of the officers involved in the incident were suffering from some form of PTSD. Twenty-nine cases were of minimal to moderate severity and 22 were moderate to severe.[61] Although there is much to learn about PTSD, it is feared that officers who suffer from it may, if left untreated, eventually become brutal in their nature. In a recent study it was concluded that an increase in the intensity of police brutality in Los Angeles in the late 1980s and early 1990s was attributed to officers suffering from PTSD.[62] It has been suggested that officers suffering from the disorder might have a tendency to vent personal anger and frustration on citizens through the use of violence while conducting their duties.

Law Enforcement in Critical Life Events

More than persons in nonpolice professions, police officers are at a much greater risk of experiencing psychological traumas in their jobs. Accidents, humanmade and natural disasters, and shootings are all examples of situations in which police are involved more frequently than the average citizen. Recent research has shown that **critical incident stress** resulting from such experiences affects up to 87% of all emergency workers at least once during their careers.[63]

The emotional impact of a shooting incident has been recognized as the most traumatic experience a law enforcement officer can face during his or her career. Researchers have recently examined the police officer's emotional and physical reactions following such instances. For example, in a sample of 86 officers, 18 reactions were recorded, including a heightened sense of danger, anger, nightmares, isolation/withdrawal, fear and anxiety about future situations, sleep difficulties, flashbacks/intruding thoughts, emotional numbing, depression, alienation, guilt/sorrow/remorse and the so-called "mark of Cain" (an assumption that others blame them), sexual dysfunction, problems with regulations/authority figures, insecurity, and suicidal thoughts.[64] Such problems are being treated with greater understanding through the use of therapy and peer support programs.

It is important for police managers to have a means by which to assess stressors and somehow gauge the magnitude of each. Sewell has provided a tool to do that using a survey instrument called the Law Enforcement Critical Life Events Scale.[65] The scale consists of 144 stressful events, the most highly stressful event being the violent death of a partner in the line of duty and the least stressful being completion of a routine report. Respondents are instructed to rate each event from 1 (low) to 100 (high) in terms of professional stress readjustment. Stress readjustment was defined as "the amount and duration of change in one's accustomed pattern of work resulting from various job-related events . . . it measures the intensity and length of time necessary to adjust to an event within one's professional life."

Results of Sewell's research using the scale indicated that the events requiring the greatest amount of readjustment are events concerned with violence or threatened violence, personnel matters, or ethical concerns. Also included in these events are criminal indictment of a fellow officer and police-related civil suits. One other event also ranked high in the list of stressors: assignment away from family for a long period of time. The events requiring the least amount of readjustment afterward involve community relations, legal/judicial concerns, or administrative and operational concerns. Each of these events could be defined as routine and include overtime duty and court appearances.

POLICE BURNOUT

The nature of effective policing requires teamwork, and officers who go out on their own to complete a task are often criticized by others for "cowboying" the situation. As a result, officers tend to become critical of one another, and such criticism tends, in and of itself, to be a great source of stress for officers seeking acceptance by their peers. Conversely, it is also generally held that once an officer is accepted by his or her peers, a positive sense of job satisfaction results. In comparison, when an officer becomes unmotivated, dysfunctional on the job, or is generally considered as "deadwood," fellow officers become resentful when such a person is a member of their team. This complacent attitude is one characteristic of some older officers looking forward to retirement, but often of younger officers as well. This complacency and lack of interest in one's work is sometimes referred to as *burnout*.

Defining Burnout

Police work is typical of that in other action-oriented professions that see a high degree of burnout. The role of police officers places them in a professional "fast lane" where they must regularly deal with conflict, confusion, long hours, and little recognition for a job well done. They must deal face to face with persons who are mentally unstable, violent, or manipulative in nature, and while doing so, they must uphold the image of the "tough cop."

Burnout has been defined as "to fail, to wear out, or become exhausted by making excessive demands on energy, strength, or resources."[66] It could be said that burnout also includes emotional withdrawal from one's work due to excessive stress or dissatisfaction. This occurs when the job is no longer fun and the person feels locked into a particular employment niche from which they feel they can't get free.

Effects of Burnout

It is also common that a person suffering from burnout does not realize it is happening. Indeed, its onset can be so gradual as sometimes to be difficult to detect. Reese suggests that burnout is a disease of overcommitment, which, ironically, results in a lack of commitment.[67] He goes on to say that the transactional definition of *burnout* consists of three stages:

1. Stress: Imbalance between resources and demands
2. Strain: Immediate, short-term emotional response to this imbalance
3. Defensive coping: Changes in attitude and behavior

It could be said that burnout is a coping mechanism that employs several unproductive measures, such as blaming others, isolating emotions, never being available, and lowering personal goals to avoid the chance of failure. Symptoms of police burnout fall into three principal categories:

1. *Emotional.* This category includes mental fatigue, apathy, and irritability. Police officers who fall within this stage find themselves being restless, highly sensitive, and defensive in nature. They often become insubordinate to superior officers and exhibit varying degrees of paranoia.
2. *Behavioral.* It is an easier task to identify behavioral signs of burnout, such as social isolation and withdrawal. A typical reaction is to resort to alcoholism or substance abuse as an outlet. Other indicators include excessive gambling, promiscuity, spending sprees, deteriorating physical appearance, and poor personal hygiene.[68]
3. *Physical.* It is thought that this stage of burnout can be very dangerous. It occurs when an officer dwells on illness and/or is excessively absent from work. Other indicators include headaches, insomnia, weight gain or loss, vomiting, or diarrhea. These, and more, result from the psychological burdens of stress on the officer.

Clearly, the physical, psychological, and performance-related problems associated with stress create an alarming problem for police administrators. As mentioned, the key to dealing effectively with these problems is early recognition and treatment of them. The attrition rate in policing is already unacceptably high, so managing predictable consequences of the job, such as stress, must be at the top of every chief officer's list of agency priorities.

REDUCING STRESS IN POLICE WORK

It is in the best interest of the officer, the police manager, and the police organization to seek the best ways to detect and treat the problem of stress in the profession. Hurrell and Kroes suggest that methods for reducing stress can been separated into three categories:[69] (1) eliminating the stressors, (2) increasing coping abilities, and (3) offering counseling for stressed officers.

Eliminating the Stressors

Of the three types of methods designed to reduce stress, the identification and elimination of stressors is considered the most effective. Officers on the beat are probably the best source of information regarding what stressors impinge on their work, so an effective way to begin is to assemble a group of officers and discuss their stress-related problems. Once identified, ideas need to be developed on how best to eliminate the sources of stress.[70] It should be noted that this is probably an oversimplified method of dealing with stress, but it is beneficial in getting officers to talk about their problems and understand that others might be experiencing similar difficulties.

Increasing Coping Abilities

It has been said that most people have within them an untapped resource with which to deal with stress. Yet, this resource will remain untapped if the person is unaware of how to utilize himself or herself to the fullest. It is likely that officers should be trained in how to understand their own reactions to various stimuli. For example, because officers interact with the general public on a daily basis, it is important for them to be able to understand how such factors as personality, motivations, cognition, emotion, and fear affect human behavior. This approach helps officers recognize and understand stress awareness and how to improve their interpersonal skills in handling daily conflict situations.

Offering Counseling for Stressed Officers

A third method of reducing stress in police officers is for the police agency to implement a program that offers professional counseling. Both sudden crises and gradual buildups of stress may contribute to the need for professional help. Although most communities have mental health professionals available, it is always a good idea for the individual law enforcement agency to employ a full-time psychologist who can be available when needed. It has even been suggested that law enforcement officers should be afforded free mental health care as a form of compensation for the stress incurred on the job.

For such programs to be successful, it is important for police managers to emphasize to officers the fact that such services are strictly confidential and that they should be able to visit therapists during on-duty hours.

In Retrospect

Modern police work is characterized by a tapestry of duties, responsibilities, and professional obligations. It has been said that the only thing a police officer can predict about his or her job is unpredictability. Police officers must work in an ever-changing environment that often results in serious threats to their safety. In addition to unpredictable tactical situations such as responding to crimes in progress, many insidious threats also exist.

These include stress reactions to diet, shift changes, and pressures of the job, as well as social pressures related to gender, race, and family problems. Together these create a "mortality framework" that may be conducive to adverse occupational reactions. Officers must be aware of the many occupational dangers inherent in their role as public protectors and deal with them successfully to ensure their effectiveness as police officers.

Improve Your Professional Vocabulary

burnout	general adaptation syndrome	operational stress
critical incident stress	internal stress	posttraumatic stress disorder
external stress	job-related stress	

Discussion Questions

1. In what ways can police officers reduce their vulnerability to being killed in the line of duty?
2. What are the various ways in which police mortality is evident?
3. Explain and define the term *stress*.
4. Explain the term *general adaptation syndrome*.
5. List and discuss various factors that may affect the problem of stress in the life of a police officer.
6. Sharon Martin identified three types of male attitudes toward female officers. List and explain them.
7. Why does stress in police officers pose such a serious problem for police agencies?
8. List and explain some of the psychological ramifications of stress in policing.
9. Define and discuss the problem of posttraumatic stress disorder.
10. Define the term *burnout* and discuss how it relates to stress in policing.

Notes

1. Law Enforcement Officers Killed Summary: 2006, FBI, (2007).
2. Ibid.
3. Ibid.
4. Guralnik, L. (1963). Mortality by occupation and cause of death among men 20–64 years of age, 1950. *United States Public Health Service Vital Statistics Special Report,* 3. Washington, DC: U.S. Government Printing Office.
5. Newland, N. A. (1993, November). Line-of-duty deaths: Preparing for the worst. *FBI Law Enforcement Bulletin,* 7–9.
6. Pinizzotto, A. J., & E. F. Davis. (1992, December). Cop killers and their victims. *FBI Law Enforcement Bulletin,* 10.
7. Cowan, A. L. (2008). Suicide bigger threat for police than criminals. *New York Times*; Published: April 8, 2008; Centers for Disease Control website accessed January 7, 2009 (http://www.cdc.gov/ncipc/dvp/Suicide/default.htm).
8. Jones, C., & G. Fields. (1999, June 1). Preventing officers from aiming guns at themselves. *USA Today,* p. 14A.; Also see The National P.O.L.I.C.E. Suicide Foundation, 2008 (http://www.psf.org/ accessed January 9, 2009).
9. Baker, T. E., & J. P. Baker. (1996, October). Preventing police suicide. *FBI Law Enforcement Bulletin.* FBI web site: http://www.fbi.gov/leb/Oct966.txt.
10. The National P.O.L.I.C.E. Suicide Foundation, 2008 (http://www.psf.org/ accessed January 9, 2009). See http://www.drugabuse.gov/DirReports/DirRep298/DirectorRepIndex.html.
11. Jones, C., & G. Fields. (1999, June 1). Preventing officers from aiming guns at themselves. *USA Today,* p. 14A.
12. Volanti, J. M. (1995, February). The mystery within: Understanding police suicide. *FBI Law Enforcement Bulletin,* 19–23.
13. Selye, H. (1973, November/December). The evolution of the stress concept. *American Scientist, 61,* pp. 692–699.
14. Selye, H. (1950). *The physiology and pathology of exposure to stress.* Montreal, Quebec, Canada: ACTA.
15. Balkin, J. (1988, March). Why policemen don't like policewomen. *Journal of Police Science and Administration,* p. 30.
16. Martin, S. E. (1980). *Breaking and entering: Policewomen on patrol.* Berkeley, CA: University of California Press, 79–108.
17. Weisheit, R., & S. Mahan. (1988). *Women, crime and criminal justice.* Cincinnati, OH: Anderson.
18. Daum, J. M. (1994, September). Police work from a woman's perspective. *Police Chief,* 46–49.
19. Ibid.
20. Johnson, K. (1998, December 3). Survey: Women muscled out by bias, harassment. *USA Today,* p. 1A.
21. Ibid.
22. Horn, P. (1980). *Women in law enforcement,* 2nd ed. Springfield, IL: Charles C Thomas.
23. Johnson, K. (1999, November 12). Women not making top police ranks. *USA Today,* p. 14A.
24. Ibid.
25. Wexler, J. G., & D. D. Logan. (1983). Sources of stress among women police officers. *Journal of Police Science Administration, 11,* 46–51.
26. Martin, S. E. (1992). The changing status of women officers. In I. L. Moyer, ed., *The changing roles of women in the criminal justice system.* Prospect Heights, IL: Waveland Press.
27. Remmington, P. W. (1983). Women in the police: Integration or separation. *Qualitative Sociology, 6*(2), 118.

28. Martin, S. E. (1992). The changing status of women officers. In I. L. Moyer, ed., *The changing roles of women in the criminal justice system.* Prospect Heights, IL: Waveland Press.

29. Breece, C., & G. Garrett. (1975). The emerging role of women in law enforcement. In J. Linton, ed., *Police roles in the seventies: Professionalization in America.* Aurora, IL: Social Science and Sociological Research, 13; Koenig, E. J. (1978). An overview of attitudes toward women in law enforcement. *Public Administration Review, 38*(3), 267–275; Milton, C. H. (1978). The future of women in policing. In A. W. Cohen, ed., *The future of policing.* Thousand Oaks, CA: Sage.

30. Weisheit, R., & S. Mahan. (1988). *Women, crime and criminal justice.* Cincinnati, OH: Anderson.

31. Rossi, P. H., et al. (1974). *The roots of urban discontent: Public policy, municipal institutions and the ghetto.* New York: Wiley.

32. Black, D. (1980). *The manners and customs of the police.* San Diego, CA: Academic Press.

33. Cole, G. F. (1998). The *American system of criminal justice*, 5th ed. Pacific Grove, CA: Brooks/Cole, 291.

34. Territo, L., & H. J. Vetter. (1981). Stress and police personnel. *Journal of Police Science and Administration, 9*(2), 195–207.

35. Ibid.

36. See: "http://www.drugabuse.gov/DirReports/DirRep298/DirectorRepIndex.html". See also National Institute on Drug Abuse. (1998, February). *The NIDA director's report to the National Advisory Council on Drug Abuse.* NIDA site. Washington, DC: U.S. Government Printing Office.

37. Ibid.

38. Ibid.

39. Harpold, J. A., & S. L. Feemster. (2002, September). Negative influences of police stress. *FBI Law Enforcement Bulletin,* 1–7.

40. Ibid.

41. Selye, H. (1950). *The physiology and pathology of exposure to stress.* Montreal, Quebec, Canada: ACTA.

42. Selye, H. (1974). *Stress without distress.* Philadelphia: J. B. Lippincott.

43. Hurrell, J. J., & W. H. Kroes. (1975). *Job stress and the police officer: Identifying stress reduction techniques.* Washington, DC: U.S. Government Printing Office.

44. As found in Stratton, J. (1978, April). Police stress: An overview. *Police Chief,* pp. 58–62.

45. Blackmore, J. (1978). Are police allowed to have problems of their own? *Police, 1,* pp. 47–55.

46. Hurrell, J. J., & W. H. Kroes. (1975). *Job stress and the police officer: Identifying stress reduction techniques.* Washington, DC: U.S. Government Printing Office.

47. Wambaugh, Joseph. *The Onion Field.* (New York, NY: Delacorte Press, 1973), 3–4.

48. Hurrell, J. J., & W. H. Kroes. (1975). *Job stress and the police officer: Identifying stress reduction techniques.* Washington, DC: U.S. Government Printing Office.

49. Goolkasian, G. A., R. W. Geddes, & W. DeJong. (1985). Coping with police stress. In *Critical issues in policing: Contemporary readings.* Prospect Heights, IL: Waveland Press.

50. Dietrich, J. F. (1989, November). Helping subordinates face stress. *Police Chief.*

51. Jacoby, J. H. (1975). Reducing police stress: A psychiatrist's point of view. In J. J. Hurrell & W. H. Kroes, eds., *Job stress and the police officer.* Washington, DC: U.S. Government Printing Office.

52. Guralnik, L. (1963). Mortality by occupation and cause of death among men 20–64 years of age, 1950. *United States Public Health Service Vital Statistics Special Report, 3.* Washington, DC: U.S. Government Printing Office.

53. Grencik, J. M. (1973). In Peter Pitchess, ed., The psychological fitness of deputies assigned to the patrol function and its relationship to the formulation of entrance standards for law enforcement officers. *LEAA Final Report.* Washington, DC: U.S. Government Printing Office.

54. Kroes, W. H., B. L. Margolis, & J. J. Hurrell, Jr. (n.d.). *Job stress in policemen: Research paper.* Cincinnati, OH: Behavioral and Motivational Factors Branch, National Institute for Occupational Safety and Health.

55. Finn, P. (1997). *Reducing stress: An organization-centered approach.* FBI Law Enforcement Bulletin, August. FBI website: http://www.fbi.gov/leb/aug975.txt.

56. Penk, W., L. Vasser, & S. Willy. (1981). Post-traumatic stress. In Anderson, et al., eds. (1995), *Stress management for law enforcement officers.* Upper Saddle River, NJ: Prentice Hall.

57. Inciardi, J. (1990). *Criminal justice,* 3rd ed. Orlando, FL: Harcourt, Brace.

58. Helzer, J., L. Robins, & L. McEvoy. (1987, December). Posttraumatic stress disorder in the general population. *New England Journal of Medicine,* 1630–1634.

59. Solomon, R. M. (1988, October). Post-shooting trauma. *Police Chief,* pp. 40–41.

60. Goolkasian, G. A., R. W. Geddes, & W. DeJong. (1985). Coping with police stress. In *Critical issues in policing: Contemporary readings.* Prospect Heights, IL: Waveland Press.

61. Mantell, M. R. (1989, February). Study of the San Ysidro massacre. *Police Chief.*

62. Territo, L., & H. J. Vetter. (1981). Stress and police personnel. *Journal of Police Science and Administration, 9*(2), 195–207.

63. Pierson, T. (1989, February). Critical incident stress: A serious law enforcement problem. *Police Chief, 56*(2), 32–33.

64. Solomon, R. M., & J. M. Horn. (1986). Post-shooting traumatic reactions: A pilot study. In J. T. Reese & H. A. Goldstein, eds., *Psychological services for law enforcement.* Washington, DC: U.S. Department of Justice, Federal Bureau of Investigation, 333–393.

65. Sewell, J. D. (1983). The development of a critical life events scale for law enforcement. *Journal of Police Science and Administration, 11*(1), 109–116.

66. Cherniss, C. (1980). *Staff burnout.* Thousand Oaks, CA: Sage.

67. Reese, J. T. (1982, June). Life in the high-speed lane: Managing police burnout. *Police Chief, 49*(6), pp. 49–53.

68. Ibid.

69. Hurrell, J. J., & W. H. Kroes. (1975). *Job stress and the police officer: Identifying stress reduction techniques.* Washington, DC: U.S. Government Printing Office.

70. Ibid.

CHAPTER | **14**

Current Challenges
and Future Directions

This chapter will enable you to:

- Realize the extent of emerging technology on police work.
- Understand the social concerns of future technology on police work.
- Understand how mobile communications will affect future policing efforts.
- Realize the possible impact of information management on crime and criminality.

- Understand constitutional concerns relating to the development of new crime-fighting technologies.
- Recognize the different types of terrorism and what trends to expect in the next decade.

In May 2002, David L. Smith of New Jersey was sentenced to 20 months in federal prison and fined $5,000 for creating Melissa, a computer virus that caused $80,000,000 in damages to computer networks and businesses in 1999. Smith was also liable for state fines in excess of $150,000.

Smith created the Melissa virus and disseminated it from his home computer through e-mail. The virus appeared on thousands of e-mail systems on March 26, 1999, disguised as an important message from a colleague or friend. It sent an infected e-mail to the first 50 e-mail addresses on users' e-mail lists, outdating antivirus software and infecting computers using Windows operating systems and other Microsoft programs. The Melissa virus was able to spread very quickly by overloading e-mail servers, which resulted in the shutdown of networks and significant costs to repair or cleanse computer systems.

In state and federal court, Smith described how he, using a stolen America Online account in his own account with a local Internet service provider (ISP), posted an infected document on the Internet newsgroup Alt.sex. The posting contained a message that enticed readers to download and open the document with the hope of finding passwords to adult content websites; it read, "Here is that document you asked for . . . don't show anyone else ;-)."

Downloading and opening the message caused the Melissa virus to infect the victim computers. The virus altered Microsoft word-processing programs such that any document created using the programs would then be infected with the Melissa virus. The virus also lowered macro security settings in the word-processing programs.[1]

The story of David Smith and his Melissa computer virus is instructive in that it shows us the manner in which computer crimes can be committed. While this chapter is concerned with current issues and future developments in the area of policing, it will also focus on technology advancements for modern police.

To many people, the task of foreseeing future events should be left up to fortune-tellers and science-fiction writers. As difficult as it is to predict future events and developments, it is strategically important to at least attempt to do so in order to anticipate crime trends and community needs. Successfully anticipating trends and developments in policing will benefit many different constituencies throughout a community and the criminal justice system. Specifically, police managers must have the ability to predict crime trends in order to request resources such as new equipment, additional personnel, and specialized training.

Police officers are in need of information regarding trends in policing to better plan their careers and to anticipate problems that may be new to the community and therefore require special attention. City planners and their state and federal counterparts will benefit from understanding future trends to be better able to anticipate budgetary, personnel, and policy changes that might be required. People in virtually every component of the criminal justice system rely on their ability to predict crime trends and changes in technology and public sentiment to facilitate the timely movement of offenders through the system.

The general public perhaps has the greatest curiosity about what crime trends are on the future's horizon for two important reasons. First, technological developments are of interest to the average citizen because of the financial support required in adopting certain technologies. Second, great concern exists regarding the impact that new technology might have on personal freedoms enjoyed by the citizenry.

Some experts predict that the criminal justice system of the future will closely resemble the system we know today. Police work will still be driven by constitutional mandates and will respond to case law and court precedents. Police will continue to work in conjunction with the courts, correctional system, and juvenile justice system. Although new issues will emerge, they will be dealt with under the larger premise of how to protect society as a whole while ensuring individual constitutional freedoms. The dynamics of just how this will be accomplished will hinge on the social philosophies of the dominant political party. Perhaps one of the greatest changes will be the evolving demographics of our neighborhoods and communities. Police departments are challenged to strive to reflect their own personnel and the community in which they serve. In doing so, the public will feel more a part of their police department, and vice versa, resulting in greater understanding of community needs.

Many such issues of past decades are unresolved and continue to plague society today. However, there exist new and uncharted areas of crime control that may also generate considerable concern. One such area is the field of molecular biology, the study of the genetic and chemical basis for human behavior and identification techniques through the use of body fluids. Some experts have predicted that ultimately such studies may become the basis for behavior modification or control in treating criminals and violent offenders. In 1998 scientists made headlines across the globe by cloning a sheep. While cloning is another new and uncharted field, questions of scientific ethics and the possibility of criminal pursuits must be considered and debated. Whether traditional or futuristic, it is clear that certain issues are more likely to present greater concerns than others. This chapter is dedicated to discussing some of the more significant issues confronting us in the twenty-first century as they relate to current and emerging technological advances.

THE POLICE AND TECHNOLOGY

The field of police work has long made use of technological developments. As we learned in Chapter 2, police departments adopted the use of automobiles and radios in order to increase the effectiveness of their patrols, including better response time to crimes in progress and emergencies.

Would-be technology affected the investigation of crime as early as 1911, when fingerprint evidence was first used to convict offenders.

Today, police officers seek to collect fingerprints, fibers, blood, fluids, and materials to be analyzed through forensic methods in order to identify and convict criminal offenders. Police officers also use polygraphs, the technical name for "lie detectors," which measure a suspect's heart rate and other physical responses as he or she responds to questions. Although polygraph results are typically not admissible as evidence, police officers have often used these examinations on willing suspects and witnesses as a basis for excluding some suspects or for pressuring others to confess. More recently, a new deception-detection device has been employed for the same purposes; the voice stress analyzer. This device consists of specially designed lie-detection software installed on a laptop computer that gives the criminal investigator a computer readout of the stress in a suspect's voice as he or she is questioned.

Several issues arise as police adopt new technologies. First, questions about the accuracy and effectiveness of technological developments persist, even though the developments were originally embraced with great confidence. For example, despite the historic use of fingerprint evidence in court by police and prosecutors, the accuracy of such evidence has been questioned. In 2002, a federal judge ruled that expert witnesses could compare crime-scene fingerprints with those of a defendant, but they could not testify that the prints definitely matched. The judge pointed out that, unlike DNA evidence, fingerprint-evidence processes have not been scientifically verified, the error rate for such identifications has never been measured, and there are no scientific standards for determining when fingerprint samples "match." Prosecutors later persuaded the judge to reverse his original decision and admit the expert testimony about a fingerprint match, but the judge's first decision raises the possibility that other judges will scrutinize fingerprint evidence more closely.

Second, some worry that new technologies will create new threats to citizens' constitutional rights. As police gain greater opportunities for sophisticated electronic surveillance, for example, new questions arise about what constitutes a "search" that violates citizens' reasonable expectations of privacy. The development of technology for the interception of e-mail messages by law enforcement agencies provides an illustration of new situations that were not foreseeable in prior decades.

Tools for Investigation

One of the most rapidly spreading technological tools for law enforcement officers is the computer, especially portable computers in patrol cars. Computers provide for instant electronic communication, which permits the radio airwaves to be reserved for emergency calls rather than for requests to check license numbers and other routine matters. Computers also give officers quick access to databases and other information sources that help identify suspects. Depending on the software used and the organization of databases, many officers can make a quick check of individuals' criminal histories, driving records, and outstanding warrants.

With more advanced computers and software, some officers can even receive mug shots and fingerprint records on their computer screens. Advances in technology provide a variety of possibilities for improving officers' abilities to evaluate evidence at the scene of an event. With mobile scanners, officers can potentially run a quick check of an individual's fingerprints against the millions of fingerprint records stored in the FBI's database. The Seal Beach, California, Police Department has worked with high-tech companies to develop streaming video capabilities that can permit officers to view live video from crime-scene cameras as they approach the location of an incident. For example, if officers can tune their computers to the surveillance cameras that are standard features of banks and convenience stores, they can see the details of an unfolding robbery in progress as they approach the scene of an emergency call. Thus, technology can improve the safety and effectiveness of police officers, especially in their crime-fighting role.

Advances in mobile computer technology raise questions about the development of law enforcement databases. The FBI has developed a significant database of fingerprints. Today, a

FIGURE 14.1 Modern-day police officers rely heavily on technology such as video surveillance to spot and document persons suspected of criminal activity.

national database of DNA records is operational, although some questions remain about which offenders should be required to submit samples. Local police departments may have **crime-mapping** databases that provide updated information about crime trends, especially the locations of recent criminal events. As police officers sought the sniper who terrorized Washington, D.C., in October 2002, new debates emerged about whether there should be a national database of ballistic evidence. Advocates argued that every gun sold should undergo a firing test so that its ballistic "fingerprint" could be stored in the database, just in case the weapon was later used in a crime.

Opponents claimed that this would be an undesirable step toward national gun registration and that such a database would be useless because the ballistic characteristics of a gun's fired bullets change as the gun is used over time. The usefulness of these databases depends on the accuracy of technology to match evidence with stored information and the accessibility of database information to police departments and individual officers. In addition, as indicated by the debate about ballistic evidence, the nature and use of evidence databases will be affected by public policy debates about what information can be gathered and how it will be used.

Computers have become especially important for investigating specific types of crimes, especially cybercrimes, which are crimes based on computer activity. Many police departments have begun to train and use personnel to investigate people who use computers to meet children online in order to lure them into exploitive relationships. Computer investigations also involve pursuing people who commit identity theft, steal credit card numbers, and engage in fraudulent financial transactions using computers.

Police have begun using surveillance cameras in many ways. American cities increasingly use surveillance cameras at intersections to monitor and ticket people who run red lights or exceed speed limits. In Scotland, England, and Australia, law enforcement officials have adopted the use of surveillance cameras that permit police to monitor activities that occur in downtown commercial areas or other selected locations. Officials in a control room can watch everyone who passes within the camera's fields of exposure. Advances in camera technology can enable these officials to see clearly the license plate numbers of cars and other specific information. American cities such as

New York and Washington, DC have considered experimenting with this approach to fight crime in specific areas. However, civil libertarians complained that constant surveillance by government intrudes on the privacy of innocent, unsuspecting citizens and that there is insufficient evidence that this surveillance leads to reduced crime rates. There are also allegations in some British cities that bored officers in the control booth spend their time engaged monitoring attractive women and ignore or hide evidence of police misconduct that is caught on camera.

Many American law enforcement officials have experimented with other surveillance and detection technologies. The National Institute of Justice is providing funding to help scientists develop devices that will assist the police. For example, scanners are being developed that will permit officers to detect whether individuals are carrying weapons, bombs, or drugs. Some of these devices detect foreign masses hidden on the human body, and others detect trace particles and vapors that are different from those associated with human bodies and clothing.

Such scanners are used at airports, prisons, schools, and stadiums. However, officers on the streets will eventually need to use smaller, more mobile versions, especially if a handheld device should be pointed at an individual passerby to detect whether that person is carrying weapons or contraband.

At the 2001 Super Bowl, police officers used a surveillance system with **facial-recognition technology** in an attempt to identify people being sought on outstanding warrants. The police claimed that the cameras and facial-recognition software permitted them to identify 19 people wanted for crimes. Casinos in Atlantic City also use facial-recognition technology with surveillance cameras to identify people whom they know to be skilled at cheating. Conceivably, the system could also be used at airports to identify terrorists attempting to enter the country.

This technology poses problems, however. It cannot identify faces and match them with database pictures quickly enough to prevent suspects from disappearing into a crowd, thus requiring officers to search for them. Additionally, questions persist about the accuracy of facial-recognition technology. According to one researcher who has tested some systems, "one of every 50 people looks like Carlos the Jackal [the infamous terrorist], and the real Carlos the Jackal has only a 50 percent chance of looking like himself."[2]

Researchers claim that **iris-recognition technology**, which examines the interior of the eye and matches its unique characteristics with information in the database, is much more accurate than facial-recognition technology or technologies that attempt to match voices, fingerprints, or the palm of the hand. Such iris-recognition technology was employed throughout the fictional, futuristic world in the Steven Spielberg film *Minority Report*. It is not clear, however, that such technology could be developed for use in police surveillance. Furthermore, iris-recognition technology would require the development of an entirely new type of database containing records of people's eyes. As with other developing technologies, significant questions arise about the costs of developing and producing new scientific devices for wide distribution. Even if the scientific community develops new technologies that might benefit policing, the expense of implementing these devices may be far more than individual cities and counties can afford.

Recently, the U.S. Supreme Court has indicated that it will look critically at some new police technologies. In the case of *Kyllo* v. *United States* (2001), law enforcement officials pointed a **thermal imaging** device at a house to detect unusual heat sources that might indicate marijuana being cultivated under "grow lights." Their efforts led to a search of a home and the discovery of 100 marijuana plants. In the minority opinion, Justice Scalia declared the use of the device in this matter to be an illegal search. According to Scalia, "Obtaining by a sense-enhancing technology any information regarding the interior of the home that could not otherwise be obtained without physical intrusion into a constitutionally protected area constitutes a search" and is, therefore, covered by the limitations of the Fourth Amendment—especially the warrant requirement. Thus, it is not clear how judges will evaluate the constitutionally permissible uses of new technologies.

Scientists are working to develop technology to detect deceptions that suspects might use when questioned by the police. Polygraph tests are considered unreliable, because some people may be very calm when they lie, and thereby avoid detection, whereas some other people may be very nervous when being asked questions. Thus, truthful people may look like liars on a polygraph test if their palms sweat and their heart rates increase as they answer. One approach to investigation is the use of a thermal imaging camera that can detect blushing in the faces of people who answer questions in an untruthful manner. Critics warn, however, that this technology may simply reproduce the problems with polygraphs by looking only at physical responses, which vary by individual.

An alternative technology detects people's brain-wave responses to words and images. The suspect wears an electronic headband while being shown words or images flashed on a screen. If the suspect shows a brain-wave response to words or pictures that would be familiar only to the witness or perpetrator of a crime, then law enforcement officials might be able to move forward with an investigation that ultimately solves the crime.

Weapons Technology

As we learned in Chapter 7, police officers have been sued in many cases when they injured or killed people without proper justification. Some of these lawsuits have resulted in cities and counties paying millions of dollars to people who were injured when police used guns or nightsticks improperly or in an inappropriate situation. To avoid future lawsuits, departments have given greater attention to the training of officers. They have also sought alternative nonlethal weapons that could be used to incapacitate or control people without causing serious injuries or deaths. Traditional nonlethal weapons, such as nightsticks and pepper spray, can be used only when officers are in close contact with suspects, and they are not suitable for all situations an officer faces.

Police officers need to have the ability to incapacitate agitated people who are threatening to harm themselves or others. This need arises when they confront someone suspected of committing a serious crime as well as when they are attempting to control a crowd causing civil disorder. They also seek to enhance their ability to stop criminal suspects from fleeing. A variety of nonlethal weapons have been developed to accomplish these goals. Police use some of the weapons widely, whereas other weapons are still undergoing testing and refinement.

Projectile weapons shoot objects at people the police wish to subdue. Some nonlethal projectiles, such as **rubber bullets**, can travel a long distance. Others are employed only when the suspects are within a few yards of the officers. Rubber bullets have been used for many years. Although they are generally nonlethal, they can cause serious injuries if they hit someone in the eye or elsewhere in the head. Many departments have turned to the use of **beanbags**, small canvas bags containing tiny lead beads that are fired from a shotgun. They are intended to stun people upon impact without causing lasting injury. Several police departments in the Los Angeles area, however, have abandoned the use of beanbags because of concerns about injuries and a few deaths caused by these projectiles as well as dissatisfaction with their accuracy when fired at a target.

Other departments have begun to use air guns that shoot **pepperballs**, small plastic pellets that are filled with a peppery powder that causes coughing and sneezing upon release after the suspect is stunned by the impact of the pellet. Officers can also fill the pellets with green dye in order to mark and later arrest individuals in an out-of-control crowd. For suspects who are close at hand, many police departments use the **Taser**, a weapon with prongs that sends an incapacitating electric jolt to people upon contact. Other weapons under development either shoot nets that can wrap around individual suspects or spray a fountain of foam that covers the suspect in layers of paralyzing ooze.

The development of new, nonlethal weapons has undoubtedly saved officers from firing bullets in many situations in which they previously would have felt required to shoot threatening suspects. However, as with all technologies, these weapons do not magically solve the problem of incapacitating suspects safely. Mechanical problems or misuse by officers may make the new weapons ineffectual. In addition, officers may act too quickly in firing a nonlethal weapon in situations where patient communication and persuasion might have been more appropriate. In such situations, needless minor injuries may be inflicted, or the targeted person may become more enraged and thus more threatening to the officers who later must transport the person to jail. Moreover, there is a limited number of weapons that an officer can carry in his or her arms. The existence of nonlethal weapons will not ensure that such weapons are actually handy when officers must make difficult, on-the-spot decisions about how to handle a threatening situation.

Mobile Communications

In the earliest days of policing, before automobiles and two-way radios, watchmen walked their beats with virtually no way of communicating with headquarters or other officers for assistance. Soon the call box was developed, which consisted of a signaling lever that indicated the presence of an officer at his prescribed post. In 1880, telephones were put in call boxes and provided for two-way communication between the officer and the station house. By the early twentieth century, police cars and radios once again revolutionized the capabilities of police officers to cover a substantially larger beat, increase the frequency of patrol, and respond quickly to calls for assistance. In addition to automobiles, police departments today use motorcycles, jet skis, bicycles, airplanes, and helicopters.

Not only are walkie-talkies and car radios commonly used, but also are cellular telephones, paging devices, and even in-car computer terminals, which enable officers to query license registrations and criminal histories. The negative side of the technological revolution is that although such devices enhance police apprehension capabilities, they also enhance the criminal's ability to avoid detection. In particular with regard to drug traffickers, mobile phones, pagers, computer bulletin boards, and an array of other sophisticated technology have been seized by drug enforcement officials over the past decade. As new technology is developed and as criminals use that technology in their illicit enterprises, police agencies must have the resources to understand and counter such capabilities quickly.

POLICE ELECTRONIC SURVEILLANCE

The capabilities of police to conduct surveillance have been greatly enhanced by new electronic technologies, such as imaging technology, computers, remote sensing, and related advancements. The task of electronic surveillance includes both sensing techniques and the ability to aggregate computerized records on suspected criminal activity. Although many different types of surveillance techniques are employed by police agencies, the most common is the wiretap. Although wiretapping has been a source of controversy for over 65 years, the Supreme Court finally ruled in 1967 that wiretapping was a breach of the Fourth Amendment and that it may be unreasonable if the subjects have a **reasonable expectation of privacy** in the area or in the activity under surveillance (*Katz* v. *United States*, 1967).

Electronic Surveillance Technologies Used by State and Federal Police Agencies

- Closed-circuit television
- Light vision systems and image intensifiers
- Parabolic microphones
- Miniature transmitters
- Electronic beepers
- Telephone taps and recorders
- Pen registers
- Computer usage monitors
- Electronic mail monitors
- Cellular radio interception
- Satellite beam interception
- Pattern recognition systems
- Intruder detector systems that identify vibrations, ultrasound, and infrared radiation

Today, wiretapping by police organizations can be done only under certain procedural safeguards set out in Title III of the 1968 Omnibus Crime Control Act. Under this law, wire tapping of conversations is prohibited except under court order or when consented to by one party involved in the conversation. Court orders must be requested by high-level prosecutors and be related to one of several specific crimes outlined under law. In addition, court orders must be based on probable cause that a specific person who is the target of the surveillance has committed the offense. Many states have passed their own wiretap legislation, which is often modeled after the federal act. This authorizes state and local officers to conduct wiretaps provided that they meet a specific set of legal criteria.

In 1998, public attention was drawn to the subject of police electronic surveillance when a federal judge in Boston scrutinized the legality of a number of FBI wiretaps. The cases included a Mafia initiation ceremony involving the Raymond "Junior" Patriarca crime organization that resulted in the arrests of 21 defendants and wiretaps involving convicted New York Gambino family boss John Gotti, who was convicted of murder and racketeering in 1993. Under federal law, a wiretap must be the last resort for investigators, and the judge had concerns that all other investigative leads had not yet been exhausted at the time of the wiretaps.[3] Of course, any time a judge rules a wiretap illegal, any defendants convicted from that evidence would have grounds for appeal and may possibly be freed.

Carnivore: The Internet "Sniffer"

With the increased use of computers and the Internet, police have observed the increasing exploitation of computers, networks, and databases to commit crimes. Criminals have been using computers to send child pornography to each other using anonymous, encrypted communications; hackers have broken into financial service companies' systems and stolen customer home addresses and credit card information; criminals use the Internet's inexpensive and easy communications to commit large-scale fraud on victims all over the world; and terrorist bombers have planned their strikes using the Internet.

Investigating and deterring such wrongdoing requires tools and techniques designed to work with new evolving computers and network technologies. The systems employed must strike a reasonable balance among competing interests—the privacy interests of telecommunications users, the business interests of service providers, and the duty of government investigators to protect public safety.

In response to a critical need for tools to implement complex court orders, the FBI developed a software program called "Carnivore." **Carnivore** is a very specialized network analyzer or "sniffer" that runs as an application program on a normal personal computer under the Microsoft Windows operating system. It works by "sniffing" the proper portions of network packets and copying and storing only those packets that match a finely defined filter set, programmed in conformity with the federal court order. This filter set can be extremely complex, providing the FBI with an ability to collect transmissions that comply with "pen register" court orders, "trap and trace" court orders, "Title III" interception orders, and so on.[4]

Carnivore is a small-scale device intended for use only when and where it is needed. In fact, each Carnivore device is maintained at the FBI Laboratory in Quantico, Virginia, until it is actually needed in an active case. It is then deployed to satisfy the needs of a single case or court order. Upon expiration of the order, the device is removed and returned to Quantico.

CONCERNS ABOUT CARNIVORE   While Carnivore was sold to the public as a crime-fighting tool, by mid-2000 it fell under considerable criticism by the media. Beginning with an article published in the *Wall Street Journal,* critics argued that the FBI was able to surveil almost anyone's e-mail without seeking legal authorization to do so. Furthermore, there were charges, that the FBI fought in court, to keep Carnivore information secret from the public, and that any documents released by the FBI were heavily edited. Still, another concern was that even the simplest encryption programs can undermine Carnivore's capabilities. In fact, according to an independent report issued by the Illinois Institute of Technology Research Institute (IITRI), free encryption software available over the Internet can make Internet communications unreadable to Carnivore, and thus many of the largest, most technically sophisticated ISPs are immune to Carnivore.

By late 2000 the FBI responded to privacy and technological concerns about Carnivore. In a letter to the editor of *USA Today*, John E. Collingwood, assistant director of the FBI, defended the use of the computer software by claiming it represents technology that can be more effective in protecting privacy and enabling lawful surveillance than can alternatives.[5]

- The supervising judge can, and does, independently verify that traffic collected is only what was legally authorized.
- Operating Carnivore introduces no operational or security risks to the ISP network where it is installed.
- Properly configured, Carnivore accumulates no data other than that which passes its filters, and it restricts data available to the FBI to specific types from or to specific users.

Carnivore does not read all incoming and outgoing e-mail messages and does not have nearly enough power to spy on almost everyone with an e-mail account.

Concerns over government surveillance capabilities have continued into the twenty-first century. Whether it be the federal government or local and state police agencies, the public has an ongoing concern about the capabilities of government to surveil private communications. However, with growing technology and the abilities of criminal elements to make use of such technologies, the

---

A Closer Look

Surveillance Technology at the Borders

During the spring of 2009, U.S. agents along the Canadian and Mexican borders began using a controversial machine that is designed to "read" the personal information contained in some government-issued ID cards—such as passports and driver's licenses—as travelers approach a checkpoint. The Homeland Security Department says the new practice will tighten security and speed the flow of traffic. Privacy advocates are concerned that the technology could make Americans less secure because terrorists or other criminals may be able to steal the personal information off of the ID cards remotely. The concern is that the cards are vulnerable to being cloned or having their codes broken.

Machines are in place at five crossings: Blaine, Washington; Buffalo; Detroit, Novalis, Arizona; and since C. Grove, California. The federal government requires that anyone who crosses the border must show a passport or another government documents proving citizenship and identity.

The technology is being used in conjunction with new government passports, pass cards and driver's licenses embedded with computer chips that contain the holder's name, date of birth, nationality, passport or ID number and a digitized photo. The personal data can be "read" via a radio frequency identification machine as the person approaches a border crossing checkpoint. By the time a car stops at the customs booth, the agent will have the photos and information of everyone in the car. If a name is on a watch list or database, the person will be questioned.

Privacy advocates argue that terrorists or other criminals can use their own machines in a process called "skimming" to read the information from as far as 50 feet. They argue that the chips create the potential for a whole surveillance network to be set up. For example, police could use the chips to find criminals, abusive husbands to fund their wives, and stores to track customers.

The Department of Homeland Security defends the use of the chips in that personal information is not revealed to machine readers—just the code, that then shows the information on the border agents' screens. The cards also come with protective sleeves for when they are not in use.

Thematic Question

While we are all aware that border protection is a high priority of the U.S. government, where should the line be drawn as far as government surveillance of its citizens—absent an immediate threat to national security?

Source: http://www.dhs.gov/index.shtm (accessed January 4, 2009).

police are obligated to identify constitutionally acceptable ways in which such criminal activities can be identified and controlled.

Data Mining

Of the many questions that presented themselves in the aftermath of the September 11, 2001 terrorist attacks on New York City and Washington DC, many people were asking the question, "What would've happened if the FBI and the Central Intelligence Agency (CIA) had shared information about possible terrorists residing in the United States?" If Zacarias Moussaoui's computer would have been searched, what would we have learned? Raising particular concern are two messages intercepted by the National Security Agency (NSA) from pay phones at al-Qaeda-controlled Pakistan on September 10, 2001. The messages read, "The match begins tomorrow" and "tomorrow is zero hour."

The messages were not translated until September 12. However, given the CIA's knowledge that the two hijackers were in the United States and had previously been linked to al-Qaeda, the messages could conceivably have been an important piece of intelligence. They could have prompted the agency to make computerized cross-references of the two men's records—credit card accounts, frequent flyer programs, cell phone calls, etc. By "connecting the dots" the CIA may have noticed that these two individuals and 17 others who had been in close contact with each other were flying on the same day at the same time on four different airplanes.[6]

The practice of "connecting the dots" is called **data mining**. It is a technique that uses information technology to determine patterns and links in existing data to predict behavior. In the corporate world, businesses have long used data mining to anticipate future buying patterns by consumers based on their past purchases. The technique has a shorter history in law enforcement, but improved data mining software holds great promise for the future of crime fighting.

While data mining has been used in many areas of crime fighting, the technology's greatest potential seems to be counterterrorism. FBI computers are continuously tracking and cross-checking vast quantities of private information on terrorism suspects: e-mails, Internet chat rooms, instant messages, and telephone conversations. The law permits the FBI to obtain the records of credit card companies, telephone companies, businesses, hospitals, ISPs, and educational institutions when such records are needed for international terrorism investigation.[7]

The way this information is obtained is by **national security letter (NSL)**. For example, if the FBI suspects a particular terror suspect has been using the Internet, it can send an NSL to an ISP requesting data on that suspect's e-mails, websites visited, and other personal records. NSLs may be used only in conjunction with "international terrorism cases," meaning that they are unavailable for other criminal investigations. Because they do not require the approval of a judge, the NSLs have proven to be an invaluable investigative tool for federal agents.

The NSL is a powerful investigative tool because it does not require judicial oversight. As such, possibilities exist for abuse of this investigative method. For example, in 2007, suspicions of government abuse of expanded data-gathering capabilities were confirmed. The FBI admitted it had exceeded its authority with regard to NSLs. Based on FBI records, it violated the rules of NSL use more than 1,000 times between 2000 and 2007. Among its transgressions, the FBI issued NSLs a part of investigations that were not connected to international terrorism, made false allegations on many of the documents, and improperly obtained educational records from a North Carolina university. In addition, the FBI obtained billing records and subscriber information from telephone companies without even issuing NSLs as required by law.

Once the scandal became known, FBI Director Robert Mueller III said abuses were the result of honest mistakes rather than intentional circumvention of the law.[8] That explanation did not sit well with members of Congress. In a congressional hearing, Senator Pat Leahy, a Democrat from Vermont, asked Mueller, "What kind of management failures made it possible for the FBI to send out hundreds of [NSL's] containing significant false statements?" Leahy threatened a reexamination of the "broad authorities we've granted to the FBI" under the USA PATRIOT Act.[9]

Scanning Technology

Recent technology advances in the design of microchips are being put to work in devices that verify the identity of persons seeking access to controlled or sensitive data or to secured areas. Such devices include an apparatus that reads fingerprints and palm prints as well as voice and retinal blood vessel patterns. One such device that has been commercially successful is one that reads hand geometry (the length, curvature, and webbing between the fingers). Data from hand geometry can be stored on a special computer card or in the memory of a microcomputer attached to the machine. Such devices are currently being used in nuclear facilities, government installations, automatic teller machines, and even in the cafeteria of a large university.

A system for analyzing handwriting by computer is currently under development and would have the capability to analyze a signature using a variety of characteristics, such as speed, pressure, and conformation, and compare it with the authorized signature on file. The commercial business world can also benefit from this technology in the areas of banking and credit card use. Although scanning technology is intended for use by businesses where the security of access is concerned, it is hard to say just how such technology will be applied to the field of criminal investigation and policing.

CRIME AND THE INFORMATION BOOM

There are those who predict that computer crime and crimes committed across the Internet will become law enforcement's biggest problem in the future. The statistics supporting the potential for criminal behavior with computers is staggering. At the end of 1996, it was estimated that there were more than 13 million host computers dedicated to Internet connectivity. There are an estimated 1 billion computer users with Internet access.[10] Virtually every **white-collar crime** has a computer or telecommunications link. Given the expanse of computer networks, even small crimes can have big payoffs. *Salami slicing*, for example, involves a thief who regularly makes electronic transfers of small change from thousands of accounts to his own. Most people don't balance their ledger to the penny, so the thief does well for himself or herself.

A more targeted approach involves stealing industrial secrets and passwords. Stealing and reselling long-distance calling codes is also big business. When people are billed monthly, thieves can make thousands of dollars because the victim doesn't find out until it is too late. Drug dealers launder their proceeds through cyberspace and commonly use the Internet to relay messages. Terrorists realize that computers are the nerve centers for the world's financial transactions and communications systems. Authorities are on guard about the possibility that terrorist hackers will tap into Fedwire, the Federal Reserve's electronic funds-transfer system, or vital telephone switching stations.

Child-pornography criminals often make use of the Internet to provide leads and images. Police investigators are now being trained in how to analyze evidence, track credit card fraud, and apply constitutional search-and-seizure techniques when they find evidence of crime on computer bulletin board systems. Indeed, computers pose special problems for police because investigations rely so heavily on paper trails, and in cyberspace, there aren't any. Police are finding that when they begin inquiries for crime in cyberspace, they face an unfriendly environment. Cyberspace, especially the Internet, involves thousands of people who embrace the notion of a culture that is hostile to authority and fearful of what could appear to be an intrusion by police or government agencies. Possibly the clash between computer technocrats and police could be attributed to the inexperience of the latter.

It is clear that keeping up with cybercriminals is one of the greatest challenges facing police. Budgets will be strained while pressures will be placed on long-protected notions of privacy, property, and limits of free speech. Indeed, the rights of many will be at stake.

INVASIONS OF PRIVACY

In this day and age, one's chances of finding work, getting a mortgage, or qualifying for health insurance may become anyone's business because almost anyone with a computer, modem, and telephone can search through cyberspace and locate the most private of personal information on almost anybody. A reasonably accurate profile of one's financial status and credit card history can be gleaned from zip codes, Social Security numbers, and records of credit card use. As commercial transactions increase through online services, more information will be available to strangers. This raises one of the most pressing issues for average Americans, as personal information acquired through commercial transactions will routinely be sold to marketers. This can be a problem for many people for many reasons. For example, suppose that sales data from an adult novelty store became available to police. Could such information be cataloged and possibly keep someone from getting a job as a policeman later? The question arises: Who is the rightful owner of the information? Other interesting questions present themselves: What if incorrect and harmful information seeps into personal databases? How can this be controlled, and by whom? How can perpetrators be caught and punished?

Encrypting Data

Today, police are becoming increasingly concerned about criminals who use cryptography to send and receive uncrackable secret communications. Some criminal investigations would no doubt be halted in their tracks, and expertise in cryptography will rapidly become available to all criminals. But cryptography might become necessary to conduct legitimate business in order to protect corporate assets. Would it be possible or realistic somehow to permit legitimate businesses to use the technology while keeping it away from criminals? It isn't likely, since encryption is necessary for e-mail, commonly used by tens of millions of people daily. Without encryption, e-mail messages would virtually be an open book for the cyberworld to see. Police are challenged with the increasing use of encryption because they need to constantly learn new ways to break the codes. The FBI won a small battle in 1996 when Congress passed the Digital Telephone Act, which allows future communications systems to be accessible to wiretaps.

Yet another facet of information technology will be a great concern to police of the twenty-first century—**anonymous re-mailers**. These are free e-mail-forwarding sites in Europe and elsewhere that can convert return addresses to pseudonyms and render e-mail untraceable. Anonymity is crucial for whistleblowers and people expressing unpopular views against repressive governments, but it raises other problems. Anonymous re-mailers, outside the jurisdiction of U.S. police, are being used by electronic vandals to threaten victims or send **mail bombs**, which are composed of thousands of gibberish messages. They are used either to clog a person's e-mail box or to jam his or her computer system. Even if legislation were passed to curb the spread of cryptography, it would be difficult, if not impossible, to enforce.[11] Cryptography may become even more popular once digital cash, the equivalent of real money exchanged via computer, is developed.

One of the more disturbing realities of the computer age is that people bound by hate and racism are no longer separated by time and space. Frustrations can be shared daily through computerized meetings, increasing the incidence of hate crimes. Perhaps the best example of problems policing cyberspace is in the difficulty of policing pornography on the Internet. In 1996, a Memphis, Tennessee, jury convicted a couple in Milpitas, California, of violating obscenity laws. A federal postal inspector downloaded pornographic pictures via computer modem from the couple's California-based bulletin board. The Memphis jury decided that the couple violated a number of local community standards. At that time, there were no easy solutions for cyberspace problems because the First Amendment, which was designed to protect offensive speech, is a double-edged sword. On one hand, the Internet encourages debate and healthy discussion, but it also allows everyone a platform. At first, many people tended to embrace it, but then a certain degree of fear became present. The question is: How should we respond to that fear?

A Closer Look

Legal Safeguards for Federal Electronic Surveillance

The FBI performs interceptions of criminal wire and electronic communications, including Internet communications, under authorities derived from Title III of the Omnibus Crime Control and Safe Streets Act of 1968, commonly referred to as "Title III," and portions of the Electronic Communications Privacy Act of 1986, or "ECPA." Such federal government interceptions, with the exception of a rarely used "emergency" authority or in cases involving the consent of a participant in the communication, are conducted pursuant to court orders. Under emergency provisions, the attorney general, the deputy, or the associate attorney general may, if authorized, initiate electronic surveillance of wire or electronic communications without a court order, but only if an application for such order is made within 48 hours after the surveillance is initiated.

Federal surveillance laws apply the Fourth Amendment's dictates concerning reasonable searches and seizures and include a number of additional provisions that ensure that this investigative technique is used judiciously, with deference to the privacy of intercepted subjects and with deference to the privacy of those who are not the subject of the court order.

For example, unlike search warrants for physically searching a house, under Title III, applications for interception of wire and electronic communications require the authorization of a high-level Department of Justice (DOJ) official before the local U.S. Attorney's Office can make an application to a federal court. Unlike typical search warrants, federal magistrates are not authorized to approve such applications and orders; instead, the applications are viewed by federal district court judges. Further, interception of communications is limited to certain specified federal felony offenses.

Applications for electronic surveillance must demonstrate probable cause and state with particularity and specificity the offenses being committed, the telecommunications facility or place from which the subject's communications are to be intercepted, a description of the type of conversations to be intercepted, and the identities of the persons committing the offenses and anticipated to be intercepted. Thus, criminal electronic surveillance laws focus on gathering hard evidence—not intelligence.

Applications must indicate that other normal investigative techniques have been tried and have failed to gather evidence of crime, will not work, or are too dangerous, and must include information concerning any prior electronic surveillance regarding the subject or facility in question. Court orders are initially limited to 30 days, with extensions possible, and must terminate sooner if the objectives are met. Judges may, and usually do, require periodic reports to the court, typically every seven to ten days, advising the court of the progress of the interception effort. This assures close and ongoing oversight of the electronic surveillance by the U.S. Attorney's Office handling the case and frequently by the court as well. Interceptions are required to be conducted in such a way as to "minimize the interception of communications not otherwise subject to interception" under the law, such as unrelated, irrelevant, and noncriminal communications of the subjects or others not named in the application.

To ensure the evidentiary integrity of intercepted communications, they must be recorded, if possible, on magnetic tape or other devices, so as to protect the recording from editing or other alterations. Immediately upon the expiration of the interception period, these recordings must be presented to the federal district court judge and sealed under his or her directions. The presence of the seal is a prerequisite for their use or disclosure, or for the introduction of evidence derived from the tapes.

Applications and orders signed by the judge are also to be sealed by the judge. Within a reasonable period of time after the termination of the intercept order, including extension, the judge is obligated by law to ensure that the subject of the interception order, and other parties as are deemed appropriate, are furnished an inventory that includes notice of the order, the dates during which the interceptions were carried out, and whether the communication was intercepted. Upon motion, the judge may also direct that portion of the contents of the intercepted communication be made available to the affected person for his or her inspection.

The illegal, unauthorized conduct of electronic surveillance is a federal criminal offense punishable by imprisonment for up to five years, a fine, or both. In addition, any person whose communications are unlawfully intercepted, disclosed, or used, may recover civil action damages, including punitive damages, as well as attorneys' fees and other costs against the person or entity engaged in the violation.

TWENTY-FIRST-CENTURY ORGANIZED CRIME

Now that we've discussed the advantages that technology promises police in the future, we must consider how criminals will make use of it to further their criminal endeavors. Let's consider some possibilities as they might relate to organized crime.

Information Theft

One thing is certain—for generations, organized crime has had the uncanny ability to identify social patterns and trends and find a place for moneymaking somewhere in that niche. The best example is what appears to be of the future—information management. After all, with today's satellites, telecommunications, microwave towers, and computers, the information superhighway seems to be open to virtually anyone. As many corporate moguls have learned, the strategic use of information can be a source of power. Of course, organized crime organizations will still practice violence and intimidation as always, but they will also make use of information to enhance the power they already possess. Does this mean that tomorrow's gangsters will be college-educated and computer-literate? Chances are that the answer is yes.

R. H. Moore predicts that the top target of twenty-first-century organized crime will be financial institutions.[12] Clearly, financial revenues from drug trafficking have, over the years, made Colombian cartels international players in global finance. Many business losses, sometimes larger than the budgets of entire countries, are often blithely written off by drug cartels. Banks will most likely be handling increased amounts of customer information, which will prove not only valuable to them but to criminal organizations as well. As a result, criminal organizations will carefully place moles in financial institutions to provide information such as computer passwords and access codes, which allow criminals to infiltrate accounts without casting suspicions on their operatives.

Today, highly skilled computer hackers are employed by organized criminals to penetrate targeted institutions. They will be able to change bank records, credit card accounts and reports, and to alter criminal, educational, and military records. It is possible that anyone's personal records will be subject to deletion or alteration for criminal purposes. Some people have even suggested that with the advent of DNA technology, which has been touted as the primary method of identifying people in the twenty-first century, a criminal service could develop where one's genetic identity could be altered—for a price, of course.

Cybercrime

On the morning of May 4, 2000, a computer virus called the "love bug" zoomed around the world, causing an estimated $10 billion in damage. The virus originated in the Philippines, where suspects Onel de Guzman and his friend, Michael Buen, both 23 years old, were arrested.[13] Experts marveled how the two suspects were such "average computer enthusiasts" and how simple the virus was for them to create. Once developed, they hacked their way into four accounts with the Sky Internet ISP to release the virus. The ISP was able to trace the bug to the phone number for de Guzman's apartment.

The structure of the virus was simple. For example, it would immediately go into the victim's Microsoft Outlook, find all the addresses there, and resend itself to all of those addresses. Computer experts reported that it took fewer than 20 lines of code to accomplish that. Corporations and other business entities moved quickly by shutting down e-mail servers and warning workers. Within half a day antidotes were available. But by then the love bug had already been a sensation—interrupting work for millions of people.

In the twenty-first century a new form of criminality has loomed, creating untold options for criminal entrepreneurs and new challenges for police. With the personal computer now occupying most households and mainframe computers acting as the epicenter of almost all Fortune 500 companies, the problem of computer crime or **cybercrime** is now a mainstream social problem. According to one definition, *cybercrime* is defined as "the destruction, theft or unauthorized use, modification, or copying of information, programs, services, equipment or communication networks."[14]

For obvious reasons, cybercrime has had a relatively short history. While electronic crime has a problem for decades, it wasn't until the 1970s that a new term entered the public lexicon—**hacker**. Early hackers began using school computers for a number of misdeeds—the least of which was altering grades. By the end of the 1980s, modems (devices linking computers to telephone lines) and computerized bulletin board services emerged.

While the first generation of hackers posed a degree of mischief, their emergence was only to set the stage for a far more insidious type of computer crime. Many large corporate computers were "hacked" not as a prank, but as a target of large-scale theft. Indeed, computers have provided opportunistic criminals a new genre with which to ply their crimes, and many of today's criminals are quite computer literate. One early example of cybercrime involves the planting of an unauthorized program known as a **Trojan horse**—a program that automatically transfers money to an illegal account whenever a legal transaction is made. To many thieves and hackers, this was akin to striking pure gold.

Today, cybercrooks have masqueraded as financial advisers or licensed brokers on the Internet and solicited investments in fictitious mutual funds.[15] In some cases, cybercrooks have attempted to extort money from their victims. In one of the biggest cases of **cyberextortion**, a computer hacker stole credit card numbers from an online music retailer—CD Universe—and released thousands of them on a website when the company refused to pay $100,000 ransom. In January 2000, the *New York Times* reported that the hacker claimed to have taken the numbers of 300,000 CD Universe customers. The hacker turned out to be a 19-year-old from Russia going by the name Maxim.[16] We will now take a closer look at yet another emerging area of cybercrime—software piracy.

Software Piracy

No one knows the actual cost of software piracy, but a study by the Software Publishers Association (SPA) claims that $7.4 billion worth of business application software was counterfeited in 1993—a figure nearly equal to the total legitimate revenues for the entire industry in that year.[17] The problem can be illustrated as we consider the Kerry Miller case:

> The company's website appeared to be legitimate. It offered a variety of software with brand-name labels such as Microsoft and Corel. The street address was in North Carolina, accompanied by a contact phone number and e-mail addresses for customer service. On the surface, the Online Software Club of America was no different from hundreds of other companies selling software via the Internet. It wasn't even unusual that one man, Kerry Miller, out of an apartment in North Carolina, ran the small business. But what set it apart is that some of its products were illegal copies of the most popular computer programs. These included Microsoft Word and Corel WordPerfect office software. Customers who purchased the counterfeit product sometimes ended up with faulty software and oftentimes couldn't get technical help or upgrades when new versions came out. Their expenses mounted when they had to pay full price to replace the counterfeit product with the legally produced software.

Since the problem of software piracy was first identified, efforts to police it were discouraging at best. Until the late 1990s, software pirates would mainly use flea markets or off-brand stores to sell their products. Today, they are online with websites and classified ads that look no different from legitimate retailers. Efforts by software makers and police to crack down on illegal software merchants and contractors are becoming more common.

In some cases, suspicion is growing that proceeds from sales of counterfeit products are financing organized crime. For example, in August 1999, U.S. marshals seized counterfeit software and business records from the Online Software Club and its owner Kerry Miller. Miller claimed he had a 60 to 70% profit margin on products he sold and was reaping $250,000 in net sales every month. Miller marketed his wares by sending out messages making offers like: "Would you like to stop paying retail prices for name brand software??? Savings as much as 50 to 75% off retail." The

Warning Signs of Counterfeit Software

- "Too good to be true" prices for software
- Gold or silver CDs
- Products missing key elements such as users' manuals, certificates of authenticity, or end-user license agreements. Pirates often sell only the CD-ROM in a jewel case without retail packaging
- Backup disks or CD-ROMs with handwritten labels
- Watermarks that are simulated with ink on the surface or embossed
- Poor imitations of security features, such as the hologram on the hub of the Windows 98 CD that says "genuine" when tilted in light
- Low-quality print and letters that aren't evenly spaced. Counterfeits often have a difficult time replicating the fonts, artwork styles, and registered trademarks that Microsoft uses
- Products marked with phrases that do not describe the transaction, such as: "for distribution with a new PC only," "special CD for licensed customers only," "not for retail," or "academic price—not for use in a commercial environment"

Counterfeiters often use these types of phrases to fool consumers into believing they are getting a genuine product that was overstocked or otherwise deserves to be discounted.

e-mail offered a version of Microsoft Office 97 sold for $124.95 compared to the real Office 97, which would have cost about $400 in stores. Miller said Microsoft was mistaken in that he, like Microsoft, was also a victim of the counterfeiter.[18]

Miller began his business in February 1999 after finding software wholesalers online. Miller claimed he bought from people who advertised that they sold 100% genuine Microsoft products, adding that he halted his business as soon as Microsoft contacted him. Following a trail of e-mail from Miller, police in Austin, Texas, seized hundreds of copies of counterfeit Microsoft and Corel software from a warehouse apparently operated by several online software suppliers.[19]

Microsoft also seized what it claimed was illegal software from the Discount Software Club operating out of St. Louis, Missouri. This operation worked essentially like the one in North Carolina and might even have used the same suppliers of counterfeit software. But experts acknowledge that even if court orders were able to shut down these operations, new ones could crop up almost immediately.

For software publishers, the scope of the problem is staggering. In addition to the loss of revenue, software manufacturers point to the ill will that piracy creates among retailers who are angry because they see a competitor undercutting their prices and among consumers who expect that the name such as Microsoft on a package guarantees a certain quality.

The Business Software Alliance (BSA), an industry organization that combats software copyright violations, estimates that over 1 million websites offer pirated software, a figure that has increased from 100,000 in 1996. Estimates are that the industry loses $11 billion each year to people who mass-produce counterfeit copies of Microsoft Office or other popular programs and sell them to unsuspecting customers.[20] The fastest way to find pirated software may be to visit one of the online auction sites. The Software Information Industry Association of America conducted a survey in August 1999 that estimated that 60% of software sold on such sites is counterfeit.[21]

The Appearance of Legitimacy

More than anything else, it is the goal of organized crime leaders to make their organizations appear legitimate in the eyes of the public. Colombian cartels already have considerable stock holdings in some of the largest Fortune 500 companies in the world. In addition, Japan's premiere organized crime group, the yakuza, is thought to have major stock and real estate holdings in virtually all parts of the world. Many Italian American crime families have long been successful in infiltrating large-scale industries such as solid-waste hauling, the restaurant business, and the garment industry.

In the years to come it is likely that large criminal organizations will have controlling interests in some of the world's largest multinational corporations. Industrial espionage by such corporations will know no ethics, as corporate computer hackers will use modern technology for stealing plans, strategies, formulas, and other valuable information possessed by competitors.

Satellite Technology

Moore predicts that since satellite-imaging services are becoming increasingly available on the commercial market, organized crime organizations of the future will own their own communications satellites.[22] Such a communications network would enable large-scale crime organizations such as those involved in drug trafficking or money laundering to own their own secure information systems, free from surveillance or detection by police authorities. Other criminal enterprises, such as sports gambling and prostitution, could also be enhanced with the use of a privately owned satellite. With such technology, criminal organizations could operate from sites where law enforcement agencies are sympathetic and would fix sporting events worldwide from horse racing to school sports. Such an operation was discovered in 1992 in the Dominican Republic, where a $1 billion gambling operation was fixing sporting events in the United States.

Indeed, there is no reason to believe that the huge amounts of money earned by large-scale organized crime organizations will not be put to use to purchase whatever they need to make themselves as invulnerable as possible. All the technology will serve one distinct purpose—to allow the organized crime organization to better provide illegal goods and services.

TERRORISM

As a criminal activity, **terrorism** and the prevention of further acts of terrorism became a primary concern of American policing following the September 11, 2001 attacks on the World Trade Center and the Pentagon. However, there is no single uniform definition of terrorism that is applicable to all places and all circumstances. Some definitions are statutory in nature, whereas others were created for such practical purposes as gauging success in the fight against terrorism.

One key definition provided by the federal Foreign Relations Authorization Act defines terrorism in terms of four primary characteristics. The act says that terrorism is premeditated, politically motivated, violent, and committed against noncombatant targets. On the other hand, the FBI defines terrorism as "a violent act or an act dangerous to human life in violation of the criminal laws of the United States or any other state designed to intimidate or coerce a government, the civilian population, or any segment thereof, in furtherance of political or social objectives."

It is important to distinguish between two major forms of terrorism: international and domestic. The distinction is generally made in terms of the origin, the base of operations, and objectives of a terrorist organization. International terrorism is the unlawful use of force or violence by a group or individual who has some connection to a foreign power or whose activities transcend national boundaries and are against people or property in order to intimidate or coerce the government, the civilian population, or any segment thereof, in furtherance of political or social objectives. In contrast, domestic terrorism refers to the unlawful use of force or violence by a group or individual based and operating entirely within the United States and its territories and whose acts are directed at elements of the U.S. government or population.

International Terrorism

U. S. concern about international terrorism extends across the globe. For example, in addition to the ongoing threat of al-Qaeda, Iran is also known to support Iraqi Shia militia groups and terrorist groups such as Hizballah and non-Shia Palestinian terrorist organizations. All of these groups pose a concern for U.S. safety and national security. Despite calls from al-Qaeda's Ayman Al-Zawahiri to Palestinian terrorist groups to join the global jihad, most Palestinian groups have focused their attacks on Israel. Additionally, the ongoing factional in-fighting between Hamas and Fatah elements in the Palestinian territories has consumed the attention of most of the Palestinian organizations. This activity surged in early 2009 with Hamas' military attack on Israel.

The threat of International terrorism can be illustrated by the two August 7, 1998, car bombs that exploded in the U.S. Embassies in Kenya and Tanzania, leaving more than 260 people dead and 5,500 injured, proving to be one of the decade's most lethal terrorist attacks. Shortly after the bombings, police in Tanzania and Kenya began rounding up suspects, but one person surfaced as the mastermind of the attack: Osama bin Laden. On August 20, 1998, acting on intelligence information that bin Laden was planning terrorist training at a secret complex in eastern Afghanistan, the United States fired 75 Tomahawk cruise missiles from Navy ships in the Arabian and Red Seas. The missiles, a retaliatory measure, landed on targets in both Afghanistan and Sudan.

According to intelligence reports, the training complex included a command center, an ammunition depot, and four training centers. At the camp, terrorists learned to handle explosives, run obstacle courses, practice on firing ranges, and operate armed personnel carriers and tanks. U.S. National Security Adviser Sandy Berger was quoted as saying that "[t]his is the largest terrorist training camp in the world." Bin Laden, a Saudi-born terrorist, was known by terrorist experts to have assembled a large-scale international terrorism network, and he has directed his followers to kill Americans: civilian or military, adult or infant. His goal: to get the United States to abandon its allies, friends, or interests in the Middle East, the Persian Gulf, and Africa.

Like many other terrorist leaders, bin Laden justified his crimes by hiding behind the religious cloak of Islam. But ironically, Muslims have been among the most tragic victims of terrorism in Egypt, Israel, the West Bank, Algeria, Lebanon, and elsewhere. Ten of the 12 people killed in the Tanzania bombing were Muslims, as were many of the more than 260 killed in Kenya.

In November 1998, the U.S. government charged bin Laden with the August Embassy bombings in East Africa and offered an unprecedented reward of $5 million for information leading to his arrest. The 238-count indictment stated that bin Laden and others have financed, trained, and ordered terrorist attacks against the United States since 1991.[23]

Terrorist groups are active throughout the world, and the United States is not their only intended target. Terrorist groups operate in South America, Africa, the Middle East, Latin America, the Philippines, Japan, India, Ireland, England, Nepal, and some of the now-independent states of the former Soviet Union.

In 2001, terrorist Osama bin Laden showed the world how easy it can be to strike at American interests on U.S. soil when members of his organization allegedly attacked the World Trade Center and the Pentagon using commandeered airliners, killing approximately 3,000 people.

The attack was allegedly coordinated by bin Laden's host terrorist organization, al-Qaeda, a fundamentalist Islamic terrorist group operating out of Afghanistan under the protection of the Taliban regime that controlled that country. Much has been written about the specific events of that day, but for our purposes the important points to be emphasized are that (1) large-scale terrorist attacks had occurred within the borders of the continental United States and (2) the government of the United States responded by initiating massive new security measures domestically and a "war" on terrorism internationally.

Following the 9/11 attacks, the United States federalized airport security; began a massive sweep that resulted in the detaining of thousands of immigrants and foreign citizens living in the United States; began a process of reorganizing American intelligence services; and initiated the first comprehensive investigation of international money laundering ever undertaken by federal law enforcement. These developments had profound impacts on the organization of crime internationally and the commitment of the U.S. government to pursuing types of organized criminality that previously had been largely ignored. Crimes such as arms trafficking, money laundering, alien smuggling, and the production of weapons of mass destruction suddenly became investigative priorities.

American Policing under Fire

Policing Terrorism and Protecting Civil Rights

On a number of occasions throughout this book the subject of terrorism has been discussed, along with its impact on American policing. Among the many questions asked in the aftermath of the September 11, 2001, terrorist attacks, many citizens have wondered whether America was properly prepared or if better, more effective laws should have been in place to prevent acts of terrorism.

Just five days after September 11, 2001, U.S. Attorney General John Ashcroft met with congressional leaders to request that law enforcement agencies be given more authority to follow and apprehend those suspected of terrorist activities. In response to Ashcroft's request, Congress enacted legislation giving the government new powers to monitor electronic communications among terrorism suspects and to wiretap any telephones that might be used by terrorists. Specifically, legislators expanded the FBI's ability to use Carnivore, the agency's Internet wiretap system. The bill also allowed for law enforcement agents to detain terrorism suspects for up to seven days without filing charges against them, and made it a crime to harbor terrorists.

Law enforcement agencies such as the FBI often take measures to expand their authority in hopes of being better prepared to fight crime and apprehend criminals. Often, law enforcement administrators justify such requests as being necessary to face specific challenges presented by specific criminals—in this case terrorists. For example, suicide terrorism is particularly suited to frustrating law enforcement efforts. That is, perpetrators do not need a plan or an escape route. Additionally, they do not need to be rescued by associates, and there's no risk of being captured and questioned by law enforcement agents.

Support for stronger measures is not, however, universal. Many people feel that one of the casualties of the "war against terrorism" will be long-cherished civil liberties. So, how differently are Americans willing to see their civil liberties treated? In other words, how much freedom are we willing to trade for national security? With regard to privacy, most Americans seem relatively untroubled by the prospect of more thorough screening processes and a greater law enforcement presence in airports and on planes. Another concern, however, is surveillance capabilities of the police, as more law enforcement agents are able to listen in on telephone conversations, and have greater access to information in personal computer systems.

In the struggle against terrorism, the primary focus of antiterrorism efforts has been fundamentalist Islamic extremists, particularly Saudi Arabian Osama bin Laden and his al-Qaeda terrorist organization. Osama bin Laden is believed to be primarily responsible for the bombing of the World Trade Center in 1993 and the bombing of the embassies in Kenya and Tanzania in 1998, in which 260 people were killed and thousands injured, and the attack on the USS *Cole* in Yemen in 2000, which left 17 Americans dead and 19 wounded. He is also the primary suspect in the September 11 tragedy. Each of the 19 hijackers believed by the FBI to have been responsible for those attacks was of Mid-Eastern descent.

In the aftermath of the 1993 World Trade Center bombing and the 1995 destruction of the Alfred P. Murrah Federal Building in Oklahoma City, by American citizen Timothy McVeigh, President Clinton signed the Antiterrorism and Effective Death Penalty Act of 1996 into law. This law, among other things, allows the government to hold foreign nationals indefinitely if they are suspected of terrorist activity. The law establishes special "removal courts" to oversee such proceedings, and such courts may hear evidence against suspected terrorists without making the evidence available to that person. Since the passage of the Act in 1996, nearly all the "secret evidence cases" brought under its authority have involved Arab or Muslim immigrants.

In the week following the September 11 tragedy, the FBI investigated 40 "hate crimes" against Arab Americans and those mistaken for Arab Americans. So in the context of the fight against terrorism, the "balancing act" discussed in Chapter 1 of this text is essential to an understanding of how the law enforcement community will respond to this threat.

The U.S. government also responded internationally. An extended air campaign was launched against the Taliban government in Afghanistan, which had harbored Osama bin Laden's al-Qaeda organization.

Domestic Terrorism

During the 1960s and 1970s, domestic terrorism in the United States required the expenditure of considerable criminal justice resources. Groups such as The Weathermen, Students for Democratic Society, and the Symbionese Liberation Army—as well as other radical groups—routinely challenged the authority of federal and local governments. Their activities resulted in bombings, kidnappings, and shoot-outs across the nation. During the 1980s, acts of domestic terrorism declined, and the national focus fell on international terrorism instead. The war in Lebanon, terrorism in Israel, bombings in France, Italy, and Germany, and the many violent offshoots of the Iran–Iraq and Gulf wars occupied the attention of the media and concerned citizens as well. For the most part, efforts by the FBI, the CIA, and other agencies served to prevent the spread of terrorism to U.S. soil.

However, in 1995 a powerful terrorist truck bomb devastated the Alfred P. Murrah Federal Building in downtown Oklahoma City. One hundred sixty-eight people died, and hundreds more were wounded. The targeted nine-story building had housed offices of the Social Security Administration, the Drug Enforcement Administration, the Secret Service, and the Bureau of Alcohol, Tobacco, and Firearms, and a day-care center called America's Kids. Twelve hundred pounds of explosives had been left in a rental truck on the side of the building. The blast, which left a crater 30 feet wide and 8 feet deep and spread debris over a 10-block area, demonstrated just how vulnerable the United States is to terrorist attack.

In 1997, a federal jury found 29-year-old Timothy McVeigh guilty of all 11 counts charged against him, ranging from conspiracy to first-degree murder, in the Oklahoma City bombing. Jurors concluded that Timothy McVeigh had conspired with Terry Nichols, a friend he had met while both were in the army, and with unknown others to destroy the Murrah Building. McVeigh was the first person under federal jurisdiction to be put to death since 1963. Terry Nichols was later convicted of conspiracy in the bombing and of eight counts of involuntary manslaughter.

Some experts believe that the Oklahoma City attack was modeled after a similar bombing described in *The Turner Diaries*, a novel used by extremist groups to map their rise to power. Just as Hitler's biography *Mein Kampf* served as a call to arms for Nazis in Europe during the 1930s, *The Turner Diaries* describes an Arian revolution that occurs in the United States during the 1990s, in which Jews, African-Americans, and other minorities are removed from positions of influence in government and society. In 2003, Eric Rudolph was arrested by the FBI for his role in the 1996 Olympics Centennial Park bombing in which one person died and 111 were injured, an attack that many antiterrorism experts believe was the work of a larger separatist organization.

Active fringe groups include those espousing a nationwide "common-law movement," under which the legitimacy of elected officials in government is not recognized. An example is the Republic of Texas separatists, who took neighbors hostage near Fort Davis, Texas, in 1997 to draw attention to their claims that Texas was illegally annexed by the United States in 1845. Although not necessarily bent on terrorism per se, such special-interest groups may turn to violence if thwarted in attempts to reach their goals.

The Use of Chemical and Biological Weapons

Terrorists' limited use of chemical and biological weapons, along with the almost nonexistent use of nuclear material is for the most part technical. The scientific literature is replete with the technical problems inherent in the production, manufacture, storage, and delivery of each of the three categories of unconventional weapons.

The manufacture of nuclear weapons is not that simple, nor is delivery to their target. Nuclear material, of which a limited supply exists, is monitored by the UN-affiliated International Atomic Energy Agency. Only governments can legally produce it, so that even in this age of proliferation, investigators could trace those abetting nuclear terrorists without great difficulty.

Chemical agents are much easier to produce or obtain but not as easy to keep safely in stable condition, and their dispersal depends largely on climactic factors. The terrorists behind the 1996 attack in Tokyo chose a convenient target (a subway) where large crowds of people gather. In addition, anthrax spores sent through the U.S. mail in the aftermath of the September 11 attacks demonstrated the relative ease by which dangerous chemicals could be delivered to targets.

Biological agents, on the other hand, are far and away the most dangerous, because they could kill hundreds of thousands, whereas chemicals would kill only thousands. They are relatively easy to produce, but storage and dispersal are even trickier than for nerve gases—a class of phosphorus-containing organic chemicals (organophosphates) that disrupt the mechanism by which nerves transfer messages to organs.

The risk of contamination for people handling biological agents is high, and many of the most lethal bacteria and spores do not survive well outside the laboratory. Given the technical difficulties, terrorists are probably less likely to use nuclear devices than chemical weapons and least likely to attempt to use biological weapons. But difficulties can sometimes be overcome, and the choice of unconventional weapons will in the end come down to the specialties of the terrorists and their access to deadly substances.

Fighting Terrorism

Although terrorism represents a difficult challenge to all societies throughout the world, open societies of the Western world are potentially more vulnerable than totalitarian regimes like dictatorships. Democratic ideals of the West restrict police surveillance of likely terrorist groups and curtail luggage, vehicle, and airport searches. In addition, press coverage of acts of terrorism encourages copycat activities by other fringe groups and communicates information on techniques that seem to

---

A Closer Look

The Threat of Biochemical Weapons

Here's how you would die: Tiny particles of anthrax, normally a disease that afflicts cattle, are sprayed over your city from a high-tech aerosol canister released in midair. They drift down in a seemingly innocuous cloud but lodge deep within your lungs. Days, even weeks, later you feel no symptoms, only a slight fever and fatigue. Then, abruptly, you go into toxic shock, with high fever and internal congestion and bleeding. Once the acute symptoms appear, it is too late for any therapy. You are dead within a few days.

Some might argue that the threat of biological weapons (as well as nuclear and chemical weapons for that matter) is more a concern for the military than the criminal justice system. But as of the late 1990s, the lines have become blurred, primarily because criminal groups operating in Europe, the Middle East, and Russia have been documented as having access to such weapons and demonstrating their willingness to sell them to the highest bidder. This could include other criminal groups from terrorist states such as Iran, Iraq, Libya, and Syria. Hence the roles of the military and those of domestic law enforcement are crossing in some cases. In a speech in Kansas City in 1997, President Clinton commented on the biochemical threat by saying ". . . we must not allow the twenty-first century to go forward under a cloud of fear."

Admiral William Owens, former chief of staff, commented that biological weapons are enormously simple to make. An accident in 1979 in a Soviet biological warfare plant in Sverdlovsk—now called Ekaterinburg—released tiny bits of anthrax, killing nearly 100 people who lived downwind of the plant. Then, in 1995, the Japanese cult Aum Shinrikyo left plastic bags filled with sarin, a nerve gas, in the Tokyo subway. A dozen people died and more than 5,000 were hurt.

Surprisingly, the toxin was only 25% of military strength—otherwise the toll would have been considerably higher.

The range of theoretical villains is far-reaching and includes North Koreans to disgruntled U.S. neo-Nazis. According to the Stimson Center, at least six nations possess biological and chemical weapons: Egypt, Libya, Taiwan, China, North Korea, and Syria. A number of others have chemical arsenals: South Korea, Ethiopia, India, Pakistan, Vietnam, and Myanmar (Burma). But despite being subjected to the toughest sanctions and scrutiny in history, Iraq is believed to pose the greatest threat.

But, experts say that the biggest threat could come from individuals, not nations—because nations employing such weapons in war would face disproportionate retaliation. On February 19, 1998, one such incident occurred in Las Vegas, Nevada, where two men were arrested for possessing the deadly germ anthrax for use as a weapon. The two men had attempted to arrange a lab test of the substance, but through the tip of an informant, federal agents seized ten bags marked "biological." Following their arrest, their beige Mercedes was sealed in plastic and hauled off to a military base for tests to confirm whether the material carried inside was, in fact, a germ warfare agent. Fortunately, the chemicals were found to be harmless animal vaccines designed to protect animals against anthrax. While charges against both subjects were dropped, the specter of biological weapons in the United States sent chills throughout the nation and confirmed that Americans are still very concerned about this new-age public-safety threat. The Nevada anthrax scare was not all that unique because in 1997 alone, the FBI reported that there were 40 threats of biological weapons in the United States.[24]

work. Laws designed to limit terrorist access to technology, information, and physical locations are stop-gap measures at best. The Federal Terrorist Firearms Detection Act of 1988 is an example. Designed to prevent the development of plastic firearms by requiring handguns to contain at least 3.7 ounces of detectable metal, it applies only to weapons manufactured within U.S. borders.

In 1996, the Antiterrorism and Effective Death Penalty Act became law. The act provided for the following:

- It bans fund-raising and financial support within the United States for international terrorist organizations.
- It provides $1 billion for enhanced terrorism-fighting measures by federal and state authorities.
- It allows foreign terrorism suspects to be deported or to be kept out of the United States without the disclosure of classified evidence against them.
- It permits the death sentence to be imposed upon anyone committing an international terrorist attack in the United States in which a death occurs.
- It makes it a federal crime to use the United States as a base for planning terrorist attacks overseas.
- It orders identifying chemical markers known as "taggants" to be added to plastic explosives during manufacture.
- It orders a feasibility study on marking other explosives (other than gunpowder).

Prior to the events of September 11, 2001, the National Commission on Terrorism released its report, countering the changing threat of international terrorism. The commission, created by House and Senate leaders in 1998 in response to the bombings of U.S. embassies in Kenya and Tanzania, was led by former U.S. ambassador-at-large for counterterrorism L. Paul Bremer. The commission's report, which now seems to have presaged the attack on the World Trade Center and the Pentagon, began with these words: "International terrorism poses an increasingly dangerous and difficult threat to America." The report identified Afghanistan, Iran, Iraq, Sudan, and Syria as among state sponsors of terrorism and concluded, "The government must immediately take steps to reinvigorate the collection of intelligence about terrorist plans, use all available legal avenues to disrupt and prosecute terrorist activities and private sources of support, convince other nations to seize all support for terrorists, and insure that federal, state, and local officials are prepared for attacks that may result in mass casualties."[25]

Following the 2001 attacks, Congress enacted and the president signed the USA PATRIOT Act. The act, which is discussed in some detail in Appendix A, created a number of new crimes, such as terrorist attacks against mass transportation and harboring or concealing terrorists. Those crimes were set forth in Title 8 of the act, titled "Strengthening the Criminal Laws against Terrorism."

The State and Local Police Response to Terrorism

Federal law enforcement agencies are not alone in responding to the threat of terrorism. And, of course, nowhere is the threat of terrorism being taken more seriously than in New York City, which established a Counterterrorism Bureau. Teams within the bureau have been trained to examine potential targets in the city and to attempt to insulate the targets from possible attack. Viewed as prime targets are the city's bridges, the Empire State Building, Rockefeller Center, and the United Nations building. Investigators have been assigned overseas to work with the police in several foreign cities, including cities in Canada and Israel. Detectives have been assigned as liaisons with INTERPOL in Lyon, France, and with the FBI. The city is now recruiting detectives with language skills from Pushtun and Urdu to Arabic, Fujianese, and other dialects. The existing New York City police intelligence division has been revamped, and agents are examining newspapers and monitoring Internet sites.[26] The department is also setting up several backup command centers in different parts of the city in case a terrorist attack puts the headquarters out of operation. Several backup senior command systems have been created so that if people at the highest levels of the department are killed, other individuals will be ready to assume their jobs.

The Counterterrorism Bureau has assigned more than 100 city police detectives to work with the FBI as agents of the U.S. Joint Forces Command. In addition, in the intelligence division

700 investigators now devote 35% to 40% of their resources to counterterrorism, up from about 2% before January 2002. The department is also drawing on the expertise of other institutions around the city. For example, medical specialists have been enlisted to monitor daily developments in the city's hospitals to detect any suspicious outbreaks of illnesses that might reflect a biological attack. And the police are now conducting joint drills with the New York Fire Department to avoid the problem in communication and coordination that marked the emergency response on September 11.[27]

COMMUNITY POLICING AND THE FUTURE

One of the underlying themes of this book has been the importance of community policing and how many problems between the public and the police can be identified and resolved through a proactive community policing philosophy. Community policing (discussed in Chapter 9) goes one step beyond the problem-solving philosophy and attempts to construct a partnership between the community and the police. Under this philosophy, the police department is more decentralized than in the past, as well as being more open to establishing interpersonal relationships between virtually all segments of society. Included in this philosophy is the concept that the police are social service agents as well as law enforcers.

In this role they will interact more frequently with social service organizations, such as rape crisis shelters, group homes for the homeless, drug-rehabilitation centers, and residential homes for juvenile delinquents. But John Crank suggests that decentralization has had some unexpected consequences because no one anticipated the enormous growth in organizational complexity that has accompanied decentralization.[28] Rather than reducing the size of the bureaucracy, it added a dimension of geographic complexity. For example, when Kansas City shifted its command to substations, the entire command structure previously in place in the headquarters was copied at each substation. As a result, there were 14 independent Kansas City police organizations, each with organizational chart, personnel systems, and command hierarchy. The city replaced three chiefs in four years in an attempt to find one with the tenacity and tough-headedness to take over the police department.

According to many police and public administrators, community policing is working and crime rates are down. The question is: Will they continue to fall? As of this writing, what is desperately needed is scientific research to determine for sure that community policing is working as well as hoped. In the meantime, although some cities continue to experience a great deal of hostility between the police and the community, it is likely that in the coming years even those cities will bridge the communication gap. But some experts predict that police officers of the future may actually become more impersonal than officers of today because of technological developments. In her book *Crimewarps: The Future of Crime in America*, Bennett speculates that "crime fighting strategies will be displaced by leaner, more focused and less personal tactics."[29]

Although community policing encourages more involvement between the police and the community, Bennett cautions that technological advances may foster a less personal stance by police agencies. After all, police in the 1980s and early 1990s adopted aggressive police tactics such as directed patrol, gang sweeps, and crackdowns—all of which tended to alienate many segments of the community. It is likely that in the future such tactics will be replaced by electronic tracking of criminals through the use of computers, resulting in a more efficient police force but not one that is necessarily more public-relations oriented. So, the compelling challenge to police administrators of the future is the continued development of new community policing strategies to nurture and prolong positive feelings of unity between police professionals and the citizenry.

Community policing must also incorporate consideration for special populations within the community. These include the elderly, mentally ill, and intoxicated and homeless persons. Not only is there a need for these populations to be considered a part of the community, but there is also a need for special training in handling calls involving them. As it stands, most officers today lack sufficient sensitivity and technical training to deal adequately with such calls. Included in future police training should be adequate familiarization among officers regarding social service agencies in the community that can aid and benefit the facilitation of this type of public complaint.

In Retrospect

Although there are indications that many aspects of modern policing are paving the way for a more tranquil future, some experts are suggesting that the future will be anything but tranquil. Two such futurists, Alvin and Heidi Toffler, suggest that we are heading into some of the most turbulent years in the history of our country. They note that our transportation system, postal system, and educational system are in crisis simultaneously.

Prospective employees face a world in which there is an ever-increasing emphasis on skills, training, and education. Persons at the opposite end of the social spectrum, with no such skills, may be forced into the illegitimate economy and criminal wrongdoing. Police agencies and the criminal justice system will be called upon to deal with the situation, and according to the Tofflers, the very survival of our democracy rests with the criminal justice system's ability to respond properly to these crises.[30]

Certainly, new technology will introduce new weapons and methods for police and criminals alike. Some futurists talk about a future in which electronic brain stimulation will be used to control behavior 24 hours a day and there will be undersea and space prison colonies.[31] In addition, there will be breakthroughs in genetics, new materials, software, and thousands of new discoveries that will have an impact on our society.

Along with such innovations will come intense political, moral, and legal debates regarding their application in modern law enforcement and crime control. For example, what new potential invasions of privacy will become technologically possible? What biomonitoring technologies should be admitted as evidence? In what way will such breakthroughs affect interpretation of the Bill of Rights and the Constitution? In what manner will criminal codes need to be restructured to address the use of new technologies? It's ironic that one of the most redeeming aspects of U.S. society is its commitment to individual freedom. Yet in times of rising crime and increased violence on the streets, the public cries out for more repressive, antidemocratic measures.

As important as it is to identify crime trends as a predictor of behavior, futurists warn that trends fail to provide any way in which accurate predictions for the future can be made. In other words, identifying a trend doesn't help at all in predicting the future. Instead, police administrators at all levels should dedicate resources for probing the future and implementing their findings into decision making at all levels within the department. The Tofflers suggest that police managers consider the following examples of questions regarding the future:

- What should a community's law enforcement budget be?
- How should law enforcement officers be trained?
- What new technologies will the police face and need?
- What new forms of organization will have to be created?
- How should forces be deployed?
- What provisions should be made for the continual updating of missions?

Answers to these and other important questions are essential in the future structuring, understanding, and implementation of public-safety measures in a society that is not victimized by, but rather is the beneficiary of, its police.

Improve Your Professional Vocabulary

anonymous re-mailers
beanbags
Carnivore
crime mapping
cybercrime
cyberextortion
data mining

facial-recognition technology
hacker
iris-recognition technology
mail bombs
national security letter
pepperballs
reasonable expectation of privacy

rubber bullets
Taser
terrorism
thermal imaging
Trojan horse
white-collar crime

Discussion Questions

1. Describe the role of technology in policing and how that role has changed since the twentieth century.

2. Explain, in your opinion, the future changes that can be anticipated with regard to the nation's drug problem.

3. In a general sense, discuss the role and concerns of futuristic technology in police work.

4. Compare and contrast the various information technologies that are on the horizon for modern policing.

5. What futuristic technologies are now being used by the criminal element?

6. Define the term "white-collar crime" and explain why it is such an area of concern for the twenty-first-century police administrator.

7. Explain how terrorism will create unique problems for domestic policing.

8. According to futurists Alvin and Heidi Toffler, in what ways will technology affect modern society and its police?

9. Discuss the various concerns civil libertarians have about the increased use of technology by the police.

10. Compare and contrast the pros and cons of a few of the newer nonlethal weapons used by some law enforcement agencies.

Notes

1. Department of Justice press release, "Creator of Melissa computer virus sentenced to 20 months in federal prison," May 1, 2002, available at http://www.usdoj.gov. Accessed August 1, 2007.

2. Meyer, C., & T. Gorman. (2001, February 2). Criminal faces in the crowd still elude hidden I.D. camera security. *Los Angeles Times,* p. 1.

3. Fitzgerald, A. (1998, April 14). Judge weighing legality of FBI's Mafia wiretaps. *USA Today,* p. 12A.

4. www.fbi.gov.

5. Evidence of FBI evasions feeds carnivore doubts. (2000, November 30). *USA Today,* p. 16A.

6. Horsenball, Mark, & Evan Thomas. (2006, May 22). Hold the phone. *Newsweek,* pp. 29–30.

7. 50 U.S.C. Section 1861 (b) (2) (a), Amended by the US Patriot Improvement and Reauthorization Act of 2005, Section 106 (b).

8. Quoted in Schmitt, Richard B. (2007, March 28). FBI has some explaining to do. *Los Angeles Times,* p. 12.

9. Ibid.

10. Pilant, L. (1997, August). Fighting crime in cyberspace. *Police Chief,* pp. 26–43.

11. Sussman, V. (1995, January 23). Policing cyberspace. *U.S. News & World Report.*

12. Moore, R. H. (1994, September/October). Wiseguys: Smarter criminals and smarter crime in the 21st century. *The Futurist,* pp. 33–37.

13. Maney, K., & P. McMahon. (2000, May 15). "Love bug" virus created in ordinary petri dish. *USA Today,* pp. 1A–2A.

14. Perry, R. (1986). *Computer crime.* New York: Franklin Watts.

15. Rosnoff, S. M., et al. (1998). *Profit without honor.* Upper Saddle River, NJ: Prentice Hall.

16. Hacker's ransom. (2000, January 11). *USA Today, Nationline,* p. 3A.

17. Pirates cheat computer software industry out of billions by illegal copying, study says. (1994, July 5). *The Houston Post,* p. C9.

18. Ibid.

19. Ibid.

20. Levy, D. (1999, September 22). Software piracy ahoy. *USA Today,* p. 1B; also see http://www.bsa.org/country.aspx?sc_lang=en (accessed January 14, 2009)

21. Ibid.

22. Moore, R. H. (1994, September/October). Wiseguys: Smarter criminals and smarter crime in the 21st century. *The Futurist,* pp. 33–37.

23. Katz, J. (1998). *Seduction of crime.* New York: Basic Books.

24. Slavin, B. (1997, November 26). Biochemical weapons: Poor man's nukes. *USA Today,* p. 17A; The Associated Press. (1998, February 21). Two charged for possessing anthrax. *USA Today, Nation;* Kasindorf, M. (1998, February 23). Test results weaken anthrax case. *USA Today,* p. 4A.

25. National Commission on Terrorism. (2000). *Countering the changing threat of international terrorism.* Washington, DC: U.S. Department of State.

26. Rashbaum, W. K. (2002, July 15). Terror makes all the world a beat for New York police. *New York Times,* p. B-1; Baker, A. (2002, August 6). Leader sees New York Police in vanguard of terror fight. *New York Times,* p. A2.

27. Flynn, S. (2003, January–February). America the vulnerable. *Foreign Affairs, 81,* 60; White House press release, November 11, 2002, http://www.whitehouse.gov/news; The section on homeland security relies heavily on "The Department of Homeland Security," www.whitehouse.gov/deptofhomeland/.

28. Crank, J. (1995). The community-policing movements of the early twenty-first century. In J. Klofas & S. Stojkovic, eds., *Crime and justice in the year 2010.* Belmont, CA: Wadsworth, 107–112.

29. Bennett, G. (1987). *Crimewarps: The future of crime in America.* Garden City, NY: Anchor Books/Anchor Press, imprint of Doubleday.

30. Toffler, A., & H. Toffler. (1990, January). The future of law enforcement: Dangerous and different. *FBI Law Enforcement Bulletin,* 7–12.

31. Ibid.

APPENDIX A

Selected Provisions from the USA Patriot Act of 2001

Title II—Enhanced Surveillance Procedures Section 203. Authority to Share Criminal Investigative Information.

(b) AUTHORITY TO SHARE ELECTRONIC, WIRE, AND ORAL INTERCEPTION INFORMATION—LAW ENFORCEMENT—Section 2517 of title 18, U.S.C., is amended by inserting at the end the following:

"(6) any investigative or law enforcement officer, or attorney for the government, who by any means authorized by this chapter, has obtained knowledge of the contents of any wire, oral, or electronic communication, or evidence derived therefrom, may disclose such contents to any other Federal law enforcement, intelligence, protective, immigration, national defense, or national security official to the extent that such contents include foreign intelligence or counterintelligence (as defined in section 3 of the National Security Act of 1947 (50 U.S.C. 401 (a)), or foreign intelligence information (as defined in subsection 19 of section 2510 of this article), to assist the official who is to receive that information in the performance of his official duties. Any federal official who receives information pursuant to this provision may use that information only as necessary in the conduct of that person's official duties subject to any limitations on the unauthorized disclosure of such information."

Sec. 213. Authority for Delaying Notice of the Execution of a Warrant.

Section 3103 a. of title 18, United States Code is amended—

(1) by inserting "(a) In General—" before "in addition": and (2) by adding at the end the following:

"(b) Delay—with respect to the insurance of any warrant or court order under this section, or any other rule of law, to search and seize any property or material that constitute evidence of a criminal offense in violation of the laws of the United States, any notice required, or that may be required, to be given may be delayed in—" (1) the court finds reasonable cause to believe that providing immediate notification of the execution of a warrant may have an adverse result (as defined in section 2705); "(2) the warrant prohibits the seizure of any tangible property, any wire or electronic communication (as defined in section 2510), or, except as expressly provided in chapter 121, any stored wire or electronic information, except where the court finds reasonable necessity for the seizure"; and "(3) the ward provides for the giving of such notice within a reasonable period of its execution, which period may thereafter be extended by the court for good cause shown."

WHAT THIS MEANS

Prior to the enactment of the USA PATRIOT Act, government agencies already had the authority, in limited situations, to delay notification for searches of some forms of electronic communications that were in the custody of a third party. (Delayed notification searches are sometimes called "sneak and peak" searches.) Previous law, according to the U.S. Department of Justice,[1] was a mix of inconsistent rules, practices, and court decisions varying widely from jurisdiction to jurisdiction. The lack of uniformity was said to have hindered the investigation of terrorism cases and other nationwide investigations.

The USA PATRIOT Act attempts to resolve this problem by amending title 18, section 3103, of the U.S. Code to create a uniform standard authorizing courts to delay the provision of required notice if the court finds "reasonable cause" to believe that providing immediate notification of the execution of the warrant may have an "adverse result" (such as endangering the life or physical safety of an individual, flight from prosecution, evidence tampering, or witness intimidation) or might otherwise seriously jeopardize an investigation or unduly delay a trial. This section of the USA PATRIOT Act is primarily designed to authorize delayed notice of *searches*, rather than delayed notice of *seizures*.

SEC. 216. MODIFICATION OF AUTHORITIES RELATING TO USE OF PEN REGISTERS AND TRAP AND TRACE DEVICES.

(b) Issuance of Orders.—

(1) In General—section 3123 (a) of title 18, U.S.C., is amended to read as follows:

(a) In General—

"(1) Attorney for the Government.

—upon application made under section 3122 (a) (1), the court shall interconnect apartheid order authorizing the installation and use of a pen register or trap and trace devices anywhere within the United States, if the court finds that the attorney for the government has certified to the court that the information likely to be obtained by such installation and use is relevant to an ongoing criminal investigation."

WHAT THIS MEANS

Although Congress enacted a pen/trap statute in 1986 (which made possible the collection of non-content traffic information associated with communications, such as the phone number dialed from a particular telephone), it could not anticipate the dramatic expansion in electronic communications that would occur in the next 15 years. Thus, the 1986 statute (18 U.S.C. 3127) contains certain language that appeared to apply to telephone communications and that did not unambiguously encompass communications over computer networks.

Section 216 of the USA PATRIOT Act updates the pen/trap statute in three important ways: (1) the amendments clarify that law enforcement may use pen/trap orders to trace communications on the Internet and other computer networks; (2) pen/trap orders issued by federal courts have nationwide effect; and (3) law enforcement authorities must file a special report with the court whenever they use a pen/trap order to install their own monitoring device on computers belonging to a public provider.

SEC. 219. SINGLE-JURISDICTION SEARCH WARRANTS FOR TERRORISM.

Rule 41 (a) of the Federal Rules of Criminal Procedure is amended by inserting after "executed" the following: "and (3) in an investigation of domestic terrorism or international terrorism (as defined in section 2331 of title 18, U.S.C.), by Federal magistrate judge in any district in which activities related to the terrorism may have occurred, for the search of property or for a person within or outside the district."

WHAT THIS MEANS

Under prior law, Rule 41 (a) of the Federal Rules of Criminal Procedure required that a search warrant be obtained within a district for searches within that district. The only exception was for cases in which property or a person within the district might leave the district prior to execution of the warrant. The rule created what some saw as unnecessary delays and burdens in the investigation of terrorist activities and networks that spanned a number of districts, since warrants had to be obtained separately in each district. Section 219 purports to solve that problem by providing that, in domestic or international terrorism cases, a search warrant may be used by a magistrate judge in any district in which activities related to the terrorism have occurred for a search of property or persons located within or outside of the district.

SEC. 224. SUNSET.

(a) In General—except as provided in subsection (b), this title and the amendments made by this title (other than sections 203 (a), 203 (c), 205, 208, 210, 211, 213, 216, 219, 221, and 222, and the amendments made by those sections) shall cease to have an effect on December 31, 2005.

WHAT THIS MEANS

None of the provisions shown in this section are scheduled to expire in 2005.

CIVIL RIGHTS IMPLICATIONS

Although many aspects of the USA PATRIOT Act have been criticized as potentially unconstitutional, section 213, which authorizes delaying notice of the execution of award, may be the most subject to challenge. The ACLU maintains that under this section, law enforcement agents could enter a house, apartment, or office with a search warrant while the occupant is away, search through his or her property, and take photographs without having to tell the suspect about the search until later.[2] The ACLU says that this provision will mark "a sea change in the way search warrants are executed in the United States." The ACLU also believes that the new provision is likely to be illegal because the Fourth Amendment to the Constitution protects against unreasonable searches and seizures and requires the government to both obtain a warrant and give notice to the person whose property will be searched before conducting the search. The notice requirement enables the suspect to assert his or her Fourth Amendment rights. A person with notice, for example, might be able to point out regularities in the warrant, such as the fact that the police are at the wrong address or that because the warrant is limited to a search for a stolen car, the police have no authority to be looking in dresser drawers. In a covert search warrant, there are no clear limitations on what can be searched. According to the ACLU, section 213 has taken what had previously been an extremely limited authority and expanded it so that it is now available in any kind of search (physical or electronic) and in any kind of criminal case.

The ACLU also questions the constitutionality of section 216, "Modification of Authorities Relating to Use Pen Registers and Trap and Trace Devices."[3] That section essentially says the courts shall use search warrants whenever a qualified prosecuting attorney, acting in an official capacity, certifies that the warrant is needed. This requirement effectively eliminates judicial oversight in the issuance of such warrants and mandates that courts issue warrants under specified circumstances rather than assess the lawfulness of warrant requests.

The Supreme Court has yet to rule on the constitutionality of "sneak and peak" searches or on section 213 requirements.

SUMMARY

Weeks after the USA PATRIOT Act became law, U.S. Attorney General John Ashcroft announced that he was using the authority of his office to allow federal corrections officials and select others to listen in on certain telephone communications between jailed suspects accused of terrorism and their lawyers—without obtaining prior approval by a judge. The Justice Department said that communications between inmates and their lawyers would be monitored when "reasonable suspicion exists to believe that a particular inmate may use communications with attorneys or their agents to further or facilitate acts of terrorism."[4]

Ashcroft's decision, which raised questions in Congress, effectively ended the long-standing tradition of lawyer–client confidentiality for telephone conversations with federal prisoners.

Following Ashcroft's announcement, President George W. Bush signed an executive order allowing secret military tribunals to try foreign terrorism suspects at home or abroad without many of the constitutional protections given to defendants in the federal court system. The president's order effectively removed suspected foreign terrorists from the jurisdiction of the federal court system. Bush said that the order was required to avoid having to prosecute accused terrorists under court rules that might result in the disclosure of state secrets or make the United States more vulnerable to terrorism.

Notes

1. References to the Department of Justice in this box are derived from *U.S. Department of Justice Field Guidance on Authorities*. Enacted in the 2001 Anti-Terrorism Legislation (Washington D.C.: DOJ, no date). Posted at http://www.epic.org/terrorism/DOJguidance.pdf. Accessed November 16, 2002.

2. Much of the information in this paragraph is taken from American Civil Liberties Union, *How the Anti-Terrorism Bill Expands Law Enforcement "Sneak and Peek" Warrants*.

3. American Civil Liberties Union, *How the Anti-Terrorism Bill Limits Judicial Oversight of Telephone and Internet Conversations*.

4. Glaberson, W. (2002, November 12). Experts divided on new anti-terror policy that scuttles lawyer-client confidentiality. *New York Times*.

APPENDIX B

Sample Police Academy Curriculum

Many criminal justice students preparing to enter a career in police work are curious about the subjects taught in a police academy. The following is the basic police academy curriculum for the Vermont State Police, which will give you a good idea of how police academies are structured.

Vermont State Police Basic Police Academy Curriculum Summary

Curriculum Summary	Hours	Percent of Time
COMMUNICATION		
Courtroom Demeanor	8	
Conflict Resolution	8	
Handling the Emotionally Disturbed	4	
Interpersonal Communication	8	
Media/Police Relations	2	
NCIC and VCIC	4	
Police Ethics	8	
Notetaking/Study Habits	4	
Report Writing	32	
Stress Management	8	
Sexual-Harassment Policy	2	
Total	**88**	**11%**
CRIMINAL LAW		
Criminal Law	48	
Introduction to Fish and Wildlife Law	2	
Introduction to Liquor Control	2	
Introduction to Federal Agencies	2	
Juvenile Law and Procedure	8	
Police Liability	4	
Use of Vermont Statutes	2	
Total	**68**	**9%**
DEFENSIVE TACTICS		
Firearms	56	
Nonlethal Use of Force	40	
Impact Weapon Certification	4	
Oleoresin Capsicum Certification	4	
Total	**104**	**13%**
INVESTIGATIVE PROCEDURES		
Accident Investigation	40	
Case Problems and Case Preparation	24	
Domestic Violence Response Training	12	
Drug Identification and Investigation	8	
Interview and Interrogation Techniques	16	
Sexual-Assault Investigation (Adult/Child)	24	
Death Investigation	8	
Victims Assistance Program	2	
Court Diversion	2	
Hate-Crimes Investigation	8	
Total	**144**	**18%**

(continued)

Vermont State Police Basic Police Academy Curriculum Summary (*Continued*)

Curriculum Summary	Hours	Percent of Time
MOTOR VEHICLE LAW		
Motor Vehicle Law	40	
Hazardous Material Recognition	8	
Total	**48**	**6%**
PHYSICAL FITNESS		
Nutrition Information	4	
Physical Assessment	6	
Physical Training	96	
Total	**106**	**13%**
POLICE PATROL TECHNIQUES		
Advanced Defensive Driving	24	
Bloodborne Pathogens	2	
Crime Prevention and Community Policing	8	
Community Policing Project	10	
Patrol Procedures	132	
Teambuilding and Problem Solving	16	
Occupant Protection Usage and Enforcement	4	
Total	**196**	**24%**
OTHERS		
Administrative/Staff Time	8	
Notetaking and Study Habits	4	
Alcohol Services Act	2	
Drill and Ceremony	10	
History and Principles of Policing	6	
Core-Value Training	2	
Final Examination	2	
Total	**34**	**5%**
Total Hours for Basic Training	**788**	**99% (rounded)**
POST-BASIC INSTRUCTION		
D.W.I Enforcement	32	
V.I.N. Verification	4	
Basic Fingerprinting Techniques	4	
Doppler Radar Operation	8	
First Aid	4	
C.P.R.	12	
Total Post-Basic Training	**64**	
Total Hours for Basic Training	**852**	

GLOSSARY

1983 Action   A frequently used civil remedy for police misconduct found in the 1964 federal Civil Rights Act.

Actual injury   A legal term referring to the real harm suffered by a plaintiff of a lawsuit.

Affirmative action   A hiring policy whereby employers must take active steps to ensure equal employment opportunity and to redress past discriminatory practices.

Anonymous re-mailers   Free e-mail forwarding sites in Europe and elsewhere that can convert return addresses to pseudonyms and render e-mail untraceable.

Assault   To intentionally put someone in fear of immediate battery or to threaten someone while having the apparent ability to carry out that threat.

Backup   A term of art in policing that refers to officers who provide safety and cover for other officers.

Battery   Intentional, nonconsensual bodily contact that a reasonable person would consider harmful.

Beanbags   Small, less-than-lethal canvas bags containing tiny lead beads that are fired from a shotgun.

Beats   Sectors or divisions in which patrol officers work.

Bivens action   A civil action/complaint for which a federal officer can be sued for violations of constitutional rights.

Blue flu   A type of planned job slowdown where a majority of a police force calls in sick.

Blue Wall of Silence   A protective code of silence among police officers.

Bobbies   The original term given to police officers in England's Metropolitan Police Department in 1829.

Broken windows theory   A crime theory that uses broken windows as a metaphor.

Burnout   To fail, to wear out, or become exhausted by making excessive demands on energy, strength, or resources.

Carnivore   An FBI investigative database designed to monitor e-mail.

Certification   The process of official approval of a police recruit's qualifications for public service.

Civil Rights Act of 1964   Federal law that prohibits discrimination based on race, color, religion, sex, or national origin.

Coercive force   The improper level of force used by police officers with the goal of gaining compliance of a suspect.

Collective bargaining   A method that enlists large numbers of employees who seek similar work-related benefits.

Color of state law   Legal term referring to officers who act wrongfully under the guise of their office.

Community policing   A policing philosophy whereby the police come together with the community to fight crime.

Compensatory damages   Designed to restore or compensate a victim for expenses, time off work, and so on.

Consent decree   A legal term referring to a judicial decree expressing a voluntary agreement between parties to a suit, especially an agreement by a defendant to cease activities alleged by the government to be illegal in return for an end to the charges.

Constable   An officer of the common law, who was paid privately by people and who wanted to escape the obligatory civic duty of police service.

Crime mapping   Use of databases that provide information on crime trends.

Crime prevention   Specific goal to reduce the need to commit crime by providing opportunities for success and achievement.

Criminal law   Acts of criminality in U.S. society.

Critical incident stress   Physical trauma policemen may suffer that is caused by disastrous situations encountered in the field.

Cybercrime   Crimes using the computer and Internet.

Cyber-extortion   Using the Internet to extort money or services.

Data mining   The process of extracting hidden patterns from data.

Deadly force   Actions of police officers that result in the killing of a person.

Decertification   A process whereby a police officer is stripped of their ability to remain employed as a police officer.

Deep Pockets   A term referring to a party in a lawsuit that is more likely to afford payment of a large settlement or monetary damages.

Differential response   Police department distinguishes between different calls for service so it can respond more quickly to the most serious incidents.

Directed patrol   Concept that requires officers to spend an allotted amount of their time in a specific area, usually one that is considered a high-crime area.

Dirty Harry problem   A phenomenon where rogue police officers ignore procedure.

Discretion   Choices or options available to police officers.

Enhanced system   To encourage higher education among peace officers, to lower training costs to police agencies, to increase local involvement in the delivery system, to increase the labor pool, and to avoid duplication of recruitment training.

Entrapment The procurement of a person to commit a crime that he or she did not contemplate or would not have committed for the sole purpose of prosecuting him or her.

Equal Employment Opportunity Act of 1972 Extended the 1964 Civil Rights Act and made its provisions, including Title VII, applicable to state and local governments. The EEOA expanded the jurisdiction and strengthened the powers of the federal Equal Opportunity Employment Commission.

Espionage Criminal acts that threaten the sovereignty of a nation.

Exclusionary rule Identified under *Weeks* v. *U.S.* (1914) and *Mapp* v. *Ohio* (1968), a judge-made law designed to thwart illegal efforts by police officers to arrest, seize property, or otherwise obtain evidence against people without sufficient probable cause.

External stress Stress caused by external stimuli.

Extralegal factors Factors external to the law that influence people, based on race, gender, etc.

Facial-recognition technology A visual surveillance system used to identify people wanted for crimes.

Field training program A term referring to basic, on-the-job training received by police recruits before they are permitted to work alone.

Fleeing-felon rule An old enforcement doctrine whereby police officers were legally authorized to employ the use of deadly force in apprehending fleeing felons.

Foot patrol Police patrol external of police vehicles.

Forseeability Reasonable anticipation that an arrestee's condition creates a hazard in a given circumstance.

Frankpledge system System that was based on an organization of tithings.

Full enforcement Police policy requiring complete enforcement of all laws in conjunction with constitutional standards.

Gallows humor A term referring to the dark humor often used by police officers.

General adaptation syndrome A model used to describe the biological reaction to sustained and unrelenting physical stress. This model has three phases: alarm reaction, resistance, and exhaustion.

G-men Old crime-fighting image of FBI agents.

Grass-eater Officers who, respectively, simply accepted whatever corrupt money came their way as opposed to those who actively sought out corruption opportunities.

Graying of America Term referring to the aging U.S. population.

Hacker One who illegally breaks into a computer program.

Hot spots Places where crimes are likely to occur.

Hue and cry A public summons for help.

Impossible mandate Expectation that police must serve many masters: the public, prosecutors, politicians, criminals, victims, judges, and so on.

Incident-driven policing Calls for service are the primary instigators of action.

Injunction An equitable remedy in the form of a court order, whereby a party is required to do, or to refrain from doing, certain acts.

In-service training Police training to keep officers current in their fields: patrol, investigation, crime prevention, juveniles, and so on.

Instinct The inherent disposition of a police officer toward a particular situation or behavior of persons.

Internal affairs unit An investigative unit within a law enforcement organization that investigates allegations of misconduct by officers.

Internal stress Stress caused from functional duties, policies, and procedures that have been implemented as a part of a department's standard operating procedure.

Invocation discretion Situations in which the officer chooses to invoke or use criminal law and thus issues a citation or makes an arrest.

Iris-recognition technology Electronic method for examining the interior of the eye and matching unique characteristics with a database.

Job-related stress A condition in which a function or combination of functions on the job interact with the worker to upset his or her psychological or physiological equilibrium.

Legal duty A term referring to the statutory responsibility of a public servant to carry out their duties.

Mail bombs Electronic vandals using anonymous re-mailers send these, which are composed of thousands of gibberish messages.

Majority rule Those in power determine the manner in which resources will be used to achieve social ends such as national security, transportation, medical care, and crime control.

Meat-eater Officers who actively seek out corruption opportunities.

Minimization A legal requirement forcing police officers to take every possible measure to monitor only those conversations that are criminal in nature during the course of electronic surveillance.

Minority rights The rights of the people, regardless of who is in power.

Miranda warning The reading of a suspect's constitutional rights before questioning.

Mission The guiding principle behind most police agencies, which guides their function and helps to establish their enforcement priorities.

Mollen Commission formally known as The City of New York Commission to investigate allegations of police corruption and the anti-corruption procedures of the police department. Former Judge Milton Mollen was appointed in July 1992 by then New York City Mayor David N. Dinkins to investigate corruption in the New York City Police Department.

Moral career Theory in which people pass through various stages of rationalization to more serious misdeeds in a graduated and systematic way.

National Security letter A form of administrative subpoena used by the United States Federal Bureau of Investigation and reportedly by other U.S. Government Agencies including the Central Intelligence Agency and the Department of Defense. It is a demand letter issued to a particular entity or organization to turn over various record and data pertaining to individuals.

Night watch Justice–constable system, in which the constables, who were appointed by the local justices, patrol their parishes during the day. At night, men of the watch were charged with patrolling deserted streets and maintaining street lamps.

Noninvocation discretion Circumstances whereby the officer could employ the law but elects not to.

Normative sponsorship theory Theory that most people are of good will and that they will cooperate with others to facilitate the building of consensus.

Operational stress Stress that results from police officers' confronting the daily tragedies of life on the street. It is logical to assume that dealing with liars, thieves, murderers, drug dealers, and the like on a regular basis tends to make officers cynical about persons not associated with police work.

Pepperballs Small, nonlethal, plastic pellets filled with peppery powder that causes coughing.

Pervasive organized corruption Situations in which corruption is not only widespread but in which both police officers and those who corrupt them are organized. This type of corruption may extend into the department's highest ranks and permits the influence of organized crime in law enforcement.

Pervasive unorganized corruption Occurs when a large percentage of the department is corrupt, but officers act independently and there is little if any collusion among them.

Physical evidence Tangible evidence collected from the crime scene.

Plain view Several conditions must exist for items to be seized. First, the officer must lawfully be present at the location to be searched. Second, the item seized must have been found inadvertently, and finally, the item is contraband or would be useful as evidence of a crime.

Police lineup The placing of suspects together with several other people, and the victim or a witness is allowed to view them and pick out the suspect.

Police subculture Police often feel a sense of social isolation from the rest of society, creating a definite subculture.

Polygraph A lie detector.

Positional asphyxia Occurs when a person's body position interferes with his or her ability to breathe.

Posse comitatus Authority to coordinate the activities of all other police agencies (Latin for "power of the country").

Posttraumatic stress disorder A disorder that occurs after a traumatic event such as rape, combat, a natural disaster, serious threat to the safety of loved ones, or seeing another person maimed or killed.

Preventive patrol Routine or random patrol.

Principle of accountability A term referring to civilian review and the responsibility of police to be accountable to the public they serve.

Proactive Encounters initiated by police action.

Proactive prevention measures A police recruitment strategy whereby measures are taken to minimize chances of hiring a high-risk or problem officer.

Probable cause A reasonable good faith in the legality of the action taken.

Problem-oriented policing Takes the view that underlying social conditions cause crime.

Procedural laws Deals with elements of fairness under the law and the manner in which the police enforce substantive laws.

Project DARE (Drug Abuse Resistance Education) Project where specially trained uniformed officers visit the classrooms of grade schools.

Proximate cause A legal term referring to an event sufficiently related to a legally recognizable injury to be held the cause of that injury.

Punitive damages Considerably more severe damages that are designed to impose a financial punishment on the defendant. It is not uncommon for both compensatory and punitive damages to be assessed, especially if there are "willful and malicious" aspects to the defendant's behavior in question.

Reactive Police encounters in response to citizen complaints.

Reasonable expectation of privacy A legal test which is crucial in defining the scope of the applicability of the privacy protections of the Fourth Amendment to the United States Constitution.

Rectitude issues The professional set of values of a police officer that include obeying the law and respecting the constitutional rights of citizens.

Response time Time between a call for service and police arrival on the scene.

Reverse discrimination When employers practice preferential hiring and promotional opportunities for minorities to counter past inequities in employment practices.

Rogues gallery Forerunner of today's police "mug book" and consisted of detailed descriptions of known criminals and their hideouts.

Rotten apple A uniformed officer who accepts an occasional bribe while on such assignments as traffic patrol.

Rubber bullets Nonlethal projectiles shot at people to subdue them.

Saturation patrol   Heavy police patrol concentration in specified areas.

Sectors   The divisions or zones that police officers are assigned to; also help determine allocation.

Selective enforcement   Enforcement of some of the laws some of the time against certain people.

Shakedown   The common practice of holding "street court," where minor traffic tickets can be avoided with a cash payment to the officer and no receipt given.

Shift work   Work that typically involves shifts of duty, for example, from 4 to 12 (4:00 P.M. to 12 midnight) and weekends and holidays.

Slave patrols   Police during the 1800s, who in rural areas were charged with tracking and apprehending slaves who had escaped from plantations and farms.

Special duty   Applied when police have reason to believe that an arrestee presents a danger to himself or herself.

Standard operating procedures   Written policies that provide operational guidance to police officers.

Statute of Westminster   A law of old England requiring men to serve on *posse comitatus.*

Stop and frisk   Pat down of suspects for weapons.

Strategic policing   Concept that emphasizes an increased capacity to deal effectively with nontraditional crimes.

Street people   Term that refers to the mentally ill, public drunks, and homeless.

Substantive laws   Laws that identify unlawful behavior and that provide penalties for violations of the law.

Surveillance   The surreptitious observation of persons, places, or things by law enforcement officers.

Sworn personnel   Part- or full-time police officers who are assigned ranks and are charged with enforcing the law.

Taser   A weapon with prongs that sends an incapacitating electric jolt.

Team policing   The reorganization of conventional patrol strategies into an integrated and adaptable police team assigned to a permanent district.

Terrorism   Violent criminal behavior to achieve some political end.

Thermal imaging   Detection of unusual heat sources that might indicate the cultivation of marijuana under "grow lights."

Thief-taker   Reward given to the Runners, the unofficial police without regular pay, upon the capture of criminals.

Tithings   Collectives of ten families in old England.

Title VII   Prohibits discrimination based on race, color, religion, sex, or national origin for private employers with 15 or more employees, governments, unions, and employment agencies.

Totality of the circumstances   Policy stating that it must be shown that the officer's words or actions would have led a reasonable person to believe that he or she was not free to leave before an attempted seizure of the person occurs.

Trojan horse   A computer virus that destroys data.

Vicarious liability   The extension of civil liability to supervisors is known as the doctrine of respondent superior.

White-collar crime   Professional/corporate crime.

Zero tolerance   A public policy position that views minor crimes as seriously as big crimes.

INDEX

("b" indicates boxed material; "f" indicates a figure; "t" indicates a table)

PHOTO CREDITS

Chapter 1: Page 2, Tony Freeman - PhotoEdit Inc.; Page 14, Picture Desk, Inc./Kobal Collection; Page 15, Cherokee County Sheriff's Dept\ AP Wide World Photos; Page 17, Kayte M. Deioma\PhotoEdit Inc.; Page 19, Mikael Karlsson\Arresting Images.

Chapter 2: Page 24, Monika Graff\The Image WorksPage 30, NORMAN NICHOLLS\Photolibrary.com; Page 32, (c)Hirz/Archive Photos; Page 39, (c) Bettmann/CORBIS/All Rights Reserved; Page 41, Evans (AG)\Getty Images Inc. - Hulton Archive Photos; Page 45, Steve Jessmore\AP Wide World Photos; Page 47, CORBIS- NY.

Chapter 3: Page 52, CLAVER CARROLL\Photolibrary.com; Page 60, 63, AP Wide World Photos; Page 71, Ronnie Kaufman - Corbis/Bettman.

Chapter 4: Page 86, Spencer Grant\PhotoEdit Inc.; Page 108, Najlah Feanny\CORBIS - NY.

Chapter 5: Page 114, A. Ramey\PhotoEdit Inc.; Page 123, AP Wide World Photos; Page 126, A. Ramey\PhotoEdit Inc.

Chapter 6: Page 146, AP Wide World Photos; Page 155, Winchester Sun, James Mann\AP Wide World Photos; Page 158, Mikael Karlsson\ Arresting Images.

Chapter 7: Page 164, Gregory Bull\AP Wide World Photos; Page 168, Doug Kanter\Corbis/Bettman.

Chapter 8: Page 184, Mikael Karlsson\Arresting Images; Page 190, Bob Daemmrich Photography, Inc.; Page 198 (a) TASER International (NASDAQ: TASR), (b) Photo Courtesy of Taser International via Getty Images.

Chapter 9: Page 210, 222, Najlah Feanny-Hicks\CORBIS - Bettman.

Chapter 10: Page 240, Jack Haley/Daily Messenger\AP Wide World Photos; Page 244, Jack Parsons\Omni-Photo Communications, Inc.

Chapter 11: Page 254, Mark Richards\PhotoEdit Inc.; Page 257, AP Wide World Photos.

Chapter 12: Page 280, Dwayne Newton\PhotoEdit Inc.; Page 283, Bob Daemmrich\PhotoEdit Inc.

Chapter 13: Page 304, Getty Images, Inc.; Page 310, AP Wide World Photos; Page 315, Los Angeles Police Historical Society; Page 316, AP Wide World Photos.

Chapter 14: Page 338, Rick Friedman\CORBIS- NY; Page 342, Michel Setboun\CORBIS - Bettman.